ASHGATE
RESEARCH
COMPANION

THE ASHGATE RESEARCH COMPANION TO FEDERALISM

ASHGATE
RESEARCH
COMPANION

The *Ashgate Research Companions* are designed to offer scholars and graduate students a comprehensive and authoritative state-of-the-art review of current research in a particular area. The companions' editors bring together a team of respected and experienced experts to write chapters on the key issues in their speciality, providing a comprehensive reference to the field.

Other Research Companions available in Politics and International Relations:

The Ashgate Research Companion to Political Leadership
Edited by Joseph Masciulli, Mikhail A. Molchanov and W. Andy Knight
ISBN 978-0-7546-7182-4

The Ashgate Research Companion to Ethics and International Relations
Edited by Patrick Hayden
ISBN 978-0-7546-7101-5

*The Ashgate Research Companion to the Politics of Democratization in Europe
Concepts and Histories*
Edited by Kari Palonen, Tuija Pulkkinen and José María Rosales
ISBN 978-0-7546-7250-0

The Ashgate Research Companion to Federalism

Edited by

ANN WARD and LEE WARD
Campion College, University of Regina, Canada

ASHGATE

© Ann Ward and Lee Ward 2009

All rights reserved. No part of this publication may be reproduced, stored in a retrieval system or transmitted in any form or by any means, electronic, mechanical, photocopying, recording or otherwise without the prior permission of the publisher.

Ann Ward and Lee Ward have asserted their right under the Copyright, Designs and Patents Act, 1988, to be identified as the editors of this work.

Published by
Ashgate Publishing Limited
Wey Court East
Union Road
Farnham
Surrey GU9 7PT
England

Ashgate Publishing Company
Suite 420
101 Cherry Street
Burlington,
VT 05401-4405
USA

www.ashgate.com

British Library Cataloguing in Publication Data
The Ashgate research companion to federalism. - (Federalism studies)
1. Federal government
I. Ward, Ann, 1970- II. Ward, Lee, 1970-
321'.02

Library of Congress Cataloging-in-Publication Data
The Ashgate research companion to federalism / [edited by] by Ann Ward and Lee Ward.
    p. cm. -- (Federalism studies)
Includes bibliographical references and index.
ISBN 978-0-7546-7131-2 -- ISBN 978-0-7546-8989-8 (ebook) 1. Federal government. I. Ward, Ann, 1970- II. Ward, Lee, 1970-

JC355.A79 2009
320.4'049--dc22

2008053459

ISBN 978 0 7546 7131 2
eISBN 978 0 7546 8989 8

Mixed Sources
Product group from well-managed forests and other controlled sources
www.fsc.org Cert no. SA-COC-1565
© 1996 Forest Stewardship Council

Printed and bound in Great Britain by
MPG Books Group, UK

Contents

Notes on Contributors	*ix*
Acknowledgements	*xv*
About the Editors	*xvii*

Introduction to the Volume
    Ann Ward and Lee Ward   1

PART 1: CLASSICAL AND JUDEO-CHRISTIAN IMAGES OF FEDERALISM
Introduction to Part 1   11

1. Nascent Federalism and its Limits in Ancient Greece:
   Herodotus and Thucydides   15
   Ann Ward and Sara MacDonald

2. Before Federalism?
   Thomas Aquinas, Jean Quidort and Nicolas Cusanus   31
   Nicholas Aroney

3. The Reformational Legacy of Theologico-political Federalism   49
   Shaun de Freitas and Andries Raath

PART 2: THE ORIGINS OF MODERN FEDERALISM
Introduction to Part 2   71

4. Johannes Althusius:
   Between Secular Federalism and the Religious State   75
   Bettina Koch

5	Early Dutch and German Federal Theory: Spinoza, Hugo, and Leibniz Lee Ward	91
6	Montesquieu on Federalism and the Problem of Liberty in the International System: Ancient Virtue and the Modern Executive Ann Ward and David S. Fott	107
7	Federalism and David Hume's Perfect Commonwealth Will R. Jordan and Scott Yenor	121
8	Jean-Jacques Rousseau and the Case against (and for) Federalism Daniel E. Cullen	137
9	Kant and Federalism Joseph M. Knippenberg	151

PART 3: FEDERALISM AND THE EARLY AMERICAN REPUBLIC

Introduction to Part 3 — 169

10	"A System Without a Precedent": The Federalism of the *Federalist* Papers Quentin Taylor	175
11	The Antifederalists and Tocqueville on Federalism: Lessons for Today David Lewis Schaefer	193
12	Thomas Jefferson's Enlightenment Idea of Federalism Peter McNamara	209
13	Tocqueville on Federalism as an American Accident Peter Augustine Lawler	225
14	John C. Calhoun's Federalism and its Contemporary Echoes James Read	245
15	A More Perfect Union: Secession, Federalism, and Democracy in the Words and Actions of Lincoln William Mathie	261

Contents

PART 4: EUROPEAN FEDERALISM
Introduction to Part 4 — 279

16 Confederation, Federal State, and Federation: Around Louis Le Fur — 283
    Guillaume Barrera

17 Looking into Medusa's Eyes: Carl Schmitt on Federalism — 297
    Nicolas Patrici

18 Altiero Spinelli and European Federalism — 315
    Roberto Castaldi

19 Polyvalent Federalism:
    Johannes Althusius to Edvard Kardelj and Titoism — 331
    Matthew McCullock

20 A "European" Federalism:
    From Altiero Spinelli to the EU Constitutional Treaty — 351
    Francesca Vassallo

21 From Laeken to Lisbon: Europe's Experiment with Constitutional Federalism — 367
    Martyn de Bruyn

PART 5: CONTEMPORARY THEORIES OF FEDERALISM
Introduction to Part 5 — 385

22 The Covenant Tradition of Federalism:
    The Pioneering Studies of Daniel J. Elazar — 391
    Glenn A. Moots

23 William Riker's "Rationalist" Federalism — 413
    Benjamin Kleinerman

24 Theories of Fiscal Federalism and the European Experience — 425
    Alberto Majocchi

25 Postmodern Federalism and Sub-State Nationalism — 441
    Greg Marchildon

PART 6: REGIONAL EXPERIENCES OF FEDERALISM
Introduction to Part 6   459

26   Federalism in Africa: An Indigenous Idea with a Colonial History   463
      Sara Jordan

27   Australian Federalism: An Innovation in Constitutionalism   485
      Haig Patapan

28   India: A Model of Cooperative Federalism   503
      Akhtar Majeed

29   Federalism: The Latin American Experience   517
      Julián Durazo Hermann

30   Federalism or Islam? Ibn Khaldun on Islam and Politics   535
      Khalil Habib

31   The Rehnquist Court and the "New Federalism"   551
      Jack Wade Nowlin

Conclusion   567
      Ann Ward and Lee Ward

Index   *571*

Notes on Contributors

Nicholas Aroney is Reader in Law and Fellow, Centre for Public, International and Comparative Law, at the University of Queensland. Dr Aroney has published extensively in constitutional law and legal theory, with particular emphasis on comparative federalism, constitutional interpretation and implied rights. His most recent major publications are *The Constitution of a Federal Commonwealth: The Making and Meaning of the Australian Constitution* (Cambridge University Press, 2008) and a jointly edited collection of essays, *Restraining Elective Dictatorship: The Upper House Solution?* (University of Western Australia Press, 2008).

Guillaume Barrera is Professor of Philosophy in Lettres supérieures at the Lycée Fustel de Coulanges, in Strasbourg, France. He is an alumnus of the ENS (1988), graduated with the agrégation in philosophy (1993), and received his doctorate in political philosophy from the EHESS (Paris, 2000). He has published articles, translations, and book reviews, especially on and around Montesquieu, including an edition of the "Essay on the Causes that can Affect Spirits and Characters" (Montesquieu, *Oeuvres complètes*, T.IX, Oxford, Voltaire Foundation, 2006). His book on the politics of Montesquieu is to appear in the Gallimard Edition series "L'Esprit de la cité" (Paris, 2009).

Roberto Castaldi is Research Fellow at the Sant'Anna School of Advanced Studies in Pisa and the Centre for Federal Studies of Turin. He is editorial coordinator of the *Bibliographical Bulletin of Federalism*. His research focuses on supranational federalism, European integration, nationalism, interdependence and globalization theories. He has published articles about Kant, Hamilton, Spinelli and Elias, and the book *Federalism and Material Interdependence*, Milan, Giuffrè, forthcoming; and as editor *Immanuel Kant and Alexander Hamilton, Founders of Federalism*, forthcoming.

Daniel E. Cullen is Associate Professor of Political Science at Rhodes College in Memphis, Tennessee. He is the author of *Freedom in Rousseau's Political Philosophy* (Northern Illinois University Press, 1993) and has written essays on liberal education, democratic theory and the thought of Rousseau. His current research interests include the relation of liberal education and civic education and a comparative study of Adam Smith and Jean-Jacques Rousseau.

Martyn de Bruyn is an Assistant Professor in Political Science at Northeastern Illinois University. He previously served as Regional Visiting Fellow at the Institute for European Studies at Cornell University. His research is focused on European Union politics with a particular interest in federalism, referendums, and constitutional development. He is currently working on a project on the effectiveness of European Affairs Committees in holding national governments accountable in the European policy arena.

Shaun de Freitas is an Associate Professor in the Department of Constitutional Law and Philosophy of Law, University of the Free State (South Africa), and lectures in Public Law. He has an interest in the relationship between religion and the law; and has contributed to scholarship with special emphasis on pre-modern and modern contributions to constitutional theory. He is also presently busy with his doctorate on republicanism.

David S. Fott is Associate Professor of Political Science at the University of Nevada, Las Vegas. He received his BA *summa cum laude* from Vanderbilt University and his AM and PhD from Harvard University. Fott is author of *John Dewey: America's Philosopher of Democracy* (Rowman & Littlefield, 1998), as well as articles on Dewey, Montesquieu, and Jane Austen. He is currently translating Cicero's *On the Republic* and *On the Laws* (Focus Publishing, forthcoming) and writing a book on Cicero's political philosophy.

Khalil Habib earned his PhD in philosophy from Boston University. He is an Assistant Professor in the philosophy department at Salve Regina University, Newport Rhode Island, where he also teaches in the university's Core Program. He works in the history of political philosophy and ethics, Islamic philosophy, and philosophical literature. His work has appeared in *Ancient Philosophy*, *Contemporary Philosophy*, *The Polish Journal of Philosophy*, and *The Review of Metaphysics*. He is a regular co-chair for the Student Conference on US Affairs (SCUSA) at West Point, Middle East Gulf States table. Since 2007, he has served as Faculty Mentor of the United States Military Academy's *Undergraduate Journal of Social Sciences*, West Point. He is currently working on a co-edited volume on ancient and modern cosmopolitanism.

Julián Durazo Hermann is a Professor of Comparative Politics at Université du Québec à Montréal (UQAM). He holds a PhD in Political Science from McGill University (2006) and a licenciatura in International Relations from El Colegio de México (1999). He has published extensively on federalism and subnational politics in Latin America.

Sara Jordan is Assistant Professor in the Department of Politics and Public Administration at the University of Hong Kong. Her research specialties include non-western political philosophy, particularly as applied to matters of political and civil service ethics. Her recent research focuses on the role of competing and complimentary philosophical traditions in the quest to define a global ethic for politics, a topic on which she is currently completing a book manuscript.

Will R. Jordan is Associate Professor of Political Science at Mercer University. He has published articles on David Hume's political thought in *The Review of Politics* and *Perspectives on Political Science*. He is currently interested in, and working on, the political thought of Henry Adams.

Benjamin Kleinerman received his BA in Political Science from Kenyon College and his PhD in Political Science from Michigan State University. A former Visiting Scholar in the Program on Constitutional Government at Harvard University, Professor Kleinerman has also taught at Oberlin College and the Virginia Military Institute. Currently working on a book on discretionary executive power in the American Constitution to be published by the University Press of Kansas, he has written articles on the subject appearing in *Perspectives on Politics* and *American Political Science Review*.

Joseph M. Knippenberg is Professor of Politics at Oglethorpe University, where he has taught since 1985. He is Editor (with Peter A. Lawler) of *Poets, Princes, and Private Citizens: Literary Alternatives to Postmodern Politics* (Rowman & Littlefield, 1996). His scholarly work has appeared in a variety of journals and edited volumes. He is also an Adjunct Fellow of the Ashbrook Center for Public Affairs and serves on the American Academy for Liberal Education's Council of Scholars.

Bettina Koch is Assistant Professor of Political Science at Virginia Tech. She is author of *Zur Dis-/Kontinuität mittelalterlichen politischen Denkens in der neuzeitlichen politischen Theorie: Marsilius von Padua, Johannes Althusius und Thomas Hobbes im Vergleich* (Berlin: Duncker & Humblot, 2005). Koch has published articles on late medieval and early modern political theory. Her research interests include history of political thought, medieval and early modern political theory, and comparative political theory, focusing on the comparison of Western and Middle Eastern political concepts.

Peter Augustine Lawler is Dana Professor of Government at Berry College. His most recent book is *Homeless and at Home in America* (St Augustine's Press, 2007); some of his others include *Stuck with Virtue* (Intercollegiate Studies Institute, 2005), *Aliens in America* (Intercollegiate Studies Institute, 2002), and *Postmodernism Rightly Understood* (Rowman & Littlefield, 1999). He is Executive Editor of the scholarly quarterly *Perspectives on Political Science*, a member of the President's Council of Bioethics, and recipient of the 2007 Weaver Prize in Scholarly Letters.

Sara MacDonald coordinates and teaches in the Great Ideas Programme at St. Thomas University, NB, Canada. She has most recently published a book on Hegel entitled *Finding Freedom: Hegel's Philosophy and the Emancipation of Women* (McGill-Queen's University Press, 2008). She has also published on Montesquieu and is currently working in a number of areas, including a manuscript concerning modern misreading of Hegel and articles regarding Thomas Hobbes' reception of the thoughts of St. Augustine and the relationship between John Locke and Richard Hooker.

Akhtar Majeed is Professor of Political Science and Director of the Centre for Federal Studies at the Hamdard University in New Delhi (India) and is also the Editor of the bi-annual *Indian Journal of Federal Studies*. He has been Theme Coordinator (Distribution of Responsibilities) of the Global Project "Federalism in the 21st Century" of the Forum of Federations, and coordinator of a number of programmes in Competence-Development in Federal Governance, for various countries.

Alberto Majocchi is Professor of Public Finance at the University of Pavia, Faculty of Economics. He has taught at the Universities of Venice, Leuven, Varese and Castellanza and he has been Visiting in the Universities of Cambridge and York (UK). Since March 2003 he has been President of the Institute for Studies and Economic Analyses in Rome. His main fields of interest are economic policy in the European Union, fiscal federalism and environmental economics.

Greg Marchildon is Canada Research Chair in Public Policy and Economic History at the University of Regina's Johnson-Shoyama Graduate School of Public Policy. In the 1990s, he served as Deputy Minister of Intergovernmental Affairs and Secretary to the Cabinet in the provincial government of Saskatchewan. In 2001–2002, he was Executive Director of a federal Royal Commission on the Future of Health Care in Canada. He is the author of numerous books and articles on Canadian public policy and federalism.

William Mathie teaches political philosophy in the Political Science Department at Brock University in St. Catharines, Canada. He was a founder of the Great Books/Liberal Studies Program at Brock University. He has recently published essays on Hobbes, Tocqueville, Newman, political philosophy and the Bible, and George Grant. He is currently working on two projects: a book-length treatment of Hobbes's role as an inventor of the modern understanding of politics, and a study of the political rhetoric of Lincoln.

Matthew McCullock is a temporary lecturer in Politics at the Department of Politics, International Relations and European Studies, Loughborough University. His main research interests are the writings of Johannes Althusius and the history of Yugoslavia. He has previously published on Althusius' Calvinist Right of Resistance and the relevance of Althusius' thought to a post-Westphalian order (with Emilian Kavalski). He also has a forthcoming book chapter exploring the notion of identity and the failure of Socialist Yugoslavia (with Silvia Susnjić).

Notes on Contributors

Peter McNamara teaches political science at Utah State University. He has written on Adam Smith, Alexander Hamilton, John Locke and Friedrich Hayek. He is currently working on the subject of liberalism and the problem of human nature.

Glenn A. Moots is an Associate Professor at Northwood University in Midland, Michigan. He has also taught at Louisiana State University, Walsh College, and Saginaw Valley State University. He writes on the intersection of religion and politics, including interdisciplinary and historical approaches to liberalism. He is at work on book-length studies of both early modern resistance theory and political covenanting. He has been both a Salvatori and a Calihan Fellow.

Jack Wade Nowlin is Associate Professor of Law and Jessie D. Puckett, Jr., Lecturer in Law at the University of Mississippi School of Law. Professor Nowlin received a PhD in Politics from Princeton University and a JD from the University of Texas School of Law. Nowlin's book chapters have appeared in *That Eminent Tribunal: Judicial Supremacy and the Constitution* (Princeton University Press, 2004) and *Liberalism at the Crossroads* (Rowman & Littlefield, 2nd Edition, 2003). His articles have appeared in the *Illinois Law Review*, the *Notre Dame Law Review*, the *Connecticut Law Review*, and the *Kentucky Law Journal*.

Haig Patapan is Professor in the Department of Politics and Public Policy, Griffith University, Australia. His research interests include political theory, leadership and democratic governance. He is the author of *Judging Democracy* (Cambridge UP, 2000) and *Machiavelli in Love: the Modern Politics of Love and Fear* (Lexington, 2006); co-editor of *Globalization and Equality* (Routledge, 2004); *Westminster Legacies: Democracy and Responsible Government in Asia and the Pacific* (UNSW Press, 2005); and most recently, *Dissident Democrats: the Challenge of Democratic Leadership in Asia* (Palgrave, 2008).

Nicolas Patrici is a PhD Candidate at the Pompeu Fabra University, Spain and currently is a Visiting PhD Researcher at Leiden University, the Netherlands. Patrici's dissertation deals with the relationship between liberalism and political theology. Patrici's most recent publications are "Niccolò Maquiavelli e la 'res publica' nell il secolò XXI" in *Revista Il Ponte*. LXIII nn. 8–9, August–September 2007 Firenze, Italy, and "Qué Fundó Hobbes: Notas a las lecturas de L. Strauss" in Bermudo, J. (ed.), *Del Humanismo al Humanitarismo*, Horsoi, Barcelona, 2006.

Andries Raath is Senior Professor in Constitutional Law and Philosophy of Law at the University of the Free State in South Africa. He has 30 books and approximately 250 contributions to scholarly journals on law, federalism and theologico-politically related themes to his credit. He is currently involved in projects on theological political federalism in the early modern period. He specializes on studies in Cicero, Luther, Bullinger and the work of the Dutch author Ulrich Huber.

James Read is the author of three books: *Power versus Liberty: Madison, Hamilton, Wilson and Jefferson* (Univeristy of Virginia Press, 2000), *Majority Rule versus Consensus: The Political Thought of John C. Calhoun* (University Press of Kansas, 2009), and *Doorstep Democracy: Face to Face Politics in the Heartland* (University of Minnesota, 2008), as well as several articles and book chapters. He is Professor of Political Science at the College of St. Benedict and St. John's University in Minnesota, and has also been Visiting Professor of Political Science at University of California-Davis.

David Lewis Schaefer is Professor of Political Science at College of the Holy Cross in Worcester, MA, where he teaches courses on political philosophy and American political thought. Among the books he has authored are *Illiberal Justice: John Rawls vs. the American Political Tradition* (University of Missouri Press, 2007) and *The Political Philosophy of Montaigne* (Cornell University Press, 1990). Besides his scholarly writings, he has contributed opinion journalism to such periodicals as *Wall Street Journal*, *The New York Sun*, and *National Review Online*.

Quentin Taylor is Associate Professor of History and Political Science at Rogers State University, Claremore, Oklahoma. He is the author of a number of books and articles on major political thinkers, including *The Essential Federalist* (Madison House, 1998), *The Other Machiavelli* (University Press of America, 1998), and *The Republic of Genius: A Reconstruction of Nietzsche's Early Thought* (University of Rochester, 1998). Currently Dr. Taylor is a Scholar-in-Residence at Liberty Fund, Inc.

Francesca Vassallo is Assistant Professor, Department of Political Science, University of Southern Maine. Her research interests are French political activism, European comparative political behaviour and European Union enlargement. She has published articles in *French Politics*, *Journal of Contemporary European Studies* and book chapters in edited volumes on Turkey's EU accession process and the failed EU Constitution. Her current project is a book manuscript on French styles and levels of political activism.

Scott Yenor is Associate Professor of Political Science at Boise State University. He has published articles on David Hume, Alexis de Tocqueville, the American presidency, Willa Cather, and the separation of church and state. He is currently writing a book on how modern philosophers have understood family and married life.

Acknowledgements

The Editors would like to thank the Humanities Research Institute at the University of Regina, the Dean of Campion College at the University of Regina and the Government of Saskatchewan's Student Employment Program for their generous financial support for this project. We would also like to thank Mr Kristopher Schmaltz for his excellent assistance with respect to the formatting and preparation of this manuscript. A special thank you also is due to Dr Søren Dosenrode, the Series Editor for Ashgate, whose great enthusiasm for the study of federalism and unfailing support for this project made this Research Companion possible.

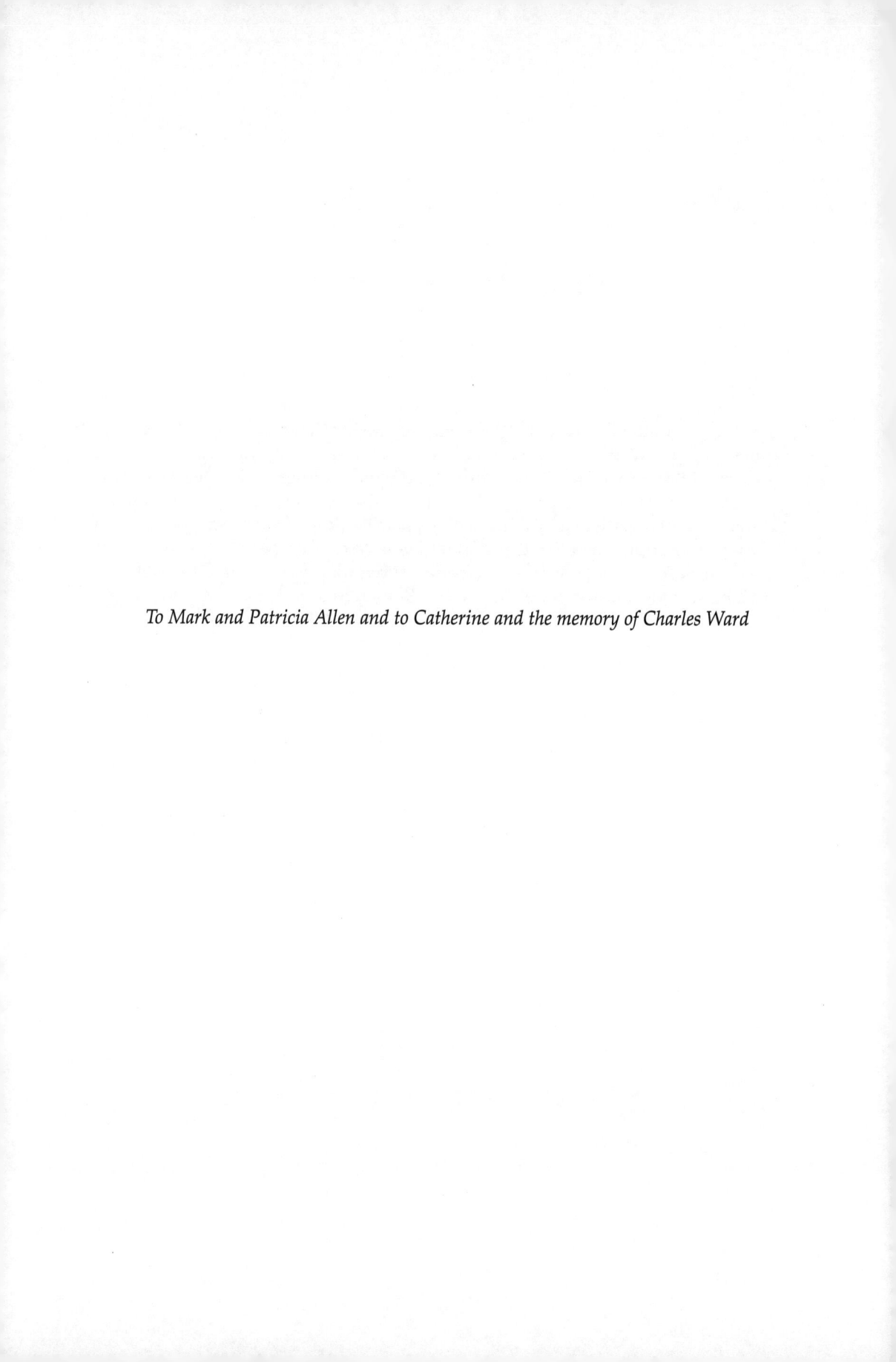

To Mark and Patricia Allen and to Catherine and the memory of Charles Ward

About the Editors

Ann Ward is an Associate Professor of Philosophy and Classics and Political Studies at Campion College, University of Regina in Canada. Her BA (Honours) is from the University of Toronto, her MA is from Brock University, and she received her PhD from Fordham University in New York City. Her previous positions have been at Converse College, Kenyon College, Ashland University, and the University of Nevada, Las Vegas. She has published articles on Herodotus, Aristotle, and Kierkegaard. She is the author of *Herodotus and the Philosophy of Empire* (Baylor University Press, 2008), and she is the editor of two volumes: *Matter and Form: From Natural Science to Political Philosophy* (Lexington Books, forthcoming), and *Socrates: Reason or Unreason as the Foundation of European Identity* (Cambridge Scholars Publishing, 2007). Her research interests are the ancient historians, ancient political philosophy, late modern and nineteenth-century political thought, and feminist philosophy. She is also on the Board of Advisory Editors for *The European Legacy: Toward New Paradigms*.

Lee Ward is an Associate Professor in the Department of Political Studies at Campion College at the University of Regina. He received his BA (Hons.) from the University of Toronto, an MA from Brock University, and a PhD in Political Science from Fordham University in New York City. He previously taught in the Department of Political Science at Kenyon College in Gambier, Ohio and was the Bradley Post-doctoral Fellow in the Program in Constitutional Government at Harvard University. His primary research interests are early modern political thought and liberal constitutional theory. He is the author of *The Politics of Liberty in England and Revolutionary America* (Cambridge, 2004) and has written articles on John Locke, Aristotle, Plato, Montesquieu, and Algernon Sidney that have appeared in the *American Political Science Review*, the *Canadian Journal of Political Science, Publius: A Journal of Federalism, The Journal of Moral Philosophy*, the *American Journal of Political Science, Interpretation: A Journal of Political Philosophy, Ratio Juris: An International Journal of Jurisprudence and Philosophy of Law*, and the *International Philosophical Quarterly*.

Federalism Studies
Series Editor: Søren Dosenrode

The end of the Cold War profoundly altered the dynamics between and within the various states in Europe and the rest of the World, resulting in a resurgence of interest in the concept of federalism. This shift in balance has been further fuelled by the increase in the number of conflicts arising from the disaffection of the diverse ethnic or religious minorities residing within these states (e.g. Sudan, Iraq). Furthermore, globalization is forcing governments not only to work together, but also to reconsider their internal roles as guarantors of economic growth, with regions playing the major part.

It is the aim of the series to look at federal or federated states in historical, theoretical and comparative contexts. Thus it will be possible to build a common framework for the constructive analysis of federalism on the meta-level, and this in turn will enable us to identify and define federal tradition traditions, and develop the theoretical.

This unique and ground-breaking new series aims to promote a complete and indepth understanding of federalism by collectively bringing together the work of political scientists, lawyers, historians, economists, sociologists and anthropologists, and with this in mind, contributions are welcomed from authors in all of these disciplines. But whereas the federal approach is the crank of the series, it does not mean that contributions must adhere to the federal approach; critical contributions are welcome too.

Also in the series

Green Leviathan
Inger Weibust
ISBN 978 0 7546 7729 1

Defunct Federalisms
Edited by Emilian Kavalski and Magdalena Zolkos
ISBN 978 0 7546 4984 7

Approaching the EUropean Federation?
Edited by Søren Dosenrode
ISBN 978 0 7546 4244 2

Introduction to the Volume

Ann Ward and Lee Ward

This research companion is designed to serve the needs of scholars interested in the theory, practice, and historical development of the principle of federalism. As such, it is hoped that it will engage researchers from a variety of specialties, perspectives, and disciplines including political theory, comparative politics, public policy, and intellectual history. Not only does this volume aim to supply a range of interpretations on the topic of federalism, it seeks to allow the researcher the flexibility to focus on chapters of specific interest to their research program, while also providing a clear overview of the academic and policy debates that characterize the field of federalism studies more generally.

The rationale for this volume rests on two fundamental premises. The first is the continuing relevance of federalism studies today and for the future. The complex political, social, and economic developments in recent times have only deepened and intensified the revival of interest in federalism that Daniel Elazar identified more than 40 years ago. The dynamic character and intrinsically flexible properties of federalism as a principle of political and social organization have brought federalism to the forefront of constitutional debates in innovative and unprecedented ways. Even a cursory glance at world politics today reveals federalism assuming renewed importance as a potential means of economic and political development in some nations, and as a promising instrument for conflict management in others. Whether it is the introduction of federal elements in old unitary states such Spain and the United Kingdom, the adaptation of intergovernmental relations in established federal states like Canada, or the great controversy surrounding the federal, or quasi-federal, trajectory of European integration, the meaning of these events for political life is unmistakable: federalism matters as much, or even more, now than it ever has.

The second premise of this volume is that the conceptual flexibility intrinsic to the idea of federalism means that federalism studies is by its very nature a "cloak of many colors." Any attempt to confine such a complex and dynamic concept as federalism to a single authoritative definition is deeply problematic. As Michael Burgess recently reminded us "there is, as yet, no fully fledged theory of federalism" (Burgess 2006, 1, 2–4). Federalism seems to be the kind of political phenomenon that cannily eludes and frustrates grand theoretical system-building, even as it so naturally invites theoretical reflection upon the most fundamental questions about the proper organization of the social and political institutions at the center of human life. This volume does not attempt to establish, propose, or defend a specific definition or conception of federalism. In each chapter of this volume, the authors have their own operating assumptions, explicit or implicit, about the meaning of federalism, and thus the volume strives to mirror the diversity of thought on the subject. While there is considerable overlap and conceptual agreement among the various contributors, there is no procrustean effort to provide a single authoritative idea of federalism. Rather the ambition for this volume is of a different sort; namely, to create a research companion of unparalleled scope and depth including the offerings of more than 30 scholars from nine countries and five continents with a range of different fields of expertise examining a variety of aspects of federal theory and practice. Our aim is to reflect as far as possible the rich conceptual diversity in federalism studies.

This is not to suggest that federalism or federalism studies are simply blank slates open to every imaginable interpretation and conceptual construction. This volume operates on the basis of two fundamental propositions. First, with respect to the idea of federalism, we propose that it is a multi-dimensional concept including both a theoretical and practical aspect, as well as a normative and empirical dimension. Practically from the beginning of the history of political thought, theorists have speculated about recognizably federal themes, just as for centuries peoples have instituted federal and quasi-federal political arrangements. This dual theoretical–practical nature produces important normative and empirical elements in the concept of federalism studies. Although it is natural to compartmentalize theoretical and practical issues given the wide range of topics covered by the field of federalism, the comprehensive scope of this research companion affords the luxury of integrating the theories and practices of federalism in a single volume. At some level, structural, legal and institutional questions about the division of power in a state and theoretical propositions concerning the nature of sovereignty inevitably point beyond themselves to fundamental issues of moral and political philosophy considering such values as liberty, tolerance, and civic engagement. Yet in another sense federalism is inextricably linked to empirical analysis. It is hard to imagine an aspect of political theory more dependent on, and modulated by, political practice than federalism. As this volume clearly demonstrates, any effort to grasp the meaning of federalism must include an understanding not only of its adaptation to a variety of local conditions, traditions, histories, and stages of economic development, but also of federalism's capacity to transform itself in the face of the ever changing dynamics of political life.

The second proposition this volume advances relates to the role of theory in federalism studies more generally. There has been much debate recently about whether federalism studies is a field "theory rich, or theory poor." This reflects an underlying concern in some quarters that the prodigious quantity and high quality of empirical studies of federalism makes treatment of theoretical issues pale by comparison. This volume hopes to demonstrate that federalism is a field "theory rich" in several senses. First, many of the offerings in this volume draw heavily from the rich body of theoretical reflection on federalism produced in the English-speaking world over the past 50 years. Theorists such as K.C. Wheare, William Riker, Daniel Elazar, Michael Burgess, Thomas Hueglin, and Ronald Watts inform and provide the conceptual ballast for many of the contributions to this volume. These scholars and their influence clearly belie any suggestion that federalism is a study theory poor.

Moreover, this volume strives to reconnect, or perhaps reacquaint, contemporary thinking on federalism with the vast theoretical resources discoverable in the history of political thought. There are Parts covering thinkers and topics ranging from classical antiquity and medieval political theology through to early modern history and political philosophy, as well as the modern American, European, and international theories and experiences of federalism. These chapters promise to approach familiar subjects from a fresh perspective, as well as provide an introduction of sorts to exciting federal dimensions in thinkers hitherto neglected in federalism studies. Finally, this volume builds upon, and draws connections between, the work of scholars exploring the rich elements of both the Anglo-American and Continental traditions of political thought. Indeed, the broad scope of this research companion allows it to move even further to suggest possibilities and limits of federalism in the context of indigenous thought and experience outside of the western tradition by turning to Africa and the Islamic world. As this study hopes to demonstrate, federalism studies is a field marked by diffuse and often untapped theoretical sources, and this broadening and deepening of philosophical reflection on federalism can complement our growing awareness of political practice in federal systems.

Naturally, any attempt to encapsulate an idea as broad and influential as federalism in a single volume inevitably confronts certain limitations. First of all, while many of the chapters throughout the research companion explore and acknowledge the enormous contribution of empirical studies to research involving such topics as fiscal federalism (e.g. Chapter 24) and intergovernmental relations (e.g. Chapter 25), the primary focus of the volume is on historical and conceptual analysis. As such, the volume considers but does not focus on analysis of a number of recent path breaking empirical studies on the workings of federalism with respect to the efficient provision of public goods and different national experiences of subnational fiscal discipline (Rodden 2006), the management of territorially, culturally, linguistically, and ethnically divided societies (Amoretti and Bermeo 2004), or with respect to the functioning of intrastate relations in different federal systems (Bolleyer 2006). Although these developments in empirical research are not the focus of this volume, these important recent studies suggest exciting new possibilities for federalism studies that complement the historical and theoretical emphasis of this research companion.

The obvious attraction and value of the comparative approach to federalism presents a second kind of limitation. While Part 6 of this volume examines a number of important case studies of federalism in the international context, the length constraints placed even on a comprehensive volume of this nature makes any sustained effort to develop comparative analysis difficult. Thus, while this volume offers an overview of the comparative approach to federalism, it does not attempt to replicate the several important, and highly detailed, studies in comparative federalism that have appeared in recent times (e.g., Watts 1999, Wachtendorfer-Schmidt 2000, Hueglin and Fenna 2006, Burgess 2006, Lazar and Leuprecht 2007). There is also the difficulty of incorporating new research into ongoing projects that are near completion. For instance, Daniel Ziblatt's recent work demonstrating the crucial role played by the infrastructural capacity of subnational units as a factor in the emergence of federal states represents an important development that many federalism scholars have not had time yet to assimilate into their work (Ziblatt 2006). With respect to this book and the others indicated above, we strongly encourage the researcher and student of federalism to consult these works and to reflect upon their findings.

Another limitation facing even a volume with a strong conceptual and historical focus is, of course, the difficulty in deciding which thinkers and traditions require close examination and which will not receive as much attention. The criterion for selection of topics in this volume is primarily a consideration of what is necessary to keep an already large volume to a manageable size. Arguably historical figures such as Georg Waitz and James Bryce, as well as more recent thinkers such as Carl Friedrich, K.C. Wheare, Rufus Davis, Preston King, Ivo Duchacek, Michael Burgess, Ronald Watts, and others, could each certainly warrant an entire chapter dedicated to an examination of their work. Perhaps the same can be said with respect to the anarcho-federalist and Marxist federalist traditions. While we fully appreciate the contribution to the development of federalism studies by these thinkers and schools of thought, it is simply impossible to afford every important aspect of federal theory the close attention it deserves while maintaining the coherence and fluency of the volume. Happily, however, these thinkers and their impact on the contemporary understanding of federalism are considered throughout the chapters and provide crucial reference points for the various discussions in the volume. In our effort to combine the goals of comprehensiveness and attention to detail we have tried to strike a balance, which we hope will prove to be intelligible and sensible to the reader.

This research companion is divided into six Parts. Each Part begins with a substantive introduction outlining its contents. Therefore, in this general introduction it is perhaps best to simply explain the rationale for the structural design of the volume. The intention is to allow for the exploration of federalism in all its multifarious character paying attention both to theory and practice, as well as its historical development as a concept and the various regional experiences of federal systems. The first Part, "Classical and Judeo-Christian Images of Federalism," provides a suggestive and atypical starting point for our analysis. While federalism is usually associated with the rise of the modern nation-state idea in the seventeenth century, this Part begins by examining pre-modern treatments of recognizably federal themes in Greek antiquity, medieval Christianity, and Reformation political theology. The classical and Judeo-Christian traditions not only included rich sources of reflection on the moral foundations of political community; they also generated motifs, concepts, and practical debates about the articulated arrangement and division of political power that will be familiar to a modern audience. Whether it is the ancient Greek notions of alliances and leagues, the biblical ideal of covenant, or medieval debates about the complex compound nature of the relation of the church and political society, there is clear evidence of "federal thinking" that reflects both the limits and possibilities of federalism in the pre-modern world. This Part suggests that the principle of federalism, in some form, has an older and more diverse origin than is often recognized.

The second Part, "The Origins of Modern Federalism," brings us to more familiar ground for federalism studies. There is little doubt that federalism first emerged as a sustained subject of substantive theoretical reflection and practical political experience in the modern period. The seventeenth century notably witnessed the rise of the modern nation-state with a definite and distinct conception of sovereignty. This period also arguably marks the genesis of the modern conception of federalism. This Part proposes that sovereignty and federalism in their recognizably modern form share a common ancestry and to some extent a causal relation. The dominant idea of unitary sovereignty championed in the sixteenth and seventeenth centuries by Jean Bodin, Thomas Hobbes, and Samuel Pufendorf, and modified by the English Whigs to produce the doctrine of parliamentary sovereignty, inspired a strong reaction and counter-tradition of federal theory as a response to the modern unitary state and the theoretical and practical problems associated with it. The early modern federalists in Europe considered in this Part reflect various concerns including the need to explain the political obligations of religious minorities in heterogeneous monarchies, to provide a theoretical account of the complex system of diffuse power inherited from feudalism, and most notably an abiding fear that excessive concentration of power in a polity is a threat to liberty and enlightenment. Federalism in early modern Europe was, then, a diverse subject and a flexible concept employed to rehabilitate ancient ideas of confederation, establish new principles of association for old heterogeneous political entities, and to control some of the more destructive and authoritarian tendencies in the modern Leviathan.

Parts 3 and 4 turn to the American and Continental inheritors of the early modern tradition of federal thought. In "Federalism and the Early American Republic," our authors examine the impact of the Revolution that established the first modern federal state created by constitutional design. Between the Founding and the Civil War period American statesmen and thinkers fused federal theory and practice in unprecedented ways. The model of "constitutional federalism" they produced derived from a complex variety of influences including both the colonists' long experience of local self-government under British imperial rule, and the intense theoretical debates between Federalists and the inaptly named Anti-federalists over the correct arrangement and division of political power in a compound republic. As several of the chapters in this Part make clear, national politics in the United States in the first century of its existence was dominated by fierce debates about the nature of American federalism produced by the issues of slavery and territorial expansion. The thought and experiences of Americans in the early republic illustrate both the great dangers and possibilities confronting federal states in the modern period.

Part 4, "European Federalism," examines the Continental tradition of federal thought and practice ranging from the nineteenth century through to present-day battles over the meaning of European integration. For much of this period Continental political theory was characterized by the deep antipathy to federalism originating in the French revolutionary idea of the unitary state and the drive toward centralization associated with the nineteenth-century age of nationalism. However, this Part reveals a rich and textured federalist sub-tradition in European political thought at this time. In the Frenchman Louis Le Fur, the German Carl Schmitt, the Italian Alterio Spinelli, and the Yugoslav Edvard Kardelj, Europeans find indigenous sources of sophisticated federal theory that would prove to be quite distinctive from the older American version of constitutional federalism. This vital sub-tradition supplies important theoretical resources for Europeans trying to conceptualize the federal, or quasi-federal, character of recent moves toward greater European Union integration. The proposed changes to EU institutions and the relations of member states to European bodies have already produced serious reflection on the evolving concept of "treaty federalism" emerging as an alternative to traditional American constitutional federalism. As the concluding chapters in this Part amply demonstrate, both the supporters and opponents of greater European integration offer arguments that could have a serious impact on our understanding of federalism in the future.

The fifth Part, "Contemporary Theories of Federalism," serves two functions. First, it provides chapters dealing with the work of two of the most important federal theorists in recent times – William Riker and Daniel Elazar. With these two thinkers, we can see how federalism was incorporated into very different emerging theoretical perspectives, rational-choice theory and covenant theology respectively. These chapters offer detailed studies explaining the significance of Riker's and Elazar's work and their impact on federalism studies. This Part also offers insights into the interplay of theory and practice in federalism by which theoretical innovations often arise in response to practical policy conditions. In chapters treating fiscal federalism and the changing nature of intergovernmental relations in "post-modern" federal states, we see how federal theory has adapted to, and will likely continue to evolve in the face of ever changing economic, social and political conditions.

The final Part, "Regional Experiences of Federalism," presents a comprehensive survey of a variety of federal systems in a global context. In order to express the sense of federalism as a cloak of many colors, this Part includes not only probing treatments of recent developments and contemporary issues of federalism in familiar case studies such as the United States, Australia, and India. It also considers less familiar, and less obvious, examples of the actual practice or potentiality for federalism in different regions of the world. One chapter examines Latin American federalism and the role a renewed conception of federalism is playing to promote democratization and economic development in countries such as Mexico and Brazil. There are also innovative chapters reflecting upon the limits and possibilities for federalism in Africa and the Islamic world. At a time when federalism is held out by some as a potential solution for deep constitutional and political problems and conflicts in developing nations as varied as South Africa, Sudan, post-war Iraq, and Afghanistan, these chapters inquire: Are there indigenous federal elements in the political culture of these regions? Why has federalism historically not been successful in these places before and what are the chances there for flourishing federal systems in the future? With this concluding Part, we re-examine some of the oldest and most successful federal states, even as we look towards emerging new frontiers for federalism studies on the horizon.

This research companion is a comprehensive examination of a political idea whose importance in our world is immense. Offering a close examination of the past, a broad survey of the present and a penetrating look to the future, this volume considers federalism in its varied contours and subtle shades. In order to serve the needs of researchers and students of federalism alike, it strives to reflect in full measure the complexity of the principle to which it is devoted.

References

Amoretti, Ugo M. and Nancy Bermeo, eds (2004), *Federalism and Territorial Cleavages*. (Baltimore: Johns Hopkins University Press).
Bolleyer, Nicole (2006), Federal dynamics in Canada, the United States, and Switzerland: how substates' internal organization affects intergovernmental relations, *Publius: The Journal of Federalism* 36:4, 471–502.
Burgess, Michael (2006), *Comparative Federalism: Theory and Practice*. (New York: Routledge).
Hueglin, Thomas O. and Alan Fenna (2006), *Comparative Federalism: A Systematic Inquiry*. (Peterborough, ON: Broadview Press).
Lazar, Harvey and Christian Leuprecht, eds (2007), *Spheres of Governance: Comparative Studies of Cities in Multilevel Governance Systems*. (Kingston: Queen's Policy Studies).
Rodden, Jonathan A. (2006), *Hamilton's Paradox: The Promise and Perils of Fiscal Federalism*. (New York: Cambridge University Press).
Wachtendorfer-Schmidt, Ute, ed. (2000), *Federalism and Political Performance*. (London: Routledge).
Watts, Ronald L. (1999), *Comparing Federal Systems*, 2nd Edition. (Montreal & Kingston: McGill–Queen's University Press).
Ziblatt, Daniel (2006), Structuring the state: the formation of Italy and Germany and the puzzle of federalism. (Princeton: Princeton University Press).

PART 1
CLASSICAL AND JUDEO-CHRISTIAN IMAGES OF FEDERALISM

Introduction to Part 1

This Part explores the roots of federal theory and practice in classical Greek antiquity and medieval and Reformation Europe. In Chapter 1, Ann Ward and Sara MacDonald consider the writings of Herodotus and Thucydides to discover what can be learned from the ancients about the origins of nascent federal structures and their collapse into empire. Ward and MacDonald argue that the alliance of Greek cities formed during the Persian Wars to save Greece from subjection to the Persian Empire, recorded by Herodotus in the *Histories*, resembles the federal republic described by Montesquieu in the *Spirit of the Laws*. Moreover, as Montesquieu argues that successful federal polities should be grounded in republican institutions, Herodotus points to Athens and its democratic regime as the locus of the Greek federal alliance formed to resist the Persians. The Athenian democracy is grounded in *isegorie*, or the equality and freedom of speech, which, Herodotus suggests, signals the withdrawal of the divine and the emergence of the human as the source of politics. The democracy's transition from a divine to a naturalistic basis of politics allowed the Athenian mind to grasp other universal truths, such as the universal nature of human beings. In his account of the battle of Marathon, Herodotus shows that the Athenians, seeing the human being in its universality, can look on the other and see themselves. This ability allows the Athenians, as demonstrated by Herodotus in his account of the Greek mission to Gelon of Syracuse, to overcome their desire for honour and yield the leadership of the Greek alliance to the Spartans. The Greek federal alliance is thereby formed and endures long enough to save Greece from subjection to Persia.

Turning to Thucydides' *Peloponnesian War*, Ward and MacDonald argue that Athens' naturalistic and demystified view of the cosmos, which upheld the Greek alliance during the Persian Wars, causes the collapse of such federal structures into empire after those wars. Four episodes are considered: the Athenian address to the Spartans, Pericles' funeral oration, the Mytilenean debate, and the Melian dialogue. Thucydides' narrative of these four episodes shows that with the withdrawal of the divine and the defeat of the Persians, the desire for honour resurfaces in Athens and becomes attached to a desire for freedom ungrounded in any principle of moderation to determine what this freedom is for. Such an honour-driven and unconditioned pursuit of freedom leads Athens into an imperial policy that seeks one power after another as it subordinates the claims of justice to those of expediency. Thus, by the time of the Melian dialogue we see Athens descend into the cruelty and barbarism of genocide and mass enslavement. Athens' enslavement of other Greek cities leads to its confrontation with Sparta during the Peloponnesian War and the eventual destruction of its democratic regime at home.

Ward and MacDonald argue that the instability and collapse of nascent federalism and democracy in the Greek world does not lead the ancient writers to long for a return to the piety of the pre-democratic condition. In order to limit the almost limitless desire for freedom and domination that arose in Athens, Ward and MacDonald suggest that Herodotus and Thucydides point ahead to the type of discursive philosophy found in the Platonic dialogue to provide principles of moderation that can guide freedom, and thus preserve federal structures and the democratic institutions on which they are built.

In Chapter 2, Nicholas Aroney finds the origins of federalism not in classical Greek politics, but rather in the thought of medieval, Catholic Europe. According to Aroney, *federalism*, understood to designate a certain body of ideas having significant influence on modern political organizations known as *federations*, has its root in the medieval political philosophy of the thirteenth-century Catholic theologian and saint Thomas Aquinas. As a set of ideas originating with Aquinas, federalism, Aroney argues, is premised on human reason and divine revelation, political philosophy and political theology. Aquinas attempts to synthesize classical political philosophy with Christian revelation. Thus, while in agreement with Aristotle that specifically human ends could be realized in the *polis*, Aquinas goes further and proposes that humanity's ultimate end is eternal life, as revealed in sacred scripture. Aquinas, therefore, departs from Aristotle in developing a conception of the separation between church and state, in which the church wields spiritual authority and is responsible for the salvation of the soul, and the state wields temporal authority and is responsible for civil welfare. Moreover, whereas Aristotle philosophized simply about the *polis*, Aquinas addresses a wide range of both private and public associations that formed "societies" within the larger societies of church and state. Church and state possessed a "unity of order" in which households, neighbourhoods, villages, cities and provinces in the case of the state, and parishes, dioceses and archdioceses in the case of the church, each possessed a degree of both self-sufficiency and interdependence within the larger body.

Aroney argues that the theories of separation of church and state and the "unity of order" developed in the thought of Aquinas and adopted and expanded upon by Jean Quidort and Nicolas Cusanus of the conciliar movement of the fourteenth and fifteenth centuries, had significant impact on modern thinking about federalism. Specifically, these theories divide power between, and hence limit the jurisdiction of, two important authorities: the Church, headed by the Pope, and the state, usually understood as headed by the Holy Roman Emperor. Moreover, the "unity of order" leaves room for the independent operation of constituent units at different levels within church and state, while at the same time allowing the integration and participation of these units in the operation of the whole.

Shaun de Freitas and Andries Raath, in Chapter 3, turn to Reformation covenantal political theology in sixteenth- and seventeenth-century Europe to explore the roots

Introduction to Part 1

of the federal tradition in modern law and politics. De Freitas and Raath argue that the set of ideas embodied in the term "federalism" were first expressed in the term "covenantal". "Covenantal" is derived from the idea of the biblical covenant between God and the descendents of Abraham that emphasized the rule of God's law over the nation of Israel, and elevated that community's sense of responsibility toward God. The covenantal political perspective of the biblical text was revitalized in Europe during the Reformation. Crucial to this revitalization was a sixteenth-century thinker from Zurich, Heinrich Bullinger, who proposed that the reformed "Christian Covenanted Community" was a restoration of the biblical covenant in the Europe of his day. Such a covenant, according to de Freitas and Raath, denotes a bilateral and conditional relationship between God and man and between man and man. The nation is understood to be in covenant with God, and the government is understood as required to facilitate the keeping of the conditions of the covenant; to aid God's people, in their judicial and civil life, and to fulfill God's law in the Christian Commonwealth.

Thinkers such as Philippe Duplessis-Mornay and Johannes Althusius furthered Bullinger's thought by developing the concept of a dual covenant within the covenantal ideal. There is a covenant between God and king in which the king or magistrate is obliged to govern justly, thus procuring the glory of God, and a covenant between king and people in which the people agree to obey the king or magistrate provided his rule is and continues to be just. De Freitas and Raath emphasize that in the covenant between king and people the king is understood as the first to promise, and the people only after such promise is made, thus adding an important democratic element to covenantal political theology. Seventeenth-century Scottish political theorist and political actor Samuel Rutherford, de Freitas and Raath argue, forms the apex of the biblically founded covenantal-political paradigm. Guided by Rutherford, the *Solemn League and Covenant*, the document that was produced by the Westminster Assembly of Scottish, English and Irish reformers in 1643, is a continuation of the theological political federalism of early reformers such as Bullinger, Mornay, and Althusius. Moreover, Rutherford deepens the democratic strain introduced into covenantal political thought. King and people are in a mutual covenant with God in which the king receives the crown on condition that he compel obedience to the true (reformed) religion, and the people are obliged to *compel* the king to preserve the true religion against heresy and idolatry. Rutherford points to such revolutionary precedent as the people directing the government's actions because failure to do so in this context would sever the nation's covenant with God.

De Freitas and Raath argue that the covenantal political theology of Reformed Christianity contributed to the modern development of federalism precisely because it bridged the medieval separation between church and state. The state was reconceived as a polity in direct covenant with God, thus transferring emphasis from unlimited state sovereignty in its separate sphere to magisterial power subject to the law of God and limited by the people.

The chapters in this Part point to both the tension and interdependence between reason and revelation as the grounds for federal ideas and institutions. Ward and MacDonald look back to the reason embodied in the classical regime as that which can allow for federal polities to form, and point to the reason of classical political philosophy as that which can prevent their demise. Aroney then turns to the synthesis of the classical political philosophy of Aristotle with the divine revelation of the Bible found in the thought of Thomas Aquinas to explain the origins of federalism. For Aroney, Aquinas' theological-philosophical reflections on federalism bridge the divide between medieval and modern political thought and practice. De Freitas and Raath conclude the Part by considering the rejection of classical politics and philosophy altogether in favour of the biblical tradition in the theological-political thought of Reformation Europe. Christian reformers developed a covenantal political theology to ground the new Christian Commonwealth dedicated to preserving the new religion and which, de Freitas and Raath argue, serves the basis for the modern theories and practices of federalism that were to arise.

Nascent Federalism and its Limits in Ancient Greece: Herodotus and Thucydides

Ann Ward and Sara MacDonald

The writers of Greek antiquity are not typically regarded as shedding light on the possibilities and limits of federal structures. However, renewed consideration of the Greek historians Herodotus and Thucydides show that the ancients have much to teach us about the origins of federal polities and the centripetal forces that pull them apart and cause the collapse into empire. In the *Histories*, Herodotus, like Montesquieu, suggests that it may be necessary that federal polities be composed solely of republics rather than monarchies or some combination of the two (Montesquieu 1989, 132–33). It is to such republican or democratic institutions in Athens that we turn when considering the account of the war between Persia and Greece in Herodotus' history. The federal alliance of Greek cities formed to save Greece from subjection to the Persian empire is cemented by an oath, pointing to a foundation in the gods to limit the alliance. However, Herodotus shows that within its leading city, Athens, there is a withdrawal of the divine and the emergence of the human as the source of politics. Herodotus suggests that the democracy's transition from a divine to a naturalistic basis of politics gives the Athenian mind access to other universal truths, such as the universal nature of human beings. As a result, the Athenians, seeing the human being in its universality, can look on the other and see themselves. This allows the Athenians to lay aside their desire for honour and yield the formal command of the Greeks to the Spartans. The Greek federal alliance is thereby formed and endures long enough to triumph over the Persians.

Consideration of Thucydides' *Peloponnesian War* reinforces the theme of Athenian impiety. Thus, Thucydides shows that Athens' activities are directed by a desire for freedom ungrounded in any principle of moderation with which to determine what this freedom is for. Athens, therefore, soon engages in a quest for freedom from all limitations, even of the federal alliance itself, dominating and enslaving all of its members. Athens' naturalistic and demystified view of the cosmos, which allowed it to uphold the Greek alliance during the Persian wars, causes its destruction after those wars. Pursuing an immoderate freedom understood as power and domination, Athens embarks on an imperial project of its own. The imperialism of Athens leads to its confrontation with Sparta in the Peloponnesian War, and its eventual defeat and destruction of its democratic regime. The ancients, therefore, suggest that in the absence of the gods or a powerful common enemy, another principle of moderation is needed to limit the desire for freedom and preserve federations and the democratic institutions in which they are grounded.

Nascent Federalism in the *Histories*

In the *Histories* Herodotus reports that Xerxes, after ascending the Persian throne, declared his intention to bridge the Hellespont and drive his forces through Europe into Greece (7.8).[1] Xerxes explained to the Persian nobility, "if we subdue [Athens] and their neighbours in the land of Pelops … we shall show to all a Persian empire that has the same limit as Zeus's sky … the sun will look down upon no country that has a border with ours, but I shall make them all one country, once I have passed in my progress through Europe" (7.8). Upon learning of Xerxes' coming invasion and wishing to resist, Herodotus tells us that, "all the Greeks who were of the better persuasion assembled together and exchanged their judgments and their pledges with one another" (7.145). They also did away with all internal enmities and wars, the most important at the time being that between Athens and Aegina. According to Herodotus, "[t]he thought behind all this … was that the entire Greek people might somehow unite and take common action, since the invaders threatened all Greeks alike" (7.145).

The epoch-making clash between the Persian Empire and the Greek world is thus initiated, the account of which is the centrepiece of the broad political panorama of Herodotus' *Histories*. Moreover, the alliance of Greek cities formed to save Greece from subjugation to Persia resembles the federal republic described by Montesquieu as "a society of societies that make a new one", federating for the purposes of external force and collective security, and which, according to Montesquieu, "made Greece flourish for so long" (Montesquieu 1989, 131). The key difficulty that had to be overcome if this Greek federal polity was to take shape was the controversial question of leadership. Who would lead the Greeks in their struggle against Persian imperialism, and thus who would be accorded the first in honour among them? The most logical choice would have been the Athenians, as they contributed the largest contingent of ships to the Greek fleet and it was in their ships that the outcome of the war was decided. As Herodotus asserts, "[i]f there had been no opposition to Xerxes at sea … all of Greece would have been subdued by the Persians. So … a man who declares that the Athenians were the saviors of Greece would hit the very truth" (7.139). Yet, despite being the premier

---

1 Herodotus, *The History*. David Grene trans. (Chicago: University of Chicago Press, 1987), 446. All subsequent citations will be taken from this edition.

naval power in Greece and thus responsible for preserving Greek freedom against the Persian threat, the allies, according to Herodotus, "refused to follow the Athenians as leaders; unless a Laconian was in the chief position, they declared that they would break up the projected force" (8.2). Faced with such opposition, the Athenians yielded the formal command of the fleet to the Spartan Eurybiades, allowing the Greek alliance to form. The Athenians gave way to the Spartans in this matter because, Herodotus claims, "they thought what mattered most was the survival of Greece and knew very well that if there was a dispute about the leadership, Greece would perish" (8.2) (but see Harrison 2002, 574). The Athenians, therefore, to borrow a concept from Robert Cooper, engaged in a "postmodern" federal policy in which they spoke "multilaterally", as it were, to further their ability to in fact act "unilaterally" in the service of Greece (Cooper 2002).

What is it about the Athenians that allows them to conceal or soften their power to officially take orders from others and thus effectively cooperate with their allies? This is the question that is explored below. It will emerge that, for Herodotus, Athens' ability to yield the formal leadership of the alliance to the Spartans arises from their democratic regime. It is therefore to the nature of the democracy in Athens that we shall turn first.

Democracy and Speech in Athens

During the reign of Xerxes' father Darius in Persia, Athens was freed from her tyrants. The Alcmaeonidae, a prominent Athenian family under the leadership of Cleisthenes, played a key role in this transition. According to Herodotus they bribed the Pythian priestess to order the Spartans, whenever they came to Delphi, to free their city (5.62, 5.63, 5.66). The Spartans, obeying the Pythia, raised an army under King Cleomenes and entered the city of Athens, expelling the tyrant Hippias and his family after 36 years of tyrannical rule (5.63, 5.64). However, after the expulsion of the tyrants factious war broke out in Athens between Cleisthenes of the Alcmaeonidae and Isagoras (5.66). When losing to Isagoras in the struggle for supreme power, Cleisthenes, according to Herodotus, took the common people (*demou*), previously "deprived of all rights", into partnership (5.66, 5.69). This added power of the people allowed Cleisthenes to defeat Isagoras, from which the democratic regime emerged.

In order to win the people to his side, Herodotus says that Cleisthenes divided the tribes of Athens into ten from four, and, expelling the old Ionian tribal names, renamed all the tribes except one after native Athenian heroes (5.66). With his account of Cleisthenes' renaming of the tribes, Herodotus shows patriotic sentiment at the foundation of the new regime. Thus, the Athenians support their regime not because it is a product of the divine, but because they believe it is "theirs". Athenians believe it is theirs, Herodotus indicates, in two ways. First, with the renaming of the tribes the regime is understood as Athenian, or native. Second, after the expulsion of the tyrants, Athens is characterized by *isegorie*, or the equal right of free speech (5.78). All, therefore, share equally in deliberation, and thus all, it is thought, participate equally in the city's decisions (5.78) (but see Ostwald 1969, 147, 153–57; Vlastos 1973, 172–74). The Athenians themselves are the regime, and the human is brought to light as the source of politics. Thus, what people say of the regime, that "it is ours", and what it actually is, a product of human agency, come together. The ability to capture what the regime is in speech allows the Athenians to internalize their regime. They believe it to be something within themselves and not a product of something outside of themselves. This internalization leads to their willingness at both the battle of Marathon and the battle of Salamis to forsake their city walls and therewith Athens' physical location (6.103; 8.40–41). Athenians become characterized by motion because their city is not in its external manifestations but in themselves or their mind – Athens becomes an "idea". The Athenians have external motion, manifested in their ships, but internal rest; they have an "idea" of the city within themselves.

The democracy founded by Cleisthenes through the institution of *isegorie* or the equality and freedom of speech provides the basis for the rise of Athens as a military power. Herodotus reveals the connection between free speech and military effectiveness when reflecting on the new democracy's defeat of the invading Boeotians and Chalcidians (5.74, 5.77). Of this double victory, Herodotus remarks:

> *So Athens had increased in greatness. It is not only in respect of one thing but of everything that equality and free speech [isegorie] are clearly a good [spoudaion]; take the case of Athens, which under the rule of [tyrants] proved no better in war than any of her neighbors but, once rid of those [tyrants], was far the first of all.*
>
> *What this makes clear is that when held in subjection they would not do their best, for they were working for a taskmaster, but, when freed [eleutherothenton], they sought to win, because each was trying to achieve for his very self.* (5.78)

Herodotus indicates in this passage that the internal freedom reflected by *isegoria* is better than tyranny because it supported the Athenian superiority in war (see Forsdyke 2001, 348; Raaflaub 2004, 59–61, 86; Euben 1986, 368–69; but see Fornara 1971, 48–99; and Pelling 2002, 131, 150–53). The expulsion of the tyrants and the institution of *isegorie* meant that now each person, when fighting for the city, fought for themselves rather than the tyrant. Each felt a sense of ownership in the regime, and that the city served their interests (see Ostwald 1969, 159–60). This identification of the city with the self drastically improved the fighting spirit and hence the military effectiveness of the Athenians. Thus, Herodotus indicates that the community of speech – or the democratic regime – shared by all and reflecting the soul, allowed each and was used by each to pursue his own private advantage (Benardete 1969, 146).

Marathon, Gelon and the Emergence of the Human

In his account of the expulsion of the tyrants and the introduction of democracy in Athens, Herodotus points to the unity of self-interest with the city's interest as an explanation for the connection between democracy and Athenian military superiority. Yet, another more fundamental cause of this connection, made possible by equality and freedom of speech, is the Athenian mind's access to universal truths, such as the nature of the human qua human.

Herodotus reveals the potential of the Athenian regime to make possible the mind's access to universal or natural truth in his account of the battle of Marathon (see Thompson 1996, 37–44). According to Herodotus, the Persian King Darius, ostensibly to punish those Greeks who took part in the Ionian revolt and the burning of Sardis, sent a Persian expedition under the command of Datis and Artaphrenes against Greece, "with instructions to enslave Athens and Eretria and to bring the slaves before him" (5.102, 5.105; 6.94). However, Herodotus says that the real reason for the expedition was Darius' desire to conquer those Greeks who had refused to give him earth and water and thereby subjugate all of Greece (6.44, 6.48–49, 6.94). Thus, after subduing the Greek islands of Naxos, Delos and Carystus, and then conquering and enslaving the Eretrians, Datis and Artaphrenes put ashore in Attica just north of the city of Athens and, accompanied by the recently expelled tyrant Hippias, encamped at Marathon (6.96, 6.97, 6.99, 6.101).

On learning of the Persian position at Marathon, Herodotus says, "the Athenians too marched out to Marathon" under the leadership of their "ten generals", the most important of whom was Miltiades (6.103). Having been refused help by the Spartans who said they would not leave their territory during the Carnea festival, the Athenians, according to Herodotus, were joined at Marathon by the Plataeans (6.105–106, 6.108). On the day in which it was Miltiades' turn to command the troops, the battle lines were drawn up, and the Athenians and Plataeans charged and routed the Persians under Datis and Artaphrenes (6.111–12).

Herodotus maintains that one of the chief reasons that the Athenians won a great victory over the Persians at Marathon was that, of the Greeks, they were "the first to face the sight of the Median dress and the men who wore it. For till then, the Greeks were terrified even to hear the names of the Medes" (6.112). The Athenians were able to hear Persian names and see Persian clothing and thus to face the Persians as Persians, or the Persians in their particularity or otherness. Moreover, the Athenians, characterized by a democratic regime in which the human comes to light as the source of politics, were able to look on the men who wore Persian clothing without fear as well, and thus were able to look on the Persians not only as Persians, but also as human beings like themselves. They could see the Persians "naked", as it were, or the universality of human nature that lies concealed beneath the convention of "clothing". In other words, Herodotus indicates that the Athenians at Marathon were victorious because they could look on the other and see the same. They could look on that which was particular and foreign and see the universal characteristics that they shared.

In his account of the Greek mission to Gelon of Syracuse, Herodotus illustrates the connection between the Athenian ability to see themselves in the other and their ability to give the appearance of a relative equality among the Greeks by obeying the Spartans. After learning of Darius' son Xerxes' intention to subjugate all of Greece, those Greeks, as mentioned previously, who wished to preserve their freedom, ended all enmities and wars between themselves and formed an alliance to resist the Persian onslaught (7.145). They also sent envoys to various other Greek cities with an invitation to join them in their fight against the Persians. One such city was Syracuse, ruled by the powerful tyrant Gelon (7.145). Upon arriving in Syracuse the Spartan envoy Syagrus spoke first, assuring Gelon that Xerxes planned to subdue all of Greece, and that if he defeated the Spartans in battle Xerxes would quickly move on to Syracuse and all of Sicily. The only way, therefore, to repel the attack of the "barbarian", was for all of Greece to draw together, thus being "fighters of consideration for any invader" (7.157). Gelon offered to help the Greek cause by supplying men and equipment, but on condition that, "I [Gelon] shall be the Captain and leader of the Greeks against the barbarian. On no other condition will I myself go or send any others" (7.158). Infuriated, Syagrus burst out and said, "Loud will be the lamentation of Agamemnon, son of Pelops, if he heard the leadership had been taken from the Spartans ... If you do not think fit to obey our orders, do not come to our help" (7.159).

Gelon, angrily rebuffed by the Spartan envoy, modified his condition, proposing that, "you [Spartans] lead the land army and I the fleet. Or if it is your pleasure to command the fleet, I am willing to take the land army" (7.160). However, Herodotus says, "the messenger from Athens answered before he of Lacedaemon could do so" (7.161). This Athenian envoy spoke to Gelon as follows:

> *As long as you were demanding the command of all the Greek host, we of Athens were content to keep silent, knowing well that the Laconian was able to make an answer for both of us. But since now, when you are turned aside from the project of commanding the whole, you are demanding the command of the fleet, here is this for you: even if the Laconian were ready to surrender this to you, we are not. This command is ours, providing the Lacedae-monians do not want it. If they want to have the command, we will stand down for them, but we will not yield the command at sea to anyone else (7.161)*

Unable to acquire a leadership position and facing another Carthaginian invasion, Gelon did not join the Greek alliance against the Persians.

Herodotus' account of the Greek mission to Gelon of Syracuse reveals important differences between Spartans and Athenians. The Spartans, interrupted by the Athenians before they could respond to Gelon's second proposal because they "were ready to surrender" the command of the fleet to him, are not aware that the Athenians will resist this demand. Herodotus indicates, however, that the Athenians, "knowing well that the Laconian was able to make an answer for both", are aware that the Spartans will resist Gelon's demand to command the whole of the forces. Herodotus therefore illustrates that whereas the Spartans do not know and understand the Athenians, the Athenians know and understand the Spartans. In contrast to the Spartans, the Athenians know the other; they can put themselves, intellectually, in the other's place, or walk in their shoes, as it were. Moreover, Herodotus shows that the Athenian ability to put themselves intellectually in another's place is related to their ability to give up their pride or their desire to be seen as first. The Spartans, outraged at the suggestion that they obey the orders of others, rebuff Gelon's proposal to command the whole because under no circumstances will they give up the command that they desire to anyone. The Athenians, on the other hand, although they too rebuff Gelon, are willing to give up the command of the fleet to the Spartans. Herodotus therefore illustrates that unlike the Spartans, who are primarily motivated by pride or their self-regarding desire for honour, the Athenians are willing to "stand down for them". Swallowing their pride and yielding the formal command of the fleet to the Spartans because the allies refused to obey their direct orders, the Athenians kept the Greek allies united against the imperial threat from Persia.

An Athenian Turn to Empire?

The Athenians, in their desire to save Greece from being absorbed into the Persian Empire, accept a Spartan leadership that brings the Greek alliance into being. The outward semblance of equality that conceals or softens Athens' actual superiority causes a federal structure to take shape that allows the Greeks to cooperate effectively in repelling the Persian invasion. Yet can Athenian moderation outlive this immediate threat to Greece? Or will their strength finally manifest itself in a turn to an imperial project of their own? Herodotus seems to concede as much when he admits that the Athenians accepted Spartan leadership "only so long as they had urgent need of the others, as they later proved. For as soon as they had driven out the Persians and were fighting for his territory rather than their own, the Athenians stripped the Lacedaemonians of their primacy" (8.3). Herodotus further reveals the imperialist impulse at work in Athens by leaving the Athenian fleet, after their victory against the Persians in the battle of Mycale at the close of the *Histories*, attacking and subjugating the Greek city of Sestos in the Chersonese (9.114–20). Thus, Herodotus suggests that what allows Athens to preserve the freedom of Greece can also make Athens imperial thereby destroying the freedom of Greece. After the withdrawal of the divine and the external power of Persia, will the Athenians, lacking a principle of moderation, attempt to impose on the political world the universality that their regime allows them to grasp in the natural world? (See Immerwahr 1966; Forsdyke 2006, 230, 232; Stadter 2006, 248 and Moles 2002, 36–39, 42, 51.) It is to explore the question of Athenian imperialism that we now turn to Thucydides.

Thucydides and the Failure of the Delian League

In Thucydides' *Peloponnesian War* we learn that the Delian league, the alliance of Greek cities that formed after the victory in the Persian wars, falls subject to the whims of Athens. With freedom as its goal, Athens ultimately seeks to be free from all limitations, even the limits of justice (see Strauss 1989, 89). Lacking a common understanding of even the political good, let alone the good in and of itself, to serve as a principle of moderation limiting and directing the activities of the league, the basis of rule quickly deteriorates to the subjective decisions of whoever is able to gain sufficient power. Not surprisingly, perhaps, a similar corruption within Athens itself results in Athens' fall from the height of its democratic golden age to being conquered by Sparta. Thucydides, therefore, teaches that freedom, especially when enmeshed in a desire for honour, is an insufficient principle for guiding participation in and the activities of both alliances and states.

Looking back to the beginning of the Delian league and even to claims made by states during the Peloponnesian War, it might seem inaccurate to say that no principle directed the aims of the alliance. Instead, a number of goals are present at the inception of the league (see Larson 1940). For example, we find out from Aristotle, although notably absent from Thucydides' account, that when deciding the terms of the alliance, participants swore an oath, "to have the same enemies and friends" (Aristotle 1984, XXIII, 5), thereby subjecting the actions and ends of the alliance to the gods. According to Aristotle, then, the league begins in recognition of an eternal principle beyond its own self-interest that ought to limit and direct the league's activities, thus allowing the alliance to be maintained and justice, presumably, to be served.

Yet in Thucydides' version the oath and the gods, at least for the Athenians, are strikingly absent (Boucher 1998, 79; Csapo and Miller 1998; Forde 1986, 436–37). Thucydides narrates the "ostensible" purpose of the league as being to regain what was taken by Persia during the previous war (1.96).[2] Further, throughout Thucydides' history, it appears as generally understood that member states joined the alliance for the sake of their freedom, and it is the quest for power and absolute freedom that seemingly govern the activities of Athens (3.10, 5.100, 5.112, 6.76) (see Kagan 1969, 31–33; Kagan 1991, 96–97; Larson 1940, 190–192; Tritle 2006, 135–36). Thus, Pericles tells us, and all Athenians, "happiness is freedom" (2.43). Hence, while the Spartans consult oracles and the barbarians offer sacrifices, the Athenians ground the purpose of their activities in the desire for freedom, but without any external principle with which to determine what this freedom is for, it quickly becomes a quest for freedom from all limitations, even those rationally determined to be good. Seeking freedom, Greek states join Athens in an alliance, but Athens will seek freedom from the limits of the alliance itself, dominating and enslaving all of its members (see Forde 1986, 442; Kagan 1969, 38–40; Rawlings 1977, 1–8).

---

2   Thucydides, *The Peloponnesian War* (Cambridge: Hackett Publishing, 1998). All subsequent citations will be taken from this edition.

Hence, although Athens has already acquired its empire and thus seemingly negated the grounds of equality that united the members of the Delian league at the beginning of the Peloponnesian War, we can see through the course of Thucydides' narrative the grounds for the decline of the league and, ultimately, Athens, by means of the reactions of Athenians to a few pivotal events preceding and during the war. Explicitly, we see a continuous decline in the attempt to even explain Athenian activities in the name of justice in four episodes, beginning with the Athenian address to the Spartans, and continuing through Pericles' funeral oration, as well as the Mytelene debate and Melian dialogue.

Athenian Envoy at Sparta

In the first book of the Peloponnesian War an Athenian envoy tries to persuade Sparta from acting on complaints from Carthage about Athenian imperialism. In Sparta on other business and, presumably, not formally prepared to defend the activities of Athens, the envoy speaks perhaps more candidly than they might otherwise. Correspondingly, as both Thucydides and the Athenians themselves note, their purpose in speaking is not as much to defend themselves against the complaints of Carthage, but to remind Sparta of their power and thus suggest that a war may not be in Sparta's self-interest (1.72–73). Yet, despite even this, in this early account, the Athenians begin speaking about the justice of their actions and the justice of their empire. Indeed, in their first argument, the envoys turn to the account of justice that Thucydides suggests initiated the Delian league, receiving what they are owed or what they merit. Given the great sacrifices the Athenians made, including the destruction of their city, and the great risks they took during the Persian War for the sake of the "general good", Athens, we are told, deserves its empire (1.73–75; alternatively, see Orwin 1986, 75–76). Only after posing this consideration of justice does Athens turn to what are the more likely causes of its rule: fear, the desire for prestige and self-interest (1.75–76). Yet, as the Athenians explain, these causes, grounded in human nature, bind all human activities; as such, the empire is not only just, it is necessary. Indeed, despite being buffeted by the force of human nature, Athenians strive to act justly even when their own strength would allow them the power of tyrants. For rather than ruling the empire by arbitrary force, Athens, at this stage, continues to rule according to law (1.77). Athens thus deserves praise rather than complaint, for, "all are entitled to praise whenever they follow human nature by ruling others and end up behaving more justly than their actual power dictated" (1.76).

Thus, at this early juncture, although the Athenians introduce contingent factors that significantly reduce their responsibility for their previous actions, they desire to at least cloak the rule of the empire in justice. As we shall see, however, once one's understanding of the principles of justice are compromised by forces considered more necessary, particularly that of self-interest, choosing justice over and against understood self-interest becomes more and more improbable (see Boucher 1998, 68).

Pericles' Funeral Oration

The clearest account of the purpose of justice, at least as it exists for the Athenians, is most apparent in Pericles' funeral oration wherein he presents an account of the war in terms of Athens' virtue and its consequent honour. With numerous casualties and their city currently under siege by the Spartans, Pericles redirects the sentiments of Athenians away from their immediate self-interest and loss, to the perhaps greater or at least larger cause: the "good" of the city itself. However, the means by which he does this is by appealing to a higher order of self-interest: the honour each individual will achieve by means of his city's greatness. Thus Pericles exhorts:

> *wonder ... at the city's power as you actually see it each day and become ... her lovers, reflecting whenever her fame appears great to you that men who were daring, who realized their duty, and who honored it in their actions acquired this, men who even when they failed in some attempt did not on that account think it right to deprive the city of their virtue, but to offer it to her as their finest contribution. For in giving their lives in common cause, they individually gained imperishable praise. (2.44)*

Moreover, Pericles indicates the grounds upon which the greatest honour can be achieved: the continued freedom of Athens and the subsequent freedom awarded to her citizens (Finley 1942, 149–50). Thus, Pericles praises the city's ancestors for their bravery in maintaining the city's freedom (2.36). He also notes that Athens' current greatness stems, at least in part, from its democratic form of government, wherein equal opportunity for all is protected, individual merit rewarded and private choices respected (2.37). Indeed, individual citizens of Athens, more than any other city, enjoy the freedom that comes with being self-sufficient; having enjoyed the benefits of the city, they more than any other men have developed the necessary skills and talents, private and public, to live in independence (2.41). Finally, encouraging those left behind to continue the fight of those they now honour, Pericles urges them to "judge that happiness is freedom" and freedom requires courage (2.43). Hence, even though Athens is subsequently devastated by a plague and with the continuation of the Spartan siege such that Athenians seek to come to terms that will end the war, Pericles is able to restrain their anger and exhort them to activities that he believes serve the common good. Consequently, he is elected general and Athenians "considered him the most valuable man for the needs of the whole city" (2.65).

Nonetheless, and as perhaps the emphasis Thucydides places on the ensuing plague suggests, this median account of virtue presented to Athenians is insufficient to ensure or even direct Athenians to justice (see Monoson and Loriaux 1998, 288–90). Pericles is singularly able to encourage Athenians to sacrifice their immediate self-interest and even survival, for the good of the city and the honour this activity will subsequently afford them (see Finley 1942, 146–49; Kagan 1991, 7; Woodhead 1970, 49). However, the nature of this political good can neither direct Athenians to actions that are good in and of themselves nor even secure the end that Pericles seeks, the good of Athens (see Forde 1986, 438–39; Podoksik 2005, 23–30; Strauss 1989, 87). Without an account of why freedom is necessary and to what end this freedom is to be directed, the quest for freedom can easily become a quest for absolute license regardless of the ends or aims of one's activities.[3] While Pericles exhorts the benefits of freedom for Athens from Persian or Spartan rule and encourages citizens to limit their freedom for the sake of this, ultimately the principle of freedom he expounds for the state and which the state inculcates in its citizens comes to be the only grounds of its and their activity. Thus Athens builds an empire to achieve greater power and acquire greater and greater freedom from external influence, while individuals in the city – Alcibiades most notably – seek to rid themselves of all limits as well, including those that the city would place on them.

Mytilenean Debate

By the time the Mytileneans revolt from the empire, Athens' understanding of its power and freedom is, for practical purposes, unlimited. Thus, although the Athenians have second thoughts about their decision to kill all the men of this state and sell all women and children into slavery, the grounds upon which they finally reverse their decision have little to do with justice. The question becomes not whether it is just to commit what will in effect be genocide, but rather, whether or not it is useful for Mytilene to be destroyed (see Podoksik 2005, 32). Indeed, although both Kleon and Diodotus speak about what is just in the given situation, they each conclude, albeit oppositely, that regardless of whether it is just or unjust, the Athenians only have one choice. Thus Kleon argues that the Athenians have to enforce their initial decision to kill all the adult males and enslave the rest of the community, for if the Mytileneans revolted justly, then the Athenian empire is unjust and should not balk about further unjust actions. However, if the Mytileans revolted unjustly, then this punishment is indeed just (3.40). Correspondingly, while Diodotus says that only the men in charge of the revolt should be punished, he concludes by arguing that if the majority of Mytileans did not act unjustly, it would be unjust to punish them, and even if they did revolt unjustly, the good of the Athenian empire requires Athens to overlook the injustice of their act (3.47). Hence, while it is possible that the decision to spare the lives of majority of the Mytileneans

---

3   Thus in Book 9 of *The Republic* Socrates describes the evolution of democracy to tyranny.

is made on the grounds of justice, both speakers make it equally possible for the consideration of justice to be entirely inconsequential to the debate (see Grene 1950, 29; Mara 2001, 826, 828).

The Melian Dialogue

Not surprisingly then, by the time of the Melian dialogue the relevance of justice has become much vaguer or perhaps sharper, depending on how one assesses the situation. Consistent with the initial envoy's account at Sparta, the Athenians insist that the strongest always rule the weakest, indeed even the gods admit this necessity (5.89, 105). Prior to the war, Athenians claimed to be just because, although the strongest, they still treated the weak with more justice than their strength required. However, the Melians are not graced with Athens' mercy. Instead, refusing to subject themselves to the Athenian empire, seeking instead to retain their freedom, Melos is laid to siege by Athens and ultimately conquered, with all adult males slaughtered and women and children enslaved (5.116). Interestingly, Athens, at this stage, is no longer moved by the earlier accepted arguments regarding expediency, seemingly believing that their strength is limitless and the safeguards of reason are no longer required (5.98, 5.100; see Liebeschuetz 1968, 74; Podoksik 2005, 38). Athens, at this stage, compares its activities to those of the gods. Being the strongest, they too are compelled to rule; compelled, ironically, to be free while subjecting all others to their power (5.105). Internally, this becomes a problem when Athenians make the same argument with respect to their fellow citizens.

Alcibiades and Athens' Destruction

Seeking the freedom of one's city by means of strengthening its power for the sake of a citizen's self-interest, particularly honour, might satisfy the desires of a civically minded individual or a person with limited desires. However, for one whose *eros* is as infinite as that of Alcibiades, Pericles' speech logically suggests seeking one's own freedom as a way to even greater honour. While it certainly is honourable for a city to acquire self-sufficiency comparable to the gods, surely it is an even greater thing for an individual to achieve. Thus, although Thucydides tells us that had the Athenians been able to bear Alcbiades' rule, they would have won the war, he also indicates that in doing so, they would have subjected themselves to a tyrant (6.15). Alcibiades most clearly demonstrates the true nature of his intentions when, having been called to trial by his countrymen, he turns to Sparta, seeking the enslavement of his homeland. One might argue that Athens' ultimate defeat comes, at least indirectly, from the acts of Alicbiades, and Alcibiades is the result of the philosophy of freedom the city itself promulgates (see Orwin 1986, 81).

Freedom is often the stated political goal of modern political regimes and their alliances. Yet as Thucydides demonstrates through the demise of Delian league and fall of Athens, such an account of justice is insufficient for governing a federation and a regime. Alcibiades, the most concise and tragic example of rule of the strongest, demonstrates how destructive such a goal can be unless it is bound by further considerations of the politically good.

Conclusion

Consideration of Thucydides' history, especially Pericles' funeral oration, shows that the problem of honour, eschewed by the Athenians during the Persian wars, resurfaces in Athens during the Peloponnesian War. The desire for honour, as Thucydides indicates, causes the collapse of the Delian league into an Athenian empire after the Persians are defeated. It is evident, therefore, that the democracy, in the absence of a powerful external threat like Persia, can be just as subject to the calls of honour as the Spartans of Herodotus' history. Moreover, Thucydides reveals that the Athenian desire for honour becomes attached to a desire for freedom, driving an imperial policy that subordinates the claims of justice to those of expediency and power; the power of Athens over other cities and ultimately the power of individuals, such as Alcibiades, over other individuals within Athens.

This brings us to another more fundamental cause of the instability and ultimate collapse of federalism and democracy in the Greek world towards which the ancient writers point. As consideration of the narrative of Herodotus shows, the movement from divine to human foundations of the democratic regime allows the universality of human nature to be revealed. Athenians win a great victory over the Persians at Marathon because they were the first to face the sight of Persian dress and the men who wore it without fear. Athenians, in other words, could see the Persians "naked", or as human beings like themselves who shared the same nature. Yet, as Thucydides illustrates, by the time of the Peloponnesian War it is apparent that the nature of the human grasped by the Athenians has more to do with the body than the soul. Athenians explicitly perceive human beings in terms of their interests, based in the body, that suggests the pursuit of one power after another as expedient if not just. Thus, in the Mytilenean debate Diodotus must cloak an argument for justice within an argument for interest to save Mytilene. Yet, when we get to the Melian dialogue, Thucydides lets us see Athens using Diodotus' rhetoric of interest and expediency not to pursue justice but rather the unjust and genocidal policy of Kleon. Thucydides therefore suggests that in order to prevent the democracy from descending into such cruelty and barbarism, a direct rather than indirect discourse on justice eventually has to emerge.

Could Thucydides have in mind the type of dialogic discourse between Socrates and his interlocutors recorded by Plato in the *Republic*? In this dialogue Socrates and his interlocutors try to work through the question of "What is justice?" and whether or not it makes a human being happy. During the course of the dialogue the mind is turned toward consideration of the soul, and ultimately to rational contemplation of the soul's ascent to what is universally good. We may speculate, therefore, that the ancients, in the absence of a pious respect for the gods, point us toward a form of discursive philosophy that brings the soul and the good to light as a principle of moderation that guides freedom and preserves federal structures and the democratic institutions upon which they are built.

References

Aristotle (1984), *The Politics and the Constitution of Athens* (Cambridge: Cambridge University Press).
Bakker, E.J. et al. (eds) (2002), *Brill's Companion to Herodotus* (Leiden: Brill).
Benardete, S. (1969), *Herodotean Inquiries* (The Hague: Martinus Nijhoff).
Boedeker, D. and Raaflaub, K. (eds) (1998), *Democracy, Empire and the Arts in Fifth-Century Athens* (Cambridge: Harvard University Press).
Boucher, D. (1998), *Political Theories of International Relations* (Oxford: Oxford University Press).
Cooper, R. (2002), The New Liberal Imperialism, *The Observer*, April 7, in Hirsh, M. (2004), *At War With Ourselves: Why America is Squandering its Chance to Build a Better World* (Oxford: Oxford University Press).
Csapo, E. and Miller, M.C. (1998), Politics of time and narrative, in Boedeker and Raaflaub (eds) (1998), *Democracy, Empire and the Arts in Fifth-Century Athens* (Cambridge: Harvard University Press).
Dewald, C. et al. (eds) (2006), *The Cambridge Companion Herodotus* (Cambridge: Cambridge University Press).
Euben, P. (1986), The Battle of Salamis and the origins of political theory', *Political Theory* 14:3, 359–90.
Finley, J.H. Jr. (1942), *Thucydides* (Harvard: Harvard University Press).
Forde, S. (1986), Thucydides on the causes of Athenian imperialism, *The American Political Science Review* 80:2, 433–48.
Fornara, C.W. (1971), *Herodotus: An Interpretive Essay* (Oxford: Oxford University Press).
Forsdyke, S. (2001), Athenian democratic ideology and Herodotus' *Histories*, *American Journal of Philology* 122:3, 329–58.
—— (2006), Herodotus, political history and political thought, in Dewald et al. (eds) (2006), *The Cambridge Companion Herodotus* (Cambridge: Cambridge University Press).
Grene, D. (1950), *Greek Political Theory* (Chicago: University of Chicago Press).
Harrison, T. (2002), 'The Persian Invasions', in Bakker et al. (eds) (2002), *Brill's Companion to Herodotus* (Leiden: Brill).
Herodotus (1987), *The History* (Chicago: University of Chicago Press).
Immerwahr, H.R. (1966), *Form and Thought in Herodotus* (Cleveland: Press of Western Reserve University).

Kagan, D. (1969), *The Outbreak of the Peloponnesian War* (Ithaca: Cornell University Press).
—— (1991), *Pericles of Athens and the Birth of Democracy* (New York: The Free Press).
Larson, J.A.O. (1940), The constitution and original purpose of the Delian League, *Harvard Studies in Classical Philology* 51, 175–213.
Liebeschuetz, W. (1968), The structure and function of the Melian Dialogue, *The Journal of Hellenic Studies* 88, 73–77.
Mara, G.M. (2001), Thucydides and Plato on democracy and trust, *The Journal of Politics* 63:3, 820–45.
Meckler, M. (ed.) (2006), *Classical Antiquity and the Politics of America* (Texas: Baylor University Press).
Moles, J. (2002), 'Herodotus and Athens', in Bakker et al. (eds) (2002), *Brill's Companion to Herodotus* (Leiden: Brill).
Monoson, S.S. and Loriaux, M. (1998), The illusion of power and the disruption of moral norms: Thucydides' critique of Periclean policy, *The American Political Science Review* 92:2, 285–97.
Montesquieu (1989), *The Spirit of the Laws* (Cambridge: Cambridge University Press).
Orwin, C. (1986), Justifying empire: the speech of the Athenians at Sparta and the problem of justice in Thucydides, *The Journal of Politics* 48, 72–85.
Ostwald, M. (1969), *Nomos and the Beginnings of Athenian Democracy* (Oxford: Oxford University Press).
Pangle, T. (ed.) (1989), *The Rebirth of Classical Political Rationalism* (Chicago: Chicago University Press).
Pelling, C. (2002), Speech and action: Herodotus' debate on the constitutions, *Proceedings of the Cambridge Philological Society* 48, 123–58.
Podoksik, E. (2005), Justice, power and Athenian imperialism: an ideological moment in Thucydides' *History*, *History of Political Thought* XXVI:1, 21–42.
Raaflaub, K. (2004), *The Discovery of Freedom in Ancient Greece* (Chicago: University of Chicago Press).
Rawlings, H.R. III (1977), Thucydides on the Purpose of the Delian League, *Phoenix* 31:1, 1–8.
Stadter, P. (2006), Herodotus and the cities of mainland Greece, in Dewald et al. (eds) (2006), *The Cambridge Companion Herodotus* (Cambridge: Cambridge University Press).
Strauss, L. (1989) Thucydides: the meaning of political history, in Pangle (ed.) (1989), *The Rebirth of Classical Political Rationalism* (Chicago: Chicago University Press).
Thompson, N. (1996), *Herodotus and the Origins of the Political Community: Arion's Leap* (New Haven: Yale University Press).
Thucydides (1998), *The Peloponnesian War* (Cambridge: Hackett Publishing).
Tritle, L.A. (2006), 'Thucydides and the Cold War', in Meckler (ed.) (2006), *Classical Antiquity and the Politics of America* (Texas: Baylor University Press).
Vlastos, G. (1973), *Platonic Studies* (Princeton: Princeton University Press).

Woodhead, A.G. (1970), *Thucydides on the Nature of Power* (Cambridge: Harvard University Press).

Further Reading

Blosel, W. (2007), The Herodotean picture of Themistocles: a mirror of fifth century Athens, in Luraghi (ed.) (2007), *The Historian's Craft in the Age of Herodotus* (Oxford: Oxford University Press).

Bowden, H. (2005), *Classical Athens and the Delphic Oracle: Divination and Democracy* (Cambridge: Cambridge University Press).

Griffin, J. (2006), Herodotus and Tragedy, in Dewald et al. (eds) (2006), *The Cambridge Companion Herodotus* (Cambridge: Cambridge University Press).

Hart, J. (1982), *Herodotus and Greek History* (New York: St. Martin's Press).

Hunter, V. (1982), *Past and Process in Herodotus and Thucydides* (Princeton: Princeton University Press).

Luraghi, N. (ed.) (2007), *The Historian's Craft in the Age of Herodotus* (Oxford: Oxford University Press).

Marincola, J. (2006), Herodotus and the poetry of the past, in Dewald et al. (eds) (2006), *The Cambridge Companion Herodotus* (Cambridge: Cambridge University Press).

Mikalson, J.D. (2002), Religion in Herodotus, in Bakker et al. (eds) (2002), *Brill's Companion to Herodotus* (Leiden: Brill).

Munson, R.V. (2005), *Black Doves Speak: Herodotus and the Languages of Barbarians* (Cambridge: Harvard University Press).

Orwin, C. (1994), *The Humanity of Thucydides* (Princeton, New Jersey).

Robertson, N. (1987), The true meaning of the "Wooden Wall", *Classical Philology* 82:1, 1–20.

Saxonhouse, A.W. (1996), *Athenian Democracy: Modern Mythmakers and Ancient Theorists* (Notre Dame: University of Notre Dame Press).

—— (2006), *Free Speech and Democracy in Ancient Athens* (Cambridge: Cambridge University Press).

Scullion, S. (2006), Herodotus and Greek religion, in Dewald et al. (eds) (2006), *The Cambridge Companion Herodotus* (Cambridge: Cambridge University Press).

Thomas, R. (2006), The intellectual milieu of Herodotus, in Dewald et al. (eds) (2006), *The Cambridge Companion Herodotus* (Cambridge: Cambridge University Press).

Before Federalism? Thomas Aquinas, Jean Quidort and Nicolas Cusanus[1]

Nicholas Aroney

Introduction

The names of Thomas Aquinas, Jean Quidort and Nicolas Cusanus are not usually associated with federalism. Federalism is widely thought to be a modern political invention, whereas these three writers are conventionally classified as strictly medieval, and between the modern and the medieval there is a vast gulf, it is said (Beer 1986; Beer 1993, ch. 1). But what precisely is the difference between the medieval and the modern, and how does it apply to federalism? While much thought and discussion has been given to this question of difference, relatively little has been devoted more specifically to the issue as it relates to federalism. This is an extraordinary omission because among the many dimensions of our modern ideas about politics and government, federalism is a concept which bridges both worlds (Hueglin 1999).

In this chapter, I am concerned with political ideas and institutions and their development through time. My intention is to focus upon several pre-modern writers and, in particular, Thomas Aquinas, as a means of drawing attention to the respects in which federalism as a political idea and a form of political organization bridges the divide between the medieval and the modern. It is not my intention to grapple directly with the question of what actually distinguishes the medieval from the modern, but it is to be hoped that my analysis of the federal idea and its development through time might shed some light upon this question.

---

[1] This chapter restates and develops arguments first advanced in Aroney (2007), Subsidiarity, federalism and the best constitution: Thomas Aquinas on city, province and empire, *Law and Philosophy* 26:2, 161–228.

To refer to federalism in this way courts the danger of anachronism. To speak in terms of an "-ism" is to adopt a decidedly modern idiom (Hopfl 1983). *Foedus* was a term known to medieval writers, but its use was usually technical in the sense of the Roman and civil law idea of a treaty between nations (Kunkel 1973, 38). Cognates of the word, such as *confederatio*, were also known (and in fact used by Aquinas) to refer loosely to agreements, pacts or covenants of various kinds, but without the specific associations of the modern usage. In modern usage, by contrast, a sharp distinction is usually drawn between the treaties and covenants of international law, and the founding compacts and constitutions of nation-states, and it is only with respect to the latter that the term "federal" is used, usually in order to distinguish federal states from unitary states. It is only in relatively very recent times, with the emergence of the European Union that the word "federal" has sometimes been associated (controversially) with a community of states founded upon international treaties (Aroney 2005). These distinctions and these developments need to be kept in mind when trying to trace an intellectual history of the federal idea.

In terms of modern usage, following the lead of Preston King and others (King 1982; Burgess 2006, 47–48; Watts 1999, 6–7), in this chapter I use the term "federalism" to designate a certain body of ideas, while I reserve the term "federation" to refer to a particular form of political organization influenced by those ideas. My concern in this chapter is not directly with the more technical distinction between federation and confederation, nor with the (problematic) use of the idea of sovereignty to draw distinctions in this field (see Friedrich 1968, ch. 2; Davis 1978, 215), although some mention of these matters will have to be made towards the end of the discussion.

My argument is that when our modern conception of federalism and the contemporary institutions with which we associate this idea are closely analyzed, a number of distinct elements become apparent, and when we look to see whether these elements exist in the political philosophies of the medieval past, both continuities and discontinuities can be identified. Which of these elements is the most significant is a highly controversial question, not unrelated to the problem of the medieval and the modern noted above. In this chapter, I limit my argument to the demonstration of the continuities and discontinuities specifically in relation to Thomas Aquinas and several other late medieval and early modern writers, while gesturing only tentatively in relation to the more debatable question of what is significant or decisive in this context.

Before turning to the relevant texts, it is necessary to make one last preliminary observation regarding the provenance of the present inquiry. Especially as we consider the relationship between medieval and modern political thought, it is important that we do not get confused about what we mean by political philosophy and how philosophy thus conceived might be distinguished from theology. It is conventional, since at least Thomas Aquinas, to understand the distinction between theology and philosophy as a difference between systematic thought founded upon premises supplied by a divine revelation and systematic thought founded upon premises discovered (or else constructed) by human reason. Given the specific subject matter of this chapter, however, my concern cannot be with philosophy alone, but must be with systematic thought founded on premises delivered by both human reason and divine revelation. For if this is not conceded, much of the political thought of medieval times will be excluded from consideration, and we will be left with an attenuated picture of the history of the federal idea. Similarly, my concern also has to be with systematic thought about all forms of social organization, not just the political. For if we do not follow Aquinas in traversing the domestic, the economic, the social, the ecclesiastical and the political, our picture will be incomplete and particular similarities between medieval social theory and later federal thought will be overlooked.

Defining Federalism

Definitions of federalism and federation break down into three basic categories. One of the most common approaches focuses upon the idea of a distribution of powers between central and regional governments, prescribed in a written document (usually called a constitution) and typically enforced by an independent judiciary. There are several variations on this theme, many of them appealing to the idea of coordinate or mutually independent governments operating in legally defined spheres (e.g., Finer 1974, 208–11; Riker 1975, 101; Dahl 1986, 114).

A second approach to defining federalism emphasizes, not so much the division of powers between central and regional governments, as the idea of several governments (or several political communities represented by such governments) participating in a system of government in which they each share and to which they each are submitted (King 1982, 77). Systems of "federal representation" and "intergovernmental cooperation" in this sense can be institutionalized in different ways, depending for example upon whether it is the governments, legislatures or voting public in each political community who choose those who will represent the community in the governing institutions of the entire federal system (Aroney 2006, 287–91, 325–29).

A third approach to defining federalism, while it generally acknowledges the importance of the two elements described above, is more concerned with the political sources from which the federal system derives its origin and, more specifically, the nature of its founding agreement (Elazar 1995–1991). Recalling that the English term "federal" is derived from the Latin *foedus*, this approach emphasizes the idea that federal systems of government find their origin in a federating agreement or covenant. A federating agreement such as this presupposes the prior, independent existence of certain constituent political communities, and it sets out what they agree shall be the institutional conditions of federal union, including the distribution of powers, the representative institutions of the federation and the processes by which the federal constitution can be altered in the future (Aroney 2006; cf. Hueglin and Fenna 2006, chs 5–7, 9–10).

The central advantage of this third approach is that it has greater explanatory power. Not only does it incorporate a wider range of features of existing federal systems (Watts 1999, 7), including what Daniel Elazar called "self-rule" and "shared-rule" (Elazar 1987, 12), it sheds light on the relationship between the formative ideas and institutional processes by which a federal system comes into being and the distribution of powers, the representative institutions and the amendment formulas adopted thereunder (Aroney 2006, 320–35). Focusing on only one element – the distribution of powers, for example – shuts out from consideration other elements which are equally typical of federal systems and, in so doing, obscures important similarities between the federations of the present and the political institutions and ideas of the medieval past. In this chapter I am therefore interested in all four of these elements: the formative grounds of the system, the configuration of power between the various spheres of government, the representation of the constituent communities within the decision-making institutions of the system as a whole, and the authoritative processes by which the entire arrangement can be altered in the future. When the political ideas and institutional arrangements of both the past and the present are assessed with these four indicia in mind, a much wider range of potential continuities and discontinuities comes into view. It is on the basis of these criteria that I will proceed to analyze the systematic reflection on problems of human organization and community in the thought of Thomas Aquinas and several other late medieval and early modern publicists, all with a view to identifying the extent to which "federal" ideas and institutions can be identified in these writers, as well as the extent to which they cannot.

Thomas Aquinas

Space does not permit detailed contextualization of the social and political thought articulated by the thirteenth-century theologian and philosopher St Thomas Aquinas. Thomas was born in Naples around 1225, the son of Landulph, Count of Aquino in the kingdom of Naples, and Theodora, Countess of Teano, through whom he was related to the Hohenstaufen dynasty of Holy Roman emperors. He commenced studies at the University of Naples, where his precocious talents soon began to be noticed. Soon thereafter, having come under the influence of the Dominicans, he joined their order – against his family's wishes. He went on to study in Cologne under Albertus Magnus, whom he later accompanied to the University of Paris, where he soon distinguished himself as a controversialist and a scholar. During the extraordinarily productive career which followed, Aquinas thereafter held lecturing and professorial positions at Cologne, Bologna, Naples, Paris, Rome and elsewhere. In his day, great controversy attached to his attempts to synthesize the received theology of the Church with the recently recovered philosophical and political writings of the Greek philosopher Aristotle. Among his works, Aquinas is best known for his massive systematic exposition of theology, the *Summa Theologiae*, and his earlier apologetic work, the *Summa contra Gentiles*, together with numerous treatises on disputed topics and commentaries on the works of Aristotle and particular biblical and theological writings, as well as (part of) a treatise *On*

Kingship. Today, Aquinas's erudition, philosophical sophistication and profound influence is widely acknowledged and he has been officially regarded within the Roman Catholic Church as its foremost theologian and philosopher (Leo XIII, *Aeterni Patris*, 1879).

A central motif of Aquinas's thought lay in his attempt to synthesize the deliverances of natural human reason with the propositions of Christian revelation in a manner which admitted the findings of reason as regards those matters falling within the proper scope of each of its sciences, but which preserved the ultimate unity of the truths known by both reason and faith, and yet insisted that revealed truths exceed those truths that can be known by reason (*ScG*, 1.9.1; 1.3.2, 4; 1.7.3).[2] For Aquinas, philosophy is especially concerned to discover the nature of things "in themselves", whereas theology begins with the knowledge of God and understands all things in relation to Him (*ScG*, 2.4.2). Moreover, because philosophy considers creatures as they are in themselves, he concluded that there are "different divisions of philosophy according to the different classes of things" (*ScG*, 2.4.1, 5).

Aquinas's observations and conclusions about matters of politics and social organization need to be understood with this background in mind. Indeed, many of his most important propositions relating to such matters were written in the context of specifically theological enquiries and, even in those cases where the basic considerations were fundamentally philosophical in character, his conclusions were still shaped, sometimes critically, by theological premises. Perhaps the most important example of this for present purposes concerns the way in which Aquinas adopted and developed Aristotle's theory of the *polis* (roughly translated, "city-state"). Aristotle had said that it is in the *polis* that human beings realize their chief end and highest good (*Politics*, I.1, 1252a). Notably, Aquinas was able to agree with this, provided that the proposition could be limited to its proper domain: political science regards humanity in itself and deals only with specifically human ends, whereas sacred theology concerns humanity's ultimate end without qualification, and therefore transcends it. Aquinas could therefore affirm that cities or states (*civitates*) exist to pursue the ultimate ends of human life, considered in themselves. But he was careful to point out that "the ultimate end of the whole universe is considered in theology, which is the most important without qualification" (*ScG*, 3.17; *Eth.*, I.2.13 [31]).[3]

Aquinas's attempt to integrate Aristotle's political thought into a medieval intellectual and cultural context also required important adjustments in order to make room for the institutions of the Church at a parochial, diocesan and catholic scale, as well as the cities, kingdoms and provinces of the Holy Roman Empire (compare Nederman 1987; Blythe 1992, 46). Classical antiquity had no conception of church and state as separate institutions, but the seeds of the idea were in Christianity from the very beginning (Mark 12:17; Acts 5:29). Combined with the

---

2 *Summa contra Gentiles* (1259–1265). Unless indicated otherwise, in-text references to Aquinas's works are to the book, section and paragraph numbers. For more on this motif, see Fortin 1987.

3 *Sententia libri Ethicorum* (1271–1272).

Roman law idea of *jurisdictio* and related concepts, medieval jurists developed the idea that church and state, as well as particular institutions within church and state, possessed distinct and limited jurisdictions (Tellenbach 1993, 309; Berman 1983, 205–15). Aquinas followed this lead by drawing a definite distinction between spiritual and temporal authority. In those matters which affect the salvation of the soul, he said, spiritual power is to be obeyed, whereas in those matters which concern the civil welfare, the temporal should be obeyed (Sent., II.44 ex. ad 4).[4] There is some dispute over the precise lines that Aquinas would draw between the temporal jurisdiction of the state and the spiritual jurisdiction of the church. There are passages, such as the one just cited, which can be interpreted to suggest that the pope's authority extends, at least in some specific contexts, into temporal affairs, and there are others which can be interpreted to suggest that the legitimate concerns of a king include the spiritual well-being of his subjects (*De Regno*, I.16.2 [115]).[5] Wherever the line was to be drawn, however, Aquinas clearly thought that there was such a line, and that church and state had distinct and by implication limited jurisdictions. And, while the nature and functions of each was unique, there was a sense in which they each confronted one another on an equal basis: Aquinas appears to have classified them both as "public associations" and as "perfect communities" (*Impugn.*, II.2, ad 9; *ST*, II–II, 31.3 ad 3; 43.8; Finnis 1998, 226, n 31).[6]

Aristotle considered the polis to be a composition of households, clans and villages (*Politics*, III.9, 1280b). The latter, he said, are formed to secure the bare necessities of life, whereas the *polis*, being self-sufficient, is concerned with securing the good life (*Politics*, I.1–2, 1252a–1252b). The *polis* is therefore prior to families and villages in nature or essence, just as the whole is prior to the part. For, as Aristotle put it, man is by nature a political animal, whose end is fulfilled only in the *polis* (*Politics*, I.2, 1253a; III.6, 1278b). Subject to the qualification that we are here concerned with "human affairs" and with the order of "nature" (see *Eth.*, I.9.10–11 [112–113]), Aquinas again agreed with the general thrust of these propositions. But there were important differences in exposition and detail. When commentating on Aristotle's *Ethics*, Aquinas emphasized that human communities such as political societies are "wholes" which possess not an "absolute unity", but rather a "unity of order" (Gilby 1958, 251–6; Eschmann 1947, 29–34). This meant that political communities consist of parts that in some respects have an operation independent of the whole, while in other respects participate in the operations of the whole community (*Eth.*, I.1.5 [5]; Finnis 1998, 24–5). Notably, the Aristotelian text upon which Aquinas commented here made no explicit mention of the question of the relationship of the whole to its parts (*Nic. Ethics*, I.1, 1094a1–18). Yet Aquinas considered it necessary to insist that, while a political community is a composition of households, this does not mean that the political community is an absolute

---

4   *Scriptum super Sententiis magistri Petri Lombardi* (1256).
5   *De Regno ad regem Cypri* (c. 1267).
6   *Contra impugnantes Dei cultum et Religionem* (1256); *Summa Theologiae* (1265–1268, 1271–1273). In-text references to the *ST* are to the Question and article, with references to specific arguments or answers dealt with in each article as applicable.

unity in which the household has no powers of independent operation. While such a conclusion is generally consistent with Aristotle's own view (see *Politics*, I.2, 1252b, 1253a; II.2, 1261b), Aquinas's emphasis on the idea that the state is a unity of order laid the foundation for several significant ways in which he departed from Aristotle.

Firstly, rather than follow Aristotle by always defining human beings simply as a "political animals", Aquinas usually preferred the designation "political and social" or simply "social", and added that human nature is not only political or civil, but also profoundly "domestic" (see, e.g., *ST*, I, 96.4; I–II, 61.5, 72.4, 95.4; *De Regno*, I.1.3 [4], I.13.2 [94]; *ScG*, III.85.11; *Eth.*, I.1.4 [4]), VII.6.7 [1391], VIII.12.18 (1719–20); *Pol.*, I.1.29 [37]).[7] Compared to Aristotle, Aquinas thus placed relatively greater emphasis on the various "non-political" forms of human association and community (compare Scully 1981; Finnis 1998, ch. 7; Aroney 2007, 177–79). Indeed, Aquinas said that it is one of the hallmarks of a tyrant that he deliberately undermines all forms of social solidarity among his subjects, preventing them from joining in various kinds of compacts and associations (*confederationes*) between individuals and families by which social friendship, familiarity and trust is generated (*De Regno*, I.4.7 [27]).

Secondly, although Aquinas generally followed Aristotle in regarding self-sufficiency to be an essential characteristic of the *polis* or *civitas* which distinguishes it from a mere household or neighbourhood (*Pol.*, I.1.3 [11], I.1.7–9 [15–17], I.1.23–25 [31–33], I.1.30–32 [38–40]; *ST*, I–II, 90.3 ad 3, II–II, 47.11, 50.1),[8] he elsewhere treated self-sufficiency in relative terms, saying that households and neighbourhoods can possess a kind self-sufficiency themselves, and adding that wider political units such as provinces, kingdoms, nations and, by implication, the empire and indeed the entire universe as a whole, possess degrees of self-sufficiency and completeness which surpass that of an individual city.[9]

The general principle seems to have been that, as Aquinas put it, "a government is the more perfect according as it is more universal, extends to more matters, and attains a more ultimate end" (*ST*, II–II, 50.1). The implications of this principle were stated plainly in *De Regno*, where Aquinas described the self-sufficiency of the various forms and degrees of human society (*De Regno*, I.2.4 [14]). Whereas an isolated individual, he said, is not self-sufficient, a solitary household enjoys a degree of self-sufficiency, particularly with regard to the giving of birth to offspring and the provision of food. Likewise, a particular street or neighbourhood within a city will be self-sufficient in respect of the particular trade that is practised there and, in turn, a city is by comparison self-sufficient in respect of all the necessities of

---

7   *Sententia libri Politicorum* (1269–1272).
8   Note that *Sententia libri Politicorum* and *Sententia libri Ethicorum* were expositions of, and not commentaries upon, Aristotle's *Politics* and *Ethics*.
9   On cities and provinces, see *De Regno*, I.2.4 [14]; on cities and kingdoms, see *De Regno*, I.14.5 [100]; on nations, see *Quaestiones Disputatae de Veritate* (1256–1259), 5.3 co; and on the universe as a whole, see *ST*, I–II, 91.1, 21.4, 100.5; *ScG*, I.42, 70–71, 78, 85–86, 93, 102, II.39, 42, III.64, 98.

life – but not, it seems, absolutely so. Rather, a province is even more self-sufficient than a city, particularly in respect of its capacity to defend the community against its enemies. Thus, although Aquinas followed Aristotle in progressing from household to city, as well as in distinguishing the city as a perfect and self-sufficient community, he here diverged from Aristotle in identifying a relative self-sufficiency in the household and neighbourhood and an even greater self-sufficiency in the province (Woolf 1913, 274–75; Gierke 1968, 96).

While Aristotle could write simply of the *polis*, Aquinas appears to have been acutely conscious of the fact that he had to address a wide range of both private and public forms of human association and government. As far as public associations were concerned, sometimes he used generic terms, such as "civic community", "political society" and so on, and referred to cities, kingdoms and provinces interchangeably – for what he had to say in these cases applied to them all without distinction (Finnis 1998, 219). But at other times, as has been seen, Aquinas referred to cities, kingdoms and provinces distinctly, for what he had to say about each one was different. Moreover, while Aquinas's picture was undoubtedly hierarchical (e.g., *ST*, I, 108.1–8, 112.1–4; cf. Beer 1986), it was a hierarchy which included a remarkable diversity of jurisdictions. Thus, although Aquinas regarded human beings and angels to be part of the one hierarchy of rational creatures under God, he maintained that there is a real sense in which they live under different hierarchies (Murphy 1997), just as those, he said, "that cannot be governed in the same way by a prince belong to different principalities" and, therefore, "under one king there are different cities, which are governed by different laws and administrators" (*ST*, I, 108.1; see also *ST*, I, 22.1 res; *Impugn.*, II.3; *ScG*, II.15.4, III.98.1; *De Malo*, I.1 res).[10] Aquinas also often had occasion to remark about the superior power of the emperor over a proconsul and of a proconsul over a governor and, likewise, the power of the pope over every other spiritual power in the church (*ST*, I–II, 19.5, 96.5; II–II, 69.3, 104.5; *De Regno*, II.3.12 [112]). Yet, elsewhere, he pointed out that "the subjects of one city or kingdom (*civitate vel regno*) are not bound by the laws of the sovereign of another city or kingdom, since they are not subject to his authority" (*ST*, I–II, 96.5 res).

Thus, thirdly, Aquinas developed a typology of kinds and forms of society which, while distinguishing "public" societies such as cities, provinces and kingdoms, from "private" societies such as households, business partnerships, craft guilds and religious associations, nonetheless classified them all as particular kinds of "society" (*Impugn.*, II.2, co; see also *Impugn.*, II.3, ad 6; *Pol.*, I.1.23 [31]).[11] These various forms of society Aquinas saw as possessing both a degree of separateness and independence from one another and a degree of integration and interdependence. An individual can be a member of a particular private society which, to a certain extent, governs itself, he said, while at the same time by virtue of that membership that individual

---

10 In *Quaestiones de quodlibet*, II, 5.1 res., Aquinas likewise described and limited the authority of the head of a household to matters pertaining to the management of the home, and that of a king to those matters pertaining to the government of the realm.
11 On medieval guilds in particular, see Berman 1983, 390–92; and Black 1984.

may be a member of a wider public society of which the smaller society is a part and in which governing institutions its representatives participate (*Impugn.*, II.2, ad 2). Aquinas here seems to have had a conception of both an inclusive membership in a set of integrated societies, and a conception of membership of several private or public societies separately and simultaneously, including a conception of dual citizenship of different cities (*Impugn.*, II.2, ad 3).

Finally, this idea of a plurality of communities of a political, ecclesiastical, social and economic nature, themselves composed of smaller constituent communities, extended for Aquinas to at least the beginning of the idea that this implies a kind of elective, corporate representation of the smaller community in the governing institutions of the larger. This conception Aquinas appears to have derived from certain texts of the Old and New Testaments in which the idea of the nation of Israel as constructed out of a plurality of tribes, clans and families (*ST*, I–II, 105.1 res., citing Exodus 18:21 and Deuteronomy 1:13, 15), parallels the idea of the church as a universal community constructed out of a plurality of dioceses and parishes (*Impugn.*, II.3; *Expositio in Lucam*, commenting on Luke 10:1), each in a sense self-governing, but also subject to a hierarchy of courts of appeal, themselves constituted by representatives of the constituent communities. Even the pope was presented here as a limited monarch, constrained by the fundamental beliefs, standards and institutions of the Christian faith (*Impugn.*, II.3). Similarly, while in some contexts Aquinas clearly favoured monarchical rule (*ScG*, IV.76.4; *De Regno*, I.3.1–4 [15–19]), he was acutely conscious of the propensity of kings to fall into tyranny, and he suggested several ways in which the authority of a king ought to be tempered, including the formation of compacts (*pacta*) which place constitutional limits on his power, mechanisms by which a tyrannical king can be deposed and systems of "mixed government" which enable all to have a "share" in ruling (*Pol.*, II.7.4 [245]; *De Regno*, I.7.1–12 [41–52]; *ST*, I–II, 95.4 and 105.1).[12]

Approximating Federalism

How close was this to modern federalism? A number of features of Aquinas's social thought stand out. First, there is Aquinas's recognition that society as a whole consists of a multiplicity of groups of a familial, social, economic, religious and political character, each possessing its own unique functions and jurisdiction. Especially as regards the institutions of church and state, Aquinas conceived of a "unity of order" which leaves room for constituent units at different levels to have an independent operation, while at the same time participating in the operations of the whole. Thus, Aquinas said that the subjects of one city or kingdom are not bound by the laws of another, and he wrote about the limitations on power to which even the pope (and by implication, the emperor) are subject. At the same time, however, he drew attention to the superior power of emperors and popes

---

12 See, further, Tierney 1979; Blythe 1992; Murphy 1997; Aroney 2007, 198–220.

over their subordinates in certain respects, and the similar power of proconsuls and bishops over those of inferior rank. An individual, according to Aquinas, may be a member of a particular corporation quite independently of the larger organization of which that corporation is a part, but in other cases membership in a constituent body necessarily entails membership in the larger one. Aquinas accordingly drew a picture of state and church constructed out of a plurality of villages and parishes, cities and dioceses, provinces and archdioceses, with the suggestion that in certain respects these communities are self-governing, in other respects they are subject to the authority of the governing institutions of the communities of which they are a part, and yet in each case there is a sense in which each smaller community is represented in the wider institutions charged with the government of the whole. Aquinas thus had a conception, similar to modern federalism, of a jurisdictional distribution of competencies between the parts and the whole, as well as a conception of corporate representation of the constituent bodies in the larger bodies of which they are a part.

In what way was Aquinas's social thought, nonetheless, conceptually distinct from modern federalism? Obviously, Aquinas's ideas were not limited to the "political" narrowly conceived. The specific institutions were different and the number and complexity of levels of government was relatively greater. Furthermore, while both the empire and the church allowed significant degrees of autonomy to their constituent parts, they were more hierarchical and aristocratic in character than could be said of most modern federations. While medieval government was clearly representative, it was certainly not democratic in the modern sense of the word. However, probably the most significant difference between Aquinas's social thought and modern federal ideas is that Aquinas did not understand these interrelationships to have been founded upon a series of federating covenants between the constituent units, but rather saw it as an outworking of the natural order of things. It was only in the context of his discussion of the constitutional limits upon the power of a king and the capacity of subjects to resist a tyrannical king that Aquinas discussed, in passing, the existence of certain pacts or agreements between king and people, to which the king may be held to account.[13] This is significant, but apart from this, Aquinas's social and political thought was not explicitly covenantal, a characteristic which goes to the very core of what distinguishes his thought from that of modern federalism.

Later theologians and canonists, some of them associated with the conciliar movement of the fourteenth and fifteenth centuries, developed the ideas of jurisdictional diversity and corporate representation in greater detail than Aquinas had (Tierney 1968; Black 1979). Jean Quidort (*c.* 1255–1306) set forth in *De potestate regia et papali* (*c.* 1302) a very detailed treatment of church and state which covered their distinct origins, jurisdictions, powers and relationships. The separate jurisdictions of archbishops, primates and pope were particularly distinguished (*De potestate*, X.119, XXV.251), but most originally, John argued that, on analogy with the representation of the elected elders of the tribes of Israel in the Sanhedrin

---

13   *De Regno*, I.7.1–12 [41–52].

(Deuteronomy 1:15), the various provinces of the Church should be represented within the governing institutions of the church as a whole (*De potestate*, XIX.207). Pierre D'Ailly (*c.* 1350–1420) and Jean Gerson (1363–1429), writing about a century later, repeated the same basic idea, D'Ailly emphasizing that it was the role of the college of cardinals, as representatives of the church, to temper the power of the pope (Blythe 1992, 246, 251). Similarly, in *De Concordantia Catholica* (*c.* 1433), Nicolas Cusanus (1404–1464) closely developed the idea of the corporate representation of the provinces in the councils of the church, extending the analysis to the representative roles of priests, bishops, archbishops, metropolitans and pope, each within their respective synods at a parochial, diocesan, metropolitan, provincial and universal level (*De Concord.*, II.1.71) and envisaging a similar representative arrangement of governors, counts, marquesses, dukes, kings and emperor in the temporal sphere (*De Concord.*, III.1.292; III.7:350; III.12:377–8; III.25.469–72; III:35.527). In both spheres, Cusanus insisted upon the election of rulers by representatives of the constituent jurisdictions, such as the election of the pope by the cardinals as representatives of the provinces (*De Concord.*, II.18.163–65) and the election of the emperor by the princely electors within the empire (*De Concord.*, III.4:325, 332, 338). Fundamental to the conciliar ideas proposed by these writers was the proposition that the fundamental locus of authority in the church rests, not with the pope, but with the *congregatio fidelium*, the entire body of the church, represented in its councils (Tierney 1968, 4–6). However, while the Councils of Constance (1414–1418) and Basel (1431–1435) marked the high point of conciliarism within the Roman Catholic Church, the movement was condemned at the Fifth Lateran Council (1512–1517).

While it has been argued, with some force, that the political thought that emerged from the Reformation during the sixteenth and seventeenth centuries drew very significantly on late conciliarist ideas (Oakley 1962), the decisive break with the Roman papacy occasioned by the Reformation gave Reformed theologians, jurists and publicists the opportunity to develop and vigorously promote the idea that both church and state ought, for fundamentally biblical reasons, to be understood as a composition of constituent communities at a local, regional and national level (e.g., Rutherford 1644a; Rutherford 1644b). The basic idea here was of a *consociation* or *federation* (both terms were used) of constituent communities, governed under a system of representative councils and graded courts, united on the basis of a common profession of faith or a common allegiance, and adopted by oath in the form of a covenant. The *Vindiciae contra Tyrannos* (1579) forcefully argued, for example, that the legitimate political authority of a king rests upon a series of covenants he has entered into with representatives of the people in their various towns and provinces, and that it rests with duly constituted inferior magistrates to resist, if necessary, a tyrannical king. The most systematic statement of the theory was set forth by Johannes Althusius (1557–1638) who founded his socio-political theory upon the general proposition that organized society is properly built up through a succession of compacts among constituent elements: starting with families and kinship groups, then guild associations and corporations, through villages, towns and cities, and culminating in entire provinces confederated together to form a universal political association or commonwealth (Althusius 1614). In Althusius, one encounters a conception of society that is thoroughly federalized in its familial, social, economic, ecclesiastical and political relations.

The social contract theory of Thomas Hobbes (1588–1679) and John Locke (1632–1704), while in certain respects similar to the covenantalism of Rutherford and Althusius, was nonetheless significantly different. Hobbes, like Althusius, wrote of a "covenant" or "social contract" lying at the foundation of political society, but Hobbes's compact was but a single agreement, entered into by all the individuals in a certain territory, who commit themselves to an absolute subjection to a single, common power: "*one* Man or *one* Assembly of men, that may reduce all their Wills, by *plurality* of voices, unto *one* Will", as Hobbes put it (*Leviathan*, II:17). For Hobbes, this "Leviathan" or "Mortall God" is "called Soveraigne, and said to have Soveraigne Power" (*Leviathan*, II:17), whether such government be in the form of monarchy, aristocracy or democracy (*Leviathan*, II:19). In a Hobbesian democracy, the singularity of the will of the sovereign is guaranteed through strictly majoritarian rule (*Leviathan*, II:18). And, according to Hobbes, under the unitary authority of the sovereign, all other groups are absolutely subject (*Leviathan*, II:20), just as all minor covenants are regarded as absolutely inferior to the social contract (*Leviathan*, II:18). Hobbes admitted that there may be within a political society various towns, provinces, universities, colleges or churches, each with their distinct laws and customs, but for Hobbes these are all ultimately and absolutely subject to the superior will of the sovereign (*Leviathan*, II:20). Leagues or covenants among subjects are in fact dangerous, he said, and therefore unlawful (*Leviathan*, II:20). Accordingly, "things that weaken or tend to the dissolution of a commonwealth" include the opinion that the sovereign is subject to civil law and that the sovereign is divided (*Leviathan*, II:1). Among them also is "the immoderate greatness of a Town" or a "great number of corporations; which are as it were many lesser Commonwealths in the bowels of a greater, like wormes in the entrayles of a naturall man" (*Leviathan*, II:29).

Hobbes was of course an extreme case, but a unitary conception of political society is also to be discerned in John Locke's *Second Treatise of Government*. For although Locke's scheme very clearly allowed a diversity of associations and institutions to operate freely within society, these associations were nothing other than expressions of the autonomous rights of individuals and were therefore strictly private in character. Political society, for Locke, is founded upon a social contract between individuals, not a federal compact between smaller constituent political communities (*Second Treatise*, §4). Locke envisaged the possibility of a league, and even a confederation, created by the exercise of the "federative power" of the commonwealth, but this did not create a political society in any significant sense analogous to our modern idea of federation (*Second Treatise*, §145). Locke's theory was likewise consistent with a form of political decentralization through the exercise of the community's primordial power to decide what "form" of government "they think good" (*Second Treatise*, §132). Indeed, Locke explicitly considered the case of subordinate communities such as cities (*Second Treatise*, §133), and discussed the status of the subordinate magistrate (*Second Treatise*, §210). However, as his discussion of these possibilities makes clear, Locke, like Hobbes, considered that true political society is *unitary* in its essential nature, with the legislative power in each society being *supreme over all subordinate institutions*, and expressing its will by *simple majority vote* (*Second Treatise*, §96, §134).

On this general approach to political philosophy, there are only two possible kinds of "federal" government, broadly conceived. The first is a confederation of independent states through which individual political societies agree to cooperate and yet retain their unique status as sovereign nation-states. The second is a situation where a unitary state decides to adopt a decentralized system of government, perhaps even going so far as to guarantee to the local or regional units of government certain spheres of independent operation. However, it is not possible on the basis of classical social contract theory to conceive of a political system which falls between these two possibilities. And yet, classic modern federations such as the United States, Switzerland and Australia partake of both sets of characteristics. All three came into being through agreements among constituent states and show the marks of this in their representative institutions, configurations of power and amending formulas. Thus, all three constitutions: (1) provide for the special representation of the states or cantons in the federal legislature, (2) assume that state or cantonal power is original and general, whereas federal power is specifically granted and (3) require state or cantonal approval of constitutional changes and, in certain cases, the consent of individual states. However, at the same time, all three exhibit characteristics which distinguish them from mere confederations. Thus, in all three systems: (1) ultimate interpretive authority is vested in the governing institutions of the whole (federal courts in the United States and Australia, the federal legislature in Switzerland) and (2) the constituent states are not (as it has turned out) free to secede from the federation on their own motion.

To explain the features of modern federations in their covenantal foundations, representatives structures, configurations of power and amendment formulas, one must look, therefore, to theories which pre-date classical liberal theories of politics (where the only really essential elements in politics are the individual and the state). In Rutherford, Althusius and other post-Reformation jurists, publicists and theologians, one meets with a vision of society founded upon a succession of covenants, and which, while not democratic in the modern sense, is thoroughly federal in terms of its covenanted foundation, representative structures, configuration of power and amendment processes. In Cusanus and others associated with the conciliarist movement, one finds a vision of church and state which, though not founded upon a succession of covenants, is nonetheless systematically federal in structure, especially in terms of its systems of corporate representation and jurisdictional diversity. Similarly in Thomas Aquinas, although one does not find a covenantal motif, one does encounter a far-reaching jurisdictional diversity and the beginnings of the idea of corporate representation, both of which are necessary, if not sufficient, indicators of the existence of a federal system of government in the modern sense of the word.

References

Original Sources

Althusius, J. (1614), *Politica methodice digesta et exemplis sacris et profanis illustrata*, 3rd Edition. (Herborn), translated: Carney, F. (1995), *Politica: An Abridged Translation* (Indianapolis: Liberty Fund).
Aquinas, T. (1256–1259), *Quaestiones Disputatae de Veritate*, translated: Mulligan, R.W. (1952), *St. Thomas Aquinas: Truth* (Chicago: Henry Regnery Company).
—— (c. 1267), *De Regno ad regem Cypri*, translated: Phelan, G. and Eschmann, I.Th. (1949), *On Kingship, to the King of Cyprus* (Toronto: Pontifical Institute of Mediaeval Studies).
—— (1263–1271), *De Malo*, translated: Oesterle, J. (1993), *St. Thomas Aquinas: On Evil* (University of Notre Dame Press).
—— (1256), *Contra impugnantes Dei cultum et Religionem*, translated: Procter, J. (1902), *An Apology for the Religious Orders* (London: Sands & Co).
—— (1263–1264), *Expositio in Lucam*, Guarenti, A. (ed.), 2nd edition (Taurini-Romae: Marietti, 1953).
—— (1256–1259, 1269–1272), *Quaestiones de quodlibet*, translated: Edwards, S. (1983), *St. Thomas Aquinas: Quodlibetal Questions 1 and 2* (Toronto: Pontifical Institute of Mediaeval Studies).
—— (1256), *Scriptum super Sententiis magistri Petri Lombardi*, translated: Molloy, M. (1985), *Civil Authority in Medieval Philosophy: Lombard, Aquinas and Bonaventura* (Lanham: University Press of America).
—— (1271–1272), *Sententia libri Ethicorum*, translated: Litzinger, C.I. (1993), *Commentary on Aristotle's Nicomachean Ethics* (Notre Dame: Dumb Ox Books).
—— (1269–1272), *Sententia libri Politicorum*, translated: Lerner, R. and Mahdi, M. (eds) (1963), *Medieval Political Philosophy: A Source Book* (Ithaca: Cornell University Press).
—— (1265–1268, 1271–1273), *Summa Theologiae*, translated: Fathers of the English Dominican Province (1947–1948), *Summa Theologica* (London: Burns & Oates).
—— (1259–1265), *Summa contra Gentiles*, translated: Rickaby, J. (1905), *Of God and His Creatures: An Annotated Translation (with Some Abridgement) of the Summa contra Gentiles of Saint Thomas Aquinas* (London: Burns and Oates).
Aristotle (1984), *The Politics*, translated: Lord, C. (Chicago: University of Chicago Press).
—— (2000), *Nicomachean Ethics*, translated: Crisp, R. (Cambridge: Cambridge University Press).
Cusanus, N. (c. 1433), *De Concordantia Catholica*, translated: Sigmund, P. (1991), *A Catholic Concordance* (Cambridge: Cambridge University Press).
Duplessis-Mornay, P. and Languet, H. (attrib.) (1579), *Vindiciae contra Tyrannos*, translated: Garnett, G. (1994), *Brutus: Vindiciae, contra tyrannos or, Concerning the Legitimate Power of a Prince over the People, and of the People over a Prince* (Cambridge: Cambridge University Press).

Hobbes, T. (1991), *Leviathan*, Tuck, R. (ed.) (Cambridge: Cambridge University Press).
Leo XIII (1879), *Aeterni Patris: On the Restoration of Christian Philosophy*.
Locke, J. (1992), *Two Treatises of Government*, Laslett, P. (ed.) (Cambridge: Cambridge University Press).
Quidort, J. (c. 1302), *De potestate regia et papali*, translated: Watt, J.A. (1971), *John of Paris: On Royal and Papal Power* (Toronto: Pontifical Institute of Medieval Studies).
Rutherford, S. (1644a), *The Due Right of Presbyteries: or, A Peaceable Plea for the Government of the Church of Scotland*.
—— (1644b), *Lex, Rex, or The Law and the Prince; A dispute for the Just Prerogative of King and People*.

Secondary Literature

Aroney, N. (2005), Federal constitutionalism/European constitutionalism in comparative perspective, in Gert-Jan Leenknegt (ed.), *Getuigend Staatsrecht: Liber Amicorum A. K. Koekkoek* (Wolf Legal Publishing, Tilburg).
—— (2006), Formation, representation and amendment in federal constitutions, *American Journal of Comparative Law*, 54:1, 277–336.
—— (2007), Subsidiarity, federalism and the best constitution: Thomas Aquinas on city, province and empire, *Law and Philosophy* 26:2, 161–228.
Beer, S. (1986), The rule of the wise and holy: hierarchy in the Thomistic system, *Political Theory*, 14:3, 391–422.
—— (1993), *To Make a Nation: The rediscovery of American federalism* (Cambridge: Belknap Press).
Berman, H. (1983), *Law and Revolution: The formation of the western legal tradition* (Cambridge: Harvard University Press).
Black, A. (1979), *Council and Commune: The conciliar movement and the fifteenth century heritage* (London: Burns & Oates).
—— (1984), *Guilds and Civil Society in European Political Thought from the Twelfth Century to the Present* (London: Methuen).
Blythe, J. (1992), *Ideal Government and the Mixed Constitution in the Middle Ages* (Princeton: Princeton University Press).
Burgess, Michael. (2006). *Comparative Federalism: Theory and Practice* (New York: Routledge).
Dahl, R.A. (1986), Federalism and the democratic process, in *Democracy, Identity and Equality* (Oslo: Norwegian University Press).
Davis, S.R. (1978), *The Federal Principle: A journey through time in quest of a meaning* (Berkeley: University of California Press).
Elazar, D.J. (1987), *Exploring Federalism* (Tuscaloosa: University of Alabama Press).
—— (1995–1999), *The Covenant Tradition in Politics*, 4 vols. (New Jersey: Transaction Publishers).

Eschmann, I.Th. (1947), Thomistic social philosophy and the theology of original sin, *Medieval Studies*, 9, 19–55.
Finer, S.E. (1974), *Comparative Government* (London: Allen Lane).
Finnis, J. (1998), *Aquinas: Moral, Political and Legal Theory* (Oxford: Oxford University Press).
Friedrich, C.J. (1968), *Trends of Federalism in Theory and Practice* (London: Pall Mall Press).
Gierke, O. von (1968), *Political Theories of the Middle Age*, Frederick Maitland (trans.) (Cambridge: Cambridge University Press).
Gilby, T. (1958), *The Political Thought of Thomas Aquinas* (Chicago: University of Chicago Press).
Hopfl, H.M. (1983), 'Isms', *British Journal of Political Science*, 13:1, 1–17.
Hueglin, T.O. (1999), *Early Modern Concepts for a Late Modern World: Althusius on community and federalism* (Waterloo: Wilfrid Laurier University Press).
—— and Fenna, A. (2006), *Comparative Federalism: A systematic inquiry* (Peterborough: Broadview Press).
King, P. (1982), *Federalism and Federation* (Baltimore: Johns Hopkins University Press).
Kunkel, W. (1973), *An Introduction to Roman Legal and Constitutional History*, Kelly, J.M. (trans.), 2nd edition (Oxford: Clarendon Press).
Murphy, M. (1997), Consent, custom, and the common good in Aquinas's account of political authority, *The Review of Politics*, 59:2, 323–50.
Nederman, C. (1987), Aristotle as authority: alternative Aristotelian sources of late medieval political theory, *History of European Ideas*, 8:1, 31–44.
Oakley, F. (1962), On the road from Constance to 1688: the political thought of John Major and George Buchanan, *The Journal of British Studies*, 1:2, 1–31.
Riker, W.H. (1975), Federalism, in Greenstein, F.I. and Polsby, N.W. (eds), *Handbook of Political Science*, Vol. 5 (Reading: Addison-Wesley).
Tellenbach, G. (1993), *The Church in Western Europe from the Tenth to the Early Twentieth Century*, T. Reuter (trans.) (Cambridge: Cambridge University Press).
Tierney, B. (1968), *Foundations of the Conciliar Theory: The Contribution of the Medieval Canonists from Gratian to the Great Schism* (Cambridge: Cambridge University Press).
—— (1979), Aristotle, Aquinas, and the ideal constitution, *Proceedings of the Patristic, Medieval and Renaissance Conference*, 4, 1–11.
Watts, R.L., (1999), *Comparing Federal Systems* (Kingston: McGill-Queen's University Press).
Woolf, C.N.S. (1913), *Bartolus of Sassoferrato: His Position in the Political Thought of his Time* (Cambridge: Cambridge University Press).

Further Reading

Original Sources

Althusius, J. (1614), *Politica methodice digesta et exemplis sacris et profanis illustrata*, 3rd edition (Herborn), translated: Carney, F. (1995), *Politica: An Abridged Translation* (Indianapolis: Liberty Fund).
Aquinas, T. (c. 1267), *De Regno ad regem Cypri*, translated: Phelan, G. and Eschmann, I.Th. (1949), *On Kingship, to the King of Cyprus* (Toronto: Pontifical Institute of Mediaeval Studies).
—— (1265–1268, 1271–1273), *Summa Theologiae*, translated: Fathers of the English Dominican Province (1947–1948), *Summa Theologica* (London: Burns & Oates).
Cusanus, N. (c. 1433), *De Concordantia Catholica*, translated: Sigmund, P. (1991), *A Catholic Concordance* (Cambridge: Cambridge University Press).
Duplessis-Mornay, P. and Languet, H. (attrib.) (1579), *Vindiciae contra Tyrannos*, translated: Garnett, G. (1994), *Brutus: Vindiciae, contra tyrannos or, Concerning the Legitimate Power of a Prince over the People, and of the People over a Prince* (Cambridge: Cambridge University Press).
Quidort, J. (c. 1302), *De potestate regia et papali*, translated: Watt, J.A. (1971), *John of Paris: On Royal and Papal Power* (Toronto: Pontifical Institute of Medieval Studies).
Rutherford, S. (1644), *Lex, Rex, or The Law and the Prince; A dispute for the Just Prerogative of King and People*.

Secondary Literature

Aroney, N. (2007), Subsidiarity, federalism and the best constitution: Thomas Aquinas on city, province and empire, *Law and Philosophy* 26:2, 161–228.
Beer, S. (1986), The rule of the wise and holy: hierarchy in the Thomistic system, *Political Theory*, 14:3, 391–422.
Berman, H. (1983), *Law and Revolution: The formation of the western legal tradition* (Cambridge: Harvard University Press).
Blythe, J. (1992), *Ideal Government and the Mixed Constitution in the Middle Ages* (Princeton: Princeton University Press).
Elazar, D.J. (1995–1999), *The Covenant Tradition in Politics*, 4 vols (New Jersey: Transaction Publishers).
Finnis, J. (1998), *Aquinas: Moral, Political and Legal Theory* (Oxford: Oxford University Press).
Fortin, E. (1987), St. Thomas Aquinas, in Strauss, L. and Cropsey, J. (eds), *History of Political Philosophy*, 3rd edition (University of Chicago Press).
Gierke, O. von (1968), *Political Theories of the Middle Age*, Frederick Maitland (trans.) (Cambridge: Cambridge University Press).

Gilby, T. (1958), *The Political Thought of Thomas Aquinas* (Chicago: University of Chicago Press).
Hueglin, T.O. (1999), *Early Modern Concepts for a Late Modern World: Althusius on community and federalism* (Waterloo: Wilfrid Laurier University Press).
Murphy, M. (1997), Consent, custom, and the common good in Aquinas's account of political authority, *The Review of Politics*, 59:2, 323–350.
Oakley, F. (1962), On the road from Constance to 1688: the political thought of John Major and George Buchanan, *The Journal of British Studies*, 1:2, 1–31.
Scully, E. (1981), The place of the state in society according to Aquinas, *The Thomist*, 45, 407–29.
Tierney, B. (1968), *Foundations of the Conciliar Theory: The contribution of the medieval canonists from Gratian to the Great Schism* (Cambridge: Cambridge University Press).
Tierney, B. (1979), Aristotle, Aquinas, and the Ideal Constitution, *Proceedings of the Patristic, Medieval and Renaissance Conference*, 4, 1–11.
Woolf, C.N.S. (1913), *Bartolus of Sassoferrato: His position in the political thought of his time* (Cambridge: Cambridge University Press).

The Reformational Legacy of Theologico-political Federalism

Shaun de Freitas and Andries Raath

Introduction

The terms *federalism* and *covenantal* are virtually interchangeable, and it is the academic specialization in the fields of theology and politics that has contributed to the separation in meaning of these two terms. Federalism entails, *inter alia*, an understanding of the relationships between God and the world, and among humans as based on covenants, including the understanding that the inner nature of social groups and the relationships among them are understood as covenantal (McCoy and Baker 1991, 11–13). This is quite similar to a more secular view as postulated by Friederich, in which federalism primarily entails the process of federalizing a political community which, in turn, entails the process by which a number of separate political communities enter into arrangements for, *inter alia*, working out solutions (McCoy and Baker 1991, 13–14).

The political connotations regarding the covenant have been approached from a myriad of angles in political history. Like organicism, contractualism formed an important underlying insight regarding the nature of the social bond (North 1990, 35–36), reflecting a particular view of the cosmos, which in turn undergirds a particular view of society. The idea of the biblical covenant not only emphasized the relevance of God's law (as stated in scripture), but also gave such law a conditional role which elevated the community's sense of responsibility towards God. On the other hand, adherents to a more enlightened and secular social contract theory relied heavily on reason as the measure for the content of the law, coupled with the absence of a conditional and responsible approach towards God. Gough's *The Social Contract* (1936) provides, mainly from a secular approach, a good indication of the importance of contractual thought throughout the history of political theory. Elazar's *Covenant and Polity in Biblical Israel* (1995) and his *Covenant and Commonwealth* (1996), on the other hand, provide a good biblical exposition on the political implications of covenantal thought.¹ Therefore, in both secular and traditionally religious circles, covenantal or contractual connotations played an integral role in political and constitutional theory throughout the ages. In addition, the theological approach to the covenant varied from support of a single covenant, applicable to both the individual and society, to the postulation of a more dispensational approach to the covenant (accompanied by a passive regard for the law), which consequently had an influence on Christian political and constitutional theory.

The idea of having parties enter into an agreement with one another accompanied by specific conditions, responsibilities and consequences, formed an integral facet of political and constitutional theory throughout history. The contractual and covenantal political paradigm was in itself a norm to be ascribed to the dictates of natural law, whether from a divine or rational perspective. Since early times, political theory included contractual ideas. According to Cicero, for example, a commonwealth is not a collection of people brought together in any particular way, but an assemblage of people in large numbers associated in an *agreement* with respect to justice and the *partnership* of the common good (Cicero *De re Publica*, 1948 [*DRP*], I. xxv. 39). Rather striking in Cicero's covenantal thought are the references to *covenanting* with the gods (God). Alluding to oath-taking as the mechanism for invoking the "higher" authority of the gods, Cicero makes social covenanting the means for assuring man's well-being in civil society (DRP II. vii. 16). The social covenant of men is only binding and enforceable if a vow to God *binds* the covenanting parties. The vow to God is in effect a contract (DRP, II. xvi. 41).² However, according to Elazar, the idea of the "social contract" was rejected by the most prominent and historically influential philosophers in favour of more organically based conceptions of political life, rooted in ideas of natural law, or what is "right" by nature (Elazar 1996, 39). Evans also observes that social contract theory was not the work of secular theoreticians and that the feudal order was, in a legal context, an intricate network of contracts within a political era that was saturated with its precepts (Evans 1994, 68–169) – the origins of the social contract were medieval and religious (Evans 1994, 184; see also Elazar 1996, 3).

---

1   For further discussion of Daniel Elazar's contribution to federalism studies, see Chapter 22 in this volume.
2   Implicated in Cicero's reference to covenanting with "God" is the question regarding the extent to which Cicero's religion had a deistic connotation. In *Justice and Equity in Cicero*, Van Zyl states that there is little doubt that Cicero considered religion to play a highly significant role in politics. According to Van Zyl, the functional and almost practical way in which Cicero refers to God or the gods does cast certain doubt as to the depth of his religious feelings. However, the pre-eminence of the divinity of nature and of man's soul was far too deeply ingrained in Cicero to admit of religious superficiality (1991, 55). On the other hand, direct references to God by Cicero do indicate some degree of acceptance of God's existence, for example Cicero's statement in *On the Commonwealth*: "the true law is an expression of the purpose and rule of God" (Hall 1996, 16). This in turn supports Romans 2:14–15 and is indicative of God's light in the hearts of men, although this light is not necessarily the light of salvation, and although this light shines brighter in some than in others.

THE REFORMATIONAL LEGACY OF THEOLOGICO-POLITICAL FEDERALISM

The Reformation contributed to the revitalization of the covenantal (contractual) political perspective from a biblical point of view, the context of Europe at the time being most conducive to this revitalization. According to Elazar, "the only record we have of a fully covenantal civilization is that of ancient Israel as portrayed in Scripture" (Elazar 1996, x). This entailed an understanding of God's political interaction with man by means of the covenant as political mechanism. Silving states that mankind has not invented any notion which would exceed in scope the democratic thought contained in the idea of the state contract, and that the appearance in the Bible of that idea is therefore one of the most puzzling phenomena in the history of ideas. The novelty of the Biblical idea on the covenant lies in the notion of the state contract as both a *historical* and *ethical* foundation of all law and government (Silving 1953, 1130–31). Politically the covenant idea, according to Elazar, has within it the seeds of modern constitutionalism in that it implies the accepted limitation of power on the part of all the parties to it – a limitation not inherent in nature but involving willed concessions. In the community's covenantal relationship with God, the leaders who bind themselves through the covenant limit their powers, by serving the people in accordance with the terms of the Covenant (which is God's law) (Elazar 2006a, 5). Also, the office of magistracy serves as the hub of conditions pivotal to the covenant. The office of magistracy implies an ordinance that is instituted by God and which bears a holy nature that cannot be equated with the sinful nature of the person of the magistrate. Popularity was not the measure of the covenant, but the law, and any activity seriously contrary to the law, would justify resistance due to the breaching of covenantal terms. The covenant therefore serves as an important political tool towards the furtherance of effective governance. In this regard also, McAllister's idea of the state as a moral person, "that is, a being which can and ought to be conscious of its duties, and which for the fulfilling of these duties is responsible before God and mankind" (McAllister 2001, 29–30), attains deeper meaning within the context of the idea of the biblical covenant. Embedded in the principle of God's divine and absolute sovereignty in the formation of all events (excluding sin) throughout history, is found the political and jurisprudential-relevant scriptural emphasis on the covenant between God and community, where the latter is both obligated and responsible for the accomplishment of the scripturally devised conditions directed at it. Deuteronomy postulates the theology of an omnipotent, living God who intervenes in history, directs it, and has chosen Israel to be His people for His reasons. This God has covenanted with Israel to require them to hearken to and to keep a certain constitution so as to achieve a certain way of life, that He will hold them and their descendents accountable for the fulfilment of their side of that covenant, that He is a God who loves, seeks and does justice and expects His covenant partners to do the same.[3] The Book of Joshua, among others, tells the story of Joshua's acquisition of a mandate from God who renews His promise and restates the conditions that must be met by the Israelites.[4] The Book of Judges is replete with the theme of the political covenant, written in

---

3 Elazar 2006b, 13; also see 3, 6, 8, 12, 14, 16 and 18–20.
4 Elazar 2006a, last accessed 3 January 2007, 11; also see 20–21, 23, 40, and 42.

the spirit of covenantal religion in the covenantal polity.[5] Pertaining to Psalm 89, Elazar comments that this psalm integrates time and eternity, heaven and earth, nature and man, the nations and Israel, God's justice and wrath, punishment and redemption, all within the covenantal framework, which is a recurrent theme of the Psalms.[6] Moses, acting under a divine commission, proposed to the nation the question of whether they would receive Jehovah for their king, and submit to His laws. By the voluntary consent of the nation Moses made God king. This led to the establishment of idolatry as a crime, and hence idolatry is called by the Hebrew writers "the transgression of the covenant" – it was a breach of the fundamental compact between the Hebrew people and their chosen king.[7] Although there are various strong covenantal connotations in the Bible such as Genesis 9 (Noah), and Genesis 15; 17 (Abraham); the most important covenant in the Old Testament is that of Sinai (Exodus 19 and further). Although the latter is viewed as God giving his law to the Jews, the larger picture reflected the calling of Israel by God to be a loyal nation to God – this new relationship being viewed as a covenant (Alexander and Alexander 2004, 210).

The Hebrew language uses the word *berith* ("covenant") to denote an international treaty as well as a covenant between God and His people. There were also many similarities between covenants in the near-Eastern world (during the time of the Old Testament) and covenants in the Old Testament. The purpose of a treaty in Old Testament times was to guarantee the absolute loyalty of a vassal king (or vassal state) to the other party (or state) to the covenant. In this regard the treaty's wording points to expectations of absolute loyalty: Deuteronomy, for example, has many indications of this. Part of the covenant format included a stipulation that stated the reciprocal responsibilities of the parties, as well as punishments and blessings if the vassal disobeyed or obeyed the treaty (Alexander and Alexander 2004, 210). Also, in this regard, treaties as well as covenants included the basis of the stipulation being the undeserved favour of the ruler. Stipulations or laws follow after the vassal is reminded of that which the ruler has done for the vassal. It is expected of the vassal to obey the stipulations out of thanksgiving and appreciation. Also in the Old Testament, the law follows on grace: on the grounds of the manner in which God freed Israel, Israel is encouraged to obey God.[8] The prophets remind the people that the covenant relationship contains responsibilities as well as privileges, as witnessed in Amos 3:2 (Alexander and Alexander 2004, 211).

---

5   Elazar 2006c, 8. Also see 9 and 15–19.
6   Elazar 2007, 17.
7   Wines 2007.
8   See Deuteronomy 28:15–68 indicating God's punishing Israel if they broke the covenant.

The Reformational Contribution to the Idea of the Biblical Covenant

The revitalization of the idea of the *Christian Covenanted Community* had its roots in early Reformational thought. Sixteenth-century Zurich revived the idea of the biblical covenant, which entailed on the one hand, the covenant, which expresses God's universality and His involvement in human affairs; and, on the other, the provision of the form for man's communal involvement in, and response to, God's promises and blessings, with the focus on man's obedience to God. Scotland, in the year 1643, heralded Samuel Rutherford's *magnum opus* on political thought, and more specifically, his theologico-political federalism. Approximately a century prior to this and quite a distance to the East, in Zurich, the emergence of a unique reformed line of thinking had occurred in the person of Heinrich Bullinger (1504–1575). Bullinger produced the first work that organized the understanding of God, creation, humanity, human history and society around the covenant, which may be defined as a *bilateral* and *conditional relationship between God and man*. This is regarded as the point of origin or the *fountainhead of federalism* and has increasingly come to permeate the world in the four-and-a-half centuries since its publication (McCoy and Baker 1991, 9).[9] To Bullinger, scripture, together with its *conditions*, confirmed the covenant between God and man. This was the covenant taught by the prophets and the apostles (McCoy and Baker 1991, 20). Baker states:

> *Bullinger's approach was biblical and historical rather than systematic and static. For this reason, in order to understand the full importance of the covenant in his thought, his conception of the covenant in history, from Adam to his own day, must be clarified. For Bullinger discovered the prototype for the Reformed community of his own day in the history of God's people within the covenant, especially during the Old Testament period (Baker 1980, 53; also see 107 and 163).*

To Bullinger, the Bible was a most important source also referring to the various church fathers in order to demonstrate that the covenant was not an innovation, but the very fabric from which the history of salvation was woven through the centuries, from Adam to his own day; also citing Augustine, Irenaeus, Tertullian, Lactantius and Eusebius for patristic support (McCoy and Baker 1991, 14–15). In fact, Irenaeus was the only church father who hinted at a *conditional* covenant (Elazar 1996, 31). The record of the covenant was to be found in Genesis 17:1–14, from which it is deduced that God has acted according to human custom at every point. First, the passage explains who bound themselves together, namely, God and the descendants of Abraham. Second, the text states the *conditions* under which they bound themselves together, specifically, that God wished to be the God of

---

[9] The authors refer here to the treatise entitled *De testamento seu foedere Dei unico et aeterno* ("The One and Eternal Testament or Covenant of God").

the descendants of Abraham and that the descendants of Abraham ought to walk uprightly before God. Third, it is explained that the covenant is made between them forever. And finally, the entire covenant is confirmed with a specific ceremony in blood (McCoy and Baker 1991, 104).[10] This *contractual* nature of covenantal thought pointed to the distinction between the covenant idea as emphasized by Bullinger on the one hand and by Augustine and Calvin on the other, the latter two not thinking in terms of a bilateral covenant (McCoy and Baker 1991, 23).

The concept of federalism in this context primarily denotes the relationship between God and man and between man and man, as a bilateral and conditional relationship (McCoy and Baker 1991, 12, 20, 23–25). Bullinger did not posit a second political covenant; his was a single covenant (Baker 1980, 176)[11] which, in turn, implied other sub-covenant structures within a political paradigm, such as between the supreme magistrate and the people. A nation is in covenant with God, and government is there to facilitate the required *conditions* of this covenant. God's people needed the magistrate and his laws to govern every aspect of life. The Christian magistrate was sovereign in Christian societies, and it was his duty to enforce the *conditions* of the covenant. The covenant was therefore the cornerstone of the Christian state (McCoy and Baker 1991, 26–27). The magistrate aided God's people in keeping the condition of love within the external church or the Christian Commonwealth, this covenant condition clearly having to do with *judicial* or *civil things*. This, to Bullinger, was part of the enforcement of the duties of piety; these *judicial* or *civil* precepts were necessary for the holiest churches, so much so that they could not exist comfortably without them. Bullinger saw the Old Testament judges and kings as models for New Testament Christian government (Baker 1980, 92). The magistracy and the church were the institutions of the covenant (Baker 1980, 107; also see 120–21). In fact, Bullinger interpreted the Reformation within the larger context of the covenant as a *restoration of the covenant*, similar to such restoration in the Old Testament under Hezekiah, Jehoshaphat and Josiah (Baker 1980, 100). To Bullinger, *true reform meant the restitution of the covenant* and the restoration of the ancient religion of the patriarchs and Christ, the pattern of which was found in the Old Testament. Restitution of the covenant between a people and God encompassed both ecclesiastical and civil, therefore encompassing all matters in society (Baker 1980, 102). As God had a remnant of seven thousand faithful (1 Kings 19:18), so He had a remnant in Bullinger's time (Baker 1980, 101).

---

10 Also see Baker 1980, 76, where Bullinger, discussing the Hebrew word *berith*, emphasizes the conditional nature of covenants, where each side promises something to the other. God makes His covenant with the human race from the very beginning, binding Himself to man and agreeing to certain conditions to be witnessed, *inter alia*, by Adam, Noah, Abraham, Moses and Daniel.

11 Bullinger applied the one covenant to both religious and civil life; the conditions of the covenant related both to matters of faith and to public policy and justice within the community. Therefore, even though Bullinger did not refer to a purely political covenant, the political implications of the covenant were inherent in what might be called his political theology (Baker 1980, 176).

Following the theologico-political federalism of Bullinger, was Philippe Duplessis-Mornay's (1549–1623) work, *Vindiciae Contra Tyrannos* ("A Defence of Liberty Against Tyrants"), published anonymously in 1579 (McCoy and Baker 1991, 47). The idea of the vertical covenant entails a *covenant between God and the king* (Duplessis-Mornay 1924, 70–71). In the covenant between God and king, the latter is *obliged* with the utmost of his abilities to procure the glory of God: God is the proper revenger of this covenant (Duplessis-Mornay 1924, 176; see also 70–74). Inherent in the covenant between the king and the people is the requirement that the people, by way of stipulation, need a *performance of covenants*, and the king promises the same. According to the law, the *condition of a stipulator is more worthy than that of a promiser*. Here, the people ask the king whether he will govern justly, upon which the king promises to do so. In turn, the people answer that, while the king governs justly, they will obey him. In this covenant, the king aims at profiting the people and the people become the lawful punisher in this covenant (Duplessis-Mornay 1924, 71 and 175–76). Mornay summarizes this horizontal covenant by saying that there is a *mutually obligatory contract* between the king and subjects which requires the people to obey faithfully and the king to govern justly; and for the performance whereof the king promises first and afterwards, the people (Duplessis-Mornay 1924, 180–81; 199 and 212).[12]

To Johannes Althusius (1557–1638), the "biblical grand design" for humankind is federal, in that it is based, *inter alia*, upon a network of covenants beginning with those between God and human beings and eventually weaving a web of human, especially political, relationships in a federal way (Elazar 1995, xxxvi). To Althusius, the covenants of humanity exist within the covenant of God and are limited by the Divine covenant. This view is to be anticipated and understood with precision in terms of the tradition of federal theology and ethics in which Althusius was immersed at Herborn. People in covenant and rulers in covenant are also bound to the more comprehensive covenantal order of God (see McCoy 1988, 197; also see 158–59). Althusius introduced the doctrine of *symbiotic association* – the community of men living together and united by real bonds which a *contract of union*, expressed or implied, institutionalized (Carney ix, 1964). The constituting of the supreme magistrate is the process by which he assumes the imperium and administration of the realm conferred by the body of the universal association, and by which the members of the realm *obligate* themselves to obey. Alternatively, it is the process by which the people and the supreme magistrate enter into a *covenant* concerning certain laws and *conditions* that set forth the form and manner of imperium and subjection, and faithfully extend and accept oaths from each other to this effect. In this *reciprocal contract* between the supreme magistrate as the *mandatory*, or *promisor*, and the universal association as the *mandator*, the *obligation* of the magistrate comes first, as is customary in a *contractual mandate* (Carney 1964, 116). No realm or commonwealth had ever been founded or instituted except by *contract* entered into one with the other, by covenants agreed upon between

---

12 For more on the theologico-political federalism of Duplessis-Mornay, see de Freitas 2003, 35–45.

subjects and their future prince, and by an established *mutual obligation* that both should religiously observe. Althusius adds that there are many precepts, examples and rational evidences of constituting a supreme magistrate by such a covenant or *contract* between the supreme magistrate and the ephori, who represent the entire people of the associated bodies (Carney 1964, 117–18).[13]

Samuel Rutherford and Scottish Reformational Thought

Nearly a century prior to the Westminster Assembly (1643–1646), Knox's political thought expressed clear indications of an adherence to the *theologico-political federalism* of Bullinger. Knox's theology remained closely aligned to Bullinger's views, and Bullinger's political views remained an integral part of Knox's political theology.[14] The reason for this is mainly to be found in the major impact that Bullinger's views of the covenant had on Knox's theology and his commitment to the idea of the covenanted Christian community (Raath and de Freitas 2002, 70).[15] Knox's political thought stemmed from the theological premise that the elect had entered into a *league and covenant* with God, which bound them to the divine will as revealed in His Word. This concept was to be witnessed in the *Common Band* or *covenant*, dated 3 December 1557, which signalled the emergence of Protestantism as an organized political force in Scotland. For at the heart of the band lay a pledge to fulfil the law of God. Its signatories, similar to the covenantal thought of Knox, confessed that they "aught, according to our bonden deutie, to stryve in our Maisteris caus, evin unto the death", and promised "befoir the Majestie of God … that we (by his grace) shall with all diligence continually apply our whole power, substance, and our verray lyves, to manteane, sett forward, and establish the most blessed word of God and his Congregation" (Mason 1983, 99–100).[16]

The idea of "banding" together in loyalty to a common enterprise was familiar enough to sixteenth-century Scots, and there is evidence of its use in both social and political contexts in pre-Reformed times. However, the transferring of the band of 1557 to a religious sphere effectively transformed the traditional concept

---

13 For more on Althusius' theologico-political federalism see de Freitas 2003, 46–51.
14 For more on Bullinger's covenantal thought, see Raath and de Freitas 2001, 285–304.
15 In the words of Greaves: "Modern scholarship on John Knox has tended to ignore his development of the covenant concept and his place in the covenant tradition. This is especially surprising because of the significance of the covenant idea for seventeenth-century Scottish history. The covenant, moreover, became a basic theme of English and American Puritan thought in the century following Knox's death. During the early years of the formulation of the covenant concept in English Puritanism, Knox was a revered figure" (Greaves 1973, 23; also see 26–27 and 29).
16 Mason also refers to Lord James Stewart (the future Regent Moray), himself the signatory to a band made in the presence of God and binding him to the aims of the congregation which was aware of the obligations and imperatives stemming from a covenant with God (Mason 1983, 101).

into a concrete expression of the league and covenant envisaged by Knox. Mason adds that, although it remains unstated, it seems reasonable to suppose that, like Knox, its signatories viewed adherence to divine law as part of their *contract* with God which promised them in return the assurance of eternal salvation (Mason 1983, 100).[17] Although Knox never fully developed a covenant theology, the concept of the covenant is nevertheless a controlling factor in his thinking, whether he is writing of individuals or of nations (Bell 1985, 41).

In addition, we find that the federal theology in Scotland, first expounded by Rollock in 1596, now realized its finest hour in such men as Rutherford, David Dickson, James Durham, Patrick and George Gillespie, as well as through its inclusion in the Westminster documents. The theological, political and social thought of their day was deeply engraved with the covenant/contract notion (Bell 1985, 70). The period from Knox to Rutherford was submerged within a federal-theological-medium which was inseparably accompanied by federal political implications. The custom of *banding* or *bonding* became common amid the disorders of medieval Scottish life. These *bands* were a source of political ideas and practices disturbing to monarchical power, with their emphasis on *shared authority, local initiative, voluntary commitment* and *mutual contractual obligations* (Maclear 1965, 69–70). Although the Protestant band of 1557 has been called the first covenant, the term was not specifically applied to a political band until 1596 when the General Assembly called for a covenant in opposition to James VI's indulgent policy toward the Catholic earls (Maclear 1965, 71–72). In the words of the ministers who protested to the king's representative in 1606: "This solemn covenant the king, and all his subjects, at his command, had renewed with God Almighty, that they should adhere constantlie to the true Reformed Religion, and established discipline of this Kirk …; and let the King take to heart what befell the posteritie of King Saul, for his breake[ing] of not such an oath as the covenant of God with Scotland" (Maclear 1965, 72).

The Puritans were English Protestants who thought that the Church of England as established under Henry VIII and Elizabeth retained too many vestiges of Rome. In the 1640s and 1650s, they reorganized not only the church but also the government of England, and for 11 years ran the country without a king. Three particular ideas lay at the root of Puritan political thought, even when they were not mentioned, namely: the idea of calling, *the idea of covenant* and the idea of the separate spheres of church and state (Morgan 1965, xiv–xv). The transition from medieval to modern times, as has often been suggested, was marked by a transformation in which one man's relationship to another ceased to depend so much on the estate or station in life occupied by each, and came to be based more on whatever covenant, that is, *contract* or *agreement*, might exist between them. Many

---

17   Hulse states: "Characteristic of the Scottish Reformation was the manner in which the godly banded themselves together under the Lord by solemn oath for mutual assistance and support in the defence of the gospel and the advance of the reformation. The earliest known bond or 'covenant' was made under the leadership of John Knox in 1556" (Hulse 2000, 192).

sixteenth- and seventeenth-century Protestants, and especially Puritans, thought about their relationship with God as though it were based on a covenant (Morgan 1965, xx). Morgan further states that English and Scottish Protestants seem to have been especially taken with the notion of a national covenant, and even tended to look upon themselves as an elect nation, as the successors of Israel. Though they had to acknowledge that many among them gave no perceptible evidence either of faith or of outward obedience to God's commands, they viewed every failure as a threat to their standing with God. Under Elizabeth they kept hoping for reforms that would assure His continued favour. With the arrival of the Stuarts, that hope grew increasingly dim, and preachers warned of the wrath to come upon a people who broke their covenant (Morgan 1965, xxii).

Samuel Rutherford (1600–1665), one of the most prolific political theorists of seventeenth-century Britain, substantially contributed towards the continuation of the legacy of theologico-political federalism postulated by the early reformers such as Heinrich Bullinger, Philippe Du Plessis-Mornay and Johannes Althusius.[18] In fact, Rutherford formed the apex on theory regarding a biblically founded, covenantal-political paradigm. Although the covenantal political legacy continued from Europe to New England, there would be no Reformed political theorist beyond Rutherford that would postulate, defend and even further so earnestly and substantially, the importance of the covenant for political and constitutional theory. Rutherford's political theory formed the apex of a reformed and biblical covenantal political theory at a time when John Milton was following Buchanan's political approach, supporting a leniency to a secularist and popularist influence on Christian political theory, and which assisted in providing a theological and political platform for the Enlightenment.[19] It was the latter that eventually progressed leaving behind the legacy of the reformed theologico-political federalists.

The Westminster Assembly first met on 1 July 1643, and herein the Scots participated on the basis of a religious covenant (Toon 1973, 38). The content of the Solemn League and Covenant attests to the fact that the participants of this assembly emphasized man's *obligation* towards God and *in return* for the accomplishment of these obligations, God's favour was bestowed upon man (Hetherington 1856, 130, 132). Therefore, man was understood as having a *duty to perform* towards God, and man's consequent obedience or resistance concerning this duty would respectively determine either God's blessing or wrath. It is in the document of the Solemn League and Covenant that the reformed groups within Scotland, England and Ireland made known to God that they would abide by His precepts in order to win the favour that God promised to bestow on those that were faithful. This important document was framed by Alexander Henderson, moderator of the assembly (Hetherington 1856, 124) and one of the six Scottish Commissioners present at the assembly, which is also a clear indication that the other Scottish Commissioners present at the Assembly shared in this covenantal thought. It is clear that Bullinger's federal thought was never alien to Rutherford (McCoy and

---

18   See de Freitas 2003.
19   For more on this, see Raath and de Freitas 2005, 301–21.

Baker 1991, 43).[20] Rutherford, following the Huguenots, points to the covenants in the Old Testament, maintaining that there is indeed a covenant between king and people, and, further, that king and people are pledged to God to preserve the true religion (Gough 1936, 93). According to Gough:

> *Where, then, it may be asked, is this covenant? There may, indeed, be no "positive written covenant", though Rutherford refuses to admit this definitely; at any rate, he contends, "there is a natural, tacit, implicit covenant", which ties the king by the nature of his office. "And though there were no written covenant, the standing law and practice of many hundred acts of parliament is equivalent to a written covenant"* (Gough 1936, 94).

With regard to the covenant between God and king, Rutherford makes it clear that the covenant between the king and the people was clearly distinguished from that of the king's covenant with the Lord (Rutherford 1982, 54(1)–54(2)). The political covenant apparently derived its force from the covenant with God and this God was real, historically realized in Scotland's covenants (Maclear 1965, 80; see also Rutherford 1982, 57(1)–57(2), 58(1), 60(1)).

Concerning the specific nature of the covenant according to Rutherford, Flinn states that it was an oath between the king and his people, laying, by reciprocation of bands, mutual civil obligation upon the king to the people, and the people to the king (see Flinn 1978–1979, 63).[21] This civil covenant made between the king and the represented people was not the same as the covenant made between the king and the Lord (2 Kings 11:17). The former was made and ratified publicly and was solemnly made in the house of the Lord; and if the obligations of a covenant were broken, then those who broke it could be disciplined according to the oath made to God (Flinn 1978–1979, 63). Concerning the covenant between God and the people in general (which includes the king), Rutherford refers to Jehoida, who made a covenant between the Lord and the people, including the king. The covenant between God and man is *mutual*; indeed it is so mutual that if the people break the covenant, God is no longer bound to fulfil His part of the agreement, Rutherford adding that the covenant gives to the believer a sort of action of law to plead with God in respect of his fidelity to stand to that covenant that binds him by reason of his fidelity (Rutherford 1982, 54(1)–54(2)). Rutherford refers to this same covenant when distinguishing between the *indebtedness* between God and the king on the one hand, and between God and the people on the other (Rutherford

---

20 See Raath and de Freitas 2001, 285–304 and de Freitas 2003.
21 To these theologico-political theorists the oath is not merely a ceremony but the outward declaration to the people (that have elected the king) by the king and in which his commitment to the covenant is sworn and confirmed in front of the people, who act as witnesses to such an oath. The people also confirm outwardly their acceptance of such an appointment to the crown by allowing such an oath to take place (see Rutherford 1982, 106(1), 126(2), 129(1), 133(2), 199(2), 200(1)–200(2), 201(1), 202(1), 219(2), 229(2)–230(1)).

1982, 56(1); also see 57(1)). A people in covenant with God, though mortal in its individuals, cannot die (Rutherford 1982, 78(2)). In fact, Rutherford in his letters frequently spoke of Scotland's covenant with the Lord, viewing King Charles I as the king of a nation in covenant with God, as having been *obliged* to prosecute heresy and idolatry with the same zeal as Old Testament rulers; however, King Charles I, having done the opposite, *severed the nation's covenant* with the Lord (Coffey 1997, 165, 168). Rutherford also produces historical evidence from acts of parliament, confessions of faith, coronation oaths and custom to claim a written Scottish covenant, and he also argues that the covenant need not be written, with nature and scripture remedying the defect (Maclear 1965, 76).

The covenant is made between the king and the people, between mortal men. However, they bind themselves before God to each other, adding that the *obligation* of the king in this covenant flows from the peculiar national *obligation* between the king and the estates (Rutherford 1982, 56(2)). In fact, the precise *mechanism* by which governments were founded was that of a covenant between king and people (Coffey 1997, 163). To Rutherford, natural law, scripture and history all combined to prove that government must rest on a covenant between king and people. Rutherford clearly distinguishes between this covenant, and the covenant between God on the one side and the king and people on the other, referring to Joash who made another covenant with the people. Whoever made a promise to another, gave to that other a sort of right or jurisdiction to challenge the promise (Rutherford 1982, 57(1); also see 60(1), 130(1), 198(2), 199(2), 200(1), 202(1), 219(2)). The general covenant of nature is presupposed in making a king, where there is no written or social covenant, confirming a covenant structure between the king and people (Rutherford 1982, 59(2)). If the king, because of the mere fact of being a king, was exempt by privilege from all covenant obligation to his subjects, then no law of men could lawfully reach him for any *contract* violated by him; then he could not be a *debtor* to his subjects if he borrowed money from them. Therefore, according to Rutherford, there must be a covenant obligation between the king and the people (Rutherford 1982, 60(2)). Rutherford refers to Romulus who covenanted with the people, and Xenophon who said there was a covenant between Cyrus and the Persians; he also refers to Gentilis and Grotius who prove that kings are bound to perform oaths and *contracts* to their people (Rutherford 1982, 61(1)–61(2)). The covenant between the king and people is reported in 17 Deuteronomy, and just as David was limited by covenant, so were the rest (Rutherford 1982, 62(1)).[22] According to Rutherford, the people give themselves *conditionally and covenant-wise* to the king, as to a public servant, and patron and tutor (Rutherford 1982, 82(1)), and they do not break their covenant when they put in action that natural power to conserve themselves (Rutherford 1982, 84(1)). The king accepts the crown upon the tenor of a *mutual covenant* in which he must govern according to the law (Rutherford 1982, 106(1)). The people are bound in this covenant no less than the

---

22 This was in answer to the objection by Arnisaeus saying that although few of the kings, as David and Joash, made a covenant with the people; it does not mean that this was a universal law.

king, and the king's duty is to compel them to *observe the terms* of this covenant: "Each may compell the other to mutuall performance" (Maclear 1965, 77).

The king cannot be above the covenant and law made between him and his people (Rutherford 1982, 126(2)). If the people had known that the king would turn tyrant, there would have been much ignorance in the contract between the people and the king (Rutherford 1982, 128(1)). All laws of kings, who are rational fathers, and so lead and guide the people by laws which propagate peace and external happiness, are contracts of king and people, and the king at his coronation-covenant with the people, gives a most intense consent to be a keeper of all good laws (Rutherford 1982, 129(1)). Referring to Galatians 3:15, Rutherford states that no man can annul a confirmed covenant, and that the king at his coronation must place himself under the law by a covenant. This relationship between the king and people is a *contract* which cannot be dissolved unless by the joint *consent* of both, in instances where the *conditions* of such *contract* are violated by neither side (Rutherford 1982, 200(1)–201(1)). Rutherford also emphasized that even the kings of Scotland are obliged to swear and make their faithful covenant to the true Church of God, so that the *bond and contract shall be mutual and reciprocal* between the prince and people (Rutherford 1982, 219(2)–220(1)). In fact, this horizontal covenant was also extended by Rutherford in order to accommodate a *bilateral* and *conditional* agreement between nations. In 1639 Rutherford was called to the chair of divinity at the University of St. Andrews. From that post, he continued as part of the leadership that led to the Solemn League and Covenant (1643), uniting the Scottish Covenanters and the English Puritans in a federal pact with powerful political, ecclesiastical and military dimensions and which eventually led to the overthrow of Charles I (McCoy and Baker 1991, 43). Referring to the National League and Covenant, Rutherford states that God severely avenged and plagued *breach of covenant*, and adds that the Lord has not "unstamped" His divine Image of making just laws upon any nomothetic power of the most free and independent kingdoms on earth so that the *breach* of lawful promises, covenant, *contracts* (which are against the Law of God, nature and of nations), should or could be the subject matter of any nomothetic power (Rutherford 1649, 267).

Although theologico-political federalism became less popular from the middle of the seventeenth century, its legacy reached the shores of early American history, hereby playing an important role in the political processes of the "New World". Theologico-political federalism is therefore undoubtedly part of the history of the Founding Fathers. Before landing, 41 male passengers (under Brewster and Bradford) assembled in the main cabin of the *Mayflower*, and signed an agreement known as the Mayflower Compact, and according to McCoy and Baker, the compound of theological, communal, political and economic dimensions of the federal tradition is nowhere represented in such brief compass as in the said Compact (McCoy and Baker 1991, 82–83). Federal thought had, by the end of the sixteenth century, become pervasive in the Reformed communities of Europe, and therefore it is not surprising to discover that federalism was brought over to the New World with the earliest settlements of people of Reformed faith. Most of the leaders of the New England colonies adhered to one or other version of federal theology and politics. Anyone seeking to find representatives of liberal democracy as understood in the twentieth century among the New England leaders was doomed to disappointment (McCoy and Baker 1991, 81). For these leaders, the covenant was a way of expressing the relation between God and humans and also at the same time an understanding of the appropriate political order within the Divine human covenant. Persecuted by the church and government of Elizabeth, separatists in great numbers fled to the European continent, many of them settling in Amsterdam and Leiden. The Leiden congregation decided to send part of its membership to America, and in 1620, this group set out under the leadership of William Brewster and William Bradford, and established the colony of Plymouth. This group became known as the Pilgrims (McCoy and Baker 1991, 81–82). There were also political theorists such as Locke, who accommodated a theory of the social compact to build a political community (and postulated a contract or covenant among a group of free individuals, who first joined in a social contract, agreeing to be one people, and then made a second, governmental contract, in which they chose rulers and imposed limits on them); such theorists did not mention God as participant in either covenant. Government existed, not to help the people please God and fend off His wrath, but simply to help them to protect their lives, liberties and properties against each other. Morgan adds that such protection was a function and duty of government for the seventeenth-century Puritan too, but for him it had been achieved when his rulers, in performance of their callings, limited the depravity of his neighbours, thus fulfilling the nation's covenant with God (Morgan 1965, xli–xlii).

Regarding eighteenth-century America, Wood states that the Americans, like Old Testament Israel, were God's chosen people and bound to him by a "visible covenant" (Wood 1969, 115). Donald Lutz and Charles Hyneman conducted an exhaustive 10-year research of approximately 15,000 political documents of the Founding era (1760–1805) and found among others, that the authors referred most frequently to the sections in the Bible on covenants and God's promises to Israel, as well as to similar passages in Joshua I, II Samuel, I and II Kings, and to Matthew's Gospel (Jacobs 1999, 68). The communities that first came to New England were heavily drawn to the covenantal doctrines of the Old Testament, with specific emphasis on the authority of the congregation in the election of ministers. This resulted in the view that a congregation was a body politic, comprised of members who, by means of a willing covenant made with their God, were under the government of God (Evans 1994, 188; also see 189–93). Bamberg states that John Adams, one of the foremost theorists of the American Revolution during the eighteenth century, was influenced by the contractual thought of Rutherford (Bamberg 1996), amongst others. While the framers of the American constitution believed in the authority of "the people", they did not believe that simply conferring power on an elected body was in itself a solution to anything. The ultimate issue for the framers was not where the power came from, or by whom it was wielded, but what was done with it, and it is the latter that allows for freedom as opposed to oppression (Evans 1994, 253). The idea of the biblical covenant played a vital role in this regard. Rossiter states that Thomas Hooker, "in placing a little more emphasis on the covenant of man to man than on that of man to God ... on the New Testament than on the Old ... pried open a door that later generations of New England churchgoers swung wide for liberty" (Rossiter 1953, 19).[23]

Conclusion

The biblical covenant model is based on creationism (not realism or nominalism) and the philosophy of such a model asserts an absolute separation of being between God and any aspect of the creation. Therefore, covenantalism is a separate philosophical system altogether (North 1990, 36–37). Mason states that public covenanting is a moral duty, incumbent upon the church in every age. The change which the Lord has made in the outward ordinance of his worship under the different dispensations does not alter anything regarding the moral obligation (Mason 1799, 12). This public covenanting is exercised by the church, a company of visible believers in Jesus, who subject themselves to God's Word (Mason 1799, 7). Therefore, it also makes sense that a nation that has come to accept the Gospel comes to receive the truths of Christ and submits to His laws, and consequently bound by covenanting nationally with Him, swears an oath of national allegiance to the Lord, as did the house of Israel and the house of Judah in the land of Canaan (Mason 1799, 60). It was especially the Scottish Puritans, more specifically Rutherford, who attempted to instill this paradigm during a climate where Christianity reached its zenith in Europe. The Reformation substantially contributed not only to the revitalization but also to a clear postulation of the biblical message related to the covenant in a political context. The idea of theologico-political federalism formulated by Bullinger was developed by Reformed thinkers in Europe (Althusius) and Scotland (Rutherford) into a powerful tradition of limited government; it shifted the political focus from secular sovereignty to the Reformed idea of office limited by law, and transferred the emphasis from unlimited government to magisterial power subject to the law of God. Ultimately the idea of the covenant and its formulation as a political concept gave rise to the development of the federal tradition in law and political systems. The legacy of the Reformation to the furtherance of political theory is legion. However, it is the idea of the biblical covenant that requires renewed emphasis. The covenant remains central to the political community, serving not only as political instrument, but also as a moral requirement for the effective functioning of society. Encapsulated in this principle and norm is a constitutional government, where a sense of accountability, responsibility and obligation are heightened, and where the ends of society are provided with an added sense of awareness as to the purpose of man's existence.

---

[23] Rossiter confirms Hooker's emphasis on the covenant between man and man, instead of between man and God (Rossiter 1953, 26).

References

Alexander, P. and Alexander, D. (2004), *Handboek by die Bybel*, 3rd Edition (Wellington: Lux Verbi. BM). Original edition published in English under the title *The Lion Handbook to the Bible* (Oxford: Lion Publishing, 1973).

Baker, J. W. (1980), *Heinrich Bullinger and the Covenant* (Ohio: Ohio University Press).

Bamberg, S. (1996), A footnote to the political theory of John Adams, *Vindiciae contra*, *Premise*, 3:7.

Bell, M. C. (1985), *Calvin and Scottish Theology. The doctrine of assurance* (Edinburgh: The Handsell Press).

Carney, F. S. (1964), *The Politics of Johannes Althusius*, abridged translation by Frederich S. Carney of the third edition of Johannes Althusius's *Politica Methodice Digesta, Atque Exemplis Sacris et Profanis Illustrata*, including the prefaces of the first and second editions and with a preface by C. J. Friedrich (London: Eyre and Spottiswoode).

Coffey, J. (1997), *Politics, Religion and the British Revolutions. The mind of Samuel Rutherford* (Cambridge: Cambridge University Press).

Cicero, M. (1948), *De re Republica and De Legibus*, translation by Clinton Walker Keyes (London: Heinemann).

De Freitas, S. A. (2003), *Samuel Rutherford on Law and Covenant: The impact of theologico-political federalism on constitutional theory* (Master of Law Thesis, University of the Free State).

Duplessis-Mornay, P. (1924), *A Defence of Liberty Against Tyrants or Of the lawful power of the Prince over the People, and of the People over the Prince*, edited by Laski, Harold J. A translation of the *Vindiciae Contra Tyrannos* by Junius Brutus, with a historical introduction by Harold J. Laski (London: G. Bell and Sons).

Evans, M. S. (1994), *The Theme is Freedom* (Washington, DC: Regnery Publishing).

Elazar, D. J. (1995), Althusius' grand design for a federal commonwealth, Preface in an abridged translation by Frederick S. Carney of Johannes Althusius's *Politics Methodically Set Forth and Illustrated with Sacred and Profane Examples* (Indianapolis, ID: Liberty Fund), xxxv–lvii.

—— (1996), *Covenant and Commonwealth. From Christian separation through the Protestant Reformation. The covenant tradition in politics* Vol. II, (New Brunswick, NJ: Transaction Publishers).

—— (2006a), The Book of Joshua as a political classic (Jerusalem Centre for Public Affairs), http://www.jcpa.org/dje/articles2/joshua.htm [website], accessed 23 December 2006, 1–51.

—— (2006b), Deuteronomy as Israel's ancient constitution: some preliminary reflections (Jerusalem Centre for Public Affairs), Daniel Elazar Papers Index <http://www.jcpa.org/dje/articles2/deut-const.htm> [website], accessed 28 December 2006, 1–24.

—— (2006c), The Book of Judges: the Israelite Tribal Federation and its discontents (Jerusalem Centre for Public Affairs), Daniel Elazar Papers Index <http://www.jcpa .org/dje/articles/judges.htm> [website], accessed 28 December 2006, 1–21.

—— (2007), Dealing with fundamental regime change: the biblical paradigm of the transition from tribal federation to federal monarchy under David (Jerusalem Centre for Public Affairs), Daniel Elazar Papers Index <http://www.jcpa.org/dje/ar ticles2/regimechange.htm> [website], accessed 3 January 2007, 1–19.

Flinn, R. (1978–1979), Samuel Rutherford and puritan political theory, *Journal of Christian Reconstruction* 5, 49–74.

Gough, J. W. (1936), *The Social Contract. A critical study of its development* (Oxford: Clarendon Press).

Greaves, R. L. (1973), John Knox and the covenant tradition, *Journal of Ecclesiastical History* 24:1, 23–32.

Hall, D. (1996), *Savior or Servant? Putting government in its place* (Oak Ridge: The Covenant Foundation).

Hetherington, W. H. (1856 reprint edition of the 3rd edition), *History of the Westminster Assembly of Divines* (Edmonton: Still Waters Revival Books).

Hulse, E. (2000), *Who are the Puritans? ... and what do they teach?* (Great Britain: Evangelical Press).

Jacobs, P. J. D. (1999), *The Influence of Biblical Ideas and Principles on Early American Republicanism and History* (PhD Dissertation, Faculty of Theology of the Potchefstroom University for Christian Higher Education).

Maclear, J. F. (1965), Samuel Rutherford: the law and the king, in *Calvinism and the Political Order*, edited by George L. Hunt, (Philadelphia: The Westminster Press), 65–87.

Mason, A. (1799), *Observations on the Public Covenants, betwixt God and the Church. A Discourse* (Glasgow: E. Miller).

Mason, R. (1983), Covenant and commonwealth: the language of politics in Reformation Scotland, in *Church, Politics and Society: Scotland 1408–1929*, edited by Norman Macdougall (Edinburgh: John Donald), 97–126.

McAllister, D. (2001), The true idea of the state, *The Christian Statesman* 144, 1, 26–30.

McCoy, C. (1988), The centrality of covenant in the political philosophy of Johannes Althusius, *Rechtstheorie*, 13, Beiheft 7, 187–99.

—— and Baker, W. (1991), *Fountainhead of Federalism. Heinrich Bullinger and the Covenantal Tradition*, with a translation of the *De testamento seu foedere Dei unico et aeterno*, 1534 by Heinrich Bullinger, (Louisville: Westminster/John Knox Press).

Morgan, E. S. (ed.) (1965), *Puritan Political Ideas 1558–1794* (The Bobbs–Merrill Company).

North, G. (1981), Comprehensive redemption: a theology of social action, *Journal of Christian Reconstruction* 8:1, (1981).

—— (1990), *Millennialism and Social Theory* (Tyler, TX: Institute for Christian Economics).

Raath, A. and de Freitas, S. (2001), Theologico-political federalism: the office of magistracy and the legacy of Heinrich Bullinger (1504—1575), *The Westminster Theological Journal* 63, 285–304.

—— (2002), Calling and resistance: Huldrych Zwingli's (1484–1531) political theology and his legacy of resistance to tyranny, *Koers* 66:1.

—— (2005), Theologically united and divided: the political covenantalism of Samuel Rutherford and John Milton, *Westminster Theological Journal* 67, 301–21.

Rossiter, C. (1953), *Six Characters in Search of a Republic* (New York: Harcourt, Brace & World).

Rutherford, S. (1982), *Lex, Rex* (Harrisonburg, VA: Sprinkle Publications).

—— (1649), *A Free Disputation Against Pretended Liberty of Conscience* (London: Printed by RI. for Andrew Crook).

Silving, H. (1953), The jurisprudence of the Old Testament, *New York University Law Review* 28, 1129–48.

Toon, P. (1973), *Puritans and Calvinism* (Swengel, PA: Reiner Publications).

Van Zyl, D. (1991), *Justice and Equity in Cicero* (Pretoria: Academica).

Wines, E. C. (2007), The Hebrew republic, http://www.contramundum.org/books/republic.pdf [website], accessed 14 May 2007.

Wood, G. S. (1969), *The Creation of the American Republic, 1776–1787* (Chapel Hill, NC: The University of North Carolina Press).

Further Reading

Bierma, Lyle D. (1983), Federal theology in the sixteenth century: two traditions?, *Westminster Theological Journal* 45, 304–21.

Bullinger, Heinrich (1849–1852), *The Decades of Henry Bullinger*, 4 volumes, translated by H. I. and edited for the Parker Society by Thomas Harding (Cambridge: Cambridge University Press).

Church, William F. (1941), *Constitutional Thought in Sixteenth-Century France. A Study in the Evolution of Ideas* (Cambridge Massachusetts: Harvard University Press).

Cowan, Edward J. (1990), The making of the National Covenant, in *The Scottish National Covenant in its British Context*, edited by John Morrill (Edinburgh: Edinburgh University Press), 68–89.

Danner, Dan G. (1981), Resistance and the ungodly magistrate in the sixteenth century: the Marian exiles, *The Journal of the American Academy of Religion* 49, 471–81.

Elazar, Daniel J. (1995), *Covenant and polity in biblical Israel. Biblical foundations and Jewish expressions. The covenant tradition in politics* Vol. I (New Brunswick, NY: Transaction Publishers).

Figgis, John N. (1914), *The Divine Right of Kings*, 2nd edition (Cambridge: Cambridge University Press).

Ford, John D. (1994), *Lex, Rex iusto posita*: Samuel Rutherford on the origins of government, in *Covenant and Commonweal: The language of politics in Reformation Scotland*, edited by Roger Mason (Cambridge: Cambridge University Press), 262–90.

Franklin, Julian H. (1969), Introduction, in *Constitutionalism and Resistance in the Sixteenth Century. Three treatises by Hotman, Beza, and Mornay*, translated and edited by Julian H. Franklin (Western Publishing), 11–46.

Gray, John R. (1939), The political theory of John Knox, *American Society of Church History* 8, 132–47.

Hagen, K. (1972), From testament to covenant in the early sixteenth century, *Sixteenth Century Journal* III (April), 1, 1–24.

Henderson, George D. (1937), The Covenanters, in *Religious Life in Seventeenth-Century Scotland* (Cambridge: Cambridge University Press), 158–89.

Hetherington, William M. (1991), *History of the Westminster Assembly of Divines*, reprint of the third edition, 1856 (Edmonton: Still Waters Revival Books).

Hopfl, Harro and Thompson, Martyn P. (1979), The history of contract as a motif in political thought, *The American Historical Review* 84, 4 (October), 919–44.

Hueglin, Thomas (1979), Johannes Althusius: medieval constitutionalist or modern federalist?, *Publius* (Fall), 9–41.

Hüglin, Thomas O. (1988), "Have we studied the wrong authors?" On the relevance of Johannes Althusius as a political theorist, *Rechstheorie*, Beiheft 16, 219–40.

Knox, John, (1995), *A Brief Exhortation to England, for the Speedy Embracing of the Gospel Heretofore by the Tyranny of Mary Suppressed and Banished* 1559, edited by Kevin Reed (Dallas, TX: Presbyterian Heritage Publications).

Lyall, Francis (1979), Of metaphors and analogies: legal language and covenant theology, *Scottish Journal of Theology* 32, 1–18.

Moltmann, Jürgen (1994), Covenant or leviathan? Political theology for modern times, *Scottish Journal of Theology* 47, 19–41.

Murray, R. H. (1926), *The Political Consequences of the Reformation. Studies in Sixteenth-Century Political Thought*. (London: Ernest Benn).

Pearson, A. F. Scott (1928), *Church and State. Political aspects of sixteenth-century Puritanism* (Cambridge: Cambridge University Press).

Raath, Andries and de Freitas, Shaun (2001), Heinrich Bullinger and the Marian exiles: the political foundations of Puritanism, *Journal for Christian Science*, 3rd and 4th Quarter, 61–87.

—— (2002), Calling and resistance: Huldrych Zwingli's (1484–1531) political theory and his legacy of resistance to tyranny, *Koers* 66 (1), 45–76.

—— (2005), Theologically united and divided: the political covenantalism of Samuel Rutherford and John Milton, *Westminster Theological Journal* 67, 301–21.

—— (2006), The Covenant in Ulrich Huber's enlightened theology, jurisprudence and political theory, *Acta Theologica*, 26, 2, 199–226.

—— (2005), Resistance, rebellion and a Swiss Brutus?, *The Historical Journal* 48, 1, 1–26.

Reid, W. Stanford (1988), John Knox's theology of political government, *Sixteenth Century Journal*, 19, 4, 529–40.

Steele, Margaret (1990), The "Politick Christian": the theological background to the National Covenant, in *The Scottish National Covenant in its British Context*, edited by John Morrill (Edinburgh: Edinburgh University Press), 31–67.

Von Gierke, Otto (1966), *The Development of Political Theory*, translated by B. Freyd (New York: Howard Fertig).
Weir, David A. (1990), *The Origins of the Federal Theology in Sixteenth-Century Reformation Thought* (Oxford: Clarendon Press).

PART 2
THE ORIGINS OF MODERN FEDERALISM

Introduction to Part 2

This Part examines the origins of modern federalist thought in seventeenth- and eighteenth-century Europe. This seminal period in the history of political thought witnessed the rise of modern natural rights philosophy with its profound reconsideration of the relation of the individual to government, and the emergence of the Bodinian and Hobbesian doctrine of absolute and indivisible sovereignty associated with the emergence of the modern nation-state. As the following chapters demonstrate, this was also the period that saw a parallel intellectual track of innovative reflections on the federal principle produced by several theoretical concerns including the inability of the modern sovereignty doctrine to account for the diffuse system of rule in existing compound states, the effort to make sovereignty doctrine cohere with key aspects of classical philosophy and reformed theology, as well as the dangers posed to liberty internally and to peace and progress internationally by prevailing notions of the unitary nation-state. Pre-modern ideas of alliances, compound associations, and covenant were modified, and in many cases radically transformed, in the intellectual context created by the new doctrine of sovereignty. Thus was modern federalism born.

In Chapter 4, Bettina Koch examines Johannes Althusius' innovative concept of "consociational" federalism. Koch considers both the secular and religious aspects of Althusius' federal theory, and suggests that it represents a theoretical bridge between pre-modern and modern thought. On the one hand, Althusius presented levels of consociation including the family, city, province, and realm that were based on the distinctively modern idea of consent and resembled the much later principle of subsidiarity. On the other hand, Althusius' notion of multiple layers of government with authority in their own sphere of competence rested not on a modern natural rights doctrine, but rather on fundamentally pre-modern theological and philosophical assumptions about teleology and the duty of the supreme ruling power to preserve religious orthodoxy in the various associations composing the realm. In the tension between these two propositions, the interrelation of independent political entities, on the one hand, and the tendency towards unification on the basis of religion, on the other, Koch discerns a clear departure from medieval constitutionalism and a movement towards modern federalism.

In the following chapter, Lee Ward examines some of the major theoretical challenges to the modern sovereignty doctrine posed by heterogeneous, compound political associations such as the Dutch Republic and the German Holy Roman

Empire that were based, however vaguely, on a territorial division of power. For many Dutch and German thinkers of the early modern period, the territorial independence of the Dutch provinces, German princes, and imperial cities meant that for all practical purposes sovereignty in the Bodinian or Hobbesian sense was difficult, or even impossible, to locate. Ward finds in Spinoza's account of federal aristocracy not only a theoretical defense of the Dutch Republic, but more importantly serious philosophical reflection on the federal possibilities in a democratized natural rights based account of sovereignty. In Ludolph Hugo's attempt to redefine the German Empire on the basis of a "double government" model including both estate governments and imperial authority autonomous in their respective spheres, Ward identifies an innovative early effort to fashion a conception of divided sovereignty compatible with a form of federalism. Finally, Ward interprets Leibniz's effort to harmonize territorial independence and imperial authority to be a groundbreaking account of the theoretical limits of sovereignty and presentation of a flexible conception of political union that could be set to explaining a federal system. While none of these early Dutch and German thinkers could be said to have developed a fully fledged theory of federalism, Ward proposes that they highlighted the central conceptual problems that later federal theory would have to address.

Chapter 6 is Ann Ward and David Fott's examination of the federal dimension in Montesquieu's classic treatise *The Spirit of the Laws*. Ward and Fott's careful analysis of Montesquieu's teaching on the difference between ancient and modern conceptions of liberty reveals the vital political preconditions underlying his account of modern "political liberty". This account climaxes in Montesquieu's treatment of the modern English commercial republic, the regime of liberty par excellence. However, as Ward and Fott reveal, Montesquieu recognized serious dangers in his consideration of the much-admired English constitutional separation of powers. Montesquieu relates that the English separation of power is undermined by the problematic relation of the armed forces to the civilian government, especially the military's instinctive hostility toward the legislative branch. It is in the context of the danger posed to liberty by unchecked executive control of the military that Ward and Fott reconsider Montesquieu's famous discussion of "federal republics" in Book 9 of *The Spirit of the Laws*. They argue that the federal "society of societies" typically associated with antiquity, actually forms the basis for Montesquieu's solution to the problem of the military in the modern constitutional regime. In supra-national structures and alliances Montesquieu proposes a recognizably federal remedy to this problem that provides support for the domestic separation of powers and for international security as well.

In Chapter 7 Will Jordan and Scott Yenor explore David Hume's federal proposal in his "Idea of a Perfect Commonwealth." Jordan and Yenor observe the striking character of this writing in Hume's corpus. While Hume's influence on the moral philosophy of the American Framer's is well documented, federalism is not a subject typically associated with early modern England. Moreover, they note the curious fact that Hume's only foray into abstract, speculative political philosophy – rare for such a philosophic skeptic – had to do with federalism. They contrast the

Introduction to Part 2

federalism of Hume's "Perfect Commonwealth" with his account of the imperfect, feudal federalism of the pre-Tudor period in England and identify the "revolution in manners"; the movement from martial virtues to softer commercial mores that Hume believed made an improved federal system ideal for liberty. Yenor and Jordan reveal the strikingly national character of Hume's federal system, one that proposes to make republican government possible over a large territory by building national institutions on the foundation of scores of county governments with autonomy over local matters and considerable agency in the creation and enactment of national legislation. Jordan and Yenor affirm Hume's rightful place as a federal thinker of the first order.

In Chapter 8, Daniel Cullen examines the ambiguous, and ultimately very fruitful, role of federalism in the thought of Jean-Jacques Rousseau. As Cullen observes, Rousseau is not often thought of as a federal thinker. His preference for small, homogeneous, and intensely patriotic republics as the seedbed for healthy citizenship is usually seen as contradictory to the cosmopolitanism and pluralistic diversity associated with federalism. However, Cullen argues that Rousseau took federalism, both in terms of its limits and possibilities, much more seriously than scholars typically suppose. Indeed, Cullen suggests that Rousseau believed the federalist model is analogous to the domestic social contract. Both reflect the centrality of voluntary, but essentially artificial, associations in Rousseau's political theory. In Rousseau's reflections on international relations in particular, Cullen finds numerous structural similarities between his account of federal and "national" union. According to Rousseau, national identity, no less than federal identity, is the product of laws, customs, and mores of human contrivance. As Cullen demonstrates, for Rousseau the prospects of either a federal states of Europe as envisioned by the Abbé de St. Pierre, or of legitimate domestic civil association based on the social contract are equally unlikely: and for the same reasons. The challenge for political society *tout court*, understood federally or nationally, is, in Rousseau's view, the immense difficulty in making citizens out of mere human beings. For Cullen, the great value in studying Rousseau's theory of federalism is not only in assessing his prescriptions for a particular federal state such as Poland, or even his judgment on the prospects for international peace through a federation of states. Rather in paying careful attention to Rousseau's reflections on the nature of federalism, we begin to discern his understanding of the essence of the political problem.

The final chapter in this Part brings us to the federal ideas of Immanuel Kant. Joseph Knippenberg continues the theme of exploring the role of the principle of federalism in international relations that we saw in earlier chapters on classical Greece, the German Empire, Montesquieu and Rousseau. As Knippenberg demonstrates, Kant employed federal thinking to ground his account of a league of republican states that could in theory operate on a global context. Drawing from the rich early modern natural rights tradition, Kant advanced a federation of free states not only as an effective means to secure international peace and preserve domestic freedom, but also as the logical extension and institutional expression of the moral imperative derived from human rational dignity. Federation unites the

Kantian ideals of freedom and moral responsibility more fully, and in service of an end more clearly discernible to human reason, than any other or previous form of political association. In distinguishing between Kant's idea of federation and more contemporary institutions such as the United Nations and NATO, Knippenberg clearly identifies the profoundly federal element in Kant's seminal arguments for cosmopolitanism and enlightenment.

In the range of ideas and thinkers spanning from Althusius to Kant, we see the origins of the distinctly modern idea of federalism familiar to theorists and political practitioners today. Whether it be in response to problems and concerns raised by the doctrine of sovereignty, or to the dangers posed to domestic freedom and international peace, in this period federalism emerged, arguably for the first time in history, as a serious alternative to the unitary state among a broad collection of thinkers living in diverse political contexts.

Johannes Althusius: Between Secular Federalism and the Religious State

Bettina Koch

Johannes Althusius's (1557/1563(?)–1638) federal theory has a somewhat peculiar status within the literature on federalism. While Otto von Gierke celebrated Althusius as a thinker who systemizes existing federal doctrines and condenses them into a coherent theory (Gierke 1981 [1980], 243–4), Carl Joachim Friedrich, the editor of the (incomplete) Latin edition of Althusius's *Politica*, characterizes Althusius's theory as "consocialism" rather than "federalism" (Friedrich 1932, lxxxviii). Patrick Riley (Riley 1976, 34) even doubts that it is justified to call Althusius's theory "federalism." Riley argues that Althusius describes and defends "a system of medieval constitutionalism." Riley's assessment of Althusius's theory, however, is based on a narrow understanding of federalism, which is geared towards the American federal model (Hueglin 1979, 40).

Consequently, to approach Althusius's federalism it is necessary to address his theory from a broad perspective. For Thomas Hueglin and Alan Fenna, Althusius's "consocial federalism," which they distinguish from "republican" and "socio-economic federalism" (Fenna and Hueglin 2006, 86), outlines quite a number of principles and characteristics reflected nowadays in the political system of the European Union (96). One of the key terms in Althusius's theory is consociation (*consociatio*) (Blickle 2002, 226; Zwierlein 2005, 143). Although the Althusian consocial federalism has a number of implications for contemporary EU federalism, it emerges from Reformed thought. As Daniel Elazar points out, Althusius's federal ideas rely heavily on the scriptural tradition, mainly the Old Testament (Elazar 1997, 210).

While the religious and secular aspects of Althusius's theory are well captured in Elazar's concept of covenant theory, recent scholarship on Althusius focuses either on a secular reading of his federal political theory or emphasizes his religious thought. Although modern scholars can legitimately draw the distinction between these two aspects of his theory, for Althusius religion and politics are inseparable.

His concept of *censura* serves as link between these spheres, which are separated in modern politics (Bianchin 2005, 93). Literally, *censura* means censorship or judgment. In the context of Althusius's theory, it refers to the institutionalized supervision of public decency. Moreover, Althusius understands divine law and, in particular, the prescription of the Decalogue fundamental to all human communities (Althusius 1981a, præfatio).

This chapter reflects on both the secular and the ecclesiastical aspects of Althusius's theory. First, this chapter distils Althusius's secular federal theory; second, it analyzes how Althusius's religious ideas fit into his concept of consocial federalism. It will be shown that, although Althusius believes the commonwealth cannot exist without religion, his religious thought undermines some of his federal ideas.[1] Nonetheless, the interdependence of both the religious and the secular spheres is essential for Althusius's general understanding of politics.

Secular Federalism

Althusius reveals the basic principle of his political theory in his definition of politics. For Althusius, politics is the art of consociation (*ars consociandi*). Politics teaches us how to establish and preserve a social and symbiotic life among human beings (Althusius 1981a, I, §1). The consocial life of the members is established through a pact (*pactum*) based on the consent of all. The consociates share goods, services, and law (*res, opera*, and *lex*) (Althusius 1981a, I, § 6–7, § 31). The end of consociation is a sacred, just, proper, and happy community, not lacking anything necessary or useful, in which the citizens show piety towards God and justice to each other (Althusius 1981a, I, § 3 and § 30). Althusius, however, does not only consider politics as *ars consociandi*; every political entity he describes is composed of different parts, forming one body. Each part has its own rights and has the responsibility to support the other parts within its power (Althusius 1981a, I, § 34). The underlying principle is the idea of subsidiarity. While usually associated with nineteenth-century Catholic social doctrine, the doctrine itself is much older and fully developed in Althusius's theory, although he neither knows nor uses the term "subsidiarity" (Hueglin 2005, 65). The same applies to the term "federalism." Althusius does not know or use any term that translates directly into federalism. He rather speaks about *confœderatio* in the meaning of alliance. Nonetheless it is justified to call his entire theory federal, since Althusius's idea of *confœderatio* points to modern concepts of federalism (Malandrino 2005, 187).

Following Aristotle, Althusius assumes humans' deficiency. Both humans' deficiency and humans' sociability make it necessary for them to live in a community. Althusius even considers the life of an eremite, hermit, or monk not only contrary to human nature, but also a heresy (Althusius 1981a, I § 28, I § 32). Moreover, it

---

1   For a treatment of Althusius' impact on modern federal theory, see Chapter 19 in this volume.

is necessary to control humans' pride and fierceness (*superbia* and *ferocia*) though reason, law, and governance (Althusius 1981a, I, § 38).

Applying these basic principles, Althusius develops his political system from the smallest unit, the family, to the largest entity, the commonwealth (*politia*). Althusius's theory is based on the idea of free consociations, first of individuals, then of larger groups or corporations. Departing from the Aristotelian tradition, Althusius considers family or kinship part of the political. While still calling the family a private consociation, it nonetheless belongs for Althusius to the political. Family is the seed (*seminarium*) of all further private and public consociations. Therefore, it follows that Althusius considers the family as the first consociation. For Althusius, one has to distinguish between the two aspects of the first consociation: the economic and the political. Politics is about just and pious symbiosis; its end is maintaining symbiotic life and the commonwealth. Consequently, the symbiotic aspect of family consociation is political (Althusius 1981a, III, § 42).

The nucleus of family consociation is the relationship between husband and wife. Both are symbiotically joined individuals, forming one body. Its foundation is symbiotic law (*ius*) and mutual services. Althusius defines symbiotic law as those rights each one has to grant to the other for the individual and common benefit. All members share the same burdens; they are joined through mutual love and support. They build a community of goods (*bonorum*) and rights (Althusius 1981a, II, § 4–6; II § 46). The consent between the symbiots Althusius calls mutual alliance and concord (*confœderatio* and *conspiratio*) (Althusius 1981a, II, § 8). In this first consociation, the main principles for all further consociation are already laid out: a consociation is based on mutual consent and shared rights and services among parts. Although the first consociation possesses already a political characteristic, it is only sufficient with respect to its particular purpose. To have a fully politically sufficient entity and to fulfill all human needs, further consociation is necessary.

The second consociation that Althusius describes is the *collegium*. The *collegium* also marks the transition from the private to the public sphere. It comes into being when the heads of each family leave the private sphere of the family to found public communities, which Althusius calls *collegia* (Althusius 1981a, IV, § 1). Each *collegium* builds "a body organized by assembled persons according to their own pleasure and will to serve a common utility and necessity in human life. That is to say, they agree among themselves by common consent on a manner of ruling and obeying for the utility of both of the whole body and of its individuals" (Althusius 1995, IV, § 1).

If one ignores restrictions emerging from the early modern moral and religious background that would not allow, for instance, gay consociations or gambling *collegia*, then one could argue that at least in theory every head of a household can consociate with other heads of households in any kind of *collegium*, independently of the *collegium*'s actual purpose. The *collegium* must only serve their members' interests and – in a broader sense – the commonwealth's needs. This rule applies at least as long as the *collegium*'s general rules do not violate the commonwealth's common law. Althusius's conception and use of the term of common law – *jus commune* or *lex communis* – is not consistent. In a general sense, it refers to a kind of constitutional law, although Althusius uses also here the term fundamental law – *lex fundamentalis*. In addition to its general meaning, common law appears also in the context of charity (Althusius 1981a, XXI, § 20) or in his discussion of the rights that are expressed in guild books (Althusius 1981a, IV, § 17; Koch 2005, 190–1, 200, 211).

Althusius does not have every kind of *collegium* in mind; he thinks merely about professional consociations. This becomes obvious through Althusius's explicit reference to corporate books, in which the rules of these consociations have been set down. In addition to the *liber collegiae*, he also uses the German term *Zunftbuch* (Althusius 1981a, IV, § 17). Nonetheless, the basic character of these consociations depends on the *collegium*'s derivation from the free will of its members and its own rights and rules.

With the exception of Althusius's discussion of the provinces – this chapter does not appear in the first edition of the *Politica* – the pattern of consocialization remains basically the same. While the family and the *collegium* do not represent self-sufficient consociations, the *collegia* consociate to a self-sufficient entity that Althusius calls *politeuma*. The term *politeuma* refers to the ambiguity of secularity and religion in Althusius's theory. The term initially appears in the first chapter of the *Politica*, "De generalibus Politicæ," in which Althusius outlines with reference to Plutarch and to Philipians 3:20 three different meaning of the term *politica* (polity). Following the Apostle Paul ("our *politeuma* is in heaven"), Althusius regards *politeuma* to be citizenship in a commonwealth. Second, *politeuma* also refers to administration and rule, while in a third sense it denotes the order and constitution of the commonwealth (Althusius 1981a, I, § 5; Schwemer 2000, 228–36). Consequently, the political-legal as well as the religious are inherent in the *politeuma*.

The *politeuma* or city is composed out of different *collegia*. This consociation is the result of the members' free will. The members are families and *collegia*. These communities, which have been founded to fulfill particular purposes, lose neither their individual status nor their particular rights – at least as long as their rights remain in keeping with the common law (Althusius 1981a, V, § 1). This means they retain their status of autonomy. Although a *collegium* is composed out of its individual members, Althusius does not regard a *collegium* as a group of individuals. Rather, each consociation forms a body or corporation. The communication with other consociations and within larger consociations composed out of different communities works through representation. Consequently, political participation is only possible through the organization of and within groups.

For Althusius, human consociations cannot exist without governance. Therefore, the *collegium* needs a superior. The superior who is called "director" or "prefect" is elected by its members by common consent and "is provided with administrative power over property and functions pertaining to the *collegium*" (Althusius 1995, IV, § 6). He has coercive power over the individual members, but he remains inferior to the united *collegium* (Althusius 1981a, IV, § 7; IV, § 22). This principle also applies to the city or *politeuma*. The consociated body, again, is established by the consent of its members. Moreover, this community continues to require the consent of the individuals, at least when governance is addressed. All superiors must take an oath that they will fulfill their offices according to the law of the community; in turn, each individual citizen is required to take an oath of fidelity and obedience (Althusius 1981a, V, § 23). In this sense, the *politeuma* can be described as *coniuratio*, a union confirmed by oath. "The prefect or superior of the city is the administrator and leader of the citizens, having authority and power over individuals by general mandate of the organized community, but not over the group" (Althusius 1995, V, § 49).

The prefect as the *politeuma*'s representative is usually elected by senators, not by the whole people. "The senate is a *collegium* of wise and honest select men to whom is entrusted the care and administration of the affairs of the city" (Althusius 1995, V, § 54). The senators are "elected by the senatorial *collegium*, or by specified electors designated by the community." Although Althusius gives examples how this designation works in some communities, he does not reveal his specific preferences (Althusius 1981a, V, § 60). Since he understands the senate as a *collegium*, the appointment of the head follows the same principles as used in other *collegia*. Both prefect and senate govern together. Usually, their decisions are made by the vote of the majority. In some cases at least, a two-thirds majority is required (Althusius 1981a, V, § 62).

The whole *politeuma* is a consociation of diverse groups. In addition to government, the main principle that applies here is consent. Furthermore, the city, again, is a community possessing its own right, since "[m]en assembled without symbiotic right (*jus symbioticum*) are a crowd" (Althusius 1995, V, § 4). The whole community is a *persona representata* that represents its members collectively, not individually (Althusius 1981a, V, § 9). In this way the whole *politeuma*, although emerging from diversity, is considered a homogeneous unity. We can view such unity in Althusius's description of citizens: "For citizens enjoy the same laws (*leges*), the same religion, and the same language, speech, judgment under the law, discipline, custom, money, measure, weights, and so forth" (Althusius 1995, VI, § 40).

However, the homogeneity of the *politeuma* does not violate or suppress the individual character of each consociation out of which the city is composed. With some reservations, this is also true for the provinces. The provinces remain nonetheless a special case. Althusius follows here mainly the historical examples of the German *Stände* (estates). Although the provinces are again a free consociation of their members, the members or their representatives do not elect the provincial prefect. The prefect of the province receives his office from the supreme magistrate and the ephors of the realm, as will be addressed below (Althusius 1981a, VIII, § 50). Furthermore, and this is a reference to the Frisian realities, he considers the farmers as one of the groups that should be represented in the province's *major collegia* (Althusius 1981a, VIII, § 40).

On the top level, which Althusius calls *politia* or universal consociation, the previous principles apply again. For Althusius the *politia* is a polity in the full sense. In the universal consociation, "people are united in one body by the agreement of many symbiotic [consociations] and particular bodies, and brought together under one right." This right Althusius describes as the "fundamental law" under which the universal consociation has been constituted. It is the foundation of the realm based on the "consent and approval of the members of the realm. By this law all the members have been brought together under one head and united in one body" (Althusius 1995, XIX, § 49). The *politia*'s responsibilities are defined by the first and the second tables of the Decalogue. While the first table contains mainly the foundation of the realm's religious administration, the second table defines aspects of secular administration (Althusius 1981a, XXIX, § 1). For Althusius, secular administration pertains mainly to justice, public decency, war and peace, and the general council (*consilium universale*). The general council, which is the representative organ of the realm's members, is the origin of the *politia*'s law and right; the *summus magistratus* and the ephors interpret and apply it (Althusius 1981a, XXXIX, § 4; § 9). The general council's responsibility is to make laws concerning religion, worship, war and peace, taxation, coinage, commerce, tyranny, public goods, and all further rights and privileges belonging to the realm (Althusius 1981a, XXXIII, § 1).

In the *politia*, "the ownership of the realm belongs to the people, and administration of it to the king" (Althusius 1995, IX, § 4), since the people as a whole cannot exercise *jus majestatis* on their own. At least as concerns the secular administration of the realm, the principles of Althusius's consocial federalism remain consistent. The following Figure 4.1 summarizes and illustrates these federal principles.

While Althusius develops his secular consocial federalism from the bottom to the top, religion belongs to the *politia*'s responsibilities. Consequently, religion has an impact on all consociations described before. It is necessary to discuss the religious design of Althusius's theory in order to establish whether the religious dimension undermines some of the (secular) federal principles.

The Religious State

The right of the realm is not limited to the welfare of the political body; it also covers the soul's welfare. The ecclesiastical right of sovereignty Althusius calls "Jehovah's business" (Althusius 1981a, IX, § 33). To what extent the welfare of the soul belongs to the *politia* becomes clear from statements like "the worshippers of the true God are to be defended and protected in the realm, even if they are few in number and there are many who profess another religion" (Althusius 1995, IX, § 41) and "it is not permitted that everybody should be free to enjoy his religion in total opposition to the Christian faith," since diverse churches would destroy the unity (Althusius 1995, IX, § 45).

This principle is also reflected in the supreme ruling office. For Althusius the relation between the ecclesiastical and the secular administration of the realm is already described in the Old Testament through the example of Moses and Aaron (Althusius 1981a, XXVII, § 5). As was already indicated, the ruler (Althusius uses the term *summus magistratus*) is the defender of faith. Therefore, it is crucial that the ruler is at minimum a Christian. If he is a member of a confession not

JOHANNES ALTHUSIUS

Althusius's system

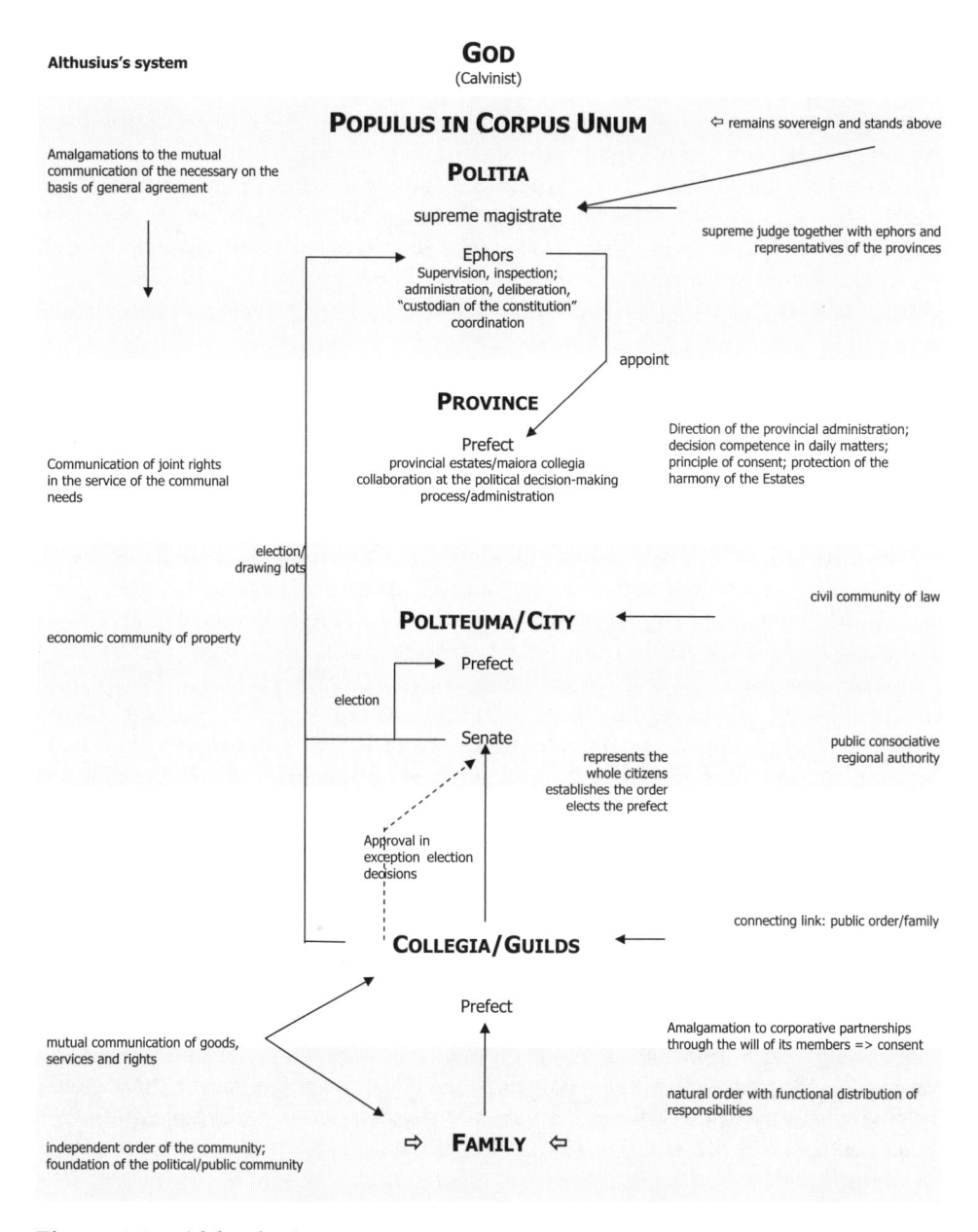

GOD
(Calvinist)

POPULUS IN CORPUS UNUM ⇐ remains sovereign and stands above

POLITIA

Amalgamations to the mutual communication of the necessary on the basis of general agreement

supreme magistrate

supreme judge together with ephors and representatives of the provinces

Ephors
Supervision, inspection; administration, deliberation, "custodian of the constitution" coordination

appoint

PROVINCE

Prefect
provincial estates/maiora collegia
collaboration at the political decision-making process/administration

Communication of joint rights in the service of the communal needs

Direction of the provincial administration; decision competence in daily matters; principle of consent; protection of the harmony of the Estates

election/drawing lots

POLITEUMA/CITY

civil community of law

economic community of property

Prefect

election

Senate
represents the whole citizens
establishes the order
elects the prefect

public consociative regional authority

Approval in exception election decisions

COLLEGIA/GUILDS

connecting link: public order/family

Prefect

mutual communication of goods, services and rights

Amalgamation to corporative partnerships through the will of its members => consent

natural order with functional distribution of responsibilities

independent order of the community; foundation of the political/public community

⇨ **FAMILY** ⇐

Figure 4.1 Althusius's system

considered to be the true orthodox religion, he cannot exercise all rights of the realm (Althusius 1981a, XIX, § 87; Koch 2004, 29), since Althusius considers it as one of the ruler's duties not only to preserve and to defend the religious orthodoxy, but also to spread it (Althusius 1981a, XXVIII, § 13). Furthermore, it is the ruler's duty to protect the citizens from harm and disadvantage in their life. Since he has regard for the citizens' bodies and souls, he also must take care for their eternal life (Althusius 1981a, XXIX, § 1). This is important for the citizens' welfare as well as for the welfare of the whole commonwealth. For Althusius, a pious life and the fear of God are the origins of all happiness. If the ruler or the citizens disregard God, Althusius fears, harm to the realm may occur. If the *summus magistratus* or the inhabitants of the commonwealth do not live piously, God might punish the whole realm for the misdeeds of its members (Althusius 1981a, XXVIII, § 8–9).

These ideas depend on Althusius's conception of mankind. Althusius takes it for granted that the perfect human condition has been destroyed through the Fall of Man (Althusius 1981b, 971). Nonetheless, all natural laws – through divine creation – are engraved in the human heart and should prevent people from doing evil (Althusius 1981a, XXI, § 31). Usually, however, these natural laws are submerged. Men concern themselves with worldly matters and are unable to live according to their original nature, thus committing evil deeds. Humanity has lost its natural desire for purity. Education is necessary to bring natural law to light and to bring the human soul back towards its original perfection (Althusius 1981b, 971–2). Man can only receive this kind of instruction in human society. Therefore, God created mankind also as a social being. The necessity of human community Althusius explains not only by referring to biblical sources, he also explicates the conditions of human existence through the use of Ciceronian and Aristotelian arguments (Althusius 1981a, I, § 4).

To enable human beings to live in community, Althusius considers people's inequality necessary. People must have different talents and qualities. This is not only crucial because people have to fulfill different tasks in society; it is chiefly the result of God's will. The differences in human talents enable some people to govern and others to be governed (Althusius 1981a, I, 12). Consequently, all human society has to reflect and has to be arranged according to human nature. Merio Scattola (Scattola 2002a, 368) even posits Althusius's belief in a preexisting human society. Humans cannot create or even choose among different alternatives, they have simply to discover and to imitate the pre-existing (divine) order. In a society established according to human nature, man is enabled to fulfill his main purposes. First of all, through the exchange of goods, rights, and services with his fellow consociates, he overcomes some of his deficiencies. Furthermore, he receives instruction (*disciplina*) necessary to gain true knowledge of God (Althusius 1981a, I, § 15). Moreover, through the second table of the Decalogue, man is committed to charity to his neighbours (Althusius 1981a, I, § 23). Consequently, Althusius considers a human society well established if it enables its citizens to have a happy and useful life in both physical and spiritual senses. In this commonwealth the common welfare, the protection of human society, and the worship of God in peace and according to orthodoxy are all guaranteed (Althusius 1981a, I, § 30).

This understanding of the human condition is not only reflected in Althusius's principle of consociation, it also indicates the necessity – by divine creation – of a diversification of human society. At the same time, it illustrates the need for religious orthodoxy. Although Althusius usually speaks about the "true orthodox religion," by which he means Calvinism, he nonetheless does not reject other Christian confessions. How Althusius integrates not only diverse political consociations, but also some different confessions while retaining at the same time religious orthodoxy, must now be addressed.

Although Althusius makes a clear distinction between the realm's secular and its ecclesiastical administrations, his outline of these two spheres is – at least for a post-modern reader – somewhat confusing. One reason for this confusion is the modern distinction between religion and politics. For Althusius, this distinction does not exist, since he considers "a sound worship and fear of God in the commonwealth […] the cause, origin, and foundation of private and public happiness" (Althusius 1995, XXVIII, § 8). This confusion, which is partly caused through a not always comprehensible classification of "secular" and "ecclesiastical," becomes in particular obvious in chapter XXX of the *Politica*, *De censura* (On Censorship).

Although Althusius includes this chapter in his discourse on secular administration, he addresses topics that he could have discussed with good reason in his analysis of ecclesiastical administration. In chapter XXX, he addresses aspects of public decency (*censura*). The meaning of *censura* Althusius defines as follows:

> *Censorship is the inquisition into and chastisement of those morals and luxuries that are not prevented or punished by laws, but which corrupt the souls of the subjects or squander their goods unproductively (Althusius 1995, XXX, § 1).*

Although usually exercised by members of the church council, Althusius ascribes the custody of *censura* to the supreme magistrate (Althusius 1981a, XXX, § 1). For Althusius, immoral deeds, although not necessarily contrary to law, have to be punished, since they could be the origin of greater harm to the commonwealth and could even lead to its ruin (Althusius 1981a, XXX, § 2). Consequently, because the well being of the whole community is concerned, the magistrate (of a city) has to appoint official inspectors, teachers, and guardians (Althusius 1981a, XXX, § 3). In Althusius's time, the censorship and inquisition of morals was usually in the responsibility of a sacred *collegium* or the presbytery. How theological and political aspects are conflicted becomes obvious not only through the nature of the officials who are entrusted to examine and punish immoral deeds, but also through the punishment of these deeds:

> *Whoever does not obey it is forbidden by it to attend sacred services, so that he becomes ashamed by this disgrace and exclusion, 1 Cor 5. If he is contemptuous of this exclusion and excommunication, he is accused of the contemptuous offense by an officer of the court before the magistrate, by whom he is deservedly punished, Mt 18 (Althusius 1995, XXX, § 4).*

1 Corinthian 5 cites "sexual immorality [...] of a kind that is not found even among pagans; for a man is living with his father's wife." 1 Corinthians 11 offers an enlarged catalogue of moral misdeeds: "But now I am writing to you not to associate with anyone who bears the name of brother or sister who is sexual immoral or greedy, or is an idolater, reviler, drunkard, or robber. Do not even eat with such a one." These are, more or less, also the deeds Althusius lists in his chapter on *censura*. In Matthew 18, the consequences for these deeds are foreshadowed: "If your hand or your foot causes you to stumble, cut it off and throw it away [...]" (Mt 18:8). In Matthew 18 one also finds guide for dealing with sinners:

> *If another member of the church sins against you, go and point out the fault when the two of you are alone. [...] If you are not listened to, take one or two others along with you, so that every word may be confirmed by the evidence of two or three witnesses. If the member refuses to listen to them, tell it to the church; and if the offender refuses even to listen to the church, let such a one be to you as a Gentile and a tax collector (Mt 18:15–17).*

Althusius, however, goes one step further. It is no longer the individual member of the community, who is responsible for his and his neighbors' morality; rather, he transfers the responsibility to a committee. If someone is suspected of immorality, the committee's members are allowed to investigate. Nonetheless, the different steps as described by Matthew are applied here, too: "[F]irst admonition, then corrective actions or fines, and lastly, if these are disregarded, excommunication, *Mt 18; Lev 19; Gal 6*. Such ecclesiastical discipline is rightly called the teacher of virtue, the custodian of faith, the walls and bulwark of piety, and the bond and sinew of the church" (Althusius 1995, XXX, § 28).

In addition to the deeds already addressed in the quoted passages from Corinthians, Althusius considers the following deeds as subject to *censura*: licentiousness, unlimited striving for profit, dissolution, love of extravagance, passion for splendor and grandeur, idleness, irregular attendance at holy services, and luxury (Althusius 1981a, XXX, § 7–8; § 10–11; § 15–17).

Although most of these deeds are not explicitly ecclesiastical, the consequences are always the same. The culprit has to suffer exclusion from the sacraments and from the sacral community. In the medieval view of excommunication, the "sinner" loses his civil status; in Althusius's Calvinist view the results are identical. Since fellow citizens are thereafter forbidden to share a table or trade with the punished, the condemned person is no longer either a member of the sacral community, nor a full member of the political community.

The consequences are even more serious or grave if the sinner violates not only morality, but the substance of faith. In chapter XXVIII of the *Politica, De administratione ecclesiastica* (On Ecclesiastical Administration), Althusius draws a general distinction between two kinds of heresies: "For there are some heresies that tear up the foundation of faith, such as Arianism and the like. But there are others that, although they err in certain articles of the faith, do not overthrow the foundation, such as the Novatians and similar heresies" (Althusius 1995, XXVIII, § 56).

For the first kind of heresy that destroys the foundation of the faith, Althusius recommends the magistrate to exile their adherents. Alternatively, the magistrate could put them in prison or punish them by the sword. All contacts with followers of these heresies are forbidden to the citizens of the realm, since the faithful could be easily infected, ruined, or corrupted (Althusius 1981a, XXVIII, § 57).

The more restrained versions of heresies are not punished that heavily, since they do not corrupt the foundation of religion. How the commonwealth should behave towards them depends primarily on the heretic himself. If he insists on his heresy, then he should be excommunicated. But the heretic has the chance to revise his errors. As long as the heresy is not manifest, the errant believer should not be blamed and condemned in public. Furthermore, the heretic should not be excluded from the Church and from sacral service (Althusius 1981a, XXVIII, § 58). Moreover, the magistrate has the opportunity to allow these kinds of beliefs, as long as the members of the different confessions do not blame each other in public. This is in particular advisable if the true orthodox religion is not flourishing in the realm (Althusius 1981a, XXVIII, § 59, § 63).

If one looks a bit closer at Althusius's outline of the commonwealth's behavior towards different religious groups, at least to those not considered fundamental heresies, then it becomes clear that Althusius is an advocate of a territorial separation between different religions, although they are accepted in the realm. Moreover, he intends to vest these groups with different rights. Jews, for example, should be allowed to live in the magistrate's dominion and territory, and, although they are allowed in theory to live according to their religious laws, it should not be permitted to them to have synagogues. Members of the true orthodox religion are neither allowed to enter into wedlock with Jews or to share their religion and rites (Althusius 1981a, XXVIII, §§ 53–54). The same rules apply to Catholics. They are allowed to live in the realm, but they are not allowed to have churches or to marry members of the true orthodox religion (Althusius 1981a, XXVIII, § 57). It is important to note that Althusius gives only common rules or advice here. Finally, he prefers "theologians [to] determine how far it is permitted to have private contact with infidels, atheists, impious men, or persons of different religions by distinguishing between the learned, the faithful, the uneducated, and the weak, and the purposes for which the contacts are to be held" (Althusius 1981a, XXVIII, § 55).

This, however, addresses mainly actual political practices. The Althusian political program looks slightly different. Although the *summus magistratus* should nourish the Christian faith in the realm, the ecclesiastical duties, which are under the magistrate's supervision, include the introduction, conversation, defense, and transmission of the true orthodox religion (Althusius 1981a, XXVIII, § 13). To fulfill these duties properly, the magistrate has to establish a sacred ministry and schools. The ministry has to choose suitable teachers to spread the word of God and to worship Him. Moreover, the ministry or the magistrate is expected to develop an orthodox canon of faith of the true orthodox religion (Althusius 1981a, XXVIII, §§ 25–27).

The second duty, the establishment of schools, is not to be considered primarily an attempt to fight early modern illiteracy. The main purpose is religious indoctrination:

> For the school is the laboratory of good and pious citizens, and the seedbed of honorable arts and customs. Indeed, it is the armory of the church and commonwealth. Arms of every kind are produced in it not only for defending the true and sincere worship of God against heretics, but also for defending and conversing the welfare and soundness of the commonwealth. A school is indeed the only means by which the pure and uncorrupted knowledge and worship of God is conserved and transmitted to prosperity (Althusius 1995, XXVIII, § 33; Hollenstein 2004, 7–22).

Since in the schools the only religion taught is the "true orthodox religion," and other religious groups, although tolerated in the realm, are not allowed to establish schools of their own, this politics of common religious education leads finally – at least in theory – not just to the dominance of the one true confession, it, furthermore, at least ultimately, could lead to an exclusive religion in the entire realm.

The same ministry that is responsible for the schools and their supervision has also to take care about the books and manifests distributed in the realm or province. In particular, those books should be allowed that spread the true orthodox religions. The ministry or an entrusted assembly should "provide that useful books on orthodox religion are produced, printed, published, and sold in the realm, and likewise that distinguished and excellent men useful to the church and the commonwealth are attracted to the realm or province" (Althusius 1995, XXVIII, § 43).

Conclusion

Many of Althusius's religious suggestions correspond to early modern realities and partly to his politics as city syndic of Emden. To find them outlined by Althusius is not necessarily surprising. The question to be addressed here is whether and to what extent his religious thought has an impact on the principles of his (secular) consocial federalism as outlined in the first part of this chapter.

If one briefly summarizes Althusius's theory, then one finds at first a commonwealth composed out of different entities. Each of these entities – family, *collegium*, city or *politeuma*, or province and *politia* – has different ends and therefore singular constitutions and rights. These rights remain untouched, even if these consociations consociate in larger entities. Human beings and diverse groups remain free to found new consociations and to join larger units in the realm. This principle does not violate any religious premise. The units even remain more or less independent in the formulation of their own law – as long as their laws are not violating the realm's common law.

However, as in particular Althusius's discussion of *censura* shows, in the commonwealth not only "laws" in the literal meaning of the word are effective; in addition to the written laws, which describe what is allowed and what is a punishable deed, a moral code is applied. Although actions contrary to this code are not necessarily unlawful, they nonetheless influence the culprit's civil status, since these deeds can be punished with excommunication and therefore with exclusion from the body of faithful citizens. This could lead, as to some extent is intended by Althusius, to a unification of the citizenry as established in Althusius's definition of citizenship in the *politeuma*.

This unification, on the other hand, is limited. Althusius's whole theory is based on the idea of human nature through divine creation. Although men are created equal concerning their natural rights, they are not equal regarding their abilities and talents. Without these differences, the whole community could not exist at all. But if, to return to Althusius's definition of citizens, all members of a *politeuma* should have the same religion, then it must be possible either to exclude some inhabitants from citizenship or to divide the realm into different religious territories to ensure that every smaller entity (*politeuma*) can fulfill its orthodox religious needs. The diversity of the whole and its federal principles would nonetheless remain.

Therefore, secular consocial federalism and religious orthodoxy do not stand in true contradiction in Althusius's theory, although some conflicts might emerge in practice. Finally, through the interaction of the independent political entities and the tendency towards unification in terms of religion, the realm's federal diversity might be softened over the time, although it can never vanish totally. Therefore, it is justified to conclude that, although Althusius's religious thought has some impact on his secular federalism, his religious ideas do not really harm Althusius's consocial federalism as outlined in *Politica Methodice Digesta*.

References

Althusius, J. (1932), *Politica Methodice Digesta of Johannes Althusius*, C. J. Friedrich (ed.), (Harvard, MA: Harvard University Press).
—— (1981a), *Politica Methodice Digesta atque Exemplis Sacris et Profanis Illustrata*, 2nd reprint of the 3rd edition, Herborn 1614 (Aalen: Scientia).
—— (1981b), De Utilitate, Necessitate et Antiquitate Scholarum, in Althusius, *Politica Methodice Digesta*.
—— (1995), *Politica: an abridged translation of "Politics methodologically set forth and illustrated with sacred and profane examples"*, F. S. Carney (ed. and trans.), (Indianapolis, IN: Liberty Fund).
—— (2003), Politik, übersetzt von Heinrich Janssen, in Auswahl hg., überarbeitete und eingeleitet von Dieter Wyduckel (Berlin: Duncker & Humblot).

Behnen, M. (1984), Herrscherbild und Herrschaftstechnik in der "Politica" des Johannes Althusius, *Zeitschrift für Historische Forschung* 10, 417–72.

—— (1997), Status Regimis Provinciae: Althusius und die "freie Republik Emden" in Ostfriesland, in Duso et al. (eds) (1997).

—— (2002), Herrschaft und Religion in den Lehren des Lipsius und Althusius, in Bonfatti et al. (eds) (2002).

Bianchin, L. (2005), "Censura," in Ingravalle et al. (eds) (2005).

Black, A. (1984), *Guilds and Civil Society in European Political Thought from the Twelfth Century to the Present* (Ithaca, NY: Cornell University Press).

Blickle, P. (2002), Die "Consociatio" bei Althusius als Verarbeitung kommunaler Erfahrung," in Blickle et al. (eds) (2002).

—— et al. (eds) (2002), *Subsidiarität als rechtliches und politisches Ordnungsprinzip in Kirche, Staat und Gesellschaft: Genese, Geltungsgrundlagen und Perspektiven an der Schwelle des dritten Jahrtausends* (Rechtstheorie, Beiheft 20; Berlin: Duncker & Humblot).

Bonfatti, E. et al. (eds) (2002), *Politische Begriffe und historisches Umfeld in der Politica Methodice Digesta des Johannes Althusius* (Wolfenbütteler Forschungen 100; Wiesbaden: Harrassowitz).

Carney, F. et al. (eds) (2004), *Jurisprudenz, Politische Theorie und Politische Theologie: Beiträge des Herborner Symposions zum 400. Jahrestag der Politica des Johannes Althusius 1603–2003* (Beiträge zur Politischen Wissenschaft 131; Berlin: Duncker & Humblot).

Chupp, J. and Nederman, C. J. (2004), The Calvinist background to Johannes Althusius's idea of religious toleration, in Carney et al. (eds) (2004).

Dahm, K.-W. et al. (eds) (1988), *Politische Theorie des Johannes Althusius* (Rechtstheorie Beiheft 7; Berlin: Duncker & Humblot).

Duso, G. (1997), Mandatskontrakt, Konsoziation und Pluralismus in der politischen Theorie des Althusius, in Duso et al. (eds) (1997).

—— (2002), Herrschaft als *gubernatio* in der politischen Lehre des Johannes Althusius, in Bonfatti et al. (eds) (2002).

—— et al. (eds) (1997), *Konsens und Konsoziation in der politischen Theorie des frühen Föderalismus* (Rechtstheorie Beiheft 16: Berlin: Duncker & Humblot).

Elazar, D. (1997), Althusius and federalism as grand design, in Duso et al. (eds) (1997).

—— et al. (eds) (2000), *The Covenant Connection: From Federal Theology to Modern Federalism* (Lanham, MD: Lexington Books).

Feuerherdt, E. (1962), *Gesellschaftsvertrag und Naturrecht in der Staatslehre des Johannes Althusius* (Köln: Diss).

Friedrich, C. J. (1932), Introduction, in Althusius (1932).

—— (1975), *Johannes Althusius und Sein Werk im Rahmen der Entwicklung der Theorie von der Politik* (Berlin: Dunker & Humblot).

Gelderen, M. van (2002), Der moderne Staat und seine Alternativen: Althusius, Arnisaeus und Grotius, in Bonfatti et al. (eds) (2002).

Gierke, O. von (1966), *The Development of Political Theory*, B. Freyd (trans.) (New York, NY: Norton).

—— (1981 [1980]), *Johannes Althusius und die Entwicklung der naturrechtlichen Staatstheorien: Zugleich ein Beitrag zur Geschichte der Rechtssystematik*, 7th edition. (Untersuchungen zur deutschen Staats- Rechtsgeschichte, Alte Folge 7; Aalen: Scientia).

Hengel, M. et al. (eds) (2000), *La Cité Dieu/Die Stadt Gottes* (Wissenschaftliche Untersuchungen zum Neuen testament 129; Tübingen: Mohr Siebeck).

Hollenstein, H. (2004), Schule und Erziehung bei Althusius, Clavin and Comenius in ihrer Bedeutung für die Gemeinschaftsbildung, in Carney et al. (eds), 7–22.

Hueglin, T. O. (1979), Johannes Althusius: medieval constitutionalist or modern federalist?, *Publius* 9, 9–41.

—— (1991), *Sozietaler Föderalismus: Die politische Theorie des Johannes Althusius* (Europäisches Hochschulinstitut, Serie C: Politik- und Sozialwissenschaften 13; Berlin: de Gruyter).

—— (1999), *Early Modern Concepts for a Later Modern World: Althusius on community and federalism* (Waterloo, ON: Wilfrid Laurier University Press).

—— (2000), Covenant and federalism in the politics of Althusius, in Elazar et al. (eds) (2000).

—— (2005), Althusius in question: interpretation and relevance, in Ingravalle et al. (eds) (2005).

—— and Fenna, A. (2006), *Comparative Federalism: A systematic inquiry* (Peterborough, ON: Broadview Press).

Ingravalle, F. et al. (eds) (2005), *Il Lessico Della Politica di Johannes Althusius: L'arte della simbiosi santa, giusta, vantaggiosa e felice* (Firence: Olschki).

Janssen, H. (1992), *Die Bibel als Grundlage der politischen Theorie des Johannes Althusius* (Europäische Hochschulschriften, Reihe XXIII: Theologie, 445; Frankfurt/M.: Lang).

Kappelhoff, B. (1994), *Emden als quasiautonome Stadtrepublik 1611 bis 1749* (Leer: Rautenberg).

Koch, B. (2004), Religion as a principle of political order? Comparing Marsilius of Padua and Johannes Althusius, in Carney et al. (eds) (2004).

—— (2005), *Zur Dis-/Kontinuität mittelalterlichen politischen Denkens in der neuzeitlichen politischen Theorie: Marsilius von Padua, Johannes Althusius und Thomas Hobbes im Vergleich* (Beiträge zur Politischen Wissenschaft 137; Berlin: Duncker & Humblot).

Lengen, H. van (ed.) (1995), *Die "Emder Revolution" von 1595: Kolloquium der Ostfriesland-Stifung am 17. März 1995 zu Emden* (Aurich: Ostfriesland-Stiftung).

Malandrino, C. (2002), "Die Subsidiarität in der Politica" und in ihrer politischen Praxis des Johannes Althusius, in Blickle et al. (eds) (2002).

—— (2005), Foedus (Confoederatio), in Ingravalle et al. (eds) (2005).

Menk, G. (1995), Zwischen Westeuropa und dem Heiligen Römischen Reich: Das Leben und die politische Theorie des Johannes Althusius, in Lengen (ed.) (1995).

Möller, B. (ed.) (1978), *Stadt und Kirche im 16. Jahrhundert* (Schriften des Vereins für Reformationsgeschichte 190: Gütersloh: Mohn).

Oestreich, G. (1969a), *Geist und Gestalt des frühmodernen Staates: Ausgewählte Aufsätze* (Berlin: Duncker & Humblot).

—— (1969b), Die Idee des religiösen Bundes und die Lehre vom Staatsvertrag, in Oestreich (1969).

Reibstein, E. (1955), *Johannes Althusius als Fortsetzer der Schule von Salamanca: Untersuchungen zur Ideengeschichte des Rechtsstaates und zur altprotestantischen Naturrechtslehre* (Freiburger rechts- und staatswissenschaftliche Abhandlungen 5; Karlsruhe: C. F. Müller).

Riley, P. (1976), Three seventeenth century German theorists of federalism: Althusius, Hugo and Leibniz, *Publius* 6, 7–41.

Scattola, M. (2002a), Subsidiarität und gerechte Ordnung in der politischen Lehre des Johannes Althusius, in Blickle et al. (eds) (2002).

—— (2002b), Von der *maiestas* zur *symbiosis*. Der Weg des Johannes Althusius zur eigenen politischen Lehre in der dritten Auflage seiner *Politica methodice digesta*, in Bonfatti et al. (eds) (2002).

Schilling, H. (1978), Reformation und Bürgerfreiheit: Emdens Weg zur calvinistischen Stadtrepublik, in Möller (ed.) (1978).

Schwemer, A. M. (2000), Himmlische Stadt und himmlisches Bürgerrecht bei Paulus (Gal 4,26 und Phil 3,20), in Hengel et al. (eds) (2000).

Scupin, H. U. (ed.) (1973), *Althusius-Bibliographie: Bibliographie zur politischen Ideengeschichte und Staatslehre, zum Staatsrecht und zur Verfassungsgeschichte des 16. -18. Jahrhundert* (Berlin: Duncker & Humblot).

Skillen, J. W. (2000), From Covenant of Grace to Tolerant Public Pluralism: The Dutch Calvinist Contribution, in Elazar et al. (eds) (2000).

Villani, A. (1993), Annotazione sulla *Politica* di Althusius: La "simbiosi" fra tradizione e modernità, I 7, 295–306.

Wyduckel, D. (1997), Föderalismus als rechtliches und politisches Gestaltungsprinzip bei Johannes Althusius und John C. Calhoun, in Duso et al. (eds) (1997).

—— (1988), Auswahlbibliographie zu Leben und Werk des Johannes Althusius, in Dahm et al. (eds) (1988).

Zwierlein, C. (2005), Consociatio, in Ingravalle et al. (eds) (2005).

Further Reading

Carney, F. S. (1995), Introduction in Althusius (1995).

Hueglin, T. (1979), Johannes Althusius: medieval constitutionalist or modern federalist?, *Publius* 9, 9–41.

—— (1999), *Early Modern Concepts for a Later Modern World: Althusius on community and federalism* (Waterloo, ON: Wilfrid Laurier University Press).

Ingravalle, F. et al. (eds) (2005), *Il Lessico Della* Politica *di Johannes Althusius: L'arte della simbiosi santa, giusta, vantaggiosa e felice* (Firence: Olschki).

Riley, P. (1976), Three seventeenth century German theorists of federalism: Althusius, Hugo and Leibniz, *Publius* 6, 7–41.

Early Dutch and German Federal Theory: Spinoza, Hugo, and Leibniz

Lee Ward

The United Provinces of the Netherlands and the German Empire stood out in the seventeenth century as rare examples of federal forms of government in an age dominated by centralized monarchies and the doctrine of indivisible sovereignty created to legitimize the post-feudal state. In the United Provinces and the post-Westphalian German Empire, Benedict Spinoza, Ludolph Hugo, and Gottfried von Leibniz were important theorists who articulated federal systems that were both challenged by, and simultaneously a challenge to, the prevailing conception of sovereignty.

These seventeenth-century Dutch and German thinkers tried to determine whether the United Provinces and the German Empire could be reconciled with the modern doctrine of sovereignty. In the process of addressing issues pertaining to the relationship of the central government to its constituent members, and the nature of the internal constitutional arrangements within their regimes, Spinoza, Hugo and Leibniz asked crucial theoretical questions such as: What is a State? And are the United Provinces and the German Empire states according to prevailing legal philosophy? Where is sovereignty located in these regimes? And does the predominant notion of supreme power adequately reflect heterogeneous, compound political structures such as the United Provinces and the German Empire?

While it is doubtful whether these Dutch and German thinkers of the seventeenth century presented a fully developed federal theory, they and their homelands are a valuable study as a crucial stage in the development of modern federalism. In Spinoza, Hugo, and Leibniz we see an articulation of the challenge to indivisible sovereignty posed by pluralistic political associations based, however vaguely, on a territorial division of power. In their efforts to find a new vocabulary and theoretical explanation for the United Provinces and the German Empire these early federalists made considerable conceptual strides that would inform later American and European views of the possibilities and limits of federalism. While the history and theory of seventeenth-century Germany and the Netherlands seems alien to many in the English-speaking world today, it is perhaps useful to recall that later federal thinkers in Europe and America were intimately familiar with the complexities, and especially the vices, of the Dutch and German systems.[1] The theory and practice of seventeenth-century Dutch and German federalism arguably highlighted the central problems that later federal theory would have to address.

Sovereignty in the United Provinces and the German Empire

The German Empire and United Provinces were both political arrangements of remarkable complexity. The seventeenth-century German or Holy Roman Empire had two main features. The empire was a heterogeneous political form composed of a dizzying array of over 300 estates including seven electors and hundreds of princes and independent cities all combined within the loose association of the Empire. It was also an elective monarchy that placed imperial authority in the conjoint power of the emperor and the Diet representing the various estates.

Two formative events account for the gradual transformation of the empire from a fairly unitary state in its ninth-century original to an emphatically decentralized arrangement of sovereign or semi-sovereign states. First, in the Golden Bull of 1356 Emperor Charles IV settled the composition of the Electoral College, and formally recognized the complex process of election involving the plethora of German princes, counts, and independent cities such as Hamburg, Lubeck, and Frankfurt. In the aftermath of the Golden Bull, the Emperor agreed to share many executive and judicial functions with the Diet, and all imperial legislation required the consent of the representatives of the estates. Second, the Reformation of the sixteenth century shattered the formal unity of the empire as the Emperor came to be seen as the leader of the Catholic faction and the Protestant princes and cities rejected imperial authority not only over religious matters, but also on a wide range of issues previously held to be a function of the central administration of the empire. The Peace of Westphalia of 1648, which finally ended over a century of religious turmoil, left the Emperor badly diminished and recognized the princes and territories as more or less fully sovereign states.

The German Empire possessed some features of statehood such as a common head and a capacity for common action albeit tortuously consensus based. Moreover, it had a common legal framework, could provide somewhat for common defense, and the central government played a role settling disputes among the constituent members of the empire. However, the state personality of the empire was seriously limited by the constant evolution of territorial sovereignty (Wilson 2006, 573). The nature of the claims of territorial sovereignty was by no means uniform as the various princes and cities often enjoyed distinct privileges, but the

---

1   For example, no less than 13 of the 85 *Federalist Papers* contained discussions of the United Provinces or the German Empire.

ultimate effect was to diminish the power of the imperial authority and produce endless disputes about supremacy in the empire. Given the amorphous character of imperial authority and the steady growth of territorial power such debates were likely inevitable.

In its own way the United Provinces was as complex as the German Empire of which it had once been a part. The logic of the Dutch revolt of the 1570s was essentially a defense of local rights and privileges, notably but not uniquely religious, against the centralizing project of Spanish rule. The Union of Utrecht of 1579 that bound the seven northern provinces of the Netherlands was described in terms of a military alliance of independent provinces that swore to a perpetual union for the purpose of common defense. The internal tension in the notion of a union constructed for the sake of preserving provincial independence would predictably be one of the central features of political life in the Dutch Republic.

The Englishman William Temple shrewdly observed that the United Provinces are a "Confederacy of Seven Sovereign Provinces" in which "each of these Provinces is likewise composed of many little States or Cities, which have several marks of Sovereign Power within themselves, and are not subject to the sovereignty of their Provinces" (Temple 1972, 52). Temple captured the essential characteristic of the Dutch Republic: it was a state form in which sovereignty by any conventional measure was difficult to locate. The general government (States-General) had no legislative, judicial, or taxation power and had only limited control even over military policy, the presumptive rationale for the union in the first place. The provinces dominated the States-General government as each province was equally represented, most matters required unanimity, and the delegates to the general government were selected by the provincial-states and operated as agents under strict instructions from their principals. Finally, the provincial-states controlled taxation by which power they, particularly Holland, supplied the general government and could effectively hold it hostage.

However, the provincial-states were themselves composed of delegates appointed by the city assemblies under the same rule of instructions governing delegates to the States-General, and typically operated on the basis of unanimity and equality of the constituent members. Each city had its own magistrates as well as legislative and judicial power generally not subject to the provincial-states. The city councils of regents were thus the real source of power in the Dutch Republic.

The only other quasi-national institutions in the Dutch Republic were the Stadtholderate and the Grand Pensionary. The Stadtholderate identified with the House of Orange was at least formally little more than the military commander appointed by each of the separate provinces. However, the real strength of the Stadtholder lay in his power as a symbol of national unity and in his role as the champion of formidable interests such as the orthodox Calvinist clergy, the rural nobility, smaller provinces wary of Holland's dominance and the urban multitudes largely excluded from a share in government by the oligarchy of regents. Because of its wealth and power, the Grand Pensionary or chief advocate of Holland held unique status in the Republic and as representative of the regent class of urban commercial elites, he was a natural rival of the Stadtholder. The ascendancy of

Oldenbarnevelt in the early republic and DeWitt in the stadtholderless period from 1650–1672 revealed the potential strength of this position. However, their demise in 1619 and 1672 respectively at the hands of the Orange faction indicate its clear limits. Arguably the power of both the Stadtholder and the Pensionary was rooted in the economic and cultural reality of Dutch society rather than the formal structures of the republic. With its weak national institutions, its lack of any system of national legislation or courts, and provincial estates dominated by fiercely independent cities, the United Provinces appear to be even less state-like than the German Empire.

For Dutch and German thinkers in the seventeenth century struggling to provide a coherent account of the rules governing their political associations, the task was given considerable urgency and complexity by the emergence of the doctrine of sovereignty originating from Jean Bodin's *Six Books of the Republic* (1576). Bodin's account of sovereignty had four main features. First, he identified sovereignty in the power of the agencies of government rather than the constituent authority of the general community or the fundamental rules a community agreed to recognize (Franklin 1991, 308). First, for Bodin, sovereignty was personal, active, and exclusive by nature. Second, sovereignty is necessarily absolute in the sense that every political system required a supreme power that can give orders to all and receive commands from none. Third, Bodin insisted that sovereign power cannot be shared by separate agents or distributed among them. Unitary sovereignty logically required the consolidation of power in a single ruler or ruling group. Fourth, in Bodin's formulation of sovereignty the notion of constitutionalism became deeply suspect. While Bodin made gestures toward natural law and fundamental customary law, there are by definition no limits on sovereign power that can be enforced by an independent agent in the body politic.

Bodin's theory of absolute and indivisible sovereignty was completely discordant with the German imperial monarchy universally recognized to be limited and with the Dutch federation of sovereign provinces. The predominant response to Bodin among Dutch and German academics produced a body of public law that was both profoundly influenced by Bodin, and yet strove to counter his claims regarding the indivisibility of sovereignty. This response took two main forms. First, the Political Aristotelians inspired by the spirit of northern European humanism elaborated a system of mixed constitutionalism or *respublica mixta* broadly analogous to the German and Dutch situations. Their interpretation of Aristotelian regime typology showed a clear preference for mixed over pure forms and focused on the idea of shared sovereignty or rights of sovereignty distributed among several agents (Bodeker 2002, 219–20). In Holland, Burgersdijk maintained the superiority of the *respublica mixta* and argued that the United Provinces constituted a transformation from monarchy to a mixed republic. In Germany thinkers such as Keckerman, Kirschner, Arnisaeus, and Besold offered some version of the mixed sovereignty argument according to which the Emperor shared some functions of sovereignty with the Diet and estates (Franklin 1991, 318–28). However conceived, the *respublica mixta* was used primarily to explain the mixture of monarchical and aristocratic elements in the imperial constitution, rather than its federal dimension.

The second major response to Bodin in the Dutch and German world was the natural jurisprudence of Hugo Grotius (1583–1645) and Samuel Pufendorf (1632–1694). Grotius retained elements of Aristotelian teleology and natural sociability, but decisively rejected the mixed regime model of the Political Aristotelians. In *De Jure Belli ac Pacis* (1625) Grotius elaborated a natural law based conception of sovereignty that departed from Bodin in key respects. He accepted Bodin's idea of sovereignty as a function of supreme power arguing: "That is called Supreme, whose acts are not subject to another's power ... the common subject of Supreme Power is the State" (Grotius 2005, 259). However, Grotius broke with Bodin's notion of indivisibility by claiming that the form and extent of sovereignty is determined by voluntary compact rather than any inherent absolutist logic in the principle of sovereignty itself. He distinguished between two types of sovereignty: full right and usufructuary right. The full right of sovereignty approximates the Bodinian ideal and involves the complete alienation of a people's freedom to a sovereign power. In this form of compact the people "transfer the right of governing" to another "without reserving any share of that right to themselves" (2005, 261). For all practical purposes, Grotius narrows the form of contractual absolutism to the particular case of conquest. Sovereign right by usufruct, on the other hand, is for Grotius the most common title to sovereign power. In this case, the people may "reserve certain acts of sovereignty to themselves" in the act of contracting (305–06). By the flexible terms of usufructuary contractual arrangement, supreme power can be "divided ... either amongst several persons, who possess it jointly, or into several parts, whereof one is in the hands of one person, and another in the hands of another" (306). The effect of Grotius' usufructuary right is to allow for a theory of limited monarchy that retains the Bodinian notion of supremacy, but jettisons the principles of absoluteness and indivisibility.

Grotius' flexible theory of sovereignty was designed at least in part to demonstrate that the Dutch Republic is a sovereign nation in international relations. On historical grounds Grotius affirms that the federation is grounded in the principle of provincial sovereignty. However, his reflections on compact and sovereignty produce a narrow interpretation of federalism as an alliance of sovereign states: "Several states may be linked together in a most strict alliance, and make a compound ... and yet each of them continue to be a perfect state" (260). For Grotius, divided sovereignty could only pertain to the distribution of sovereign functions within a state. The territorial division of power was not only a much lesser theoretical concern; it was a proposition difficult to adjust to his account of sovereignty. In this respect, Grotian natural law practically limited federalism to an alliance of fully sovereign states.

Samuel Pufendorf was both one of the leading natural law theorists in seventeenth-century Germany and an astute observer of the theoretical predicaments confronting the German Empire in the new era of sovereignty. He accepted the formal principle of Bodinian sovereignty as a function of ruler agency, but he framed sovereignty in the context of a natural law theory informed by the insights of Grotius and Hobbes. To the Grotian notion of compact, Pufendorf assimilated the Hobbesian imperative of the primacy of self-preservation deduced from reflection upon the state of nature and proposed a multi-stage series of compacts in order to explain the transition from the state of nature to civil society (Hunter 2001, 186–7). However, with respect to the actual properties of sovereignty, Pufendorf retained the Bodinian idea that every form of government required an "absolute" supreme power located somewhere in the legal order (Pufendorf 1934, 7.4.11). In Pufendorf's voluntarist conception of law, the source of legal and moral obligation derives from the relationship of a superior to an inferior, and thus there can be no higher authority in any system than the supreme legislative power.

The central thrust of Pufendorf's teaching on sovereignty is that limited monarchy is compatible with supreme power. The monarch may be bound by certain fundamental laws and in some areas required to govern with consent of popular or noble assemblies, and yet the state still represents a single moral entity: "supreme sovereignty without division or opposition, is exercised by one will in all parts of the state" (Pufendorf 1934, 7.6.10, 7.7.5). He dismissed mixed republics as unstable, "irregular" forms of government that fluctuate between the logical imperatives of their constituent elements. Limited monarchy, as opposed to mixed monarchy, is a regular regime type because it is regulated by fundamental laws that either circumscribe sovereign power or allow the establishment of compound sovereign structures bound by the laws governing their association. Whereas mixture implies uncertainty about the location of sovereignty in competing claims to rule, the principle of regularity ensures that the location of sovereignty is easily identifiable, even if the supreme power involves a complex dynamic of conjoint power.

With regards to the German Empire, Pufendorf's theory of sovereignty was hardly encouraging. In his influential study *The Present State of Germany* (1667), he stigmatized the post-Westphalian imperial order as a "monstrosity" (Wilson 2006, 565). It was a monstrosity because of the irregularity produced by the territorial governments holding a share of sovereign power independently of the common head. This problem was only compounded by the imperial government's weakness and incapacity to compel obedience by the constituent members of the empire. As such, the empire is not one but a variety of state forms fluctuating between a pure alliance or confederacy of sovereign states and a limited monarchy involving the Emperor and the Diet. The mix of powers and functions in the empire without solid legal foundation inevitably produced instability and made sovereignty difficult to locate.

Pufendorf rejected further evolution toward a federal structure of territorial states because, like Grotius, he believed that sovereignty is government over individuals and federalism is an alliance of independent states requiring unanimity in collective decision-making. The inadequacy of this arrangement for an empire composed of over 300 states was obvious. Thus, he advocated reforming or regularizing the empire by encouraging the territorial states to surrender a large measure of their sovereignty to an Emperor who has agreed to limits established by fundamental written laws. Given the political reality of the empire this accommodation was never likely to occur.

Early Dutch Federalism

By the latter decades of the seventeenth-century, the natural jurisprudential account of sovereignty and federalism championed by Grotius and Pufendorf came to supplant the *respublica mixta* as the dominant philosophical paradigm among Dutch and German intellectuals trying to interpret the United Provinces and the German Empire. However, despite the pervasive influence of the modern conception of sovereignty formulated by Bodin and modified by Grotius and Pufendorf, a small group of Dutch and German thinkers in this period sought to develop an alternative account of sovereignty and federalism more consistent with the political and constitutional reality of these regimes. In the Netherlands the most prominent of these early federalists were Pieter de la Court (1618–1685) and Benedict Spinoza (1632–1677).

Writing in the context of the Stadtholderless period (1650–1672), the Leiden merchant de la Court re-examined republicanism and the federal nature of the United Provinces. In *The True Interests and Political Maxims of the Republic of Holland* (1662) there is a clear presentation of the Dutch Republic as a form of confederate republic. The central themes of the work are hostility to the stadtholderate and monarchy generally, on the one hand, and a radicalization of the particularist principles of the Union of Utrecht, on the other. With the renaissance ideal of civic republicanism firmly in mind, de la Court argued that republicanism is rooted in the independence of city-states, and thus federal republicanism can mean only an alliance of self-governing cities (Haitsma 1980, 140). As an implacable opponent of the stadtholderate, de la Court roundly rejected the notion of the mixed republic. Monarchy, in any form, he held to be synonymous with militarism and centralizing tendencies inimical to the Dutch commercial spirit and tradition of local autonomy (de la Court 1972, 209). de la Court accepts the Bodinian idea of indivisible sovereignty, but precisely for this reason concludes that republics have to be small self-governing entities (Haitsma 1980, 160). In the Dutch context this meant that the union was essentially a collection of independent city-republics. He not only insisted that Holland free itself from dependence on the other provinces by fortifying its borders, but went one step further to argue that in principle "every city in Holland can defend itself" (de la Court 1972, 204–05, 307). On the central question of the internal character of the Union, de la Court believed that the real danger lay in the claims to increased power in the national government that he believed could only strengthen the Stadtholder and hurt Holland. For this reason he proposed proportional representation in the States-General as a means to defend the cities of Holland against the coercive power of the central government. This provincialism was at core a reflection of the commitment to a version of civic republicanism that made even the loosely bound United Provinces seem like a seedbed for centralized monarchy.

The most theoretically sophisticated effort to reconsider the republican and federal character of the United Provinces was that of Spinoza. Spinoza's project needs to be understood in both its historical and philosophical context. As an associate of DeWitt during the stadtholerless period, and the republic's most celebrated *philosophe*, Spinoza's direct political aim was to provide a theoretical account of the Dutch Republic that would counter the various forces of political and religious reaction grouped around the Orange camp. After the collapse of the stadtholderless republic in 1672, Spinoza's project assumed a new sense of urgency as he sought to counter the excessive pessimism of demoralized republicans who despaired of ever establishing a successful republic in modern conditions (Gross 1996, 123). To them, Spinoza maintained that the Dutch republican experiment can be revived, but it needs a more solid theoretical foundation than the renaissance humanism of de la Court. Significantly, Spinoza's most extensive reflections on federalism occur in the context of this effort to revivify and rationalize Dutch republicanism.

Spinoza's considerations on federalism also need to be understood in the larger context of his role in the development of modern natural rights philosophy. His major innovation was to produce a decisive break from the contractual tradition of Hobbes, Grotius, and Pufendorf. Spinoza agreed with Hobbes in many respects. He argued that natural rights are based on passions or "affects," and like Hobbes derived the character of the state from the nature of individuals. Spinoza also echoed Hobbes' claim that self-preservation is the primal core of moral right.[2] Spinoza broke from Hobbes, as well as Grotius and Pufendorf, with his argument that the democratic foundation of the state in consent does not disappear in the civil compact. Individuals retain natural rights in the state, especially a right of rebellion and the right to have some influence over public affairs (TPT 17.214). For this reason democracy emerges as the strongest and most rational regime in Spinoza's analysis because it is the system of government that most accurately reflects the basic truth that "the right of the commonwealth is determined by the common power of the multitude" (PT 3.9). Insofar as the foundation of the state is the multitude, then the stability of the regime requires integrating the multitude into the legislative process as much as possible.

The implications of Spinoza's account of sovereignty with regard to the possibility of federalism are complex. On its face, Spinoza's conception of popular sovereignty seems to exclude both mixed constitutionalism and divided sovereignty (Bodeker 2002, 225, 228). The supreme authority in any regime is subject only to the limits of its own power as it is: "the mind of the dominion, whereby all ought to be guided" (PT 4.1). The marks of sovereignty thus appear to be the exclusive preserve of the supreme authorities. Yet there is also in Spinoza's account of sovereignty an inherent tension between its reliance on a realistic assessment of the dynamics of power, on the one hand, and its insistence on the formal unity of sovereignty, on the other. The more sovereignty reflects the whole of society, the more difficult it is to conceive of its actual, as opposed to formal, unity, and thus the more complicated it will be to organize the power of the state in practice (Balibar 1998, 57). Actual political practice in the Dutch Republic clearly suggests possibilities for structuring supreme power that do not obviously flow from the logic of indivisibility. Thus,

---

2   Spinoza (1951), *Theologico-Political Treatise*, chapter 16, page 200 and *Political Treatise*, chapter 2, section 5 (hereafter in text and notes TPT chapter.page and PT chapter. section).

Spinoza's natural rights philosophy not only does not preclude, but also seems to actually require, a flexible approach to constitutionalism in order to identify and understand the democratic forces immanent in actual states.

It is in this pragmatic spirit that Spinoza offers his reflections on federalism in the Hebrew Republic of the Old Testament, the contemporary Dutch Republic, and in his account of a generic federal aristocracy loosely based on the United Provinces. In the Hebrew Republic the formal unity of sovereignty is guaranteed by "the power of God, which has sovereign right over all things." However, in actual practice "the Hebrews ... retained absolutely in their own hands the right of sovereignty" (TPT 16.200, 17.220). The Hebrew Republic was in essence an alliance in which "the different tribes should be considered rather in light of confederated states than of bodies of fellow citizens." While the Hebrews had a source of unity in "God and their religion," each tribe was fully sovereign with "complete control over all civil and military affairs" (TPT 17.224). Spinoza explicitly links this highly decentralized system of "confederated states" with that of the United Provinces when he insists that the Hebrews "were in fact in much the same position ... as the United States of the Netherlands" (TPT 17.224).

Spinoza's expression of the parallel between the Hebrew and Dutch republics raises a number of issues relating to his analysis of federalism. First, while he insists that for the Dutch "the rights of sovereign power have always been vested in the States," he seems to exaggerate the independence of the Dutch provinces by implying that they enjoyed "complete control over all civil and military matters" (TPT 18.244). For republicans like de la Court it was precisely the power that the States-General, and more ominously the Stadtholder, had over military policy that posed the chief danger to republicanism in Holland. In contrast to the rhetoric of perpetual union contained in the Union of Utrecht, Spinoza highlights Dutch particularist tendencies by arguing that all alliances are by nature revocable because if the basis in necessity or advantage is removed "the compact thereby becomes void" (TPT 16.208). The implication of Spinoza's discussion of the nature of alliances is that the Dutch polity is internally, and perhaps unnaturally, torn between the logic of union and its commitment to an extreme form of provincial sovereignty.

Spinoza's fullest treatment of federalism contained in chapter 9 of the *Political Treatise* describes an arrangement that is not a confederation of states, but rather a union of cities in which "all the cities are mutually associated and united, not as under a treaty, but as forming one dominion" (PT 9.4). In the framework of Spinoza's regime typology the aristocratic republic of one city and that of many cities share the same basic laws relating to the fixed ratio of subjects to patricians and age requirements for office. The government of both rests on a city assembly selected by cooptation that appoints its own magistrates from the ranks of the assembly. The unique feature of the federal aristocracy is that it includes a number of cities "so united, that each of them may yet remain as far as possible, independent" (PT 9.4). This union has two main features. First, a national Senate and court of justice provide the means by which the cities are "bound into one dominion" (PT 9.4). Both the Senators and the federal judges are appointed by the patricians of each city and represent their cities on the basis of their proportional share of national population. In this scheme the city councils have the sole power to tax and have supreme authority to legislate on matters of civic concern, however the national Senate is authorized "to manage the common business of the dominion" (PT 9.5, 8). Both the city councils and the "great Senate" are supreme within their jurisdictions.

The second main feature of Spinoza's federal republic is the interaction of the central government and the constituent members. The Senate and a committee of consuls drawn from the Senate govern national affairs, however the councils of all the cities occasionally can assemble as the "supreme council of the dominion" in order to decide by the majority of cities on major constitutional change or appointments of general and ambassadors (PT 9.6). Every citizen of the union has the right to appeal decisions of their city court to the "supreme court of the dominion" (PT 9.12). Finally, there is a "council of syndics" appointed by the cities as non-voting members of the federal Senate, who are charged "to see that the constitution is kept unbroken" and supplied with a body of troops to execute their duty (PT 9.10, 8. 23–5). Thus, in contrast to the United Provinces the legislative, executive, and adjudicative functions of the union government reach individuals, not just member polities (Gross 1996, 132). The city councils remain the supreme power in the ultimate sense, although their role is largely passive as electors of senators, syndics, and judges, and only rarely activates independently on matters of significance to the union as a whole.

Spinoza lauds the federal aristocratic republic as superior to its non-federal counterpart because "liberty under this dominion is common to more" (PT 9.15). With this he rejects both the small republic of de la Court and the notion of indivisible sovereignty. In the federal aristocratic republic the unity of power and the unity of population are approximated by a much more consolidated government than the United Provinces or even each provincial-state. His democratic conception of sovereignty allows for the creation of federal institutions with a jural link to the people as a whole, and thus for a version of sovereignty compatible with the territorial division of power. While the federal aristocracy may simply be an idealized version of the Dutch Republic, it also holds more radical potentialities as a reinterpretation of the nature of the union in terms of a multitude of citizens as opposed to a federation whose members are sovereign provinces. Spinoza's presumptively pragmatic constitutional theory may be more subversive of Dutch political conventions than he initially suggests.

Early German Federalism

German political thought throughout much of the seventeenth century was dominated by the debate between the Political Aristotelians and the natural lawyers led by Pufendorf. Ludolph Hugo (1630–1704) and Gottfried Wilhelm von Leibniz (1646–1716) stand out in this period for proposing ways to reconsider sovereignty and federalism in the context of the political reality of the empire. Hugo's *De Statu*

Regionum Germaniae (1661), written while he served as Vice-Chancellor of Hanover, was the first comprehensive interpretation of the federal nature of the German Empire post-1648. Hugo's analysis was unique in the sense that it focused on the constitution of the territorial governments as opposed to the imperial authority. He reinterpreted the empire in terms of the relation between the imperial "super-state" and the territorial "sub-states" (Eulau 1941, 650–5). Arguably, Hugo was the first German thinker to pose the central questions relating to the conflict between the prevailing idea of statehood and the undeniably federal character of the empire. Hugo identified three forms of composite political arrangements. First, there is the "confederated league," which is not a civil union because "the union contracted by treaty does not become the master of states, but the states are masters of the treaty" (Riley 1973, 111).[3] The confederated league approximates the narrow conception of federalism associated with Grotius and Pufendorf defined by the full sovereignty and equality of the constituent members. Hugo puts the United Provinces and Swiss Confederacy in this category. The second arrangement he adduces is the decentralized state in which local administration cannot be considered a state because the sub-national units or provinces "could not really even seem to be separate civil societies" (111). The primary example is the ancient Roman Empire.

The German Empire is neither a federation as traditionally understood nor a unitary empire-state along the lines of its putative ancient Roman progenitor, but rather a third category that Hugo terms "double government" [*duplex regimen*] (109). He describes the division of power between the imperial whole and its parts as a body composed of two state forms. Double government arises "when the civil power is somehow divided between the highest and lowest governments, so that the higher manages those matters pertaining to the common welfare, the lower to the things pertaining to the welfare of the individual regions" (112). The territorial governments constitute "a certain special civic body" for which since it "corresponds by some analogy to the highest civil power, it follows that the form of this governing must by the same token be considered a state government" (110, 112). Both forms of government are state-like, but not in the same way for while the territories "lack free and complete power ... their power is still universal and wide enough to take something of the highest power." (112). In contrast to the confederate league, double government involves clear subordination of part to whole. However, unlike the decentralized state, the territorial governments share some aspect of the "highest power." Their power and rights appear to differ in degree, if not in kind.

Hugo's argument for this division of power in some sense foreshadows the modern concept of devolution by establishing jurisdictional division of power based on whichever state form proved most capable of handling certain matters. As he relates, many of "the things required by the needs of the citizen's life cannot be seen to properly through a universal authority ... but should be handled by some lesser civil bodies" (113). Accordingly, the territorial states normally should

---

3 All quotations by Hugo are from the translation of *De Statu Regionum Germaniae* in Riley 1973.

have control over criminal law and the higher government over issues of foreign relations and war and peace. However, Hugo acknowledges that the principles governing an arrangement of powers based on efficiency must be flexible and thus no jurisdictional claim is absolute. For instance, while foreign affairs and matters relating to religious supremacy are typically assigned to the higher power, in the conditions of the empire since 1648 considerable independence has been prudently left to the territories. Hugo retained the logic of supremacy and subordination but in a form attenuated by the political reality in the empire, for while the territories can legislate for themselves, he suggests that these laws should comply with imperial legislation and be subject to oversight by the imperial courts.

By focusing on the constitution of the estates, Hugo highlights the territorial nature of the division of power, while separating this issue from the perennial question about who exercises sovereignty in the empire as a whole. He was inclined to view imperial sovereignty resting in a combination of the Emperor and the Diet, but opinions on this issue were not prejudicial either way to his argument for the federal division of power. Hugo's major theoretical achievement lay in reconsidering the meaning of statehood in light of the dual character of the empire, and providing an account of a federal political arrangement in which the constituent members can be considered states without reducing the central government to a mere alliance of states (Riley 1973, 112). With Hugo the concept of a state composed of states first became a plausible explanation of German political reality.

Hugo certainly challenged prevailing notions of the empire, however it was Leibniz who developed perhaps the most radical reinterpretation of federalism in seventeenth-century Germany. As official historian of Hanover, Leibniz was commissioned by Hugo to render an opinion on the question of whether the German territories have the right to send representatives to peace negotiations involving the empire and foreign powers. In *De Suprematu Principum Germaniae* (1677), Leibniz provided a theoretical defense of his two-fold political project. First, he sought to redefine the concept of sovereignty in order to allow German princes like Hanover to be treated as sovereigns in international negotiations. Second, he aimed to dilute the conception of sovereignty to make it consistent with the allegiance a sovereign might owe a universal power such as the Emperor or the Papacy (Leibniz 1970, 111). With this complex strategy, Leibniz tried to meld the traditional incommensurables in German history; namely, territorial independence and imperial authority, in order to enhance the empire's capacity to establish peace and order in the heart of Europe.

The first element of Leibniz's argument was his effort to reinterpret sovereignty so that this concept could be defined narrowly and applied broadly. He defines a territory as any area served by a common administration composed of an "aggregate of laws and rights" (114). Territorial "hegemony" is essentially a function of the exercise of executive "right of enforcing and coercing" and judicial power in "deciding cases and handing down judgments" (115). When Leibniz applies these criteria to the context of the empire, he determines that the princes may be called supreme in their territories, and thus in a tolerable sense are sovereign: "Persons only are called sovereigns or potentates who hold a larger territory and can lead out an army" (116). In this minimalist notion of sovereignty practically any civil authority that can maintain order in a given territory, as the well-armed German princes and cities manifestly could, is entitled to recognition of sovereignty.

In order to explain how this greatly diminished idea of sovereignty coheres with the political arrangement of the empire, Leibniz established a crucial distinction between a confederation and a union. A confederation is a mere alliance "entered into by words alone" (117). This verbal agreement produces a loose military alliance in which armed forces are joined only in emergencies and each member retains full independence. In a union, however, a new civil person is formed as "several territories … unite into one body with the territorial hegemony of each preserved intact" so that "the union notwithstanding there still remains in each region that which I have called supremacy" (116). Union also requires that a common administration be formed "with some power even over the members; which power obtains as a matter of ordinary law" (117). The union government is supreme in matters that "concern the public welfare" of the whole.

Leibniz's key point is that in a union several territories can be united into one body without diminution of territorial supremacy in any of the parts. He also, however, affirms that the union possesses state attributes in its own right. The test of statehood in the union is measured by the effectiveness with which its laws pertaining to the general welfare are accepted throughout the union (Eulau 1941, 656). Leibniz claims that by this measure, in some respects the German Empire is more tightly bound than the United Provinces because of the imperial court system and imperial legislation, but in other ways the German princes have more independence than the Dutch provinces "who are granted much less right of war, peace, treaties and ambassadors than are ours" (111). He presents the idea of union as flexible, and admits that political maturity and compromise are likely necessary features of federal unions characterized by "demands, negotiations and discussions" (119). Leibniz frames his idea of the federal union as a middle ground between absolute sovereignty theory in which "liberty or supremacy are abrogated in the individual members," and those including Grotius who "conceding liberty of the individual members, have thought that there is constituted not one state, but merely an alliance" (Riley 1973, 117). The former makes federalism impossible and the latter relegate it to a form of international relations.

The final element of Leibniz's federal account of the German Empire is his subordination of sovereignty to the concept of *majestas*. It is to *majestas*, rather than sovereignty, that Leibniz ascribes "the right to command without being subject to commands" (Riley 1973, 115). *Majestas* assumes metaphysical proportions far more exalted than territorial hegemony, and thus this highest form of political authority belongs exclusively to the heads of universal associations like the Emperor or the Pope and not to the nation-state. The effect of this diminution of sovereignty by *majestas* is to make sovereignty a relative term, and thus to narrow the difference between federal and non-federal arrangements (Riley 1973, 116). Leibniz observes that even centralized monarchies are a kind of Pufendorfian "monstrosity" in which the central government has to negotiate with cities, regional assemblies, and the church (Leibniz 1970, 119–20). The suggestion that there is no supreme power in any state that does not still have obligations to a higher authority rejects the very essence of sovereignty as understood since Bodin. In one sense Leibniz's argument for *majestas* is simply a legacy of the medieval conception of the papal plenitude of power, but in another sense this old idea had very innovative implications as applied to the division of power within the empire after 1648 where in principle the doctrine of sovereignty would no longer be an obstacle to federal possibilities that combine territorial independence and imperial authority.

Leibniz's major theoretical achievement perhaps lies in recognizing the difficulty in trying to formulate a new understanding of federalism within the confines of the modern doctrine of sovereignty (Riley 1973, 88). He saw that indivisible sovereignty is incompatible with the territorial division of power in the German Empire, which is manifestly neither an alliance of fully independent states nor a unitary state. By locating *majestas* in a supra-governmental category with greater metaphysical sources of legitimacy than those available to the nation-state, Leibniz disconnected government and supremacy in the full sense and thus arguably invented an idea of sovereignty compatible with a flexible theory of coordinate powers foreshadowing recognizably modern forms of federalism.

Conclusion

German and Dutch federal theory was largely marginalized in the intellectual climate of seventeenth-century Europe dominated by the sovereignty doctrine. The following century would see the transformation of Bodinian ruler sovereignty into popular sovereignty in a process arguably started by Spinoza, but clearly radicalized by Rousseau in his argument for the indivisible and indestructible general will. On the level of theory, many continental thinkers embraced this philosophy and its antipathy to federalism, even as the French Revolution dismissed federalism in practice because of its association, however unfairly, with feudalism and the discredited *ancien regime*. Only in the nineteenth century would Europe experience a sustained revival of interest in federal theory as von Gierke, Bryce, Le Fur, and others would re-examine earlier federal theory with an eye to modern developments that would have a great impact in Germany in particular and its later history as a federal state (Riley 1973, 99). For this reason alone a study of early German and Dutch federal thought is a worthwhile task.

Perhaps more importantly, however, early Dutch and German federal theory may provide us with a glimpse into the intellectual genesis of American federalism. While we must be careful neither to overstate nor to underestimate the achievements of thinkers like Spinoza, Hugo, and Leibniz with respect to federalism, it seems clear that the full development of modern federalism as a form of government over individuals, rather than a system of states, would need to wait until 1787. And we are well advised to recall that to the American Framers the United Provinces and the German Empire were largely seen as cautionary tales about the dangers attending the federal system they envisioned for the young republic (Madison

2001, esp. #19–20). However, perhaps the major achievement of the early Dutch and German federal thinkers lay in their ability to raise the questions that needed to be addressed if federalism were ever to progress as a concept beyond the limits imposed by the doctrine of sovereignty. They intelligently probed the idea of constitutionalism either to find the theoretical limits of sovereignty as in the case of Leibniz, or with Hugo to provide a functional basis for divided sovereignty, or to explore the federal possibilities in a thoroughly democratized notion of sovereignty *à la* Spinoza. In this respect, the Dutch and German federal arguments of the seventeenth century highlighted the conceptual challenges and problems later federalists would have to resolve.

References

Balibar, Etienne. (1998), *Spinoza and Politics*. Trans. Peter Snowdon (New York: Verso).

Bodeker, Hans Erich. (2002), Debating the *respublica mixta*: German and Dutch political discourse around 1700, in *Republicanism: A Shared European Heritage*, Vol. I. Martin van Gelderen and Quentin Skinner, eds (Cambridge: Cambridge University Press), 219–46.

Court, Pieter de la. (1972) [1662], *The True Interests and Political Maxims of the Republic of Holland* (New York: Arno Press).

Eulau, Heinz H.F. (1941), Theories of federalism under the Holy Roman Empire, *American Political Science Review*. Vol. 35, No. 4 (August): 643–64.

Franklin, Julian H. (1991), Sovereignty and the mixed constitution: Bodin and his critics, in *Cambridge History of Political Thought, 1450–1700*. J.H. Burns, ed. (Cambridge: Cambridge University Press), 298–328.

Gross, George M. (1996), Spinoza and the federal polity, *Publius*. Vol. 26, No. 1 (Winter): 117–35.

Grotius, Hugo. (2005) [1625], *The Rights of War and Peace, Three Volumes*. Richard Tuck, ed. (Indianapolis: Liberty Fund).

Haitsma, Eco Mulier. (1980), *The Myth of Venice and Dutch Republican Thought in the Seventeenth Century* (Assen: Van Corcum).

Hunter, Ian. (2001), *Rival Enlightenments: Civil and metaphysical philosophy in early modern Germany* (Cambridge: Cambridge University Press).

Leibniz, Gottfried Wilhelm von. (1970) [1677], De Suprematu Principum Germaniae, in *The Political Writings of Leibniz*. Patrick Riley, ed. (Cambridge: Cambridge University Press), 111–20.

Madison, James and Alexander Hamilton, John Jay. (2001) [1788], *The Federalist Papers* (Indianapolis: Liberty Fund).

Pufendorf, Samuel. (1934), De Jure Naturae et Gentium, Libri Octo. Vol. I photographic reproduction of the edition of 1688, Amsterdam, and Vol. II, translation of the text by C.H. and W.A. Oldfather. (Oxford: Clarendon Press).

Riley, Patrick. (1973), The origins of federal theory in international relations theory, *Polity*, Vol. 6, No. 1 (Autumn): 87–121.
Spinoza, Benedict. (1951) [1670, 1677], *A Theologico-Political Treatise and A Political Treatise*. R.H.M. Elwes, ed. (New York: Dover).
Temple, Sir William. (1972) [1672], *Observations Upon the United Provinces of the Netherlands*. George Clark, ed. (Oxford: Clarendon Press).
Wilson, Peter H. (2006), Still a monstrosity? Some reflections on early modern German statehood, *The Historical Journal*, Vol. 49, No. 2, 565–76.

Further Reading

Bodin, Jean. (1962) [1576], *The Six Books of a Commonweale*. R. Knolles, trans. K.D. McRae, ed. (Cambridge, MA: Harvard University Press).
Bryce, James. (1926), *The Holy Roman Empire*. (London: MacMillan).
Drischler, William Fr. (2006), *The Political Biography of the Young Leibniz in the Age of Secret Diplomacy*. (Charleston, SC: BookSurge Publishing).
Gelderen, Martin van. (2002), Aristotelians, Monarchomachs and Republicans: Sovereignty and the *respublica mixta* in Dutch and German political thought, 1580–1650, in *Republicanism: A Shared European Heritage, Vol. I*. (Cambridge: Cambridge University Press), 195–217.
Grotius, Hugo. (2006) [1609], *Commentary on the Law of Prize and Booty*. Martine Julia van Ittersum, ed. (Indianapolis: Liberty Fund).
Israel, Jonathan. (1995), *The Dutch Republic: Its rise, greatness, and fall, 1477–1806*. (Oxford: Clarendon Press).
Moore, James and Michael Silverthorne. (1995), Protestant theologies, limited sovereignties: Natural law and conditions of union in the German Empire, the Netherlands, and Great Britain, in *A Union for Empire: Political Thought and the British Union of 1707*. John Robertson, ed. (Cambridge: Cambridge University Press), 171–97.
Prak, Martin. (2005), *The Dutch Republic in the Seventeenth Century: The golden age*. (Cambridge: Cambridge University Press).
Price, J.L. (1998), *The Dutch Republic in the Seventeenth Century*. (New York: St. Martin's Press).
Pufendorf, Samuel. (2007) [1667], *The Present State of Germany*. Michael Seidler, ed. (Indianapolis: Liberty Fund).

Montesquieu on Federalism and the Problem of Liberty in the International System: Ancient Virtue and the Modern Executive

Ann Ward and David S. Fott

In *The Spirit of the Laws*, Montesquieu recognizes that unlike the modern commercial nations of his time, the small city-republics of Greek antiquity demanded political virtue of their citizens. The context that propelled the ancient republic toward this demand for excessive virtue was the chaos of the international system. The ever-present insecurity within the international system meant that individual liberty and self-fulfillment had to be suppressed for the sake of political survival.

In modernity the rise of the large nation-state opens up new possibilities. The larger populations of modern nations make war at once less frequent and less burdensome on each individual citizen. This greater stability within the international system allows modern nations, such as England and America, to aspire not to political virtue but rather to the political liberty of their citizens, with the accompanying pursuit of economic prosperity. For Montesquieu the core of the problem in modernity involves relations between the armed forces and the legislative and executive branches of government. Montesquieu asserts that the army will have contempt for the senate but respect the executive. This hostility implies that power over the military must be placed solely in the hands of the executive branch. Yet, one may question whether a civilian executive with unchecked authority over the military is in fact less dangerous to the liberty of the citizens than an executive in uniform.

This chapter will conclude by exploring the possibilities for the preservation of liberty suggested by Montesquieu's discussion of what he calls the "federal republic." A federal republic is a "society of societies": a collection of sovereign states that confederate for the purpose of achieving collective security. Montesquieu therefore points us in the direction of supranational federal structures and organizations for the sake of preserving political liberty. International alliances can provide security to citizens while simultaneously restraining the sweeping power of a single executive that can threaten their liberty.

Ancient Virtue

In *The Spirit of the Laws*, Montesquieu, reflecting on democracy, claims, "The political men of Greece who lived under popular government recognized no other force to sustain it than virtue. Those of today speak to us only of manufacturing, commerce, finance, wealth, and even luxury" (*SL* 3.3, 22–33).[1] As this quote indicates, Montesquieu believes that unlike the modern commercial nations of his time, the free cities of Greek antiquity demanded virtue of their citizens. Montesquieu explains what he means by a free city or a "popular government" in Greece in his discussion of the natures and principles of government in books two and three of *The Spirit of the Laws*. The "nature" of each government, according to Montesquieu, "is that which makes it what it is," or "its particular structure" (*SL* 3.1, 21). In other words, it is who rules (the many, the few, or one) and how they rule (by law or arbitrarily, beyond law). The "principle," or what Montesquieu sometimes calls the "spring," of each government is "that which makes it act," or "the human passions that set it in motion" (*SL* 3.1, 21). The principle is, therefore, the primary motivation for the actions of the people living under a particular government.

Montesquieu's classification of regimes includes three basic varieties. One variety is despotic; its nature is the rule of one person without the restraint of law, and its principle is fear. Monarchical government, on the other hand, is characterized by the rule of one person according to "fixed and established laws," with honor as its principle (*SL* 2.1, 10). The third variety of government is republican, which, according to Montesquieu, can have two "natures" or forms. Either a part of the people rules, which Montesquieu calls "aristocracy" (*SL* 3.4, 24) and what we today would call "representative democracy," or "the people as a body, ... have the sovereign power," identified simply as "democracy" by Montesquieu and what we today have come to call "direct democracy" (*SL* 3.2, 21). According to Montesquieu, the latter type of republican government, exemplified by Athens and Sparta in ancient Greece, had virtue as its principle.

The virtue that is the spring of republican government is distinguished by Montesquieu in the foreword to his work both from "moral virtue," which he associates at the end of book one with the rational self-knowledge of the ancient philosophers, and from "Christian virtue" (*SL* Author's Foreword, xli). Rather,

---

1   Montesquieu 1989, bk. 3, chap. 3, 22–23. All future references to *The Spirit of the Laws* will be to this edition and will be made in parentheses with this format: (*SL* book. chapter, page). Reproduced with permission of Cambridge University Press.

Montesquieu refers to a passion, not for a transcendent supernatural being or the Church that represents this divinity on earth, but for one's fellow citizens and their laws; it is "love of the homeland, that is, love of equality," which he calls *"political virtue"* (*SL* Author's Foreword, xli, italics in original) (see Rahe 2001, 73 and Pangle 1973, 64–5).

Political virtue is, therefore, the passion of patriotism. The "political good man," according to Montesquieu, "is the man who loves the laws of his country and who acts from love of the laws of his country" (*SL* Author's Foreword, xli–xlii). Montesquieu refines what he means by political virtue in book three when he discusses why virtue is less needed in a monarchy than in a republic: in contrast to monarchy, where the one who executes the laws is not subject to the laws himself, in a republic "the one who sees to the execution of the laws feels that he is subject to them himself and that he will bear their weight" (*SL* 3.3, 22). Thus in a republic, because the people both make and obey the laws simultaneously, they must possess the self-control, or virtue, that would allow them to pass measures to restrict themselves as well as others.

What does such republican self-control consist of? What is needed to achieve it? Montesquieu suggests the answers to these questions when he clearly states what he regards as the lack of political virtue in his day. We have already noted his contrast between the political men of ancient Greece, who relied on political virtue to sustain their republics, and the political men of "today," who speak only of "manufacturing, commerce, finance, wealth, and even luxury." It is thus clear that modern nations lack political virtue in Montesquieu's eyes because they are commercial or dedicated to wealth and material prosperity. Moreover, Montesquieu claims, "When … virtue ceases, ambition enters into those hearts that can admit it, and avarice enters them all. … One was free under the laws, one wants to be free against them. Each citizen is like a slave who has escaped from his master's house. What was a *maxim* is now called *severity*; what was a *rule* is now called *constraint*; what was *vigilance* is now called *fear*. There, frugality, not the desire to possess, is avarice. Formerly the goods of individuals made up the public treasury; the public treasury has now become the patrimony of individuals" (*SL* 3.3, 23).

The disappearance of political virtue and the emergence of vice are thus characterized by Montesquieu as the rise of ambition and avarice, or the desire for power and physical pleasure. This results in a desire for freedom understood as lawlessness and licentiousness, for self-fulfillment rather than self-restraint or self-government. In such a situation individual goods are no longer dedicated to the public treasury; rather the wealth of the state is bilked for personal profit. Montesquieu's point is that the corruption of political virtue occurs when self-interested individualism emerges, or the spring of human action becomes the desire for personal satisfaction: the satisfaction of our desire for power or to be recognized as first in pre-eminence, of our desire for personal pleasures, and of our desire for personal material prosperity. It follows that the political virtue of the ancient republics entailed the suppression of individual self-interest and desire in favor of dedication to the public good.

In book four Montesquieu suggests that the political virtue needed to sustain a republic is almost unnatural in the demands it makes on the individual (Rahe 2001, 73–5 and Pangle 1973, 80–2). Its hardship results from the fact that "political virtue is a renunciation of oneself, which is always a very painful thing" (*SL* 4.5, 35). Moreover, this suppression of individual self-identity means that in a republican government, "the full power of education is needed" (*SL* 4.5, 35). Montesquieu then discusses the institutions established by ancient legislators to educate their people toward political virtue. Those established by Lycurgus, famous lawgiver of the Spartans, as described by Plutarch in his *Life of Lycurgus*, are singled out by Montesquieu for special praise (*SL* 4.6, 36–7). The laws of Crete, according to Montesquieu, were the model for those given to Sparta by Lycurgus, and the communal institutions of Plato's *Republic* were a further refinement of those of Sparta. Since Plutarch's *Life of Lycurgus* is the reference point of Montesquieu's assessment of the education needed to make citizens politically virtuous, we will briefly digress to discuss the institutions described therein.

With regard to economic arrangements, Plutarch writes that Lycurgus redistributed wealth to ensure an equality of property among Spartan citizens, the purpose of which was to create unity or a familial feeling within the city (*Lives*, 227).[2] In addition, Lycurgus abolished money or the use of gold and silver within the city, and along with this prohibited all foreign trade and commerce with other cities (*Lives*, 229, 231). All those who practiced a moneymaking trade, such as manual artisans, were banned from citizenship, and all farming was done by "helots," a non-citizen slave class who worked the land (*Lives*, 279). The only occupation open to citizens was war or the life of a soldier. The result of these economic reforms was to turn Sparta into a non-commercial, homogeneous, and highly militaristic society closed to the corruption of the outside world.

Plutarch also discusses the social reforms instituted by Lycurgus. Two of the most notable of these reforms were the institution of "common wives" and "common children" (*Lives*, 251, 253). Lycurgus made it possible for a husband to ask a promising young man in the city to sleep with his wife; Lycurgus even encouraged that to happen. If a young unmarried man noticed a married woman with "good genes," so to speak, he could solicit her husband's permission to have intimate relations with her. The aim of these rather open relationships was to subject erotic attachments to the public good, or to ensure that excellent children were produced for the city. Moreover, when such children were born, parents were not allowed to educate them in any way they wished, but boys were taken away from their families at seven years of age and raised in common public schools at the expense of the city until their early twenties (*Lives*, 257). This publicly run educational system administered a very harsh and rigorous physical training program, the purpose of which was to prepare the boys to be good soldiers; by purposely underfeeding them, it even created the conditions that required the boys to steal to survive (*Lives*, 261). Plutarch maintains that, like physical training, the

---

2   Plutarch 1914. All future references to Plutarch's *Lives* will be to this edition and will be made in parentheses with this format: (*Lives*, page).

habituation to theft was meant as preparation for battle against the city's enemies. After having undergone and survived this common education provided by the city, adult men were required to attend "common meals" (*Lives*, 233, 237). Lycurgus mandated that all male citizens were to eat their meals among their companions in common eating "societies," usually composed of groups numbering from ten to twelve men.

The institution of common wives and common children in Sparta stopped just short of the abolition of the private family altogether in what Montesquieu says was an attempt to "raise a whole people like a family" (*SL* 4.7, 38). Moreover, common meals aimed to suppress private indulgence in pleasure and encourage friendship and fellow feeling. Taken together, Plutarch concludes that the economic and social reforms of Lycurgus had as their ultimate end the total socialization of Spartan citizens (*Lives*, 279, 283). Any desire for individual liberty and identity was to be suppressed so that Spartans would be totally dedicated to their city and thereby unbeatable in war. As Montesquieu notes, Greek society, with Sparta as its highest exponent, almost collapsed political virtue with military virtue. This made Greek men harsh toward enemies, but potentially brutal among themselves. According to Montesquieu, "One did not want the citizens to work in commerce, agriculture, or the arts; nor did one want them to be idle. They found an occupation in the exercises derived from gymnastics and those related to war. The institutions gave them no others. One must regard the Greeks as a society of athletes and fighters. Now, these exercises, so appropriate for making people harsh and savage, needed to be tempered by others that might soften the mores" (*SL* 4.8, 40–1). Music, Montesquieu claims, was the means that the Greeks chose to counterbalance the brutality produced by their military education. An education in music supplemented the education to war in order to soften the soul and make decent political life possible.

The institutions conducive to the creation and maintenance of political virtue, Montesquieu concludes, "can have a place only in a small state ... The laws of Minos, Lycurgus, and Plato assume that all citizens pay a singular attention to each other" (*SL* 4.7, 38). The people of a large state cannot satisfy that assumption. But earlier in book three, Montesquieu suggests that not only did smallness of size *allow* the ancient republics to develop political virtue, but that smallness also *required* virtue of them. For instance, speaking of the military greatness of Athens during the Persian and Peloponnesian wars, Montesquieu says that Athens "had 20,000 citizens when it defended the Greeks against the Persians, when it disputed for empire with Lacedaemonia, and when it attacked Sicily" (*SL* 3.3, 23). It had the same number when it was later conquered by Philip of Macedon. "It was always as easy to triumph over the forces of Athens as it was difficult to triumph over its virtue" (*SL* 3.3, 23). The political virtue of the Athenians, Montesquieu argues, is what allowed them to defend the collective freedom of their city against foreign domination and even to pursue empire; the loss of this virtue led to the conquest of Athens and to the destruction of her way of life. The ever-present threat of war made political virtue or its absence the key to either freedom and empire or subjection and destruction (see Pangle 1973, 54–5, 57).

Montesquieu is suggesting that the context that propelled the ancient republic toward the demand for political virtue was the chaos of the international system. The reality of a multitude of small, sovereign, but highly competitive cities, all struggling for power and preeminence, produced an international disorder rather than order. Constant warfare made the continual supply of citizen-soldiers prepared to sacrifice themselves in battle a priority for the city. For Montesquieu, the ever-present insecurity within the international system meant that individual liberty and self-fulfillment had to be suppressed in order to develop a political virtue necessary for political survival (but see Pangle 1973, 83–9).

Political Liberty and the Modern Executive

Montesquieu's discussion of the political virtue of the ancient republics naturally leads to the question of their disappearance. Why do Europeans in Montesquieu's day live their lives in large monarchical states, seemingly without virtue, rather than in small self-governing cities as they did in the past? Montesquieu suggests an answer to this mystery when he opens book nine with the claim, "If a republic is small, it is destroyed by a foreign force; if it is large, it is destroyed by internal vice" (*SL* 9.1, 131). The disadvantages of the republican form of government are thus twofold. If the republic is small – and, as Montesquieu suggests elsewhere, "[i]t is in the nature of a republic to have only a small territory" – it will be conquered by a greater power (*SL* 8.16, 124). Small republics dedicated to political virtue are in the end too small to defend themselves. If, on the other hand, the republic is large, virtue cannot be maintained, and it will collapse due to internal vice.

Montesquieu indicates what he means by vice in this context at the end of book four, when he says that, whereas in a small republic "silver must be banished" in order to maintain virtue, "in large societies, the number, the variety, the press and the importance of business, the ease of purchases, and the slowness of exchanges, all … require a common measure" (*SL* 4.7, 38, 39). Money, Montesquieu therefore suggests, is the "common measure" or universal means that citizens use to relate to, and interact with, one another when they are all isolated individuals. This in turn reinforces greed and the pursuit of private wealth, and the vast economic inequality that results further divides the citizens from one another and eventually from concern for their country altogether (see Larrere 2001, 337–8). According to Montesquieu, "[i]n a large republic, there are large fortunes, … ; at first a man feels he can be happy, great, and glorious without his homeland; and soon, that he can be great only on the ruins of his homeland" (*SL* 8.16, 124). These defects of republican government lead human beings to live under monarchy in a territory that, although not as extensive as a vast empire, is much larger than the city republics of antiquity. In a moderately large nation governed by a single executive, people can defend themselves from foreign aggression without being destroyed by the necessary internal vice of private greed (see Larrere 2001, 338–9).

The large nation-state of modernity thus seems to rise out of the ruins of the political virtue of old. But Montesquieu indicates that new possibilities have emerged that were foreclosed to the small republics of antiquity. The larger size and populations of modern nations make war, although by no means absent from the world stage, at once less frequent and less burdensome on each individual citizen (but see Hulliung 1976, 173–4). The most promising result of this greater stability within the international system, Montesquieu suggests, is that it allows modern nations to aspire, not to political virtue, but rather to what Montesquieu calls "political liberty." In book eleven Montesquieu defines political liberty as "the right to do everything the laws permit" (*SL* 11.3, 155). It is thus doing what the laws allow, or more precisely being ruled by law, rather than by either a single person, as in a despotism, or by the majority of persons, as in a democracy. Montesquieu emphasizes the distinction between political liberty and majority rule when he says that "in democracies the people seem very nearly to do what they want, [because] liberty has been placed in this sort of government and the power of the people has been confused with the liberty of the people" (*SL* 11.2, 155).

Montesquieu further refines his definition of political liberty by maintaining that it is "that tranquillity of spirit which comes from the opinion each one [i.e., each citizen] has of his security, and in order for him to have this liberty the government must be such that one citizen cannot fear another citizen" (*SL* 11.6, 157). The political liberty of the citizen is thus the peace of mind that comes due to the belief that one is safe against oppression and violence; freedom from the feeling of fear is thus the core political value (Pangle 1973, 45–6, 89–92, 107–17). This is an understanding of liberty with a highly subjective element: it implies that the end of government is to ensure not only that the citizens *are* in fact secure against oppression, but also that they *feel* secure against oppression.

How can such a subjective understanding of liberty flourish among citizens of a modern nation? Montesquieu instructs his readers that we must first perceive that there are three different functions or "powers" of government: the legislative power, the executive power, and "the power of judging" or the judicial power (*SL* 11.6, 156, 157). He then asserts that if the legislative and executive powers are fused in a single body or person, "there is no liberty, because one can fear that the same monarch or senate that makes tyrannical laws will execute them tyrannically" (*SL* 11.6, 157). Moreover, if the judicial power were united with either the legislative or executive, political liberty would be equally threatened. In short, Montesquieu declares, "All would be lost if the same man or the same body of principal men, either of nobles, or of the people, exercised these three powers: that of making the laws, that of executing public resolutions, and that of judging the crimes or the disputes of individuals" (*SL* 11.6, 157). Political liberty therefore requires the separation of the powers of government so that power can check power to ensure that the citizens are not oppressed, and do not fear that they will be oppressed. According to Montesquieu, political liberty "is present only when power is not abused, but it has eternally been observed that any man who has power is led to abuse it; he continues until he finds limits" (*SL* 11.4, 155). Hence citizens will have that "tranquillity of spirit" that comes with freedom from fear only when the powers of government are so arranged in different hands as to check and balance one another.

Montesquieu asserts that only one nation in the world has this separation of powers and checks and balances as its constitution or particular structure of government: England. In the English constitution the legislative power is divided into two bodies: the House of Commons, which is composed of representatives of the people, and the House of Lords, which is composed of the body of nobles. The executive power is vested in a hereditary monarch whose person is held "sacred," and the judicial power is placed in juries or temporary tribunals composed of "persons drawn from the body of the people at certain times of the year in the manner prescribed by law" (SL 11.6, 162, 158).

This brief overview of the structure of the English government naturally raises the question of where it fits into Montesquieu's earlier classification of regimes in book two. Montesquieu had defined republican government as either the rule of the people, "direct democracy," or the rule of part of the people, "representative democracy" or "aristocracy." Likewise, monarchical government was defined as the rule of one person according to law, and despotic government the rule of one without law. Under what variety would we place the English government described in book eleven? The House of Commons and the House of Lords seem to resemble representative democracy and aristocracy respectively. England's hereditary monarch, on the other hand, seems to resemble Montesquieu's understanding of monarchy. But juries "drawn from the body of the people," or the separate judicial power, seem to represent something completely new not discussed by Montesquieu before. If they do have a place in the earlier classification, they would seem closest to direct democracy. Finally, nothing in the English constitution appears to resemble the despotic form of government. The answer to the above question, therefore, seems to be that the English constitution fits into none of the previously defined varieties. It appears, rather, to be a new form of "mixed regime," as it were.

The distinctiveness of the English government from all previous forms further clarifies the fact that political liberty, the end that the English government secures, is something quite different from political virtue. With a new regime, both in history and in Montesquieu's work, a new end has come in sight: political liberty (see Rahe 2001, 71–2, 81, 84, 87, 90 and Courtney 2001, 278).

The mixed regime of the English nation, in Montesquieu's eyes, has clearly made great advances over the republics of antiquity with respect to the liberty of the citizen. But Montesquieu also suggests that this modern regime has not ensured that the threat to political liberty has disappeared entirely (Ward 2007, 558, 560–68; Krause 2000, 233, 239–43, 251). The potential threat to liberty posed by the English regime is initially pointed to in the discussion of the nature of monarchy in book two. Monarchy is the regime in which "one alone governs by fundamental laws," such fundamental laws "necessarily assum[ing] mediate channels through which power flows" (SL 2.4, 17–18). These mediate channels are "intermediate, subordinate, and dependent powers," the most natural of which, according to Montesquieu, is the nobility (SL 2.4, 18). Thus, "the nobility is of the essence of monarchy, whose fundamental maxim is: ... *no nobility, no monarch*; rather, one has a despot" (*SL* 2.4, 18). This argument is complex, as it is not the nobility that is the depository of the nation's laws thereby checking the capricious will of the monarch. Rather, given the "ignorance, ... laxity, and ... scorn for civil government" natural to the nobility, the depository of the laws "can only be in the political bodies, which announce the laws when they are made and recall them when they are forgotten" (*SL* 2.4, 19). Thus, popular assemblies, such as the House of Commons in England, are needed to remind monarchs of the laws and their people's ancient rights in order to prevent the slide into despotism.

The nobility, however, and other intermediate ranks between monarch and people cannot simply be dispensed with. Speaking of European states that had contemplated abolishing the power of the lords, Montesquieu says, "they wanted to do what the Parliament of England did. If you abolish the prerogatives of the lords, clergy, nobility, and towns in a monarchy, you will soon have a despotic state or a popular state" (*SL* 2.4, 18). Thus, Montesquieu implies that there can be no mixture of monarchy and democracy without nobility. When a monarch exists, they can only be prevented from acting arbitrarily beyond law by the nobles, or the few wealthy families with real political power in the nation. The people, represented in popular assemblies, although attached to the law are not strong enough themselves to keep the monarch within its bounds. The people rely on the nobility to prevent despotism. Yet, what of England in which the Commons has stripped the nobility of any real power? Montesquieu suggests that England is really a popular or democratic state cloaked in monarchical forms (Krause 2000, 237). The Commons does not wish to share real power with the king, but rather to preserve all to itself. Thus, Montesquieu asserts, "In order to favor liberty, the English have removed all their intermediate powers that favored their monarchy. They are quite right to preserve that liberty; if they were to lose it, they would be one of the most enslaved people on earth" (*SL* 2.4, 18–19). In removing the intermediate powers that formed their monarchy, they have actually removed their monarchy, as a real power rather than a symbolic power, as well, and have thereby preserved their liberty and prevented the lurch into despotism. Thus, the English, taking away all real power from the nobles, at the same time had to take away all real power from the monarch if the monarchy was not to become a despotism. Indeed, Montesquieu suggests that if the Commons were to allow the monarch real power in the absence of the power of the nobles, the English, of all people, would be most lacking in liberty.

Returning to Montesquieu's discussion of the English regime in book eleven, he suggests that the core of the problem in modernity has to do with the relations between the armed forces and the executive branch of government (but see Rahe 2001, 83; Krause 239–41, 248–50; and Pangle 1973, 133–7). According to Montesquieu, the armed forces should be made "directly dependent on the executive power" to the exclusion of the legislative branch of government (*SL* 11.6, 165). The reason for this preference given to the executive is that "[t]he army will always scorn a senate and respect its officers. It will not make much of the orders sent from a body composed of people it believes timid and, therefore, unworthy to command it" (*SL* 11.6, 165). The only explanation Montesquieu gives for this hostility between army and legislature is the rather vague statement that the army's "concern is more with action than deliberation" (*SL* 11.6, 165). We may speculate, based partly on what Montesquieu suggests throughout *The Spirit of the Laws* about the pacifying effect of commerce, that the senators' timidity could be the result of their being moneymakers. Nonetheless, Montesquieu makes clear his belief that in modern nations command over the military must be placed solely in the hands of the executive branch. Indeed, this is one of the key reasons Montesquieu gives for why a separate and independent executive branch must exist in modern nations as opposed to a simple reliance on legislative supremacy.

If the legislature denies to the executive sole control over the military, Montesquieu argues that one of two undesirable consequences will ensue: "either the army must destroy the government, or the government must weaken the army" (*SL* 11.6, 165). Then either the nation will be left without arms as the legislature purposely weakens the military to defend itself, or a military dictatorship will be established as the officers of the army usurp the powers of government from the legislature. Placing the armed forces in the hands of an independent executive, Montesquieu suggests, is supposed to pre-empt these two dark possibilities. Yet, one may question whether a civilian executive with almost unchecked and sweeping authority over the military is in reality any less dangerous to the political liberty of the citizens than an executive in uniform (see Montesquieu 1973, 187 and Courtney 2001, 275). How can that "tranquillity of spirit which comes from the opinion each one has of his security," which in turn requires that the government "be such that one citizen cannot fear another citizen," not be extinguished when the entire armed might of a society is in the hands of one person and the rest feel threatened?

We cannot be sure how grave a threat to political liberty Montesquieu would consider that question to represent. Admittedly, in book nineteen he considers two factors that would possibly mitigate the threat of an army in the hands of a single executive: (1) the balance of power between legislative and executive and (2) the commercial spirit (Rahe 2001, 95–6; Courtney 2001, 286–87; Mansfield 1993, 213–46; and Hulliung 1976, 206–10). On the latter point, he writes about a country such as England, "This nation, made comfortable by peace and liberty, freed from destructive prejudices, would be inclined to become commercial" (*SL* 19.27, 328). Later he adds, "If this nation sent colonies abroad, it would do so to extend its commerce more than its domination" (*SL* 19.27, 328). But it is possible to question whether Montesquieu, in making England his model, overestimates the extent to which England has solved the problem of establishing political liberty. Can Montesquieu offer further guidance on that problem?

Federalism and the Move toward Internationalism

We infer from Montesquieu's argument that the exigencies of war and the need to use force in the international system leave us with two choices detrimental to liberty: either the harsh suppression of individuality required of the virtuous citizen-soldier of the ancient republic, or the assumption of sweeping power over the armed forces of a society by an independent executive of a modern nation. We will conclude, however, by exploring a third alternative suggested by Montesquieu: the "federal republic," which he treats of in book nine (but see Ward 2007, 552, 555, 568; Shklar 1990, 268, 278 and 1987, 124; Nelson, 1987, 112 and Wolfe 1977, 427–45).

As discussed previously, Montesquieu opens book nine with the defects of republican government. A small republic will eventually be destroyed by conquest; a large one will eventually collapse due to internal vice. Both defects tend to the rise of monarchy in moderately large states so that people can defend themselves without being destroyed by vice from within. Montesquieu concludes, "[I]t is very likely that ultimately men would have been obliged to live forever under the government of one alone if they had not devised a kind of constitution that has all the internal advantages of republican government and the external force of monarchy. I speak of the federal republic" (SL 9.1, 131).

Montesquieu describes the federal republic as a "society of societies that make a new one," or an "agreement by which many political bodies consent to become citizens of the larger state that they want to form" (SL 9.1, 131). It is thus a "confederation" not of individuals but of societies or states; the member-states are the citizens of the new republic that is brought into being to obtain the advantages of monarchy without having to give up their republican forms of government. The advantages of monarchy are size, which makes the federal republic "able to resist external force," and security against conflict between or within the member-states themselves (SL 9.1, 132). For instance, Montesquieu argues that if one state within the federal republic attacked another, the remaining states could come to the victim's aid. Moreover, if rebellion or usurpation occurred within one or more of the member-states, the rest could come in and quell the insurrection and restore the republican form of government to the threatened members. Federal republics prevent war between, and chaos and dictatorship within, the member-states.

Montesquieu proceeds to discuss two examples from history of the structure of a federal republic: one ancient, the republic of the Lycians, and one modern, the republic of Holland. The Lycian republic, with respect to representation, was composed of 23 cities, the large ones having three votes in the "common council," and the medium cities two and the smaller cities, one (SL 9.3, 133). Thus the Lycians took account of population in the distribution of representatives, thereby moving toward the concept of a union of individuals rather than cities. Regarding the internal administration of the Lycian republic, the "common council" reached into the internal affairs of member-cities and appointed their judges and magistrates. With this significant aspect of centralization, combined with its principle of representation, it appears that the federal republic of the Lycians, in contrast to Montesquieu's initial description, moved toward becoming a society of individuals rather than of societies or political bodies. It aimed toward being one large state ruled by a single central government rather than an alliance of multiple, self-governing entities cooperating together for the common good of all. Surprisingly, Montesquieu says, "If one had to propose a model of a fine federal republic, I would choose the republic of Lycia" (SL 9.3, 133). Indeed it is the Lycian republic described by Montesquieu that Alexander Hamilton praises in *Federalist 9*, encouraging his fellow Americans to replace the Articles of Confederation with the much stronger Union proposed by the new constitution drafted in Philadelphia in 1787 (Hamilton et al. 2003, 44).

The republic of Holland, the modern example of a federal republic that Montesquieu chooses to discuss in detail, is composed of seven provinces of varying size. Yet each receives one vote in the common council. Thus, unlike the Lycian republic that moved toward representation by population, the Dutch republic adheres to the principle of the equality of states. Moreover, with respect to internal administration, each town or province, not the central government as was the case in the Lycian republic, chooses its own magistrates. The republic of Holland, in contrast to that of the Lycians, remains a society of societies rather than of individuals, and the member-states retain their sovereignty as opposed to being subordinated to a single central government. Rather than resembling the single nation created by the federal constitution of the United States, as the Lycian republic does, the federal republic of Holland appears closer to a supranational structure such as the European Union or an international organization such as the United Nations. Moreover, when speaking of whether federal republics can be a mixture of republics and principalities or whether all the member-states should be purely republican in nature, Montesquieu states that, "Germany is composed of free towns and small states subject to princes. Experience shows that it is more imperfect than the federal republics of Holland and Switzerland" (SL 9.2, 132). If Germany in contrast to Holland is an "imperfect" federal republic, the logical conclusion is that Holland is "perfect" or at least close to it (see Montesquieu 1973, 158–9; but see Pangle 1973, 134).

How do we choose between the "fine" federal republic of the Lycians clearly preferred by Alexander Hamilton at the time of American founding, and the closer to "perfect" federal republic of the Dutch? Perhaps it is the historical context within which the choice must be made that is the key. If the chief danger to the political liberty of the citizen is the potential for internal chaos and conflict, as was produced by the Articles of Confederation making the relations among the American states resemble the competitive strife among ancient Greek cities, one would probably side with Alexander Hamilton and his preference for a union of individuals under a strong national government. Since Hamilton also advocated an energetic president for America, such a union would be compatible with a strong executive. But if the chief danger to the political liberty of the citizen is a powerful independent executive of a modern nation who has sweeping control over the armed forces of the state, one would probably choose a "society of societies" aiming at liberty by pursuing collective security through international alliances and organizations.

Each of the two federal republics is instructive. Lycia pushes us to focus on creating a single nation; Holland makes a single nation such as England, recognizing that it has not fully solved the problem of creating political liberty, look outward toward creating international alliances. Montesquieu, we conclude, might well advise us to look outward in the direction of the international community in order to protect political liberty against the dangers of powerful modern executives, rather than inward toward strengthening national institutions in isolation from the world (see Ilgen 2006, 11, 12–14, 17–18; but see Hulliung 1976, 175). The spirit of Montesquieu's argument is to suggest that supranational federal structures and international alliances and organizations can provide security to citizens against foreign aggression, while simultaneously restraining or making unnecessary the sweeping power of a single executive who can threaten their liberty. Security and liberty can be combined.

References

Bock, G. et al. (eds) (1990), *Machiavelli and Republicanism* (Cambridge: Cambridge University Press).
Carrithers, D. W. et al. (eds) (2001), *Montesquieu's Science of Politics: Essays on the Spirit of the Laws* (Lanham: Rowman and Littlefield).
Courtney, C. P. (2001), Montesquieu and English Liberty, in Carrithers et al. (eds) (2001).
Elazar, D. J. (ed.) (1987), *Federalism as Grand Design: Political philosophers and the federal principle* (Lanham: University Press of America).
Hamilton, A. et al. (2003), *The Federalist Papers* (New York: Signet Classic).
Hulliung, M. (1976), *Montesquieu and the Old Regime* (Berkley: University of California Press).
Ilgen, T. L. (ed.) (2006), *Hard Power, Soft Power and the Future of Transatlantic Relations* (Aldershot: Ashgate Publishing Limited).
—— (2006), The Atlantic Alliance and the integration of Europe, in Ilgen (ed.) (2006).
Krause, S. (2000), The spirit of separate powers in Montesquieu, *The Review of Politics* 62:2, 231–65.
Larrere, C. (2001), Montesquieu on economics and commerce, in Carrithers et al. (eds) (2001).
Mansfield, H. C. (1993), *Taming of the Prince: The ambivalence of modern executive power* (Baltimore: Johns Hopkins University Press).
Montesquieu (1973), *Persian Letters* (London: Penguin Books).
—— (1989), *The Spirit of the Laws*, trans. Anne M. Cohler, Basia Carolyn Miller, and Harold Samuel Stone (Cambridge: Cambridge University Press).
Nelson, R. (1987), The federal idea in French political thought, in Elazar (ed.) (1987).
Pangle, T. L. (1973), *Montesquieu's Philosophy of Liberalism: A commentary on the Spirit of the Laws* (Chicago: University of Chicago Press).
Plutarch (1914), *Lives*, vol. 1, trans. Bernadotte Perrin (London: William Heinemann).
Rahe, P. A. (2001), Forms of government: Structure, principle, object, and aim, in Carrithers et al. (eds) (2001).
Shklar, J. N. (1987), *Montesquieu* (Oxford: Oxford University Press).
—— (1990), Montesquieu and the new republicanism, in Bock et al. (eds) (1990).

Ward, L. (2007), Montesquieu on federalism and Anglo-Gothic Constitutionalism, *Publius: The Journal of Federalism* 37:4, 551–77.
Wolfe, C. (1977), The Confederate republic in Montesquieu, *Polity* 9:4, 427–45.

Further Reading

Baum, J. A. (1980), *Montesquieu and social theory* (Oxford: Pergamon Press).
Boesche, R. (1990), Fearing monarchs and merchants: Montesquieu's two theories of despotism, *The Western Political Quarterly* 43:4, 741–61.
Carrithers, D. W. (2001), Democratic and aristocratic republics: Ancient and modern, in Carrithers et al. (eds) (2001).
Courtney, C. P. (1963), *Montesquieu and Burke* (Oxford: Blackwell).
Krause, S. (1999), The politics of distinction and disobedience: Honor and the defense of liberty in Montesquieu, *Polity* 31:3, 469–99.
—— (2002), The uncertain inevitability of decline in Montesquieu, *Political Theory* 30:5, 702–27.
Mason, S. M. (1975), *Montesquieu's Idea of Justice* (The Hague: Martinus Nijhoff).
Riley, P. (1973), The origins of federal theory in international relations ideas, *Polity* 6:1, 87–121.
Shackleton, R. et al. (eds) (1988), *Essays on Montesquieu and the Enlightenment* (Oxford: Voltaire Foundation at the Taylor Institution).
Waddicor, M. H. (1970), *Montesquieu and the Philosophy of Natural Law* (The Hague: Martinus Nijhoff).

Federalism and David Hume's Perfect Commonwealth

Will R. Jordan and Scott Yenor

Alexander Hamilton bemoans, in *Federalist* No. 9, the disappointing record of republican forms of government. It is impossible, he writes, "to read the history of the petty republics of Greece and Italy without feeling sensations of horror and disgust at the distractions with which they were continually agitated, and at the rapid succession of revolutions by which they were kept in a state of perpetual vibration between the extremes of tyranny and anarchy." Given this record of factious instability, Hamilton fears that republican government and, more importantly, the principle of civil liberty will be sacrificed to the more reliable principle of political order. Yet Hamilton urges his readers not to lose faith in republican forms. "The science of politics," in his view, "like most other sciences, has received great improvement. The efficacy of various principles is now well understood, which were either not known at all, or imperfectly known to the ancients." This new science of politics includes the separation of powers, institutional checks and controls, and the principle of representation – all of which tend to mollify factious tendencies of popular government. Also among the discoveries of this new science is what is now known as federalism, the "enlargement of the orbit" of republican systems through the "consolidation of several smaller States into one great Confederacy" (Hamilton, Madison, Jay 1999, 39–41).

One significant contributor to this new science of politics, joining thinkers such as John Locke and Montesquieu, is David Hume. Hume's influence on the framers of the US Constitution is well documented,[1] but few have seen the connection between Hume's national federalism and the Framers' federalism. It would probably be an overstatement, especially in view of what this volume brings to light, to call Hume the "Father of Federalism." Yet it is evident that Hume thought about many of the issues confronting the American Founders as they attempted to combine national government with state sovereignty. Hume's essay "Idea of a Perfect Commonwealth" describes how a large federal republic might be able to

---

1   See, for example, Adair 1974, and Balog 1990.

produce "all the advantages both of a great and a little commonwealth" (*E*, 525).² What are the advantages of commonwealths great and small? How can national and sub-national governments be combined in order to achieve these desiderata?

This chapter evaluates Hume's "perfect" commonwealth by considering how its account of federalism is grounded in his understanding of human nature and his appreciation for how this nature manifests itself in different historical settings. The federalism of Hume's perfect commonwealth is best understood in opposition to the imperfect, feudal federalism that Hume describes most fully in the early volumes of his *History of England*. Hume's perfect federalism is as much a matter of a properly constituted public opinion as it is an institutional achievement, which suggests that the institutions of federalism are not transferable to all times and places; however, when the time is ripe, a division of state and national sovereignty can be accomplished as long as the national government has sufficient means (both institutional and in opinion) to protect itself from encroachments of sub-national governments. For Hume, federalism serves the purpose of refining public opinion as opposed to encouraging civic efficacy or cultivating republican virtue or fostering administrative efficiency.

Before describing the institutional arrangements of Hume's perfect commonwealth, we do well to appreciate how uncharacteristic it is for Hume to take up the idea of a perfect commonwealth.³ In the essay's title, the words "idea" and "perfect" strike a discordant note, coming as they do from a thinker rightly known for his aversion to "abstract speculative principles" and for his appreciation of the role that custom and habit play in human life.⁴ For example, in his account of the English Civil War, Hume derides the speculative fantasies put forward by the parties of the day: "Every man had framed the model of a republic; and however new it was, or fantastical, he was eager in recommending it to his fellow citizens, or even imposing it by force upon them" (*H*, 6.3).⁵ Hume dismisses such speculation as being "too perfect for human nature" (*H*, 5.532) and fears that it serves to loosen the salutary "bands of society" (*H*, 6.4). In another example, Hume describes the British system of government as an uneasy balance between an absolute monarchy and a republic. If forced to choose between the two extremes, Hume would choose absolute monarchy. While admitting that liberty is preferable to slavery and that popular government could be "imagined more perfect" than absolute monarchy, Hume asks his reader to consider "what kind of republic we have reason to expect. The question is not concerning any fine imaginary republic, of which a man may form a plan in his closet" (*E*, 52). Hume concludes that, as a matter of practice, any pure republican experiment in Great Britain would likely produce another Cromwell.

---

2   *E* refers to Hume 1987.
3   One scholar, James Conniff (1980), goes so far as to argue that the entire essay was ironic.
4   See Hume's essay "Of Parties in General" (*E*, 60–2). See also Livingston 1984.
5   *H* refers to Hume 1983, cited by volume and page number.

Despite his contempt for those who try to reduce "fine imaginary republics" to practice, this is what Hume seems to do in "Idea of a Perfect Commonwealth." Hume opens the essay by admitting that wise magistrates, aware of the authority of long-established forms, will not "tamper ... or try experiments merely upon the credit of supposed argument and philosophy" (*E*, 512). How, then, does Hume justify his composition of a perfect commonwealth? He does so first by asking, "as one form of government must be allowed more perfect than another, independent of the manners and humours of particular men; why may we not enquire what is the most perfect of all?" (*E*, 513). Such an inquiry will be useful if, in some future age, "an opportunity might be afforded of reducing the theory to practice, either by a dissolution of some old government, or by the combination of men to form a new one, in some distant part of the world" (*E*, 513). This argument has a certain prophetic charm, written less than 30 years before the American Revolution.

Hume's second defense is bolder; no thinker before him has succeeded in providing a helpful model for practice. He rejects Plato's *Republic* and More's *Utopia* out of hand, for "all plans of government, which suppose great reformation in the manners of mankind, are plainly imaginary" (*E*, 514). He contends that James Harrington's *Commonwealth of Oceana* is the "only valuable model" yet produced, but proceeds to list three major defects that render it inconsistent with itself (*E*, 514–5).[6] A defense of a perfect commonwealth is both useful and necessary, having never been done properly. While these claims may be overdrawn for rhetorical effect, they reveal one of the guiding principles of Hume's analysis. His plan will not suppose "great reformation in the manners of mankind." This claim is true in one sense, and somewhat misleading in another, as we shall see.

Hume's Perfect Commonwealth

While federalism is one of the distinguishing characteristics of Hume's perfect commonwealth, Hume's "ideal" federalism does not involve the "consolidation of several smaller States" that Hamilton described in *Federalist* No. 9. Hume begins instead with one existing state of substantial size – "Great Britain and Ireland, or any territory of equal extent" (*E*, 516) – and divides it into 100 counties.[7] By an existing state, Hume means more than a consolidated land mass. An existing state has a distinctive national character or a peculiar set of manners (*E*, 197–9), and the citizens of the nation are loyal to it before they are loyal to any sub-national political entities, be they regional, tribal, or feudal. The nation for which Hume

---

[6] Hume thinks that Harrington's *Oceana*, by giving the senate the power to initiate legislation, gives far too much power to that body. Describing how the senate would effectively hold all legislative power, Hume suggests that Harrington himself would find this "to be an inconvenient form of government" (*E*, 516).

[7] Smaller states could be subdivided into fewer counties, but Hume sets the minimum number at 30 (*E*, 516).

draws his perfect commonwealth constitutes, more or less, a nation in opinion and has an established national character. Note the priority of the national to the local: the nation already exists and, much as Napoleon did 60 years later, Hume divides the nation into districts after the consolidation of the nation. As he presumes that local attachments do not pose a serious political problem, the task Hume sets for himself in his essay is much easier than the task actually faced by the American Founders, beset as they were by the sovereign claims of existing states and the problem of strong local attachments.

Instead of attempting to harmonize discordant states, Hume's essay aims at overturning the strong prejudice against the sustainability of a large republic. He notes that there exists a "falsehood of the common opinion, that no large state, such as France or Great Britain, could ever be modelled into a commonwealth, but that such a form of government can only take place in a city or small territory" (E, 527). This falsehood, cultivated by thinkers such as Montesquieu, would prevail long enough to animate much of the anti-Federalist resistance to the US Constitution three decades later.[8] Hume's perfect commonwealth uses republican forms at both the county and national level, and does so to sustain those forms over the larger territory.

Hume's large state is divided into 100 counties, each becoming "a kind of republic within itself" (E, 520). Every county is then subdivided into 100 parishes. In each parish the citizens meeting a property qualification annually vote for a county representative.[9] Two days later, the 100 representatives from each county gather "in the county town, and chuse by ballot, from their own body, ten county magistrates, and one senator" (E, 516). Once concluded, these elections produce 100 senators, 1,100 county magistrates, and 10,000 county representatives.[10] The 100 senators, one from each county, meet in the capital and are "endowed with the whole executive power of the commonwealth" (E, 516). They fill the offices of the various administrative councils,[11] and enjoy the "the power of peace and war, of giving orders to generals, admirals, and ambassadors, and, in short, all the prerogatives of a British King, except his negative" (E, 516–7). The senate also enjoys the power to initiate legislation, although the ultimate legislative power of the commonwealth belongs to the county representatives, who, meeting in their

---

8   See, for example, Storing (1981), chapter 3.
9   Hume sets the property qualification at "twenty pounds a-year in the county, and … 500 pounds in the town parishes" (E, 516).
10 The odd number here is 1,100 county magistrates. Every county has ten magistrates, but the senators are also counted in this total.
11 The senators would elect, from their own body, the following officials: a protector, two secretaries of state, a council of state, a council of religion and learning, a council of trade, a council of laws, a council of war, a council of admiralty, and a commission of the treasury. Each council would include five members, though the commission of the treasury would include seven (E, 518). In all, Hume identifies 40 offices to be filled by the 100 senators.

separate counties, vote on legislation sent down by the senate.[12] A bill becomes law when it is approved by a majority of the counties.

Compared the American Founders, Hume appears to be less interested in drawing spheres of sovereign authority between the national and sub-national governments. It seems that the national legislature can act on any matter, and through the councils, which serve as the administrative units of the realm, can give orders on all matters affecting commerce, trade, foreign policy, war, the structure of the armed forces, religion, learning, and the integrity of inferior offices. Despite the fact that there is only one branch of government at the national level, Hume sees his ideal commonwealth embodying a system of checks and controls; the system operates vertically instead of horizontally. For the most part, the senate proposes while the counties dispose, though counties can work around this channel with a complicated bypass procedure.

Each county is a "kind of republic within itself," as we have mentioned, and each possesses a reservoir of sovereignty. The county magistrates try all crimes in the county, and would name tax officials, parish ministers, and officers of the militia, "colonels and downwards" (E, 520–1). The county representatives possess an independent power to make all bylaws for the county. All of this would seem to empower the counties to dominate the tenor of the government, and if it was combined with a pervasive local spirit, it no doubt would. Such a system would prove unworkable were the localities jealous of their prerogatives, such as the American states were at the time of the Founding.

Hume thwarts any centrifugal drift by giving the senate a veto over all county bylaws,[13] a species of national negative not dissimilar to the one proposed (unsuccessfully) by James Madison at the US Constitutional Convention.[14] This national negative, which Hume defends as a way of determining "what agrees with general interest" (E, 525), swings the institutional balance away from anything resembling independent, sovereign counties. In fact, Hume sees his plan as avoiding an overly decentralized form of federalism. The counties in his plan, when compared to the commonwealth of the United Provinces, "are not so independent of each other, nor do they form separate bodies so much as the seven

---

12 So that the senate would not have a preemptive veto on legislation, Hume includes a bypass procedure making it extremely easy for the counties to call pending legislation down to the representatives (E, 517). Also, the magistrates could vote in lieu of the representatives on some legislative matters, but this decision is ultimately up to the representatives themselves, as only five out of the 100 would be able to request that the larger body decide the matter.
13 A county bylaw can also be annulled by any other county (E, 520). This seems like a dangerous opportunity for provincial obstructionism. In practice, however, it is not difficult to see how cooperative arrangements would necessarily emerge. For a discussion of the conditions necessary to promote cooperation see Axelrod 1985. The prevailing national character also works to mitigate the dangers here.
14 We are not aware of any treatment tracing Madison's national negative to Hume's "Idea of the Perfect Commonwealth," though Adair (1974) shows that Madison's *Federalist* No. 10 was profoundly influenced by that essay.

provinces; where the jealousy and envy of the smaller provinces and towns against the greater, particularly Holland and Amsterdam, have frequently disturbed the government" (*E*, 526).[15] Hume's rejection of the Dutch model reflects his goal of creating a federal republic that will remain "steady and uniform, without tumult and faction" (*E*, 527). A national negative is possible because of the solid nationality of his ideal commonwealth. The Constitutional Convention rejected Madison's national negative partly because the jealous states thought it tilted power too much to the national government. Hume's national commonwealth would be less in need of a national negative because of its pre-existing nationality; Madison's national negative may have been essential, but it was unacceptable precisely because it was so essential. Hume and Madison both sought to tilt authority toward the national government, but Hume found it easier to assume conditions of national cohesion than Madison had in forging such conditions in a real commonwealth.

Given this national tilt, why was Hume interested in forming a commonwealth that maintains a local government within a national government? It seems somewhat out of character that Hume sees a *small* commonwealth as "the happiest government in the world within itself," and this because "every thing lies under the eyes of the rulers" (*E*, 525). According to Hume, such republics are easy to form because the citizens hold "the same notions of government, the natural equality of property favours liberty, and the nearness of habitation enables the citizens mutually to assist each other" (*E*, 528).[16] Along with these advantages, however, Hume identifies several intrinsic, and fatal, disadvantages to small republics. First, they are vulnerable to predation by larger states (*E*, 525). Second, as Hamilton argues in *Federalist* No. 9, the internal politics in small republics are dangerously unstable. Hume writes: "Democracies are turbulent. For however the people may be separated or divided into small parties, either in their votes or elections; their near habitation in a city will always make the force of popular tides and currents very sensible" (*E*, 528). As befits a thinker who founds his moral philosophy on the notion of sympathy,[17] Hume is sensitive to how easily human beings are influenced by the judgments and passions of those around them. The contagion of passion becomes especially problematic when it is combined with intentional deception, which Hume argues is easily used by the ambitious few against the ignorant "lower sort" (*E*, 522). As a result of these factors, small republics are always vulnerable to the forces of "intrigue, prejudice, or passion" which "hurry them into ... measures against the public interest" (*E*, 528). Confronted by these tendencies, Hume favors a large federal republic, "modelled with masterly skill" (*E*, 528).

---

15   Hume also criticizes the scheme of the United Provinces for giving each province a "negative ... upon the whole body of the Dutch republic, with respect to alliances, peace and war, and the imposition of taxes" (*E*, 526).
16   See Storing (1981), chapter three, to see how all of these themes were advanced by Anti-Federalist defenders of the small republic.
17   See Book III of Hume's *Treatise* (2000). For one of many scholarly treatments see Capaldi 1989.

We see here that Hume's institutional plan is shaped by his observations on human nature, much as Madison's defense of the separation of powers bespeaks a view of government as the greatest reflection on human nature. Hume begins his essay "Of the Independency of Parliament" by declaring that "it is ... a just *political* maxim, that every man must be supposed a knave" (*E*, 42). While he casts doubt on whether each man is in fact a knave, Hume suggests that, in large bodies, partisan interest and approval have a troubling tendency to relax the restraint of honor, making men "more more honest in their private than in their public capacity" (*E*, 43). As a result, there are several institutional mechanisms in Hume's perfect commonwealth designed to counteract man's cabalistic tendencies. Worried about faction and intrigue in his senate, for example, Hume includes multiple procedures for removing individual senators: by a vote of the counties; by the senate itself; or through the efforts of a unique oversight institution, the court of competitors. The court of competitors would be composed of any candidate for senate who lost the election but garnered more than one-third of the votes. This body "has no power in the commonwealth. It has only the inspection of public accounts, and the accusing of any man before the senate" or, if rebuffed by the senate, before an ad hoc court (*E*, 519–20). Hume envisions the court of competitors as providing all of the benefits of the British government's salutary "opposition of interests," without the "endless factions" bred by such opposition (*E*, 525).

Hume also takes into account that a citizen's station in society affects his capacity for, and interests in, political life. Hume takes a dim view of the political and intellectual abilities of the "lower sort of people." Most are "wholly unfit for county-meetings, and for electing into the higher offices of the republic." He also suggests that their ignorance makes them easy targets for deceptive and ambitious "grandees." While he is no friend of direct democracy, Hume does contend that this sort of citizen has a political talent that can be of service in a well-modeled republic. "The lower sort of people and small proprietors are good judges enough of one not very distant from them in rank or habitation; and therefore, in their parochial meetings, will probably chuse the best, or nearly the best representative" (*E*, 522). They therefore can be trusted to elect the 10,000 county representatives, the legislative body in the commonwealth.

The issue of trust is important here in another sense. Hume suggests that the people are trustworthy in a way that the ambitious few are not. Recalling an axiom of Harrington, he remarks that "all free governments must consist of two councils, a lesser and greater; or, in other words, of a senate and people. The people ... would want wisdom, without the senate: The senate, without the people, would want honesty" (*E*, 523). Accordingly, Hume relies on the people, through annual elections, to prevent both the tyrannical combination and the factious division of the senate (*E*, 523–4).

Returning more specifically to the issue of federalism, we can see how the issues of government size and proximity intersect with Hume's observations about human nature. The small republic is attractive because people can be trusted to make decisions about those "not very distant from them," and because nearness of habitation fosters similitude of thought and mutual assistance (*E*, 522, 528).

However, this same nearness of habitation leads to the harmful contagion unleashed by "popular tides and currents" (*E*, 528). Hume's remedy is to extend the sphere of government in such a way that it enjoys the benefits of the small republic while avoiding its vices.

We can now appreciate the real benefits derived from dividing the republic into 100 counties. Hume suggests that increasing the size of the republic, making its parts more "remote and distant," helps to mitigate the spread of dangerous popular passions (*E*, 528). If this new, larger republic wants to reap the benefits provided when electors choose representatives "not very distant from them," an extremely large representative body would be needed. Hume's representatives number 10,000. The problem of popular passion seems to be merely deferred. Hume, citing Cardinal de Retz, contends that "all numerous assemblies, however composed, are mere mob, and swayed in their debates by the least motive …. When an absurdity strikes a member, he conveys it to his neighbor, and so on, till the whole be infected."[18] Hume remedies this by having the 10,000 representatives meet in their 100 separate counties, as voting is done by county. Instead of an unruly debate among 10,000, Hume's perfect commonwealth relies upon 100 separate debates occurring simultaneously on the same piece of legislation. "Separate this great body; and though every member be only of middling sense, it is not probable, that anything but reason can prevail over the whole. Influence and example being removed, good sense will always get the better of bad among a number of people" (*E*, 523). Hume makes the same argument in his essay "Of the First Principles of Government," when he notes that "though the people, collected in a body like the Roman tribes, be quite unfit for government, yet when dispersed in small bodies, they are more susceptible both of reason and order; the force of popular currents and tides is, in a great measure, broken; and the public interest may be pursued with some method and constancy" (*E*, 36).

Hume's perfect commonwealth makes use of federalism to reap the "advantages both of a great and a little commonwealth" (*E*, 525). Strong and united in its foreign policy,[19] the commonwealth nonetheless encourages the local governments favorable to the development of liberty (*E*, 528). Taking advantage of nearness of habitation in electing representatives, the commonwealth nonetheless avoids the contagion of passion which all too easily infects democratic bodies. Hume's counties act as buffers or breaks to popular passions; "intrigue, prejudice, or passion" might poison one or even a handful of counties, but it would be very difficult to affect a

---

18   One cannot help but think here of Publius' famous dictum: "Had every Athenian citizen been a Socrates, every Athenian assembly would still have been a mob" (Hamilton, Madison and Jay 1999, 310).

19   Hume makes the senate essentially absolute with respect to foreign policy (*E*, 524), and relies upon a decentralized militia on the Swiss model, with the caveat that each year "an army of 20,000 men be … drawn out by rotation, paid and encamped during six weeks in summer; that the duty of a camp not be altogether unknown" (*E*, 521). This addition seems to garner some of the advantages of a standing army, while avoiding the concomitant centralization of power.

majority of the counties at the same time and in the same way (E, 528). Perhaps most importantly, Hume's perfect commonwealth does not seem to rely upon a "great reformation in the manners of mankind" (E, 514). It is designed to operate with representatives of "middling sense" (E, 523) and is not endangered by either widespread ignorance (E, 522) or powerful personal ambition (E, 525–6).[20]

When we compare Hume's imaginary republic with Madison's experience trying to get his colleagues to accept a national negative, we notice that it is impossible to argue a nation into existence. Institutions cannot survive without a supportive foundation in public opinion. Hume, of course, does not just assume the existence of a national character. The development of a distinctive national character and identity is a central theme in his monumental *History of England*. Interestingly, the *History* also provides a description of a radically different kind of federalism, one inimical to civil liberty. Hume allows us to see how the federalism of the feudal order is overcome, creating the conditions for England's system of liberty as well as Hume's ideal commonwealth.

Feudal Federalism in the *History of England*

At the beginning of the first Tudor volume of his *History of England*, Hume informs his readers that "here … commences the useful, as well as the more agreeable part of modern annals; … whoever carries his anxious researches into preceeding periods is moved by a curiosity, liberal indeed and commendable; not by any necessity for acquiring knowledge of public affairs, or the arts of civil government" (H, 3.82). Hume interestingly seems to ignore his own advice; the earliest, pre-Tudor volumes of the *History* were the last to be written. These early volumes, far from useless, are essential in understanding Hume's theory of political and economic development; he records in detail how the English people emerged from their rude and barbarous past, charting a path to "the most perfect and accurate system of liberty that was ever found compatible with government" (H, 2.525). More important for our purposes is the fact that the ancient English constitution provides a model for a kind of federalism radically different from the one described in "Idea of a Perfect Commonwealth." The ancient English monarch was a centralizing force, while the great barons enjoyed a significant amount of independent authority over their holdings. For the sake of convenience, we refer to this federalism, which prevailed between the Norman Conquest and the rise of the Tudors (1066–1485 AD), as feudal federalism.

As Hume describes it, feudal federalism tipped the balance of power away from the national government headed by the monarch toward local control exercised by barons. Though even the greatest baron could "never lose view entirely of those principles of the feudal constitution, which bound him, as a vassal, to submission

---

20 Indeed, the only ambition that seems to trouble Hume is when the entire commonwealth is united in an ambitious project of conquest (E, 529).

and fealty towards his prince" (*H*, 1.464), the constitution as a whole gave barons the lion's share of political power. Feudal governments had "so strong a bias towards aristocracy, that the royal authority was extremely eclipsed in all the European states, and, instead of dreading the growth of monarchical power, we might rather expect, that the community would every where crumble into so many independent baronies, and lose the political union, by which they were cemented" (*H*, 1.464). The baron's power over those underneath him was based on military might and the provision of some services. Providing protection for vassals and serfs dependent upon him, and realizing that the monarch himself was dependent upon the military retainers that only the baron could provide, the baron "considered himself as a kind of sovereign within his territory; and was attended by courtiers and dependants more zealously attached to him than the ministers of state and the great officers were commonly to their sovereign" (*H*, 1.485).

Though powerful and martial monarchs were sometimes able to overawe individual barons, Hume provides many more examples of powerful barons dictating policy to the crown.

> *The great nobility were a kind of independent potentates, who, if they submitted to any regulations at all, were less governed by the municipal law, than by a rude species of the law of nations. The method, in which we find they treated the king's favourites and ministers, is a proof of their usual way of dealing with each other. A party, which complains of the arbitrary conduct of ministers, ought naturally to affect a great regard for the laws and constitution, and maintain at least the appearance of justice in their proceedings: Yet those barons, when discontented, came to parliament with an armed force, constrained the king to assent to their measures, and without any trial or witness or conviction, passed, from the pretended notoriety of facts, an act of banishment or attainder against the minister, which, on the first revolution of fortune, was reversed by like expedients.* (*H*, 2.179)

Given this state of affairs, it is far from surprising that the feudal state was "so little favourable to ... true liberty" and "still more destructive of the independence and security" of the people (*H*, 1.463). Hume criticizes feudal federalism for encouraging oppression, disorder, crime, and poverty; justice was for sale, and neither lives nor property were effectively secured (*H*, 1.485). The Magna Charta, so often portrayed as a boon to the birth of liberty, was, in Hume's judgment, merely a codification of the aristocratic character of the feudal constitution. Aristocratic control brought with it local control.

The demise of feudal federalism was a necessary and positive development for the British constitution. It is in the demise of feudal federalism that we find lessons that apply to Hume's perfect commonwealth. Feudal federalism was not replaced at a stroke by a liberal and equitable constitution. Instead, an intervening step was required which swung the federal balance decisively towards the nationalizing power, ushering in a period of absolute monarchy. Hume goes to great lengths to emphasize the unlimited character of Tudor rule,[21] and he recognizes that the creation of a strong monarchy came at the expense of the barons. The Tudors acquired an authority "almost absolute" and used that power "to pull down those disorderly and licentious tyrants, who were equally averse from peace and from freedom" (*H*, 2.525). Hume fully grants that the Tudor government was oppressive, but, in describing Henry VII's reign, notes that "it was so much the less burthensome, as, by his extending royal authority, and curbing the nobles, he became in reality the sole oppressor in his kingdom" (*H*, 3.49). A national control wielded by an absolute monarch is preferable to feudal federalism because the source of the tyranny is physically more distant and hence more benign. Hume explains this in more detail when discussing Elizabeth's reign: "the power of the prince ... entered not into every part of the administration; ... the freedom from faction, the quickness of execution, and the promptitude of those measures, which could be taken for offence or defence, made some compensation for the want of a legal and determinate liberty" (*H*, 4.370). If a small republic is the happiest of governments because "every thing lies under the eye of the rulers" (*E*, 525), a small tyranny is the most miserable for the same reason. When dealing with arbitrary governments, Hume would tilt the federal balance toward the center, taking advantage of the inefficiency and incapacity that come with distance. What little power the barons retained under the Tudors allowed them to be a salutary check on royal power.

This discussion of the ancient English constitutions brings us to Hume's more fundamental point. According to Hume, all of these ancient arrangements are flawed because their success ultimately depends on the character of the governors. A recurring theme in the early volumes of the *History* is how much the regime changed depending upon the abilities and disposition of the sovereign. In the Anglo-Saxon period, for example, Hume notes that the king was only "considered as the first among the citizens; his authority depended more on his personal qualities than on his station" (*H*, 1.161). Similarly, not even the Tudor constitution fully satisfies Hume's definition of a civilized monarchy as one "which enables the government, by the force of its laws and institutions alone, without any extraordinary capacity in the sovereign, to maintain itself in order and tranquility" (*H*, 3.24). A government falling short of this standard is only as good as its ruler, a situation that Hume finds precarious. In many ways, the central story of Hume's *History* is the process by which the English constitution advanced beyond these necessarily unstable forms (including both feudal federalism and centralized, absolute monarchy) and attained a "regular and equitable plan of liberty" (*H*, 2.525).

This theme relates back to Hume's perfect commonwealth in several important ways. Hume points out in his essay "That Politics May be Reduced to a Science"

---

21 Hume's primary aim here is to debunk the Whig historians' view that the ancient, pre-Stuart constitution was a paradigm of liberty. To emphasize the arbitrary quality of the Tudor monarchy, Hume, after a discussion of Elizabeth's powers, states, "thus we have seen, that the most absolute authority of the sovereign ... was established on above twenty branches of prerogative, which are now abolished, and which were, every one of them, totally incompatible with the liberty of the subject" (*H*, 4.367).

that he would be "sorry to think that human affairs admit of no greater stability, than what they receive from the casual humours and characters of men" (*E*, 15). He goes on to point out that all absolute governments are dependant upon human character, but that "a republican and free government would be an obvious absurdity, if the particular checks and controuls, provided by the constitution, had really no influence, and made it not the interest, even of bad men, to act for the public good" (*E*, 15–6). According to Hume, the advantage of republican government is that its checks and controls render individual character unimportant; the system works even with bad men. This issue plays an important role in "Idea of the Perfect Commonwealth." In a two paragraph section near the essay's conclusion, Hume addresses a topic that seems out of place: he examines two possible alterations to the British government, neither of which seems related to the surrounding discussion of the perfect commonwealth. As soon as he has suggested these alterations, however, he dismisses them. One of the reasons he gives for rejecting them is that "the king's personal character must still have great influence on the government" (*E*, 527). This brings to an abrupt close the short discussion of the "most perfect model of limited monarchy" (*E*, 526).

Hume, in rejecting the perfect limited monarchy, has highlighted some of the chief advantages of his perfect commonwealth: personal character does not have a great influence, and extraordinary talents are not required. We have already discussed how Hume's federal republic does not suppose a great revolution in human manners, but this conclusion adds another dimension. Hume's perfect commonwealth not only can function given the presence of certain human vices, like ignorance and ambition, but it is designed to make human character more or less superfluous. When discussing how to avoid faction in the senate, for example, Hume suggests that regular rules be adopted for assigning the major administrative offices: "Almost any man, in a senate chosen so regularly by the people, may be supposed fit for any civil office. It would be proper, therefore, for the senate to form some *general* resolutions with regard to the disposing of offices among members" (*E*, 524). From this, we can conclude that the senators are essentially interchangeable; special abilities or temperaments are not required for any of the offices, though not just anyone would be selected by the counties to be senators.[22] Hume's perfect commonwealth is "civilized"; order and tranquility reign without any dependence on human character. The federal arrangements are part of a larger system of checks and controls that make this possible.

Before embracing this conclusion, we need to reconsider how the defects of feudal federalism were remedied. It was not simply a matter of redesigning institutions or

---

22 Interestingly, Hume makes an exception for "critical times" (*E*, 524). Related to this, Hume seems to suggest that human ambition is such that it can be satisfied through regular institutional channels. He makes a similar argument when discussing his "perfect limited monarchy," recommending that "turbulent" members of the House of Commons be pacified by giving them a peerage (*E*, 527). It is not clear how a man of truly great ambition would fit in Hume's commonwealth, especially in "critical times."

adding checks and controls. In fact, Hume attributes the fall of feudal federalism to a remarkable change in manners among the barons. They began to value wealth more for the luxury it would buy than for the military vassals it would keep.

> *The manners of the age were a general cause, which operated during this whole period, and which continually tended to diminsh the riches, and still more the influence, of the aristocracy, anciently so formidable to the crown. The habits of luxury dissipated the immense fortunes of the ancient barons; and as the new methods of expence gave subsistance to mechanics and merchants, who lived in an independent manner on the fruits of their own industry, a nobleman, instead of that unlimited ascendant, which he was wont to assume over those who were maintained at his board, or subsisted by salaries conferred on them, retained only that moderate influence, which customers have over tradesmen, and which can never be dangerous to civil government. (H, 4.384)*

Hume suggests that this revolution in manners was the "chief cause" of the political realignment introduced by the Tudors (*H*, 4.385) and represents a necessary step in civilizing the English constitution.

This revolution in manners was profound. Hume suggests that it ushers in a new type of man. The warlord gives way to the industrious tradesman. Competition on the field of battle gives way to competition in the marketplace. Idleness gives way to industry, and servitude to independence. Hume argues that "it must be acknowledged, in spite of those who declaim so violently against refinement in the arts, or what they are pleased to call luxury, that, as much as an industrious tradesman is both a better man and a better citizen than one of those idle retainers, who formerly depended on the great families; so much is the life of a modern nobleman more laudable than that of an ancient baron" (*H*, 3.76–7).[23] It is impossible to imagine Hume's commonwealth functioning without these better men and better citizens. They end up being the backbone of a new, more widespread and somewhat thinner, ethos of nationality necessary to sustain a federal government. The willingness of each man to submit to legal forms rather than resort to a "rude species of the law of nations" (*H*, 2.179) is only the most clear example of how the ideal commonwealth depends on this revolution in manners.

Conclusion

While Hume's perfect commonwealth does not propose a "great reformation in the manners of mankind," it presupposes that such a reformation has taken place and

---

23 Hume gives a similar version of this argument in his essay "Of Refinement in the Arts" (*E*, 277–8). For a scholarly treatment of the importance of this revolution in manners for instituting a modern republic see Lerner 1987.

that a better citizen and man have emerged through the workings of history. The independence and modest ambition of the "industrious tradesman" are compatible with Hume's system in a way that the servile and disorderly life of the idle retainer is not. While it is true that Hume goes to great lengths to construct a system that does not depend on individual character, a close reading of his *History* reveals the extent to which character counts – the character of the people develops so that the character of the rulers becomes less and less relevant.

At the end, what is most striking about Hume's modern federalism is its national character. Not only does the national government possess a national negative over all county actions, but the senate also has the power of initiating national legislation and there seem to be no sovereign limits on national power (as there is in the US Constitution). These national institutions could only be sustained in a country that has a truly national public opinion. The presence of such opinion makes Hume's task of building the institutions of a national government much easier than that which faced the American Founders. The Founders debated where to draw the line between state and national sovereignty, but for Hume this is not much of an issue. The national government is simply sovereign, and the national negative is uncontroversial. What does this show? It is much easier to assume a nation than to build one. Hume's *History* reveals an acute awareness of this fact.

What overarching purpose is served by the federal arrangements of Hume's perfect commonwealth? Hume does not design his system to cultivate republican virtue or tighten civic bonds. Nor does he pursue federalism for the sake of administrative efficiency or accountability. Instead, Hume's federalism is one that refines public opinion through the mechanisms of representation and the partition of popular passions. By frustrating the natural courses of public opinion, Hume hopes to guarantee that it will coalesce in support of his large federal republic.

References

Adair, Douglass. (1974), "That politics may be reduced to a science": David Hume, James Madison, and the Tenth Federalist, in *Fame and the Founding Fathers: Essays by Douglass Adair*. 93–106. (New York: W.W. Norton & Co).
Axelrod, Robert. (1985), *The Evolution of Cooperation*. (New York: Basic Books).
Balog, Frank D. (1990), The Scottish Enlightenment and the liberal political tradition, in *Confronting the Constitution*. Edited by Allan Bloom. (Washington DC: AEI Press).
Capaldi, Nicholas. (1989), *Hume's Place in Moral Philosophy* (New York: Peter Lang).
Conniff, James. (1980), The Enlightenment and American political thought: A Study of the origins of Federalist Number 10, *Political Theory* 8:3:381–402.
Hamilton, Alexander, James Madison, and John Jay. (1999), *The Federalist Papers*. Edited by Clinton Rossiter. (New York: Mentor).

Hume, David. (1987), *Essays, Moral, Political, and Literary*. Edited by Eugene F. Miller. (Indianapolis: Liberty Fund).
—— (1983), *History of England: from the Invasion of Julius Caesar to The Revolution in 1688*. Six volumes. (Indianapolis: Liberty Fund).
—— (2000), *A Treatise of Human Nature*. Edited by David Fate Norton and Mary Norton. (Oxford: Oxford University Press).
Lerner, Ralph. (1987), *The Thinking Revolutionary: Principle and practice in the New Republic* (Ithaca: Cornell University Press).
Livingston, Donald W. (1984), *Hume's Philosophy of Common Life* (Chicago: University of Chicago Press).
Storing, Herbert J. (1981), What the Anti-Federalists were for, in *Volume 1 of the Complete Anti-Federalist* (Chicago: University of Chicago Press).

Further Reading

Capaldi, Nicholas and Donald W. Livingston, eds. (1990), *Liberty in Hume's History of England* (Dordrecht: Kluwer Academic Publishers).
Danford, John W. (1990), *David Hume and the Problem of Reason: Recovering the human sciences* (New Haven: Yale University Press).
Livingston, Donald W. (1998), *Philosophical Melancholy and Delirium* (Chicago: University of Chicago Press).
Manzer, Robert A. (1996), Hume's constitutionalism and the identity of constitutional democracy, *American Political Science Review* 90:488–96.

Jean-Jacques Rousseau and the Case against (and for) Federalism

Daniel E. Cullen

Rousseau's Federal Political Science

Despite his reputation as a utopian thinker, Rousseau was never enthralled by the prospect of cosmopolitanism or world government. The last best hope for humanity was that "men" might become "citizens," which is to say, members of particular societies whose moral existence depended on the energy produced by its very exclusivity: "Patriotism and humanity are … two virtues incompatible in their very tendencies [*énergie*], especially in a whole people. The Legislator who desires to achieve the two will obtain neither one" (Rousseau 1964, 706n). The same considerations would appear to exclude the possibility of federalism defined as "a comprehensive system of political relationships" combining "self-rule and shared rule within a matrix of constitutionally dispersed powers" (Elazar 1987, 1). Although it recognizes the logic of progressive political unity, federalism stops short of the universal state; but, to the extent that the members of a federal association remain divided peoples, *plures* within a more comprehensive *unum*, the federal vision seems to run afoul of the Rousseauian principle of undivided sovereignty. Federalism is customarily regarded as an arrangement for a pluralistic society of diverse peoples aiming at a union of parts which does not concern itself with the internal affairs of the latter. From a Rousseauian point of view, federalism seems to offers contract without transformation of the contracting parties, and it appears less as a vision of the good society than a testament to the inability of a pluralistic society to be a good society. Federal polities limit governmental power by dispersing it among administrative levels with independent sources of authority; such defensive measures typically aim at preserving the diversity of political entities (especially ethnic minorities) who distrust a more comprehensive union. The goal of federalism thus appears to be the toleration of difference rather than the overcoming of difference in a wider unity (Cf. Walzer 2007, 168–182). Whereas

Tocqueville admired the way in which the American federal system preserved the virtues of small republics within a union that conferred the advantages of greater size, power, and wealth (Tessitore 2004, 63), Rousseau viewed those "gains" as corrosive of the virtues they ostensibly served. American federalism is predicated on an extended commercial republic.

Most interpreters of Rousseau have thus concluded that his thinking about federalism cannot ultimately be reconciled with his political science as a whole, especially given his preferred model of the small, homogeneous, and intensely patriotic state (Hoffman 1965, 72–82). As we have seen, Rousseau's insistence on the inviolability of sovereignty appears to exclude the very possibility of a federal arrangement which rests on the sharing of legislative powers (Windenberger 1900). Rousseau seems to have regarded federalism as a last resort that might preserve as much as possible the political integrity of the small state (Vaughan 1915, 95–102). In the most thorough treatment to date of Rousseau as a "theorist of federalism," Patrick Riley (1973) observes that "the absence of a developed federal theory" suggests "that the problem did not interest him very much, that it was a question of constitutionalism or of international relations too far removed from his real concerns … for him to write a treatise about it. To this one can add that the subject not only did not engage his full interest, but that it ran counter to some of his most cherished later principles" (5). For Riley, Rousseau's "nationalism," his preference for the moral qualities of small and cohesive republics, made it impossible for him to takes federalism seriously at the national level since the latter implied a dual citizenship at odds with his profound critique of human dividedness (9, 17). One might argue, however, that it is this concern over a divided existence that leads Rousseau to take federalism seriously in the first place.

In a fragment written at the time of the *Social Contract*, Rousseau explained:

> *The cause of human misery is the contradiction between our condition and our desires, between our duties and our inclinations, between nature and social institutions, between man and citizen; make man one, and you will make him as happy as he can be. Give him entirely to the state or leave him entirely to himself, but if you divide his heart, you tear it, and do not imagine that the state can be happy when its members so suffer (Rousseau 1964, 510).*

Rousseau's political thinking is focused on the problem of the historical transformation of "men" into divided "bourgeois selves" and the possibility of its reversal by their becoming "citizens," which is to say, by becoming a unified whole or by acquiring an artificial integrity in a new identity within civil society (see Cullen 1993, 70–116). The international condition manifests a similar dividedness or contradiction, leavings states with one foot in and one foot out of the state of nature:

> *The first thing I notice upon considering the position of the human race is a manifest contradiction in its constitution, which makes it always vacillate. From man to man, we live in the civil state and subject to its laws; from*

people to people, each citizen enjoys natural freedom: which at bottom renders our situation worse than if these distinctions were unknown. For, living in the social order and in the state of nature at the same time, we are subject to the inconveniences of both, without finding security in either of the two (Rousseau 2005, 62).

This mixed condition is as intolerable as the situation of "men" in the final stage of the state of nature, which drives them to change their way of life in order to preserve it (Rousseau *Social Contract* [SC] I.6); Rousseau explores the possibility of federalism for the same reason he searches for a new form of association "taking men as they are and laws as they can be" (SC I, preface). The challenge of federalism is not qualitatively different than the problem of social contract simply; the fragility of either solution is attributable to the same difficulties: the divisive passions of men, the weakness of reason, the inefficacy of natural right, and the incomplete and imperfect operation of *droit politique*.

Riley's careful treatment of Rousseau's ambivalence about federalism (in either its national or international mode) errs in one significant matter: the subject is neither far from Rousseau's real concerns, nor counter to his central principles; indeed, Rousseau grapples with the problem of federalism at the same time as he developed his political principles in their mature form. One need not speculate about the existence of a lost manuscript on international relations, federalism, and war to conclude that Rousseau considered these topics because they were relevant to his understanding of the logic of civil association (see Cobban 1934; Roosevelt 1990, 9–17). Rousseau's interest in the project of the Abbé de St. Pierre and in the problem of international relations generally can be explained by the vivid way in which they illuminate the problem of the social condition as such.[1] For Rousseau, the relation (or, more precisely, the absence thereof) of states affords the clearest view of the prepolitical state of nature. If one recalls the meaning of the Latin word *foedus* (a contract or treaty) Rousseau's whole political science can be characterized as "federal," for politics is the art of agreement; moreover, it was thinking through the problem of the relation of states that led Rousseau to his mature formulation of the principles of social contract and the art of association.

The principles of political right emerge as Rousseau attempts to explain the rights of war and peace among sovereign states in his fragmentary essays on war, and in his redaction of the writings of the Abbé. The *Social Contract* itself resumes a discussion of "federation," applying it first to individuals and sketching its extension to states in a sequel which was not completed.[2] The very epigraph to the *Social Contract*: *foederis aequas, Dicamus leges* – "In an equitable federation we will make laws" – indicates that the essence of federalism is the act of association,

---

1   Rousseau originally entitled his fragment on war: "That the State of War Is Born Out of the Social State." The reference to *'état social"* was crossed out in the manuscript. (See Rousseau 1964, 601 n.1.)
2   Roger Masters echoes Riley's suggestion that Rousseau failed to complete the planned discussion of international affairs out of lack of interest. (Rousseau 1978, 163 n.144)

whether of peoples or individuals. Similarly, Rousseau's first interlocutor in the *Social Contract* is Grotius, whose treatise on "The Right of War and Peace" provides a foil for Rousseau's own doctrine of the radical artificiality of human conventions. As Vaughan has shown, Rousseau's reflections on "the principles of war" treat it as a relation exclusively between states and not between natural individuals. Rousseau holds that, properly understood, war is not aimed at destruction, but at vindicating the *status* of equality by the reassertion of equal national rights (Vaughan 1915, 282–292). The key insight is that the relation of "moral" or artificial beings can be detached from the aggressive motives of men as they are; the sheer artificiality of the state permits one to think both of its indefinite extension or its combination with others in federal relations. There is no reason *in principle* to limit the agreement of subjects to a particular territory, although there are, of course, practical considerations which govern the optimal size of a state (see Roosevelt 1990, 58). As Rousseau presents it, the federalist model is analogous to the domestic social contract wherein each individual pledges his cooperation and entrusts his individual "powers" to the association in return for security of his rights and property. The members of a federal association are normally considered to be sovereign entities who have prior rights, interests and perhaps a cultural identity which they seek to preserve; but federal relations are essentially political in Rousseau's strict sense: matters of voluntary agreement in which the goal is to prefer the general good of the *corps politique* to the particular interest of lesser bodies.

The central concern of Rousseau's political thought from start to finish is the art of association. On the individual and national level, the political problem arises from the need for and the obstacles to a political unity that will be both legitimate and reliable:

> *I assume that men have reached the point where obstacles to their self-preservation in the state of nature prevail by their resistance over the forces each individual can use to maintain himself in that state. ... Now since men cannot engender new forces, but merely unite and direct existing ones, they have no other means of self-preservation except to form, by aggregation, a sum of forces that can prevail over the resistance; set them to work by a single motivation; and make them act in concert. (SC I.6. 1978, 52–53)*

In parallel fashion, the obstacles to the preservation of states are such that only a more general association can preserve them. Having imagined the establishment of the national polity out of a social contract, Emile's tutor wonders,

> *whether the establishment of society accomplished too much or too little; whether individuals – who are subject to laws and to men, while societies among themselves maintain the independence of nature – remain exposed to the ills of both conditions without having their advantages; and whether it would be better to have no civil society in the world than to have many. Is it not this mixed condition which participates in both and secures neither ...? Is it not this imperfect and partial association which produces tyranny and war;*

> *and are not tyranny and war the greatest plagues of humanity? (Rousseau 1979, 466)*

As he will later suggest in the "Geneva Manuscript" (GM), a draft version of the *Social Contract*, the art of association is Rousseau's comprehensive solution to the disordered condition which human history has brought about:

> *although there is no natural and general society among men, although men have become unhappy and wicked in becoming sociable, although the laws of justice and equality mean nothing to those who live both in the freedom of the state of nature and subject to the needs of the social state ... let us attempt to draw from the ill itself the remedy that should cure it. Let us use new associations to correct, if possible, the defect of the general association (GM I. 2. Rousseau 1978, 162).*

In his "Abstract" of the Abbé de St. Pierre's *Project for Universal Peace* Rousseau depicts the international condition of sovereign states in a way that precisely mirrors the natural predicament which the Rousseauian social contract and the art of association propose to remedy. Individuals find themselves in a divided condition: "each of us is in the civil state with his fellow citizens and in the state of nature with all the rest of the world." The only hope of overcoming these "dangerous contradictions" is through "a form of confederative government, which, uniting Peoples by bonds similar to those which unite individuals, equally subject them to the authority of laws" (Rousseau 2005, 28). Rousseau notes that informal confederations may arise, drawing divided peoples into "common relations" on the basis of shared customs and commerce, and Europe in fact has become a "society of peoples" which enjoys a relative equilibrium. Yet its political practice remains violent and inhumane because, Rousseau explains, "every union formed or maintained by chance" cannot endure. The absence of "public right" leaves European states in a *de facto* condition of war (29, 31–32). No spontaneous adjustment of interests is to be expected without the intervention of political art. The imperfect socialization of European peoples leaves them worse off than would the state of nature; and yet the remedy might, against all odds, be drawn from the sickness itself.

In language approximating the formula of the *Social Contract*, Rousseau describes the "perfection of the federal union" as the creation of a moral and collective body, "begun by fortune" but "completed by reason" which unites the European states into a "true Body politic," a "real confederation" (36). Essential to the completion of this task is a force sufficient to compel cooperation for the common good, to prevent members from preferring their particular interest to the general interest. In effect, the members of the perfected federation must be forced to be just, or forced to be free (SC I.7). Rousseau poses two questions concerning the prospective federation:

1. Would it proceed reliably to its goal of peace?
2. Is it in the interest of the Sovereigns (as opposed to their peoples) to create the union?

Rousseau agrees with the Abbé that, once established, the federation would remove the seeds of war from its body; and he concludes that the sovereigns cannot reasonably expect to prevail if they merely assert their interests through aggression. But what is needed most is security that the agreement will be kept by others, and Rousseau argues that far from diminishing the rights of sovereignty, dependence on a common tribunal would strengthen them by guarantees against foreign invasion and domestic rebellion: "there is a great deal of difference between depending on someone else or only on a Body of which one is a member and of which each is the leader in his own turn; for in this latter case one does nothing but secure one's freedom by the pledges one gives for it; it would be alienated in the hands of a master, but it is strengthened in those of Associates" (Rousseau 2005, 44; cf. Rousseau 1978, 53, 56). So it is that the inconveniences engendered by "the absolute and mutual independence of all sovereigns in the imperfect society" of Europe ought to force these realistic sovereigns (who are not "men as they ought to be, good, generous, disinterested and loving the public good out of humanity") to consult their reason and assure their (enlightened) self-interest (49).

In his own "Judgment" of the Abbé's plan Rousseau acknowledges that one has every reason to expect that the real interest of sovereign leaders will be defeated by their apparent interest. Kings will bridle at being "forced to be just," and they will fail to see the wisdom of a federal arrangement; predictably, "the sum of particular interests" will "outweigh the common interest" (Rousseau 2005, 54, 56). In Rousseau's view, the Abbé "saw rather well the effect of things if they were established," but he misjudged the means for establishing them (57). The problem of founding the federal order mirrors the problem of founding as such. As the *Social Contract* explains, the emergent order requires that "the effect become the cause," that the cooperative spirit which the new institution would produce would have to preside over the founding of the institution itself: "men would have to be prior to the laws what they ought to become by means of the laws" (SC II.7). The interest of citizens is always a modest one: they desire only "to be governed justly and peacefully;" the vanity of kings is a larger obstacle (Rousseau 2005, 78). But none of these considerable difficulties amount to a reason in principle why federalism is excluded by considerations of national sovereignty or, more strongly, by the power of nationalism.

The Political Character of Nationalism

My concern here is not to suggest that Rousseau held any utopian hope for the achievement of a European union, or even that he reduced the problem to a lack of good will; his realism is much more pronounced than he is typically credited for.[3] What I hope to demonstrate is rather that Rousseau's theory of federalism is consistent with his political theory generally, and that in each case he approaches the problem of association by emphasizing the artificiality of political relations. The first point to emphasize is that Rousseau's concern for national unity and patriotic sentiment does not spring from a principled attachment to "cultural particularity" for its own sake. While Rousseau often appears as the eulogist of nationalist enthusiasm (Cobban 1934, 178), his brand of nationalism is political rather than "ethnic" and is focused squarely on the requirements of maintaining attachment to (the artificial) laws and the political freedom which only those laws can sustain.[4] Remarking on the tension between the idea of a federation and the total identification of the citizen with the *patrie*, Pierre Hassner (1997) emphasizes how the classic dilemma of federations (that they risk becoming too much or too little) becomes acute in Rousseau's case, forcing him to retreat to a conventional nationalism in circumstances in which the general will cannot be expected to prevail; but Hassner himself notes that Rousseau's nationalism is primarily political, and that peoples are molded by legislation and education, not the other way around (208–209). Rousseau writes, "It is neither walls nor men that constitute the fatherland. It is laws, mores, customs, government, constitution, the manner of beings which results out of all this. The fatherland lies in the relations of the state to its members; when these relations change or are destroyed, the fatherland vanishes." (quoted in Hassner 1997, 209–210) As Marc Plattner (1997) has argued, Rousseau believed in nation-building in the contemporary sense of constructing a national identity not on the basis of ancient ties of blood or soil, but through political mobilization and the construction of a new political consciousness, or as Rousseau would say, a "national education" (194). Properly understood, nationalism can be viewed "as a step on the road to cosmopolitanism," for the essence of politics is the extension and overcoming of parochial attachments in favor of more general ties; thus even nationalism points in the direction of internationalism (196).

National identity is thus a political construct even as it functions as a limitation on the latter. Peoples must be suited for legislation, and as Rousseau remarks in his *Plan for a Constitution for Corsica*, "the first rule we have to follow is the national

---

3   See his critique of the Abbé's *Polysynody* which emphasizes that even the proposal of general plans is far from guaranteed to serve the interest of the state. "Indeed, the greatest good of the State is not always such a clear thing, nor one that depends as much as one might believe on the greatest good of each part; as if the same state of affairs could not have an infinity of different orders and connections more or less strong among them, which cause just as many differences in the general plans." (Rousseau 2005, 95–96)
4   See Kelly, Rousseau 2005, xix.

character;" but it is clear that the national character can be reconstructed where it is unavailable or found wanting (Rousseau 2005, 133). Legislators determine what laws are suitable for peoples. Even the national identities of the Corsicans and the Poles, two rare examples of healthy peoples in modern conditions, are the effects of legislation (Plattner 1997, 192). National institutions form, not merely reflect, the genius of particular peoples who appear in this light as malleable matter. Nature does set limits to the dimensions of "well-formed" states which must be neither "giants or dwarfs," and it is the task of the political theorist to "find the proportion most advantageous to the preservation of the State" (SC II.9).

> *What people then is suited to legislation? One that, though already bound by some union of origin, interest or convention, has not yet born the true yoke of laws. One that has neither customs nor superstitions that are deeply entrenched. One that does not fear being crushed by a sudden invasion and can, without becoming involved in its neighbors' quarrels, resist each of them by itself or use the help of one to drive away another (SC II.10).*

Rousseau's view of nation-building (of which federalism is a part) is firmly rooted in the primacy of political considerations over prepolitical claims of identity. Rousseau's skepticism concerning the formation of any general society of the human race and a system of universal peace among nations does not detract from the essential recognition that the condition of "men as they are" points toward its solution in "laws as they might be." Political facts, however recalcitrant, must be interpreted by reference to correct principles of political right, not vice versa. Rousseau's thinking about the constitution of political bodies oscillates between the fatalism of a socially evolved condition in which "our needs bring us together in proportion as our passions divide us," and the optimism of legitimate politics (GM I.2; see Roosevelt 1990, 75–76). The people's true interest, like the interests of sovereign states in the Abbé's treatise, is to submit themselves to equal rules of justice; but men as they are remain disinclined to trust. The possibility of "new associations" which could cure the evils of social life as they have developed depends on the habits of citizenship. It is the actual experience of a common life that progressively nurtures in a people its apprehension of a general will and yet the latter must be available at the founding of the association. This conundrum of the contractual or covenantal relationship accounts for the deeply paradoxical character of Rousseau's theorizing. How do individuals initially consent to associate, to identify themselves as "we," when they must be already disposed to that perspective to make the initial choice? For Rousseau, it is not enough to say that it would be rational to do so and presume their consent; he accuses Diderot of this very error (GM I.2). Political logic reveals that general rules indeed ought to prevail over private desires, and that particular societies should defer to the larger ones that contain them, but Rousseau is wary of the posture of the cosmopolitan who feigns the motivation of universal brotherhood (see Roosevelt 1990, 82–89). Rousseau reiterates a familiar dilemma: "We conceive of the general society on the basis of our particular societies; the establishment of small republics makes us think about the larger one; and we do not really begin to become men until after we have become citizens" (GM I.2 quoted in Roosevelt 1990, 82).

The conundrum notwithstanding, Rousseau does concede that the duties of "men" take precedence over those of the citizen. The latter are primary only in the sense that we must be citizens first for the habit of generalization (that is, the voluntary submission to equal rules of justice) to develop; but it remains true that those very norms carry us beyond (national) citizenship to the supranational obligations of men while stopping short of an unreal cosmopolitanism. The flexibility and relative expansiveness of political relations explains Rousseau's otherwise strange prescription for the Polish constitution.[5] If the Poles cannot retrench their boundaries, the only way to invest the large Polish state with "the stability and vigor of a small republic" is through "perfecting the system of federative Governments." This decentralization will concentrate the energies of the particular provinces and necessarily threaten the unity of the general Polish nation; but it need not destroy it, for the provincial bodies may remain mindful of their paramount obligation to the larger whole through the bond of "common legislation" (Rousseau 2005, 184). The political relation, in the final analysis, trumps lesser identifications and qualifies even the most vibrant nationalism. Following the logic of his theory of the artificial character of the body politic, Rousseau departs from the classical model of citizenship. As Plattner explains, "The ancient Spartan was a Greek, but he was first and foremost a Spartan. By contrast, a Pole or a Corsican educated under the legislation proposed by Rousseau would regard himself as a citizen not of the town or province where he lives but of Poland or of Corsica" (Plattner 1997, 194). The crucial point is that the definition of the nation is politically determined, and the principle of legitimacy is not identification with the *patrie* but conformity to the general will. It is true that Rousseau would rely on patriotism to instill the disposition to obey the general will, but he is careful to avoid the romantic idea that cultural uniqueness is desirable for its own sake, as an expression of a natural wholeness superior to the artificiality of civilized life.[6]

One can agree with Hassner that Rousseau's effort to conceive of a federal polity while preserving a patriotic model of citizenship generates a tension in his thought; but the vision is not simply contradictory when viewed in the context of Rousseau's basic political assumptions. The national state already gives us an idea of an even more general society, he argues. Reflection on the nature of law reveals that its object must always be general, and this concept in turn discloses the fundamental maxim of justice, which is also the moral result of social contract: "each man prefers the greatest good in all things" (GM II.4). Effective natural right is thus politicized from the beginning, a point that eluded Diderot who looked for a prepolitical source of unity in human reason alone, believing that people could intuit principles of justice that would lead us to prefer the general will (Roosevelt 1990, 89). Rousseau argues, to the contrary, that the disposition to will the general is an acquired habit; it does

---

5 The following discussion is heavily indebted to Smith 2003 and Plattner 1997.
6 See the excellent treatment of this subject in Velkley 1997, 69–75.

intrinsically tend toward an increasing "universality," but the habit arises out of political practice itself:

> *Extend this maxim to the general society of which the State gives us an idea. Protected by the society of which we are members or by the one in which we live, the natural repugnance to do evil is no longer counterbalanced in us by the fear of being wronged, and we are simultaneously moved by nature, by habit, and by reason to treat other men approximately as we do our fellow citizens. From this disposition, transformed into actions, arise the rules of rational natural right, different from natural right properly so called, for the latter is based only on a true but very vague sentiment that is often stifled by love of ourselves (GM II.4).*

"Rational natural right" expresses a second nature, a politicized and not merely socialized one. Law precedes justice; only after we have developed the habit of generalizing, which the discipline of law instills in us, can we extend ideas of justice to a "more general society." One might say that the trajectory of generalization is always toward a more perfect union, that extended political consciousness can only be nurtured, in Roosevelt's phrase, "from the inside out" (Roosevelt 1990, 82).

The principles of political right derive from and point toward the activity of federation qua association. If we return to Rousseau's reflections on the Abbé de St. Pierre's vision for a European federation, we see that the crucial problem is the contradiction of an imperfectly politicized relation among the states of Europe. Federalism is nothing more than a form of social contract among societies, and the same logic that applies to the association of individuals applies to it. The criticisms that Rousseau directed to Diderot are recapitulated against the Abbé's assumption that one could rely on an appeal to the reason of sovereigns as if they were already part of a legitimate order (Cf. Manent 2001, 297–298).

The task then is to find the appropriate convention, which must be the work of art rather than nature. The case for a European federation tracks closely the argument of the *Social Contract*. The equality of all states would be established morally (artificially) as a matter of legitimacy in the same way that the social contract restores the natural equality among men that has been distorted in social evolution. By agreeing to a condition of mutual dependence, the sovereign states enhance their individual security in collective security. Of course the plain interest of sovereigns in uniting in a new association that would preserve, protect, and defend the rights of each is hindered by the perversity of actual sovereigns in clinging to their absurd and worthless privileges. Unlike the Abbé, Rousseau sees no necessity for common sense to prevail. Still, in distilling the Abbé's proposal into a reasonable set of articles of agreement, Rousseau pursues the question "whether the undertaking is possible or not" judging by "the nature of things" (Rousseau 2005, 38). If one leaves aside the illegitimate interests of princes in pursuing self-aggrandizing projects at the expense of their peoples, Rousseau finds that there is no necessary conflict between the goals of the federation and the original or internal sovereignty of the member states. Just as the social contract leaves each individual "as free as he was before," by guaranteeing each against unjust domination by others, the collective security established by the federation need not impinge on national sovereignty. Rousseau's framing of the problem echoes the opening of the *Social Contract*:

> *If there is some way of resolving these dangerous contradictions [being in the civil condition with our fellow citizens but in the state of nature with all others] this can only be by a form of confederative government, which, uniting Peoples by bonds similar to those which unite individuals, equally subject both of them to the authority of Laws. (Rousseau 2005, 28)*

What prevents sovereigns from mustering the political will to prefer their real interest to their apparent one is the same fatality that besets Diderot's utopian vision. The *amour-propre* of princes makes it doubly difficult to "separate themselves from themselves" and see the good which eludes them.

> *It would be necessary that the sum of particular interests not outweigh the common interests and that each believe he sees the greatest good that he can hope for himself in the good of all. Now it is asking for a concurrence of wisdom in so many heads and a concurrence of relations in so many interests, that one must hardly hope for the fortuitous harmony of all the necessary circumstances from chance; nevertheless, if a harmony does not take place, force is the only thing that can take its place. (Rousseau 2005, 56)*

Rousseau does not expect kings to become philosophers, but his sharp criticism of their blindness cannot help but make one wonder whether republican governments would be as insensitive to the needs of their peoples. However that may be, Rousseau limits himself to showing, not that the perfection of supranational association is possible, but only that it is necessary.

One can see how Rousseau's experimentation with federalist ideas nurtured the thinking on civil association that would eventually appear in the *Social Contract* (Cobban 1934, 187). The structural similarities between the federal and the "national" union are numerous: a deliberate act of political will (rather than a spontaneous or evolutionary accord of interests); equal rights, mutual dependence; a controlling force to guarantee the keeping of agreements; the exchange of a practically useless freedom for a legitimate freedom to act within one's own sphere, subject only to equal consideration of others. The only route forward for both men and states "as they are" is "to draw from the ill itself the remedy that should cure it," and "find in perfected art the reparation of the ills that the beginnings of art caused to nature" (GM I.2; cf. Rousseau 2005, 183, 205). The complex double movement from man to citizen and citizen to man which our second nature requires points toward the possible reconciliation of national citizenship and, in appropriate circumstances, a federal unity.

I conclude, *contra* Riley, that Rousseau's idea of federalism is not incompatible with his mature principles of political right; its prospect is as unlikely as is that of the legitimate domestic civil association, *and for the same reasons*. To Hassner's question, "Isn't there a tension between the very idea of a federation and the total identification of the citizen with his fatherland and fellow citizens?" one may reply, not necessarily, given that it is the particular political identity which nourishes the art of generalization in the first place: we must be citizens first in order to become men.

The Rousseauian social contract aims to transform the social state in such a fashion that men recover the equivalent of the advantages they forfeited in leaving the natural condition of independence. As is the case with men, the disposition of sovereign states is not naturally inclined toward cooperation, but it isn't in principle refractory to it. Like natural man, the sovereign state is not naturally suited to interdependence; but once circumstances make it inevitable, the establishment of a "moral and collective" existence is superior to an association that "offers no real union among the individuals who compose it" (GM I.2; see Halbwachs 1943, 43, 47, 159). It is also the case, Rousseau declares in his *Discourse on Political Economy*, that "all political societies are composed of other, smaller societies of different types, each of which has its interests and maxims. ... The will of these particular societies always has two relations: for the members of the association it is a general will; for the larger society it is a private will" (Rousseau 1978, 212). The problem of foreign relations is no different than that of domestic relations: "the will of the State, although general in relation to its members, is so no longer in relation to other States and their members, but becomes for them a private and individual will ..." (Rousseau 1978, 212). The conclusion is that every political society is the same, and every one is equally artificial. Politics is, at every level, a matter of constructing a larger identity through the art of association.

Rousseau's effort to solve the political problem (of guaranteeing freedom in social circumstances which necessarily undermined it) required that abstract principles of political right be instantiated in a particular community with what we would today call an "ethnic identity" or feeling of solidarity. Only in such an association would freedom within community be both "legitimate and reliable" (SC I. preface). Democracy and political right rest on an assumption of equality and therefore generality or universality; but humanity seems always and everywhere divided into partial nations or peoples united by affective bonds (language, religion, customs) and, often, by a reflexive hostility toward outsiders. And yet the world is not naturally "peopled" in the way theorists of nationalism usually suggest. Peoples are essentially political; they must be theoretically conceived or redescribed as the addressees of a system of legislation; that is to say, the nation is justified or legitimated ultimately by conventions that trace back to the unaligned individual self and the sovereignty of the general will. While it may be true that for Rousseau democracy depends on the nation, the goal of democracy is not to preserve national identity; cultural nationalism is always a means, never the end, of Rousseauian politics. His exploration of federalism is likewise pragmatic; like the social contract itself, it is a matter of necessity rather than choice. The requirements of the transition from the state of nature to the civil condition apply to states in the same way as they do to individuals, and thinking through the problem of federalism is a way of looking at the condition of the souls of men as they are writ large. The limitations of federalism are the limitations of political association itself.

References

Cobban, Alfred (1934), *Rousseau and the Modern State* (London: Allen and Unwin).
Cullen, Daniel E. (1993), *Freedom in Rousseau's Political Philosophy* (DeKalb: Northern Illinois University Press).
Elazar, Daniel (1987), Viewing federalism as grand design, in Daniel Elazar (ed.), *Federalism as Grand Design* (Lanham MD: University Press of America).
Halbwachs, Maurice (ed.) (1943), *Rousseau: Du Contrat Social* (Paris: Editions Montaigne).
Hassner, Pierre (1997), Rousseau and the theory and practice of international relations, in Clifford Orwin and Nathan Tarcov (ed.), *The Legacy of Rousseau* (Chicago: University of Chicago Press).
Hoffman, Stanley (1965), *The State of War* (New York: Praeger).
Manent, Pierre (2001), *Cours Familier de Philosophie Politique* (Paris: Gallimard).
Plattner, Marc (1997), Rousseau and the origins of nationalism, in Clifford Orwin and Nathan Tarcov (ed.), *The Legacy of Rousseau* (Chicago: University of Chicago Press).
Riley, Patrick (1973), Rousseau as a theorist of national and international federalism, *Publius*, 3 (Spring): 5–17.
Roosevelt, Grace (1990), *Reading Rousseau in the Nuclear Age* (Philadelphia: Temple University Press).
Rousseau, Jean-Jacques (1964), *Oeuvres Completes*, Volume III (Paris: Gallimard).
—— (1978), *On the Social Contract with Geneva Manuscript and Political Economy* ed. Roger D. Masters. Trans. Judith R. Masters. (New York: St. Martin's).
—— (1979), *Emile or On Education*. Trans. Allan Bloom. (New York: Basic Books).
—— (2005), *The Plan for Perpetual Peace. On the Government of Poland, and other Writings on History and Politics, The Collected Writings of Rousseau*, Vol. II, ed. Christopher Kelly. Trans. Christopher Kelly and Judith Bush (Hanover and London: University Press of New Hampshire).
Smith, Jeffrey A. (2003), Nationalism, virtue, and the spirit of liberty in Rousseau's Government of Poland, *The Review of Politics*, 65 (Summer): 409–437.
Tessitore, Aristide (2004), Alexis de Tocqueville on the Incommensurability of America's Founding Principles, in Peter Augustine Lawler (ed.), *Democracy and Its Friendly Critics* (Lanham, MD: Lexington Books).
Vaughan, C. E. (1915), *The Political Writings of Rousseau*, Volume 1. (Cambridge: Cambridge University Press).
Velkley, Richard (1997), The tension in the beautiful: on culture and civilization in Rousseau and German philosophy, in Clifford Orwin and Nathan Tarcov (ed.), *The Legacy of Rousseau* (Chicago: University of Chicago Press).
Walzer, Michael (2007), *Thinking Politically* (New Haven: Yale University Press).

Windenberger, J. L. (1900), *Essai sur le système de politique étrangère de J.-J. Rousseau: La République Confédérative des Petits Etats* (Paris: Alfonse Picard et Fils).

Further Reading

Cobban, Alfred (1934), *Rousseau and the Modern State* (London: Allen and Unwin), Chapter 6: Rousseau and the Nation State.
Hassner, Pierre (1961), Les Concepts de Guerre et de Paix Chez Kant, *Revue Francaise de Science Politique* 11 (September).
—— (1997), Rousseau and the theory and practice of international relations, in Clifford Orwin and Nathan Tarcov (ed.), *The Legacy of Rousseau* (Chicago: University of Chicago Press).
Hinsley, Francis H. (1962), *Power and the Pursuit of Peace* (Cambridge: Cambridge University Press), Chapter 2: Rousseau.
Hoffman, Stanley (1965), *The State of War* (New York: Praeger), Chapter 3: Rousseau on War and Peace.
Plattner, Marc (1997), Rousseau and the origins of nationalism, in Clifford Orwin and Nathan Tarcov (ed.), *The Legacy of Rousseau* (Chicago: University of Chicago Press).
Riley, Patrick (1973), Rousseau as a theorist of national and international federalism, *Publius*, 3 (Spring): 5–17.
Roosevelt, Grace (1990), *Reading Rousseau in the Nuclear Age* (Philadelphia: Temple University Press).
Vaughan, C. E. (1915), *The Political Writings of Rousseau*, Volume 1 (Cambridge: Cambridge University Press), 95–110.

Kant and Federalism[1]

Joseph M. Knippenberg

Introduction

Immanuel Kant was born in Königsberg, Prussia (now Kaliningrad) on April 22, 1724, lived his entire life in his hometown, and died on February 12, 1804. He was educated at the Albertina University of Königsberg, became a lecturer there in 1755, and was appointed Professor of Logic and Metaphysics in 1770. He was a prolific and conventional academic philosopher until, around 1770, an encounter with the writings of David Hume "interrupted [his] dogmatic slumber."[2] After a fallow period of more than a decade, Kant published his *Critique of Pure Reason* (first edition, 1781; second edition, 1787), followed by the *Critique of Practical Reason* in 1788, and the *Critique of Judgment* in 1790. Kant's "critical turn" inaugurated a new period of philosophical productivity in the course of which he devoted himself to articulating the limits of our rational and intellectual faculties in such a way as, above all, to reconcile the apparently contradictory claims of science and morality.[3]

Kant's purpose, as he put it in a preface to the first *Critique*, was to "deny knowledge in order to make room for faith,"[4] showing how modern scientific accounts of causality and materialism could be understood so as to permit us still to have conceptions of God, freedom, and the immortality of the soul, all of

---

1   I presented a preliminary version of this chapter as a lecture at Mercer University in Macon, GA. I am grateful to Will Jordan and Matthew Oberrieder for their invitation to give the lecture and their hospitality on that occasion.
2   Kant's admission can be found in his introduction to his *Prolegomena to Any Future Metaphysics* (1783); see Kant (1902). The passage can be found in Kant (1968), vol. IV, 260.
3   The classic German biography is Vorländer (1986). Three recent English treatments of his life and work are Kuehn (2002); Wood (2004); and Guyer (2006).
4   Kant (1965), 29; in the standard pagination of Kant's works, the passage is found at page Bxxx (that is, page xxx of the B [second] edition).

which are necessary, he believed, to sustain human dignity and the moral life. It is not possible, he argued, for "pure reason" definitively to affirm or deny these conceptions, which leaves it open for practical (moral) reason to operate *as if* they exist. In undertaking this project, limiting the claims of science so as to preserve the claims of morality, Kant acted on a long-standing commitment, which he made upon encountering the work of Jean-Jacques Rousseau sometime after 1762:

> *I am by inclination an investigator. I feel a thirst for knowledge and ... the deep satisfaction of every step forward. There was a time when I believed that all this could be the honor of mankind and I despised the people, who know nothing. Rousseau has set me right [or straight] .... I learned to honor mankind and that I would be less worthy than the average worker if I did not believe that [philosophy] could contribute to what really matters, restoring the rights of mankind.*[5]

We can better understand the practical and theoretical significance of Kant's critical turn by sketching Thomas Hobbes's mechanistic alternative.[6] For Hobbes, everything can be explained in terms of matter in motion: our actions (visible motions) are the products of our appetites and aversions (invisible motions), which, in turn, are the products of external stimuli. As every action is necessarily the effect of a previous cause, freedom can only mean the absence of external impediments to action, not a "free will" that might serve as the ground or locus of moral responsibility. In Hobbes's world, human dignity has a very narrow meaning and human worth is not infinite; rather, we are worth precisely what others would give us for our services. In other words, our worth is dependent upon our value in the marketplace. As Hobbes puts it, a good general is worth a lot in time of war, but in peacetime the price we would pay for his services would be lower.[7]

A Hobbesian political system depends heavily upon passions and interests, above all the passions of the subjects and the interests of the rulers. If the ruler wishes to maximize his power to satisfy his interests, he must maximize the collective power to which he has access. The enlightened pursuit of his self-interest requires that he prevent his subjects from harming one another and that he encourage their industry so that they will produce as much wealth as possible. The best way to make people behave well, Hobbes says, is to rely on their most intense and reliable passion, the fear of violent death. The powerful state excites in its subjects a fear of apprehension and punishment that leads them to behave well toward one another and to obey the ruler. The external effect – "law and order" – is produced by the external cause – an intimidating police power.

---

5   This is my translation of a passage from Kant's *Bemerkungen* [Remarks] on his *Observations on the Feeling of the Beautiful and the Sublime* (1764). An accessible English edition of these *Bemerkungen*, found in his *Nachlaß* (unpublished notes) is Kant (2005). For extended discussions of Kant's encounter with Rousseau, see Shell (1980) and Velkley (1989).
6   Thomas Hobbes (1994).
7   See Hobbes (1994), ch. x, 51.

Hobbes is at pains to insist that the fear of violent death is a reliable – nay, the *most* reliable – instrument of public policy. Faced with the realistic prospect of violent death, most people most of the time will act as the one who threatens them wishes. But what if some people – a small minority – care more about honor than death, if, in the words of an old television advertisement, some few would rather fight than switch? Hobbes's response is that a sufficiently powerful state can effectively deal with these outliers, killing them, if need be.

But if the proud, ambitious people are not deterred by the fear of violent death or killed, what then? Hobbes has to concede that either the ambitious will themselves seize power or they will be a permanent thorn in the side of the ruler. In the former case, he can argue that the new rulers will be most successful if they follow his advice, prudently using the levers of power to maintain order. If, in the end, the "exceptional" adopt his methods, his argument is vindicated. After all, what generally works is for all intents and purposes true.

In the latter case, Hobbes would advise the ruler to maintain order by depriving the ambitious of their followers. If the latter can be convinced that what matters most is personal security, not the honor of a leader or the opinion he is promoting, then the ambitious man's capacity for political mischief is minimized. Stated another way, managing a state requires not just effectively using the instruments of fear, but also encouraging the recognition and pursuit of *enlightened* self-interest. In Hobbes's view, we can be consistently and thoroughgoingly "materialist" if only we are enlightened. In order effectively to be ruled as Hobbes would have us ruled, we must be persuaded of the "effectual truth" of his materialist point of departure.

But there, as Kant would argue, lies the rub. Thoroughgoing materialism can be proven no more definitively than can its "spiritualist" opposite. A politics that ultimately depends upon enlightenment for its success is already not thoroughgoingly materialist. Genuine "realism" requires something else.

Kant's Alternative to Hobbesian Realism

Kant is clearly aware of and to a limited extent agrees with the position articulated by Hobbes.[8] He refers, for example, to "the *unsocial sociability* of men, that is, their tendency to come together in society, coupled, however, with a continual resistance which constantly threatens to break this society up" (IUH, 44). And, just as Hobbes does, he remarks that "the depravity of human nature is displayed without disguise in the unrestricted relations which obtain between the various nations" (PP, 103).

---

8   I shall cite all Kant's short political writings in the body of the paper. All can be found in Kant (1991b). IUH is "Idea for a Universal History with a Cosmopolitan Purpose" (1784). TP is "On the Common Saying: 'This May Be True in Theory, But It Does Not Apply in Practice'" (1793); and PP is "Perpetual Peace: A Philosophical Sketch" (1795). See, in this case, TP, 73.

For Kant, as for Hobbes, the state of nature is a state of war (cf. PP, 98).⁹ War, he says at another point, "seems to be ingrained in human nature" (PP, 111). Indeed, in one respect Kant could be said to be almost more Hobbesian than Hobbes himself. The latter denies that there is a *summum bonum*, or greatest good, on which all human beings can agree, but insists that, in effect, violent death is for everyone the *summum malum*.¹⁰ In the course of agreeing with the first part of this proposition – that "as far as happiness is concerned, [men's] will cannot be brought under any common principle nor thus under any external law harmonizing with the freedom of everyone" (TP, 73–74) – Kant implies that there is no "empirical" basis for union or community, not even a universal natural aversion to death. There is no sure-fire purely "natural" way of overcoming the sources of our conflict.

This is not to say that Kant thinks that union or community is impossible, either in theory or in practice. He writes extensively in his moral works about the "Kingdom of Ends," a comprehensive *moral* community in which each member respects everyone else, where everyone regards everyone else as an end in himself.¹¹ This conception is an idea that can guide our approach to political life, even if no actually existing community fully embodies it.¹² The task of applying this idea in practice falls to the "moral politician" (PP, 118), who possesses "the art of utilizing nature for the government of men" (PP, 117), but recognizes that this is only part, not "the whole of practical wisdom" (PP, 117).¹³ The moral politician understands our unsocial sociability and knows how to channel our passions and ambitions into an institutional system that, by compelling everyone to respect everyone else, serves to protect our rights. While Kant says that "the problem of setting up a state can be solved even by a nation of devils (so long as they possess understanding)" (PP, 112), he also insists that moral people have a *duty* (cf. PP, 109) to use natural mechanism to overcome our natural tendency to conflict.

Stated another way, much of Kant's institutional political science is not much different from that of his liberal predecessors, like Locke and Montesquieu. He appreciates the importance of separation of powers and checks and balances in enabling people to respect one another's rights and to live together peacefully.¹⁴ Indeed, he goes so far as to define a republic as a form of government in which

---

9   See also Kant (1998), 108n.
10 See Hobbes (1994), ch. xi, 57, and compare with chs. xiii, 75; xiv, 79; and xv, 100.
11 See, for example, Kant (1964), 100–103, as well as Kant's discussion of an "ethical community" in Book III of Kant (2005). See also Korsgaard (1996). I have discussed these themes in Knippenberg (2001), 58–101.
12 See Nussbaum (1997), 36: It is this deep core [of Stoicism] that Kant appropriates – the idea of a kingdom of free rational beings, equal in humanity, each of them to be treated as an end no matter where in the world he or she dwells. In Kant as in Stoicism, this idea is less a specific political proposal than a regulative ideal that should be at the heart of both moral and political reflection and that supplies constraints on what we may politically will. See also McCarthy (1997), 203.
13 See also Apel (1997), 86.
14 See, for example, Kant (1991a), secs. 48–49, 127–129.

there is separation of powers (cf. PP, 101).[15] Human beings, he says, are animals who need masters, but their masters are also animals who need masters (cf. IUH, 46–47). The task, he says, is "to arrange [the state] in such a way that [men's] self-seeking energies are opposed to one another, each thereby neutralizing or eliminating the destructive effects of the rest" (PP, 112). The moral politician who builds these institutions must have "a correct conception of the nature of a possible constitution, great experience tested in many affairs of the world, and above all else a good will prepared to accept the findings of this experience" (IUH, 47).

What distinguishes Kant's moral politician from his classical liberal counterparts is that his vision does not end simply with the construction of an institutional edifice that provides security or prosperity. Instead, the relative peace facilitated by liberal institutions is intended to enable people to devote themselves to moral cultivation. Rather than culminate in the pursuit of happiness, Kantian liberalism culminates in the pursuit of deserved happiness.[16] Where Hobbes, for example, believes that the maintenance of domestic peace encourages people to engage in honest industry,[17] Kant believes peace and its attendant prosperity will eventually make possible not only enlightenment but also moral development (cf. e.g., IUH, 49 and PP, 113).[18] This is, of course, the ultimate goal of the moral statesman, who recognizes a "duty to promote it by using the natural mechanism" he has come to understand (PP, 109).

Moral Development and Federalism

Indeed, it is Kant's concern with securing the political conditions of moral development that leads to his interest in federations. So long, he argues, as states are threatened with war, they must organize themselves for and devote substantial resources to national defense. Educational efforts of all sorts take a back seat, and such education as is promoted has more to do with cultivating a narrow and bellicose patriotism than with encouraging a cosmopolitan appreciation of our common humanity and a recognition of the universal character of our moral responsibility.[19]

---

15 See also Michael W. Doyle's capsule description in Doyle (1993), 186.
16 See Kant's discussion of the highest good in Kant (1998), Bk. II, as well as Knippenberg (2001).
17 See, for example, Hobbes (1994), ch. xviii, 117–118.
18 See also Kant (1951), sec. 83, 281–284.
19 To be sure, Kant believes that even in a cosmopolitan world order embodied in a federation of states there will be a certain kind of nationalism and patriotism. We will still love our homelands, but that love will be conditioned by our recognition of and respect for everyone's humanity. See Knippenberg (1989), as well as Kant (1978), 225–236. John Rawls makes much the same point in his attempt to elaborate a "law of peoples." See Rawls (1999), 40, 41, 44, as well as McCarthy (1997), 203–204.

In other words, there cannot be good – or, if you will, republican – government of any sort unless the threat of war is significantly diminished. And the instrument for the diminution of that threat is a federation. Here is how he puts it in his *Idea for a Universal History* (47):

> *The problem of establishing a perfect civil constitution is subordinate to the problem of a law-governed* **external relationship** *with other states, and cannot be solved unless the latter is also solved.*

In order to avoid the manifold inconveniences of an unstable and unsettled international arena – "[w]ars, tense and unremitting military preparations, and the resultant distress which every state must eventually feel within itself, even in the midst of peace" (IUH, 47) – states must enter into a lawful arrangement, "a federation of peoples in which every state, even the smallest, could expect to derive its security and rights not from its own power or its own legal judgement, but solely from this great federation (*Foedus Amphictyonum*), from a united power and a united will" (IUH, 47). The federation, he says, will be the product of decisions to "renounce … brutish freedom and seek calm and security within a law-governed constitution" (IUH, 48).

But while Kant operates here using the analogy of our entry from the state of nature into a civil state, as if the federation essentially comprised a world government, a global Leviathan, he also writes of discovering a "law of equilibrium to regulate the essentially healthy hostility which prevails among the states and is produced by their freedom" (IUH, 49). The "united power and … united will," the "common external agreement and legislation" (IUH, 48), lead to and are the products, not of "a cosmopolitan commonwealth under a single ruler, but [of] a lawful *federation* under a commonly accepted *international right*" (TP, 90). The federation's aim is not "to acquire any power like that of a state, but merely to preserve and secure the *freedom* of each state in itself, along with that of the other confederated states" (PP, 104).[20] Such a federation, he continues, would not have any coercive power.

Kant strongly prefers an international federation to world government because the latter, he expects, would be a "soulless despotism," a "universal despotism which saps all man's energies and ends in the graveyard of freedom" (PP, 113, 114; cf. TP, 90).[21] A central government that had effectively to attempt to project power over the entire globe could be nothing else. Kant's understanding here is a commonplace of eighteenth-century political science, which held that large states could only be governed despotically.[22] The further from the center people were, the less closely they would identify themselves with it. The less they identified themselves with the center, the more attenuated would be their allegiance and obedience to it. Since they would be less likely to obey laws voluntarily, out of

---

20 See also Kant (1991a), sec. 54, 151.
21 See also Kant (1998), 57n. For an argument that this goal is unsatisfactory according to Kant's own principles, see Lutz-Bachmann (1997).
22 See Rawls (1999), 36n40.

affection for and allegiance to a central authority, the maintenance of order would require the blunt instrument of force, rather than the more subtle instruments of civic education and the cultivation of affection. Projecting power over a large geographic area would thus require an immensely powerful army that could overawe any local efforts at resistance. The ruler or ruling authority that had such an army at its disposal could not be trusted not to abuse it, aggrandizing himself or itself at everyone's expense, rather than promoting cosmopolitan principles of right. In other words, the only effective set of checks and balances would be to give local authorities the capacity to resist any central authority, to establish a federation whose members had substantial local autonomy (including the capacity to enforce laws and to defend themselves).[23]

Kant's international federation thus resembles an international balance of power, with the noteworthy exception that, in addition to individual states seeking for their own reasons and interests to maintain the balance, there is a central organization whose purpose is to enable them to articulate the universal rational principles to which they are all supposed to subscribe. Such an organization would also help them adjudicate international disputes, albeit only before the court of international public opinion.[24] In *The Metaphysics of Morals* (1797), Kant describes this arrangement in the following way:

> *Such an association of several states to preserve peace can be called a permanent congress of states, which each neighboring state is at liberty to join. Something of this kind took place ... in the first half of the present century in the assembly of the States General at the Hague. The ministers of most of the courts of Europe and even of the smallest republics lodged with it their complaints about attacks being made on one of them by another. In this way they thought of the whole of Europe as a single confederated state that they accepted as arbiter, so to speak, in their public disputes ....*
>
> *By a congress is here understood only a voluntary condition of different states that can be dissolved at any time, not a federation (like that of the American states) which is based on a constitution and can therefore not be dissolved. Only by such a congress can the Idea of a public Right of Nations be realized, one to be established for deciding their disputes in a civil way, as if by a lawsuit, rather than in a barbaric way ... , namely by war.*[25]

Of course, these features are already sufficient to distinguish it from a "mere" balance of power.[26] States that acknowledge the existence of shared principles, an organization to articulate them, and a mechanism – however imperfect – for

---

23 See Kant (1991a), sec. 61, 156–157.
24 For one way of conceiving the role of international public opinion in a Kantian federation, see Bohman (1997).
25 Kant (1991a), sec. 61, 156–157. For a discussion of this passage, see Habermas (1997), 117–118.
26 See Bohman and Lutz-Bachmann (1997b), 1–2, 5.

resolving disputes, must already have organized themselves in accordance with those principles. They do not merely prudently pursue their interests, absent any real concern with their domestic regimes.[27] They are republics, whose republicanism may well be imperfect (after all, it developed under conditions of international instability), but which nonetheless acknowledge the authority of cosmopolitan principles of right and the importance of an organization that embodies them, even if it lacks – and indeed *ought* to lack – the power definitively and effectively to enforce them.[28]

The organization Kant proposes is distinct from the two principal sorts of contemporary treaty arrangements with which we are familiar. It is not like a collective security arrangement such as that offered by the United Nations or like a collective defense arrangement such as that offered by NATO.[29]

Let me explain, beginning with collective security arrangements. Although the United Nations is ostensibly committed to the protection of both the human rights of individuals and the autonomy of member states, there is effectively no requirement that members have a republican form of government that would tend to protect these rights or respect that autonomy.[30] Claims about the autonomy of states often – at least in practice – trump any other consideration, making the UN's promotion and protection of human rights for the most part ineffective.[31] By contrast, a common commitment to republicanism is at the core of Kant's federation. As a result, in Kant's federation, the principal protection for human rights comes not from the declarations of the international body (which would have limited impact on a non-republican regime bent on asserting and protecting its interests) nor from the sanctions incompletely pursued and enforced by its members (who, after all, still have their own national economic and political interests at heart), but rather from the internal arrangements of the member states, all of which are set up so as to uphold the dignity of their citizens and to promote the cultivation of a public sphere – a civil society, if you will – marked by respect for the dignity of all. By protecting the integrity of the member states from external threats and by providing a quasi-legal framework by means of which to attempt to resolve international disputes, Kant's federation works to eliminate, or at least to diminish,

---

27 See Doyle (1993), 182–185.
28 See Mulholland (1990), 370: Kant's insight into the problem of international law ... is that there can be no rule of law and no peace unless states can be trusted to commit themselves to law without there being an international executive force to ensure obedience to law through force. States, however, can be trusted only if they themselves manifest in their internal constitution that they are – at least in spirit – republican.By contrast, Jürgen Habermas argues that the logic of individual rights ought to drive us in the direction of a global republic. See Habermas (1997), 128–130.
29 For a different view, see Doyle (1993), 187.
30 Even Habermas, who favors a quite robust world government, recognizes the difficulty in having non-republican members of the federation. See Habermas (1997), 134. See also Rawls (1999), 3–4, 59–70, and McCarthy's criticism of this position in McCarthy (1997).
31 For a contrasting argument, see Honneth (1997), 170–171.

the international instability that makes it harder for republics to maintain their institutions and educate their citizens to respect the rights of all. In other words, unlike contemporary proponents of the United Nations or of world government, Kant recognizes that the principal protection of human rights comes from the members of the federation, not from the federation itself.[32]

Another way of stating the difference is to examine the reliance of the United Nations and of Kant's federation on international agreements and international law. Both aspire to a world in which international law is obeyed and treaties are upheld. But Kant recognizes that so long as the signatories to a treaty are not republics, subject in some way to their people and to what he calls "the *formal attribute of publicness*" (PP, 125; cf. TP, 79), they will not on their own accord be inclined to live up to their agreements (cf. PP, 93–94). The interests of the rulers will predominate, and those interests typically tend toward self-aggrandizement, at the expense both of their subjects and of other states. By contrast, in a republic there are mechanisms that make it difficult for the government to operate secretly and without the consent of the governed.[33] While it is surely not impossible to excite a people about its own selfish interests, to be pursued at the expense of others, the fact that the people have to bear directly the cost of this pursuit makes them somewhat less likely to be enthusiastic about it (cf. PP, 95; IUH, 47; and TP, 90–91).[34] This mechanism, animated in the first place by people's self-interest, also leaves room for arguments from "cosmopolitan" principle (cf., e.g., PP. 130), as well for the development of what Kant calls a *sensus communis*.[35] As a result, republics are more likely to uphold treaties and other attempts to impose a quasi-legal structure

---

32 For a different view, see Habermas (1997), 127–131.
33 Doyle describes these as the hallmarks of "republican caution;" see Doyle (1993), 190. See also Habermas (1997), 123–126.
34 See also Kant (1979), 165. For a different view that makes much more of the bellicose nationalism to which republics are said to be prone, see Habermas (1997), 120–121.
35 See Kant (1951), sec. 40, 136–137:
   [U]nder the *sensus communis* we must include the idea of a sense *common to all*, i.e., of a faculty of judgment which, in its reflection, takes account (*a priori*) of the mode of representation of all other men in thought, in order, as it were, to compare its judgment with the collective reason of humanity, and thus to escape from the illusions arising from the private conditions that could easily be taken for objective .... This is done by comparing our judgment with the possible rather than the actual judgments of others, and by putting ourselves in the place of any other man, by abstracting from the limitations which contingently attach to our own judgment ....
   However small may be the area or the degree to which a man's natural gifts reach, yet it indicates a man of *enlarged thought* if he disregards the subjective private conditions of his own judgment, by which so many others are confined, and reflects upon it from a *universal standpoint* (which he can only determine by placing himself at the standpoint of others).
   Bohman makes much of this passage, following the suggestion of a political theory based in Kant's understanding of aesthetic judgment, developed in the first instance by Hannah Arendt and Ronald Beiner. See Bohman (1997), 185–186, as well as Arendt (1982) and Beiner (1983).

on international affairs. Kant's emphasis on the importance of republics as constituents of an international federation thus follows from his realistic appraisal of the conditions of international law-abidingness. A federation that permits non-republics to join admits into its bosom the states that will undermine or destroy it. So long as they are not republics, such states remain inimical to the spirit of the federation, in theory and very likely in practice.

The organization that Kant recommends can also be distinguished from a NATO-style collective defense arrangement. While the latter is restricted to republics in a particular geographic area, enabling them to make common cause against those that would threaten their security, Kant's federation is expansive, committed to the promotion and spread of republican principles. Whereas a NATO-like organization helps republics defend themselves in a permanently dangerous world, Kant's federation aims at the long-term transformation of the world, making it less dangerous because it is increasingly comprised of republics that have joined it.[36] That does not mean that Kant approves of intervention for the sake of what we call "regime change." Indeed, he explicitly eschews such methods (cf. PP, 96, 118).[37] But he certainly would not eschew the peaceful promotion of republican principles, using instruments of "public diplomacy," like Radio Liberty and the erstwhile United States Information Agency, as well as organizations like the National Endowment for Democracy. In addition, he relies on the informal contacts encouraged by commerce (and required by the cosmopolitan principle of hospitality) to spread awareness of the universal principles of right.[38] Kant's federation thus does not merely defend the territorial integrity of a geographically concentrated or culturally related set of member states; instead or in addition, it promotes the universal idea of republicanism. Membership in his federation would be open to republics anywhere in the world.

Federalism and History

Kant's international federation thus seems to be the result of an odd combination of "realism" and "idealism." He recognizes the predominance of interest in politics and consequently of our "unsocial sociability." But rather than leaving us with a barely contained Hobbesian war of all against all, Kant promotes an apparently breathtakingly ambitious ideal, in which states enter into an arrangement by means of which perpetual peace is in principle possible. If we can understand how he combines these two elements – a "realistic" understanding of the selfishness and violence inherent in human nature and an "idealistic" aspiration to have us govern ourselves by reason – we will have gone a long way toward understanding how

---

36 To be sure, Kant concedes that the prospect of war can never be altogether extirpated and hence will always be on the horizon. See PP, 105.
37 See also Kant (1979), 153.
38 See PP, 105–108.

Kantian internationalism can be a sober corrective to the liberal internationalism predominant today.

On a number of occasions in his writings, Kant argues that nature or history paves the way for the perpetual peace of the international federation. For example, in his *Idea for a Universal History* (1783), he says the following (IUH, 47):

> *Wars, tense and unremitting military preparations, and the resultant distress which every state must eventually feel within itself, even in the midst of peace – these are the means by which nature drives nations to make initially imperfect attempts, but finally, after many devastations, upheavals, and even complete inner exhaustion of their powers, to take the step which reason could have suggested to them even without so many sad experiences – that of abandoning a lawless state of savagery and entering a federation of peoples in which every state, even the smallest, could expect to derive its security and its rights, not from its own power or its own legal judgment, but solely from this great federation ..., from a united power and the law-governed decisions of a united will.*

In his essay on *Theory and Practice* (1793), he concisely summarizes a similar argument in this way: "[S]heer exhaustion must eventually perform what goodwill ought to have done but failed to do" (TP, 90). In his famous essay on *Perpetual Peace* (1795), he supplements these accounts by arguing that nature causes both our propensity to conflict and the occasions for it – "*linguistic* and *religious* differences" that "occasion mutual hatred and provide pretexts for wars" (PP, 113–114) – and yet at the same time puts in train the developments that pave the way for peace, by encouraging the growth of culture and the spread of "the *spirit of commerce*" (PP, 114). The way in which our passions and interests work themselves out in history – or, if you will, nature – "guarantees" that we will arrange ourselves into republics and arrange our republics into a federation. We merely have to be prudent, properly understanding and pursuing our self-interest when the time is ripe.

This last point deserves some emphasis, for Kant does not simply expect an international federation to arise "automatically," as it were, without the prudence and foresight of a "moral politician" (PP, 118), who works on its behalf. History does not work inexorably through entirely impersonal forces; rather, it gives the "moral politician" confidence that his efforts to promote decent ends will not be undertaken in vain.[39] He still has to assess his circumstances, size up the various forces and personalities at work, and figure out how best to pursue and promote his decent ends. Absent such a figure, who is – as Kant says, quoting Scripture[40] – "*wise as* [a serpent] ... *and harmless as* [a dove]" (PP, 116), the institutional arrangements that historical developments *make possible* will not *actually* come into being. Enlightened self-interest is, in the end, insufficient. There has to be someone who actually and actively works toward the moral end.

---

39 See Knippenberg (1993).
40 Matthew 10:16.

At the same time, however, absent the circumstances that follow, say, from an exhausting series of wars, the moral politician cannot produce the effects he so earnestly wishes. He cannot conjure a federation out of thin air. The man and the circumstances have to match. Hence Kant writes consistently of the need for gradualism, of taking steps toward a more decent world when, and only when, they are actually possible. He does not demand the impossible, nor does he countenance the use of impermissible (e.g., unjustly violent or underhanded) means to achieve desirable ends.[41] Just as Kant praises moral politicians, he blames "despotic moralists," who seek prematurely and violently to accomplish morally desirable ends (PP, 119; cf. 122).

In sum, Kant "realistically" pays attention to how the circumstances that arise and develop naturally may both obstruct and facilitate action on behalf of federalism. He would have "realism" chasten the "idealistic" moral politician, but only to the extent of giving him the patience to await the propitious confluence of circumstances, of which he could, and indeed should, take advantage.

Conclusion: The Distinctiveness of Kantian Federalism

I have sought to make the case that Kant's conception of federalism offers a number of distinctive contributions to our understanding of the subject, especially as it is discussed in the contemporary world. To state his distinctiveness formulaically, he is more realistic than most idealists and more idealistic than most realists.

Above all else, his realism consists in two related arguments. In the first place, he recognizes that any law – political or moral – is addressed to people who have passions and interests. The law may be unconditional and obligatory, but, absent the appropriate institutional mechanisms for enforcement, we cannot expect that it will reliably or predictably be obeyed. The only possibly non-despotic enforcement mechanisms are those employed by a properly constructed republic. In other words, universal laws will be obeyed when republics are so constructed as voluntarily to enforce them. Any other attempt to secure obedience will fail, either because despotic states will not willingly cooperate or because the global state necessary forcibly to compel obedience will itself be a despotism that ultimately will not care about enforcing genuinely universal law. In practice, then, only republics will be likely to uphold universal law. As well, only republics will see the benefit of creating a federation as a means of resolving conflicts, making it easier for them to uphold universal law. Kantian realism teaches that a successful international federation will consist only of republics. To borrow a catchphrase from contemporary activists, for Kant, peace begins at home.

---

41   To be sure, he can live with, even if he does not approve of, results obtained unjustly. The revolution that produces a republic may be wrong, but we are not obliged to restore the despot to his throne. See PP, 118.

In the second place, Kantian realism teaches that only a moral politician will have the incentive and the practical wisdom to use the forces of nature or history to establish a federation. He will recognize and resist the temptation to act as a despotic moralist, compelling people before they are ready to act on their own. He will not establish a global tutelary state, since he knows that that can only be a despotism; he knows that the temptation to abuse such immense power cannot reliably be resisted. Stated another way, it is his morality that makes him approach his task realistically or responsibly. It is his morality that makes him attend carefully to the conditions that promise success and that makes him work toward the construction of a republic and a federation that protect human rights and human dignity.

But the realism of the moral politician does not leave him indifferent to the prospect of a better future. Recognizing "realistically" that all human beings are capable of acknowledging the authority of the moral law, even if at the moment they do not all heed it, the Kantian moral politician keeps his goal in mind as he speaks and acts in the world. He does not act precipitously and prematurely, but he is always on the lookout for circumstances that presage enlightenment and political and moral improvement.

Historical developments make such improvements possible, but they do not make them necessary. The moral politician has to seize the moment, capitalizing on the natural forces and arranging them in such a way as to facilitate the attainment of rational, and hence moral, ends. This reliance on moral action and openness to moral development are, in the end, the truly distinctive features of Kantian federalism. It demands the allegiance of decent human beings, not simply because peace and order are goods,[42] but because they are the prerequisites for serious moral cultivation.

References

Apel, K-O. (1997), Kant's "Toward Perpetual Peace" as historical duty from the point of view of moral duty, in Bohman, J. and Lutz-Bachmann, M. (eds), *Perpetual Peace: Essays on Kant's Cosmopolitan Ideal* (Cambridge, MA: MIT Press).

Arendt, H. (1982), *Lectures on Kant's Political Philosophy*, ed. Beiner, R. (Chicago: University of Chicago Press).

Beiner, R. (1983), *Political Judgment* (Chicago: University of Chicago Press).

—— and Booth, W.J. (eds) (1993), *Kant and Political Philosophy* (New Haven: Yale University Press).

Bohman, J. (1997), The public spheres of the world citizen, in Bohman, J. and Lutz-Bachmann, M. (eds), *Perpetual Peace: Essays on Kant's Cosmopolitan Ideal* (Cambridge, MA: MIT Press).

---

42 Kant jokingly notes at the beginning of *Perpetual Peace* that one can have perpetual peace in a graveyard (93). This, of course, is not the kind of perpetual peace that he has in mind.

—— and Lutz-Bachmann, M. (eds), (1997a), *Perpetual Peace: Essays on Kant's Cosmopolitan Ideal* (Cambridge, MA: MIT Press).
—— (1997b), Introduction, in Bohman, J. and Lutz-Bachmann, M. (eds), *Perpetual Peace: Essays on Kant's Cosmopolitan Ideal* (Cambridge, MA: MIT Press).
Doyle, M.W. (1993), Liberalism and international relations, in Beiner R. and Booth, W.J. (eds), *Kant and Political Philosophy* (New Haven: Yale University Press).
Guyer, P. (2006), *Kant* (New York: Routledge).
Habermas, J. (1997), Kant's idea of perpetual peace, with the benefit of two hundred years' hindsight, in Bohman, J. and Lutz-Bachmann, M. (eds), *Perpetual Peace: Essays on Kant's Cosmopolitan Ideal* (Cambridge, MA: MIT Press).
Hobbes, T. (1994), *Leviathan*, ed. Curley, E. (Indianapolis: Hackett).
Honneth, A. (1997), Is universalism a moral trap? The presuppositions and limits of a politics of human rights, in Bohman, J. and Lutz-Bachmann, M. (eds), *Perpetual Peace: Essays on Kant's Cosmopolitan Ideal* (Cambridge, MA: MIT Press).
Kant, I. (1902), *Prolegomena to Any Future Metaphysics*, trans. Carus, P. <http://www.mnstate.edu/gracyk/courses/phil%20306/kant_materials/prolegomena1.htm#info> [website], accessed May 15, 2008.
—— (1951), *Critique of Judgment*, trans. Bernard, J.H. (New York: Hafner).
—— (1964), *Groundwork for the Metaphysic of Morals*, trans. Paton, H.J. (New York: Harper and Row).
—— (1965), *Critique of Pure Reason*, trans. Smith, N.K. (New York: St. Martin's).
—— (1968), *Kants Werke* (Berlin: Walter de Gruyter).
—— (1978), *Anthropology from a Pragmatic Point of View*, trans. Dowdell, V.L. (Carbondale: Southern Illinois University Press).
—— (1979), *The Conflict of the Faculties*, trans. Gregor, M.J. (New York: Abaris).
—— (1991a), *The Metaphysics of Morals*, trans. Gregor, M.J. (Cambridge: Cambridge University Press).
—— (1991b), *Political Writings*, ed. Reiss, H., trans. Nisbet, H.B. (Cambridge: Cambridge University Press).
—— (1998), *Religion within the Boundaries of Mere Reason*, trans. and ed. Wood, A. (Cambridge: Cambridge University Press).
—— (2005), *Notes and Fragments*, ed. Guyer, P., trans. Bowman, C., Guyer, P., and Rauscher, F. (Cambridge: Cambridge University Press).
Knippenberg, J.M. (1989), Moving beyond fear: Rousseau and Kant on cosmopolitan education, *Journal of Politics* 51, 809–827.
—— (1993), The Politics of Kant's Philosophy, in Beiner, R. and Booth, W.J. (eds), *Kant and Political Philosophy* (New Haven: Yale University Press).
—— (2001), Liberalism and religion: The case of Kant, *Political Science Reviewer* 30, 58–101.
Korsgaard, C. (1996), *Creating the Kingdom of Ends* (Cambridge: Cambridge University Press).
Kuehn, M. (2002), *Kant: A Biography* (Cambridge: Cambridge University Press).
Lutz-Bachmann, M. (1997), Kant's idea of peace and a world republic, in Bohman, J. and Lutz-Bachmann, M. (eds), *Perpetual Peace: Essays on Kant's Cosmopolitan Ideal* (Cambridge, MA: MIT Press).

McCarthy, T. (1997), On the idea of a reasonable law of peoples, in Bohman, J. and Lutz-Bachmann, M. (eds), *Perpetual Peace: Essays on Kant's Cosmopolitan Ideal* (Cambridge, MA: MIT Press).

Mulholland, L. (1990), *Kant's System of Rights* (New York: Columbia University Press).

Nussbaum, M. (1997), Kant and cosmopolitanism, in Bohman, J. and Lutz-Bachmann, M. (eds), *Perpetual Peace: Essays on Kant's Cosmopolitan Ideal* (Cambridge, MA: MIT Press).

Rawls, J. (1999), *The Law of Peoples* (Cambridge, MA: Harvard University Press).

Shell, S.M. (1980), *The Rights of Reason* (Toronto: University of Toronto Press).

Velkley, R. (1989), *Freedom and the End of Reason: On the Moral Foundation of Kant's Political Philosophy* (Chicago: University of Chicago Press).

Vorländer, K. (1986), *Kants Leben*, 4th Edition (Hamburg: Felix Meiner Verlag).

Wood, A.W. (2004), *Kant* (Oxford: Wiley-Blackwell).

Further Reading

Beiner, R. and Booth, W.J. (eds) (1993), *Kant and Political Philosophy* (New Haven: Yale University Press).

Bohman, J. and Lutz-Bachmann, M. (eds), (1997), *Perpetual Peace: Essays on Kant's Cosmopolitan Ideal* (Cambridge, MA: MIT Press).

Delsol, C. (2008), *Unjust Justice: Against the Tyranny of International Law*, trans. Seaton, P. (Wilmington, DE: ISI).

Kant, I. (1991), *Political Writings*, ed. Reiss, H., trans. Nisbet, H.B. (Cambridge: Cambridge University Press).

Knippenberg, J.M. (1989), Moving beyond fear: Rousseau and Kant on cosmopolitan education, *Journal of Politics* 51, 809–827.

Korsgaard, C. (1996), *Creating the Kingdom of Ends* (Cambridge: Cambridge University Press).

Rawls, J. (1999), *The Law of Peoples* (Cambridge, MA: Harvard University Press).

Shell, S.M. (1980), *The Rights of Reason* (Toronto: University of Toronto Press).

PART 3
FEDERALISM AND THE EARLY AMERICAN REPUBLIC

Introduction to Part 3

Quentin Taylor, in Chapter 10, analyzes the uniquely American theory of federalism articulated in the *Federalist* papers. Writing under the collective pseudonym of "Publius," Alexander Hamilton, James Madison, and John Jay, Taylor argues, developed a number of key concepts in their defense of the federal union embodied in the new Constitution. First, unlike the Articles of Confederation, the new Constitution would not be a mere compact of states, but rather, by means of ratification through special conventions, the Union and the national government found therein would be grounded in the consent of the people. The people, not the states, were thus recognized as the fountain of all legitimate authority. Second, the federal structure envisioned in the Constitution provided for an extended republic that would serve as the antidote to faction and the threat of tyrannical majorities that it spawned, thus being the safeguard of liberty and ensuring responsible rule. Third, the national government would not exercise authority over states but rather act directly on persons, thereby preventing the descent into civil war and ensuring the needed "energy" in government. The concept of "energetic government" focused on two key areas of expanded national authority: security and taxation. The final arbiter in disputes between the national and state governments was the "disposition of the people." Publius, according to Taylor, therefore recognized the importance of the civic virtue of the people in preserving the balance of power within the federal system.

Taylor argues that the concept of civic virtue introduces us to Hamilton's unique "psychology of federalism." Hamilton suggests that divided sovereignty between state and national governments also produces a split in the civic identity of the people who would be citizens of both. For Hamilton, the level of government, state or national, exhibiting better administration will harness the sentiments and earn the rational compliance of the people. Having substituted "goodness of administration" for "delegated powers" as the basis for political legitimacy, Hamilton predicts that the national government will be better administered, thus betraying what Taylor argues is a strikingly nationalist vision of the federal union. Madison, on the other hand, is more conciliatory. The federal system arising out of the Constitution is neither entirely national nor fully federal but rather a mixture of both that Madison describes as a "compound republic." An example of the mixed nature of the Constitution is the judicial power of the national government outlined in Article III. Taylor argues that Article III envisions a system of "judicial federalism" in which state and national courts possess exclusive jurisdiction in certain areas and share jurisdiction in others. Thus, the America federalism embodied in the Constitution does not merely divide power between state and national governments, but integrates both levels of government into a system of mutual dependence.

David Lewis Schaefer, in Chapter 11, analyzes the Antifederalist opposition to the Constitution in light of Alexis de Tocqueville's account of its practical operation before the Civil War. Schaefer argues that the Constitution, according to Tocqueville, actually accommodated the concerns of the both the Antifederalists and their Federalist opponents. Schaefer identifies four core arguments made by the Antifederalists against the Constitution. First, the national government, too remote from the people to command their voluntary compliance, would rely on force to ensure obedience thereby resulting in the loss of liberty. Second, Congress would be dominated by a "natural aristocracy" whose ambitious glory seeking would lead to expensive and risky schemes of national aggrandizement adverse to the interests of most citizens. Third, by habituating the people to subservience to a powerful national government, the Constitution would undermine the moral character necessary for a free people. Fourth, the federal judiciary, through the exercise of "judicial review," would expand federal authority at the expense of state governments.

Tocqueville, writing of its operation in 1830, suggests that the American federal system actually combined the freedom of small nations, desired by the Antifederalists, with the military and economic strength of large ones, desired by the Federalists. For Tocqueville, the decentralized administration of the federal system allowed for local self-government that encouraged the love of free institutions and the moral habits necessary to sustain them, and which the Antifederalists believed were so crucial. Moreover, Tocqueville argued that the aristocratic outlook and inherent conservatism of the legal profession in America meant that the federal judiciary was not a threat, but rather a bulwark to the federal system and the moral basis of freedom. Schaefer concludes, however, that the judicial branch of government in the twentieth century was transformed from an aristocratic and conservative body into a progressive, activist judiciary. In seeking to institutionalize the preferences of cosmopolitan "elites" against the values of "ordinary" Americans, the judiciary has been the source of an excessive centralization and the rise of the "tutelary" despotism that Tocqueville feared.

In Chapter 12 Peter McNamara discusses Thomas Jefferson as both a theorist and practitioner of federalism. McNamara argues that Jefferson's theory of federalism, intimately connected with his republicanism and his natural rights philosophy, is a body of ideas that unmistakably originates in the Enlightenment. For Jefferson the two threats to liberty were the natural tendency of governments toward centralization and monarchy, and the corruption of the people toward an apathetic indifference to political affairs. The republican response proposed by Jefferson was to make government power responsive to majority will. However, to ensure that majority will was reasonable and just, institutions and practices such as agrarianism, public education, freedom of speech and the press, and most importantly citizen

INTRODUCTION TO PART 3

participation in local government, were required to ensure that the people shared a uniformity of opinion on broad political principles. The need for active citizen participation gave rise to Jefferson's idea of a unique federal structure in which power was divided by function into different levels of government, down to the county that could be further subdivided into wards small enough such that every citizen could attend and act on public business. Jefferson, according to McNamara, believed that a federal republic so organized would ensure the security, liberty, and happiness of the citizens. With respect to the federalism of the American Constitution in particular, Jefferson developed a strict constructionist doctrine of constitutional interpretation that understood the Union, in contrast to Publius, as a compact of states, thereby rejecting the nationalism of Hamilton and the original populism of Madison.

McNamara argues that in practice Jefferson, while serving as President, faced a number of challenges and threats to his theory of federalism. The role of Native and African Americans in society, the incorporation of the original western territories and the new territories acquired by the Louisiana purchase into the Union, secessionist threats, and the anti-republic tendencies of an apparently monarchist cabal of Federalists based in New England and threatening to come to power on the anti-slavery banner, all presented grave difficulties to the application of Jefferson's federal ideas. McNamara concludes that despite our postmodern distaste for universal principles and homogeneity, Jefferson's federal ideal teaches us an important negative lesson: fundamental diversity threatens federal systems such that they must either become weaker or more monarchical.

In Chapter 13, Peter Augustine Lawler argues that Alexis de Tocqueville, in 1830, presents the American federal system as an accidental constitutional outcome unlikely to endure. Tocqueville, according to Lawler, argues that the Constitution of 1787 produced an "incomplete national government." The new government was national in that it exercised direct sovereignty over individuals. Yet it was incomplete because its sphere of sovereignty was limited to national defense, foreign policy, and commerce; power over all other areas of domestic life was left to the states. This federal structure, however, was inherently unstable, and thus would either complete itself over time, becoming fully national and centralized as the Framers intended, or dissolve into full state sovereignty.

Lawler argues that these two challenges to the federal system that Tocqueville identifies have engulfed the American Union at different times in its history. The threat of dissolution reared its head during the Civil War, and the menace of centralization asserted itself after that war and continues to this day. Paradoxically, for Lawler, both dissolution and centralization have their spring from the same source. This source is what Tocqueville, in essence, would regard as the atomistic individualism of the Lockean theory of the leading Framers. Lockean theoretical individualism abstracts from human particularity and personal significance and opposes the way political liberty, nurtured at the level of the township or small local community, is actually practiced and experienced in America.

James Read, in Chapter 14, explores John C. Calhoun's theory of federalism. Read argues that "nullification" – the state's right to nullify or veto any federal law that it deems unconstitutional or harmful to its interests – is central to Calhoun's federalism. Thus, not the federal judiciary or any other federal body, but rather each individual state is the final judge of the state's constitutional rights and obligations. Moreover, nullification is the key to Calhoun's wider political theory, which insists that legitimate decisions are grounded in the consensus among all key sections and interests in the country, and not majority rule. For Calhoun, majority rule meant majority despotism, the prevention of which required that minorities be given permanent, guaranteed veto rights over collective decisions. The need to include the minority in collective decision-making reflected Calhoun's concept of the "concurrent majority." The point of the minority veto and the need for a concurrent majority, Read argues, is not to encourage stalemate at the federal level, but rather to force leaders of all key interests to negotiate in good faith, working together to pursue the common good. Calhoun's federal theory is therefore a third model of federalism distinct from both that of the Framers of the Constitution and that of the Articles of Confederation. Like the Framers, Calhoun desires an effective central government oriented toward the common good. But, like the Articles he insists on full state sovereignty and veto power over collective decisions.

Read argues that Calhoun's unique body of federal and political ideas is echoed in comparative-political theorist Arend Lijphart's "consociational" model of democracy, in contrast to the "Westminster" majority/opposition model. Moreover, Read concludes by considering recent political arrangements in Northern Ireland, the former Yugoslavia, and proposed but not implemented in South Africa, as test cases for the efficacy of Calhoun's theory of federalism. According to Read, if the disintegration of the former Yugoslavia illustrates the limit of Calhoun's federal system, the potential long-term success of the Good Friday Agreement in Northern Ireland may prove the workability of Calhoun's federal solutions. Yet the survival and health of constitutional majority rule in South Africa may show that, with enlightened statesmanship, Calhoun's prescriptions are unnecessary.

In Chapter 15, William Mathie investigates what can be learned about federalism by considering the speeches and actions of Abraham Lincoln as political actor in the seven years leading up to the Civil War, and as president during that war. Specifically, Mathie focuses on Lincoln's denial that federalism entails the right of secession and his assertion that the national executive has the right and duty to prevent the dissolution of the federal system. Mathie argues that Lincoln equated the concept of "secession" with "rebellion," and insisted, unlike Calhoun, that with regard to controversial political questions unresolved by the legal language of a nation's constitution, democracy required the final rule of the national majority. To suggest otherwise was to endorse the despotism of permanent minority rule or the anarchy of secession. Moreover, on the assumption that perpetuity is the underlying premise of all government, Lincoln argues that it was the responsibility of the nation's chief executive, provided that their power was derived entirely from the people, to transmit to their successor unimpaired by dissolution the government as it had come into their hands.

Lincoln applied his thinking on federalism to the American constitutional structure in particular by denying the sovereignty of the states and thus their

Introduction to Part 3

subsequent right to secede. What powers the states did have derived solely from the Constitution, never having been states outside the Union, and losing that status if they broke from the Union. Moreover, the division of powers in the Constitution followed the "principle of generality and locality," whatever concerned the whole being assigned to the national government, and local concerns being assigned to the state governments. Mathie suggests that for Lincoln, slavery, whether in the southern states or extended into the territories, could not in the end be regarded as a purely local issue, as it violated the equality and rights claims articulated in the *Declaration of Independence* and which the Framers intended the Constitution of 1787 to achieve.

Mathie concludes by asking whether Lincoln, in his argument for and use of executive power to preserve the Union and further the principles of the *Declaration*, was true to the federal order as expressed in the Constitution, or rather was he, as Lawler suggests, a determined centralizer. Mathie argues that light can be shed on this question by looking to the understanding and intent of the leading Framers. According to Mathie, Framers such as Madison acknowledged that, unlike the Articles of Confederation, the Constitution was partly national and thus only partly federal. It was, therefore, as Tocquville describes, an "incomplete national government." Moreover, Mathie argues that for Madison it was more important that the Constitution be republican in character rather than federal. Mathie's final conclusion, however, is ambiguous. Although Lincoln's refutation of the southern states' lawful right of secession was based on his reading of the Constitution, he ultimately justified his actions on two extra-Constitutional premises: the assumption of perpetuity underlying all government, and the duty of the president to prevent disunion based on the "sacred" oath s/he takes to uphold the Constitution.

10

"A System Without a Precedent": The Federalism of the *Federalist* Papers

Quentin Taylor

Among the many difficulties facing the delegates who assembled in Philadelphia in 1787, few were as formidable as drawing the line between the power and jurisdiction of the general government and that of the states. The idea of dividing sovereignty between two or more entities had received the stern rebuke of history and the admonishment of the best political writers. To set up a power within a power, an *imperio in imperium*, was "a solecism in politics," contradictory in theory and untenable in practice. For many the experience of the United States under the Articles of Confederation only confirmed the verdict of Clio and reinforced the received wisdom: America's brief experiment in federalism had failed. In light of this false start, the new nation's leaders faced a harrowing dilemma. Some, like Alexander Hamilton, James Madison, and John Jay, concluded that only a system that firmly subordinated the states to the central government, even to the point of reducing them to administrative districts, could overcome their centrifugal tendencies, protect liberty, and preserve the Union. The perceived need for something approaching a *consolidation* of the states under a national authority signaled a deep skepticism toward, if not a total abandonment of, the federal idea. This, however, was the minority view, both inside and outside the Federal Convention. Virtually all the delegates in Philadelphia agreed that the national government should be strengthened and the states restrained, but few were willing to go as far as Madison, and none as far as Hamilton, who was openly contemptuous of the states. Outside the Convention a truly "national" system that would turn sovereign states into mere counties was unthinkable for the vast majority of Americans. As it was, the federal compromise hammered out in Philadelphia raised cries of "consolidation" from the Constitution's opponents and nearly defeated its adoption in key states like Massachusetts, New York, and Virginia.

This state of affairs placed nationalists like Hamilton and Madison in an awkward position, both in the Convention as advocates of a supreme central government, and in the ratification contests as proponents of a compromise that left the states with a large measure of sovereignty. As the Convention completed its work neither man expressed much confidence in the long-term viability of a plan that blurred jurisdictional lines, made the states "constituent parts of the national sovereignty," and lacked an explicit mechanism for resolving disputes between the two. Shortly before he affixed his signature to the fair copy of the document, Hamilton declared that "no man's ideas were more remote from the plan than mine were known to be." For his part, Madison, who had lost a number of key battles in the Convention, feared that the failure to invest the national government with a veto power over state legislation created but another *"imperia in imperio"* that would ultimately prove fatal. John Jay, blocked from attending the Convention by suspicious colleagues in the New York legislature, also nourished shrewd reservations about the efficacy of the plan. The irony, of course, is that all three fought tirelessly for the Constitution's adoption, both in their respective state ratifying conventions and in the war of words in the press. Shortly after the document was made public, Hamilton aimed to sway opinion in New York through a series of essays that would explain and defend the Constitution's various provisions and underscore its necessity to preserve the Union, and with it the safety and liberty of the American people. To assist in this endeavor he selected fellow New Yorker, John Jay, and Virginia congressman James Madison, who collectively wrote under the *non de plume* "Publius," the founder of the Roman republic. On October 27, 1787, the first of the *Federalist* papers appeared in New York City newspapers, followed by another 84 over the next six months. While the federal nature of the Constitution is not included in the list of broad topics proposed in the first paper, the considerable space devoted to federalism throughout the series testifies to its importance. Indeed, "marking the proper line of partition, between the authority of the general, and that of the state governments" was not only a most "arduous" task for the Framers (37:182), but it presented Publius with a unique challenge as an expositor of the Constitution. His performance has occasionally been denounced as "disingenuous" and "equivocal," but it remains to this day (in the words of J. S. Mill) "the most instructive treatise we possess on federal government."

While James Madison is often credited with formulating the modern theory of federalism, it was Hamilton who first took up the pen in *Federalist* 9 to explain and defend it. Opponents of the Constitution charged that the plan violated the *federal* principle and leaned towards a *consolidated* or *unitary* form of government. In any "true" federal system, it was argued, the states would (1) possess equal representation in the national councils, (2) exercise an exclusive control over their internal affairs, and (3) maintain their sovereignty and supremacy over the central government. For Hamilton, this definition was based on a false dichotomy "between a *confederacy* and a *consolidation* of the states" and was therefore "arbitrary; ... supported neither by principle nor precedent" (9:40). Not all federated systems strictly adhered to these criteria, nor did history provide an "absolute rule on the subject" (9:41). A *confederacy* merely denotes "'an assemblage of societies,' or an association of two or more states into one state," wherein "[t]he extent, modifications, and objects, of the federal authority are mere matters of discretion" (9:41).

In place of the narrow and rigid federalism of the purists, Hamilton fashioned a broad and flexible rule that could easily accommodate the "new" federalism embodied in the Constitution.

> *So long as the separate organization of the members be not abolished, so long as it exists by a constitutional necessity for local purposes, though it should be in perfect subordination to the general authority of the union, it would still be, in fact and in theory, an association of states, or a confederacy (9:41).*

Conversely, the suggestion that the plan aimed at an "abolition" of the states was not only untrue but nonsensical, for the Constitution makes them "constituent parts of the national sovereignty" (9:41) and the general government could not function without them. This feature of the plan, often overlooked by its critics, provided an additional if not impregnable bulwark against a consolidated government. American federalism does not merely *divide* power between the national and state governments, but *integrates* these authorities into a system of mutual dependence. Given the *necessity* of the states for the full operation of the national government, any effort to abolish them would be self-defeating. In such a case, the national government "would be compelled, by the principle of self preservation, to reinstate them in their proper jurisdiction" (14:65). Moreover, the Constitution gives the states equal representation in the Senate, and "leaves in their possession certain exclusive, and very important, portions of the sovereign power," an arrangement which "fully corresponds ... with the idea of a federal government" (9:41).

A final reason Publius gives for rejecting a cramped view of federalism is practical and prescriptive, for wherever this view has prevailed "it has been the cause of incurable disorder and imbecility in the government" (9:41). In succeeding papers (Nos. 18, 19, 20) Publius makes good on his pledge to illustrate this principle with reference to a number of failed (or feckless) confederacies, ancient, medieval, and modern. His aim was not merely to evince the "*insufficiency of the present confederation to preserve the Union*" (1:4) – which was clear to virtually everyone – but also to show that the revised federalism of the Constitution was not simply an *authentic* species of federated government, but the *only* one capable of preserving the Union.

Madison's *Federalist* 10, famous for its treatment of factions, adds little to the theory of federalism *per se*, nor does the almost equally famous number 51. Both, however, develop the concept of the "extensive republic" which Hamilton briefly defended in *Federalist* 9. Drawing on the "celebrated" Montesquieu, some Antifederalists denied a republican form of government could be maintained over an extensive territory with a diverse population like the United States. In countering the claim, Hamilton sought to best the critics at their own game, citing Montesquieu's endorsement of "a CONFEDERATE REPUBLIC as the expedient for extending the sphere of popular government, and reconciling the advantages of monarchy with those of republicanism" (9:39). Madison added to the list of advantages associated with an extended republic, including a hedge against majority tyranny and a greater likelihood of obtaining "fit characters" for the national councils (10:47). The *federal* structure of the Union promises to reinforce these advantages through (1) a natural division of labor between the state and central governments, "the great and aggregate interests, being referred to the national, the local and particular to the state legislatures" (10:47); (2) the creation of a separate entity (the national government) capable of curbing the causes and restraining the effects of tyrannical majorities where they are most likely to occur (the states); and (3) large electoral districts that will enhance the prospect of selecting men of known quality for national office. In sum, federalism works in tandem with an extended territory to safeguard liberty and bolster responsible rule: it is an essential antidote to the "bane" of faction. For "[i]n the extent and proper structure of the Union," Publius concludes, "we behold a republican remedy for the diseases must incident to republican government" (10:48).

In *Federalist* 51 Madison expands on the advantages of the extended republic, identifying the *division of power* in the "compound republic" along with the *separation of powers* at both levels of government as a "double security" for popular rights. "The different governments will control each other; at the same time that each will be controlled by itself" (51:270). As in number 10, *faction* is identified as the general evil and *tyrannical majorities* as its most dangerous spawn. The large extent of the country, and the multiplicity of "interests, parties, and sects," guard against the advent of such factions *among the people*, while separation of powers and checks and balances serve a similar function *within the government*. Federalism, by dividing power and distributing it over a large area, contributes to both. Far more than a convenient way of assigning public duties, federalism makes an extended republic *workable*. "And happily for the *republican cause*," Publius proclaims, "the practicable sphere may be carried to a very great extent, by a judicious modification and mixture of the *federal principle*" (51:272). Subsequent innovations in transportation and communication may have rendered the concept of the extensive republic partially obsolete, but the remarkable spread of the "federal principle" across the continent gives Madison's words a prophetic ring.

The heart of the *Federalist's* theory of federalism unfolds between the poles of numbers 10 and 51. In paper 14 Madison answers "objections" to the extended republic, enlisting the distinction between a "democracy" and a "republic" that was central to the argument in number 10. The implication is that a union of republics is not only feasible for "the thirteen primitive states" (14:65), but may expand to incorporate others. As Hamilton observed in the previous paper:

> *Civil power, properly organized and exerted, is capable of diffusing its force to a very great extent; and can, in a manner, reproduce itself in every part of a great empire, by a judicious arrangement of subordinate institutions* (13:61).

Such diffusion would not have been possible under the flawed federalism of the Articles, but under the "new modeled" federalism of the Constitution (coupled with internal improvements) republican government can safely expand well beyond its current scope. Given the massive frontier inherited from the British, the utility of a system capable of an orderly and equitable incorporation of new states (as well as their defense) was not the least of its virtues.

Hamilton picks up the thread in *Federalist* 15, the first of eight papers aimed at demonstrating the "insufficiency of the present confederation to preserve the union" (15:68). First and foremost is "[t]he great and radical vice" of legislating for the states in their corporate identities as opposed to directly for individuals (15:71). Although Congress could *request* men, money, and supplies from the states, it had no legal means of *enforcing* compliance. As a consequence, requests were often denied or fulfilled only in part, a deficiency that had seriously hampered the war effort and perpetuated a host of "embarrassments" following the peace. More fundamentally, the inability of the national government to exercise jurisdiction over the states created "the political monster of an *imperium in imperio*," an unbridled sovereignty within a sovereignty, "which is in itself evidently incompatible with the idea of GOVERNMENT" (15:70, 71).

The specter of "the violent and sanguinary agency of the sword" sweeps through the next paper until "anarchy" "civil war" and "military despotism" have deluged the nation in blood (16:75–77). Whether by a violent or "natural death," the present confederacy (or any association based on its "idle and visionary" principles) is unsustainable and doomed to dissolution "if the federal system be not speedily renovated in a more substantial form" (16:77). This *form* is precisely the "reverse of the principle" embodied in the Confederation, the principle of a sovereign national government operating directly on individuals.

> *It must carry the agency to the persons of the citizens. It must stand in need of no intermediate legislations; but must itself be empowered to employ the arm of the ordinary magistrate to execute its own resolutions. The majesty of the national authority must be manifested through the medium of the courts of justice. The government of the union, like that of each state, must be able to address itself immediately to the hopes and fears of individuals; and to attract to its support, those passions, which have the strongest influence upon the human heart. It must, in short, possess all the means, and have a right to resort to all the methods, of executing the powers with which it is entrusted, that are possessed and exercised by the governments of the particular states (16:78).*

This compact and forceful statement of the national principle contains the linchpin of the new federalism and offers a glimpse into the underlying political psychology that Publius would develop in subsequent numbers. Without the power to act directly on persons or the capacity to legally vindicate its authority, any additional grants of power to the general government would prove empty and ineffectual. Only a truly *national* authority, backed by adequate means of enforcement could remove the "great and radical vice" of *imperium et imperio*, and substitute "the COERCION of the magistracy" for "the COERCION of arms" (16:72).

In response to the objection that obstruction on the part of a state would still entail the use of force, Publius draws a distinction between "mere NON-COMPLIANCE" (which prevailed under the Confederation) and "a DIRECT and ACTIVE RESISTANCE" (which would be required under the Constitution), and observes that state leaders would be hesitant to pursue the latter in order to defeat a lawful national measure (16:78). The related objection that a power over individuals would result in the usurpation of the "residuary authorities" left to the states is the focus of the seventeenth number. Hamilton's answer is notable not only for its exquisite condescension, but for its insight into the psychology of power. For men entrusted with the great objects of national authority – "[c]ommerce, finance, negotiation, and war" – the local and petty objects of state regulation will "hold out slender allurements to ambition" (17:80). There can be little motive to usurp powers that would prove "troublesome" and "nugatory" to exercise and "contribute nothing to the dignity, to the importance, or to the splendor, of the national government" (17:81). The integrity of the states, then, is given an additional (and ironic) support in the "charms" of *haute politique*, which absorb the attention of "minds governed by that passion" (17:80).

Indeed, it is more probable that the *states* will "encroach upon the national authorities," for they will possess a "greater degree of influence" over citizens, particularly "if they administer their affairs with uprightness and prudence" (17:81). This "superiority of influence" is rooted in a natural propensity to adhere to that which is nearest: family, district, state. (17:81). The grounds for a pronounced bias in favor of local government are many, but "the one transcendent advantage" possessed by the states is "the ordinary administration of criminal and civil justice…. [T]he most powerful, most universal, and most attractive source of popular obedience and attachment" (17:82).

In contrast to the patronizing tone of his earlier remarks, Hamilton now honors the states as (1) the primary agents of social formation, binding individuals and interests with the "great cement of society," and (2) the "immediate and visible guardian[s] of life and property,… impress[ing] upon the minds of the people affection, esteem, and reverence towards the government" (17:82). Such an "empire" over the hearts and minds of citizens will render the states a "complete counterpoise" to the pretensions of the national government, and "not unfrequently dangerous rivals" to its power (17:82). Conversely, the relatively remote, general, and indirect operation of the national government will exert a proportionately weaker attraction on the loyalties and attachments of ordinary citizens.

The use of historical analogy to illustrate "our political mistakes" in forming a union is developed in the next three numbers. In a *tour de force* of engaged scholarship, Madison presses the sordid history of European confederacies into the service of the new federalism. In each case the misfortunes of these confederacies are attributed to the "fallacious principle" upon which they were built (18:86), a principle shared by the Articles of Confederation: *imperio in imperium*, "a sovereignty over sovereigns, a government over governments, a legislation for communities, as contradistinguished from individuals" (20:99). The verdict of history, Publius pronounces, is clear. No association of states can survive unless this "repellent quality, incident to the nature of sovereignty" is replaced by a "proper consolidation" (19:93).

Having consulted history, "the oracle of truth," Publius turns to an enumeration of the more specific "defects" of the Confederation. First and "most palpable" is the absence of a provision for enforcing federal law, a "striking absurdity" that renders the "government, destitute even of the shadow of constitutional power" (21:99, 100). Second, the Articles fail to guarantee each state a republican form of government, "a capital imperfection" in view of the late rebellion in Massachusetts (21:100). The defective quota system of collecting revenue presents a third "fundamental error" (21:101), while the inability to regulate commerce among the states – an "object … that more strongly demands a federal superintendence" than any other – is a fourth (22:104). An inadequate national authority in military matters, the source of "imbecility in the union, and of inequality and injustice among the members," constitutes a fifth (22:106). The principle of equal representation in Congress, the "[s]ophistry" of its defenders aside, is yet another "poison" (22:106, 107), while the lack of a national judiciary "crowns the defects of the confederation" (22:110).

In combination these seven "material defects" not only deprive Congress of those powers necessary to govern, but undermine the powers it does possess, creating "a system so radically vicious and unsound" as to defy amendment or amelioration (22:111). Yet even if Congress *did* possess the requisite powers of a national government, its unicameral organization is "utterly improper for the exercise" thereof (22:111). Finally, the Articles are a mere *compact* among the states, which never received the consent of the people and whose provisions may be broken with impunity. A national government, Publius argues, should lay its foundations "deeper than in the mere sanction of delegated authority," and issue from the "pure, original fountain of all legitimate authority," the people themselves (22:112). The method of ratification selected by the Framers – special conventions elected by the people – will provide this sanction and give the new federalism both a *popular* and *national* foundation.

The twenty-second paper concludes the second section of the *Federalist* and marks a transition in the general sweep of the argument. Having shown the "absolute necessity for an entire change in the first principles of the system" (23:114) – that the general government must act directly on individuals – Publius turns to demonstrate the "necessity of a constitution, at least equally energetic with the one proposed, to the preservation of the union" (23:112).

The need for *energy* in government runs like a leitmotiv through the *Federalist* and constitutes a leading theme in its bold makeover of republican theory. It was precisely a lack of "energy" that had plagued Congress under the Articles and reduced the general government to a state of "imbecility." A decade of ineptitude and frustration had forced many to reconsider the conventional wisdom which associated weak government with liberty and strong government with tyranny. By insisting on a government "at least" as energetic as the one proposed by the Convention, Publius placed himself at the vanguard of the revolution in federalism. The novelty of an "energetic" central government was not lost on the Constitution's opponents, who spied in its "sweeping" grants of power a threat to both the autonomy of the states and the liberties of the people. It is not coincidental, then, that the case for "energetic" government centers on the two areas where an expanded national authority was at once most feared and most necessary – the common defense and taxation.

In papers 23–29, Publius marshals a number of arguments to support the Constitution's provisions for the "common defense." Antifederalists objected to the "unlimited" nature of this power, and specifically feared the prospect of an overbearing military establishment. In addition to evincing the illogic and folly of placing limits on an inherently "unconfined authority" (23:115), Publius dismissed the shibboleth of a standing army in time of peace and rejected alternatives to the Constitution's provisions for regulating the state militias and calling them into national service. In systematically countering the principal objections to these arrangements, Publius develops something like a theory of *military federalism*, wherein the necessities of defense and security are merged with the realities of the federal structure.

In nearly every instance in which a face-off between the national and state governments is contemplated, the decisive factor in the outcome is the *disposition of the people*. There are different ways of interpreting this projection. An uncharitable view might consider it a mere dodge or, worse still, a cynical ruse to conceal a nationalist fist in a republican glove. If Publius had simply assigned the "people" the role of *dues ex machina* without further ado there would be some ground for the charge. This, however, is not the case. The appeal to *vox populi* as a last resort is premised (often explicitly) on the fundamentally sound judgment of the "people" (or a majority of active citizens); viz., "a people enlightened enough to distinguish between a legal exercise and an illegal usurpation of authority" (16:79). In contests between state and federal governments (or in the event of attacks on liberty by either), the people will serve as the "natural guardians of the Constitution," whose preponderate weight will prove decisive (16:179). While sometimes faulted for relying too heavily on institutional safeguards to preserve a balance of power *within the national government*, Publius duly recognized the importance of a modicum of *civic virtue* to "preserve the constitutional equilibrium between the general and the state governments" (31:154).

If making the "people" the ultimate arbiter of their political fate was consistent with republican doctrine, the question of how citizens could be expected to mediate their loyalties in a compound republic was less easily answered. Just as the Constitution divided *sovereignty* between state and national entities, it split the *civic identity* of a people who would be citizens of both. This obvious (if neglected) duality presents one of the most interesting aspects of federalism. It was not neglected, however, by Publius, who in the context of exploring the dynamics of state–federal conflict, developed what might be called a *psychology of federalism*.

In *Federalist* 17 Publius provides a compelling account of the psychological bases for citizens to "feel a stronger bias" in favor of the state governments, particularly "if they administer their affairs with uprightness and prudence" (17:81). Given the proximity, immediacy, and visibility of local government, a remote and veiled national authority will simply be no match for the "affection, esteem, and reverence" of the great bulk of citizens (17:82). As an unreconstructed nationalist, Hamilton must have swallowed hard when he penned this paean to localism, but beneath his musings on the "strong propensity of the human heart" (17:81), the brilliant polemicist was burrowing away. The proviso that state governments will find especial favor if marked by *good administration* implied that they will lose favor if the reverse were true. Indeed, the natural bias in favor of the states might even be "destroyed by a much better administration" of the national government (17:81).

On one hand, Publius uses the alleged "superiority of influence" of the states – and the corollary of "an inherent and intrinsic weakness in all federal constitutions" – to justify the Constitution's grant of expansive powers to the national government, giving it "all the force which is compatible with the principles of liberty" (17:81). On the other, he opens the door to the possibility that the federal government *will* exhibit a better administration than the states, and thereby gain ascendancy in the minds of the people. One should perhaps say "probability" (as Publius does in later papers), for it is hard to imagine a worse administration than that of the states as depicted in the first section of the *Federalist*. The point is further reinforced in Madison's defense of "extensive republics," whose principal virtue is to procure "fit characters" to administer the national government.

Hamilton brings these threads together in number 27 when countering the contention that "the people will be disinclined to the exercise of the federal authority, in any matter of an internal nature" (27:132). In light of the Constitution's (1) broad, and in some cases vague and open-ended, grants of power, (2) its multiple prohibitions on the states, (3) the supremacy clause (requiring state officials to take an oath to support all federal measures), and (4) the absence of a statement of "reserved" powers, it is not surprising that concerns were raised along these lines. Hamilton side-steps the issue of internal governance and repairs to the standard of *administration* as the decisive factor in generating an attitude of compliance with federal authority: "I believe it may be laid down as a general rule, that [the peoples'] confidence in, and their obedience to, a government, will commonly by proportioned to the goodness or badness of its administration" (27:132).

Having substituted *goodness of administration* for *delegated powers* as the basis for political legitimacy, Hamilton proceeds to explain why in all "probability … the general government will be better administered" than the states (27:133). The "principal" cause is derived from "extension of the spheres of election," particularly in the method of selecting senators (27:133). As a result of this method, those sitting in the national councils will, on the whole, exhibit greater virtue, possess superior wisdom, and display fewer defects than their counterparts in the states. "Several additional reasons," rooted in the "interior structure of the [national] edifice," might be given to support the probability of better administration (27:133), but in the absence of any argument to the contrary there is no reason to presume that federal laws will meet with any more obstruction or require more coercive methods of enforcement than those of the states.

The capstone of this imposing edifice is supplied by the *supremacy clause*, which binds all state officials to lawful federal authority, so far as it operates on "the *enumerated* and *legitimate* objects of its jurisdiction" (27:135). What emerges is a strikingly *nationalist* vision of the federal union.

> *Thus the legislatures, courts, and magistrates, of the respective members, will be incorporated into the operations of the national government as far as its just and constitutional authority extends; and will be rendered auxiliary to the enforcement of its laws (27:135).*

That Hamilton attached a footnote to this sentence, vowing to refute the "sophistry" of those who claimed that "this will tend to the destruction of the State governments," is most revealing. The statement itself, indeed, the entire construction of federalism in number 27, runs against the common opinion that "Publius" soft-peddled the nationalist features of the plan. What is equally telling is Hamilton's locution; for instance, using the generic "enumerated" as opposed to the more restrictive "delegated" or "explicit" powers. Similarly, he opts for the normative "legitimate" and "just" instead of the more empirical "limited" or "finite." He even substitutes the word "objects" for "powers," a slight-of-hand worthy of a Wall Street lawyer.

If this were the final word, one might conclude that "Publius" failed to reconcile the two visions of federalism presented in numbers 17 (*federal* and *separatist*) and 27 (*national* and *integrationist*). But this is not the final word. The pledge to refute the contention that the envisioned system will "tend to the destruction of the State governments" was met, first, obliquely in number 39, and then directly in numbers 45 and 46. (Interestingly, it was Madison who took up the gauge; a fact that has given a handle to those who would cleave "Publius" in half.) The former paper is famous for its synoptic statement of the *republican* and *federal* principles underlying the Constitution. After (re)defining republican government as a system of indirect and non-majoritarian democracy, Madison turns to discover "the real character of the government" (39:196); that is, the degree to which it represents a *federal* (confederal), a *national* (consolidated), and a *mixed* (hybrid) system. With lawyerly precision he examines the government's (1) "foundation" or "establishment," (2) the "sources," (3) "operation," and (4) "extent" of its powers, and (5) its mechanism for "future changes" or amendments.

Since ratification of the Constitution will proceed through state conventions, the *establishment* of the government will "not be a *national*, but a *federal* act" (39:196). Conversely, as neither a majority of the people nor a majority of states can compel any state to join, the union will have "a *federal*, and not a *national* constitution" (39:197).

The *sources* of power (or manner in which federal officials are selected) will partake of both federal and national principles. The House of Representatives, elected directly by the people and proportional to population, will be "*national, not federal,*" while the Senate, elected by state legislature on the basis of equal representation, will be "*federal, not national*" (39:197). The source of the President's power is of a "mixed character." In the first instance, the selection is made by the states through their chosen electors (*federal*), but given the probability that no candidate will secure a majority of electoral votes (a common belief among the Framers), the choice, as provided by the Constitution, will frequently devolve to the House of Representatives (*national*), but be made on the basis of one vote per state (*federal*). Accordingly, the sources of the government's power exhibit "at least as many *federal* as national *features*" (39:197).

As for the *operation* of the government, the authority to directly legislate for individuals partakes of the "the *national*, and not the *federal* character," although states still retain their corporate identities when parties to a suit (39:198). "[I]n its ordinary and most essential proceedings," however, it will comprise "a *national* government." In terms of the *extent* of its powers, it "cannot be deemed a *national* one; since its jurisdiction extends to certain enumerated powers only, and leaves to the several states a residuary and inviolable sovereignty over all other objects" (39:198). It is therefore a *federal* government from this perspective, although disputes between the two authorities must ultimately (and of necessity) be decided by the *national* government.

Finally, the manner of amending the Constitution is "neither wholly *national*, nor wholly *federal*," but a mix of both principles (39:199). Neither a majority of the people (*national*), nor unanimous consent of the states (*federal*) is required for adoption, but rather a supermajority of the states. (Madison does not mention the national method of *proposing* amendments.)

In sum, the system of government embodied in the Constitution is, like its constituent parts, neither entirely national, nor fully federal, but a *mixture* of both. Given its striking novelty (what Madison would latter call "a system without a precedent") it is understandable that Publius had difficulty finding a name for it. While Hamilton attempted to force the new hybrid into the old category of "confederacy," glibly suggesting that the precise size and scope of the national government were "mere matters of discretion," a more candid Madison tacitly acknowledged that the national features of the plan rendered the distinction between a consolidated and a federal government obsolete, hinting that it could more accurately be described as a "mixed constitution" (40:199) or a "compound republic" (51:270). This semantic ambiguity ultimately played into the hands of the Constitution's supporters, who shrewdly adopted the name "Federalist." Opponents of the plan, the "true" Federalists, cried foul, but in the end were left with the negative sobriquet.

In succeeding papers (Nos. 41–46), Publius considers two questions regarding the powers granted to the national government, including restraints imposed upon the states: "1. Whether any part of the powers transferred to the general government, be unnecessary or improper? [and] 2. Whether the entire mass of them be dangerous to the portion of jurisdiction left in the several states" (41:207)? Having shown that the powers granted to the national authority (viz., the powers of Congress, Article I, section 8) and those denied the states (viz., Article I, section 10) are absolutely essential to the welfare of the union, he proceeds to consider the overall impact on the state's "residuary" powers. Here Madison honors the promise made by Hamilton in his footnote to number 27, countering "the supposition that the operation of the federal government will by degrees prove fatal to the state governments" (45:238). In contrast to Hamilton's quasi-psychological analysis, however, Madison provides a quantitative and structural argument to support the conclusion that

> [t]he state governments will have the advantage of the federal government, whether we compare them [1] in respect to the immediate dependence of the one on the other; [2] to the weight of personal influence which each side will possess; [3] to the powers respectively vested in them; [4] to the predilection and probable support of the people; [5] to the disposition and faculty of resisting and frustrating the measures of each other (45:239).

First, the role of the states in selecting national officials for the two political branches (directly in the case of the President and Senate and indirectly in the case of the House of Representatives) will create an "immediate dependence" (45:239) of the central government on the states. Conversely, the selection of state officials is wholly independent of the national authority. Second, the "personal influence" of state officials will far exceed that of federal officers based on the former's vast superiority in numbers, as well as the likelihood that the central government will enlist state officials in the collection of federal revenue and the adjudication of federal law (45:240). Third, "[t]he powers delegated by the proposed constitution to the federal government, are few and defined. Those which are to remain in the state governments, are numerous and infinite" (45:241). The former will be largely restricted to the "external objects" of war, diplomacy, and commerce, while the latter will encompass the remaining objects of governmental control.

Before moving to the fourth heading, Publius makes the rather dubious claim that the change proposed by the Constitution "consists much less in the addition of NEW POWERS to the union, than in the invigoration of its ORIGINAL POWERS" (45:241–42). While conceding that the power to act directly on individuals, regulate interstate commerce, and levy direct taxes represents a departure from the Articles of Confederation, he suggests that the basic objects and ends of the national authority envisioned by the Constitution are essentially the same. In contrast to Hamilton, who underscored the need for "an entire change in the first principles of the system" (23:114), Madison finds a fundamental continuity at the higher level. The "discovery" is not, however, without a Hamiltonian purpose: to catch the critics in the contradiction of implying that "the existence of the state governments is incompatible with any system whatever, that accomplishes the essential purposes of the Union" (45:242)

As for the "support of the people," Madison returns to Hamilton's premise that a "popular bias" based on propinquity will give the state governments "the advantage" over the federal authority (46:242, 243). In addition, he breaks down the bifurcated and antagonistic paradigm of state and national sovereignties (a view encouraged by Hamilton in earlier numbers), reminding the adversaries of the Constitution that both "are in fact different agents and trustees of the people, instituted with different powers, and designated for different purposes" (46:243). To assume that state and central establishments will be "mutual rivals and enemies" is simply rash, and overlooks the fact that "ultimate authority ... resides in the people alone" (46:243). Again, unless given "manifest and irresistible proofs of a better administration," "the first and most natural attachment of the people, will be to the governments of their own states" (46:243). Yet even if the people are partial to the central authority, its reach will necessarily be limited, for "it is only within a certain sphere, that the federal power can, in the nature of things, be advantageously administered" (46:244).

Given the foregoing observations, it is no surprise that the "advantage" in the "disposition and faculty of resisting and frustrating the measures" of the respective governments is given to the states as well (45:239).

With the conclusion that "the powers proposed to be lodged in the federal government, are as little formidable to those reserved to the individual states, as they are indispensably necessary to accomplish the purposes of the union" (46:248), the *Federalist*'s explication and defense of the Constitution's (non-judicial) federal arrangements is essentially complete. There are, however, a few key arguments which require comment before proceeding to Publius's discussion of the judiciary.

Earlier it was noted that the case for an "energetic" central government focused on the national defense and taxation. Having defended the former, Publius turns to uphold the Constitution's grant of an "unlimited" power to tax. Under the Articles this power had been denied Congress, which was limited to making "requisitions" on the states with no means of enforcement. Efforts to procure an independent source of revenue during the postwar years had proved futile, leaving the insolvent Congress unable to meet its most basic financial obligations. The movement for a national convention to "revise and amend" the Articles was in no small part owing to the government's mounting fiscal crisis. As "the most important of the authorities proposed to be conferred upon the union" (33:159) – and one repeatedly denounced by opponents of the plan – Hamilton felt justified in defending it at length.

His task was basically twofold: first to demonstrate that anything less than a general taxing authority was inconsistent with the objects entrusted to the national government and second, to ally fears that this authority would in time result in a "federal monopoly" (31:152). The first point was largely self-evident, based on the maxim that "every POWER ought to be proportionate to its OBJECT" (30:147). Given the unbounded nature of this object – national defense, domestic order, trade and commerce – "no possible limits" could be placed on this power beyond "a regard to the public good" (31:151). Any attempt to restrict this power to certain objects (imports) or articles (manufactures) would inevitably frustrate the government's ability to provide for present needs and future contingencies and place unfair burdens on certain sectors of the economy.

Against this bold defense of "an unqualified power" to tax (31:152), Publius reminded the critics that the states would "retain that authority" for themselves (short of foreign and interstate commerce) in the form of a "concurrent and co-equal" power (32:156). But would not the establishment of a coordinate power to tax result in endless conflicts, double taxation, and swarms of revenuers? Publius denies the presence of a "direct contradiction" in a system of concurrent power

(32:157), pointing to the example of the Roman Republic (34:162–163). As for the specter of duplication, he argues that a kind of natural division of labor will prevail, characterized by a spirit of "reciprocal forbearance" in which the federal government will limit itself to those sources of revenue least burdensome to the states (36:176). On one hand, an exclusive control over the taxation of imports will largely obviate the need for direct or "internal" taxes, while the reduced costs to the states for present necessities (e.g., defense) will restrict their revenue needs "within *a very narrow compass*" (34:163). On the other, the Constitution's requirements for proportionality in levying direct taxes on incomes and for uniformity in laying "all duties, imposts, and excises," are further guards against abuses. As for an army of tax farmers, Publius suggests that the federal government will either "wholly abstain" from sources of revenue traditionally reserved to the states, or "make use of the state officers, and state regulations, for collecting" them (36:176).

It is notable that in the midst of his defense of a general taxing power, Publius digresses to defend the *necessary and proper* and *supremacy* clauses, "the sources of much virulent invective, and petulant declamation, against the proposed constitution" (33:158). After assuring the reader that the states will retain "all the rights of sovereignty ... [not] *exclusively* delegated to the United States" (32:155), he declares that the supremacy of the Constitution (including federal law) and the authority to carry out its enumerated provisions is *implicit* in "the very act of constituting a federal government, and vesting it with certain specified powers" (33:158). Again, the central authority is limited in its objects, and the supremacy of its laws is "*expressly*" confined to it constitutional powers. Any measures adopted outside these confines "will be merely acts of usurpation, and will deserve to be treated as such" (33:161).

Hamilton's emphatic use of "*expressly*" was undoubtedly intended to underscore the limited scope of federal power and blunt the charge that the necessary and proper clause would prove a Trojan horse to the states. While this usage was technically correct, it was ultimately misleading, perhaps intentionally so. In his extended defense of the clause in *Federalist* 44, Madison notes that the use of "*expressly*" in the Articles of Confederation to restrict the powers of Congress was *not* transferred to the Constitution, primarily for fear that it would be interpreted "with so much rigor, as to disarm the government of all real authority whatever" (44:234). A similar concern led Madison to oppose the insertion of "expressly" into the Tenth Amendment, which reserved non-enumerated powers to the states and the people.

A defense of the federal government's power to regulate elections is taken up in papers 59–61. Under Article 1, section 4 of the Constitution, the states are authorized to establish the "the time, place, and manner" of electing members of Congress, with the proviso that "Congress may at any time, by law make or alter such regulations, except as to the places of choosing senators." To have left this power entirely with the states "would leave the existence of the union entirely at their mercy," for they could simply refuse to make provisions for elections (59:307). Moreover, the power to establish *uniformity* in the time of elections will ensure a more orderly process of rotation, and reduce the likelihood of an accumulation of "the same [factious] spirit in the body" that might result from a series of elections over time (61:317). At bottom, however, the reservation on the power of regulating national elections turns on a general principle: "that *every government ought to contain in itself the means of its own preservation*" (59:306). Just as each state is left a plenary power to regulate state elections, prudence dictates that the federal government must reserve a power over its own.

In *Federalist* 62 Publius expands on the anomalous method of appointing senators and the provision for equality of representation. Putting the best face on measures he had vigorously opposed in the Federal Convention, Madison claims for the former the "double advantage" of a "select appointment" of qualified persons, and a means to "secure the authority" of the states (62:320). Allowing the state governments an "agency in the formation of the federal government" also supplies a "convenient link between the two systems" (62:320). As for equal representation in the Senate, Madison betrayed his animus towards the "Great Compromise," calling the measure an "evil," albeit a "lesser" one than no compromise at all (63:320). Better to consider its "advantageous consequences" than to dwell on the "sacrifice" made by the larger states, viz., "a constitutional recognition of the portion of sovereignty remaining in the individual states, and an instrument for preserving that residuary sovereignty" (62:320).

The final pillar of the federal structure is supplied in the penultimate section of papers (Nos. 78–83), where Publius outlines and defends the judicial power of the national government. Under Article III this power would "extend to all Cases, in Law and Equity" arising under the Constitution and to "the Laws of the United States and Treaties made ... under their Authority." Federal jurisdiction would also extend to disputes involving the national government, as well as controversies between a state and a citizen of another state, between citizens from different states, and between the states themselves. The Supreme Court was given original jurisdiction over disputes among the states, and in "all Cases affecting Ambassadors, other public Ministers and Consuls." The Court's appellate jurisdiction, "in Law and in Fact," was made co-extensive with the federal judicial power, although subject to "exceptions" and "regulations" imposed by Congress. In addition to these Article III provisions, Article VI declared the Constitution, as well as federal statues and treaties, the "supreme Law of the Land."

Given the broad grant of power and the vagueness over critical details, it is little wonder that the proposed judiciary was a frequent target of Antifederalist attacks. It also left Publius at something of a disadvantage in making a case for this part of the Constitution. He was, nonetheless, able to show the necessity of a national tribunal to vindicate national law, for such a power could not be safely vested in the state courts, which would prove "a hydra in government" (80:412). As he observed in an earlier paper:

> *To avoid the confusion which would unavoidably result from the contradictory decisions of a number of independent judicatories, all nations have found it necessary to establish one tribunal paramount to the rest, possessing a general*

> *superintendence, and authorized to settle and declare in the last resort an uniform rule of civil justice (22:110).*

If the need to establish a supreme arbiter of the law was necessary in a unitary state like Great Britain, it was even more essential in a federal system of coordinate laws like the United States. Similarly, the need for impartiality in disputes involving the states and citizens of different states "speaks for itself," and necessitates federal jurisdiction over such cases (80:414).

But what of the states' jurisdiction over state law? Will it remain plenary and exclusive? Moreover, will the states exercise concurrent jurisdiction over federal law or in constitutional cases? If so will the federal courts exercise an appellate jurisdiction? In the absence of the enabling provisions that would be supplied by the Judiciary Act of 1789, Publius could not answer all of these questions definitively. He could, however, ensure that "the states will retain all *preexisting* authorities ... not ... exclusively delegated to the federal head" (82:426). Moreover, since the Constitution does not bestow *exclusive* federal jurisdiction over all cases arising under Article III, it is probable that the Framers intended for the state courts to exercise a *concurrent* power in this area. As for appeals from state courts in cases of "federal cognizance," it will be found convenient to establish "inferior" appellate courts (81:420), but there is nothing to prohibit a higher state court from adjudicating such an appeal. "All this seems to be left to the discretion of the legislature" (82:429). What is clear is that the Constitution envisions a system of *judicial federalism* in which both state and central governments possess exclusive jurisdiction in certain areas and share jurisdiction in others. Despite this division of labor, "the national and state systems are to be regarded as ONE WHOLE. The courts of the latter will ...be natural auxiliaries to the execution of the laws of the union," while appeals to the Supreme Court will "unite and assimilate the principles of national justice and the rules of national decision" (82:428).

If the provisions of the Judiciary Act tended to support Hamilton's reading of Article III, he would prove a far poorer prophet in his rejection of a bill of rights as an unnecessary and potentially dangerous accretion to a constitution of enumerated powers On the whole, however, the projection of the "compound republic" portrayed by Publius proved far more accurate than the dire predications of the critics. Indeed, the construction of federalism in the *Federalist* is particularly impressive for the same reason the creation of the Constitution was something of a "miracle."

In reviewing the achievement of the Convention, Madison compares the "science of government" to the complexities of the mind, the obscurity of language, and the promiscuity of nature. For the legislator, no less than the philosopher, the linguist, and the naturalist, the goal of attaining and communicating perfect knowledge is simply impossible, a fact which demonstrates the "necessity of moderating ... our expectations and hopes from the efforts of human sagacity" (37:182). From arranging the three branches of government to combining energy with the republican form, the Framers were like mariners on a strange sea without adequate means of navigation. To this embarrassment was "added the interfering pretensions of the larger and smaller states," which forced the Convention into some "deviations" from "theoretical propriety;" viz., the composition of the Senate (37:184). Yet "marking the proper line of partition, between the authority of the general, and that of the state governments," was perhaps the most "arduous" task of all (37:182). Here the "novelty of the undertaking" was greatest, for history offered no examples, but those confederacies "vitiated by the same erroneous principles" as the failed Articles, which "furnish[ed] no other light than that of beacons, which give warning of the course to be shunned, without pointing out that which ought to be pursued" (37:180, 181).

Madison and Hamilton have often been faulted for their performances as Publius, particularly in their treatment of federalism. It should be recalled, however, that they were projecting a system that did not yet exist beyond the four corners of the Constitution, and could hardly be expected to display a clairvoyance regarding its precise workings in practice. As Hamilton wrote near the end of the series:

> *Time only can mature and perfect so compound a system, liquidate the meaning of all the parts, and adjust them to each other in a harmonious and consistent WHOLE (82:426).*

Given the "novelty of the undertaking" (and the strain under which most of the papers were penned), what Publius said of the Framers may be aptly applied to himself: "The real wonder is, that so many difficulties should have been surmounted;" indeed, "[i]t is impossible for any man of candour to reflect on this circumstance, without partaking of the astonishment" (37:184–185).

References

Hamilton, A. et al. (2001), *The Federalist*, ed., G. W. Carey and J. McClellen (Indianapolis, IN: Liberty Fund).

Further Reading

Banning, L. (1988), The practicable sphere of a republic: James Madison, the Constitutional Convention, and the emergence of revolutionary federalism, in R. Beeman et al. (eds), 162–187.
Beeman, R. et al. (eds) (1988), *Beyond Confederation: Origins of the Constitution and American National Identity* (Chapel Hill, NC: University of North Carolina Press).
Beer, S. H. (1989), *To Make a Nation: The Rediscovery of American Federalism* (Cambridge, MA: Harvard University Press).

Benson, G. C. S. (ed.) (1962), *Essays on Federalism* (Claremont, CA: Institute for Studies in Federalism).
Carey, G. W. (1989), *The Federalist: Design for a Constitutional Republic* (Urbana, IL: University of Illinois Press).
—— (1995), James Madison and the principle of federalism, in *In Defense of the Constitution* (Indianapolis, IN: Liberty Fund), 77–121.
Diamond, M. (1962), The Federalist's view of federalism, in G. C. S. Benson (ed.), 21–64.
—— (1963), What the Framers meant by federalism, in R. A. Goldwin (ed.), 24–41.
—— (1977), The Federalist on federalism: "Neither a National nor a Federal Constitution, but a Composition of Both," *Yale Law Journal* 86, 1273–1285.
Dietz, G. (1961), *The Federalist: A Classic on Federalism and Free Government* (Baltimore, MD: Johns Hopkins Press).
Goldwin, R. A. (1963), *A Nation of States: Essays on the American Federal System* (Chicago, IL: Rand McNally).
—— and Schambra, W. A. (eds) (1987), *How Federal is the Constitution?* (Washington, DC: American Enterprise Institute).
Greene, F. R. (1994), Madison's view of federalism in *The Federalist*, *Publius* 24, 47–61.
Millican, E. (1990), *One United People: The Federalist Papers and the National Idea* (Lexington, KY: University of Kentucky Press).
Ostrom, V. (1985), The meaning of federalism in *The Federalist*: A critical examination of the Diamond thesis, *Publius* 15, 1–21.
Peterson, P. (1985), Federalism in the founding: In defense of the Diamond thesis, *Publius* 15, 23–30.
Rakove, J. H. (1996), *Original Meanings: Political and Ideas in the Making of the Constitution* (New York, NY: Vintage Books).
Riley, P. (1978), Martin Diamond's view of *The Federalist*, *Publius* 8, 77–101.
Story, H. J. (1981), *What the Anti-Federalists Were For* (Chicago, IL: University of Chicago Press).
Yarbrough, J. (1976), Federalism in the foundation and preservation of the American regime, *Publius* 6, 43–60.
—— (1985), Rethinking "*The Federalist*'s View of Federalism", *Publius* 15, 31–53.

The Antifederalists and Tocqueville on Federalism: Lessons for Today

David Lewis Schaefer

Introduction

During the 1787–88 ratification debates the so-called Antifederalists, who opposed the adoption of the American Constitution, suffered a rhetorical disadvantage owing to the Constitution's advocates having claimed the "Federalist" title for themselves – even though in the traditional usage of the term, according to which "federation" meant the same thing as "confederation," the Antifederalists more aptly merited the name (see Diamond 1992, 93–107). Indeed, even James Madison, in *Federalist* no. 39, acknowledged that the government to be established under the Constitution was only partly federal, and partly national (Hamilton et al. 1999, 210–14). But although the Antifederalists lost the debate, they made an important contribution to American constitutionalism, not only through the Bill of Rights, added in response to their demands, but also through a series of challenges that have reverberated, at varying levels of strength, throughout American political history.

No one today can reasonably doubt that it was fortunate for America, and the world, that the federal Constitution was adopted, notwithstanding the Antifederalist warnings about its dangers. Despite its largely unplanned character, our federal system enabled us, as Alexis de Tocqueville argued in *Democracy in America*, to combine the individual vigor and attachment to liberty that only small nations had previously enjoyed with the military and economic benefits for which large size was essential in the modern world (Tocqueville 2000, I.i.8, 146–9). In this manner, American federalism in its heyday proved to satisfy the legitimate concerns of the Antifederalists, while securing against the dangers of disunion and/or financial and military weakness on the international stage that the Federalists warned would ensue were the Constitution not adopted.

By the mid-twentieth century, however, the balance between federal and state authority had been transformed, in a manner that would have concerned both Tocqueville and the Antifederalists. Four causes – two of them institutional changes, the other two alterations in popular opinion – underlay this transformation. The first institutional change was the adoption following the Civil War of the Fourteenth Amendment, an essential means of establishing (in response to the Supreme Court's infamous Dred Scott decision) the primacy of national over state citizenship, and of guaranteeing the fundamental rights of all citizens against violation by the states – but one destined to have ramifications, as a result of judicial interpretation, that are unlikely to have been foreseen by its authors. The second institutional change was the Seventeenth Amendment, which by altering the mode of selecting senators from appointment by the state legislatures to direct popular election reduced the role of the states in forming the national government. Of the informal causes, the first was the debatable but popularly persuasive claim by advocates of the New Deal that modern economic conditions dictated a vast expansion of the scope of the national government beyond what the Constitutional text envisioned. The remaining cause was the legacy of racial discrimination in the South, which tarred all appeals to federalism or "states' rights" by association with racial bigotry, necessitating a national solution through the Supreme Court's antisegregation decisions beginning with *Brown v. Board of Education* (1955) along with the 1964 Civil Rights Act and the 1965 Voting Rights Act.

The transformation of American law and life over the past half-century make a return of government-sanctioned racial bigotry unlikely. Nonetheless, despite a growing literature that casts doubt about the success of New Deal and Great Society economic programs and highlights the economic and political benefits of "competitive federalism," it is improbable that the domain of federal authority will be cut back to anything approaching its pre-New Deal limits. Still, I shall suggest, some contemporary political and Constitutional difficulties invite a reconsideration of certain Antifederalist concerns.

In this chapter I first summarize the Antifederalist arguments that have had the most lasting significance. Then I discuss Tocqueville's account of how the American Constitution as of 1830 operated in such a manner as seemingly to answer the concerns of the Antifederalists as well as their Federalist opponents – even though the balance, as he acknowledged, was inherently unstable.[1] Finally, I discuss the ways in which changes in the American system of government during the twentieth century vindicated some of the Antifederalists' concerns, albeit largely in an unforeseen way.

---

1 For further discussion of Tocqueville and American federalism, see Chapter 13 in this volume.

The Antifederalist Critique of the Constitution

Among the Antifederalist charges against the Constitution, four have the greatest resonance today:

> 1.
> The Federal government will be too remote from the people to command their voluntary allegiance and law-abidingness, thus requiring the government to depend for enforcement of its laws on a standing army, with the resultant loss of liberty (see Storing (1981): "Federal Farmer," 2.8.18, 23 and "Brutus," 2.9.50).

As things turned out, of course, with the exception of the Civil War, there have been no major occasions on which the federal government had to use military force to enforce the laws. As the *Federalist* assured Americans, the federal government would ordinarily rely on the apparatus of the state governments for that purpose. And the national government could supplant the states as the primary object of citizens' attachment over time, the *Federalist* observed, only if it distinguished itself by being better administered (a result of its superior institutional construction). If that were the case, who could reasonably object?[2]

Not until after the Civil War could it be said that most Americans identified more closely with the nation than with their respective states, ultimately fulfilling the *Federalist*'s prophecy. But we can see an echo of the Antifederalists' fears in the common complaint about the size (and hence, inevitably, the sometime heavy-handedness) of the bureaucracy that must be used to enforce the enormous body of federal legislation today, as well as in the phenomenon of unfunded mandates imposed on state and local governments by Congress.

> 2.
> Because of the superior accomplishments necessary to win election to the relatively large House districts (as well as the Senate), in comparison with districts in the state legislatures, Congress would come to be dominated by a "natural aristocracy" composed of men of superior talent, whose ambition and love of glory would lead them to pursue expensive or risky schemes of national aggrandizement adverse to the interests of ordinary citizens (see Storing, 1981: "Federal Farmer," 2.8.25 and Melancton Smith, 6.12.16–17).

In support of this forecast, Antifederalists could note that one of Madison's arguments in *Federalist* no. 10 concerning the superiority of large over small

---

2   Having observed that only a superior administration of the federal government could overcome the people's bias in favor of "their local governments" (Hamilton et al. 1999, no. 17, 87), Publius proceeds ten essays later to explain why such a development is likely (no. 27, 142–3).

republics was precisely that a representative body selected from a larger number of citizens was likely to attract more capable representatives. And in defending the relatively long term of office granted to the president, along with his eligibility for re-election, Hamilton spoke of the love of fame as "the ruling passion of the noblest minds" (Hamilton et al. 1999, no. 72, 405). Even Jefferson and John Adams, longtime adversaries during the core of their political careers, agreed that a system which elevated the natural *aristoi* to positions of political power while compelling them to use that power for the public good was practically the definition of good government (Jefferson, letter to Adams, October 28, 1813, in Koch and Peden 1944, 633). Since the natural (as distinguished from conventional) aristocrats are by definition those of superior talent, who could deny the desirability of a system in which such individuals filled the country's offices to the greatest extent, while the broadly democratic Constitution (including such devices as separation of powers and checks and balances) ensured that they could use their authority only in ways that benefited the public?

Nonetheless, the Antifederalists may have had a point. Contrary to Jefferson, one cannot assume that the interests of the talented (and ambitious) few always harmonize with those of the people as a whole.[3] May not the aspirations of the few for personal and hence national greatness conflict with the desire of ordinary folk for a tranquil existence under a moderate and frugal government? As the Antifederalist "Brutus" warned, "the passion for pomp, power and greatness works as powerfully in the heart of many of our better sort, as it ever did in any country under heaven" (Storing 1981, 2.9.119).

Surveying most of America's history, one could hardly contend that the House of Representatives has been dominated by a natural aristocracy in any meaningful sense: in this respect both the Antifederalists and the Federalists underestimated the degree to which an increasingly democratic or populistic spirit would militate against any habit of electoral deference towards "the great." And although the events of the past century have compelled the United States to undertake an active role in world affairs, this very fact would appear to vindicate the Federalists' foresight in espousing a Constitution that would facilitate the long-term growth in the country's power. Nonetheless, as I shall argue further on, there is one important way in which this Antifederalist warning proved prescient, although not in the way the Antifederalists typically anticipated.

3.
A related Antifederalist fear is that the Constitution would undermine the sort of character necessary among a free people, or what the Federal Farmer calls "strong & manly habits," by accustoming them to subservience to a powerful and distant national government (Storing, 1981, 2.8.59).

---

[3] Jefferson's own warning of the need to uncover and "defeat" ambition (*Notes on Virginia*, Query XIV, in Koch and Peden 1944, 265) stands in unacknowledged tension with his concern to advance members of the natural *aristoi* to positions of power.

This is a concern I shall address in discussing Tocqueville's argument.

4.
The final Antifederalist concern meriting mention here is the one expressed by Brutus during the New York ratification campaign: that the Federal judiciary would claim the right to judge the constitutionality of both state and Federal legislation, and would use that power to expand Federal authority at the expense of the state governments. Brutus agrees with Hamilton (whose Federalist no. 78 was composed partly as a reply to him) that Federal courts will assert the power of what later came to be called "judicial review," even though this power is nowhere specified in the Constitution.[4] The courts will claim this authority over Congress itself, Brutus explains, because the "legislature must be controlled by the Constitution, not the Constitution by them." And he foresees that in exercising judicial review, the courts will interpret the Constitution by reference not only to its letter, but to what they conceive as "its reason and spirit." But the Federal courts will not be unbiased arbiters. Rather, as agencies of the Federal government, the courts will silently and imperceptibly effect the "entire subversion of the state governments." And Federal judges will be able to employ their historically unprecedented power as final interpreters of the Constitution to "mold the government into almost any shape they please" (Storing 1981, 2.9.137–44; 2.9.186–8).

Brutus' argument contains one major difficulty: as a remedy for judicial enlargement of the federal government's powers, he proposed that judicial interpretations of the Constitution be overridable by "those whom the people chuse at stated periods," just as the British Parliament traditionally held an interpretative authority superior to that of the judiciary (Storing 1981, 2.9.187, 196). But if Brutus wishes to assign this power to Congress, yet regards the chief danger of judicial abuse to be the unjustified expansion of federal power, what interest would Congress have in curbing such abuses?

Tocqueville

Although Tocqueville praised the American federal system, his account of it in Volume I of *Democracy in America*, in conjunction with his laudatory account of administrative decentralization, shows how that system originally operated in a way that addressed some of the chief Antifederalist concerns.[5] What unites Tocqueville's praise of administrative decentralization with Antifederalist thought

---

4   On the relation between Hamilton's and Brutus' treatments of the judiciary, see A. Diamond (1976), 269–79; Slonim (2006).
5   On the relation of decentralized administration to federalism for Tocqueville, see M. Diamond (1992), 144–66.

is his wish to preserve the habits of active self-government among the populace, against the ambitions of national "opinion leaders" and bureaucrats to subordinate them to centralized guidance from above.[6]

Significantly, Tocqueville titles his discussion of township government "Necessity of Studying What Takes Place in the States Before Speaking of the Government of the Union." This necessity arises, he explains, not only because the states preceded the federal government in their establishment, but more importantly because in their daily operation (at the time he was writing), "the federal government ... is only an exception; the government of the states is the common rule" (Tocqueville 2000, I.i.5, 56).

Tocqueville's account of the township (commune) emphasizes both its naturalness and its fragility. Even though the township is the sole form of political association that forms spontaneously wherever human beings gather, Tocqueville maintains, the difficulty of preserving its autonomy increases "as nations become enlightened," because highly civilized peoples find it difficult to tolerate the inefficiencies that result when local citizens, lacking special talents or expertise, administer their own affairs. Consequently, Tocqueville observes, no (Continental) European state allows municipal freedom (57).

Tocqueville acknowledges that a system of local self-government is less efficient than one that relies on a nationally centralized bureaucracy operating on the basis of rules and expertise (87). But the cost in administrative efficiency that derives from local autonomy is outweighed by its political benefits. Taking as his model the New England townships, Tocqueville observes that local institutions are a school of political freedom, habituating citizens to its "peaceful employment" (57). The dispersion of power among a number of local offices also interests more people in public affairs and engenders a "paternal pride" towards free institutions (64–5). Finally, Tocqueville argues, despite the inefficiency of local government in America, the American system, by causing people to identify with their government rather than regarding it as an alien force, enlists so much popular energy on behalf of the public good that "in the long term the general result of all the individual undertakings far exceeds what the government could do" (90–1).[7]

Tocqueville links his praise of Americans' local self-government with his account of the federal system by repeating, in discussing the latter, that "the taste for and usage of republican government are born in the townships" as well as within the state governments themselves. And he adds that "this same republican spirit, these

---

6   See, on Tocqueville's intention, Ceaser 1990, ch. 7.
7   Tocqueville's praise of the opportunity that decentralized administration affords citizens to participate in their own governance should be distinguished from recent, utopian proposals for "deliberative democracy" that entail involving the people in plebiscitary local meetings concerning national affairs (e.g., Ackerman and Fishkin 2004). Decentralized administration entails involving citizens in the decision of matters that are within their competence and that have a more or less direct connection to their own interests, such as the location of a road (II.ii.4, 487) or the curriculum of the local schools – not complex issues of national policy.

mores and habits of a free people," are in turn transferred to the Union as a whole. People's attachment to the Union is "only a summation of [the] provincial patriotism" that attaches every citizen to the "little republic" in which he resides (I.i.8, 153).[8]

Tocqueville emphasizes the novelty of the American federal system by comparison to all previous "federations" (i.e., leagues or alliances) in that the Constitution enables the federal government to address itself to the citizens themselves, rather than rely on the member states to enforce its edicts – thus averting the twin dangers of anarchy and of domination by the strongest members to which prior federations fell victim (I.i.8, 147–8, 157). But he shows how the limitation of federal authority to a few, albeit important, objects effectively answers the Antifederalists' fears by preventing "the love of glory" among individuals, and hence the sort of ambition that has destroyed previous republics, from growing to the point of threatening liberty (150–1). The novel form of American federalism, in Tocqueville's account, enables us to have our cake and eat it: combining the freedom that can be found only in small nations with the military and economic strength of large ones.

Tocqueville articulates two dangers to the preservation of a federal system like the American one, only one of which is likely to pose a threat to the United States itself. The real threat is the danger of disunion arising from the violent collision of federal law with a particular state's "interests and prejudices." Such a danger arises because even though America's founders supplied the Federal government with "money and soldiers," the individual states retained the people's "love and prejudices" (I.i.8, 157) (Tocqueville elsewhere cites the South Carolina report proclaiming the doctrine of nullification [I.ii.10, 367].) The other danger, from which America's geographic isolation fortunately preserves her, is the threat of foreign war, since Tocqueville doubts that a confederated people could successfully combat an equally powerful but more centralized nation (I.i.8, 161).

One other aspect of Tocqueville's argument merits comparison with the Antifederalist position. Like Brutus, Tocqueville attests to the enormous power of American judges, above all the "immense political power" of judicial review (I.i.6, 95). Indeed, he describes the assignment to the Supreme Court of final authority to interpret the Constitution and thereby delineate the boundaries between federal and state authority as "the most dangerous blow" to state sovereignty (I.i.8, 134). But he identifies several causes that reduce its danger. First, the power of judicial review arises only in connection with particular disputes involving individual citizens, rather than entailing the capacity "to attack laws in a theoretical and general manner." Additionally, the fact that challenges to the laws must arise out of the concern of "particular interests" affected by them saves the maintenance of the laws from direct partisan attack (I.i.6, 96–7). Finally, with respect to the prospect that most concerned Brutus, the likelihood that judges would use their power of constitutional interpretation to expand federal authority at the expense of the states, Tocqueville observes that judges' awareness that the people are more attached to the state governments deters such abuse, making judges more likely to

---

8   Cf. Burke's account of the attachment to "the little platoon we belong to in society" as the root of patriotism and philanthropy (Burke 1894, III, 292).

forsake a legitimate claim to jurisdiction than assert an improper one (Tocqueville I.i.8, 134–5).

Tocqueville's sanguineness regarding judicial restraint rests further on his account of the spirit of the American legal profession. Lawyers as a class, he remarks, have an aristocratic outlook, arising from their possession of specialized knowledge that assures them of a privileged social rank. In addition, deriving from their work "habits of order, a certain taste for forms," lawyers are "strongly opposed to the revolutionary spirit and unreflective passions of democracy," and "secretly scorn" democratic government itself (I.ii.8, 252). This antidemocratic outlook is moderated, however, by the lawyers' class interest: in the absence of a monarch or hereditary aristocracy, lawyers constitute "the only enlightened and skilled" group that the people can choose for important offices. In addition, Anglo-American common-law jurisprudence instills an attachment to precedent (254–5). Thus, whereas French lawyers' exclusion from political office under the *ancien régime* encouraged them to lead the 1789 Revolution, in America lawyers' situation as the leading political class makes innovation, let alone revolution, contrary to their interest. Hence their inherent conservatism, far from threatening American democracy, enables them to serve as the "lone counterweight" to democratic excesses, opposing a "superstitious respect for what is old" to the people's "love of novelty," moderating the people's "immense designs," and preserving a "taste for forms" in the face of popular "scorn" for them (256). One of the forms that Tocquevillean lawyers would seek to preserve, we surmise, is the federal system itself.

From Tocqueville to the New Deal

Tocqueville's observations regarding administrative decentralization, the federal system, and the role of judges and lawyers in the United States indicate that 40 years after the Constitution's ratification, the fears of the Antifederalists appeared to have been misguided. While the proper line between federal and state authority continued to be a matter of legal as well as political disputation, the federal system as a whole operated largely as the *Federalist* assured Americans it would, with matters of essentially state and local significance largely being left to the discretion of state and local governments. Indeed, Tocqueville maintained that Americans' "great fear" of political centralization was misdirected: on the contrary, the federal government was becoming "visibly weaker" (II.ii.10, 368–9). Anticipating one of the concerns that Lincoln was to express in his 1838 Lyceum Address, he observed that despite the commercial ties and growing assimilation of manners that tended to unite the American people (as Publius had forecast: Hamilton et al. 1999, no. 53, 302), the very security and prosperity that Americans now enjoyed weakened the "energy and patriotism" that had attached them to the union (Tocqueville 369–71). Hence the bitter controversies over Congress's appropriation of funds from the sale of western land and over the national bank, and the nullification crisis, the latter resolved only by the action of a president (Andrew Jackson) who otherwise flattered the people's "decentralizing passions" (372–7). The decentralization that threatened the Union was what Tocqueville termed "political" as distinguished from "administrative" decentralization, that is, a disunity regarding the most fundamental national issues, rather than inherently local ones (I.i.5, 83; on the distinction see Diamond 1992, 153–7). As the nullification controversy indicated, it was Southerners, led by "ardent and irascible men" who saw their power in the federal government steadily weakening, who threatened to destroy the Union, even though they had the most to lose from such destruction, which would leave them facing a potential race war (II.ii.10, 366–7).

The Civil War vindicated Tocqueville's judgment that a split in the Union was a more immediate threat than an excessive centralization of authority in the national government. In the aftermath of that terrible event, Americans gradually acquired the sense of national loyalty that Tocqueville had judged to be excessively weak. Ironically, however, as the danger to the American union that Tocqueville articulated at the conclusion of Volume I of *Democracy* receded, the ground was prepared for the alternative threat to democracy as such (but from which America appeared immune in Tocqueville's time) that he described in the last part of Volume II. This other, deeper problem was the growth of a centralized, "tutelary" despotism, in which even though the forms of democratic election might remain, the people lost the opportunity for genuine self-government, having their material needs filled by an omnipresent bureaucracy that spared them the need and hence the opportunity to develop their own faculties. It would be kinder and gentler than the oppressive despotism that some Antifederalists feared. But it would be no less stifling of human faculties and of the spirit of manly freedom and self-assertion.

The theoretical ground for this transformation was prepared by the Progressive movement, which disparaged the Constitutional forms of federalism as well as separation of powers as an improper restraint on the people's "will" – even as it aimed to transfer much of the business of government to "experts" insulated from direct popular control.[9] Exemplary of Progressive thought were the pre-presidential writings of Woodrow Wilson, including not only his call for the replacement of the separation-of-powers system by unitary cabinet government (or, later, through informal presidential leadership), but also his influential essay on "The Study of Administration," which argued for a separation between "politics" and "administration" such that the people would be prevented from "meddling" with the day-to-day operation of an expert, centralized bureaucracy, being limited to conveying their wishes at elections to the administrators' political superiors. Even though Wilson, a Southerner by birth, expressed some deference to the doctrine of states' rights, the logic of his position tended no less towards the abolition of federalism than towards the extension of the federal bureaucracy. That logic bore fruit in the administration of Franklin Roosevelt, who represented the New Deal as an effectuation of the policies that Wilson would have instituted as

---

9 On the antidemocratic tendency of many of the reforms advocated by the Progressives, see West 2005, 19–20.

president had his attention not been diverted by the First World War (Roosevelt 1932, 749–50). Not only did Roosevelt's program entail an enormous expansion of the federal government's scope; his counselors aspired to transfer much of the authority for the operation of government from the domain of "politics" to that of expert "administration."[10] After the Supreme Court abandoned its initial resistance to Roosevelt's disregard of Constitutional limitations on federal authority, the neardeath of federalism as a legal doctrine was signified by the Court's decision in Wickard v. Filburn (1942), upholding the government's power to punish a farmer for growing crops to feed his own animals, on the ground that his failure to purchase the feed instead had adverse effects on the economy which Congress was free to prevent under its authority to regulate interstate commerce.

The Federal System Today – Or, What Remains of It

I shall not review the process by which most presidential administrations since Roosevelt's have continued expanding the range of federal domestic programs without regard to Constitutional limitations – George W. Bush's most noteworthy contribution to that record having been the "No Child Left Behind Act," which considerably enhances the national role in supervising public schools. The serious case to be made against the expansion of federal authority is not one based on "states' rights," per se. As the Federalists hoped, in the long run (following the Civil War), as Americans' habits and mores became more homogeneous, their primary attachments indeed shifted from state governments to the national one. Nor can it be said that the Constitution specifies a particular allocation of power between federal and state authority: as Purcell (2007) demonstrates, the document itself invites dispute over that division, and hence has generated shifting currents of opinion and policy from the outset. Nonetheless, when Congress extends its authority to such essentially local concerns as public schools, a field for which it would be extremely difficult to identify any mandate among the powers enumerated in Article I, section 8, one may reasonably fear a slackening of the sense of citizen efficacy portrayed by Tocqueville, or of the proud habits of independence that Brutus was concerned to preserve.

Certainly, this expansion of federal authority has occurred with the consent of the American people as a whole. But the dynamic of that expansion, and its detrimental effect on the operation of self-government at the national level have been aptly described by political scientist Morris Fiorina (1989). The fact that the expansion of Congressional authority guarantees a heightened role for individual Congressmen as purveyors of "pork" to their respective districts, and also as interveners on their constituents' behalf with the bureaucracy that grows to administer such programs, has considerably heightened Congressmen's job security, incidentally giving them *carte blanche* to vote their particular policy preferences on matters that do not

---

10 See, on the Wilsonian roots of the New Deal approach to administration, Brand 2007.

directly affect their own districts. More fundamentally, the popular expectation that the federal government should provide assistance to relieve individuals, including the non-poor, of the need to pay for goods like health insurance, along with the demand for uniform national standards in areas like education, is reminiscent of the tutelary "nanny state" against which Tocqueville warned.[11]

It may be, as Rossum (2001, 233–4) has argued, that the expansion of Congress's authority at the expense of the states was inevitable once the institutional bulwark that the Founders created to support state interests, the selection of senators by state legislatures, was eliminated by the Seventeenth Amendment.[12] Given the Founders' distrust of what the *Federalist* dismisses as "parchment barriers" – that is, mere verbal prohibitions on violations of the Constitutional limits on government by its member institutions – it is unlikely that they would have expected a mere tradition of Constitutional reverence to prevent Americans from demanding an ever-greater range of services from Congress, let alone prevent Congressmen and presidents from complying with that demand. Nor can they have expected the courts, the least accountable branch of the federal government, to have held the line on federal expansion indefinitely, as the pre-1937 Supreme Court attempted to do.

It is striking, in this regard, in view of Brutus' concern about federal judicial power, that the most vehement proponents of restoration of Constitutional limits on Congress's powers in the name of federalism today hope for such a restoration to be brought about by the courts. For instance, Michael Greve, who seeks to restore "real federalism" on the ground that it encourages economically beneficial competition among state governments, holds that "nobody but the courts" can prevent the federal government "from trumping state competition with monopolistic schemes," and that "judicial enforcement" of the Constitution's enumeration of the federal government's powers is a "touchstone" of federalism.[13]

To rely on judicial activism to restore what Barnett (2004) calls the "lost Constitution," however, is likely to be a cure worse than the disease. This is so because the deepest value of America's federal system, and the partial local autonomy it serves to protect, lies in the area of what Tocqueville called *moeurs* (morals and mores). The primary threat to that aspect of self-government today comes from a direction not foreseen by Tocqueville or the Antifederalists: the use made by an activist judiciary since the late 1950s of the Fourteenth Amendment, in conjunction with the Bill of Rights that the Antifederalists had advocated, to undermine the capacity of elected state and local governments to maintain the

---

11 Of course nothing in the federal Constitution would have prevented state and local governments from instituting programs designed to cover expenses such as health insurance. But the need of state governments, unlike the federal government, to balance their budgets would tend to constrain these expenses, by making more manifest the connection between government spending and the taxes necessary to finance it.

12 The *Federalist* (1999, no. 59, 332) had represented state appointment of senators as the "absolute safeguard" of their interests.

13 Greve 1999, 14; see also 16 regarding the need of "an assertive role for the Court" in preserving federalism's "constitutional boundaries."

moral foundations of political freedom. The vehicle for that transformation was the doctrine that the amendment "incorporates" the guarantees contained in the Bill of Rights so as to apply them against the states.

Over the past 60 years the application of this principle, in conjunction with the Supreme Court's reading a quasi-Nietzschean doctrine of "self-actualization" into the Constitution, has involved federal judges in such enterprises as eliminating most restrictions on abortion, prohibiting religious displays on town commons or prayers at school graduations, severely limiting the capacity of local communities to ban parades by hate groups like the Nazis or the dissemination of pornography, and in other respects making themselves the overseers of daily life in ways that neither the framers of the Constitution nor the authors of the Fourteenth Amendment dreamed of.[14] It is in this sense that the Antifederalists' fears of irresponsible government by an "aristocratic" body have been fulfilled. Whereas the Anglo-American lawyers of whom Tocqueville wrote were distinguished by their innate conservatism and love of "forms," so that their aristocratic outlook actually served the cause of constitutional government, over time the grandiose ambitions and distance from, or opposition to, the concerns of ordinary citizens that the Antifederalists had feared would characterize Congress came instead to characterize federal judges and the law professors who educate them.[15]

In one of the great ironies of American constitutional history, the Bill of Rights that the Antifederalists effectively made a condition of the Constitution's ratification became the vehicle by which the selfsame judicial supremacy feared by Brutus was ultimately achieved.[16] The explanation of this paradox is that the Antifederalists did not advocate a Bill of Rights as a set of judicially enforceable limitations on state or federal governments, but rather conceived it as an educational device for the people themselves, to remind them of their rights and serve as a benchmark for

---

14 I shall not enter here into the debate over whether or how far the framers of the Fourteenth Amendment understood themselves to be incorporating the Bill of Rights guarantees against the states. While there is considerable evidence that they did understand such fundamental rights as freedom of speech and of religion as among the "privileges and immunities of citizens of the United States" that the Amendment protected, the most learned recent advocates of the incorporation thesis, such as Michael Kent Curtis and Michael Zuckert, do not maintain that its authors intended of the sorts of strained interpretations of those rights as those listed in the text. See Curtis 1986; Zuckert 1996.

15 See, on the contrast between the notion of a "living Constitution" promoted by Woodrow Wilson and Tocqueville's view of the American judiciary, Carrese 2005, 154–5. On the problematic consequences for constitutional liberty of the erosion of public morality as a consequence of judicial doctrines mandating governmental "neutrality," see Clor 1996.

16 Gary McDowell notes one prerequisite for the expansion of judicial authority in this manner that was foreseen and warned against by the Antifederalists "Federal Farmer" and "Brutus": the ambiguity of the extension of federal jurisdiction to "equity," which courts in the mid-twentieth century began to reinterpret to authorize remedies for the grievances of entire social classes, rather than only of individuals (McDowell 1982, 102–9; Storing 1981, 2.8.43, 2.9.137–8).

judging federal policies (Storing 1981: "Federal Farmer," 2.8.19, 70, 196; "Impartial Examiner," 5.14.10; I, 21, 70).[17]

Unfortunately, in a manner that substantiates the fears of Antifederalist writers as well as Jefferson and Tocqueville, over time the American people appear to have become far less concerned with usurpations of their right to self-government – opening the way for the courts, in the name of a "living" Constitution, to rewrite the rules governing their common life.[18] In effect, the courts over the past half-century have been the agency for institutionalizing the preferences of cosmopolitan "elites" at the expense of the traditional, often religiously based, mores which Tocqueville (2000, Introduction, 11; I.ii.9, 278–82, 293–5) represented as a condition of freedom. While particular constituencies have arisen in protest against judicial usurpations in particular areas – e.g., abortion – there is little evidence of widespread popular concern over the problem of judicial usurpation as such, in the name of constitutional government.

Over the past three decades the Supreme Court has intermittently engaged in a halfhearted battle to maintain vestiges of a federal system by rejecting some of the most extreme extensions of Congressional power into local affairs or over state governments themselves. Key decisions in that battle included National League of Cities v. Usery (1976) (invalidating the application of federal wage-and-hours regulations to state employees), United States v. Lopez (1995) (denying the Constitutionality of the "Gun-Free Schools Act"), and United States v. Morrison (2000) (striking down the federal civil remedy Congress authorized for "gender-motivated" violence).[19] But as the typically narrow subject-matter of these cases indicates, the courts are not going to restore the sweeping restriction on Congress's powers to those enumerated in the Constitution that would call into question such popular programs as Social Security, Medicare, or federal aid for housing and education. Any battles over the further expansion of federal authority into areas

---

17 One exception among advocates of a bill of rights is Jefferson, who favored "the legal check which it puts into the hands of the judiciary": Letter to James Madison, March 15, 1789, in Koch and Peden 1944, 462. Another precedent suggesting the power that a bill of rights would give the courts (albeit not, in this instance, ruling a legislative act unconstitutional) was the 1783 case of Quock Walker, in which Massachusetts' Supreme Judicial Court ruled that slavery was unconstitutional, based on the declaration in the newly adopted Massachusetts constitution that all men are born free and equal. But I have found no instance in Herbert Storing's (1981) comprehensive collection of Antifederalist writings of any Antifederalist who advocated a bill of rights for the purpose of judicial enforcement. (In fact, "Brutus" was apparently the only Antifederalist to foresee that federal courts would claim final authority to interpret the Constitution, a practice for which there was hardly any precedent among state courts; see Crosskey 1953, ch. 27.)
18 See Jefferson, *Notes on Virginia*, Query XVII, in Koch and Peden 1944, 277, anticipating that Americans will allow their rights to be disregarded once they become preoccupied with private economic gain.
19 For a summary and criticism of the Courts' efforts in this regard, see Rossum 2001, chs. 1 and 7; and for a more sympathetic but pessimistic overview, Rivkin and Casey 1996.

like primary and secondary education will have to be fought in the political rather than the judicial arena.

Numerous economists as well as political theorists have made a persuasive case for the benefits of a system of competitive federalism, in which the states, if left with considerable discretion over public expenditures, taxation, and social policy, can increase the choices available to citizens, and try out experiments such as welfare reform, thus enhancing both individual freedom and public policy.[20] Their argument furnishes additional ground for campaigning against further federal pre-emption in these areas. But when it comes to the judiciary, friends of federalism would accomplish more where it really matters, and have greater prospects for success (because they have potential popular majorities on their side) by battling against, rather than for, an activist judiciary. To ask the courts to step forward more actively to draw the limits of Congressional authority is inevitably to encourage judicial intervention in other areas where far more damage can be done, and has been done, to the moral foundations of self-government. Anyone who shares the concerns expressed by the Antifederalists and Tocqueville regarding political liberty and its preconditions should be far more concerned, today, with the transformation of federal jurisprudence into a vehicle for the establishment of moral libertarianism than with the expansion of Congressional power into domains formerly deemed local.

References

Ackerman, B. and J. Fishkin (2004), *Deliberation Day* (New Haven: Yale University Press).

Barnett, R. (2004), *Restoring the Lost Constitution: The Presumption of Liberty* (Princeton: Princeton University Press).

Brand, D. (2007), Progressivism, the Brownlow Commission and the rise of the administrative state, in R.J. Pestritto and T. West (eds), 137–66.

Burke, E. (1894), *Reflections on the Revolution in France*, in *Works* (12 vols.) (Boston: Little, Brown), vol. III.

Carrese, P. (2005), Montesquieu, the Founders, and Woodrow Wilson, in J. Marini and K. Masugi (eds), 133–62.

Ceaser, J. (1990), *Liberal Democracy and Political Science* (Baltimore: Johns Hopkins University Press).

Clor, H. (1996), *Public Morality and Liberal Society* (Notre Dame, ID: University of Notre Dame Press).

Crosskey, W. (1953), *Politics and the Constitution in the History of the United States* (2 vols., Chicago: University of Chicago Press).

Curtis, M. (1986), *No State Shall Abridge: The Fourteenth Amendment and the Bill of Rights* (Durham, NC: Duke University Press.)

---

20 See the references in Greve 1999, ch. 1; also chs. 2, 9.

Diamond, A. (1976), The Anti-federalist "Brutus," *Political Science Reviewer* 6, 249–82.

Diamond, M. (1992), *As Far as Republican Principles Will Permit*, ed. W. A. Schambra (Washington: AEI Press).

Fiorina, M. (1989), *Congress: Keystone of the Washington Establishment*, second ed. (New Haven: Yale University Press).

Greve, M. (1999), *Real Federalism* (Washington: AEI Press).

Hamilton, A., J. Madison, and J. Jay (1999), *The Federalist Papers*. Ed. C. Rossiter, Introduction and Notes by C. Kesler (New York: New American Library).

Katz, E. and G. A. Tarr (eds) (1996), *Federalism and Rights* (Lanham, MD: Rowman and Littlefield).

Koch, A. and W. Peden (eds) (1944), *The Life and Selected Writings of Thomas Jefferson* (New York: Modern Library).

Marini, J. and K. Masugi (eds) (2005), *The Progressive Revolution in Politics and Political Science* (Lanham, MD: Rowman and Littlefield).

McDowell, G. (1982), Were the Anti-Federalists right? Judicial activism and the problem of consolidated government, *Publius*, 12:3 (Summer), 99–108.

Pestritto, R. J. and T. West (eds) (2007), *Modern America and the Legacy of the Founding* (Lanham, MD: Lexington Books).

Purcell, E. (2007), *Originalism, Federalism, and the American Constitutional Enterprise* (New Haven: Yale University Press).

Rivkin, D. and L. Casey (1996), "Federalism (Cont'd)," *Commentary*, 102:6 (December), 47–50.

Roosevelt, F. (1932), Commonwealth Club address, in *Public Papers and Addresses*, 12 vols., (New York: Random House, 1938–50), I, 742–56.

Rossum, R. (2001), *Federalism, the Supreme Court, and the Seventeenth Amendment: The Irony of Constitutional Democracy* (Lanham, MD: Lexington Books).

Slonim, S. (2006), Federalist #78 and Brutus' neglected thesis on judicial supremacy, *Constitutional Commentary* 23:1 (Spring), 7–31.

Storing, H. (ed.) (1981), *The Complete Anti-Federalist* (Chicago: University of Chicago Press).

Tocqueville, A. de (2000), *Democracy in America*, H. C. Mansfield and D. Winthrop trans. (Chicago: University of Chicago Press).

West, T. (2005), Progressivism and the transformation of American government, in J. Marini and K. Masugi (eds), 13–32.

Zuckert, M. (1996), Toward a corrective federalism: The United States Constitution, federalism, and rights, in E. Katz and G. A. Tarr (eds), 75–100.

Further Reading

Diamond, A. S. (1976), The Anti-Federalist "Brutus," *The Political Science Reviewer* 6, 249–82.

Diamond, M. (1992), *As Far as Republican Principles Will Permit* (Washington: AEI Press), chs. 6–10.

Dry, M. (1987), Anti-Federalism in *The Federalist*: A founding dialogue on the Constitution, republican government, and federalism, in Charles Kesler (ed.), *Saving the Revolution: The Federalist Papers and the American Founding* (New York: Free Press), 40–60.

Koritansky, J. (1975), Decentralization and civic virtue in Tocqueville's "New Science of Politics," *Publius* 5:3 (Summer), 63–81.

Manent, P. (1996), *Tocqueville and the Nature of Democracy*, John Waggoner trans. (Lanham, MD: Rowman and Littlefield).

Marini, J. (1991), Centralized administration and the "new despotism," in K. Masugi (ed.), *Interpreting Tocqueville's "Democracy in America"* (Savage, MD: Rowman and Littlefield), 255–86.

McDowell, G. (1982), Were the Anti-Federalists right? Judicial activism and the problem of consolidated government, *Publius* 12:3 (Summer), 99–108.

Storing, H. J. (1981), *What the Anti-Federalists Were For* (Chicago: University of Chicago Press).

—— (1985), *The Anti-Federalist* (one-volume abridgment of Storing, ed., *The Complete Antifederalist* compiled by M. Dry) (Chicago: University of Chicago Press).

Tocqueville, A. de (2000), *Democracy in America*, Harvey Mansfield and Delba Winthrop trans. (Chicago: University of Chicago Press).

Zetterbaum, M. (1967), *Tocqueville and the Problem of Democracy* (Stanford, CA: Stanford University Press).

Thomas Jefferson's Enlightenment Idea of Federalism

Peter McNamara

It is not surprising that federalism loomed large in the mind of Thomas Jefferson. From the beginning Jefferson was accustomed to multiple identities and citizenships. The tensions between part and whole and between center and periphery pervaded his life. Born at the edge of an empire that embodied for many, Jefferson included, the Enlightenment's promises of liberty and progress and himself receiving a classical and cosmopolitan education, Jefferson nevertheless had a deep affection for his native Virginia, a high opinion of its inhabitants, and an unbounded confidence in their future prospects. The mature Jefferson would be a Virginian, an American, a distinguished member of the Republic of Letters, and a zealous advocate for mankind. Jefferson's Enlightenment idea of federalism was the critical element in his attempt to come to terms with these multiple allegiances. His successes and his failures in this attempt contain significant lessons for today.

Jefferson is notable as both a theorist and as a practitioner of federalism. Although his thinking about federalism was expounded in the course of a series of sharp political conflicts, it was not reactive or opportunistic. The striking thing is the remarkable consistency that it displays. Furthermore, few thinkers have had Jefferson's opportunity to put their theories into practice. Jefferson believed his own time to be distinguished "for it's experiments in government on a larger scale than has yet taken place" (TJ to D'Ivernois, Feb. 6, 1795; Peterson 1984, 1024). Throughout his political career Jefferson was a consistent advocate for his own particular understanding of federalism. Most importantly, as president, Jefferson put his idea of federalism into practice on the grandest scale. The purchase of Louisiana, with its doubling of the size of the country, was just the most conspicuous of Jefferson's federalism related initiatives.

This chapter considers first Jefferson's theory of federalism, before turning to Jefferson's practice. It concludes with a discussion of the legacy and any possible contemporary relevance of Jeffersonian federalism.

Jefferson's "Federative Principle"

Responding to critics of the Louisiana Purchase, Jefferson defiantly asked "[W]ho can limit the extent to which the federative principle may operate effectively?" (Second Inaugural Address, March 4, 1805; Peterson 1984, 519). Jefferson held that, contrary to the weight of received opinion, an extensive territory is not a disadvantage for republics but instead is a decisive advantage. Montesquieu's *Spirit of the Laws* had given authoritative voice to the opinion that republics must be small.[1] Large republics are so riven by division and conflict that they eventually give rise to monarchical government. But, and here was the dilemma for republicans like Jefferson, small republics are vulnerable to attack from larger powers. Montesquieu did raise, albeit briefly and vaguely, the possibility of a confederation of republics combining the advantages of a monarchy and a republic. Jefferson embraced the idea of a confederation of republics, but he did so in a way that, he at least believed, involved a refutation of Montesquieu's "brilliant fallacies." Jefferson speculated that "it will be found, that to obtain a just republic (and it is to secure our just rights that we resort to government at all) it must be so extensive as that local egoisms may never reach it's greater part; that on every particular question, a majority may be found in it's councils free from particular interests, and giving, therefore, an uniform prevalence to the principles of justice. The smaller the societies, the more violent & more convulsive their schisms" (TJ to D'Ivernois, Feb. 6, 1795; Peterson 1984, 1024).[2] It is with his disagreement with Montesquieu that we must begin in order to understand Jefferson's idea of federalism.

When Jefferson spoke of republics, he had in mind not the discredited direct democracies of antiquity, but a new kind of enlightened republicanism that made judicious use of representation. Nevertheless, in a Jeffersonian republic the people still rule. Jefferson's clearest statements on the subject come after his presidency in a series of letters, the immediate subject of which is constitutional reform in Virginia. To John Taylor, he writes that:

> *Were I to assign to this term a precise and definite idea, I would say, purely and simply, it means a government by its citizens in mass, acting directly and personally, according to rules established by the majority; and that every other government is more or less republican, in proportion as it has in its composition more or less of this ingredient of the direct action of the citizens. (May 28, 1816; Peterson 1984, 1392)*[3]

---

1 See Montesquieu (1748) 1989, Books IV–IX.
2 Jefferson here comes close to Madison's famous argument of the *Federalist*, No. 10. But Jefferson does not take the decisive step of making the national government the focal point of the argument. He envisages the nation somehow acting through the states.
3 See also TJ to P. S. de Pont Nemours, April 24, 1816 and to Samuel Kercheval July 12, 1816; Peterson 1984, 1384–88, 1395–1403.

For Jefferson, then, republicanism requires institutions that are responsive to the people's will and a people actively engaged in political affairs. Jefferson, of course, was no Leveller. He was convinced that the "natural aristocracy" of talent and virtue make the best public officials but he was also persuaded that popular election and strict accountability are the best means of securing their faithful service (TJ to Adams, Oct. 28, 1813; Peterson 1984, 1306).

Jefferson's confidence in the people was founded upon two considerations. First, and most importantly, he took great care to see that the people were virtuous and, as a result, the will of the majority reasonable. Jefferson did not believe that republicanism required the kind of self-denying Spartan virtue Montesquieu so vividly describes. He had in mind instead the more liberal kind of patriotism of an independent, educated, informed, politically engaged citizenry. Jefferson's continued advocacy of agrarianism, public education, newspapers, free inquiry and, as we will see, participation in local government were all part of his effort to preserve and enhance the political virtue of the American people. The second consideration leading Jefferson to place his trust in the people was his belief that errors made by the people were less damaging than those made by government. Errors growing out of liberty were liable to correction, whereas once power was concentrated and consolidated it was unlikely to be ever relinquished.[4] These two considerations were accompanied by two corresponding fears: first, that governments show a natural tendency towards centralization and monarchy and, second, that this natural tendency cultivates a corrupt complacency in the people.

It is in his post-presidency letters that we also find Jefferson's most elaborate discussions of federalism. In a letter to Samuel Kercheval, Jefferson explicitly links republicanism and federalism. After giving his definition of republicanism and its "mother principle," popular control, Jefferson turns to the question of how to organize the county and local governments. He exhorts Kercheval to be rigorously consistent: "Only lay down true principles, and adhere to them inflexibly." Follow principle and, he continues, "the knot unties itself." Jefferson extends the republican principle of popular control to the question of how to organize the county system. Taking the New England townships as his model, Jefferson arrives at his famous conclusion: "Divide the counties into wards of such size that every citizen can attend, when called on, and act in person." What ought to be the responsibility of the wards? The key strategy of Jeffersonian federalism is the "division and subdivision" of powers according to function (July 12, 1816; Peterson 1984, 1399–1400). As with the separation of powers, this division and subdivision of powers is qualitative rather than quantitative. Responsibility for governmental functions should fall to the level of government best suited for carrying out each particular activity. Jefferson further argues that the most efficient arrangement will be the one with the maximum possible of individual control and involvement. For Virginia he suggests the following arrangement as optimal: there should be a general federal republic of which Virginia is a sovereign part, a state republic, county republics,

---

4 TJ to Archibald Stuart, Dec. 23, 1791 and to de Tracy, Jan. 26, 1811; Peterson 1984, 983–84, 1246–47.

and ward republics. Writing to Joseph Cabell around the same time, Jefferson assigns specific responsibilities to each "republic":

> *Let the national government be entrusted with the defence of the nation, and its foreign and federal [i.e., relations among the states] relations; the State governments with the civil rights, laws, police, and administration of what concerns the State generally; the counties with the local concerns of the counties; and each ward directs the interests within itself. (Feb. 2, 1816; Peterson 1984, 1380)*

Writing to Adams a few years earlier, Jefferson assigns to the ward republics care of local schools along with "the care of their poor, their roads, police, elections, the nomination of jurors, administration of justice in small cases, elementary exercises of militia" (Oct. 28, 1813; Peterson 1984, 1308).[5] Jefferson was convinced that if a proper federal system were established *and* if a foreign policy were followed such that "our affairs be disentangled from those of all other nations, except as to commerce" then "our general government may be reduced to a very simple organization, & a very unexpensive one; a few plain duties to be performed by a few servants" (TJ to Granger, Aug. 13, 1800; Peterson 1984, 1079).

Jefferson makes at least five assumptions in this proposal. Whether or not these are realistic assumptions is a question taken up in our conclusion. First, he assumes that American affairs can be "disentangled" from the rest of the world. Second, he assumes that local concerns are truly local. There are, in other words, no negative spill-over effects between the various jurisdictions. Third, he assumes that local knowledge, as opposed to technical expertise, is the key to good administration. This is why local communities can best administer local concerns. Fourth, he assumes that devolving power to the local level will arouse vigorous political participation, not just with respect to local concerns, but in the affairs of the state and beyond. Lastly, Jefferson assumes that local majorities will provide not only an efficient but also a just administration of local matters. Where there is any doubt, Jefferson's default option is to leave power with the lower level of government or with the individual. Here Jefferson's natural rights philosophy, his republicanism, and his federalism all come together. According to the natural rights philosophy, all political power is originally held by the individual in a state of nature. It is given up conditionally and by no means completely to government. Seen in this light, Jefferson's federalism provides guidance beyond what Locke had given as to the most prudent way for an individual to give up his natural powers when making the transition from the state of nature to civil society.

---

5   In this letter Jefferson claims that his proposal in the *Notes on Virginia* for ward schools also contemplated the kind of local self-government he was now explicitly proposing. See Query XIV for the original proposal. Jefferson refers to public education and the ward system as the "two hooks" of republican government. TJ to Cabell, Jan. 31, 1814; Ford (1904) 11.302.

As with his republicanism, Jefferson's rationale for federalism is Lockean and liberal rather than classical republican. Jefferson wants to foster a virtuous and politically engaged citizenry, but his ultimate goals are fundamentally liberal.[6] His argument for preferring the federal system to a unitary system is three-fold: the security argument; the liberty argument; and the happiness argument.

Security

Jefferson believed that the federal system solved the Montesquieuean dilemma of corruption versus destruction. The combined strength of a federal union of states was sufficient for resisting threats from even the great powers. Jefferson envisaged state militias, rather than a standing army or a large navy, as being the first line of defense against invasion. This strategy highlighted the need not only for vigorous state governments but for patriotic citizens willing to serve. Perhaps even greater than the fear of European powers was the fear that disunion would set in motion a chain of events in North America that would be disastrous for peace and liberty. The disunited nations of Europe were continually at war – "exterminating havoc," as Jefferson put it in his First Inaugural (Peterson 1984, 494). A properly structured federal republic would ensure a continental peace and an international peace.[7]

Liberty

Jefferson saw a properly constructed federal republic as an indispensable support for liberty. "What has destroyed liberty and the rights of man in every government which has ever existed under the sun?" he asked Joseph Cabell. Jefferson's answer: "The generalizing and concentrating all cares and powers into one body, no matter whether of the autocrats of Russia or France, or of the aristocrats of a Venetian senate" (Feb. 2, 1816; Peterson 1984, 1380). Closely related to this danger was that of corruption, particularly in the form of a complacent people. Jefferson attributed the downfall of the Roman Republic ultimately to the "corruption vice and venality" of the Roman nation, a disorder that individual statesmen, however brilliant, were powerless to correct (TJ to Adams, Dec. 10, 1819; Cappon 1959, 549). The federative principle secures liberty by counteracting this natural tendency towards consolidation and by cultivating in the people a robust attachment to republicanism.

Jefferson regarded the states as the "surest bulwarks against anti-republican tendencies" (First Inaugural; Peterson 1984, 494). The states are close enough to the people to be trusted with the protection of the people's liberties and, furthermore,

---

6   See Yarbrough 1998. Cf. Sheldon 1991.
7   Intriguing international relations perspectives on federalism and the early republic are presented by Hendrickson 2003, Tucker and Hendrickson 1990, Onuf 2000 and Onuf and Onuf 2006.

the states (unlike the local governments) are in a powerful enough position to resist encroachments by the national government. For this reason the states must remain sovereign and independent in their respective arena, "domestic concerns." Not only this, care must be taken to ensure that in addition to written constitutional guarantees of sovereignty, state constitutional structures are strong enough to resist encroachments. Jefferson wanted to make the state governments stronger by making them more "wise" and "able." How? He recommended strengthening the executive by making it a more independent and therefore desirable office. He also recommended making legislative offices more desirable by reducing their number. The general principle at work – a sometimes forgotten component of Jefferson's republicanism – is that "Responsibility is a tremendous engine in a free government" (TJ to Stuart, Dec. 23, 1791; Peterson 1984, 984). Truly responsible public officials feel individually the rewards of success and the punishment for failure. Strong state governments can take action against corruption, whether it be in particular states or in the national capital. Jefferson made this point to Destutt de Tracy – a French political thinker greatly admired by Jefferson but who thought federalism impractical. Jefferson observed that the "republican government of France was lost without a struggle, because the party of '*un et indivisible*' had prevailed; no provincial organizations existed to which the people might rally under the authority of the laws, the seats of the directory were virtually vacant, and a small force sufficed to turn the legislature out of their chamber and to salute its leader chief of the nation" (Jan. 26, 1811; Peterson 1984, 1246).[8]

Federalism also cultivates patriotic citizens firmly attached to republican principles. Jefferson believed that where every man feels that he is a "participator in the government of affairs, not merely at an election one day in the year, but every day … he will let the heart be torn out of his body sooner than his power be wrested from him by a Caesar or a Bonaparte" (TJ to Cabell, Feb. 2, 1816; Peterson 1984, 1380). An additional benefit of vigorous local politics is that it makes possible the rapid mobilization and disclosure of public opinion through regular political channels. This is important in the course of ordinary politics, say for proposing constitutional amendments, but perhaps even more so during political crises.[9]

Happiness

The final argument in favor of federalism is the contribution it makes to the pursuit of happiness. Securing liberty makes possible the pursuit of happiness, but in addition, federalism makes it possible for all levels of government to carry out their legitimate functions well and cheaply. Inefficient government is also oppressive government. Things are done "best" and to "perfection" when they are carried out by the lowest possible level of government. This principle applies in fact to all

---

8   Jefferson thought de Tracy's *Commentaire sur l'esprit des lois de Montesquieu* (1806) "[t]he ablest work of the age." TJ to Cabell, Jan. 5, 1815; Ford 1904, 11.447.
9   See TJ to Kercheval, July 12, 1816; Peterson 1984, 1403.

human activities. "It is by dividing and subdividing these republics from the great national one down through all its subordinations, until it ends in the administration of every man's farm by himself; by placing under every one what his own eye may superintend, that all may be done for the best" (TJ to Cabell, Feb. 2, 1816, and to Kercheval, July 12, 1816; Peterson 1984, 1380, 1400).

Jeffersonian Federalism in Practice

Critical and troubling questions arise when we move from Jefferson's theory of federalism to his application of that theory. These questions bear heavily on the issues of Jefferson's legacy and contemporary relevance. Jefferson's vision of the American future as a federal and republican "empire for liberty" (TJ to James Madison, April 27, 1809; Lipscomb and Bergh 1904, 12:277) was challenged by political circumstances in three fundamental ways. The first challenge concerned constitutional structures. Jefferson found himself at odds with the Federalists regarding the interpretation of the new Constitution and especially as regards the powers reserved to the states. Second, Jefferson had to face the challenge to federalism of an increasingly large and diverse society, especially after the Louisiana Purchase. Lastly, the federal idea was challenged by the threats of war with the great powers and by secessionism, particularly in the Northeast and in the Southwest.

Jefferson was initially shocked by the work of the Philadelphia Convention. It had gone far beyond what was necessary to reinvigorate the Union. "[A]ll of the good of this new constitution," he remarked to Adams, "might have been couched in three or four new articles to be added to the good old venerable fabrick [the Articles], which should have been preserved even as a religious relique" (Nov. 13, 1787; Peterson 1984, 914). James Madison's arguments and the certain prospect of the addition of a Bill of Rights brought Jefferson around, but not completely. During the 1790s Jefferson elaborated a constitutional theory that diverged not just from Hamilton but also from his friend and political ally, Madison. As best he could Jefferson tried to establish his view as the constitutional orthodoxy.

Jefferson made two major contributions to constitutional interpretation in the 1790s. The first was his cabinet opinion on the constitutionality of a national bank. Famous for its doctrine of strict construction, the opinion is just as notable for its argument for a particular kind of federalism.[10] The central part of the opinion, where

---

10 Indeed, only the federalism argument explains the rather peculiar mode of argument Jefferson employs. Jefferson begins listing the ways in which a national power of incorporation will impact on a variety of venerable areas of *state* land law. The creation of a corporation would necessitate the holding of land and property within a state that would necessarily be exempt from state laws regarding mortmain, alienage, escheat, forfeiture, and descents. Jefferson begins and ends his opinion emphasizing these concerns. Jefferson's constitutional thought is surveyed in Mayer 1994.

he outlines his doctrine of strict construction, turns on a question of federalism. The foundation of the Constitution, Jefferson explains, is contained in the proposed Twelfth Amendment (subsequently the Tenth when ratified) to the Constitution: "all powers not delegated to the United States by the Constitution, nor prohibited to it by the states, are reserved to the states or the people." The powers delegated are those *expressly* delegated and those "necessary and proper" means for carrying out delegated powers, taking "necessary" to be "those means without which the grant of power would be nugatory." Any other mode of interpretation destroys the very nature and purpose of the Constitution which was intended, Jefferson says, "to lace them up straitly within the enumerated powers, and those without which, as means, these powers could not be carried into effect" ("Opinion on the Constitutionality of a National Bank," Feb. 15, 1791; Peterson 1984, 416, 418–19).

Jefferson clarified his understanding of the foundation of the Constitution in his draft of the Kentucky Resolutions opposing the Federalist Party's Alien and Sedition Acts. He believed these laws un-Constitutional in that they usurped state powers to make criminal law and to determine the treatment of aliens. In addition, they violated the Bill of Rights protection for free speech. Jefferson might have left matters at that, but he went further when he turned to the question of a remedy. The electoral process is the appropriate "constitutional" remedy in cases where delegated powers are abused. But where the national government exercises powers that are not delegated, action by the states, including the "natural right" of "nullification," is appropriate. Jefferson argued that the Constitution is a "compact" among the states and that it is up to the individual states to judge whether the fundamental compact has been violated ("Draft of the Kentucky Resolutions," Oct. 1798; Peterson 1984, 453). Perhaps too Jefferson believed that a change of officers following an election would be an ineffectual remedy because even new officers would be unlikely to relinquish usurped powers. Only the states, "the surest bulwarks against anti-republican tendencies," have an enduring incentive to resist encroachments by the national government. Jefferson's compact theory not only rejected Hamilton's nationalism but also departed significantly from Madison's opinions that the foundation of the Constitution was in the people of the states, not the states themselves and that, in any case, to allow an individual state to nullify an agreement made by all could only lead to anarchy.[11]

Jefferson's theory of federalism faced a second challenge in coping with the diversity and rapidly expanding size of the American empire. While not usually seen as such, the problems of Native Americans and of Africans in America were dramatic challenges to Jefferson's federal idea.[12] Jefferson rejected the idea of

---

11   See Madison to Hayne April 1830, Hunt 9.384. Madison was embarrassed by the publication of Jefferson's draft of the Kentucky Resolutions. He was unaware that it endorsed nullification. McCoy 139–51. Hamilton's popular and nationalist understanding of the Constitution is on display in the *Federalist* No. 78.

12   Important exceptions are Onuf 2000 and 2007. For this point and much of what follows we are much indebted to Onuf 2000. Onuf stresses the distinctive and paradoxical way in which Jefferson conceived the Union and American identity: a weak central

incorporating Africans into American society and implicitly the idea of an African state within the American Union. While acknowledging the Africans' right of and capacity for self-government, Jefferson believed (and is infamous now for so believing) that "political" conflicts as well as "physical and moral" differences between the races argued conclusively against any incorporation into American society (*Notes on Virginia*, Query XIV; Peterson 1984, 264). They would be a distinct people, but in a different land. The case of Native Americans was somewhat different. Jefferson held out the long term hope for their integration into the Union, but not as an independent people or state. In the meantime, Jefferson advocated their confinement to smaller areas and their separation from whites.

A less stark but nevertheless significant challenge to the federative principle arose in the western territories of the original Union. Jefferson himself was intimately involved in deliberations about how to handle the territories and especially the vital question of how to create new states as equal members of the Union. Jefferson's 1784 "Report on a Plan of Government for the Western Territory" did set a number of conditions for admission as a state, notably that new states must remain part of the Union *forever*, that their governments must be republican, that slavery be excluded, and that citizenship must be withheld from anyone holding an hereditary title. But beyond these restrictions, Jefferson favored making the conditions for admitting new states relatively easy, especially as regards the minimum population requirement. He did so despite his reservations about whether the character of westerners would sustain a republican system. His judgment favoring easy admission was based on a complex prudential calculation. Doubts about the loyalties of those in the west were balanced against his belief that making admission to statehood difficult would only engender resentment. He also believed that if new states were small they would be more likely to remain in the Union, rather than entertain hopes of independence.[13] Jefferson believed his calculation was vindicated by experience. To his mind, westerners showed conspicuously more loyalty to the Union during the Burr conspiracy, the Embargo, and the War of 1812 than many New Englanders.[14]

A more difficult problem was the incorporation of the vast territories acquired in the Louisiana Purchase. In addition to calling into question Jefferson's theory of strict construction – Jefferson had acted without congressional approval and on a matter seemingly not contemplated by the Constitution – the Purchase raised fundamental questions for a republican government. The United States acquired not just land but also persons, subjects, raised in non-republican societies and now part of the United States without their consent. Jefferson's bold statement in his Second Inaugural concealed some real concerns. The kind of immediate self-government already afforded to the western territories was out of the question. Jefferson complained that while it was widely acknowledged that "our new fellow

---

government and a strong national identity as "federalists" and "republican."
13   One new states, see TJ to Monroe July 9, 1786; Ford 1904, 131–33.
14   On the loyalty of westerners during the Burr conspiracy, see TJ to Lafayette, May 26, 1807; Ford 1904, 10.406–12. On the significance for Jefferson of the contrast between westerners and certain New Englanders, see Onuf 2000, 129–37.

citizens are as yet as incapable of self government as children, yet some cannot bring themselves to suspend its principles for a single moment. The temporary or territorial government of that country therefore will encounter great difficulty." Jefferson's preference was to place the new territories largely under the control of governors and only gradually bringing the established laws into line with American habits and law. But again Jefferson was not overly concerned. His major concerns were elsewhere: finding the precise borders of the new acquisition, particularly the disposition of Florida, and seizing the possibility the Purchase presented for moving Native Americans westward so as to make way for new settlers.

Jefferson came to take for granted that the federative principle solved the security problem not just for the United States but for all nations republican and federal in nature. Not only was a federal republic inherently strong, it could remain secure without a standing army and a large navy. Jefferson assumes that a federal republic will only be engaged in defensive wars and only very limited offensive operations. As noted above, it will for its initial defense rely on state militias manned by patriotic republican citizens. Jefferson interpreted the events of the early republic as dramatic confirmations of his optimistic view. In a letter to William Crawford soon after Jackson's victory at New Orleans a jubilant Jefferson summed things up: "It may be thought that useless blood was spilt at New Orleans. ... I think it had many valuable uses. It proved the fidelity of the Orleanese to the United States. It proved that New Orleans can be defended by land and water; that the western territory will fly to its relief (of which ourselves had doubted before); that our militia are heroes when they have heroes to lead them on; and that ... their skill in the fire-arm, and deadly aim, give them great advantages over regulars" (Feb. 11, 1815, including postscript of the Feb. 26; Ford 1904, 11:453–54).

The extraordinary paradox contained in Jefferson's belief in the strength of the federal system is that the real dangers to a federal republic are internal. These threats might come in various forms. Secessionist threats would always be a problem in a large federal republic. Jefferson was also aware that there was little that could be done in the face of such threats. For practical and sentimental reasons, Americans would be reluctant to take up arms against their brethren. While Jefferson acknowledged this as a persistent danger, particularly at the extremities, in a large and expanding federal republic, he did not regard it in any sense as a mortal weakness. In the case of westerners, good policies and careful attention to grievances would facilitate their incorporation into the Union. Furthermore, secessionist movements would likely be short-lived because in a republic they would be the products of an excess of liberty and therefore ultimately self-correcting. Jefferson at times could talk blithely about the prospect of separation but probably only because in the end he took the threat lightly.[15]

The danger from anti-republican tendencies was far more serious, especially when combined with secessionism. Jefferson's federal republic required, not quite

---

15 For Jefferson making light of the threat if disunion, see TJ to Priestly, Jan. 29, 1804; Peterson 1984, 1142. For Jefferson on the likelihood or not of disunion, see TJ to Madison, Jan. 30, 1787; Peterson 1984, 883; and to de Tracy, Jan. 26, 1811; Peterson 1984, 1246–47.

a uniformity but certainly a very widespread agreement about basic political principles. In such circumstances enemies of the Union or republicanism could then "stand undisturbed, as monuments of the safety with which error of opinion may be tolerated where reason is left free to combat it" (First Inaugural; Peterson 1984, 493). Where anti-republican tendencies and sentiments were more than mere "monuments," however, Jefferson was anything but complacent. Soon after his return from France, he became convinced that there was a dangerous anti-republican movement in the United States. It was not a mass movement but a sizable cabal of monarchists and Anglophiles who had in mind the destruction of the republic. Hamilton was the early leader of the cabal but its heart and soul was in New England's Federalist elite which, unlike Hamilton, was not dedicated to the Union. As noted above, Jefferson was confident that in a nation both republican and federal the politically healthy parts of the nation would be more than a match for corruption in any particular part, including the national government. Again he believed his theory was vindicated during the first three decades of the republic. The ordinary electoral processes at the state and national level provided one course of action for republican forces, as in the election of 1800. The threat of state resistance to unconstitutional laws, as contained in the Kentucky Resolutions, was another means. Still another was the vigorous enforcement of laws duly made by constitutional majorities. Finally, action by ordinary citizens was a powerful force. Jefferson saw the failure of Burr's schemes a vindication of the federal system. No doubt taking pride in the implicit contrast between the different outcomes of their two revolutions, Jefferson wrote to Lafayette: "A simple proclamation informing the people of these combinations, and calling on them to suppress them produced an instantaneous *levee en masse* of our citizens wherever there appeared anything to lay hold of, & the whole was crushed in one instant" (May 26, 1807; Peterson 1984, 410).

Jefferson believed that the Federalist cabal had been finally put to rest with Jackson's victory at New Orleans and the discrediting of secessionist "Hartford Convention" forces in New England. But to his despair, the Federalist party it turned out was dead in name only. The Missouri Crisis provided another and to Jefferson's mind most dangerous opportunity for the cabal to reconstitute itself. Jefferson believed that its adherents, in New England and in the national judiciary, had indeed given up on the idea of monarchy but that they had now coalesced around the idea of "consolidation": the centralization of all power in the national government. The Missouri question – whether the national government could prohibit slavery in a new state – gave the consolidationists an opportunity to combine their cause with the anti-slavery cause. For Jefferson, this was a "mere party trick" (TJ to Pinckney Sep. 30, 1820; Ford 1904, 12.165); a grab for power cloaked in the language of morality. Slavery was not the issue. The real issue was national versus state power, and in this particular case involved the "existence" of Southern whites who would be in jeopardy if the national government attempted a general emancipation.[16]

---

16 TJ to Gallatin, Dec. 26, 1820, Peterson, 1984, 1449.

Much might be said about Jefferson's consistency or otherwise on the issue of slavery as well as about his analysis of his opponents' motive and arguments. From the perspective of Jefferson's idea of federalism, however, the most important point is the reason for Jefferson's despair which, with the benefit of hindsight, proved prophetic. In his famous letter to Holmes, Jefferson remarked that "this momentous question, like a fire bell in the night, awakened and filled me with terror. I considered it at once as the knell of the Union." Jefferson believed that the consolidationists were deliberately creating a "geographical line, coinciding with a marked principle, moral and political, [that] once conceived and held up to the angry passions of men, will never be obliterated; and every new irritation will mark it deeper and deeper" (April 22, 1820; Peterson 1984, 1432). The consolidationists would ascend to power under the anti-slavery banner they had stolen from republicans in much the same way the Federalists had stolen the banner of federalism three decades earlier. A division based on "principle" shattered the uniformity of opinion necessary for the preservation and expansion of the Union. Jefferson fell into "the deepest political malaise of his entire life" (Peterson 1970, 997).

Conclusion

The essential features of Jeffersonian federalism are a strictly limited national government, strict construction of the Constitution, strong and independent states, vigorous local government, and republicanism characterizing all levels of government. Jefferson saw a written constitution as supportive of these arrangements, but just as important as words on paper were the structural checks and balances built into the federal system. Jefferson's federalism is intimately connected with his republicanism and his natural rights philosophy. Although federalism was not an end in itself, he saw it as one of the necessary and fundamental preconditions for the success of the American republican experiment.[17] The advantages of federalism are liberty, security, and happiness. Jefferson's theory emphasizes federalism's ability to take advantage of size (geographic and demographic) and homogeneity, rather than its ability to preserve or cultivate diversity. Jefferson's was quintessentially an Enlightenment idea of federalism. It was on this basis that he was able theoretically to reconcile his multiple allegiances and identities.

Did his theory bear any relation to actual practice? Was Jefferson's planned "empire for liberty" fatally flawed such that something like the Civil War was inevitable? In any case, did Jefferson's empire for liberty end with the Civil War, after which the United States became a different kind of nation, thereby robbing Jeffersonian federalism of any practical significance? And regardless of the answers to these questions, is Jefferson's Enlightenment way of thinking about federalism

---

17   Cf. Onuf 2000 who comes closest to according federalism and republicanism equal weight.

now obsolete in our post-modern world with its growing distaste for universal principles and homogeneity? Let us take up these questions in turn.

Jefferson's theory had the virtue of consistency to be sure but it clashed with political circumstances and gave rise to contradictions in such a way as to call into question its importance. To begin with Jefferson's compact theory of the Constitution and his strict constructionist mode of interpretation were at odds with the views of Hamilton *and* Madison. Perhaps he simply misunderstood what was agreed to at the Convention and at Ratification? Jefferson might respond that whatever was decided his theory was the only way to understand the constitution so that republican and federal principles might be prevail.[18] But was Jefferson's a workable theory of federalism? Hamilton and Madison (at least at the time of the *Federalist*) saw the Constitution as a dramatic and necessary departure from the Articles. The Constitution was not a compact made by the states and, furthermore, the new national government not only had new powers, some of which overlapped with state powers, it operated in a new way, directly on citizens (rather than on states). They believed this to be the only workable form of federalism.[19] Other forms of federalism would fall prey to the centrifugal forces that had destroyed earlier federal republics. Jefferson was not alone in elaborating a compact theory of the Constitution, but once his authorship and later his draft of the Kentucky Resolutions became known (in 1821 and 1832 respectively), his great authority lent tremendous weight to the compact theory. The doctrines of nullification and secession as they were later elaborated might not be Jefferson's but they were certainly derivable from his "Principles of Ninety-eight."[20]

The question of the practicality of Jeffersonian federalism recurs when we consider some of its contradictions or paradoxes. The security dilemma confronting republics is the most dramatic. Jefferson believed that the internal unity of a federal republic was the key to solving the security problem. When the nation was threatened its citizens would rally to its defense. While Jefferson interpreted the events of his day as so many confirmations of his theory, it is possible to see them in another far less comforting light. To take just one example, during his Embargo, which he saw as a peaceful alternative to war, Jefferson was forced to take measures very similar to, and some even more draconian, than those he had criticized Federalists for adopting during the so-called Quasi-war with France. To enforce the

---

18 Indeed this was his response to criticisms of his "Summary View of the Rights of British North America" in which he outlined a federal understanding of the British Empire. While his arguments may have been novel, he believed they established the only "orthodox or tenable" ground for opposition to Great Britain ("Autobiography," Peterson 1984, 9). Jefferson's visionary account of the imperial union as a collection of independent sovereignties consenting to be united in certain limited respects bears some striking similarities to his plan for the American Union.

19 It is worth noting that a leading student of American federalism could write an important book on "the meaning of American federalism" and not mention Jefferson. See Ostrom 1999.

20 For Jefferson influence on the states' rights movement, see McDonald 2000 and Peterson 1970.

Embargo he severely curtailed civil liberties, used regular military forces against civilians, and called for substantial increases in the army and navy to prepare for the advent of actual war with Great Britain or France. Ironically, resistance to Jefferson's measures was centered in New England in the very townships that were the models for his proposed ward republics.[21] These considerations lead to a further question, one raised by de Tracy and later by de Tocqueville, concerning the applicability of a federal system to a nation facing a continual threat of war. Both de Tracy and de Tocqueville answered in the negative. Jefferson's policy contortions and his unrealistic hopes of what could be expected of even patriotic Americans raise grave doubts about his positive answer to the question.[22]

Reflections such as these might lead us to conclude that Jeffersonian federalism is indeed irrelevant. Yet this is too hasty. While Jefferson's compact theory may not be compatible with a workable federalism, there are other aspects of Jeffersonian federalism that remain highly pertinent. Clearly, Jefferson's federative principle has much in common with contemporary ideas of decentralization and subsidiarity. Today these arguments tend to be cast in economic terms. Jefferson provides a richer, more political language for such arguments. Moreover, his emphasis on the importance of state and local government in promoting an active and engaged citizenry anticipates much of Tocqueville's classic defense of federalism and decentralized administration. Jefferson's federalism project takes these principles of decentralization to an extreme. Notwithstanding Jefferson's aversion to Plato's "whimsies" (TJ to Short, Aug. 4, 1820; Peterson 1984, 1436), there is a sense in which Jefferson's thinking about decentralization represents a kind of pure or ideal federalism to be brought about not by philosopher kings but by popular enlightenment – the "progress of the human mind."[23] Like Plato's best regime it is for liberal republicans an ideal to be consulted and, where possible, strived for, rather than ever actually achieved.

Plato's ideal of the best regime is also an outline of the basic contours of political life, including its limits. Jefferson's ideal points to important limits on the federative principle. Jeffersonian federalism presupposes a considerable homogeneity among citizens and a fundamental agreement on basic political principles. This observation bears on the question of Jefferson's relevance for a post-modern world. Accepting for the moment that we live in such a world, there is an important negative lesson to be learned from Jefferson's ideal. A significant diversity of opinion threatens any experiment in federal and republican principles. Jefferson blamed the Missouri crisis on resurgent Federalists, but perhaps the real and enduring lessons of this

---

21 For Jefferson's curtailment of civil liberties, see Levy 1963, 93–141.
22 See Jefferson's translation of de Tracy's *Commentaire* 1811, 82–83 and Tocqueville (1835) 2000, 159–61.
23 "[L]aws and institutions must go hand in hand with the progress of the human mind. As that becomes more developed, more enlightened, as new discoveries are made, new truths disclosed, and manners and opinions change with the change of circumstances, institutions must advance also, and keep pace with the times." TJ to Kercheval, July 12, 1816; Peterson 1984, 1402.

episode point to the difficulty of establishing a strong federal system and to the recognition that for a federal system to cope with fundamental diversity it must become either weaker or it must become more centralized – more monarchical, as Jefferson might put it. These difficult choices are still with us.

References

Cappon, L. J. (ed.) (1959), *The Adams-Jefferson Letters* (Chapel Hill: University of North Carolina Press).
Ford, P. L. (ed.) (1904), *The Writings of Thomas Jefferson* 12 Vols. (New York: Putnam's).
Hunt, G. (ed.) (1900–10), *The Writings of James Madison* (New York: Putnam's).
Hendrickson, D. (2003), *Peace Pact: The Lost World of the American Founding* (Lawrence: University Press of Kansas).
Levy, L. (1963), *Jefferson and Civil Liberties: The Darker Side* (Cambridge: Harvard University Press).
Lipscomb A. A. and Bergh, A. E. (eds) (1904), *The Writings of Thomas Jefferson* 20 Vols. (Washington DC: Thomas Jefferson Memorial Association).
Mayer, D. (1994), *The Constitutional Thought of Thomas Jefferson* (Charlottesville: University Press of Virginia).
McCoy, D. (1991), *The Last of the Fathers: James Madison and the Republican Legacy* (Cambridge: Cambridge University Press).
Montesquieu, C. S. (1748) 1989, *The Spirit of the Laws*, Anne Cohler, trans. (Cambridge: Cambridge University Press).
McDonald, F. (2000), *States' Rights and the Union: Imperium in Imperio 1776–1876* (Lawrence: University Press of Kansas).
Onuf, P. (2000), *Jefferson's Empire: The Language of American Nationhood* (Charlottesville: University Press of Virginia).
—— (2007), *The Mind of Thomas Jefferson* (Charlottesville: University Press of Virginia).
—— and Onuf, N. (2006), *Nations, Markets, and War: Modern History and the American Civil War* (Charlottesville: University of Virginia).
Ostrom, V. (1991), *The Meaning of American Federalism* (San Francisco: ICS Press).
Peterson, M. (1960), *The Jefferson Image in the American Mind* (New York: Oxford University Press).
—— (ed.) (1984), *Thomas Jefferson: Writings* (New York: Library of America).
Sheldon, G. W. (1991), *The Political Philosophy of Thomas Jefferson* (Baltimore: Johns Hopkins University).
Tocqueville, A. de (1835) 2000, *Democracy in America*, Harvey C. Mansfield and Delba Winthrop, trans. (Chicago: University of Chicago Press).
Tracy, D. de (1806) 1811, *A Commentary and Review of Montesquieu's Spirit of Laws*, Thomas Jefferson, trans. (Philadelphia: William Duane).

Tucker, R.W. and Hendrickson, D. (1990), *Empire of Liberty: The Statecraft of Thomas Jefferson* (New York: Oxford University Press).
Yarbrough, J. (1998), *American Virtues: Thomas Jefferson on the Character of a Free People* (Lawrence: University Press of Kansas).

Further Reading

Thomas Jefferson
A Summary View of the Rights of British North America (1774); Report on a Plan of Government for the Western Territory (1784); Opinion on the Constitutionality of a National Bank (1791); Draft of the Kentucky Resolutions (1798); First Inaugural Address (1801); Letters to Archibald Stuart, Dec. 23, 1791; François D'Ivernois Feb. 6, 1795; Gideon Granger, Aug. 13, 1800; Destutt de Tracy, Aug. 11, 1811; John Adams, Oct. 28, 1813; Joseph Cabell, Feb. 2, 1816; Samuel Kercheval, July 12, 1816; John Holmes, April 22, 1820. All available in: Peterson, Merrill (ed.) (1984), *Thomas Jefferson: Writings* (New York: Library of America).
Mayer, D. (1994), *The Constitutional Thought of Thomas Jefferson* (Charlottesville: University Press of Virginia).
Onuf, P. (2000), *Jefferson's Empire: The Language of American Nationhood* (Charlottesville: University Press of Virginia).
—— (2007), *The Mind of Thomas Jefferson* (Charlottesville: University Press of Virginia).
Sheldon, G. W. (1991), *The Political Philosophy of Thomas Jefferson* (Baltimore: Johns Hopkins University Press).
Tucker, R. W. and Hendrickson, D. (1990), *Empire of Liberty: The Statecraft of Thomas Jefferson* (New York: Oxford University Press).
Peterson, M. (1960), *The Jefferson Image in the American Mind* (New York: Oxford University Press).
Yarbrough, J. (1998), *American Virtues: Thomas Jefferson on the Character of a Free People* (Lawrence: University Press of Kansas).

Tocqueville on Federalism as an American Accident

Peter Augustine Lawler

Alexis de Tocqueville was easily the best friendly critic of the United States of America. In *Democracy in America*, he presents the American federal system as a sort of accidental constitutional outcome that would be unlikely to endure.[1] It was opposed by the centralizing partial truth found in the theory of the Constitution's leading Framers, which aimed at maximizing individual freedom and prosperity by unleashing the homogenizing forces of atomistic (or individualistic) egalitarianism and materialistic science. It would be opposed by the partial truth in self-understandings, such as those that animated southern aristocrats and the idealistic Puritans, which focused on proud personal significance and willful resistance to all forces of centralization. Tocqueville presents his own theory of what the unprecedented American federal system accomplished, not so much with the intention of instructing the Americans who were not his primary audience, but in order to show us how various conceptions of the human good might be harmonized, if only fortunately and temporarily (II.ii.15).[2]

Drawing upon the *Federalist*, Tocqueville describes the American Union of the Constitution of 1787 as "an incomplete national government." What made the new government decisively national – or distinguished from those created by previous federal constitutions – is that it exercises direct sovereignty over particular individuals. "In America," Tocqueville explains, "the Union has, not states, but plain citizens, for those governed." The Constitution removed a formidable barrier

---

1   The best introduction to Tocqueville's thought – including his life and times – is the "Editor's Introduction" to the Mansfield and Winthrop (2000) translation of *Democracy in America*. That's the translation I use here.
2   References to Tocqueville's *Democracy in America* are given in the text by volume, part, and chapter number. This reference, for example, is to volume 2, part 2, chapter 15. If an entire paragraph on my analysis is based on a single chapter, I put the reference at the end of the paragraph.

to the exercise of power by previous federal governments. Individuals, as "centers of resistance," are bound to be ineffective, but not so the "collective passions" of "peoples" organized into provinces. It's much easier to make individuals obey than states or provinces. That's one reason why, compared with the "feeble and powerless" federal governments of the past, the American national government "conducts its affairs with vigor and ease" (I.i.8).

The American national government is incomplete because its sphere of sovereignty or the authoritative use of power is limited. It has control over defense or foreign policy and whatever concerns commerce; everything else – the detailed regulation of domestic or ordinary life – is reserved to the states. Still, the American federal (or national) government is meant to be more "like most ordinary governments" than not; the constitutional intention is that it be able to do what it has a right to do. The weakness of past confederal authorities is that they didn't have the power that corresponded to their responsibilities, and the American system is national enough to avoid or at least substantially mitigate those weaknesses. So the word "federal" (or "confederal" – "federated with") is very misleading as a description of the American system as described in the Constitution. Tocqueville says that the word for the form of government that's not exactly national nor federal but more national than federal has not yet been invented. There is, of course, still no such word (I.i.8).

Tocqueville doesn't present the dominant Framers as regarding federalism understood as divided sovereignty as serving an enduring human good. The national government is incomplete not by their choice but as a necessary concession to the states as pre-existing proud and particular entities. Because the states couldn't be destroyed, they had to be humored. "The legislators who formed the Constitution of 1789 ... were limited," Tocqueville observed, by the fact that "[t]hey had not been charged with constituting the government of a unitary people," and so "whatever their [nationalizing] desires were, they still had in the end to partition the exercise of sovereignty." They weren't given the power to do what they wanted (I.ii.10).

But the Framers didn't produce a Constitution with the purpose of making those limits to their national intention as permanent.[3] By saying that the national government is "incomplete," Tocqueville suggests that the Constitution was constructed in a way that would facilitate its completion over time. Through the astute use of the powers over money, to tax, and to regulate commercial transactions and the necessary use of powers to defend the nation, the president and Congress – with the aid of basically nationalist judges – would make the national government more and more influential over the details of individual lives. The leading Framers aimed at a national government that would protect individual rights effectively, and they regarded both state and local government as relatively unjust and incompetent. They thought they were building as well as they could with a national or centralizing theory in mind (I.i.6; I.i.8). Tocqueville agrees with their judgment that the new Constitution was the cause of the national government

---

3 The best account of Tocqueville's view of the nationalizing intention of the leading Framers in Winthrop 1976.

being more just, moderate, wise, durable, skillful, clever, and firm than those of the states (I.i.8).

Tocqueville's Theory of American Federalism

Tocqueville stills says the Framers produced, contrary to their intention, a federal system worthy of a theory. That theory, he claims, is "entirely new." With their federal system, they managed to accomplish what was previously thought to be impossible. They combined in one Union the advantages of being a big nation with those of being a small one. Their prudent concessions to the states were accidentally the source of "one of the great discoveries of political science in our age" (I.i.8). Through the practice of statesmanship, it's possible for human beings to build better than they know. Tocqueville provides evidence, in other words, that the best theory might be reflection on sound political practice, and not a means of radically transforming that practice. Theoretical innovations, it turns out, don't have to be consciously chosen.[4]

Tocqueville, with some irony, says that the American federal system is so complicated that it actually makes Americans more enlightened. They're stuck with employing their reason daily to comprehend and use it (I.i.8). They have to think hard about their system precisely because it's far from reasonable in the senses of being either consistent or self-evident to the mind. The incoherent but beneficial mixture that is the American federal system is still theoretically pleasing to Tocqueville himself because it mirrors the complexity of the human soul. The American themselves, Tocqueville observes, tend to reject the "general ideas" of Cartesian (Lockean) theorists that don't conform to what they learned for themselves about themselves through their experience in local self-government (I.ii.9; II.i.4).

Tocqueville claims that perhaps *the* reason why the American federal system is national enough not to share the defects of previous confederation is that Americans had not really deeply connected their political freedom or habits of self-government with the states at the time the Constitution was written. Self-government, he observes, developed in America at the level of the township or small local community and had little to do with the relatively remote states. Free, local institutions are what still animate the hearts of American citizens (II.ii.4). The states, at the time of their declaration of independence, "had long been part of the same empire; therefore they had not yet contracted the habit of governing

---

[4] On the general Tocquevillian theme of "the superiority of American practice to democratic theory," see Mansfield and Winthrop 2000, 80–96. Orestes Brownson, in *The American Republic* (1866), makes more explicit and elaborate the claim that the statesmanship – as opposed to the theory – of the Framers was the cause of their building better than they know. See Lawler 2002, 42–67. Another excellent beginning to connecting Tocqueville's and Brownson's "providential" approaches on federalism, among other issues, is Hancock 2008.

themselves completely." The patriotic prejudices that citizens can't help but have weren't focused all that well on the states, much less the United States. Americans thought of themselves as citizens of England too. The complex ambivalence of American patriotism in 1776 was that it was directed, simultaneously, toward the local political community, the state, the United States conceived as a nation, and Great Britain (I.i.5; I.i.8).

Not only that, the Americans "equal in enlightenment ... felt only weakly the passions in peoples that ordinarily oppose the extension of federal power." And "the greatest citizens" – the dominant Framers – worked to combat such unenlightened passions on behalf of the nation and its principles (I.i.8). The Americans were much less parochial or particular in their attachments than people usually are, and so, guided by their theoretically minded leaders, they were much less inclined to defend their particular prerogatives against the effective achievement of some general good. The Americans came together, in constructing their Union, to a remarkable degree as one people composed of sovereign or self-governing individuals. The Constitution's creation of the incomplete national government reflected the Americans' real or at least dominant self-understanding in 1787.

Tocqueville also observes that the Americans were (at the time of the Constitution's ratification) and are (in 1830) largely of one mind when it came to religion, philosophy, morality, and language. America is more one society than European nations that are far more perfectly united politically. In a typical European nation, there is one set of laws and a single prince, but all sorts of religious, class, cultural, linguistic, and other opinionated differences. The Americans of the various states know one another – even before the Constitution – better than the people of the provinces of the highly centralized French nation know one another (I.i.8). In the crucial respects, Tocqueville suggests, there is more uniformity of opinion in America than there has been almost anywhere ever before (I.ii.7). Without employing the Declaration of Independence or revolutionary fervor, Tocqueville gives a strong argument for the conclusion that in 1787 the Americans were, in fact, one people.

The Unprecedented Combination of the Advantages of Largeness and Smallness

The theory that justifies America's federal system, in Tocqueville's eyes, has little to do with the questionable fact of American diversity or even competing patriotisms or loyalties. American federalism, as an implicit theory, aims to combine the advantages of large and small nations. Size, not diversity, matters. Small nations are full of people who are easily contented, and so they usually succeed in satisfying their modest needs. People have quite limited opportunities to seek wealth and fame, and there is no outlet for and no arousing of great ambition (I.i.8).

Small countries, with their political freedom, both acknowledge and constrain ambition or the need for personal significance, making the danger of tyranny slight. Almost all ambition is directed to real internal improvements or genuine well-being; effective human effort is not "dissipated in the vain smoke of glory. People, we can say, are more genuinely concerned with the real details of particular lives in small countries. One reason among many for the intensity of concern is that people are really more alike in wealth, desires, and mores" (I.i.8).

Tocqueville invites us to compare with the atomistic individualism or egalitarianism of emotional emptiness characteristic of despotic empire with the real or civic egalitarianism found among the Puritans. By connecting real equality, real freedom, peace, tranquility, and even prosperity with smallness, Tocqueville seems to take the side of those who defended the "small republics" that are the states and who, allegedly, were against the Federalists, meaning the nationalists.[5] The dominant Framers did not reflect sufficiently on the material and psychological conditions of real human freedom (I.i.5; I.i.8).

Tocqueville pointedly says that "freedom, to tell the truth, [is] the natural condition of small societies." "In all times," he adds, "small nations have been cradles of political freedom," and they have lost their freedom by becoming large. The truth is that "history … has not furnished an example of a great nation that has long remained a republic," and so America will be an exception only if its federal combination of the best features of smallness and greatness can really endure. Tocqueville refuses to make a definite prediction on the future of the American republic, but does say "that the existence of a great republic will always be infinitely more exposed to peril than a small one" (I.i.8).

Large nations are intrinsically restless and dynamic. So they are more exciting, display more greatness, have a more sophisticated and interesting intellectual life, and are more progressive. But because the pursuit of wealth, power, and glory are much more intense, liberty is constantly threatened by potential tyrants. Individual souls become more tyrannical as they become more constantly restless or anxiously disoriented.[6] So human misery becomes more "profound," more "depraved," "individual selfishness" more pronounced, the clash of interests more complicated, and, in general, lives are more sophisticated and alienated or "metropolitan" (I.i.8). Large republics have no choice but to rely more and more on institutional solutions to the problem of tyranny; one tyrant has to be induced to check another.[7] What animates the natural forces of resistance to tyranny diminishes; people become both too isolated or individualistic and too diversified

---

5   Alulis (1998) shows Tocqueville taking a position somewhere between the Federalists and the Antifederalists in attempting to do justice to the claims of both freedom and virtue.

6   Tocqueville, by describing, in words echoing Pascal, the extreme restlessness of the Americans in the midst of prosperity, makes it clear that, in the most important psychological respect, America is a large nation. And so he makes it clear that the most important benefit of being small has no future in America (II.ii.13). See Lawler 1993.

7   As *Federalist* 51 explains.

in terms of interests to act effectively in concert (II.ii.2–4). Tocqueville concludes that, generally speaking, "nothing is more contrary to the well-being and freedom of men than great empires" (I.i.8). The dominant Framers were wrong if they thought that institutional mechanisms designed to maintain the semblance of liberty could replace the material, communal, and psychological preconditions of political liberty (I.i.5).

Still, from another point of view, large countries promote freedom understood as aristocrats do – as manifestations of great individuality. Because the scope of action is much greater, there is much more for great men to do. Large countries, of course, also find it much easier to defend themselves. Small nations may find it easier to find freedom within, but they are easy prey for those who threaten their freedom from outside (I.i.8). Great men find their most profound satisfaction in fighting to defend large countries (II.iii.9; I.ii.2). Both sides in the great American Civil War, we remember, were, in effect, large countries.

Small countries have the advantage when it comes to political freedom and happiness, and large ones the advantages when it comes to brilliance, power, and greatness. And the federal system of the American Constitution is the source of an incomplete large nation that is free, happy, and strong, although at the expense, Tocqueville implies, of some brilliance and greatness or glory. The national government achieves the most essential advantage of bigness – defense, which includes defense of its own indispensable prerogatives. It does so, fortunately, rather easily, because America is blessed by its isolation or lack of strong, menacing neighbors. So the nation achieves its goal without burdening the states much, or really testing the constitutional theory that it is complete enough to secure the ends it has been given. Its existence is enough to keep the states from erecting commercial barriers against one another, and so in America the spirit of enterprise soars unrestrained. And ideas circulate with barely any impediment throughout the whole country (I.9.8; I.ii.10).

The individual states are free to pursue internal well-being without worrying about defense and or being tempted to enlarge themselves. The actions of the national government are important – the basic regulation of war (and peace) and commerce, but they are relatively rare. The political life that ordinarily affects most lives is reserved to the states. Ambition is relatively benign because it is both constrained by the incompleteness of the national government and broken up by the existence of many significant political units. The passion for greatness is dispersed and so to some extent dissipated (I.i.8).

Tocqueville adds that the American Union – which is in some ways a union of provinces and not of individuals – is more suitable for the cultivation of patriotism than the amorphous mass of some completely centralized great nation. In America, people find it easier to connect their own prosperity to some political community (I.i.8; II.ii.4). The small, local political communities – such as the townships – where the Americans learn to love political liberty are better protected by the states than they would be by the necessarily more general rules of a national government (I.i.5).

The atomistic individualism that turns the activity of citizens to the passivity of dependents who are easy prey for despots is much weaker in America than in very centralized eighteenth-century France (II.ii.2–4; Tocqueville 1998). Most citizens remain relatively untouched by "the general interests of the country and the glory of the nation," and so they must become citizens, so to speak, at the state and especially local level. Loyal attachment to the states, of course, can be at the expense of loyalty to the nation. But the national government, arguably, provides citizens enough tangible benefits that they can see that the freedom and happiness that they enjoy in the states depends on what they're provided by the nation. In America, "provincial patriotism" to some extent inspires "love of the common native country" that all the states share in common (I.i.8).

Tocqueville is more than a bit ironic in calling "theory" the American combination of bigness and smallness. It was pretty accidental, and, he suggests, there's not that much reason to believe that such an incoherent mixture can be durable. Is the dependence of local liberties on routine and precedent – the ordinary life of the small, political community – really compatible over the long run with a great nation's passion for innovation based on general ideas concerning technology and indefinite perfectibility (I.i.8; II.ii.3, 8, 10, 16–17, 19)? Tocqueville's constant suggestion, now confirmed by history, is that the national government is bound either to dissolve or become more complete. Its inherent intention is to become more complete, but unpredictable circumstances will determine whether it has any future at all.

The national government is, in fact, even threatened both by prosperity and the absence of external threats. The states will proudly, if wrongly, come to believe that the need for an effective Union was not as great as they originally thought. And the transfer of patriotism from the states to the nation depends on the benefits accorded by the Union being visible enough to inspire sufficient gratitude. The truth is that the Union does need to remain strong both to facilitate commerce among the states and with other nations and to deter the constant possibility of invasion, to secure peace, freedom, and prosperity. But the truth about necessity is easy to forget when people have become too accustomed to peace and prosperity. The national government is undermined whenever people aren't calculating clearly about their interests, and Tocqueville says he knows better than to rely on such calculation (I.i.8; I.ii.10).

The Federal System as Particularly American

Tocqueville goes on to question whether American federalism is really a theoretical solution in another way. It certainly can't be universalized. It works here as well as it does because of contingencies and circumstances that can't be exported elsewhere.[8]

---

8   Krislov 2001 is an able recent account of the connection between American federalism and American exceptionalism generally.

"The Constitution of the United States," Tocqueville contends, "resembles those beautiful creations of human industry that lavish glory and good on those who invent them, but remain sterile in other hands" (I.i.8). The American federal system depends on and is a reflection of the homogeneity of Americans who share the same opinions about politics, morality, and religion. The "tyranny of the majority" that incorporates the whole nation allows Americans to readily agree on fundamental issues.

The states also have the same or at least compatible interests. The American Union is held together by an obvious or somewhat natural division of labor. Tocqueville observes that the economy of the southern states is agricultural, those of the West is both agricultural and manufacturing, and those of the North predominately commercial and manufacturing. The Union is actually more an economic than political whole; the states need each other to flourish. "A tight bond," Tocqueville concludes, "exists among the material interests of all parts of the Union" (I.ii.10).

The national government has no need, usually, to impose uniformity of the states; what uniformity it needs usually comes from the fact that America is mostly one society. No other nation with powerful provinces can claim to have that advantage of social homogeneity. And, of course, the American system had not really been tested by the necessity of fighting for its survival. Whether the national government would be able to impose sufficient uniformity if confronted constantly by formidable adversaries, Tocqueville says, is unclear. One reason among many that European statesmen aren't free to choose the American federal system, he does make clear, is that they are defective when it comes to maximizing military power. The American federal system is not for a continent where war is common (I.i.8).[9]

The goodness of this form of federalism is also particularly American in other ways.[10] In America, political freedom – the activity of citizens – is threatened by centralization based on theoretical abstraction from human particularity or personal significance. The progress of civilization unleashed by the Constitution of 1787 threatens to replace the greatness of individuality with the soft despotism of individualism (II.ii.4–6). Tocqueville tends to defend any expression of human particularity rebelling against impersonal homogeneity, and the assertiveness of the states that thwarts the nationalist intention of the Framers is certainly such an expression.

The theoretical intention to complete the national government opposes the way political liberty is actually cultivated in America. The Framers of the Constitution didn't deliberately create but, in fact, ungratefully presupposed the existence of free, local, communal, "township" institutions. Free, local institutions came to America from England, where they had grown in the context of proud and barbaric feudal localism (II.ii.4; I.i.5). And the Puritans combined the egalitarian spirit of Christianity with the spirited tradition of aristocratic liberty to act, in a

---

9 For some astute contemporary analysis of the problems of applying anything like the American federal model the European context; see Stepan 1999, Kincaid 1999, and Schmitter 2000.

10 The rest of this section is generally indebted to Hancock 2002.

quite idealistic and unprecedented way, in the very small democracies of New England. The theory of the Puritans was all smallness and no bigness; it dispensed altogether with representative institutions. The personal advantages of smallness are manifested, most clearly, in an egalitarian local community (I.i.5). They are threatened as the particular, intense political life of significant persons or citizens and creatures in those communities is undermined by the abstract individual of the enlightened, "Lockean" theory of the leading Founders.

The real theory of the Constitution is actually hostile to the prior existence of other particular political units or even the unique manifestations of unpredictable greatness and misery in particular human lives. Political liberty in America depends on the modification of that abstract theory by the concrete practices of citizens, creatures, and family members, who flourish only if relatively untouched by the national government and its principled individualism.[11] The real theory of the Constitution was modified by its Framers' prudent decision – forced on them by the states – not to impose their theoretical understanding on the details of particular lives. The main danger to human liberty is that the significance given to particular entities will be eroded over time by a more complete imposition of theoretical individualism. The tension between the "general idea" of the national government and the proud particularities that proudly elude its grasp, the danger is, will be resolved in the direction of impersonal centralization (II.i.20).

More generally, Tocqueville describes the movement from the locus of political life from the local communities to the states then to the national government as part of characteristically modern or highly civilized progress and decadence. The active exercise of political liberty's natural home is in semibarbaric society, and it is, characteristically, eradicated by the progress of civilization. The Puritans, as Tocqueville describes them, were an exceedingly unusual mixture of civilization and barbarism – educated, enlightened, even scientific Englishmen building a democratic community based on the barbaric laws of the Old Testament. And the pull of the benefits of modern civilization enhanced their individual freedom at the expense of real political freedom – the freedom of citizens. The American experience confirms the general truth that the progress of civilization makes the perpetuation of any form of local independence more difficult (I.i.5).

The strong tendency of increasingly civilized societies is to be increasingly intolerant of local or communal freedom. It undermines the efficiency achieved through enlightenment, and the diversity and the parochialism of decentralized authority is at the expense of any general or uniform egalitarian understanding of justice. Any very civilized society, Tocqueville observes, is disgusted by the numerous blunders of any experiment in local government (I.i.5). The ideology of rational control – the popularized Cartesianism – characteristic of both modern egalitarianism and the modern, technological understanding of science and nature

---

11 See Lawler 2007, 152–67 for more on how Tocqueville understands the doctrine of self-interest rightly understood as a way of protecting the personal loves of Americans. For the same understanding's place in the Tocqueville's account of American as a whole, see Lawler 2008, especially 403–11.

are at odds with any form of local freedom or decentralization (II.i.1, 3, 10). The advantages of decentralization, Tocqueville explains, are *only* political,[12] and the modern tendency is to surrender the willful unpredictability of political life to the rational benefits of the sciences of economics and administration (I.i.5). He says that modern governments, as such, will grow and become more bureaucratized to promote justice, prosperity, and national defense. All decentralization in the modern world will increasingly depend upon statesmen employing the political art to resist various forms of impersonal progress, and that art is based on premises about human liberty contrary to the modern intellectual grain (II.iv.2–5).

The apolitical or materialistic view of self-interest can't help but erode the foundations of genuine self-government. The American may be compelled to connect his own good to that of his fellow citizens through the perpetuation of free, local institutions against the grain of modern individualism. But it's hard to see why a modern individual would resist with particular vigor the atrophying of those free political institutions in the centralizing interests of justice and prosperity. His tendency, Tocqueville explains, is to find political life a tiresome inconvenience that unnecessarily diverts him from success in business and industry (II.ii.14). The interests of Americans will tend to point in the direction of centralization and nationalization, and the Americans often brag that they think of nothing but their interests (II.ii.8). So we might conclude, today with history on our side, that the long-term threat to American federalism is that the national government will complete itself in pursuit of prosperity or commercial success and uniformly egalitarian justice.

Consolidation, from this view, is much more likely than disintegration. The danger is that what the Framers built better than they knew – American federalism – will be transformed according to what they thought they knew – their individualistic theory. Tocqueville, in some measure, points to this conclusion: the Fourteenth Amendment, especially as interpreted by an activist, nationalizing judiciary, would more or less inevitably combine with the ever intensifying progress of the division of labor (II.ii.20) to eviscerate the authority of and devotion to the states.

Tocqueville even foresees the change in the American Union that would be the result of the Fourteenth Amendment. He says that there are, in such a Union, certain matters that are clearly national, such as "war and diplomacy." There are others that are clearly provincial or local, such as "the budget of townships." But there are others that are mixed: they are of interest to all the nation's individuals, but there is "no necessity that the nation itself provide for them." The example he gives of such "mixed objects" are "civil and political rights." Prior to the Civil War, such rights weren't uniformly regulated by national government, and that's one reason why the preponderant force over people's lives remained with the states (I.ii.10). The Fourteenth Amendment transferred the power of regulating rights to the national government, with uniformity in mind. The states' racist denial of rights discredited the idea that states' rights is compatible with the effectual protection of individual

---

12 Diamond 2002 and Zuckert 1983 have some Tocquevillian appreciation, at least, of the political benefits of decentralization.

rights. And so the national government acquired and gradually implemented its power to Lockeanize many of the details of ordinary life.

The Tendency Toward Dissolution

Tocqueville's stronger tendency, however, is to reject any theory of more or less inevitable nationalization. He goes as far as to say that the fear of many Americans concerning consolidation is "entirely imaginary." The dominant truth is that "the federal government is becoming visibly weaker." The sovereignty of the Union, he explains, "is an abstract being," "a work of art" (I.i.8). The sovereignty of the American nation is *artificial*, whereas that of the states is much more *natural*.

The national Union attracts liberated individuals, beings who act consistently according to their interests and so are not moved by love or prejudice or natural instinct. But the states in their much more immediate and detailed enveloping of the ordinary lives of citizens will, Tocqueville says, attract the hearts of whole or real human beings. The Union only "offers a vague object for patriotism to embrace," while the sates have much more "fixed forms and circumscribed boundaries." They're also much more connected with the concrete and tangible foundations of the imagination – the soil, property, memories, and dreams. The national government will have all the advantages when it comes to guns and money, but will that power be enough to secure the loyalty of beings who are much more than merely beings with interests (I.ii.10)?[13]

Tocqueville provides contradictory evidence concerning changes in "patriotic sentiment" among the Americans since the time of the Constitution's ratification. In some ways, the American patriotism has become "less exclusive," or less attached to particular states. Mail, steamboats, and commerce have caused the Americans to know each other better, and the restlessness of the American keeps his travels from being confined to one state or even one region. On the other hand, the Constitution failed to extinguish "the individuality of the states, and all bodies ... have a secret instinct that carries them toward independence." That's especially true in America, where each citizen is particularly attached to a particular locality "habituated to governing itself." So the willfully independent and democratic Americans engage in "a great combat" from "the provinces" against "central power" (I.ii.10).

Are the Americans primarily interdependent beings with interests or willful beings asserting their often blind independence against all hierarchy and authority? There are both centralizing and decentralizing passions at work in their country. But, on balance, Tocqueville concludes, "the sentiment of independence has become more and more lively in the states," and so "the love of provincial governments" has become "more and more pronounced" (i.ii.10).

---

13   Tocqueville "expected the Union to remain weaker than the states for as long as citizens continued to be moved less by shared reasoning or common need and more by habit or passion" (Mansfield and Winthrop, 61).

The centralizing passions support the theory of the Framers; the truth is that "the goal of the federal constitution was not to create a league, but to create a national government." Their intention was to create a single people, a "national will" determined by the majority, to which all minorities – including dissident states – have the duty to submit. But the ambiguity of their real accomplishment – the incomplete national government – allowed for the development of a rival legal doctrine: the Constitution is a contract of sovereign states, and each state interprets its obligations under that contract for itself. Is America one people or is it "a league of independent peoples"? The gradual weakening of the federal government will be the cause of the growing ascendancy of the latter view, even or especially because it is contrary to the centralizing or nationalizing intention of the leading Framers (I.ii.10).

America was largely one society at the time of the Constitution's ratification, but that Constitution allowed most political life to continue to be dispersed among the states. So loyalty to the states, in Tocqueville's view, should have been expected to grow over time, largely at the expense of the national government.[14] And although the intention of the Framers was for the government to be decisively national and so indissoluble, the states increasingly tend to understand the Constitution as a confederation that *they* created as nations through *their* "free will." Tocqueville remarks that if "one of these same states wanted to withdraw its name from the contract, it would be quite difficult to prove that it could not do so" (I.ii.10).

The states as states have come to regard the Union as "useful" but not "essential" to their well-being. So any particular state would not hesitate to withdraw its consent from the constitutional contract if it suited its interests, and there doesn't seem to be any state or groups of states that would be "disposed to make very great personal sacrifices to preserve" the Union. All in all, it's easy to show that the states have numerous "immense interest[s]" in remaining united, but that the Union also might easily collapse if perceptions of interests change. In the absence of real political loyalty to the national government – deeply instinctive as opposed superficially reflective patriotism – and a willingness to fight for its perpetuation, America is in the midst of becoming less of a real nation than the Constitution itself says. That's why the very existence of the Union seems like an "accident" to Tocqueville, although republican government of some kind seems essential to the Americans' self-understanding (I.ii.10).

Tocqueville's criticism here is, in part, of the understanding of government itself as a contract rooted in individual utility or selfishness. The Framers understood the national government to be based on the free, self-interested consent of sovereign individuals. Yet they also maintained that those individuals couldn't withdraw their consent when their perception of their self-interest changed. Individuals as individuals, of course, don't have the wherewithal – the power – to exercise any right of withdrawal of their consent to government on their own. But the states are, in a way, a form of collective individuality or particularity, and patriotism itself

---

14   Maletz 1999 gives a good account of this criticism of the Framers' idea of the Union.

is, in large measure, a selfish extension of oneself. The states have what it takes to make the willful nullification of the selfish contract effective (I.ii.10).

The contractual theory of the Framers and the anarchic theory of the "nullifiers" aren't as different as it first seems. The nullifying South Carolina, Delba Winthrop notices Tocqueville showing, "speaks as if she had a copy of Locke's *Second Treatise* in her hand," and that state's resistance seems both contrary to the Framers' intent and in accordance with their Lockean principles (Winthrop 1976, 108–09). South Carolina intended no return to a state of nature, because its alternative to the national government was not the sovereignty of the individual but of its own government. But even the return to the state of nature can be justified as better than submission to a national government dominated by an oppressive majority faction (I.2.10; I.i.7).

Orestes Brownson, writing at the close of the Civil War, was even more insistent that cause of the war was the secessionist theory embraced by the leading Framers. The Lockean understanding of the American Constitution as based on the consent of "sovereign individuals" is incompatible with the idea of real loyalty to a particular nation. If individuals are sovereign, then obedience must be voluntary. A Lockean Union consists not of citizens, but of confederates, of people who use each other to advance their private interests. The Framers, Brownson observes, may have thought they "were constituting a real government," but they also thought, quite inconsistently, that they had produced "a treaty, a compact, or agreement among sovereigns" (Brownson 2003 [1866], 153). "The right of secession was certainly never contemplated by the framers of the constitution," Brownson admits, but that doesn't mean they have a coherent argument against it (Brownson, 1864).

For Brownson, the key issue is whether we have a nation or a confederation in this sense. Are Americans citizens loyal to a nation occupying territory in a particular part of the world, or are they sovereign individuals who finally, only have loyalty to themselves? For a consistent Lockean, "the right of secession" applies to all of human social life – to marriage, the family, religion, and government itself. And no nation – or no family or no church – can endure that understands itself to be composed of individuals with that right.[15]

One piece of evidence among many that Tocqueville would have echoed Brownson's explanation of this important cause of the Civil War is his refusal to find the foundation of the American nation in the revolutionary, rights-based individualism of the Declaration of Independence. In the long run, as the Tocquevillian Pierre Manent has shown us, modern individualism is at war with the very idea of the nation (Manent 2007). That's obviously true in sophisticated Europe today, but also in the autonomous, cosmopolitan theorizing of American sophisticates. American patriotism persists because the majority of Americans, even today, don't understand themselves primarily or consistently as beings with interests. They are, as they were in Tocqueville's day, the most religious – and the most loving and proud – of the modern, middle-class peoples (Lawler 2007).

---

15   See Lawler 2003, 56–71 for a fuller account of the connection between the Framers' state-of-nature individualism and the South's claim of the right of secession.

The problem of predicting whether the national government will complete itself or disintegrate altogether is connected to the psychological issue animating much of *Democracy in America*. The American moral doctrine, he observes, is "self-interest well understood." Each American complacently brags about his freedom by saying that he's always thinking about his interests, his pursuit of his own, individual happiness. He's free because he's never suckered. He proudly says he never loses his head in natural impulses such as love. But Tocqueville observes, from his aristocratic view, that the Americans *are* much better than *they* say; their bragging actually assists in masking their real love of God, their country, and each other (II. ii.8).

The Americans' love and especially their pride are evidence that they're more than they brag that they are. They have, Toqueville observes, "an immense opinion of themselves," and "they are [even] separated from all peoples by a sentiment of pride." Pride is a manifestation of individuality; it is a "decentralizing" passion; it opposes itself to the apathetic materialism that characterizes contentless individualism. Even when the Americans believe they are merely serving their interests, they're doing more than that. And so any "merely reflective patriotism" based on interests alone Tocqueville refuses to trust. The Americans are quite capable of preferring their own willfulness to what's best for their merely material interests, and so they are quite capable of choosing their prejudiced attachments to their states and localities – which are extensions of their manly attachments to their own significance as particular beings – over efficient and interdependent centralization (I.ii.10).

The history of America, for Tocqueville, will hinge, in great measure, on to what extent what Americans say about their freedom transforms who they are. If they become more exclusively beings with interests, then the national government will, in fact, complete itself over time. But a statesman – as opposed to some Lockean theorist – would doubt that words could actually defeat the heart-enlarging natural instincts we can't help but have (II.ii.4; II.ii.12; II.ii.15). As long as Americans really are more than beings with interests, interests won't really keep the Union together, and its future might well depend on whether the states or the nation inspire more effectively the deep patriotic instinct that's natural to proud and loving beings. But if Americans really do become predominately beings with interests, if the Framers' theory transforms their very beings, then interests alone might secure the Union's future. The result, however, would likely be less a proud nation than a soft despotism administered by meddlesome schoolmarms (II.iv.6).

North vs. South or the Middle Class vs. the Aristocrats

The most immediate cause of the centralization of the Fourteenth Amendment was a war between the states, one whose outcome was in doubt. *The* most significant psychological cause of that war, Tocqueville predicted in advance, is that human beings can't be counted on to act according to their interests. The people of the southern states were too proud (of their aristocratic way of life) and too scared (of what would happen if their slaves were liberated) to be able to act either reasonably or justly (I.ii.10).

The differences of interests and opinions flowing from the fact that some states allowed and others prohibited racially based slavery were a huge exception to Tocqueville's generalization that America was one society. But the threat slavery poses is not primarily through different interests or opinions. Its presence or absence has a fundamental effect on the character of human beings and so on the type of civilization they choose. "Slavery," Tocqueville explains, "does not attack the American confederation directly by its interests, but indirectly through its mores." The northerners had the middle-class characters of free beings who work, and the leading southerners had the characters of aristocrats – of beings proudly freed from work for nobler pursuits. The northerners thought of themselves as primarily beings with interests, and the southerners thought of themselves as much better than that. The northerners are proud that they have more money and are more just than the southerners, but the southerners are proud that they live more freely or nobly than northern wage slaves. The southerners – with their love of hunting and fighting – are considerably more barbaric than the northerners, but they're also more brilliant and imaginative because they think more highly of themselves and their place in the world (I.ii.10).

The fundamental division in America, from one view, is between the states that allow slavery and those that don't. From another view, the division is really regional, and the states offer the slaveholders "prepared organization[s]" with which to defend the distinctive way of life. The aristocratic opinions that correspond lower levels of power and prosperity – not to mention monstrous injustice – of the slaveholding civilization are shared by the leading citizens of all the states in the region. To some extent, "states' rights" is a vehicle for defending the southern aristocracy and its racially based slavery. But that way of life, in the short term, also functions to defend the prerogatives of the states against the project of complete nationalization. The slaveholders defend human particularity against impersonal centralization. The proud and vain assertiveness of the leading southerners, like that of all aristocrats, both promotes injustice and individuality (as opposed to individualism [II.ii.7]) (I.ii.10).

If the Union dissolves into regional confederations, Tocqueville observes, the cause will likely be southern pride and envy. As the northern states become more prosperous, the citizens in the southern states increasingly feel slighted or dishonored. They are losing their proud place in the Union, and out of both pride and fear they refuse to surrender the unjust or leisurely way of life that's the real cause of their growing political and economic inferiority. Slavery, Tocqueville pointedly observes, has a "fatal influence … on the well-being of the master himself." And "[i]t is difficult to conceive of a lasting union between two peoples when one is poor and weak, and the other is wealthy and strong." From this view it's "the very prosperity" of the North that is "the greatest danger that threatens the United States" (I.ii.10).

The southerners, for good reason, have no confidence that the powerful northerners will treat them with justice. The two peoples have come to have two different views of what justice is, and the northerners offend southern honor by holding their aristocratic and racist view of justice in contempt. It's hardly in the self-interest of the states of the South to be left alone with the slaves whom they imagine, with good reason, hate them, but their indignation still can't help but get the better of them. Rather than submit to degradation, they'll assert their particular rights. They'll defend the honor of their individual choices by defending the laws of their particular states against the perceived tyranny of the (northern) majority and the impersonal economic forces pushing toward homogenization. If the Union dissolves – and Tocqueville thinks that likely – it will be rooted in the decentralizing tendency found in human nature itself (I.ii.10).

When it comes to virtues, the northerner is strong where the southerner is weak, and vice versa. The active and industrious middle-class northerner is stronger according to the natural standards of strength and justice, and so he deserves to prevail. And prevail, Tocqueville predicts, he almost surely will. That doesn't mean that the southern states won't be allowed to separate, if that's what they want. Tocqueville also doesn't predict that the South would be doomed to defeat in some war between the states or regions. Even if southern pride is the cause of the states' separation, Tocqueville does predict, the middle-class or northern way of life will eventually dominate or become "the standard" everywhere in America (I.ii.10).

In the decisive respect, consolidation or social uniformity will happen, whether or not the Union endures. The crucial differences in laws, mores, and characters that separate the people of the northern and southern states are bound to fade away. The South's aristocratic civilization is as doomed as those once found in Europe or among the American Indians. Whether America remains one or becomes two or several nations Tocqueville regards as an "accident" or inessential to comprehending the likely future of the people of the United States (I.ii.10). America, Tocqueville would not have been surprised to see, is much less diverse in this crucial respect than it was at the time he wrote *Democracy in America*.

The association of both the southern way of life and states' rights with the defense of slavery and racism, Tocqueville suggests, will weaken the states or contribute to nationalization over the long term. The middle-class American is pretty much blind to the manifestations of human liberty and greatness found among either the Indians or southern aristocrats. All he sees is discredited indolence and injustice; aristocratic pride, for middle-class Americans, is nothing but self-serving vanity. Tocqueville's suggestion is that, over the long term, proud and loving human individuality might wither away in the service of both economic efficiency and egalitarian uniformity, whatever happens to the federal system (II.ii.16; II.iv.4–6). But Tocqueville also observes and predicts the possibility of fierce rebellions against merely middle-class life on behalf of the indestructible needs of the human soul, whether the American national government either becomes more comprehensive or disappears (II.ii.12). Great revolutions will become rare, in his view, but not impossible (II.iii.21). And so the decentralizing passions that made the American federal system necessary, from the Framers' view, and a human good, from Tocqueville's view, may or may not have much of a future.

Is There a Theory of American Federalism?

Tocqueville leaves us to reflect on the fundamental inadequacy of the American federal system. It is contrary to the theoretical intention of the leading founders. Insofar as it is supported by a theory based upon the mixture of centralizing and decentralizing passions that compose human nature, that theory is imposed from without. It is, in fact, not acknowledged as true by partisans on either side in the American debate over whether the United States is a national government or a federal league. The very existence of the federal system Tocqueville presents as an American accident with a very uncertain future.

The Constitution's Framers, by constructing an incomplete national government, built better than they knew, but even they themselves had no particular interest in perpetuating the mixture of national and federal elements they constructed. Because they overestimated the place of interests in securing people's loyalty to government, they didn't anticipate that the Union they constructed would be eroded over time by increasing political loyalty to the states. The coming of the war between the states would only have surprised Tocqueville insofar as the northern states were so resolute in resisting the Union's dissolution. His explanation for his error would begin with the observation that no one could have predicted the statesmanship of Lincoln, but he would add that even the North's victory left the country with no theory that corresponded to the good that is (in many ways was) the American federal system. We still don't know how to think about the states as indispensable parts of an American whole, just as we still don't know how to think about the relationship between human particularity – including the particularity of political life and the nation – and our general or universal principles.

References

Alulis, J. (1998), The price of freedom: Tocqueville, the Federalists, and the Antifederalists, *Perspectives on Political Science* 27:2 (Spring), 85–92.

Brownson, O. A. (1864), Are the United States a nation? *The Works of Orestes Brownson* (Detroit: Thorndike Norse, 1882–87), vol. 17 (originally published in 1864).

—— (2003), *The American Republic* (Wilmington, DE: ISI Books,) (originally published in 1866).

Deutsche, E. and Fornieri, J. (eds) (2008), *An Invitation to Political Thought* (Belmont, CA: Thomson/Wadsworth).

Diamond, M. (2002), The ends of federalism, in P. Lawler (ed.) (2002), *Tocqueville's Political Science: Classic Essays*.

Hancock, R. (2002), Tocqueville on the good of American federalism, in P. Lawler (ed.) (2002), *Tocqueville's Political Science: Classic Essays*.
— (2008), Brownson's political providence, with some preliminary comparisons with Tocqueville's providential statesmanship, *Perspectives on Political Science* 37:1 (Winter), 17–22.
Kincaid, J. (1999), Confederal federalism and citizen representation in the European Union, *West European Politics* 22 (April), 34–58.
Krislov, S. (2001), Federalism as American exceptionalism, *Publius* 31:1, 9–26.
Lawler, P. A. (1993), *The Restless Mind: Alexis de Tocqueville on the Origin and Perpetuation of Human Liberty* (Lanham, MD: Rowman and Littlefield).
— (ed.) (2002), *Tocqueville's Political Science: Classic Essays* (New York: Garland Publishing).
— (2003), Introduction to the ISI edition, Orestes A. Brownson, *The American Republic* (Wilmington, DE: ISI Books).
— (2005), *Stuck with Virtue* (Wilmington, DE: ISI Books).
— (2007), *Homeless and at Home in America* (South Bend, IN: St. Augustine's Press).
— (2008), Tocqueville, in E. Deutsche and J. Fornieri (eds) (2008), *An Invitation to Political Thought*.
Maletz, D. J. (1999), The Union as idea: Tocqueville on the American Constitution, *The History of Political Thought* 19:4, 599–620.
Manent, P. (2007), *Democracy Without Nations: The Fate of Self-Government in Europe* (Wilmington, DE: ISI Books).
Mansfield, H. and Winthrop, D. (2000), Editor's introduction to Alexis de Tocqueville, *Democracy in America* (Chicago: University of Chicago Press).
Schmitter, P. (2000) Federalism and the Euro-polity, *Journal of Democracy* 11 (January), 40–47.
Stepan, A. (1999), Federalism and democracy: Beyond the U.S. model, *Journal of Democracy* 10 (October), 19–24.
Tocqueville, Alexis de (1998), *The Old Regime and the Revolution*. A. Kahan trans. (Chicago: University of Chicago Press).
— (2000), *Democracy in America*. Harvey Mansfield and Delba Winthrop trans. (Chicago: University of Chicago Press).
Winthrop, D. (1976), Tocqueville on federalism, *Publius* 6:3, 93–115.
Zuckert, C. H. (1983), Reagan and that unnamed Frenchman (de Tocqueville): On the rationale for the new (old) federalism, *Review of Politics* 45 (July), 421–42.

Further Reading

Frohnen, B. (1993), *Virtue and the Promise of Conservatism: The Legacy of Burke and Tocqueville* (Lawrence, Kan: University Press of Kansas).
Jardin, A. (1998), *Tocqueville: A Biography*. L. Davis trans. (New York: Farrar, Straus, and Girous).

Manent, P. (1996), *Tocqueville and the Nature of Democracy*. J. Waggoner trans. (Rowman and Littlefield).

Mitchell, J. (1995), *The Fragility of Freedom: Tocqueville on Religion, Democracy, and the American Future*. (Chicago: University of Chicago Press).

Zunz, O. and Kahan, A. S. (2002), *The Tocqueville Reader: A Life in Letters and Politics* (Blackwell Publishing).

John C. Calhoun's Federalism and its Contemporary Echoes

James Read

I

This chapter explores John C. Calhoun's minority veto/consensus model of federalism, as well as some contemporary or recent political arrangements – in Northern Ireland, the former Yugoslavia, and proposed though not implemented in South Africa – that resemble what Calhoun advocated. The chapter also compares Calhoun with James Madison and with the influential contemporary comparative-politics theorist Arend Lijphart, whose concept of "consociational democracy" echoes Calhoun in important ways.

The political theory of John C. Calhoun of South Carolina (1782–1850) grew directly out of his political experience. He was born in the closing years of the Revolutionary War, was elected to Congress in 1810, and served as Secretary of War from 1817 to 1824. He served as vice-president under John Quincy Adams and then under Andrew Jackson (and politically opposed both presidents). During the late 1820s and early 1830s he fought against the high protective tariff, which he saw as economic warfare by northern manufacturers against southern agriculture; and argued for a state's right to nullify any federal law (such as the protective tariff) that the state considered unconstitutional or harmful to its interests. Nullification was a central element both of Calhoun's federalism and of his wider political theory, which insisted that decisions be made on the basis of consensus among all key sections and interests instead of through majority rule. Nullification was supposed to ensure only those laws and policies truly beneficial to all regions and interests.

Calhoun insisted that each individual state – not the federal judiciary or any federal body – was the final judge of a state's constitutional rights and obligations. The only limitation on a state's right to be final judge was the following: if three-fourths of the other states passed a constitutional amendment overriding a single state's nullification, the nullifying state must either rescind its nullification or peacefully secede from the Union.

In 1833 Calhoun became US senator from South Carolina, a position he held until the end of his life (except for a term as secretary of state). The issue that most preoccupied him from the early 1830s until his death in 1850 was slavery. He saw abolitionism as a dangerous attack on the rights and interests of the South. Calhoun sought above all to protect the interests of the (white) Southern minority of slaveholders from the actions of a (white) national majority hostile to the spread of slavery. Slaves themselves did not count as an "interest" at all in Calhoun's theory and of course had no veto rights over decisions affecting them.

Calhoun's two major works of political theory, both completed near the end of his life, were *A Disquisition on Government* and *A Discourse on the Constitution and Government of the United States*. The present chapter focuses on the intersection between Calhoun's federalism, under which each member state enjoys veto rights over decisions of the whole, and his more general consensus model of government. Calhoun clearly intended the first as a means to the second: nullification was not intended to produce weak government or engineer stalemate, but to force all key interests in the United States to work together in the common good. This problematic intersection between federalism and a consensus decision rule also characterizes the twentieth-century cases examined later in the chapter.

To understand Calhoun's federalism it is essential to distinguish it from some other varieties. The term "federal" describes many systems that function in different ways and serve very different purposes. In all federal systems constitutional powers are divided in some way between central government and member states, which retain their own distinct identities and some measure of political autonomy. A system that concentrated all power in a central government would not be federal. Nor at the other extreme would a group of states that recognized no constitutional obligations toward one another constitute a federation. But there is a large range of territory between these two poles. Federal systems vary according to *how* powers are divided between central government and states; what specific *purposes* federalism is supposed to achieve – what good is to be realized or what evil prevented; and *who decides* where the line is drawn between the respective spheres of authority.

One model of federalism, arguably the one intended by the Framers of the US Constitution and embodied in its provisions, would be the following. Those powers whose exercise directly concerns the whole political community (national defense, foreign trade, tariffs, interstate commerce, and so on) are assigned to the national government and accountable to a national majority; while those powers that principally concern each member state's peculiar interests and needs are reserved to the state and accountable to the majority within that state. Where some state law or policy interferes with a power constitutionally assigned to the national government, the state must yield, for it is encroaching on the good of the whole: that is the point of the "supreme law of the land" clause of Article VI.

In practice the line between these two spheres is not always clear, and in disputed cases the final decision must be made by some organ of the central government. As James Madison puts it in *Federalist* No. 39: "In controversies relating to the boundary between the two jurisdictions, the tribunal which is ultimately to decide, is to be established under the general government" (Madison

1999, 216). This model presupposes that there exists a national political community transcending the separate peoples of each state. It also assumes a relatively high degree of interdependence: what one member state does (or refrains from doing) can crucially affect the rights or interests of the whole.

A very different model of federalism comes closer to what has come to be called a "confederation." (The distinction between "federal" and "confederal" is not always clear cut.) The US Articles of Confederation, the governing document for the United States from Independence until 1788, exemplifies this much more decentralized model. Under the Articles, each individual state was sovereign, and one state could block decisions of the whole. This vulnerability to obstruction was one of the "defects" of the Articles that the Constitution was intended to remedy. But even after ratification of the Constitution there continued to be a strong states' rights, strict-constructionist constitutional tradition that saw the United States as a loose federation of sovereign states.

This kind of federal (or confederal) system is arguably most appropriate where citizens' attachments are overwhelmingly to their member state, not to the wider political community; and where interdependencies of interest are kept limited: member states keep the peace by staying out of one another's way. As long as interdependencies are limited, member states can implement widely varying, even contradictory, policies and laws without any pressing need to sort out the differences.

What is interesting and problematic about Calhoun's federalism is that it attempts to have the best of both models: the effective central government and orientation toward the common good that characterizes the first model, together with the full state sovereignty and veto power over collective decisions that characterize the second. Calhoun did not assume states could get along with no common policy at all on important matters. On the contrary, he assumed some urgent necessities on which "something *must* be done" and which "can be done only by the united consent of all" (*Disquisition*, in Lence 1992, 48; emphasis in original.) He believed individual states' capacity to block decisions of the whole would not prevent urgent collective action but instead ensure its fairness. Nor did Calhoun's federalism presuppose any clear line separating the jurisdiction of the federal government from that of the member states. Setting and collecting tariffs, for example, was a power clearly assigned to Congress under the Constitution and specifically denied to the states; but Calhoun believed states had the right to block the unjust exercise of a federal power. Thus Calhoun's has to be regarded as a third model of federalism, distinct from either of the other two. Whether Calhoun's model can in practice achieve the best of both worlds is of course another question.

Calhoun insisted on state veto rights over collective decisions because he believed majority rule would always lead to majority despotism, especially where there were deep (and geographically marked) divisions of interest. A majority concentrated in one region, with its own economic and social interests, would write those interests into law at the expense of a minority with different interests located in another region. Under this scenario, majority and minority were unlikely to change places under the ordinary circumstances of political competition: once a regional interest found itself in the minority it would stay there forever. The majority never has to worry about finding itself in the minority and thus has no incentive to treat minorities justly.

Standard models of democracy assume that a minority coalition can hope to become a majority by persuading enough voters in the middle to switch their political allegiances. But change of allegiance is unlikely to happen where differences between majority and minority are deeply marked. In our contemporary world this might result from nationality, language, race, ethnicity, religious differences, or a host of other causes. Calhoun himself in the antebellum US context was most concerned with differences in mode of production (northern manufacturing versus slave-plantation agriculture).

Calhoun's diagnosis of majority tyranny and proposed remedy contrasted with James Madison's well-known diagnosis and remedy in *Federalist* No. 10. Madison argued that majorities were more likely to oppress minorities in small, homogenous political communities than in extended republics which contained a large number of diverse interests, no one of them enjoying a majority. Under Madison's scenario, unjust majorities were prevented from easily forming. But Madison was still an advocate of majority rule. The right kind of institutional arrangements would produce rational, deliberate majorities – those that embody "the permanent and aggregate interests of the community" (Madison 1999, 161).

Calhoun understood Madison's argument and rejected it. Calhoun believed that a number of developments since Madison's time – including the advent of national political parties, the sharpening of divisions between industrial north and agricultural south, and above all divisions over slavery – meant that a regionally concentrated minority interest could find itself permanently facing a determined national majority hostile to its interests. In the end Madison remained an advocate of majority rule while Calhoun sought an alternative to it.

Calhoun's remedy was to insist on a consensus rule: "to give to each division or interest, through its appropriate organ, either a concurrent voice in making and executing the laws, or a veto on their execution" (*Disquisition*, in Lence 1992, 21). The minority, in short, had to be given permanent, guaranteed veto rights over collective decisions. He called this the principle of the "concurrent majority." The idea was to ensure only those laws and policies that truly benefited every "portion" or "interest" within the community. That was the point behind giving each state, as the representative of some regionally concentrated interest, veto rights over federal law. Calhoun also proposed the creation of a kind of dual presidency, one for the North, one for the South, each of whom would enjoy veto rights over executive acts (*Discourse*, in Lence 1992, 275).

Calhoun did not intend merely to engineer stalemate. Using veto rights to block a collective decision was only stage one. Calhoun believed that the crisis triggered by nullification would force stage two: the statesmen representing each "portion" or "interest" would come together, deliberate in good faith, and resolve the matter in a manner acceptable to all. "When something *must* be done – and when it can be done only by the united consent of all – the necessity of the case will force to a compromise – be the cause of that necessity what it may" (*Disquisition*, in Lence

1992, 49). He compared this decision procedure to the deliberations of a jury, which must also render a unanimous decision.

Calhoun's consensus rule does not everywhere require federalism. Calhoun considered the Roman Republic a consensus government because the senate and the people each possessed veto rights and nothing could pass that was not supported by both. But veto rights in Rome were exercised by orders (the senate and people), not geographically bounded states. In the United States, however, Calhoun believed the key interests (northern manufacturing, western farmers, southern plantation agriculture) were geographically distributed such that giving a state (like South Carolina) veto rights over federal law meant giving veto rights to the *interest* that predominated in that state. This leaves open the question: who defends those minority "portions" or "interests" that do not control any member state and thus possess no veto rights?

In what follows I describe some contemporary or recent (actual or proposed) political arrangements that resemble what Calhoun recommended. In examining these cases we should keep in mind that Calhoun himself did not seek merely to block action; he believed that the exercise of veto rights would force the leaders of each interest to deliberate together in good faith and act in the true common good. This raises the standard according to which such political arrangements ought to be judged.

II

Among contemporary political scientists Arend Lijphart is probably the one whose theoretical approach is closest to Calhoun's. Lijphart coined the term "consociational democracy" and has championed this idea both theoretically and practically for at least 35 years. The degree of Lijphart's influence is evidenced by the frequent use of the term "consociational" in the literature of comparative politics. Few other comparative political scientists demonstrate any familiarity with Calhoun, but Lijphart himself is explicit about the similarities between Calhoun's thought and his own.

By "consociational democracy," Lijphart means a "consensus model of democracy" characterized by "the cooperative attitudes and behavior of the leaders of the different segments of the population" (Lijphart 1977, 21–36). He contrasts consociational democracy with the majority/opposition model of democracy ("the Westminster model") where a majority party or coalition governs, in competition with a minority that remains in loyal opposition and that seeks to replace the majority. Lijphart argues that the majority/opposition model may be appropriate to homogeneous societies like Britain, but is not appropriate to "plural societies" – "societies that are sharply divided along religious, ideological, linguistic, cultural, ethnic, or racial lines into virtually separate subsocieties with their own political parties, interest groups, and media of communication." European nations that (at least in the 1970s) Lijphart described as "plural societies" include Belgium, the

Netherlands, Austria, and Northern Ireland; plural societies elsewhere in the world include Nigeria, Lebanon, Malaysia, and South Africa.

In a society deeply divided into segments, Lijphart argues, "the flexibility necessary for majoritarian democracy is absent" because voters' loyalties are rigid rather than fluid, and there is little chance that "the main parties will alternate in exercising governmental power." Under such conditions, "majority rule is not only undemocratic but also dangerous, because minorities that are continually denied access to power will feel excluded and discriminated against and will lose their allegiance to the regime … What these societies need is a democratic regime that emphasizes consensus instead of opposition …" (Lijphart 1984, 22–23). This consensus regime is what Lijphart means by consociational democracy.

According to Lijphart there are four essential requirements of consociational democracy: (1) "government by a grand coalition of the political leaders of all significant segments of the plural society"; (2) "the mutual veto or 'concurrent majority rule'"; (3) "proportionality as the principal standard of political representation"; and (4) "a high degree of autonomy for each segment to run its own internal affairs." (Lijphart 1977, 25).

Requirement (2) follows from the insufficiency of requirement (1), that all interests be included in a grand coalition. Lijphart observes that "participation in a grand coalition offers … no absolute or foolproof protection" to a minority, because "it may nevertheless be outvoted by the majority." (In other words, there is a difference between a minority's merely being consulted and having the right to block action.) "When such decisions affect the vital interest of a minority segment, such a defeat will endanger intersegmental cooperation. A minority veto must therefore be added to the grand coalition principle; only such a veto can give each segment a complete guarantee of political protection." Lijphart then adds that "The minority veto is synonymous with John C. Calhoun's concurrent majority" (Lijphart 1977, 37).

Lijphart addresses the chief objection to the minority veto, i.e. "that it will lead to minority tyranny, which may strain the cooperation in a grand coalition as much as the outvoting of minorities." He lists three reasons "why this danger is not as serious as it appears." All three of the reasons are drawn from Calhoun's own answer to the same objection and are supported with quotations from Calhoun's *Disquisition*. First, because it is a *mutual* veto ("Calhoun uses the term 'mutual negative'", Lijphart notes), its too frequent use can be turned against the minority's own interest. Second, "the very fact that the veto is available as a potential weapon gives a feeling of security which makes the actual use of it improbable." Finally, "each segment will recognize the danger of deadlock and immobilism that is likely to result from an unrestrained use of the veto." This is immediately supported by a quote from Calhoun: "Impelled by the imperious necessity of preventing the suspension of the action of government … each portion would regard the sacrifice it might have to make by yielding its peculiar interest to secure the common interest and safety of all, including its own, as nothing compared to the evils that would be inflicted on all, including its own, by pertinaciously adhering to a different line of action" (quoted in Lijphart 1977, 37; original passage in Lence 1992, 51). Thus

Lijphart's theory of consociational democracy resembles Calhoun's concurrent majority, not only in the method itself (the "mutual veto"), but also in the reasoning employed to answer the principal objection to the theory.

Lijphart makes clear that consociational democracy and federalism are not necessarily the same: there can be consociational systems that are not federal and federal systems that are not consociational. Whether a federal system advanced consociational goals would depend on how minority populations were distributed geographically, how federal district lines were drawn, and whether the member units possess veto power over collective decisions. But in practice Lijphart's consociational theory naturally lends itself to federalism wherever minorities are geographically concentrated rather than equally spread across the territory. In this respect too Lijphart and Calhoun are alike. For Calhoun also recognized that the relation between federalism and the consensus model was contingent rather than necessary; federalism supports the consensus model in the United States but would not have done so in the Roman Republic.

In at least one respect Lijphart's minority veto is broader than Calhoun's. Lijphart's minority veto includes both formal veto rights "anchored in the constitution" and "an informal and unwritten understanding" that governs political cooperation among the different segments; *constitutionally guaranteed* minority veto rights are essential in some countries and not in others. For Calhoun, in contrast, the minority veto always had to be a clear constitutional guarantee.

III

John C. Calhoun was of Scots-Irish descent, and his spirit seems to have presided over negotiations in his ancestral homeland. The Good Friday Agreement of 1998 attempts to resolve the longstanding and bitter conflict between nationalists and unionists in Northern Ireland through arrangements that perfectly embody Calhoun's principle of the concurrent majority. There is no evidence that Calhoun's writings were directly consulted, but Arend Lijphart's theory of consociational democracy (which in turn draws from Calhoun) was an explicit influence on the Northern Ireland settlement; this is acknowledged by both supporters and critics.[1] Thus the Good Friday Agreement will function as a test case for the theoretical prescriptions of both Calhoun and Lijphart.

The agreement requires that all "key decisions" receive majority support from both of the two key groups, the predominantly Protestant Unionists (who seek to remain part of Great Britain) and the predominantly Catholic Nationalists (who seek ultimately to join Northern Ireland to Ireland). All members of the assembly must designate themselves "nationalist," "unionist," or "other." All key legislation

---

1 On the explicit role of consociational theory in the design of the agreement, see McGarry and O'Leary 2004, 1–4 and Horowitz 2001, 38. Horowitz is critical of consociational theory but concedes its key role in shaping the agreement.

requires "concurrent nationalist and unionist majorities as well as a majority of MLAs [members of the Legislative Assembly]." (Note the use of Calhoun's own term here, "concurrent majority.") Decisions require "both an overall majority of Assembly members and a majority of both unionist and nationalist members." If a strict concurrent majority fails, there is a fallback procedure whereby legislation may be passed on the basis of "a weighted majority – the support of 60 per cent in the Assembly, including at least 40 per cent of both registered nationalists and unionists" (McGarry and O'Leary 2004, 290–1). Thus key decisions require both a majority in the assembly as a whole, and majority support (or, in the fallback procedure, near-majority support) among both the nationalist group and the unionist group, which gives each of these two groups a veto. The assembly members designated "other" such as the Northern Ireland Women's Coalition – which seeks to organize voters around issues that challenge the ideologies of both major groups – do not enjoy any veto rights.

The concurrent majority/consensus model also has been built into the executive branch, which has been described as a "diarchy" – a First Minister and a Deputy First Minister, each representing one of the two key divisions, and at least in theory of equal power. "If either the First Minister or the Deputy First Minister ceases to hold office, whether by resignation or otherwise, the other shall also cease to hold office." The purpose here is not merely to allow each to veto decisions of the other – though of course it has this effect – but also, more positively, to force the two to work together: "… this new diarchy will critically depend upon the personal cooperation of the two holders of these posts" (McGarry and O'Leary 2004, 264).

The "diarchy" executive, whether by design or chance, closely resembles Calhoun's own proposal for a dual executive for the United States, each representing one of the two great sections of the country, and "requiring each to approve all the acts of Congress before they shall become laws." (*Discourse*, in Lence 1992, 275). Recall that for Calhoun the purpose of veto powers was not merely to block action; stalemate was not the goal. The purpose was to force deliberation and cooperative action in the common good. The *intention*, at least, of the Northern Ireland diarchy – to force "personal cooperation" between top leaders of two antagonistic communities – is exactly the same.

The Agreement leaves open the key long-term question of whether Northern Ireland will remain part of Great Britain or join the Republic of Ireland. What it does instead is incorporate both of those external entities (and others as well) into the political process. This is where the federal aspect comes in. If we looked only at the parliamentary arrangements, the Northern Ireland settlement would appear to exhibit the consensus model, but not necessarily a *federal* version of the consensus model; for the nationalist and unionist groups are not cleanly separated by district lines. But in another respect it is a federal arrangement. The Agreement was from the outset pushed by outside actors – the United Kingdom and the Republic of Ireland above all, with additional participation by the European Community and the United States. Built into its operations are a network of federal and confederal arrangements between Northern Ireland and Ireland, Northern Ireland and the UK, and the UK and Ireland (McGarry and O'Leary 2004, 272–79). The Agreement itself is in effect a treaty between the UK and the Republic of Ireland, who remain its ultimate guarantors.

It is too early to judge whether the Good Friday Agreement will bring about lasting peace and effective government in Northern Ireland. If the Agreement succeeds, not only in restraining open violence, but also in creating a viable and effective political community out of two embattled groups, it will be evidence in favor of Calhoun's political theory. But some features of the Agreement limit its precedent for other deeply divided societies. If the Agreement breaks down, governance responsibilities revert to the safety net of Anglo-Irish cooperation. This removes the threat of dangerous anarchy, the "imperious necessity" that according to Calhoun (and to Lijphart, quoting Calhoun) would force all groups to work together in good faith. It would be a truer test of the theory to observe how the Agreement would work in the absence of any safety net. I am not recommending that this experiment be attempted.

In the short run even deadlock may be preferable to continued violence. But the consensus theory of government ultimately depends upon positive cooperation among leaders of conflicting groups in realizing common goals. This is the standard by which to judge the success of the consensus model in Northern Ireland and the federal arrangement that sustain it.

IV

The ill-fated former Federal Republic of Yugoslavia would seem an odd comparison for the political theory of John C. Calhoun. Calhoun's writings had no more impact on Yugoslavia than Yugoslavia (not yet existing) had on Calhoun. And yet in many respects Yugoslavia was a practical test of the consensus federalism championed by Calhoun.

Yugoslavia consisted of six republics (Serbia, Croatia, Slovenia, Bosnia, Montenegro, and Macedonia) and of two "autonomous provinces" within Serbia (Kosovo and Vojvodina). It also included a number of national groups with long histories (Croats, Serbs, Slovenes, and so on) whose demographic distribution corresponded only roughly to the republics that bore their names: thus in 1991 the population of the republic of Croatia was 78.1 percent Croat, 12.2 percent Serb, with a scattering of other groups; the republic of Serbia was 65.8 percent Serb, 17.2 percent Albanian (concentrated in Kosovo); meanwhile significant numbers of Serbs lived in Croatia and Bosnia (Woodward 1995, 33–35). In the Bosnian republic no single group composed a majority. There were also religious divisions between Catholicism, Orthodox Christianity, and Islam that did not precisely coincide with either republican boundaries or national tradition.

The consensus-based federal system adopted by Yugoslavia in the 1970s was an attempt by the communist leadership to resolve a number of governance challenges that had been building up over time. Under Yugoslavia's 1974 constitution, key decisions were to be made by a process of "harmonization of views" among the several republics rather than majority rule; each republic possessed a de facto veto over federal decisions (which could be temporarily overridden in emergencies). A rotating collective presidency was created to ensure the participation of each republic in the formation and execution of federal measures.

One purpose of the 1974 constitution was to defuse nationalist conflicts through a timely decentralization of power. All national groups were officially regarded as equal. The consensus requirement was supposed to reinforce this principle by preventing any one national group from dominating the others. The other major purpose was to resolve distributional conflicts between the *republics* (whose boundaries did not perfectly coincide with national groups). Much of Yugoslav economic development policy involved transfer of resources from wealthier republics like Slovenia to comparatively underdeveloped republics like Bosnia. This was resented by the wealthier republics, which demanded more control over the economic resources at their disposal (Burg 1983, 55–56).

The 1974 constitution provided that "decisions in the federation should be taken on the basis of harmonization [of views] and agreement among the republics ... It precludes the adoption of any policy without the complete agreement ... of all republics and provinces." This meant "explicit recognition of a principle of unanimous decision making" (Burg 1983, 110).

Though the intention of the consensus requirement was to resolve inter-republic and nationality conflicts, its actual effect was the opposite. "Although these procedures aimed to protect smaller republics and to prevent majority tyranny, they tended to end in deadlock, which could be broken only by temporary measures that delayed real agreements ... The consensual voting rules gave each party to the negotiation a veto. For those who believed their bargaining position was strong, there was little incentive to negotiate trade-offs and compromises and much potential gain from obstructionist tactics, stubbornness, or the threat of a walkout" (Woodward 1995, 60). One consequence of the inability of the federal government to make effective economic policy was to worsen the very ethnic and nationality conflicts the consensus system was intended to diffuse, and to lead increasing numbers of individuals to turn to their ethnic or national group to provide the economic subsistence and physical protection that the federal government was too weak to provide (Woodward 1995, 15–17).

When the communist monopoly of political power was broken in the late 1980s Yugoslavia attempted to establish itself as a true democracy. With respect to the federal structure, two very different reforms were proposed. One proposal (advanced by Serbia, whose motives invited suspicion) was "to improve the efficiency of the federation by giving the federal government greater authority to enforce federal acts" (Hayden 2000, 32).

The other proposal, advanced by Slovenia and Croatia, was to remodel Yugoslavia as a pure confederation, with full sovereignty for the constituent republics, an explicit and unilateral right of secession, and an absolute consensus requirement for federal action: even on matters explicitly within its jurisdiction the federal government could act only with the consent of all republics. Slovenia proceeded to act on the assumption of full sovereignty in a manner directly parallel to Calhoun's theory: by nullifying 27 federal laws and incorporating language in the Slovenian constitution giving Slovenian law precedence over federal constitution and law (Andrejevich 1990c). When the federal Constitutional Court declared Slovenia's action to be unconstitutional, Slovenia declared the Constitutional Court's decision to be unconstitutional (Hayden 2000, 44). In October of 1990 Slovenia and Croatia issued a joint declaration of "sovereignty based on a confederal arrangement" with a purely consultative parliament and a Council of Ministers in which "all decisions, with the exception of procedural decisions, would be made unanimously" (Andrejevich 1990c, 30–31).

These proposals were advanced, not with the declared aim of dissolving Yugoslavia, but at least ostensibly for the purpose of preserving Yugoslavia in a new and better form. The actual result was the breakup of Yugoslavia, which triggered a decade of civil war and ethnic cleansing in which more than a hundred thousand were killed and millions forcibly relocated or turned into refugees. It would be wrong to claim that Yugoslavia's consensus-based federal order was the chief cause of this tragedy. There were a number of causes, both old and recent, that drove the breakup of the country and the warfare that followed. However, it is clear that the consensus process established by the 1974 constitution *failed to prevent* exactly those problems it was intended to resolve. The more radical proposals put forward by Slovenia and Croatia, even if they had been accepted (the two republics declared independence before any decision was made on the proposals) would neither have saved the federation, nor made possible any series of clean, peaceful secessions for the ethnically mixed republics of the former Yugoslavia.

Calhoun's consensus model of federalism, and even his insistence on a right of secession, were intended to make the actual resort to secession unnecessary, because secession itself meant a bloody "knife of separation through a body politic … which has been so long bound together by so many ties, political, social and commercial" (Calhoun 1959, *Papers* 14:107). The case of the former Yugoslavia does not support Calhoun's faith in the workability of a federal system operating under a consensus requirement. But it reconfirms a hundred times over his observation about the bloody knife of separation.

V

Calhoun's federalism is significant, not only where it (or something like it) has been implemented, but also where it has been seriously considered; for this shows it remains a live option in the modern world. One place it was seriously considered if ultimately rejected was South Africa.

The century-long struggle that culminated in a democratic South Africa in 1994 began as a contest between racial equality and racial monopoly. But toward the end, when it was clear that racial monopoly would fall, it became a contest between majority rule and minority veto. At stake here was a real decision between two options. The aim of then-prime minister F. W. de Klerk and the ruling National

Party, in initiating the reform process in the late 1980s, was to design a government that included all races but that did not turn over full political power to a black majority. In the end it was majority rule that won out, above all because Nelson Mandela and the African National Congress refused to compromise on this point. But under different bargaining conditions and different leadership on one or both sides, some version of a permanent minority veto might have been enshrined in the new South African Constitution – as the National Party had intended from the outset of the reform process.

The form of government envisioned by F. W. de Klerk, when he commenced the reform process, was one under which "minorities have special rights, and whites special powers, in a political system constructed – as in the days of apartheid – from separate racial groups. De Klerk believed the presidency should rotate between white and non-white leaders, with matters of importance decided collectively by all of them – an arrangement that would have given whites a veto over the majority. He wanted this form of power sharing enshrined in the Constitution, forever" (Waldmeier 1997, 135). Much later, in 1993, when it was clear his original vision of power-sharing was unacceptable and the ANC had gained the upper hand, de Klerk continued to insist on high super-majority rules for important legislation and a requirement that in the cabinet (where the National Party expected to participate as a minority partner) "decisions be taken by consensus, a system that would give each party an effective veto over the others." Only at the very end did the National Party reluctantly agree to drop the minority veto "in favor of a commitment from the ANC that it would take decisions 'in a spirit of national unity'" – i.e., a promise from the majority to seek consensus rather than a constitutional right on the part of the minority to demand it (Waldmeier 1997, 178, 214).

Though the National Party's principal object was a veto for the white minority, the same proposal would have guaranteed veto rights to regionally based non-white groups such as the ethnically Zulu Inkatha Freedom Party headed by Mangosuthu Buthelezi. Because South Africa is divided not only by race but also by language and ethnicity, the minority veto was advocated by some – including Arend Lijphart – as a means of protecting the interests of all minorities, not just whites (Lijphart 1985). One proposal for a post-apartheid constitution was to grant veto rights to every group enjoying at least 15 percent in parliament (Slabbert and Welsh 1979, 153–54, citing Lijphart 1977, 37 for support, who in that passage is quoting and paraphrasing Calhoun).

Because many South African minority groups were regionally concentrated, the minority veto/consensus proposals included federal elements. In this respect it resembled Calhoun's own consensus model as applied to the geographically distributed interests of the United States. Thus the National Party's minority veto proposal would have also created (in Nelson Mandela's unfavorable characterization) "entrenched regional powers that would be binding on a future constitution." The Inkatha Freedom Party demanded not only veto rights over national decisions but also an "autonomous and sovereign" Zulu homeland. Something similar was demanded by conservative white groups uniting "around the idea of a volksstaat, a white homeland" (Mandela 1994, 525, 532).

As it turns out, though there was a reasonably high degree of consensus on the constitutional settlement itself, the actual constitution that emerged did not inscribe consensus as a permanent, constitutionally guaranteed decision rule. One of the chief arguments in favor of such a rule had always been that white South Africans would resort to civil war rather than accept the rule of a black majority whose decisions they could not block. Yet in the end Nelson Mandela was able to persuade white South Africans to turn over power peacefully without any permanent special guarantees.

This brings us to Mandela's own peculiar version of consensus-seeking politics, which played an indispensable role in the peaceful revolution that occurred in South Africa. Despite all predictions to the contrary, white South Africans did in the end allow political power to be turned over to Mandela and the African National Congress – and thus to the black majority – without civil war. Whether South African whites would have willingly turned over power to a black leader other than Mandela is an open question. Without compromising on the essential principle of majority rule, Mandela was somehow able to reassure a critical mass of white South Africans that their interests would not be overlooked and that they would be honored citizens in a new South Africa.

In his autobiography *Long Walk to Freedom* Mandela speaks about his admiration for the consensus model in traditional African governance: "The meetings would continue until some kind of consensus was reached. They ended in unanimity or not at all ... Majority rule was a foreign notion. A minority was not to be crushed by a majority" (Mandela 1994, 18–19). But his admiration for the traditional consensus rule definitely did not make Mandela into an advocate of a formal minority veto when he and the ANC began negotiating with the government in the early 1990s. (Ironically in this respect de Klerk's insistence on a formal consensus rule comes closer to the African tribal model celebrated by Mandela.) But Mandela clearly did consider it a high moral duty that a majority not crush a minority, and he knew the Afrikaners' own history and heroes well enough to be able to honor their traditions even as he challenged their regime. He did not just give verbal assurances to white South Africans; he made them believable. Calhoun's minority veto/consensus model of government absolutely depends upon enlightened statesmanship to function at all. Calhoun was not content with the merely negative step of blocking action. He believed instead that the threat of deadlock or anarchy brought about by the resort to veto rights would in turn call forth the efforts of true statesmen to resolve the crisis.

The case of Mandela and South Africa should lead us to ask whether genuinely enlightened statesmanship might make the minority veto unnecessary by achieving something approaching consensus in another way, at least during especially critical periods where consensus is indispensable. If the objection is raised that one cannot always count upon enlightened statesmanship in a system based on majority rule, the same objection holds at least equally for any minority veto/consensus model of government; for Calhoun's consensus model cannot function at all without exemplary leadership.

One might also ask the counterfactual question: what would have been the effect of a constitutionally mandated minority veto rule in a country as divided and potentially ungovernable as South Africa was in the mid-1990s? A post-apartheid South African state that was impartial with regard to race, but unable effectively to govern because every group could veto its operations on a continuing basis, would have been a disaster.

South Africa ultimately decided in favor of a limited-majority-rule model of government, despite predictions that it could never work there. And it was a decision, not a foregone conclusion: the minority veto model (with corresponding federalism elements) could have been implemented, with results about which we can only speculate.

If the Good Friday Agreement in Northern Ireland stands in the long run the best chance of proving that Calhoun's prescribed solution can work, the survival and health of constitutional majority rule in South Africa stands in the long run the best chance of proving Calhoun's solution unnecessary.

References

Andrejevich, M. (1990a), Slovenia heading toward independence, *Report on Eastern Europe* 1:13 (30 March), 36–40.

—— (1990b), Kosovo and Slovenia declare their sovereignty, *Report on Eastern Europe* 1:30 (27 July), 45–47.

—— (1990c), Crisis in Croatia and Slovenia: proposal for a confederal Yugoslavia, *Report on Eastern Europe* 1:44 (2 November), 28–33.

Burg, S. L. (1983), *Conflict and Cohesion in Socialist Yugoslavia: Political Decision Making Since 1966* (Princeton: Princeton University Press).

Calhoun, J. C. (1959), *The Papers of John C. Calhoun*, Vols 10–28, Clyde N. Wilson (ed.) (Columbia: University of South Carolina Press).

Hayden, R. M. (1999), *Blueprints for a House Divided: The Constitutional Logic of the Yugoslav Conflicts* (Ann Arbor: The University of Michigan Press, paperback ed., 2000).

Horowitz, D. L. (2001), The Northern Ireland Agreement: clear, consociational and risky, in *Northern Ireland and the Divided World: The Northern Ireland Conflict and the Good Friday Agreement in Comparative Perspective*, John McGarry (ed.) (Oxford: Oxford University Press), 89–136.

Lence, R. M. (ed.) (1992), *Union and Liberty: The Political Philosophy of John C. Calhoun* (Indianapolis: Liberty Fund).

Lijphart, A. (1977), *Democracy in Plural Societies* (New Haven and London: Yale University Press).

—— (1984), *Democracies: Patterns of Majoritarian and Consensus Government in Twenty-one Countries* (New Haven and London: Yale University Press).

—— (1985), *Power-Sharing in South Africa* (Berkeley: Institute of International Studies, University of California).

Madison, J. (1999), *James Madison: Writings*, Jack N. Rakove (ed.) (New York: The Library of America).
Mandela, N. R. (1994), *Long Walk to Freedom: The Autobiography of Nelson Mandela* (Boston, New York and London: Little, Brown and Company).
McGarry, J. and O'Leary, B. (eds) (2004), *The Northern Ireland Conflict: Consociational Engagements* (New York and Oxford: Oxford University Press).
Van Zyl Slabbert, F. and Welsh, D. (1979), *South Africa's Options: Strategies for Sharing Power* (New York: St. Martin's Press).
Waldmeier, P. (1997), *Anatomy of a Miracle: The End of Apartheid and the Birth of the New South Africa* (New Brunswick NJ and London: Rutgers University Press).
Woodward, S. L. (1995). *Balkan Tragedy: Chaos and Dissolution After the Cold War* (Washington DC: The Brookings Institution).

Further Reading

Bartlett, I. H. (1993), *John C. Calhoun: A Biography* (New York and London: W. W. Norton).
Burg, S. L. (1988), Political structures, in *Yugoslavia: A Fractured Federalism*, edited by Dennison Rusinow, 9–22. (Washington DC: The Wilson Center Press).
Calhoun, J. C. (1992a), *Fort Hill Address*, 26 July 1831, in *Union and Liberty: The Political Philosophy of John C. Calhoun*, Ross M. Lence (ed.) (Indianapolis: Liberty Fund).
—— (1992b), *The South Carolina Exposition*, 19 December 1828, in *Union and Liberty: The Political Philosophy of John C. Calhoun*, Ross M. Lence (ed.) (Indianapolis: Liberty Fund).
Ford, Lacy K. (1994), Inventing the concurrent majority: Madison, Calhoun, and the problem of majoritarianism in American political thought, *The Journal of Southern History* 60:1 (February), 19–58.
Freehling, W. W. (ed.) (1965), *Prelude to Civil War: The Nullification Controversy in South Carolina 1816–1836* (New York and Oxford: Oxford University Press).
—— (1967), *The Nullification Era: A Documentary Record* (New York: Harper & Row).
Gligorov, V. (1994), Is what is left right? (The Yugoslav Heritage), in *Transition to Capitalism: The Communist Legacy in Eastern Europe*, Janos Matyas Kovacs (ed.), 147–72 (New Brunswick NJ and London: Transaction Publishers).
Kateb, G. (1969), The majority principle: Calhoun and his antecedents, *Political Science Quarterly* 84:4 (December), 583–605.
Lerner, R. (1963), Calhoun's new science of politics, *The American Political Science Review* 57:4 (December), 918–32.
Lijphart, A. (1968), *The Politics of Accommodation: Pluralism and Democracy in the Netherlands*. (Berkeley: University of California Press).
—— (1969), Consociational democracy, *World Politics* 21:2 (January), 207–25.

McGarry, J. (ed.) (2001), *Northern Ireland and the Divided World: The Northern Ireland Conflict and the Good Friday Agreement in Comparative Perspective* (Oxford: Oxford University Press).

Niven, J. (1988), *John C. Calhoun and the Price of Union: A Biography* (Baton Rouge: Louisiana State University Press).

O'Malley, P. (2001), Northern Ireland and South Africa: "Hope and history at a crossroads," in *Northern Ireland and the Divided World: The Northern Ireland Conflict and the Good Friday Agreement in Comparative Perspective*, John McGarry (ed.), 276–308 (Oxford: Oxford University Press).

Rae, D. (1975), The limits of consensual decision, *The American Political Science Review* 69:4 (December), 1270–94.

Rusinow, D. (ed.) (1988), *Yugoslavia: A Fractured Federalism* (Washington DC: The Wilson Center Press).

Wiltse, C. M. (1949a), *John C. Calhoun, Nationalist, 1782–1828* (Indianapolis and New York: Bobbs-Merrill).

—— (1949b), *John C. Calhoun, Nullifier, 1829–1839* (Indianapolis and New York: Bobbs-Merrill).

—— (1949c), *John C. Calhoun, Sectionalist, 1840–1850* (Indianapolis and New York: Bobbs-Merrill).

15

A More Perfect Union: Secession, Federalism, and Democracy in the Words and Actions of Lincoln

William Mathie

Does federalism entail the right of secession? Might it not even define federal systems of government that their members have a qualified – or unqualified – right to secede? In 1996 the Government of Canada asked Canada's Supreme Court whether the Province of Quebec – its "National Assembly, legislature or government" – could unilaterally effect the secession of Quebec from Canada by virtue of the Canadian Constitution or international law, and if this might be justified in one but not the other of these ways, which would govern the case. The Court replied (in 1998) that even if a clear majority of those voting in a referendum on a clearly stated question approved secession, this would not in itself authorize the province to secede unilaterally (*Reference re Secession of Quebec*, 2 S.C.R. 217). On the other hand, the Court also held that this would authorize the province to proceed towards that goal through "principled" negotiations with the government and other provinces of Canada and that the other provinces and federal government "would [in this situation] have no basis to deny the right of Quebec to pursue secession ... so long as in doing so, Quebec respect[ed] the right of others." In the course of delivering its opinion, the Court added that it must be left to the political actors involved, and not the Court, to decide what was or was not a clear question and what would constitute a clear majority, and that the Court would play no role in supervising the negotiations through which secession might be effected. If the secession of Quebec cannot be effected by the unilateral action of its government, it may be brought about through negotiations that reconcile "the various rights and obligations" of "two legitimate majorities, namely the majority of the Province of Quebec and that of Canada as a whole." The Court has in this way identified a process to which Quebec and the federal and other provincial governments would become obligated by a clear vote for secession in

Quebec, what it calls "principled" negotiations. Or we might say that the Court has identified what it deems a necessary condition of secession by Quebec. But is that condition also sufficient? As the Court acknowledges, there can be no guarantee in advance that those negotiations would be successful, but the Court does not tell us what "successful" means in this case. Does it mean agreement by all of the parties engaged in those negotiations to secession and to the terms on which it is to occur? Or what one or other party to the negotiations may plausibly describe to members of their own constituency as a serious effort to negotiate? The Court does not say. It does indicate that it will not answer this question even if it should later be asked of the Court. The Court, we may add, did not find its response to the questions the government had posed it within the text of the Canadian Constitution but within its own wider understanding of the several principles implicit in the Canadian Constitution including democracy, federalism, the rule of law, and the rights of minorities.

Questions resembling those put to Canada's Supreme Court were addressed by the 16th President of the United States on the occasion of his inauguration on March 5th 1861 and a few months later on July 4th in a message to a special session of Congress convened by that president, Abraham Lincoln, to approve what he had done and proposed to do in response to the actions taken in several states to secede from the Union. In this case, however, the questions posed were not reference questions directed to a judicial tribunal abstracted from any case in law, but questions implicit in the actions of several Southern slave-holding states and in the statements made by those taking and defending those actions. And if the judgment of the Canadian Court was addressed to several audiences including the federal government and the government of Quebec and the leadership of the separatists in Quebec and Ottawa advising them in effect as to how they might or might not proceed in the pursuit of their several objectives with the Court's approval, Lincoln must say what he says on both occasions in circumstances of immense danger and uncertainty, and he too must address a complex and conflicting set of audiences. On the other hand, if the Canadian Court could define and even restrict its own future role in the actions that might surround a referendum vote seeming to support secession – holding that it could not properly say as a court whether a clear majority had voted on a clear question of secession or determine whether any subsequent negotiations between Quebec and the rest of Canada were genuine or "principled" or sufficiently attentive to the rights and obligations of all those affected by those negotiations in Quebec and the rest of the country – what Lincoln could and could not do as chief executive would be hugely affected by what he said now, though how far he could successfully carry out the intention expressed in his words was unclear enough to preclude anything like sure calculation on his part. And what he would and could do at once and over the next four years would greatly affect the understanding of what he said.

My aim in this chapter is to see what we might learn about "federalism" by considering some of the things that were said and done by Abraham Lincoln as a political actor and participant in the political struggles of the years immediately preceding the US Civil War and as president through the four bloody years of that war, but especially as he took up the duty of administering the executive power and confronted the steps taken by the political leadership in several Southern states to secede from the Union following his own election in November 1860. But why should we look for a better understanding of federalism than what is immediately available in our ordinary understanding of the thing as citizens of what is said to be a federal form of government, or as students of contemporary political science? And why should we look for that better understanding in the place suggested? My answer to the first question is that our ordinary understanding of federalism as, say, a division of powers between a central or federal government and local, provincial, or state governments treats federalism as a means without knowing what its end might be, and so is unable to adjudicate conflicts between the two levels of authority, or to say whether it is the central or local authority that ought finally to determine the boundary between central and local authority. But what of our second question? How far might we suppose the truth about federalism to be revealed by a crisis arising out of a claim to secede? And even if it be granted that the meaning of federalism might be clarified by a consideration of the question of secession, why should we suppose that we can learn anything of universal significance about the meaning of federalism from a secession crisis arising in one particular political regime in one particular time and place, much less from the words of one man exercising executive authority at the heart of that crisis and using his words not to obtain a philosophic understanding of federalism as a political phenomenon but to accomplish a variety of complex political aims? And why, finally, should we expect to learn anything of general application by reflecting upon a crisis having as much or more to do with the issue of slavery than with the meaning of federalism? For the most part, the answer to these several doubts will be furnished in the course of the discussion that follows.

Lincoln explicitly addresses the claim that the Constitution of the United States justifies secession by the states under certain conditions that those claiming to secede say have been met, and sets out his implicit understanding of federalism as it bears upon, or is the basis of, his refutation of this claim in the two major public statements he makes in the first moments and months of his presidency – in his First Inaugural on March 4th 1861 and four months later in his address to a Special Session of Congress he has convened on July 4th 1861 (Fehrenbacher 1989b). In his Inaugural address Lincoln speaks as six states have seceded, a seventh is about to do so, and an eighth deliberates doing so. He speaks at a time of great public uncertainty as to what the Union – Congress and the Executive – will do – what it can do and what it should do – in response to these actions. In the speech on July 4th he speaks after South Carolina has fired upon Fort Sumter and he has "called out the war power" (Fehrenbacher 1989b, 250). Whatever Lincoln's own expectations, intentions, and priorities he must speak in the first speech as one eager to do whatever is reasonable to avoid the use of arms while also persuading his hearers how "reasonable" is to be defined in present circumstances; in the second, he must rather win approval for what he has done already in taking up arms and for what he proposes to do in prosecution of the war that has now begun. Whatever his own estimate of this probability, what he says about secession in the first speech must be said as if he supposes that he might persuade those seceding to abandon the course of action they have begun (Jaffa 2000, 237–50). The condemnation of secession in the speech on July 4th need no longer be qualified by this assumption.

In his Inaugural Lincoln must answer those who claim already to have seceded from the Union and those contemplating doing the same, including those more and less likely to do so. So far as he can, he must dissuade those who might leave the Union, and shape the expectations of those who already have. But, of course, whatever Lincoln says to the South is heard by the North, if indeed his words are actually heard at all in the states who have already disrupted the Union. Indeed, the Northern response to what he says to the South and his account of the secessionist challenge as it emerges out of his response to that challenge must be at least as important as its affect upon actual or potential secessionists. In the second place, even as he speaks to the North, Lincoln must address a complex variety of Northern opinions and again, so far as he can, achieve control over various possible responses to the threat – and reality – of secession by several Southern states. In the third place, Lincoln must define his own role as president and secure an adequate measure of public and congressional acceptance for his understanding of that role: he must show that it is his peculiar duty as president to prevent the dissolution of the Union and identify and justify a means whereby he might fulfill that duty. And finally Lincoln must dissuade other nations from recognizing the claim of the secessionists to be an independent state.

"It might seem, at first thought, of little difference whether the present movement at the South be called 'secession' or 'rebellion.'" With this remark Lincoln begins his refutation of the "ingenious sophism" that if conceded leads logically "to the complete destruction of the Union" in his July 4th Message (Fehrenbacher 1989b, 254). The sophism is that any state of the Union may by its own decision withdraw from the Union in accordance with the national constitution and thus do so lawfully and peacefully: secession is the name given to that decision by those claiming the right to make it. The importance of what Lincoln calls a sophism from the point of view of those employing it, Lincoln says, is that the people whose support they sought would not have supported "at the beginning" what was openly acknowledged to be "rebellion." The moral sense, respect for law, and patriotism of that people could only be overcome by an "indirect" approach. The chief and perhaps whole source of the sophism that makes this indirect approach possible is, Lincoln says, "the assumption that there is some omnipotent and sacred supremacy, pertaining to a State – to each State of our Federal Union." Lincoln has already – in his First Inaugural address – defended the opposing assumption that the Union is perpetual simply because it is a national government and perpetuity is implicit in the fundamental law of all national governments, and as a proposition that is confirmed by the actual history of the American Union (Fehrenbacher 1989b, 217–18). And, in his July 4th Message, he attacks the false assumption of the sacred supremacy of the states. These arguments we may take as, in part, a response to the first and best-known statement of what Lincoln calls the ingenious sophism through which the "rebellion" was "sugar-coated." That statement declaring "the Immediate Causes Which Induce and Justify the Secession of South Carolina from the Federal Union" had been adopted on December 24, 1860 by delegates assembled in Convention for this purpose and claiming to speak for the people of South Carolina (May and Faunt 1960, 76–81).

Imitating the words and style of the *Declaration of Independence* so far as they can, the authors of South Carolina's *Declaration* claim to speak for the people of a state resuming "her separate and equal place among nations." To justify their act of secession, they appeal to three principles. Two of these, they say, were "established" by that earlier *Declaration* and by the war successfully waged for independence. The first was the claim of the colonies, uttered in the concluding paragraph of the *Declaration*, "that *they* are, and of right ought to be, Free and Independent States" (emphasis added – as Lincoln will observe, the South Carolinians substitute "they" for "these United Colonies") with the power to do all that independent states may rightly do, which the authors take to be the right of each state to govern itself. The second was "the right of a people to abolish a Government when it becomes destructive of the ends for which it was instituted." Treating this right simply as "asserted" and then "established" by the Colonies, the authors of South Carolina's declaration ignore altogether its basis as this was set out in the *Declaration* they otherwise imitate by these words:

> *We hold these truths to be self-evident, that all men are created equal, that they are endowed by their Creator with certain unalienable Rights, that among these are Life, Liberty and the pursuit of Happiness.--That to secure these rights, Governments are instituted among Men, deriving their just powers from the consent of the governed, --That whenever any Form of Government becomes destructive of these ends, it is the Right of the People to alter or to abolish it, and to institute new Government, laying its foundation on such principles and organizing its powers in such form, as to them shall seem most likely to effect their Safety and Happiness.*

The third principle to which the South Carolinians appeal is one they derive from the manner in which the Constitution was adopted. Their argument is this. The 13 states who had acquired their independence from the British Empire had – in order to do so – "entered into a League, known as the Articles of Confederation, whereby they had agreed to entrust the administration of their external relations to a common agent" while expressly reserving the rights and sovereignty of each state except as their rights were expressly delegated to that common agent, "the United States in Congress assembled." Deputies who were later appointed by the states to revise these Articles, had recommended the adoption of what became the Constitution of the United States when nine of the "several sovereign States" to whom it had been submitted should agree; this "compact" would thereupon "take effect among those concurring; and the General Government, as the common agent, [would be] then invested with their authority." The sovereignty of the states as parties to this compact is shown, the authors say, by the fact that any states not concurring would remain as they had been, "separate sovereign States, independent of any of the provisions of the Constitution" established by and among those concurring. (In the

Federalist papers #43, Madison had justified the mode whereby the Constitution was to take effect with the agreement of the people in nine of the thirteen states as this departed from the rule of unanimity set out in the Articles that were to be replaced by the Constitution. Madison had appealed first to the revolutionary right of a people to abolish or alter its government when it shall see fit but then added that a further argument might be drawn from the defective manner in which the Articles themselves had been adopted in some states. But Madison casts a different light upon the possible situation of any states who should fail to ratify and so enter into the Constitution assuming it is approved by the required number. In this "delicate" situation moderation on the part of those who have joined the union and prudence on the part of those who have not (yet) done so would be called for (Hamilton et al. 2001, 230). He adds that both those who have and those who have not ratified would remain morally related (Jaffa 2000, 379–86). That the states retained their sovereignty was, according to South Carolina explicitly confirmed by the 10th Amendment's declaration that those powers that the Constitution neither delegated to the United States nor prohibited to the states were reserved to the states or to the people. The consequence of the mode whereby the Constitution was effected, as understood by the South Carolinians, entails what they call "the law of compact." By this "law," they suppose, the failure of any of the parties to the compact to fulfill "a material part of the agreement" frees the others of their obligations, with each party to determine "the fact of failure" where no arbiter is named.

How do these principles justify secession? A condition of the compact so important that without it there would have been none was the Constitutional provision for the return of escaped slaves. The violation or disregard of this provision has released South Carolina from her obligation, the authors say. The several ends for which the Constitution was framed, as those ends are declared in its preamble – "to form a more perfect union, establish justice, insure domestic tranquility, provide for the common defence, promote the general welfare, and secure the blessings of liberty" – were to be accomplished, they add, "by a Federal Government, in which each State was recognized as equal, and had separate control over its own institutions" and under which the right of property in slaves was recognized by those provisions that gave free persons distinct political rights as well as "the right to represent" and burden of direct taxes for three-fifths of those slaves, and permitted the import of slaves from abroad for 20 years have been defeated. In fact, those ends have been defeated and the government itself has become destructive of them through the actions of non-slave-holding states in condemning slavery and denying the rights of property established in the 15 slave-holding states. And now a sectional party has found a means to subvert the Constitution in the Article that established the Executive Department through the election of a president who has been elected precisely "because he has declared that the 'Government cannot endure permanently half slave, half free,' and that the public mind must rest in the belief that slavery is in the course of ultimate extinction." That President intends, among other things, to prevent the taking of slaves into the common territories.

If his response to this argument as set out in his First Inaugural and July 4th Message is the proper place to begin our effort to see what Lincoln can tell us about federalism, we would observe that Lincoln is not the first president to address the secessionist argument we have just reviewed. Lincoln's predecessor, James Buchanan, had already done so a few weeks before South Carolina had actually adopted its Declaration, in his last State of the Union Address (Buchanan 1960, 7–54). In setting out Lincoln's answer it will be useful to contrast that answer to the one given by Buchanan. What is remarkable about Buchanan's Address is that he denies the lawfulness or constitutionality of secession and much at least of the theoretical argument upon which it is based while granting – or anticipating – much of South Carolina's complaint and denying that he, as executive, can, or that Congress should, employ force to prevent the dismantling of the Union by secession. Is there is a link between Buchanan's denial that he or Congress can do anything to prevent an action he condemns as unlawful and his implicit agreement with the substance of South Carolina's case and even the very narrow grounds on which he denies the lawful right of secession? Is there a corresponding link between Lincoln's understanding of his duty and authority as the executive and his understanding of democracy, federalism, and the status of slavery as these are to be understood within the Constitution and within the wider political and moral understanding upon which the Constitution itself rests? These are questions we must consider.

Buchanan sets out the Southern case so powerfully (and, even, in such exaggerated terms) that his condemnation of secession as unlawful and his appeal for patience could hardly have persuaded those to whom it was addressed. So Buchanan begins his account of the present crisis by condemning the North for permitting "violent agitation of the slavery question" and identifying this as the cause of widespread apprehension of slave uprisings in the South which "whether real or imaginary" have rendered half the households of the Union so insecure as to justify disunion by appeal to the concern for self-preservation which "is the first law of nature, and has been implanted in man by his Creator for the wisest purpose." How is this anxiety that would at some point, if not already, justify disunion to be overcome? Buchanan does not say other than to insist that it would "only" require the people of the North to recognize that they have no more right to condemn or interfere with slavery in the South "than with similar institutions in Russia or Brazil" (Jaffa 2000, 174). Buchanan says that all the Southerners want "is to be let alone and permitted to manage their domestic institutions in their own way" but he soon adds that they do rightly demand their equal rights in the territories – i.e. the protection of their slave property in the territories – and notes with approval the Taney Court's decision that no territorial legislature may restrict slavery. And, while pointing out that neither Congress nor any president nor the courts can be held responsible for the actions taken by various state legislatures to prevent the execution of the fugitive-slave laws, he concludes that unless the states do repeal the many unconstitutional provisions whereby they have interfered with those laws, "the injured States … would be justified in revolutionary resistance to the Government of the Union." Only when he has granted the justice of all but one, or possibly two, of the grievances he reviews, does Buchanan qualify what he has said. (The clearest exception is the complaint that a sectional party has elected a president who opposes slavery. Buchanan points out that the election of the president was in accord with the rules set out by the Constitution, and that that president has very limited powers to do mischief. He adds that the peculiar circumstances in which Lincoln was elected are unlikely to be repeated. The more ambiguous exception is the possibility of preventing Southerners from taking slaves into the territories. In this case, Buchanan must insist that the holding of the Court in the Dred Scott case will be maintained despite the election of the head of a political party whose chief campaign pledge has been to stop the extension of slavery into the territories.) The grievances Buchanan does endorse, in any case, might or even do justify revolutionary resistance to the Union but they cannot, he says, authorize the exercise of a lawful right of secession because there is no such right. And indeed Buchanan makes a strong case against South Carolina's argument albeit within very limited terms. He observes, for example, that the fierce debate at the time of its making and ratification as to whether the powers given by the Constitution to the central government were too dangerous would be senseless if it had been supposed true at that time that any state could at any time opt to secede from that Constitution. And he points out that the Articles of Confederation had claimed themselves to be perpetual, and the Constitution promised "a more perfect union." So we are left by Buchanan's argument with a refutation of the claim that there is a unilateral right of secession under the law of the Constitution and a compelling case for most of the grievances claimed by the seceders albeit as grounds for revolutionary resistance not secession. And it is in this context that Buchanan takes up the question of what can be done against acts of secession that are unlawful but perhaps justified as revolutionary resistance and concludes that as president his duty under his oath of office "to take care that the laws be faithfully executed" is not one he has the means to fulfill without action by Congress to supply those means, and further that Congress lacks the power under the Constitution to furnish such means and would be unwise to do so even if that power were authorized: "our Union rests upon public opinion, and can never be cemented by the blood of its citizens shed in civil war. If it cannot live in the affections of the people, it must one day perish. Congress possesses many means of preserving it by conciliation, but the sword was not placed in their hand to preserve it by force." Buchanan's last and only recommendation in the face of the threat or fact of unlawful, if justified, resistance by the slave-holding states is the adoption of Constitutional amendments that would recognize "the right of property in the States where it now exists or may hereafter exist," protect this right in the territories until they are admitted into the Union, and declare void all state efforts to impair or defeat the Constitutional right for the return of escaped slaves.

Like Buchanan, as we have already noted, Lincoln denies that there is a lawful right of secession: the unlawful actions of slave-holding states to remove themselves from the Union must be seen as "insurrectionary or revolutionary, according to circumstances." And like Buchanan, in his Inaugural Address Lincoln states that it is his "simple duty" under the Constitution, which is "unbroken" if the right of secession is denied, to take care that "the laws of the Union be faithfully executed in all the States." Unlike Buchanan Lincoln promises to perform this duty "so far as practicable, unless [his] rightful masters, the American people, shall withhold the requisite means, or in some authoritative manner, direct the contrary"(Fehrenbacher 1989b, 218). On the other hand, Lincoln, intends to use his power only to "hold, occupy, and possess the property and places belonging to the government, and to collect the duties and imposts" while foregoing the use of force beyond that purpose to impose federal office holders where local hostility to the Union prevents the filling of those offices by "competent resident citizens." Lincoln departs from the argument of his predecessor most importantly in addressing and opposing the claim of the secessionists that their rights under the Constitution have been denied. His argument is that revolution would be morally justified if any vital and express constitutional rights had been denied to a minority by the majority but none have. Whether fugitive slaves should be surrendered by state or national authority, whether Congress may prohibit slavery in the territories, whether it must rather protect slavery there are all questions that the Constitution does not expressly resolve. These are rather questions of the kind from which "spring all our constitutional controversies, and we divide upon them into majorities and minorities" and to reject the final rule of the majority in such controversies must be to endorse secession whose central idea is "the essence of anarchy. "A majority, held in restraint by constitutional checks, and limitations, and always changing easily, with deliberate changes of popular opinions and sentiments, is the only true sovereign of a free people" (220). Whoever rejects this principle must "fly to anarchy or to despotism" for "unanimity is impossible" and the permanent rule of the minority "wholly inadmissable." Nor may one hold that such questions are to be irrevocably settled by the Court in deciding cases brought before it. If this were granted the people would have "ceased to be their own rulers" (221). The "only substantial dispute" is the issue between that section of the country that "believes slavery is right and ought to be extended" and the other that "believes it wrong, and ought not to be extended" and this is a dispute that must be resolved by the majority. Like Buchanan Lincoln insists that the chief executive has no authority to fix terms for the separation of the states. Unlike Buchanan Lincoln observes that his own authority derives entirely from the people and that it is his duty to transmit to his successor unimpaired the government "as it came to his hands." Lincoln makes the argument we have just summarized in discharge of that duty.

Lincoln completes the argument of his Inaugural address in his message to the Special Session of Congress he has convened on July 4th of 1861. In this message Lincoln does two things. He justifies calling out the war power in response to the firing by South Carolina upon Fort Sumter and, in particular, one of his actions in doing so – the suspension of the writ of *habeas corpus* – on the basis of his understanding of his duty under the oath he has taken on becoming president, and he further defines the question posed by secession. By the former, he clarifies the special status of the executive in relation to the Constitution in the present crisis; by the latter, he sets out what he takes to be the meaning of federalism. While resisting the use of force other than to retain federal property so long as peaceful resolution could be thought possible, the issue posed by the attack at Sumter was "'Immediate dissolution, or blood'" and Lincoln's response undertaken some time prior to the meeting of Congress he now addresses was "to resist force, employed for [the Government's] destruction, by force for its preservation." Lincoln had called out the militia and appealed for additional volunteers. What Lincoln has done is remarkable only as it differs from the stated intention of Lincoln's predecessor, though Lincoln observes that the issue posed was also whether any "democracy – a government of the people, by the same people – can, or cannot, maintain its territorial integrity against its own domestic foes" (250). More remarkable in view of the question we are pursuing is the defence Lincoln furnishes for his decision to authorize the commanding general to arrest and detain those he thinks a threat to the public safety without resort to the ordinary processes and forms of law. To be sure, Lincoln sketches out an argument that might well justify his action as constitutional, but he does not leave it at this. He also argues that the one who is sworn to "take care that the laws be faithfully executed" may have the right or even duty under his official oath to disregard a single law if he believes that he can only thus prevent the whole of the laws failing in execution – as they were already in a third of the states. At the close of his Message, Lincoln describes the choice and duty that confronted him in these words:

> *He could but perform this duty or surrender the existence of the government. No compromise, by public servants, could in this case, be a cure; not that compromises are not often proper, but that no popular government can long survive a marked precedent, that those who carry an election, can only save the government from immediate destruction, by giving up the main point, upon which the people gave the election. The people themselves, and not their servants, can safely reverse their own deliberate decisions. As a private citizen, the Executive could not have consented that these institutions shall perish; much less could he, in betrayal of so vast, and so sacred a trust, as these free people had confided to him (Fehrenbacher 1989b, 261).*

Lincoln also offers a definition of federalism in his July 4th Message. He does so in the course of refuting the secessionist claim that the states only exercise a sovereign authority they have always enjoyed in removing themselves from the Union. Lincoln's response to the secessionist claim is that the states have only such powers as they enjoy by virtue of the Constitution having never been states out of the Union, and lose that status if they break from the Union, the old states became "Free and Independent States" only as United Colonies, united in making war to accomplish their independence. (So Lincoln corrects the South Carolinians who had written "they" where the authors of the *Declaration* had "these United Colonies" Fehrenbacher 1989b, 255.) If the powers enjoyed by the states are enjoyed by virtue of the Constitution, they are as marked out and distinguished from the powers of the national government in the Constitution. If we look for the principle on the basis of which this division is drawn, it is "no other than the principle of generality and locality. Whatever concerns the whole, should be confided to the whole – to the general government: while, whatever concerns only the State should be left exclusively, to the State. That is all there is of original principle about it" (257).

What Lincoln says here about the division between "National power, and States rights" states his understanding of federalism. But if this is so, it raises a number of questions. Certainly Lincoln's understanding of federalism, if that is what this is, flies in the face of the account of the purpose of Canada's federal scheme as described by the Judicial Committee of the Privy Council in 1919 in words cited with apparent approval by the Canada's Supreme Court in the Reference case *re Secession of Quebec*:

> *not to wield the Provinces into one, nor to subordinate Provincial Governments to a central authority, but to establish a central government in which these Provinces should be represented, entrusted with exclusive authority only in affairs in which they had a common interest. Subject to this each Province was to retain its independence and autonomy ...*

How far does what Lincoln calls "the principle of generality and locality" express the truth of American federalism? To what extent is the truth of federalism reflected in the understanding and practice of federalism in America? And even if we take federalism to be defined by the principle of generality and locality, how far does that justify the stand Lincoln takes in his Inaugural address and July 4th Message? How far does Lincoln's understanding of the Constitution and the question of slavery as expressed, for example, in those words cited by South Carolina, that the nation "cannot endure permanently half slave, half free," violate the rights of the states to control what is local as what concerns only them?

Does Lincoln speak the truth about the American constitution when he insists that the rights of the states are only those they enjoy by virtue of the Union and pertain only to what is of exclusively local concern? Though it is true that the colonies only became independent bodies through their united action in support of the claims made in the *Declaration of Independence*, it is also true to say that their relationship to one another under the Articles of Confederation was more or less that of parties to a league or treaty. We see this for example in their equality as members of that association, in the fact that the central agent under the Articles can deal only with the states who are its members as states and not with the individuals who are the citizens of those states, and in the rule of unanimity demanded for changes in the terms of that association. What we see in the Articles of Confederation are the features traditionally taken to define federalism, what its contemporaries and philosophers like Montesquieu meant by federalism: a means of combining the virtues of republicanism that are in this view available only in a political unit of very limited size and the means of defending those units against larger neighbors by common association for defence (Diamond 1992, 109). But this is not at all what we see in the government established under the Constitution in 1787 by those who had condemned what had existed under the Articles as entirely incompetent to obtain the ends of government all, or most, acknowledged and, in fact, as no government at all. Indeed, the primary defect of the Articles according to the devisers and defenders of the new constitution was that it could not act immediately upon individuals; one could say that the primary fault of the Articles was what had hitherto been understood as the defining principle of federalism. And finally its defenders concede that the Constitution they have made is only partly federal. Thus in the 39th *Federalist*, Madison responds to critics of the Constitution who insist that the new Constitution should be ratified only if it is federal in character because they think that it is only by being federal that a large society can be republican. His answer is to separate what the critics link. To be sure, the Constitution must be republican and it is: all powers under it are drawn from the people. But the test of federalism is secondary and no single or simple test (Hamilton et al. 2001, 193–94, 196). Federalism is no longer a critical test because in fact representation has permitted the extension of the sphere that may be encompassed by republican government and the special contribution made to the new science of politics by the American founders is the discovery that the gravest threat to liberty when the people govern themselves – tyranny by the majority – is best avoided by greatly extending the orbit. (This has been argued in the 9th and 10th *Federalist* papers. See, especially, Hamilton et al. 2001, 38.) When the federalism test is applied, the result is mixed. The Constitution is federal in the mode whereby it is to be established; partly federal, partly national when we look to the sources of the ordinary powers of government under it; national so far as the government will operate upon individual citizens – contrary to what opponents of the Constitution regard as the defining feature of federalism; federal in as much as the powers of the national government are enumerated and the states retain sovereignty over the powers not enumerated, though it is a federal tribunal that is to decide controversies concerning the line between national and state authority; and neither "wholly federal nor wholly national" in the manner whereby it may be amended. Were the devisers of the Constitution in fact authorized under the terms of the Articles of Confederation to propose a Constitution that so radically departed from the federalism of the Articles? Whether the new Constitution can be defended as a reformation or transformation of the Articles, and whether the authorization of those who met to make the new constitution extended so far as their work went, the fact that the new Constitution did not demand unanimity for its implementation and so did violate the provisions of the Articles may be dismissed by appeal to the acknowledged absurdity of permitting one state, however small and corrupt, to determine the fate of 12 (Hamilton et al. 2001, 203). Indeed, all possible formal objections to the work of the makers of the new Constitution are finally overcome by appeal to the words of the *Declaration of Independence*: rigid adherence to the forms established under the Articles of Confederation would have "rendered nominal and nugatory the transcendent the transcendent and precious right of the people to 'abolish or alter their governments as to them shall seem most likely to effect their safety and happiness'" (Hamilton et al. 2001, 205).

But if the principle of generality and locality as stated by Lincoln is consistent with the new federalism, does Lincoln correctly interpret that principle in his words as president when he argues that constitutional controversies not expressly determined by the text of the Constitution and, in particular, whether slavery may be prohibited in the territories or must rather be protected, are to be determined by the majority, and in his famous insistence as a leader of the Republican Party that the nation may not persist "half slave and half free" (Fehrenbacher 1989a, 426)? Lincoln's chief adversary in the debates from 1854 to 1860, Stephen Douglas, had argued precisely that the question of slavery belonged to the category of local questions to be resolved within each state and in the territories prior to their acceptance into the Union (Fehrenbacher 1989a, 503). Lincoln begins his Inaugural speech with words of reassurance: he has "no purpose, directly or indirectly, to interfere with the institution of slavery in the States where it exists." He has, he believes, "no lawful right to do so … and no inclination to do so." He fully accepts the words of the political platform on the basis of which he was elected that "the right of each State to order and control its own domestic institutions according to its own judgment exclusively is essential to that balance of power on which the perfection and endurance of our political fabric depends …" (Fehrenbacher 1989b, 215).

Does the intention of Lincoln to prevent the extension of slavery beyond the states where it exists threaten the "balance of power" described or violate the fundamental intention underlying the Constitution, if not its express provisions? Lincoln's understanding of that intention as stated repeatedly from his first speech against the repeal of the Missouri Compromise to the speech at Cooper Union that made him a national leader and successful contender for the Republican nomination in 1860 was that the signatories of the *Declaration* and the authors of the Constitution regarded slavery as a necessary and temporary evil (Fehrenbacher 1989a, 309–11; 1989b, 111–19). The fact that the three provisions in the Constitution dealing with slavery – the provision for the return of fugitive slaves, the forbidding of a ban on the importation of slaves for 20 years, and the counting of three-fifths of the slave population in apportioning representation and direct taxes – never use the word "slave" reflected the founders' hope that slavery would disappear and therefore ought not to be named in a document they intended to be perpetual (Fehrenbacher 1989b, 142). So did their efforts to prohibit slavery in the territories ceded to the nation by Virginia in the earliest days of the republic under the terms of the Northwest Ordinance. On the other hand, it is not clear that the framers did, or even could have done, anything in making the Constitution to assure that their hope would ever be realized. And indeed, in the last speeches he makes before his election as president, Lincoln suggests that the problem posed by slavery – the greatest threat to the preservation of the Union – has never been resolved because "our fathers" have failed to recognize the magnitude of the problem or to see that any final resolution of that problem must be based on what he calls a "philosophic public opinion" – either the property view that slavery is a good, or the opposing view that slavery is a moral evil and must not be extended. If the framers, Northerners and Southerners alike, generally saw slavery as a necessary evil, they failed to appreciate the moral difficulty of remaining content with the recognition that the basis of one's wealth was an evil, albeit a necessary one (Fehrenbacher 1989b, 134–36). The belief that slavery was a positive good, or that the *Declaration* could not have meant that "all men are created equal," or even that these words state a "self-evident lie" inevitably replaced the original view Lincoln attributes to the founders.

If Lincoln's analysis of the founders understanding and of their error and its consequence goes beyond the express terms of the Constitution, does it attack the federal character of the Constitution even as defined by the principle of generality and locality? The answer to this charge must be, I think, that if the Constitution could do nothing to accomplish the hope Lincoln attributes to its framers, neither could it consistently protect slavery to the extent demanded by slave-holding states while treating the institution as of exclusively local concern. The provision for the return of escaped slaves seems to demand not only that the states enact no laws that hindered this, but also that state authorities cooperate fully in accomplishing their recovery; this, at any rate, was the opinion of Chief Justice Taney when he dissented from a Supreme Court decision striking down a Pennsylvania law as obstructing federal laws implementing the Constitutional provision but declaring this an exclusively federal concern (*Prigg v Pennsylvania* 41 U.S. 539, 1842). So too, it is another of South Carolina's grievances that some states have granted the right of citizenship to those who can never be citizens in the view of the slave-holding states or in the view of the Court as stated in the Dred Scott case. Or consider the rule granting additional representation for three-fifths of the slave population. Whatever the fact of the matter, that provision may well be understood and accepted by Northerners in 1861 as a necessary compromise between slave-holding and non-slave-holding states at the time of the making of the Constitution. (Madison can only defend this provision by an argument he attributes to one of our Southern brethren. He notes that the argument he has devised "may appear to be a little strained in some points," and even in devising that argument has his imaginary Southerner admit that slavery depends entirely upon the law – has no basis in nature – and concede that what justifies the three-fifths rule is that the slave is partly property, partly a person. Hamilton et al. 2001, 283–86). But the same provision becomes a strong argument against the extension of slavery into the territories insofar as it asks those whose own political representation lacks this extra weight to contribute to the further reduction of their own representative weight where they are under no existing obligation to do so in order to further an institution they think unjust (Fehrenbacher 1989a, 331–32). The protection of slavery may finally require that the Constitution "expressly" affirm the right of property in slaves, as Taney, says it does. But such an affirmation would bring the Constitution into contradiction with the Declaration it was meant to realize, according to Lincoln. So the actual text must mock the Chief Justice and those who repeat what he says.

Are Lincoln's words and actions as president and as a political actor in the seven years before his election finally consistent with what is true and important about federalism, so that we may learn something worth learning from them? The framers of the Constitution condemned the Articles of Confederation because they failed to furnish the essential elements of what could properly be described as a government: in particular, the Articles failed to provide for a legislative authority that could make laws applicable to citizens as citizens, and they failed to provide for an executive. Defenders of the Articles might respond as South Carolina did in 1860 that this was not a government but a league. The response to this by the makers of the Constitution in 1787 and by Lincoln as politician and as president was that only a government could achieve a result consistent with the *Declaration of Independence*, which is for Lincoln, and even in a limited sense for the secessionists, the basis for judging the Constitution itself and the institutions and laws created under its authority. Lincoln's refutation of the claim that there is a lawful right of secession under the Constitution was based on his reading of that document and its history, and his claim that perpetuity must be the assumption underlying all government. But his understanding of his duty as the executive to do all that he can to prevent disunion unless "the people themselves" "shall withhold the requisite means, or in some authoritative manner direct the contrary" is based not merely on the Constitution itself but above all on the "sacred" oath he has taken to uphold it (Fehrenbacher 1989b, 261, 218).

References

Buchanan, J. (1960), *Works, vol. XI*, ed. John Bassett Moore (New York: Antiquarian Press).
Diamond, M. (1992), *As Far as Republican Principles Will Admit* (Washington: AEI Press).
Fehrenbacher, D. (1989a), *Lincoln: Speeches and Writings 1832–1858* (New York: Library of America).
—— (1989b), *Lincoln: Speeches and Writings 1859–1865* (New York: Library of America).
Hamilton, A., Jay, J., and Madison, J. (2001), *The Federalist Papers*, Gideon Edition (Indianapolis: Liberty Fund).
Jaffa, H. (2000), *A New Birth of Freedom* (Lanham, MD: Rowman and Littlefield).
May, J. A. and Faunt, J. R. (1960), *South Carolina Secedes* (Columbia: University of South Carolina Press).

Further Reading

Briggs, J. C. (2005), *Lincoln's Speeches Reconsidered* (Baltimore: Johns Hopkins).
Carwardine, R. (2006), *Lincoln: A Life of Purpose and Power* (New York: Knopf).
Deutsch, K. L. and Fornieri, J. R. (2005), *Lincoln's American Dream* (Washington: Potomac Books).
Diamond, M. (1992), What the framers meant by federalism, The federalist's view of federalism, and The ends of federalism, in *As Far as Republican Principles Will Admit* (Washington: AEI Press).
Fehrenbacher, D. E. (1978), *The Dred Scott Case: Its Significance in American Law and Politics* (New York: Oxford).

Jaffa, H. V. (2000), *A New Birth of Freedom* (Lanham, MD: Rowman and Littlefield).
—— (1959), *The Crisis of the House Divided* (New York: Doubleday).
Miller, W. L. (2002), *Lincoln's Virtues* (New York: Knopf).
Montesquieu, C. S., Baron de (1961), *De l'Ésprit des Lois* (Paris: Garnier).

PART 4
EUROPEAN FEDERALISM

Introduction to Part 4

This Part examines the Continental tradition of federal theory and practice as it developed from the nineteenth century through to the contemporary European Union. This Part reveals a rich stream of federalist thought in modern Europe that provides an indigenous source of federal theory, which is both distinctive from the older American tradition and contributes to recent debates about the federal, or quasi-federal, nature of European integration.

In the opening chapter of this Part, Guillaume Barrera examines Louis Le Fur and his role in the development of federal theory in the French tradition of political thought. As Barrera observes, federalism has long been seen as an alien concept in French political life deeply conditioned by the ideal of unitary sovereignty inherited from both the *ancien régime* and the Revolution. However, Barrera helps us to understand Le Fur's arguments about federalism during the Third Republic by locating his thought in the context of a rich, but often neglected, tradition of nineteenth-century federal theory spanning Constant, Rossi, Tocqueville, and Proudhon. Barrera illustrates that Le Fur's major theoretical achievement was to introduce into French juridical vocabulary the important conceptual distinction, familiar to German legal theorists, between the federal state and confederation. However, Le Fur moved beyond German legal thought by combining abstract theorizing about the doctrine of sovereignty with detailed historical inquiry about diverse forms of alliances and federations in order to articulate an account of the federal state, superior to confederations, in which member-states are neither sovereign, nor completely dependent on central government, and have distinct rights and competences, yet lack sovereign rights of war and treaties reserved for the federal government. While Barrera concludes that Le Fur did not develop a fully fledged theory of federalism, he insists that Le Fur's legacy for federalism studies lies in clearly distinguishing federal and confederal forms, and in identifying the conceptual obstacles that any future federal theory in Europe would have to overcome.

In Chapter 17 Nicolas Patrici examines German theorist Carl Schmitt's contribution to the European understanding of federalism. As Patrici observes, while the impact of Schmitt's constitutional theory, especially his doctrine of sovereignty and concept of the political, are well known, his reflections on federalism have typically been overlooked. In contrast to the common view in federalism studies, Schmitt rejects any inherent positive correlation between federalism and democracy. Indeed, Patrici argues that Schmitt saw a negative correlation with federalism being, like parliamentarism, an essentially liberal idea designed to limit and control democratic tendencies. In his critique of the troubled Weimar Republic of post–World War I Germany, Schmitt highlighted the contradiction between democracy and federalism as traditionally understood; that is between the universality of the German people as a whole and the particularity of each Land. Patrici explores Schmitt's innovative proposal for a new concept of federalism based on the democratic principle of homogeneity of a people as a whole. Schmitt's new kind of federation rested on a constitutional pact that subordinated each member state to the federal state, while also obligating the federal state to protect the existence of the member states. Patrici argues that by producing a conception of federalism compatible with his theory of the state, Schmitt not only contributed to the development of German constitutionalism, but also to the evolving conception of federalism in Europe generally.

Chapter 18 involves Roberto Castaldi's examination of the life and thought of the great Italian champion of European federalism, Alterio Spinelli. As Castaldi illustrates, Spinelli's biography reads like a history of European integration, for rarely has the life and times of one man been so closely linked to the theory and practice of federalism in post–World War II Europe. Castaldi argues that in Spinelli's colorful and eventful life as a former communist, political activist, polemicist, personal diplomat, and member of the European Parliament, the underlying intellectual continuity was his deep theoretical commitment to the "Hamiltonian" or constitutionalist strand of federalism as the vision for the future of a united Europe. In contrast to both the French inspired "Proudhonian" or global federal approach influential immediately after the war and the confederal vision that has dominated European integration for most of its history, Spinelli as far back as the 1940s championed a democratic constituent procedure to draft a federal constitution that would establish a European federal government. While some of Spinelli's major proposals have come to pass, such as the direct election of members of the European Parliament and greater monetary coordination in the form of a single currency and central bank, other features of Spinelli's vision, such as a federal constitution, have not. But perhaps Spinelli's most important legacy, Castaldi explains, was his acute sense that any successful federal project in Europe would depend on the ability to mobilize directly the European public in support of federal goals.

In Chapter 19 Matthew McCullock offers an examination of the theoretical influences on, and practical application of, Yugoslav federalism as it developed under the guidance of Tito's chief theoretician Edvard Kardelj. McCullock begins by tracing the distinctive influence of Althusius on the architects of the Yugoslav Federation. In Althusius, he argues, the Yugslavs found a version of "polyvalent federalism" that did not derive from liberal natural rights doctrine, but rather from an older idea of "consociation" originally designed to preserve the autonomy of religious and municipal self-government from the predations of centralized authority. Kardelj, in particular, turned to Althusian themes to ground the distinctively Yugoslav concept of "self-management," which emerged as a means to avoid both the conflictual system of multi-party liberal democracy and the authoritarian tendencies of single party rule. McCullock explores the links between Kardelj's "self-management" and Althusian corporatism and finds in Tito's Yugoslavia principles of consociational representation and subsidiarity that drew directly from this older federal theory. While the bloody conflicts of the 1990s may have led to the demise of the Yugoslav experiment in federalism, McCullock suggests that there are important elements of "polyvalent federalism" evident in discussions about the European Union and other complex federal systems today.

The concluding chapters in this Part turn to the longstanding and controversial debate over the federal, or quasi-federal, character of the European Union. In Chapter 20, Francesca Vassallo examines one of the central paradoxes of recent European political history; namely, that while a federal Europe was the ultimate goal for architects of the European Community such as Spinelli and Monnet, federalism as a concept has never gained common currency as a way to approach or explain European integration. This chapter considers why the European project has struggled to present a coherent and attractive conception of federalism. Vassallo traces the current idea of European federalism back to an original ambiguity in the Founders' vision of a "United Europe." This ambiguity had two dimensions. First, integration was often initially presented less as a federal project and more as an institutional response to specific problems facing post-war Europe. Second, European integration has typically involved a mixture of federal elements that diminish, and confederal elements that reinforce, national sovereignty. More fundamentally, however, Vassallo argues that the federal project in Europe has been undermined by the focus on institutional creation at the elite level and relative neglect of the need to engage the imagination and active support of EU citizens. From Spinelli's original vision of federal Europe through to Maastricht, and from the period of rapid enlargement to the collapse of the Constitutional Treaty in 2005, Vassallo sees federalism as a permanent, if often problematic, feature of the debate over the European project.

In Chapter 21 Martyn de Bruyn reflects on the meaning of the failure of the recent EU Constitutional Treaty. He examines this question in light of contemporary theories of "multilevel governance" and determines that the deep divisions within the Union over the future of Europe can best be described in the language of federalism. Supporters of the Treaty were comfortable with the idea of a European Federation, whereas its opponents or "Eurosceptics" tended to be committed to the notion of a confederation of Europe built on sovereign nation-states. de Bruyn analyzes the new approach to European integration in the Constitutional Treaty in order to compare its characteristics with the functional federalism that marked the European project for its first 50 years. He argues that the transformation from functional or treaty federalism to American-style constitutional federalism faced stiff resistance precisely because it produced heated debate over the meaning and legitimate goal of European integration. In the Lisbon Treaty negotiated in the aftermath of the failed Constitutional Treaty, de Bruyn sees a return to the older model of functional or treaty federalism. However, de Bruyn argues that despite the demise of the dream of constitutional federalism in Europe, the Lisbon Treaty represents considerable continuity with its predecessor and in some respects reflects a deepening of federal relations within the Union that will have serious repercussions for the future of the European confederal system.

16

ASHGATE RESEARCH COMPANION

Confederation, Federal State, and Federation: Around Louis Le Fur

Guillaume Barrera

> *- Le citoyen Jean-Jacques Langreneux, typographe, rue Dauphine, voudrait qu'on élevât un monument à la mémoire des martyrs de thermidor. -*
> *Michel-Evariste-Népomucène Vincent, ex-professeur, émet le vœu que la démocratie européenne adopte l'unité de langage. On pourrait se servir d'une langue morte, comme par exemple du latin perfectionné.*
>   Gustave Flaubert, *L'Éducation sentimentale* (1869)

Few European states embody the model of the unitary state as much as France. Modern and contemporary France – monarchic, republican, or imperial – was built around a dual concept that hampered enduringly the appearance of federal thought. Thus, many of the francophone partisans of federalism were of Swiss origin such as the Rousseau of the *Considerations on the Government of Poland*, Constant, Rossi, and Rougemont. This dual concept is the same idea of the state and its corollary sovereignty. In the French tradition, the state defines itself by its sovereignty, and the essence of its sovereignty, supreme power, is to be indivisible. A century after Constant had attacked these principles and demonstrated the dangers of the dogma of the general will by which the republic came to seize, in the name of national unity, a power that the kings had scarcely stopped trying to amass, one of the major legal minds of the Third Republic, Léon Duguit, still set in opposition federalism and sovereignty (Duguit 1923, 144).

Thus, people hold federalism in France to be an "unthinkable concept" (Beaud 1999). Truly, federalism seems condemned to be thought of negatively: decentralization, dual or shared sovereignty, and multiple levels of government sound like ruin to French ears. Centralization has so much weight in France, sovereignty dazzles the mind so much, that federal thought suffered from the following dialectic. First federalism and the unitary state were presented in the form of a dilemma until the former was sorted under the anarchist banner. Then came Louis Le Fur. His tour de force consisted in crossing the line of demarcation in the middle of the federal idea by introducing in this field the criterion of state controlled sovereignty. The route that follows happened to be open: it aims to think of federalism on its own terms, while giving up all unitary premises, centralist or sovereigntist. It is to walk this curved path that this chapter invites the reader.

From the Festival of the Federation to the Thesis of 1896

In the development of the Revolution, federalism, or in truth an imaginary federalism (Beaud 1999, 7), above all acted as a foil. Jacobinism defined itself by such enemies as it had need of (Ozouf 1988, 75). They thus accused the Gironde, supposed bearers of such a project, of seeking to ruin the established fact of the Revolution, for federalism would precipitate the dissolution of national unity barely established on new foundations. It will lead us back to feudalisms of all kinds that the night of August 4 had undermined. It would contradict by its principle even the effort toward legislative uniformity, this expression of the general will at the heart of the republican social contract. Against such centrifugal tendencies the Festival of Federation (14/07/1790), in a sense the opposite of federalism, celebrated the union of the social body and the universality of laws, which emanate from it and would completely animate it (Ozouf 1988, 96). Some wise readers, closer to us, on the contrary, perceived in the same feudal system or the theories of the feudal system a prefiguring of, or a space for, federalism: challenges to authority from intermediary powers were a guarantee of moderation (Baechler 1993, Ward 2007).

That which could not see the light of day politically did, however, have a place in thought: animated by the concern for liberty, for historical heritage, for a democracy rooted in local experience or for a new economic and social solution to the problems, also new, that the Industrial Revolution kept creating, Benjamin Constant in 1806, Pellegrino Rossi in 1830, Alexis de Tocqueville in 1835, and Joseph Proudhon in 1863 will each in turn defend the federal idea.

With Constant (1767–1830) as with Rossi (1787–1848), both marked by the spirit of Coppet Group, the one a vaudois and the other an adopted Genevan, federalism counterbalances as much as possible the power of a state always quick to menace the liberty of the individual or the liberty of the cantons. According to Constant, Rousseau was outraged to see the *ancien régime* in possession of an immense power, and was wrong to entrust it to the people, instead of limiting it. He thus only prolonged the despotism under a specious concept – the general will – that the *Principes de Politique* make its primary target. Proscribed in France by the Emperor, Constant therefore calls to establish a form of power that would equally avoid both despotism and anarchy through an administrative decentralization. Nothing appeared to him more sure than to defend with the restoration of municipal power and authentic "local authority" a new kind of federalism better in accord with the capacities of human attachment (Constant 1999, 1191). In the first years of the European project, another Swiss thinker, a true apostle of federalism, will transfer this municipal federalism to the "patries locales," that he will call the "régions" (Denis de Rougemont 1994, 2, 756).

Future peer of France and professor at the college of the same name, Pellegrino Rossi for his part wrote up a memorable report as a member in 1831 of the federal commission charged to revise the pact that had governed the Helvetian Confederation since 1815. This report notably advanced a distinction between two kinds of "confederation" that together appears to prefigure and correct the central thesis that Louis Le Fur will defend in 1896. For if it is true that there are some confederations where the principle states receive their rights from a central power that pre-exists them, and others in which the central powers themselves exist only by the concessions that are granted by the local sovereignties – *grosso modo* what Le Fur will name "federal states" and "confederations" – Rossi refuses to see here a sharply contrasted alternative, as Le Fur will do. Confederation for him, a term common to both, is "an intermediary state" susceptible to be identified in a large number of degrees (Rossi 1997, 12). To restore the sense of these degrees against the crudeness of stark alternatives would be one of the premier tasks assigned to a renewed federal theory (Beaud 1999, 17–18).

As for Tocqueville and Proudhon, a half century after Constant, they bring a striking convergence of diagnosis to the state of their country. According to the famous thesis of the former, the Revolution marked less a rupture than the deepening of the centralization that preceded it. The old regime had already "completely let itself go to the instinct that brings every government to want to lead all affairs alone." This is why centralization brought about by the royal administration did not perish in the Revolution, which not only destroyed the monarchy, but also the provincial institutions. On the contrary, the old centralization "was itself the start of the Revolution and its sign" (Tocqueville 1986, 989)! Having some years of an interval, Proudhon hardly sees the French sickness otherwise, and his remedy is clear: "It is not among seven or eight representatives … that the government of a country should be shared, it is among the provinces and communes: otherwise, political life abandons the peripheries for the center" (Proudhon 1999, 123).

In the thought of Tocqueville and Proudhon, federalism is thus a mirror held up to modern France, struck by a continuous evil whatever its regime. Faced with this France left bloodless by the effects of both political and administrative strangulation, Tocqueville exalts the American experience,[1] for the United States knew how to reconcile respect for self-government with unity and the external power of the Union. As for Proudhon, he searches for and thinks to find in the "federal republic" a regeneration of the sole authentic revolutionary ideal able to harmonize the principles, always active but always contrary, of liberty and authority. Their respective conceptions of federation merit a little more attention.

The thought of Tocqueville did not gravitate only towards America. Like an ellipsis, it saw itself rather having a double focus: France and the United States. The

---

1   See Chapters 14 and 25 in this volume.

federal question, and the American success in the matter, is thus thought of in terms of the distinction between administrative and political centralization. Tocqueville calls political or governmental centralization, the concentration in the same hands of the common interests of all the parts of the nation. Administrative centralization takes back to itself the special interests in some of its parts such as the communes (Tocqueville 1986, 117). In his eyes, France is centralized in these two senses, while the Americans enjoy a regime more respectful of provincial authorities. Tocqueville's understanding of American federalism – in fact very marked by the tradition of the *Federalist Papers* – really aroused some controversies. To truly grasp this, it is absolutely indispensable to put it in parallel with the judgments of *Souvenirs* and of *L'Ancien Régime et la Révolution* concerning the French situation. America from the point of view of federalism as much as democracy is the theatre of a new phenomenon. The federal power that is seen today is unprecedented. Tocqueville thus emphasizes all together the novelty, the specificity, the interest, but also the problems, in finally advancing solutions of a democratic nature capable of resolving them.

This federalism is new in the extensiveness of its competence. The states "not only consented that the federal government dictate laws to them, but also that it would execute these laws itself" (Tocqueville 1986, 164). Such a government is thus not a variant of the leagues that acted only on the confederated peoples, and not on the normal citizens. It also is superior to the confederations of the day, especially when they were loose like the Swiss. Thus in January 1848, on the eve of the reform of the Swiss federal government, Tocqueville judged the federal constitution of the Swiss, the Rossi plan (1830–31) having been rejected, as "the most imperfect of all the constitutions of this kind that have appeared up to this time in the world" (Tocqueville 1986, 1132). But he has trouble exactly categorizing the American system due to its very novelty. The specific form, nearly *sui generis*, in the end, according to Tocqueville, would deserve the name "incomplete national government." Its federal form has united and saved America, its national form manifests itself in the way it acts directly upon the governed. However, it only acts in a limited scope. Congress only rules on the principal acts of social existence, while it leaves the details of legislation to the state. Federalism in America nevertheless, but we also need to say as a result, faces a threefold problem. By establishing a sort of friction between two sovereignties, it complicates political life and supposes the practice of habits that are not enacted by law. The Mexicans, who copied American institutions to the letter, oscillate between anarchy and military despotism because the spirit of these institutions is lacking. The federal government, for another thing, is still quite weak compared to the direct monarchies of Europe. Finally, the duration of the Union will not depend solely on the excellence of its institutions; it will also depend on the change that will take place in the relations between socially and culturally heterogeneous states. The key to American democracy, the *"fait générateur"* of this regime is contained in three celebrated words: "equality of conditions." What chance, therefore, is there to harmonize a Union embracing not only one but two societies with distinct principles, one of them, the South, proclaiming natural inequality (Tocqueville 1986, 336ss)?

Happily America solved the problem of political centralization, while avoiding administrative centralization. Better still the Americans knew how to remedy inherent flaws in democracy by checks that are themselves democratic. There are none of the concessions to the corporatist spirit and organic structures that the French counter-revolutionaries will want to resuscitate sometimes under the name federation, from the First to Third Republic, from Bonald to Maurras. Rather America has institutions designed to interest the people in public life: the free press, voluntary associations, the educative function of the judiciary, and the institution of juries. Nothing here, despite the aristocratic character of lawyers, that causes fear of a return to some "feudal system."

Travelling through a capital taken over by the workers in February 1848, writing his memoirs and last great work in the growing shadow of the Prince-President and in a sort of domestic exile with Napoleon III ruling, Tocqueville was saddened to foresee in France of the 1850s a ferment of division that the Americans knew how to destroy. On the one hand, France already suffers from a double centralization that suffocates liberty and favours revolutions and coups d'état (Tocqueville 1986, 762). On the other hand, there is a sort of "servile war," a war between the classes had been sparked by the theoreticians of socialism. Their "foreign systems" bore less on the government than on the laws of society itself, but in sacrificing liberty to radical equality that will follow the destruction of private property; the socialists are preparing a monster state "master of every man" (Tocqueville 1986, 711). Tocqueville nevertheless concedes to the socialists the merit of having pointed to "the most serious object" of all thought and all political action: the modern social question and inequality.

As it happens, all the socialist theories of the day did not prefigure the statist monster that the liberal dreaded. Quite the contrary, it was to destroy this monster that Proudhon devoted his last efforts, knowing he would be regarded as a "renegade" and an "apostate" by the unitary republican descendents of the Jacobins (Proudhon 1999, 83). Written four years after the death of Tocqueville, *Du Principe Fédératif et de la nécessité de reconstituer le parti de la révolution* proposed federation precisely as the solution to a problem all at once social, economic, and political. Whereas Tocqueville treated what he had seen, Proudhon defended his visions. Federation appeared to him necessary, beneficial, and called to spread. 1848 failed to rectify 1793. Since the defeat of the Girondins, centralizing despotism had not stopped growing and liberty diminishing. Now the stakes of 1848 were immense: it is a matter of finishing with what Proudhon calls in his turn the "social war." This war pits the property owners, capitalists, and entrepreneurs against the proletariat and wage earners. The *"federation agricole industrielle"* will mark the end of it. The principles of mutuality and economic solidarity will replace the dominant "bankocracy" and stockjobbery.

Following Tocqueville, Proudhon also stigmatizes the French dual centralization. Against political centralization, he affirms that the 2nd of December coup of Louis-Napoleon Bonaparte (1851) could not have taken place if the Constitution of 1848 had given a federal structure to the country. Paris would not have dragged along the rest of France. Administrative centralization, for its part, according to Proudhon, mainly serves the interests of the bourgeoisie. "Buttress of the industrial feudal system," this centralization permits them to grab hold of power and taxation, while calmly exploiting the masses destined for the wage earning class (Proudhon 1999, 86).

To put an end to this double evil, now it is necessary to commit to a sort of "anarchy" that Proudhon assimilates into self-government. One such form of self-government signifies nothing less than the end of politics as formerly understood. For the central problem, if not the unique problem that the times force us to face up to, is the problem of labour. If political functions were brought back to private "industrial functions," from now on, the social order would only result from doing transactions and exchange in private, and each could consider himself an autocrat! Despite the fact that he aims explicitly to reconcile the principles of authority, centralized by nature, and liberty ranging from transactions to anarchy, Proudhon speaks mainly of a school of thought, before even economics, in which the ideal is to "completely do away with governmental establishment" in order "to construct society on the sole basis of ownership and free labour" (Proudhon 1999, 71). Nothing would satisfy such a view as well as federation. Proudhon's confidence, even his enthusiasm is rooted in a triple conviction: federation will always be most difficult to ignore; it is at the same time the most just and most fertile form of alliance; and it favours peace.

Federation is necessary the extent to which it answers a sort of historical law: the more a society expands, the more it has need of liberty, Proudhon thought. Its path thus leads it to the constitution of decentralization, and from decentralization to federation. What is a federation? It is a contract, not unilateral, but "bilateral and communal;" not abstract and fictional like the social contract of Rousseau, but apt to make links among the heads of families, of villages, of cantons, and of states, without going so far as stealing their sovereignty. These confederates would ally themselves for common security and prosperity. But contemporary states, for the most part monarchies, jealous of their sovereignty and worried to lose none of it, are incapable of forming a confederation, in which the principle is that the contractors always reserve to themselves a part of sovereignty and a freedom of action that is greater than what they gave up.

The central question of federalism politically is, then, the share, the extension and the competence of the state, this "great civil servant." For Proudhon it is about reducing these as much as possible in favour of liberty. To the state would come back the functions of initiative, of control, of institution, and of legislation, as it wants the principle of authority, but not of execution or universal administration. Proudhon is alarmed by the example of seeing the United States multiplying the attributes of federal authority. Himself looking deeply at this point to the difference that separates the future state from real states, he anticipates on this occasion the conceptual distinction between state and federation. While every state, according to him, is brought to annexation by its nature, confederations offer a model of peaceful expansion – an idea that we could discover already in Book 9 of the *Spirit of the Laws* (Larrère 1995). This is why Proudhon, three years before Sadowa, hopes for and advocates the reestablishment of the Scandinavian, Batavian, and Germanic

Confederations. Struck by decentralization, the great unitary states would disarm. All of Europe would gain by this: Will its future not go towards a "confederation of confederations"?

The Thesis of 1896

In some respects, Louis Le Fur (1870–1943) would share this belief in the vitality of the federal system, which he saw spreading over the largest part of the American continent, and which could return great service to central Europe and the Balkans. But the object of this brilliant and very young jurist is not to promote a particular political form, it is rather to end the vagueness that surrounds it, and introduce into French juridical vocabulary a distinction, familiar to German theorists, between the federal state (*Bundesstaat*) and the confederation (*Staatenbund*). But to think of federalism in its two forms, Le Fur believes it is good to sharpen precisely the concepts which most preceding authors would recognize as the delicate, or perhaps even shocking, character as regards federalism: the state and sovereignty.

However, contrary to what some would blame him for (Burdeau 1949, 411), Le Fur did not deliver to his readers purely abstract theoretical principles. If it is true that his conception is fundamentally marked by, and maybe mistaken for, the concept of the state, it is also preceded by a long historical inquiry into the diverse forms of alliances. According to one positivist tradition, Le Fur intended to bring out some permanent traits from the examination of facts – these facts occupy between a third and one-half of his *Thesis*! On the other hand, it is true that his manner, particularly in the sequel, has something of the scholastic to it, in the noble sense of the term. It is a continuous dialogue with actual federal jurists, especially Swiss and Germans. The *Thesis of 1896* is therefore composed this way: the first part offers a history of the federal idea, where he shows again that federative states, the original common idea, held to one or the other of these types: confederation or federal state. But the second proves to be more viable than the first, both if we hold to the same facts, but also by reason of their nature. The second part of the *Thesis* proposes a juridical theory of these two types, considered by themselves, according to internal law, and according to international public law.

History must be consulted because the dual federal form itself has a history. It is hardly possible to understand the leagues, alliances, and federations of antiquity through this dual form. Doubtless instructed by Fustel de Coulanges's *La Cité antique*, Le Fur is loathe to impose on the ancient world concepts of sovereignty and the state that do not correspond to it. Ancient and modern unions do not differ as two sorts of federal state, but rather in spite of their federal character! The feudal system likewise presents to his eyes only a vague analogy with federalism properly speaking, precisely because state and sovereignty play there more or less no role. It is only in modern history that the alternative between federal state and confederation comes to light. And the balance leans decidedly, for Le Fur, in favour of the federal state. The conviction that he takes away from his inquiry, or that guides this inquiry, is that most federal states began in the form of confederation. But the external weakness of the confederation, its powerlessness greater still to impose itself on its members very often led, by means of war, to the formation of federal states.

This was the case in Germany. The Germanic Confederation of 1815, with neither finances nor military forces, survived only a half-century. Germany is from now on a *Bund*, and a *Staat*. It is a federation under Prussian hegemony since the victory 30 years earlier of King Wilhelm I over the Emperor of Austria (1866). This is a paradoxical lesson for a jurist: a federal state can thus have its juridical basis in a treaty. Be that as it may, the Empire born in 1871 has the upper hand in military and financial questions. It settles the disputes that could suddenly materialize among the members of the *Bund*, which are dealt with moreover under the reservation that the law of the Empire always prevails over the law of the states. The form of this federal state is a hybrid, however, the weight of Prussia leads Le Fur to think that the German Federation is not a model, but rather a case of instability that should have to suffer one of the following fates: either a clearly Prussian unitary state, or a disintegration of the *Bund* under the effect of anti-Prussian spirit.

An identical victory of the federative state is manifest in the history of the Swiss and the United States. For a long time held to be an example of a confederation among free and sovereign cantons, Switzerland changed its form in 1848 and 1874. The centre and the executive power were strengthened. This is no longer the days when the cantons could block the diet by their mere absence, and Le Fur, nevertheless persuaded that democracy has deep roots in Switzerland, even believes to perceive there the beginnings of administrative centralization, if not a unitary state.

On the subject of the United States, and all the while holding the southern states to be rebels, Le Fur agrees with Jellinek in seeing the southern Confederacy, defeated in 1865, as a model of confederation of states, like the Union had been prior to 1787. In the rest, his analysis of the American Constitution and of its epigones (Mexico, Brazil, and Argentina) principally turns on the question of the "right of revision." Le Fur is not very precise about the role, the function, and the weight of the American and Mexican states. He is interested mainly in what concerns sovereignty, precisely because sovereignty characterizes the federal state. It is thus of the greatest importance to know, at all times, how the power of the federal government is determined relative to the power of its members that exercise sovereignty and participate in sovereignty – this would be only in revision – but do not possess it.

The historical part of the *Thesis* comes to a close with the contrasted picture of Europe. Le Fur, judging the "Anglo-Saxon race more than any other the declared enemy of centralization" (Le Fur 2000, 290), doubts that a federal state properly speaking could one day form an association of England and its colonies, especially as it would not be in the interest of England. As for France, virtually on the other side, it is too attached to centralization to commit one day to federal ideas. As proof, such ideas have always been understood there in a distorted way. The Federation of 1791 celebrated nothing under this name other than the unitary state. Napoleon only understood the term alliance in the spirit of hegemonic domination. Proudhon searched above all for synthesis. All the more reason, Le Fur advances, not to reject a project of decentralization – the risk of federative breakup hardly threatens France (Le Fur 2000, 298–307)!

Elsewhere the situation is more complex. In some states like Italy, trying for a confederation quite conforms to its history, or Spain, briefly involved in a federal republic project of President Pi y Margall, the balance finally titled towards the unitary state, but not without leaving an inheritance of grave questions. But the Austro-Hungarian Empire truly is instructive. For example, the relation of Hungary with Croatia and Slavonia does not hold together the unitary state, as Jellinek supposes, but rather the federal state, as is attested to by the existence of shared and superior organs among the parties in question. The "real union" of Austria and Hungary, on the other hand, would be a species of the genus confederation because it is dedicated to and respects the sovereignty of the respective member states.

Le Fur concludes his inquiry with a "critical appreciation" of the merits and defects of the federative form. To his credit, the young jurist picks up again the argument illustrated by Montesquieu, for whom the "*république fédérative*" is a "constitution which has all the internal advantages of republican government and the external force of monarchy" (*Spirit of the Laws*, IX, 1). It thus resolves in an optimal manner not only the problem of smaller states threatened by big states, but also that of an immense territory menaced with break up or drift to despotism. In fact, the federal reality lies in the plurality of states, a remedy or choice counterweight to the risks of demagoguery, caesarism, and legislative uniformity. Inversely, legislative diversity inspires fraud, or at least the ease of it, when the central power, particularly in confederations, suffers from a congenital weakness. Furthermore, confederation bears the problem of dual sovereignty, which ought never arise, to a sometime critical degree. The conclusion that Le Fur draws from history is marked by moderation: the federal form is not a panacea. It does not establish complete peace on Earth because it will never happen universally. But neither is it a purely transitory fact. If confederations tend to become federal states, it does not follow that the unitary state is the ineluctable future of the federal state. The inverse march has already been observed (Mexico and Brazil). And some federal states proved their strength and their ability to last (the United States).

Here begins the largest part of the *Thesis*, entirely devoted to defending and illustrating the distinction between confederation and the federal state. Le Fur proposes straightaway to ground this distinction between the two types of federative systems on the criterion of sovereignty. Therefore, he first works to clarify this concept in contrast to what he calls the excesses of German legal science, to which he nevertheless owes much. Taking this road, he also intersects Tocqueville's route and reproaches him for having given credit to the idea of dual sovereignty in the federal state. Against both of these, he holds sovereign a state that is not "obligated or determined except by its own will in the limits of a superior principle of right and in conformity with the collective goal that it is called to realize" (Le Fur 2000, 443). Jellinek, Rosin, Haenel, and Barel committed the error of holding sovereignty to be unlimited, while forgetting that the qualifier "supreme" is not an absolute superlative, but rather a relative one. Tocqueville, for his part, exaggerated a great deal the division of sovereignty in America because he did not see that sovereignty, all the while remaining indivisible, may not be delegated but at least may be exercised by several bodies in conjunction.

As sovereignty characterizes the state, Le Fur sees it as his duty to explain in what sense the particular states, not being sovereign, still deserve the name states! This is why he works so much to distinguish these provincial states from a unitary state. His thesis is precisely because the provincial states exercise sovereignty, while the relations of the unitary state to the inferior collectivities rest on a relation of command, these provincial states can be assumed to be represented. Le Fur nevertheless admits with the German jurists that the federal state has the right to modify freely its rights and its competences, either to limit them or to enhance them, provided that the safety of the people – *suprema lex* – demands it. The same principle, this same safety, conditions the fidelity of the federal state to uphold its commitments. Such commitments do not diminish its sovereignty, it must respect them – *pacta servanda* – but they are not held in an irreversible manner.

Sovereignty like this is a flaw in confederation. In this sense, Le Fur agrees with John Calhoun that in every federative system in which the states preserve their sovereignty, it cannot have a central sovereign state; this is to say a federal state. Or to put it another way, it would not be able to have two sovereignties on the same territory. Confederation is thus less than a state. But it is more than a simple alliance or *vinculum juris*. For, without being truly sovereign, it at least has a reality, a unity of legislative, judicial, and political powers. Juridically it has a "personality" recognized by international law. This concession has been taken by contemporary jurists to be one of the most certain claims in the *Thesis of 1896* (Beaud 2007, 85). For his part, Le Fur nevertheless shows sensitivity to the defects of such a system. While a confederation unites states remaining sovereign, it needs to recognize an equality among them, which authorizes the smallest to hold up the action of all the rest. All of its members conserve the right of nullification and secession, while the confederation has the right of exercising a constraint that merits, between sovereign states although linked, the name of war. Le Fur thus believes that confederation is a form destined to dissolve or at least to transform into a federal state.

He then sees it as his duty to explain more precisely the genesis of such a state (Le Fur 2000, 540ss). His own position rises to a refutation of Jellinek. Jellinek had been mistaken to maintain that the federal state is always born from an act. It happens that it can be born thus, but the Swiss were not really the product of the cantons, and Italian unity did not result from a treaty between states. Yet it also happens that federal states can see the light of day owing to such a treaty, as shown by American and German history. Even though it is necessary to accord a sort of *saltus* and change of regime from the ratification of a treaty to the proclamation of a constitution, a constitution is certainly not a treaty. But it could be the result of a treaty as soon as federal organs in keeping with the treaty seize the federal power and proclaim the entry in force of the constitution. Immediately, the contractual relations make way for the relations of subjection to the advantage of the federal state.

If the federal state is nevertheless distinguishable from the unitary state, it is due to its dual juridical nature. It is both a state and a federation. As a state it defines itself as a union of individuals; as a federation it unites non-sovereign collectivities. Its competence bears principally on what enhances the general and common interest. But to envisage this duality of nature from the republican point of view; that is from the point of view of the people, ultimate holders of sovereignty for the moderns, it will be said that the people exercises its sovereignty at the same time by the state, and by and in collectivities inferior to the state. This fundamentally justifies the bicameralism of federal republics.

Without doubt here Le Fur makes his most concise argument against the German juridical science. The object of the controversy is the status of the particular states in what he calls the federal state. In his eyes, Laband made a mistake in qualifying the federal state as a "republic of states" in which the state would hold the place of citizens and form an intermediary link between the federal state and the citizens properly speaking, for there are more relations between the citizen and the federal state than Laband assumes. As for mediation, it exists as much in unitary states that are decentralized, but may not be federal. On his side, Gierke went too far in appraising that in a federal state there would be basically two sorts of states. If the state defines itself by its sovereignty, only the federal state truly merits the name.

But how are we to describe the members of the federal state, if they are neither states in the strict sense nor provinces? For Le Fur, their nature always links up with the distinction between sovereignty and its execution. The federal state cannot deny the power of its members as freely as the unitary state can reduce that of its provinces. Besides, no province takes part in the formation of the will of the state in the same way as the members of the federal state. On the other hand, the unity of the federal state and the sovereignty that is recognized in it rather explains that the relations between the state and its members are distinguished a great deal from the relations that are woven between the confederation and the sovereign states that compose it. In the federal state there would be there neither the right of war, nor of legislation among states deprived of their sovereignty that will be treated as rebels, if they secede. Neither is the federal state required to treat its states in an equal manner, save for if the constitution provides for it. Le Fur looks to the guaranteed rights of the members of the German Bund as historical remainders incompatible with the modern notion of the state. The internal relations of the state are, or should be, relations of subjection and not of contract. In the end, the members of a federal state could see their rights modified or limited, against their will, according to majority rule, which does not apply to confederations because of the sovereignty of each member state.

The *Thesis* of Le Fur finishes with the central distinction envisaged from the point of view of international public right. Precisely because confederation has as its object to assure the security and protection of its parts and to enjoy a moral and juridical personality, it recognizes the rights ordinarily attached to sovereign powers: to send delegations, declare war, and conclude treaties. On its side, the federal state alone has a complete international personality; its members can never undertake such things without its control and agreement. On the contrary, they must follow the federal state in its alliances and its hostilities. Nevertheless, Le Fur has the honesty to admit that the practical manifestation is more flexible than the theory. Three federal states such as the German Empire, the Swiss, and the United States do not absolutely reserve to the federal government the exclusive right to conclude commercial treaties or treaties with bordering states.

In this section, like the preceding one, constitutional law and international law lead Le Fur to judge the federal state superior to confederation: the confederation condemned by history would only be a phase.

Against the Grain

The clarity of the distinctions, the force of the deductions and refutations are the value of this great *Thesis*. It influenced a number of French thinkers, who were often however more inspired by Le Fur to consider the state rather than to go deeper into his conception of the federative system (Carré de Malberg 1920).

But this quality has its reverse side too. If Le Fur deserves to be read today, this is not that he should be continued, but rather precisely because he combined all the obstacles that a new doctrine would have to surmount. For instance, Olivier Beaud, author of the recent *Théorie de la Fédération* (2007) basically considers the federal state and confederation as the "epistemological obstacle" par excellence, in the bachelardien sense of the term. Nothing is more useful in this respect than to reopen a thesis in which federalism is thought of under the triple concept of the state, sovereignty, and the distinction between the federal state and confederation. For by showing us that the problem is insoluble if it is posed in these terms, it forces us to pose the question differently!

Olivier Beaud endeavoured to be lavish in this effect. He virtually had to cease thinking in French in order to advance a concept of "federation" that is not conceivable as a sort of state – but a political form *sui generis* – and to reconnect finally with thinking less obsessed than Le Fur by the idea of sovereignty. For federation is a political order without sovereignty, not so much decentralized, as not centred. In a word, it is a "society of societies" as Montesquieu says, less hierarchical than horizontal (Beaud 2007, 64). It is thought that such a form has something that perplexes a mind marked by French experience. But as it happens, the experience of the European Union and its construction and *aporia* also summons the French, however reluctantly, to think about federation (Andréani 2001).

It would be unfair to him to dispatch in a few lines a work that would deserve a special study. It suffices to underline its impact by signalling in two propositions the deep causes of disagreement between its author and Le Fur. The distinction between the federal state and confederation is contrary to practice and prejudicial to the intelligence of federalism in its unity. To find this again, it would be better to follow the spirit of Rossi and his attention to degrees. Besides Le Fur's distinction betrays the spirit of an age dependent on a "doctrinal crystallization operating in the German legal science under Bismark" (Beaud 2007, 73). Beaud thus proposes to go back upstream in history and practice in order to erect a theory of "emerging federations."

Doubtless it would be necessary to leave to a philosophy of history the task of accomplishing a synthesis of these two systems of right. Tocqueville had already indicated this "instinct" of the state to concentrate all affairs to itself. Le Fur takes notes of it, Beaud deplores it. But Tocqueville had not lost hope in the human ingenuity to forge new institutions: "the human mind invents things more easily than words, from this comes the usage of so many improper terms and incomplete expressions" (Tocqueville 1986, 165).

The minds that reflect upon contemporary Europe feel the pertinence of such a judgment and the difficulty to understand what is occurring in accordance with terms that it no longer accepts.

Translated from the original French by Lee Ward

References

Andréani, Gilles. 2001. « Le fédéralisme et la réforme des institutions européennes », in *Annuaire français de relations internationales*, vol. 2.
Baechler, Jean. 1993. « Europe et fédération », *La Pensée politique*, n°1, Paris, Seuil-Gallimard, 244–259.
Beaud, Olivier. 1999. « Fédéralisme et fédération en France : histoire d'un concept impensable ? », in *Annales de la Faculté de Droit de Strasbourg*, P.U Strasbourg, n° 3, 7–82.
—— 2003. « Fédération et État fédéral », in Stéphane Rials et Denis Alland (dir.), *Dictionnaire de la culture juridique*, Paris, Puf, 711–716.
—— 2007. *Théorie de la Fédération*, Paris, Puf, collection Léviathan.
Burdeau, Georges. 1949. *Traité de science politique*, Paris, LGDJ.
Carré de Malberg, Raymond. 1962. *Contribution à la théorie générale de l'État* (1920), rééd. CNRS, 2 vols.
Constant, Benjamin. 1999. *Œuvres*, Paris, Gallimard, Pléiade.
Dufour, Alfred. 1998. *Hommage à Pellegrino Rossi*, Bâle, Genève.
Duguit, Léon. 1923. *Traité de droit constitutionnel*, Paris, de Boccard.
Larrère, Catherine. 1995. « Montesquieu et l'idée de fédération », in *L'Europe de Montesquieu*, Cahiers Montesquieu 2, 137–152.
Le Fur, Louis. 2000. *État fédéral et confédération d'États*, thèse de droit (1896), rééd. Paris, Panthéon-Assas.
Ozouf, Mona. 1988. « Fédéralisme », « Fédération », in François Furet et Mona Ozouf (dir.), *Dictionnaire critique de la Révolution française*, Paris, Flammarion, 85–95, 96–104.
Proudhon, Pierre-Joseph. 1999. *Du principe fédératif et de la nécessité de reconstituer le parti de la révolution*, Paris, Romillat.

Rossi, Pellegrino. 1997. *Per la patria commune*, (1832), édition bilingue (franco-italien), établie par L. Lacchè, Bari, Piero Laicata.

Rougemont, Denis de. 1994. *Œuvres complètes*, III, *Écrits sur l'Europe*, 2, Paris, La Différence.

Tocqueville, Alexis de. 1986. *De la démocratie en Amérique, Souvenirs, L'Ancien régime et la Révolution*, Paris, Robert Laffont.

Ward, Lee. 2007. Montesquieu on federalism and Anglo-Gothic constitutionalism. *Publius: The Journal of Federalism*, Oxford, volume 37, n°4, 551–577.

Further Reading

Aron, R. 2000–2001. « Comment étudier le fédéralisme ? », *Commentaire*, n°92, hiver, 823–831.

Beaud, O. 2007. *Théorie de la Fédération*, Paris, Puf, collection Léviathan.

Chopin, Thierry. 2002. *L'héritage du fédéralisme? Etats-Unis / Europe*. Paris, Fondation Robert Schuman.

Manent, Pierre. 1994. *An Intellectual History of Liberalism*. Trans. Rebecca Balinski. Princeton, Princeton University Press.

Nelson, Ralph. 1987. The federal idea in French political thought, in *Federalism as Grand Design: Political Philosophers and the Federal Principle*. Ed. Daniel J. Elazar, 109–164. Lanham, University Press of America.

Riley, Patrick. 1973. The origins of federal theory in international relations theory. *Polity*. Vol. 6, No. 1 (Autumn): 87–121.

17

**ASHGATE
RESEARCH
COMPANION**

Looking into Medusa's Eyes: Carl Schmitt on Federalism[1]

Nicolas Patrici

Introduction

In the last few years, discussions about federalism have become a main issue among political theorists and political scientists (Karmis and Norman 2005). Moreover, in some cases, federalism appears as an important institutional tool to guarantee political stability and to improve democracy. The positive correlation between democracy and federalism is particularly stressed when this notion is debated within the context of national or cultural pluralism, like in contemporary Europe, Canada, Bolivia or India (Requejo 2005; Kymlicka 1996, 2007; Bellamy and Castiglioni 1997; Stepan 1999; Amoretti-Bermeo 2004; Gagnon, Guibernau and Rocher 2004; Gagnon and Tully 2001).

In spite of the impact Schmitt's work on constitutional theory has had in twentieth-century political theory, and in spite of the fact that in the last years there was a revival of Schmitt's theory, not much has been said about the review of federalism present in Schmitt. More often than not, Schmitt's commentators[2] and federal theorists do not pay much attention to Schmitt's treatment of federalism. The former focus their analysis mostly on Schmitt's role in Weimar and during the Nazi period; the latter, on the other hand, focus their analysis on the institutional

---

1 I wish to thank Prof. Ferran Requejo for his helpful comments on this chapter. I also wish to thank Prof. Klauss-Jünger Nagel for the discussions about federalism in general and German federalism in particular. I would also like to thank Prof. Montserrat Herrero Lopez (University of Navarra) for the magnificent debates on Carl Schmitt's work and her invaluable comments on this chapter. However, the responsibility for the content of this chapter is mine. This chapter has been written thanks to the financial support of the Argentinean National Research Council (CONICET) and the institutional support of the Department of Political and Social Science, Pompeu Fabra University (Barcelona), the Philosophy Department of the University of Barcelona and the Faculty of Philosophy of the Leiden University (Netherlands).

2 For studies focused on Schmitt and federalism, see Ulmen (1992) and Bandieri (2002).

features of federalism. The concept of federalism is not treated extensively by Carl Schmitt. In fact this concept is hardly found in Schmitt's main works. Schmitt only refers to federalism, in a very brief way, in two of his works: *Verfassungslehre* and *Der Hüter der Verfassung*.[3]

Schmitt, contrary to current political theorists, does not find a positive correlation between federalism and democracy. He asserts that federalism not only has a negative correlation with democracy, but that it is an institutional design and a political concept that hinders democratic sovereignty. Moreover, Schmitt's statements on federalism are directly related to his critique of the Weimar Constitution. The Weimar Constitution, Schmitt argues, presupposes a contradiction: it contains the incompatible principles of liberalism and democracy. It contains a liberal legal structure but also seeks democratic legitimacy: on one hand, the Weimar Constitution implies plurality and on the other it was sustained by the proposition of the homogeneity of the German people.

In the following pages I present Schmitt's treatment of the concept of federalism and clarify the relation between Schmitt's theory of democracy and Schmitt's treatment of federalism. In order to achieve this objective, first, I present an overview of Schmitt's political theory in order to give a framework to the concept of federalism as it is developed by this author. Finally, I present the relationship Schmitt finds between federalism and his theories of the state and democracy.

Sovereignty, the Political and Democracy in Carl Schmitt's Political Thought

Schmitt's commentators (Schwab 1989; Galli 1996; Meier 1998, McCormick 1999; Mouffe 1999; Dyzenhaus 1998, 1999; Herrero Lopez 2007) have repeatedly pointed out that the question of the nature of modern politics crosscuts all of Schmitt's work. Hence, in this section, we briefly discuss and present the three main concepts of Schmitt's political theory: (a) sovereignty, (b) the political and (c) democracy. Then after presenting these three notions that are at the core of Schmitt's political theory, we will attempt to present the correlation among them.

Sovereignty

In the first page of his *Politische Theologie: Vier Kapitel zur Lehre von der Souveranitat*, Schmitt defines sovereignty with the following famous phrase: "Sovereign is he who decides on the exception" (Schmitt 2005, 5). However, the definition is more extensive: "only this definition can do justice to a borderline concept. Contrary to the imprecise terminology that is found in popular literature, a borderline concept

---

3   Bandieri (2002) pays attention to this particularity of Schmitt's work.

is not a vague concept, but one pertaining to the outermost sphere" (Schmitt 2005, 5). Thus, Schmitt posits that sovereignty is defined by the capacity to decide on the exception (*Ausnahmezustand*);[4] however, the meaning Schmitt gives to the concept "exception" (*Ausnahmezustand*) needs to be clarified.

Schmitt argues that the main aim of defining the "exception" is to be found in the dialectic between norm and exception. For Schmitt's theory, exceptional means a substance that is not included nor regulated by the norm. As it has been pointed out by Schwab (1989), "a state of emergency need not have an existing order as a reference point because *necessitas non habet legem*."[5] Thus, it should be added that when Schmitt uses the concept of "normality," he gives it a juridical meaning. Hence, normality becomes what is contained in the normative system that regulates the polity. "Normal" is the legal–juridical frame within which the political life occurs. The exception becomes a *political moment* capable of neutralizing the legal–juridical order. In the end, it becomes an extreme and radical concept in Schmitt's theory. The Schmittian approach is developed in the understanding that sovereignty is a concept correlated to the notion of exception because it is within the exception, and only by the exception, that sovereignty exists. Thus, if the exceptional neutralizes the legal–juridical order, the presence of sovereignty results in the disappearance of normality.

But what does "to decide" mean to Schmitt? To Schmitt "to decide" implies an *existential* act of differentiation. To decide becomes a dictate capable enough to create, *ipso facto*, an order. Thus, the act of deciding implies the sovereign capacity to inscribe in the borders of the legal–juridical order the outsideness that embodies the latter and gives it an existential meaning. As Agamben (2005) has pointed out the decision is neither a *quaestio iuris* nor a *quaestio facti*; it is the proper relation between the right and the fact. In other words, in Schmitt's theory to decide is equivalent to create.

Moreover, if we take into account that the exceptional situation is a situation that is not contemplated by the legal–juridical order, the impact of the exception is always destructive for the political unity. It destroys the legal–juridical order that existed before the exception and it has the power to generate a new order. However, it is not the exception itself that has the capacity to create a new order but rather the decision on the exception. As Schmitt says: "After all, every legal order is based on a decision, and also the concept of the legal order, which is applied as

---

4   *Ausnahmezustand* can be translated as "state of emergency," or as a kind of exceptional circumstances. However, as Agamben (2005) points out, it should be noticed that the term, common in German law doctrine, does not find a literal correlation in the Anglo-Saxon doctrine. Anglo-Saxon doctrine uses the term "emergency powers" or "state of emergency." It is clear that the German term *Ausnahmezustand* implies more than an emergency. It does not refer to the existing order but to a moment that transcends it. As it will be argued, for Schmitt the "exception" is equivalent to "the miracle." English translators of Schmitt use both to refer to the same phenomena. Here, we are inclined to use "exception" or "exceptional moment." For a further debate see Schwab (1989) and Agamben (2005).
5   Quoted in Schmitt (2005), 5 n1.

something self-evident, contains within the contrast of the two distinct elements of the jurist – norm and decision. Like every other order, the legal order rests on a decision and not on a norm" (Schmitt 2005, 10). Thus, the decision on the exception incarnates an existential capacity to create a new political order and to embody that new political order with an *existential substance*; an existential substance that embodies and enforces the law of the *Nomos*.[6] Sovereignty thus implies the capacity to found an institutional order while simultaneously destroying order itself. Hence, sovereignty is within the borderline of the *Nomos*.

It remains to be understood who the sovereign is. The sovereign, it was affirmed, is the one who decides on the exception. It is important to notice at this point that in Schmitt's theory there is no hierarchy (as sovereignty is not included in the legal–juridical order and therefore it cannot be part of it) that tells who the sovereign actor is. At the end of the day, it is a question of force and power. The sovereign is, in Schmitt's thought, the one who is powerful enough to emerge from the Nothing and to create, to establish, to embody, to enforce and to sustain a concrete legal–juridical order. The sovereign resembles, in Schmitt's theory, a God which emerges from the Nothing exercising an absolute power to create the institutional order from the Nothing, as Schmitt says "The exception in jurisprudence is analogous to the miracle in theology" (Schmitt 2005, 36).

In consequence, since the sovereign is the one who creates and embodies the order, it becomes, for Schmitt's constitutional theory, its unique guardian. Contrary to the classical liberal theory that supposes that the guardian of the constitutional-order has to be found in the constitution, Schmitt situates the guardian of the constitutional-order outside the positive constitution.[7] Schmitt bases his decision to assert that the sovereign, who is in the borderline of the legal–juridical order, is his guardian on the fact that the legal–juridical order cannot contain the exception in itself and that, the decision on the exception remains with the one who can claim it: the sovereign.

In order to conclude this brief presentation of Schmitt's concept of sovereignty, firstly, it should be underscored that, according to Schmitt, the sovereign emerges in the dialectic midway between normality (legal–juridical order) and the exception. Secondly, the sovereign emerges from the decision on the exception. That is to say, the sovereign creates the exception and at the same time creates the order. At the end of the day, sovereignty is a radical concept that cannot be trapped within the legal–juridical order but that cannot simply be placed outside said order either. Sovereignty rests, as it has been said, in the borderline of the legal–juridical order.

---

6   See Schmitt (1997). For an analysis of the term and its correlation with Schmitt's political theory, see Herrero Lopez (2007).
7   For a further treatment of this point see Schmitt (1996a) and Dyzenhaus (1999).

The Political

Sovereignty is, as it has been said before, at the same time, the creator, the upholder and the guardian of the legal–juridical order. And it can be affirmed that sovereignty is the creator, the upholder and guardian since it is capable of formulating a political and existential decision. Next, it needs to be clarified what is the relation between sovereignty, the existential and the political in Schmitt's theory.

Schmitt relates the act of the sovereign to an existential moment in which the political order is created through a decision on the exception. Consequently if the decision involves a decision that embodies and creates the legal–juridical order, it also becomes a political decision. However, if the political decision is in the borderline of the legal–juridical order because the legal–juridical order is created by the political decision, it has to be affirmed with Schmitt that the state presupposes the concept of the political: "The concept of the State presupposes the concept of the Political. According to modern linguistic usage, the State is the political status of an organized people in an enclosed territorial unit" (Schmitt 2007a, 19).

If the concept of the state presupposes the concept of the political, the political as such cannot be enclosed within any of the spheres of the state. Moreover, if the political supposes an existential decision that resolves an existential conflict, it cannot be enclosed in any sphere of life. It is a criterion that cannot be labelled in economic terms or in moral terms, nor in aesthetic terms. It only appears when the existential appears. The political, according to Schmitt has a particular status. And that status, as is it known, is related to the existential capacity to distinguish between friends and enemies: "The specific political distinction to which political actions and motives can be reduced is that between friend and enemy. This provides a definition in the sense of a criterion and not as an exhaustive definition or one indicative of substantial content" (Schmitt 2007a, 26).

The distinction between the friend and the foe does not correspond in Schmitt's work to a whimsical decision based on moral or aesthetic reasons. On the contrary, the political distinction between the friend and the foe implies, for Schmitt, a serious decision: it has an existential character. It is not a private distinction about what is good or bad, beautiful or ugly, or profitable or unprofitable. On the contrary, it is a public distinction that transcends all particular distinctions. As a public act, it embodies the public sphere. Moreover, the political decision is a dictate that casts and delimits the public sphere. Consequently, the political establishes the limits of the polity, and creates and enforces the law of the *Nomos*. The limit of the *Nomos* is defined by the limits of friendship. As Schmitt says: "The enemy is solely the public enemy, because everything that has a relationship to such a collectivity of men, particularly to a whole nation, becomes public by virtue of such relationship. The foe is *Hostis*, not *Inimicus* in the broader sense" (Schmitt 2007a, 28).[8] Thus, due to its public status, the political distinction can generate identity. It defines the existence of a *Nomos* in relation to *other Nomos*: "The phenomenon of the political

---

8   Cleary Schmitt's definition refers to the New Testament, particularly to Luke 6:27 and to Matthew 5:55.

can be understood only in the context of the ever present possibility of the friend-foe grouping, regardless of the aspects which this possibility implies for morality, aesthetics and economics" (Schmitt 2007a, 35).

Schmitt affirms that the existential distinction between friend and foe (*Hostis*) implies the formation of a concrete *Nomos*, the boundaries of which are delimited by the existence of the enemy that is outside the political unity and that, at the same time, provides it with its identity. The confrontation generated by the political, in Schmitt's theory, is radical. It implies an open and permanent existential conflict with the public enemy. However, the polity is sustained, in fact, by this existential and open conflict. Hence, The *Nomos* – the concrete existence of which also implies a concrete and positive legal juridical order – is embodied in and enforced and sustained by the political decision. The political decision is always a decision on the exception. It is always; it must be said, in Schmitt's case, a sovereign decision. As we have already pointed out, it is an act of *ipso facto* creation.

To conclude, the political always implies an exceptional moment that is decided by the sovereign in order to generate and enforce a *Nomos*. If the political distinction is always enforcing the legal–juridical order, the state should always presuppose the political. The existence of the state as a institutional and juridical order is sustained by and upon the political. Otherwise, the state would not be a state but just a private association based on apolitical and non-existential distinctions.

Democracy

Schmitt directly looks into the problem of democracy in his *Die geistesgeschichtliche Lage des heutigen Parlamentarismus*. In the first page of the text, Schmitt states that "the history of political and State theory in the nineteenth century can be summarised in a single phrase: the successful advancement of democracy" (Schmitt 1985, 5). Thus, for the jurist, democracy is the predominant political organization of the twentieth century.

Nevertheless, Schmitt's conceptualizations are usually built upon opposites. In the case that is about to be analyzed, parliamentarism is the political form opposite to democracy. Parliamentarism is the political form that has emerged from the reformation process in Europe. The religious pluralism that appeared during the sixteenth and seventeenth centuries suffered, according to Schmitt, a process of transformation due to the secularization process and was transformed into political pluralism – a pluralism impregnated by the logic of economic competition.[9]

---

[9] Schmitt says, in "The age of neutralization and depolitization": "In the past four centuries of European history, intellectual life has had four different centres and the thinking of the active elite which constituted the respective vanguards moved in the changing centuries around changing centres. The concepts of changing generations can only be understood from these shifting centres. It should be emphasized that the shift – from the theological to the metaphysical domain, and from there to the humanitarian-moral and finally to the economic domain – is not meant as a theory of cultural and

However, during the entirety of the reformation process and until the nineteenth century, an irrepressible magma existed: a mass with no political shape, incapable of identifying with the "interests represented" in parliament.

Parliamentarism, as a political form, implies for Schmitt an erroneous concept of representation. Parliamentary representation results in the representation of particular interests, whereas for Schmitt, representation presupposes the representation of the unit and not of the individual parts. And the unit, as it has been seen, is the product of an existential decision and not the mere sum of the individual parts. The public debate entails that all actors have the possibility to debate and to argue in public. Thus, the two principles that sustain parliamentarism are directly related to the faith in public opinion. That is to say, for Schmitt, parliamentarism is based on the faith in the reasonable competition among arguments where each argument represents a particular interest.

Cleary, Schmitt's argument implies that parliamentarism is an *apolitical* form. The apolitical nature of parliamentarism owes its existence to the fact that a political form is based on an existential decision. Thus, since it is an existential decision, it transcends the individuals and, of course, it transcends their interests as well. Schmitt's claim is that a political unity cannot exist based on the plurality of interests, but rather on the unity generated by the decision: "Political Unity is the highest unity – not because it is an omnipotent dictator, or because it levels out all other unities, but because it decides, and has the potential to prevent all other opposing groups from dissociating into a state of extreme enmity –that is, into civil war" (Schmitt 1999, 203).

Democracy, as the opposite of liberal parliamentarism, appears in Schmitt's eyes as a political form. And as a political form it should be based on a principle capable enough to provide it with unity. Thus, while parliamentarism was based on the liberal idea of pluralism and competition, democracy aims at creating an identity based on homogeneity. Cleary, for Schmitt, democracy and liberalism cannot go together. As it has been pointed out, the political form of liberal tradition – parliamentarism – is, by definition, apolitical while democracy is political: it is based on unity and creates a homogeneous identity through an existential decision between the friend and the foe.

Consequently, homogeneity must be at the core of any democratic regime. This homogeneity does not entail liberal equality – based on interest – or the liberal concept of equality among men. Homogeneity is, for Schmitt, about a substantive equality: "Every actual democracy rests on the principle that not only are equals equals but unequals will not be treated equally. Democracy requires, therefore, first homogeneity" (Schmitt 1985, 9).

Schmitt evokes the concept of homogeneity in order to claim that democracy is related to a substantial unity[10] (as opposed to the liberal concept of the equality

---

intellectual 'dominance' not as a historical-philosophical law in the sense of a law of three stages or similar constructions" (Schmitt 2007b, 82). For Schmitt's analysis of the secularization process, see Schmitt (2005) and Schmitt (2007a).

10 For a further treatment of this point see Herrero Lopez (2007).

among humankind that Schmitt finds an apolitical abstraction) that delimitates who belongs and who does not belong to the *Demos*. Thus, the boundaries of the *Demos* are delimited by an existential substance that, as it has been pointed out, is the product of the political decision. Therefore, in direct opposition to the liberal concept of equality[11] that is at the basis of parliamentarism, Schmitt claims that homogeneity is at the basis of democracy: a political concept that presupposes an existential decision. That is to say, it is political because it entails the possibility of a distinction (Mouffe 1999, 40). Thus, the *Demos* implies the substantial existence of the democratic *Nomos*. Hence, the people are *One*, and cannot be divided.[12]

Thus, the oneness of the people is prior to the conformation of the *Nomos* and, at the same time, it is the existential substance that decides the boundaries of the *Nomos*. Consequently, in a democratic *Nomos*, sovereignty is the people as a whole who, according to Schmitt, exists before the conformation of the political unity. It is the people as a whole that dictates the existence of the concrete order.

The importance of Schmitt's theory of democracy is that by identifying democracy with the homogeneity of the people, he reveals the incompatibility of democracy and liberalism. In addition, Schmitt's rationale behind the compatibility of democracy and political unity lies on the fact that the *people as a whole* is a substantial unity prior to the embodiment of the legal–juridical order. Moreover Schmitt places the being of the *Nomos* in the substantive identity of the people as a whole. This enables Schmitt to identify the people as a homogenous unity with the sovereign in a democratic *Nomos*. Therefore, the *people as a whole* is on the borderline of the legal–juridical order.

Schmitt's Analysis of Federalism

The inherent contradiction presented above had, for Schmitt, a negative and catastrophic impact on the Weimar Republic. Historically speaking, Weimer was not the first time in which the universality of the German people and the particularities of each *Land* contradicted each other. However, Weimar was the first time in which said conflict appeared within the framework of a democratic constitutional order. The first symptom of that conflict arose when the *Land* of Bavaria called for federal constitutional reform in 1924, claiming that Weimar needed a deeper federal reform to guarantee the particularities of each *Land* against the hegemony of Prussia.

---

11 "The equality of all persons as persons is not democracy but a certain kind of liberalism, not a state form but an individualistic-humanitarian ethic and *Weltanschauung*" (Schmitt 1985, 13).

12 It does not mean that any kind of pluralism exists inside the polity. The unity implies that all the members of the *Demos* share the same substantial identity and their existence as part of the *Demos* is determined by that identity. They can have different economical perspectives or different ideas of what is beauty, but they cannot have an existential disagreement.

Schmitt did not participate in the debates concerning the Bavarian case. But when in 1932 the revolt in the *Lämder* of Prussia irrupted, Schmitt did not hesitate in defending the unity of Reich by appealing to the article 48 of the Constitution of Weimar. As is well known, the article allowed the president to suspend the legal order by declaring the exception.

Particularly, in the case of the Prussian revolt, the *Reichspräsident* Field Marshall von Hindenburg suspended the legal order and authorized Chancellor of the Reich Franz Von Papen to intervene in the *Land* to restore order and public safety. By declaring the exception, the *Reichspräsident* appeared to Schmitt as the last guardian of the constitution: the representative of the people as a whole (Schmitt 1996a).[13] Thus, by resorting to the exception, Weimar faced the contradiction inherent to its own nature: the co-existence of the democratic principle of unity and that of legal pluralism (Schmitt 2004). This moment was crucial to the breakdown of Weimar.

Schmitt's theoretical analysis of federalism has to be understood within this political context. Schmitt's analysis of federalism is briefly presented in two of his works; it can be said that *Verfassungslehre* (1928) and *Der Hüter der Verfassung* (1931) constitute Schmitt's constitutional theory. Moreover, the importance of Schmitt's analysis of federalism becomes obvious when reviewing the central role these works had in Weimar's political debate. Even though the presentation of federalism was not extensive, it would be unfair to disregard it when analyzing Schmitt's constitutional theory.

In this section, we will present Schmitt's arguments on federalism and we will be able to discuss his theory on federalism in relation with his theory on democracy. This presentation is divided into four parts. First I present (a) Schmitt's characterization of the main principles of a constitutional pact and (b) the particularities Schmitt finds in a federal pact. Once these two elements are presented, I discuss (c) the problems Schmitt identifies in the federation and the way he solves them (d) by resorting to the democratic principle of homogeneity.

The Constitutional Pact

According to Schmitt, every legal–juridical order is the product of a sovereign political decision, and the sovereign is in the borderline of the legal–juridical order. In Schmitt's theory of democracy, the political order becomes a substantial political unity that is determined by the existence of the people as a whole, which is *One*, and, at the same time, the subject of sovereignty. Thus, the people as a whole is

---

13 The main debate about who has to be the guardian of the constitution involved, among others, Carl Schmitt and Hans Kelsen. Kelsen's position, contrary to Schmitt's, implied that the guardian of the constitution has to be a legal organism contemplated in the constitution. As it has been seen, Schmitt's position supposes that Kelsen's is a mere liberal-legalistic position that does not take into account the political core of the constitution. See Schmitt (1996a) and Kelsen (1931). For a complete debate on this topic see Dyzenhaus (1999).

bound to exist before the conformation of the juridical-legal order. *Il Popolo*, as a homogenous entity – that is as one – becomes the sovereign entity who founds and embodies the state.

Thus, the subject of sovereignty is bound to exist before the institution of the political–juridical order. The political and the sovereign decision appears in the borderline of the concrete legal–juridical order. Hence, Schmitt makes a distinction when it comes to the conformation of a political–juridical order. Firstly, the political entity is created by a "social contract" or "founding pact" whereby an unformed substance embodies itself in a political form. In the case of democracy, the people institute themselves as "the people as a whole," as *Il Popolo*, under a "social contract." Secondly, according to Schmitt, a "constitutional convention" appears when *il Popolo* as a whole, by a sovereign decision, dictates a constitutional order. This shows that, for Schmitt, a constitutional convention does not found the political unity but presupposes it.[14]

The Federal Pact

According to Schmitt, federalism is a concept always related to the relations between states. However, the federal agreement is not a mere treaty (e.g. The League of Nations) executed among states whereby the parties involved do not change their political status. The federal pact is a pact with a particular characteristic. The federal pact is, for Schmitt, a "status pact." And since it generates a constitution by the agreement of multiple political unities, the agreement has the power to modify the political status of each member-state. Each member has to change its constitution in order to subordinate itself to the new federal state. The federal state establishes a new and collective political status: a federal constitution.

However, once each member becomes a party to a federal state, it loses its capacity to dictate its own unity. In order to enter into the new federal state and in order to be protected by and to be ruled under the new constitution, each member-state gives up its sovereign power to the federal state. And this change of status

---

14 In the case of the constitution of the Weimar Republic, Schmitt defended the thesis that the Reich constitution of 11th of August 1919 rests on the will and the constitutive power of the German people. Schmitt based his argument in the first article of the Weimar Constitution and in its prelude. Both texts affirm that state authority derives from "the people." By defending this thesis, Schmitt is observing that the unity of the Reich is based on the homogeneity of the German people that existed before the creation of the federal agreement. Thus, the constitution had a strong democratic basis. In his analysis of Weimar's crisis, Schmitt affirms that Weimar's crisis was due to contradiction in the Weimar Constitution: it had a democratic "spirit" but it also proposed liberal institutions. The contradiction was, for Schmitt, strong enough to attempt against the unity of the Reich. In Schmitt's view, the contradiction between the democratic principles and the liberal principles the Constitution had, made it impossible to resolve the conflict between the federal prerogatives and the *Länder* in 1929–1931 that ended with Hitler in power and with the end of the Weimar Republic.

is due, for Schmitt, to the fact that the objective of a federation is the permanent union of its members. As a new state the federation *"is thus 'perpetual': it is meant to endure"* (Schmitt 1992, 30, italics in original).[15]

The federation is instituted as a political entity conformed by a plurality of sub-unities with the objective to preserve each member-state. According to Schmitt, on the internal level, the federal power as the supreme power has the duty to protect the existence of each member-state and to decide – in the name of unity – when resolving conflicts among them. As the new sovereign, the federal power has to act as a peacemaker. At the international level, the federal power has the duty and the right to defend the territory and the existence of the federation. Thus, this change in the status of member-states affects the monopoly of the *ius belli* that each member held before the federal agreement. At the end of the day, the main characteristic of the federal pact (the status) implies the resignation by each member-state of their power to exercise the sovereign power: the *ius belli*. The *ius belli* is now monopolised by the federal power. The federation is rendered the new sovereign. Schmitt says: *"As long as the federation exists, the only possibility is federal **enforcement** against individual members. If it comes to a war, the federation no longer exists in its previous form"* (Schmitt 1992, 23, italics in original).

Lastly, once the federal state is instituted and has the sovereign power, it has the right to intervene in member-states matters to guarantee the permanence of the federation. This is possible because each member-state has changed its constitutional status and handed power over to a "power" that, once instituted, transcends them.

These arguments explain that for Schmitt there is no possible difference between a confederation and a federation. According to Schmitt, both are the result of a constitutional convention that implies the change of the political status of each member-state. The classical distinction that states that a confederation is a subject of international law and a federation is a subject of political law lacks meaning for Schmitt. Both the confederation and the federation exist only if the members renounce the *ius belli*, both forms are a political unity. And, hence, both forms act in the international sphere as singly and as one state.

The institution of a federation implies, for Schmitt, a particular constitutional pact: a status pact. The status pact supposes the change of the political status of the member-states of the federation. They have renounced to their previous sovereign powers. Moreover, the federation aims at the self-preservation and the preservation of its members. In order to fulfil its aim, the federal power arises as the power that transcends each member and monopolises the *ius belli* (that is, the monopoly of the decision). As the member-states have renounced their *ius belli* and they have accepted the sovereign power of the federation, they have also renounced, according Schmitt, the possibility of secession from the federation. Since the member-states have given up their sovereignty when entering the federation they are no longer sovereign and it is the federal state now that has the duty to guarantee the internal peace and the preservation of each member-state by exercising the right to declare

---

15 Schmitt uses the German Federal Act (1815) and the Viennese Act of 1820 as examples.

the exception (*Ausnahmezustand*). Hence, the federal power holds the absolute power to intervene in the domestic affairs of the member-states. However, this intervention does reflect nor imply any kind of abuse; it is, for Schmitt, just a logical act of government in the exercise of its sovereignty.

Federal Antimonies

Schmitt finds a complex and contradictory issue in federal theory that can be presented in the form of the following question: How can it be possible that a plurality of political unities becomes *One* and remains *Many* at the same time when the central attribute of the sovereign implies the monopoly of the existential decision? Cleary, the federal agreement is in direct opposition to Schmitt's theory of the state. Thus, Schmitt observes that any constitutional theory of federalism is confronted to three main antinomies.

The first antinomy "concerns the *right of self-preservation*[16] of each member state" (Schmitt 1992, 33). The antimony arises in the fact that while the main aim of the institution of the federation is the preservation of each member-state, each member-state has to yield its right to self-preservation in favour of the federal state. That is to say, every member-state has renounced its right of the *ius belli*. Hence, the member-states have lost their sovereign capacity to dictate and to decide; they have renounced to their own capacity of self-protection.

The second antinomy concerning the right of self-determination is closely related to the first antinomy. While the member-states have entered in the federation in order to preserve their right to self-preservation and to maintain their political independence, every federation qualifies the autonomy of the member-state by exercising the right of self-determination of the federation via the federal capacity of intervention (Ulmen 1992). Thus, if the political implies the capacity of determination and the construction of the legal–juridical order, the capacity of intervention demolishes the political capacity of each member-state.

The third antinomy has a general character and questions the issue of sovereignty. It implies the possible conflict between the federation and the member-states since the existence of the federation presupposes a tension between the unity of the federation and the plurality of the member-states. In the federation, Schmitt argues, two kinds of political unities necessarily coexist: the federation and each member-state. Federal intervention may not always be enough to resolve the conflict that may arise form this double status. Thus, the survival of the federation depends upon the inexistence of "existential" conflicts – that is, pure political conflicts – within or among member-states. Thus Schmitt says: "*in a federation two types of political existence obtain- that of the federation and that of the individual member states. Both must coexist so long as the federation is desired. Neither should supersede the other; neither should be subordinate to the other*" (Schmitt 1992, 33, italics in original). However, in the context of this thin equilibrium it cannot be guaranteed that the

---

16 Emphasis in the original text.

federation will be exempt of any existential conflict since in the federation two different political units coexist and the possibility of the political conflict will be always there: "*This existential conflict is always possible wherever there are politically autonomous entities. Thus the question of sovereignty, i.e. the ultimate conflict is always remains open*" (Schmitt 1992, 34, italics in original).[17]

Lastly, the federation will only survive if the thin equilibrium between the right of the member-states and the right of the Federation is enough to avoid the existential conflict. However, the possibility of conflict is inherent to the existence of different political unities. If the existential conflict arises the federation no longer exists. For Schmitt, the federation bears, within itself, the seeds of its own self-destruction.

Solving the Antinomies

After analyzing the antinomies of the theory of federation, Schmitt affirms that these antinomies are resolved by his theory of democracy. Schmitt underscored that the main characteristic of democracy is homogeneity. Thus, when it comes to a democratic federation the last guardian of the unity is the homogenous people as a whole who has given itself a constitutional federal order. At this point, Schmitt's main critique relates to how democratic federation arises. There cannot be any conflict between member-states if the federation has been created under the supposition of the homogeneity of the people that comprise all member-states. Schmitt says: "every federation is based on an Essential presupposition – the homogeneity of all Member-States, on a substantial sameness of the member states that brings an essential consensus which in turn precludes the possibility of the extreme conflict within the federation" (Schmitt 1992, 37).

It is within the framework of this main critique that Schmitt resolves each one of the antinomies. The first antinomy, concerning the right of self-preservation of each member-state, is solved by asserting that if self-preservation implies the right to use the *ius belli* in order to protect the existence of the political unity against an existential foe, as the federation implies the homogeneity of each member-

---

17   Cleary, Schmitt is neglecting any distinction between the confederation form and the federation form. He clarifies that if the distinction were correct, the political and, thus, the existential tension that always exists inside a federation would never be understood. Moreover, Schmitt accuses on this point the classical German political Right tradition (particularly to Laband, Haener and Meyer Anschütz) of not paying attention to the "true" problem of the federation and to offer "false and dangerous answers." Moreover, Schmitt criticizes the classical theories of Calhoun and Seydel. In particular, Schmitt refers to the case of America and the American civil war. According to Schmitt, the federal negotiation in the context of the American civil war ended once the war was declared. Thus, the federation disappeared. In this particular case, the appearance of the existential conflict among the political unities ended with the destruction of the previous federation. Schmitt has the same argument when he analyzes the German Empire of 1815.

state, in a democratic federation the possibility of such an enmity is excluded. It is impossible, according to Schmitt, that the enemy of the people of one member-state does not become the enemy of the people of remaining member-states since all members share the same homogenous people. Self-preservation is guaranteed under the principle of democratic homogeneity.

The second antinomy that concerns the autonomy of each member-state is also solved by the principle of homogeneity. Autonomy can only be threatened by an alien intervention in the internal matters of the member-state. However, as the federal constitution has been transposed to the constitution of each member-state, federal intervention does not imply a threat to political autonomy. Federal intervention in internal matters of a member-state is not an alien intervention. The will of the people can never go against itself.

The third and most important antinomy is, again, solved by the democratic principle of homogeneity. Schmitt has pointed out that sovereignty is an indivisible principle. Therefore, in a democratic federation where the sovereign is the people, the possible conflict between member-states or between a member-state and the federation can never be an existential conflict, that is to say a conflict between sovereigns.[18] The question of who decides in a democratic federation always has the same answer: the people by the principle of representation. However, this does not imply that, administratively speaking, the member-states do not have a certain space of autonomy; the political decision is always in the hands of *Il Popolo*.

Conclusion

Democracy and federalism do not have, for Schmitt, a positive correlation. They are, in fact, opposite principles. While democracy is concerned with homogeneity, federalism is concerned with pluralism. At the end of the day, federalism is a political–territorial organisation correlated with the principles of liberalism.

As presented in this chapter, for Schmitt, the democratic federation implies the rise of a new kind of federation: a federation without a federal basis. It is a federation that assumes the homogeneity of the people as a whole. It is a federation in which the existence of the member-states as individual and independent political unities is excluded: "The linkage of democracy and federalism leads organizationally into

---

18 However, Schmitt cannot explain, at this point, how to solve a conflict in a plurinational federation. We should clarify: Schmitt finds the basis of the homogeneity of the people in the concept of "nation". According to Schmitt, the nation is the democratic concept *per excellence* in modern times. However he never rules out the possibility that homogeneity can be built under other precept. Cleary he follows Hobbes – and of course M. Weber – and asserts that all political order is open to transcendence, the contents of which (values) operates as a unifying element that creates homogeneity. However, Schmitt does not fill the content of transcendence. It can be argued that, the unifying element could be the nation or human rights, or, as in the case of Hobbes, that "Jesus is the Christ." See Schmitt (1996b, 1996c, 2001).

a distinctive type of state – a federal state without a federal foundation. On the surface, this is a contradiction" (Schmitt 1992, 55).

Schmitt's analysis of federalism is directly related to his theoretical effort to think through the meaning of political unity. In this sense, federalism implies a clear contradiction to Schmitt: it is at the same time plurality and unity. Moreover, a democratic federation cannot work without resorting to the democratic principle of homogeneity, but this homogeneity can only thrive in a unitary state, thus rendering pointless the plurality of member-states. This is a clear contradiction that implies that for Schmitt the democratic federation is a process, gradual but unstoppable, towards the democratic unity that embodies the modern state. When Schmitt analyzes federalism he is looking at the core of the state; he is looking at modern democratic sovereignty.

At the end of the day, Schmitt, with no fear of being thunderstruck, looks into Medusa's eyes.

References

Agamben, G. (2005), *State of Exception*. (Chicago: Chicago University Press).
Amoretti, U.N. and Bermeo, N. (2004), *Federalism and Territorial Cleavages*. (Baltimore: Johns Hopkins University Press).
Bandieri, J.L. (2002), Carl Schmitt and federalism. *Telos* 122.
Bellamy, R. and Castiglioni, D. (1997), Building the union: The nature of sovereignty in the political architecture of Europe. *Law and Philosophy* 16, 421–445.
Dyzenhaus, D. (1998), *Law as Politics. Carl Schmitt's Critique of Liberalism*. (Duke, NC: Duke University Press).
—— (1999), *Legality and Legitimacy: Carl Schmitt, Hans Kelsen and Hermann Heller in Weimar*. (New York: Oxford University Press).
Gagnon, A. and Tully, J. (2001), *Multinational Democracies*. (Cambridge: Cambridge University Press).
—— Guibernau, M. and Rocher, F. (2004), *The Condition of Diversity in Multinational Democracies*. (Montreal: McGill–Queen's University Press).
Galli, C. (1996), *Genealogia della politica: Carl Schmitt e la crisi del pensiero politico moderno*. (Bologna: Il Mulino).
Herrero Lopez, M. (2007), *El Nomos y los Político: La filosofía política de Carl Schmitt*. (Navarra: EUNSA).
Karmis, D. and Norman, W. (eds) (2005), *Theories of Federalism. A reader*. (New York: Palgrave).
Kelsen, H. (1931), Wer soll der hüter der Verfassung sein? *Die Justiz. Monatsschrift f. Erneuerung d. Deustschen Rechtwesens* t, 6, 576–628. (Berlin).
Kymlicka, W. (1996), *Multicultural Citizenship: A liberal theory of minority rights*. (New York: Oxford University Press).
—— (2007), *Multicultural Odysseys: Navigating the new international politics of diversity*. (New York: Oxford University Press).

Meier, H. (1998), *The Lesson of Carl Schmitt. Four chapters on the distinction between political theology and political philosophy*. (Chicago: Chicago University Press).
McCormick, J.P. (1999), *Carl Schmitt's Critique of Liberalism. Against politics as technology*. (New York: Cambridge University Press).
Mouffe, C. (1999), Carl Schmitt and the paradox of liberal democracy, in C. Mouffe (ed.) (1999), *The Challenge of Carl Schmitt*. (London: Verso).
Requejo, F. (2005), *Multinational Federalism and Value Pluralism: The Spanish case*. (London: Routledge).
Schmitt, C. (1985), *The Crisis of Parliamentary Democracy*. Ellen Kennedy trans. (Cambridge: MIT Press).
—— (1992), The constitutional theory of federation. G. Ulmen, trans. *Telos* 91, 26–57.
—— (1993), *Verffasungslehre*. (Berlin: Dunker & Humblot).
—— (1996a), *Der Hüter der Verfassung*. (Berlin: Dunker & Humblot).
—— (1996b), *Roman Catholicism and Political Form*. G. Ulmen, trans. (Westport, CT: Greenwood Press).
—— (1996c), *Der Begriff des Politischen*. Text von 1932 mit einem Vorwort und drei Corollarien. (Berlin: Dunker & Humblot).
—— (1997), *Der Nomos der Erde im Völkerrecht des Jus Publicum Europaeum*. (Berlin: Dunker & Humblot).
—— (1999) Ethics of State and Pluralistic State. In Mouffe, C. (ed.) (1999) *The Challenge of Carl Schmitt* (London: Verso).
—— (2001), La teoría política del Mito. Angelika Scherp, trans. In H. Orestes Aguilar (ed.) (2001), *Carl Schmitt, Teólogo de la política*. (Mexico: FCE).
—— (2004), *Legality and Legitimacy*. Jeffery Seitzer, trans. (Duke, NC: Duke University Press).
—— (2005), *Political Theology*. George Schwab, trans. (Chicago: University of Chicago Press).
—— (2007a), *The Concept of the Political*. George Schwab, trans. (Chicago: University of Chicago Press).
—— (2007b), The era of neutralization and depolitization. George Schwab, trans. In *The Concept of the Political*. (Chicago: University of Chicago Press).
Schwab, G. (1989), *The Challenge of the Exception: An introduction to the political ideas of Carl Schmitt between 1921 and 1936*. (Westport, CT: Greenwood Press).
Stepan, A. (1999), Federalism and democracy: Beyond the US model. *Journal of Democracy* 10:4, 19–34.
Ulmen, G. (1992), Introduction to "The Constitutional Theory of Federalism". *Telos* 91, 16–26.

Further Reading

Agamben, G. (1998), *Homo Sacer: Sovereign Power and Bare Life*. (Stanford: Stanford University Press).

Arato, A. (1999), Carl Schmitt and the revival of constituent power in the United States. *Cardozo Law Review* 21:5, 1739–1747.

Bendersky, J. (1983), *Carl Schmitt: Theorist for the Reich*. (Princeton: Princeton University Press).

—— (1999), The expendable Kronjurist: Carl Schmitt and National Socialism, 1933–36. *Journal of Contemporary History* 14:2, 309–328.

Berthold, L. (1999), *Carl Schmitt und der Staatsnotstandsplan am Ende der Weimarer Republik*. (Berlin: Dunker & Humblot).

Cristi, R. (1998), *Carl Schmitt and Authoritarian Liberalism*. (Cardiff: University of Wales Press).

Holmes, S. (1993), *The Anatomy of Antiliberalism*. (Cambridge, MA: Harvard University Press).

Kalyvas, A. (1999), Carl Schmitt and the three moments of democracy. *Cardozo Law Review* 21:5, 1525–1565.

Kennedy, E. (2004), *Constitutional Failure. Carl Schmitt in Weimar*. (Duke, NC: Duke University Press).

Schmitt, C. (1969), *Gesetz und Urteil*. (Berlin: Auflage).

—— (1994), *Die Diktatur*. (Berlin: Dunker & Humblot).

—— (2004), *Der Wert des Staates und die Bedeutung des Einzelnen*. (Berlin: Dunker & Humblot).

Seitzer, J. (2001), *Comparative History and Legal Theory: Carl Schmitt in First German Democracy*. (Westport, CT: Greenwood Press).

18

Altiero Spinelli and European Federalism

Roberto Castaldi

Altiero Spinelli was born in Rome in 1907, where he died in 1986. He was the most important figure of European federalism after World War II, combining idealism and realism, and changing tactics several times, but always maintaining the aim of European federation (see Paolini 1988; Levi 1990 and Graglia 2008).

In his autobiography, *Come ho tentato di diventare saggio* [As I Attempted to Become Wise], Spinelli divided his life into six action periods (1943–45; 1947–54; 1954–61; 1961–70; 1970–76; 1976–86) to which must be added his "prehistory": the period when he was a communist and was jailed by the Fascist regime, before becoming a democratic federalist.

He was brought up in a socialist family and was an early reader of Marx's and Lenin's works. In 1922 he enrolled at Rome University to study law, and in 1924 joined the Italian Communist Party (PCI). His talent was recognized by Gramsci and in 1926 became inter-regional secretary for central Italy of the youth branch of PCI, and went underground. In June 1927 he was arrested and condemned by the Fascist special tribunal to a sentence of 16 years and 8 months. He spent nine years in jail in Rome (July 1927–May 1928), Lucca (May 1928–January 1931), Viterbo (January 1931–July 1932) and Civitavecchia (July 1932–March 1937). Spinelli refused to ask for pardon and renounce his political ideas. However, different amnesties provided him some hope for early release, and he was supposed to be freed in 1937. He remained in jail until March 1937 when he was forced into confinement first on the island of Ponza (March 1937–July 1939), and then on the island of Ventotene from July 1939 up to his release with all other political prisoners in August 1943.

In prison, Spinelli studied languages, literature, philosophy, history, economics and politics, reading hundreds of books. He met some of the main leaders of the PCI and other political groups. He criticized and tried to change several party positions, until he left the PCI to join the democratic and federalist cause. He was formally expelled by the party during his confinement in Ponza. The communists tried to isolate him from all other political prisoners, but did not succeed.

In Ventotene his federalist vision took proper shape, in an intense dialogue with other political prisoners, especially Ernesto Rossi, Eugenio Colorni and Ursula Hirschmann.[1] Rossi obtained from Luigi Einaudi some Federal Union literature, mainly by Lionel Robbins, together with Einaudi's own federalist essays. Spinelli recalled this enlightening discovery of federalism as a new way to analyze political reality, and the expression of these ideas developed along with his rejection of communism. Afterwards, Spinelli devoted his life to the cause of European unity on a federalist basis, which he considered to be the most important political aim necessary to save civilization.

In the summer of 1941 Spinelli and Rossi completed the *Manifesto for a free and united Europe* (Ventotene Manifesto), with a preface by Colorni. They attributed the crisis of modern civilization to absolute national sovereignty, which had caused international anarchy and the two world wars. They proposed a European federation, in which a social reform would be possible, as the post-war main political aim. They believed that a revolutionary situation would follow the war, in which those in favour of the old sovereign nation-states and those aiming at federalizing Europe would confront each other. Later, Spinelli said the *Manifesto* contained some useful ideas and also some mistakes, due to the limited experience and information available in jail and confinement. The first illusion was that the war would create a revolutionary situation in which the creation of a European federation would be possible. This was linked to the absence of a proper geopolitical analysis and recognition that after the war the European states would fall under the control of the US and the USSR, which would allow for their quick reconstruction under the latter's hegemony. The third mistake was the idea of a federalist revolutionary party, along the lines of the Leninist tradition, which he had just abandoned. Spinelli retained other ideas from the *Manifesto*, such as the notion of the irreversible historical crisis of the European nation-states, due to their being too small to tackle the main problems of the time. He felt that the goal of a federal Europe had political, and not just ideal, salience and was a duty and a challenge for today, not tomorrow. Federalism constituted the new dividing line between progressive and conservative forces, given that the most important political problems could only find a positive solution at a higher level of government than those of the nation-states. Therefore an autonomous federalist political movement devoted to this goal was necessary.

Most political prisoners in Ventotene did not support the *Manifesto*. Even the future Italian President, Sandro Pertini, then a socialist prisoner, first signed and then withdrew his support, due to socialist party pressure. On the mainland, Ursula Hirschmann distributed the *Manifesto* and two other federalist essays by Spinelli: *The United States of Europe and the various political stands*, and *Marxist politics and federalist politics*. In Ventotene each political group organized its own canteen, and the federalist one, led by Spinelli, was the first form of federalist organization he set up.

---

[1] She was Colorni's wife, and was free, thus allowed to stay on the island and to travel on the continent. After Colorni was murdered by the Fascists in 1944, she became Spinelli's wife in 1945.

Spinelli was freed on 18 August 1943. Unlike the other political prisoners he did not have a political party waiting for him, but had to start a new political movement for the federalist political struggle he had envisaged. On 27 and 28 August 1943 Spinelli with about 20 other people founded the Movimento Federalista Europeo (MFE) in Mario Alberto Rollier's house in Milan (see Levi and Pistone 1973).

1943–1945

The first period of Spinelli's action aimed at spreading the federalist message to create a federalist supranational movement to exploit the revolutionary situation which would follow the war. He fled to Switzerland, and travelled also to France and Milan in his quest for other people ready to pursue a federal Europe to ensure peace. Spinelli wrote several pamphlets in different languages, recruited people from different countries and political backgrounds, and planned a first European federalist conference. He also contributed to *L'unità europea* [European unity], an MFE clandestine journal, which was the first to call for armed resistance to the Nazis in Italy.

Spinelli and many other Italian federalists joined the new Partito d'Azione, which accepted their international federalist vision. However, MFE remained the main instrument to spread the federalist vision to other political groups. Spinelli spent four months in France and on 22–24 March 1945 the first international federalist conference was held in Paris, in which two positions emerged: the world federalists suggested that a federal Europe could only emerge within a world federal government; the "realists" considered it more feasible to create federal institutions in Europe.

Spinelli realized that the revolutionary situation at the end of the war he had expected did not come to pass, and that in order to recruit existing political movements and elites to the federalist cause, a proper federalist culture was needed because many people could not yet detach themselves from the myth of national sovereignty. Spinelli saw little short-term chances for a federalist action and was economically hard pressed, given the end of the financial support provided by his brother Veniero and by the Partito d'Azione. He left MFE and federalist activity to work in a public enterprise, Azienda rilievo alienazione residuati (Arar), headed by Rossi, where he remained from June 1946 to June 1948.

During that period he was active in Italian political life, and joined the short-lived Movimento per la Democrazia Repubblicana (MDR), created by Parri, La Malfa and other people coming out of the Partito d'Azione, but he was not elected to the Parliament in 1948. Later on, he moved close to the Partito Socialista Liberale Italiano (PSLI) headed by Saragat. He was always trying to draw political organizations to the federalist cause and wrote several articles in favour of European unity, beginning in western Europe, and exploiting American benevolence – manifested by the Marshall Plan – rather than waiting for an unlikely international situation when all European countries could unite.

1947–1954

The day after the Marshall Plan speech, on 6 June 1947, Spinelli returned to the federalist activity. Between 1947 and 1954 he believed that the international situation, especially American foreign policy in favour of European integration against the Soviet threat, would make it possible for western European leaders to create a European federation, if properly advised and pressed by favourable public opinion. In August 1947 he failed to convince the Montreaux Congress of the Union of European Federalists (UEF)[2] to endorse the constitutionalist or Hamiltonian federalist stand, in favour of a European constituent assembly among the western European states. The French (Proudhonian) global strand of federalism, considered to be the best model upon which to organize political life at all levels, starting from its social and cultural premises, led by Alexandre Marc, was still very important at that time. However, UEF supported a western European federation that would work to democratize the Eastern European countries, so that they could join the federation.

Spinelli thus turned his attention back to MFE, which in his absence was led by Campagnolo, still waiting for an all-European union. He brought MFE to support his western vision and the Marshall Plan, and was elected secretary general in 1948. Initiatives such as the planned French–Italian Custom Union confirmed Spinelli's theory about the possibility of western European integration. At The Hague Congress, promoted by the United Europe Movement led by Churchill, Spinelli proposed a coherent federalist vision, which was not endorsed. The Congress launched a compromise proposal for a European consultative parliamentary assembly and a European Charter of Rights. This led to the Council of Europe, without any transfer of sovereignty. However, coming shortly after the signature of the Atlantic Pact, which put on American shoulders the defence of Europe, the Council of Europe and the Bruxelles Treaty provided the possibility of further European unity and independence.

Spinelli led MFE and brought UEF, at the Rome Congress in 1948, to criticize the European governments and launched the campaign for a European Federal Pact, on the basis of a report presented by Piero Calamandrei, an eminent federalist constitutionalist who drafted much of the Italian constitution. On the one hand, the federalists tried to exploit the governments' initiatives, denouncing their contradictions and indicating the possibility for improvement. Thus they asked the consultative parliamentary assembly of the Council of Europe to assume a constituent role. On the other hand, they mobilized European citizens, civil society

---

2   Created in 1946, it united the different federalist organizations in European, and had a membership of about 100,000 people.

and local political elites in favour of requesting a European constituent assembly. Spinelli always maintained the need for a democratic constituent procedure in order to draft a federal constitution establishing a European federal government.

The Campaign for a European Federal Pact to convene a constituent assembly focused on different targets according to the strength and ability of the federalist organizations in the European countries. In Italy Spinelli and MFE had collected more than 500,000 signatures from citizens, personalities and politicians including the Italian Prime Minister, Alcide De Gasperi, by October 1950. In Germany it was approved by overwhelming majorities in several local referenda and approved by the Bundestag. In France 10,000 city mayors supported it, notwithstanding the rivalries between the different French pro-European organizations. Still, by the end of 1950 it became clear that the Council of Europe would have no chance to develop a federal structure because of the veto power attributed to each state in the Ministers' Committee. However, a more promising new political platform was taking shape.

In this period Spinelli published many articles and pamphlets, especially on the German issue. He contributed regularly to *Europa federata* [Federated Europe], the new MFE journal. The reluctance of the European states to accept a fully sovereign Germany made it possible to pursue a European federation within which Germany would not represent a threat. Spinelli criticized functionalism and favoured European constitutionalism, but supported Jean Monnet's initiative leading to the Schuman Declaration on 9 May 1950, and the launch of the European Coal and Steel Community (ECSC) between France, Germany, Italy and the Benelux countries. Without Britain it was possible to start a new European platform based on the principle of the transfer of sovereignty, at least on limited grounds.

After the start of the Korean War, the US demanded German rearmament, fearing that a similar situation could evolve in Germany. France opposed such an idea. Thanks to Monnet's initiative, the French Prime Minister, Pleven, proposed a plan to create a European Defence Community (EDC), on the model of the ECSC. Spinelli saw this as a new window of opportunity for the creation of a European federation. He denounced the idea of a European army without a democratic federal government as dangerous to democracy. Indeed, nation-states should give up their useless sovereignty in the field of defence, and a fully democratic European government would be needed to control the new European army. Otherwise, the latter would only be a mercenary army at the service of the United States.

Spinelli and the federalists' actions convinced De Gasperi. Spinelli's *Memorandum relatif à la constitution de l'autorité politique européenne à la quelle l'armée européenne doit appartenir* [Memorandum on the constitution of a European political authority, to which the European army must belong] was the basis of De Gasperi's proposal to include in the Treaty establishing the EDC a particular provision – which became Article 38 of the Treaty – to create a European Political Community, based on a statute drafted by the Parliamentary Assembly of the EDC, which was thus implicitly assigned a constitutional mandate. De Gasperi requested a federal government and parliament and a federal tax as the institutional framework for the establishment of a European army.

The Italian government insisted that the process go ahead while the EDC Treaty was not yet ratified. The Parliamentary Assembly of the ECSC, which included some other members in order to make it equal with the future EDC Assembly, took the name of the Ad Hoc Assembly with the mandate to draft a project of federal or confederal union. Spinelli was very active in the Committee for the European Constitution of the European Movement, obtained the help of famous scholars such as Carl Friedrich and Robert Bowie, promoted conferences and studies about American and comparative federalism, and produced much of the material available to the Assembly. The Assembly drafted a statute providing for a quasi-federal institutional framework, with limited competences, and lacking some of those usually attributed to federations (see Preda 1990, 1994, 1996).

The end of the Korean War and Stalin's death changed the international situation, and weakened the prospects for French ratification of the EDC Treaty, notwithstanding its ratification by Germany, Belgium, Netherlands and Luxembourg, and the wide majority in favour of ratification in Italy (which waited to ratify to extract western diplomatic help on the issue of Trieste). After several changes of government due to French difficulties in the colonial wars, Schuman's party went into opposition and the Gaullists into government. In August 1954, the unusual alliance between Gaullists and communists won a vote to postpone indefinitely the ratification of the Treaty, by a slight margin. The public and parliamentary debates indicate that many French people hoped to avoid the creation of a new German army by rejecting the project of a European one (see Lerner and Aron 1957). The result, on the contrary, was the creation of a German army linked with the other western countries within NATO and the Western European Union, which remained a traditional alliance and not at all a substitute for the planned European army.

The defeat of the ECD treaty and the reconstruction of the German army spelled the end of the possibility of building a federal Europe as a solution to the German problem and an alternative to a fully sovereign Western Germany. The national solution had prevailed, and US support for European unity was weakening. The federalist organizations required a new strategy.

1954–1961

The defeat of the EDC and EPC projects ended Spinelli's actions to convince western European governments to create a federal union. De Gasperi's death further weakened the prospects of new federalist initiatives by the Italian government. The reconstruction of the nation-states had re-established vested interests in their preservation by the bureaucratic and military elites, all jealous of national sovereignty. At this time Spinelli's and Monnet's initiatives diverged (see Melchionni 1993).

Monnet continued along a functionalist perspective. He proposed an atomic energy community, and called for Spaak and the Benelux countries to proceed in the economic sector, which became the basis of the Messina conference leading to the Rome Treaties, establishing the EEC and the Euratom, also favoured by the French need to take initiative after the failure of the Suez intervention.

Spinelli tried to directly mobilize the European people, wrote a new *Manifesto dei federalisti europei*, and suggested to Spaak that a common market would fail without a democratic political authority founded on the European people's will. He strongly criticized the new communities and proposed that the federalists take "a new course of action" to mobilize widespread feelings in favour of European unity in order to challenge the nation-states' legitimacy and obtain a European constituent assembly. The new action would take the form of the European People's Congress (EPC), on the model of Gandhi's Congress Party that had led to Indian independence. It would be organized via spontaneous local elections promoted by the federalists, and would claim the right of the European people to decide which democratic institutions and competences to establish at the European level.

This new strategy implied a strong opposition to the national governments' European initiatives and a renewed autonomy of MFE from the political class. Most members active within national parties supported the governments' initiatives and left MFE, which lost much of its membership and acquired a more radical profile. UEF did not accept this new political platform, and the EPC became an organization in itself rather than simply an action, even if it was de facto organized by the federalist sections who shared Spinelli's position. After a long struggle between Spinelli's "new course of action" and the "realist" position taken by Henri Brugmans and Ernst Friedlander (who supported the Rome Treaties and the WEU), UEF split up in 1959. The sections from Germany, the Netherlands and a French association (La Fédération), which was not part of UEF, created the Action Européenne Fédéraliste and forbade their members to take responsibilities within UEF and the EPC. Some of their members and sections left and continued to operate within UEF, which in 1959 transformed itself into the Supranational European Federalist Movement, with individual members rather than national organizations, and with a European congress rather than national congresses.

The first election for the European People's Congress took place in 1957 in Turin, Milan, a few other Italian cities, Strasbourg, and about 50 small towns in Alsace, Lion, Anvers, Düsseldorf, Maastricht and Geneva. The number of cities and countries involved grew until 1962; overall 638,114 people voted in seven countries – Austria, Belgium, France, Germany, Italy, the Netherlands and Switzerland – but 455,214 of them in Italy. This action reflected the strength of the federalist organizations in the different countries, but did not manage to get a real European dimension, and did not have much political impact. The Congress delegates were received by the presidents of most national parliaments, and promoted the democratic idea of a European constituent assembly, while criticizing the idea of a directly elected European Parliament of the Communities without real powers, an idea Spinelli and the federalists came to support and to campaign for a few years later.

The success of the Common Market seemed to refute the federalists' idea that the EEC could not succeed without proper federal institutions. A new change in Spinelli's strategy was necessary.

1961–1970

Spinelli recognized that the EEC had produced a European administrative machine and some economic integration. This new platform should be exploited by the federalists, Spinelli believed, pointing out the contradictions and democratic limits of the functionalist approach and achievements. De Gaulle proposed a European confederation under French leadership. Spinelli bet on the federalist democratic alternative, trying to mobilize the democratic parties and forces around Europe and the world.

He visited the United States in June 1961, meeting – among others – Arthur Schlesinger, Zbigniew Brzezinski, Samuel Huntington and Daniel Bell, and discussed with them the project of a World Convention for Democratic Action. He always kept strong links with eminent American figures, as his letter exchanges with Henry Kissinger and others show. Back in Europe he continued his federalist activity, but was unhappy with the actions of the Congress. In 1962 he left the leadership of MFE and UEF,[3] even as he continued to contribute to federalist journals such as *Popolo Europeo* [The European People], and *Il federalista* [The Federalist]. Spinelli then took up a teaching post at Johns Hopkins University in Bologna, where he stayed until 1965 and where the Olivetti Foundation provided him the research funds to study the EEC. In Bologna Spinelli became involved in the association, journal and publisher *Il Mulino*, with which he continued to cooperate throughout his life.

In this period Spinelli created two new instruments for his public activity. In December 1963 he founded the Comitato italiano per la Democrazia Europea (CIDE) [Italian Committee for European Democracy]. This looked like an Italian version of Monnet's Action Committee, and was aimed at bringing the socialist and the centre-left Italian parties to the cause of European unity. Spinelli invited the European Commission President Hallstein, who had worked with him at the Ad Hoc Assembly, to further promote European integration and democracy by making an alliance with the European democratic forces. Hallstein rejected this perspective, but on the basis of a traditional neo-functionalist view, led the Commission to bold proposals, which led to the Empty Chair crisis, and were eventually defeated by De Gaulle's opposition. In his 1966 book *The Eurocrats*, Spinelli noted that Hallstein would have had more chance of success if he had made an alliance and invested in the relationship with the European democratic forces and parties.

In 1964 Spinelli travelled to the United States to meet, among others, Hubert Humphrey, Under-secretary of State for foreign affairs George Ball, the influential adviser to President Johnson George Bundy, and Senator Fullbright. In 1965 Spinelli founded a think tank on the Anglo-Saxon model, the Istituto Affari Internazionali (IAI) [International Affairs Institute], thanks to the financial help of the Olivetti and Ford foundations, and with some cooperation by *Il Mulino*. Spinelli directed

---

3   From then onwards Mario Albertini led MFE until his death in 1995, keeping it autonomous from all political parties.

IAI until 1970, producing studies about international affairs, the prospects for democracy, European integration and Italian foreign policy.

In 1968 Nenni, the leader of the Italian Socialist Party (PSI), became foreign minister and took Spinelli as his adviser. Their relationship had begun in 1957, when Nenni had brought the socialist congress to approve a note by Spinelli on European federation and distanced the socialists from the USSR and its intervention in Hungary. Spinelli conducted personal diplomacy for Nenni with the British and European elites, and recalled it in his diary in similar terms to the activity he had done between 1950 and 1953 around De Gasperi and Schuman. This led to the Common Italian–British Declaration about Europe on 28 April 1969, drafted by Spinelli, in which the two countries called for both economic and political integration towards European unity. A split in the socialist party drove Nenni out of office and Spinelli's influence went with him. He did not have enough time to exploit the positive political climate following De Gaulle's retirement and a new British positive attitude towards Europe. He had to find a new platform for his battle to reform the Communities towards the European federation.

1970–1976

Spinelli signalled his availability to become European Commissioner, and after some debate the Italian government designated him thanks to the support by much of the Italian Socialist Party, the Unitary Socialist Party, the Italian Republican Party, some Christian Democrats, and all the pro-European and federalist organizations. He remained in office from 1970 to 1976 as commissioner for research, technological development and industrial policy through the Malfatti, Mansholt and Ortoli Commissions. In this period he tried to lead the Commission to bold initiatives to face the collapse of the Bretton Woods system – with all its consequences: the oil shock and the energy crisis, the structural crisis of some European industries, increasing inflation and unemployment in some countries and the Italian crisis – the enlargement from six to nine member states, and the beginning of the criticism toward the only supranational European policy, the Common Agricultural Policy (CAP). He proposed to go forward with economic and monetary union, direct election of the European Parliament (EP), strengthening of the Commission and Parliamentary powers, and the beginning of regional and environmental European policies.

Spinelli participated in several federalist meetings, creating a link between his action and the federalists' campaigns to democratize the Communities. He promoted the creation of a Commission experts' group on institutional reform that would be chaired by Georges Vedel. Spinelli supported full co-decision for the Parliament within the legislative procedure, but the Vedel Report only proposed to gradually strengthen the EP with an assent procedure. Spinelli continued in his personal diplomacy with political leaders of different countries – including some Italian communists, whom he convinced to try to bring the PCI to the European cause – and wrote several essays and articles in newspapers and journals around Europe.

Two days after Nixon declared the inconvertibility of the US dollar, which spelled the end of the Bretton Woods system, Spinelli asked the Commission to propose a bold plan towards economic and monetary union. He proposed proceeding towards economic and monetary union by immediately re-modulating the parities between the European currencies; creating a European currency unit (ECU), a reserve fund to help the currencies in difficulty to keep the new parities; and establishing European control on speculative capital movements. He also proposed enlarging the fluctuation margin between the ECU and the dollar to establish a realistic new parity; looking for an international agreement to abolish tariffs and other obstacles to international trade; and coordinating economic and monetary policies and periodically readjusting their parities to ensure possible safeguards clauses in cases of serious troubles in their economic relationships. Parts of these proposals became the basis for the European Monetary System (EMS). At the same time Spinelli tried to set up new European industrial, regional and environmental policies, but the Council stopped his initiatives.

In 1972 Spinelli published *The European Adventure*, analyzing the European integration process and proposing a plan for political unity. He noticed that only during crises, such as in the early 1970s, did national governments listen to the European federalist vanguards and decide to bring Europe forward. But the 1972 Paris Summit rejected Spinelli's institutional proposals, notwithstanding his personal diplomacy with some of the main political leaders, especially in Italy, France, Britain and Germany. The national governments proclaimed the vague aim of European Union at the 1972 Paris and the 1973 Copenhagen summits. Spinelli asked the Commission in spring 1974 to take the initiative for monetary union, starting with a European constituent procedure to immediately create a European Central Bank and give the Commission the power to borrow money on the international markets to set up the new necessary industrial, regional and environmental policies, with the view to creating a European government with fiscal capacity. He continued his personal diplomacy with Aldo Moro (the Italian foreign minister), François Mitterrand (secretary of the French socialist party) and other political leaders, but complained about the Commission's lack of courage.

In 1974 the Paris Summit, thanks to new French President Valéry Giscard d'Estaing, decided to support the direct election of the EP, the regular meetings of the Head of states and governments, re-launched economic and monetary union, and asked the Belgian Prime Minister, Leo Tindemans, to prepare a report on this issue. Spinelli criticized the intergovernmental method and the fact that the Commission was not associated to the Tindemans group. He asked the Commission to propose a plan to create a European central bank endowed with parts of the national reserves, an economic planning institute of the Commission to coordinate national economic policies, to establish Community owned resources and fiscal and borrowing capacity, the transfer of economic international cooperation competence to the Community, and the launch of industrial, regional and environmental policies aimed at building European infrastructures.

Spinelli remained linked with federalist organizations. He took part in 1973 in a ceremony in Ventotene to recall the Manifesto, and in a Milan conference recalling the thirtieth anniversary of the foundation of MFE, as well as in congresses of the European Movement, and especially in the general states of the cities of Europe organized by his old federalist friend, Umberto Serafini, which asked for a constituent mandate to the EP.

In 1975 the Rome Summit set 1978 for the first direct election of the EP. However, Spinelli could not rejoice because the day before his wife, Ursula, had suffered a cerebral haemorrhage. Spinelli felt unable to continue his struggle, as his diary vividly shows. He decided not to continue as Commissioner in order to devote himself to Ursula's rehabilitation, to study and write, and thought this the end of his federalist activity.

1976–1986

Ursula's health improved, and in 1976 the PSI asked Spinelli to lead their list for the Rome council election, with the agreement that if the centre-left parties won the elections, Spinelli would become the new mayor of Rome. Spinelli refused because he was not interested and knew little about local issues, but would accept an offer which could allow him to continue his European struggle. This hinted at the national election and the possibility to be involved with the European Parliament (EP), which was still made of members of the national parliaments (MPs). The PSI refused to nominate him for the EP – it was only a few days before the final date to present the lists – and it was then that the PCI took the opportunity to demonstrate its support for a federal Europe by offering Spinelli the chance to run as an independent on its list. Spinelli accepted on condition that the PCI agree to respect his independence; namely that he would not be subordinate to any party discipline or position.

In his diary Spinelli had noted that in his European struggle he had been first offered the co-direction of the Partito d'Azione, which soon collapsed as a party for various reasons. He had then brought De Gasperi and the DC (Christian Democratic Party) to the European cause, but they never recognized their intellectual debt. Afterwards, he had convinced the socialist leader Nenni to support the European cause, but the party never understood the importance and priority of European unity. Finally the PCI gave him some credit for its European turn and offered him this post. In his activity he had always shown a willingness and capacity to cooperate with the various politicial groups from across the political spectrum in order to win them over to support a federal Europe.

The same day as Spinelli's success in the election, his beloved daughter Diana died after a long illness. Despite his grief, Spinelli became the president of the mixed group, and in 1979 was re-elected as an independent within the PCI list, and became president of the Independent Left Group until 1983. In 1978 he supported the Andreotti government's decision to participate in the EMS, against the PCI opposition. At the same time he was very active in the EP in preparing for the direct election and supporting the EMS, which it was hoped would herald the "birth" of the European people and the relaunch of monetary integration. He shared with Willy Brandt the idea of the EP as a permanent constituent assembly, but asked the EP to immediately draft a European constitution to be ratified by the national parliaments.

In 1978 Spinelli published *PCI, che fare?* about the European left aims. He favoured the "historical compromise" between DC and PCI against the terrorist Red Brigades, and even more to pursue a federal Europe, without which democracy at national level would not survive for long. In 1979 he was elected to the EP as an independent within the PCI list. His health deteriorated, but he still managed to develop a new strategy. To convince the EP of the need for a comprehensive institutional reform and constituent initiative, he first led it in the battle on the Community budget, to show that its powers were absolutely insufficient. In 1980 the EP rejected the proposed budget, asking for a change in the CAP and the further development of other European policies. The Council waited to present a new budget, happy to proceed every month with a twelfth part of the budget and to reduce the Community capacity. The EP was thus forced to accept the new budget in July. The proof of the dominance of the Council and the weakness of the European Parliament was achieved.

In June 1980, realizing the urgent need for institutional reform, Spinelli invited all MEPs to meet to define the best strategy to achieve it. Only nine MEPs answered, and started the Crocodile Club (named for the restaurant where they met). Spinelli was assisted by a small group of devoted and loyal MEPs from different political groups and a small staff of functionaries, headed by Pier Virgilio Dastoli, who worked with him daily. Their action led to the creation in July 1981 of the Institutional Affairs Committee, which elected Ferri as president and Spinelli as rapporteur. The federalist organizations also gathered support for the EP initiative. In July 1982 the EP approved a resolution on institutional reform and European Union drafted by Spinelli, on which the committee worked with specialized groups coordinated by Spinelli. In September 1983 the EP approved an outline treaty proposed by the Institutional Committee. In February 1984 the EP adopted the Treaty of European Unity, providing for EP participation in the legislative procedure together with the Council, the strengthening of the Commission, the abolition of unanimity in the Council, the principle of subsidiarity, and its ratification by the member states – without a previous intergovernmental conference (IGC) – and its entry into force as soon as member states representing two-thirds of the Community's population ratified, pending a meeting of those governments to set a date and decide their relationship with those member states unable or unwilling to ratify. Spinelli referred to Hemingway's fisherman story, suggesting that the EP had captured a big fish, but had to ensure that the sharks did not eat it all before bringing it back to the shore. He called on French President Mitterrand, who was also president of the Council at that time, to take the initiative to ratify the EP Treaty in France. In May 1984 Mitterrand addressed the EP supporting its initiative.

In April 1984 Spinelli published the first volume of his autobiography. He was then re-elected to the EP but failed to become its president. Still his candidature forced the Christian Democrats to present another strong federalist figure, Spinelli's friend Pierre Pflimlin. The Fontainebleau Summit in June 1984 created a new ad hoc committee on institutional issues. To prevent this intergovernmental committee from destroying the EP project, Spinelli convinced the Italian government to be represented by two federalists: Mauro Ferri, former president of the institutional affairs committee of the EP, and Pier Virgilio Dastoli, Spinelli's assistant. During this period, Spinelli's health deteriorated, and his daughter Eva became ill and underwent surgery in December and died in July 1985. Still Spinelli defended the EP project; pressed Pflimlin; cooperated with the Italian foreign minister, Giulio Andreotti; and influenced the Dooge committee, through Ferri and Dastoli. In June 1985 at the Milan Summit the federalist organizations promoted the largest supranational rally to support the EP project: about a hundred thousand people and hundreds of city and regional mayors and presidents with their gonfalons participated. The Council could not take a decision on the EP project, nor on the Dooge Report. The popular pressure helped the Italian government to call a majority vote, for the first time since the 1966 Luxembourg Compromise, to convene a new IGC to discuss the two projects. There was still room for hope.

The IGC did not allow the EP to participate in its meetings, and only Italy continued to support the EP project. The IGC produced the Single European Act, which was much less federalist than the proposals of both the EP and the Dooge Report. Spinelli condemned the arrogance of the Council and the IGC, and wondered if the mountain had just given birth to a mouse, and maybe a dead one. He asked the EP and the federalist organizations to learn a hard lesson and take a new initiative, calling for consultative referenda to be associated with the 1989 European election. He called for the new EP to be given a clear constituent mandate to draft a Constitution of the European Union, which would be be ratified by the national parliaments, and which would be entered into force if ratified by member states representing a two-thirds majority of the European population. Spinelli wanted to avoid a new IGC, made of diplomats meeting in secret, who defended their own authority and did not represent the European citizens. Spinelli died on 23 May 1986, unable to conduct this last struggle. Thanks to MFE mobilization Spinelli's referendum did take place in Italy, together with the European election of 1989, obtaining a staggering 88.8 per cent in favour of a constituent mandate to the EP. It did not take place elsewhere, and without Spinelli's leadership the EP has not been able to take on itself a constituent role in a bold fashion.

Since 1941 Spinelli had struggled to bring about a European federation, changing his strategy to exploit the available windows of opportunity. His books, articles and papers show the depth of his thought and the extensive network of his personal diplomacy at the highest political levels. Many of the ideas he proposed later came to pass, from the direct election of the EP, to its co-decision power; from monetary coordination to a single currency and a European Central Bank. Some of his ideas still wait to be realized and constitute the crucial issues of the contemporary European political debate: overcoming the democratic deficit and unanimity in drafting and ratifying a constitution, and involving European citizens in a democratic constituent process to give Europe a proper government. Together with Monnet he was probably the single person with the largest influence on the European integration process.

References

Graglia, P. (2008), *Altiero Spinelli*, Bologna: Il Mulino.
Lerner, D. and Aron, R. (1957), *France Defeats EDC*, London: Atlantic Press.
Levi, L. and Pistone, S. (1973), *Trent'anni di vita del MFE*, Milano: Angeli.
—— (ed.) (1990), *Altiero Spinelli and federalism in Europe and in the world*, Milano: Franco Angeli.
Melchionni, M.G. (1993), *Altiero Spinelli et Jean Monnet*, Lausanne: Fondation Jean Monnet pour l'Europe.
Paolini, E. (1988), *Altiero Spinelli. Appunti per una biografia*, Bologna: Il Mulino.
Pistone, S. (2008), *L'Unione dei Federalisti Europei*, Napoli: Guida.
Preda, D. (1990), *Storia di una speranza*, Milano: Jaca Books.
—— (1994), *Sulla soglia dell'unione: la vicenda della Comunita' politica europea (1952–1954)*, Milano: Jaca Books.
—— (ed.) (1996), *Per una costituzione federale dell'Europa*, Padova: Cedam.

Further Reading

It is impossible to provide here an accurate list of Spinelli's works. A complete index of his private archive, including articles, papers, notes and letters, is available at www.csfederalismo.it.

Other bibliographical material is available at http://www.altierospinelli.it/bibliografia/index.php.

Books by Altiero Spinelli

with Ernesto Rossi (1944), *Problemi della federazione europea*, Roma. Preface by Eugenio Colorni (reprinted 2004 Torino: Celid; and 2006, Milan: Mondadori).
(1950), *Dagli Stati sovrani agli Stati Uniti d'Europa*, Firenze: La Nuova Italia.
(1957), *Manifesto dei federalisti europei*, Parma: Guanda.
(1960), *L'Europa non cade dal cielo*, Bologna: Il Mulino.
(1960), *Tedeschi al bivio*, Roma: Opere nuove.
(1963), *Che fare per l'Europa?*, edited by Spinelli, Milano: Comunità.

(1965), *Rapporto sull'Europa*, Milano: Comunità. Also in English (1966), *The Eurocrats: conflict and crisis in the European Community, with a new epilogue*, Baltimore: Johns Hopkins University Press.

(1967), *Il lungo monologo*, Roma: Ateneo.

(1972) *L'avventura europea*, Bologna: Il Mulino. In English (1972), *The European adventure: tasks for the enlarged Community*, London, C. Knight, 1972. In French (1972), *Agenda pour l'Europe*, Paris: Hachette.

(1978), *PCI, che fare?* Torino, Einaudi.

(1979), *La mia battaglia per un'Europa diversa*, Manduria: Lacaita.

(1983), *Verso L'Unione Europea*, Firenze: Istituto Universitario Europeo. In English *Towards the European union*, Florence: European University Institute; Luxembourg: Office for Official Publications of the European Communities (French and German translations also published).

(1984) *Come ho tentato di diventare saggio. Io Ulisse*, Bologna: Il Mulino.

(1987) *Come ho tentato di diventare saggio. La goccia e la roccia*, Bologna: Il Mulino.

(1999) and (2006), *Come ho tentato di diventare saggio* (new edition in a single volume), Bologna: Il Mulino.

(1989), *Diario europeo, Volume 1: 1948–69*, Bologna: Il Mulino.

(1992), *Diario Europeo, Volume 3: 1970–76*, Bologna: Il Mulino.

(1992), *Diario Europeo, Volume 3:1976–86*, Bologna: Il Mulino.

Anthologies of Altiero Spinelli's papers and speeches

(1987), *Discorsi al Parlamento Europeo*, edited by Pier Virgilio Dastoli, Bologna: Il Mulino (French and English translations by the Communist and Affiliates Group of the European Parliament in 1986).

(1989), *Una strategia per gli Stati Uniti d'Europa*, edited by Sergio Pistone, Bologna: Il Mulino.

(1989), *Battling for the Union*, Luxembourg: Official Publications of the European Union.

(1990), *L'Europa tra Ovest ed Est*, edited by Cesare Merlini, Bologna: Il Mulino.

(1991), *La crisi degli stati nazionali: Germania, Italia, Francia*, edited by Lucio Levi, Bologna: Il Mulino.

(1993), *Machiavelli nel secolo XX (scritti del conflino e della clandestinità, 1941–44)*, edited by Piero Graglia, Bologna: Il Mulino.

(1996), *La Rivoluzione Federalista (scritti 1944–47)*, edited by Piero Graglia, Bologna: Il Mulino.

(1996), *Interventi alla Camera dei Deputati*, edited by Luciano Violante, Roma: Camera dei Deputati.

(1998), *Altiero Spinelli and the British Federalists: writings by Beveridge, Robbins and Spinelli, 1937–1943*, edited by John Pinder, London: Federal Trust.

(2000), *Europa Terza Forza (scritti 1947–54)*, edited by Piero Graglia, Bologna: Il Mulino.

(2003), *Le forme dell'Europa: Spinelli o della federazione*, edited by Luciano Angelino, Genova: Il Melangolo.
(2006), *Il linguaggio notturno*, edited by Luciano Angelino, Genova: Il Melangolo.
(2007), *From Ventotene to the European Constitution*, Edited by Agustín José Menéndez, ARENA Report No 1/07, RECON Report No 1, available at http://www.reconproject.eu/projectweb/portalproject/Report1_Spinelli.html.
(2007), *Carteggio, 1961–1971 / Pietro Nenni, Altiero Spinelli; a cura di Edmondo Paolini*, Roma: Editori riuniti.

# Polyvalent Federalism: Johannes Althusius to Edvard Kardelj and Titoism

Matthew McCullock

Introduction

The aim of the chapter is to both historically and theoretically explore Titoist federalism, but more importantly attempt to identify how it was influenced by the work of Johannes Althusius. Consequently, the chapter has two specific aims and a more general aim. Specifically, the chapter aims to examine a comment made by the leading Yugoslav constitutionalist Jovan Djordjević to Daniel Elazar in 1973. Speaking of the theoretical influences on Titoism as a model of federal constitutionalism, Djordjević noted the influence Althusius had had on the constitutional writers in Yugoslavia, especially as a counter-balance to Marxism (Elazar 1990).

The second specific aim is to further the ideas first discussed by Djordjević in an article he wrote in 1975. Entitled *Remarks on the Yugoslav Model of Federalism*, Djordjević explored the potential of a new form of federalism, which was being explored by the Yugoslavs: "polyvalent federalism." Djordjević argued that this form of federalism had traits of Althusius, whose understanding of federalism is deeper than that of other federal authors (1975: 78). Despite the promise for federal theory that polyvalent federalism displays, it has never been explored in the academic literature. Thus, this chapter intends to explore this neglected area of federal theory, by elaborating upon Djordjević's work.

The general aim centers on the idea of "rediscovery" of political writers. The first case is that of Johannes Althusius (1557–1638), who despite being described as a major scholar of modern federalism exists only on the periphery of federal discussions. There have been recent authors, most notably Frederick Carney, Daniel Elazar, and Thomas Hueglin, who have explored the rich potential of Althusius, but he still remains relatively unknown to the majority of students of federalism.

The second rediscovery is that of Edvard Kardelj (1910–1979). In a position as Tito's right hand, his left hand, and, occasionally, even Tito's head (Stanković 1981: 68), Kardelj was the key player in the theoretical evolution of Titoism as a political ideology. In addition to being the author of a wealth of constitutions, constitutional amendments, and other legal documents, Kardelj also offers a fascinating theoretical model of federal constitutionalism based not on the "traditional" guises of the individual and the social contract, but on functional and practical representation in self-managing communities, that has not received the attention it deserves.

In order to achieve these aims the chapter will proceed as follows: firstly, the chapter opens with a few comments on the term "polyvalent," as despite being common parlance in scientific discourses, the use of the term is a relatively recent phenomena in political discourses; secondly, a mini introduction to Althusian political theory is essential to "contextualize" the discussion; thirdly, and with the aim of rehabilitation in mind, Edvard Kardelj as a man and theoretician will be introduced, most notably by means of *Ways of Democracy in a Socialist Society*, in which he offers a thorough defense of the Yugoslav politic and economic system; fourthly, the discussion will focus on the Althusian influences in three key areas of the constitutional system: the "interpretation of the individual," the articles of the 1974 constitution, and the structure and relationships established by the constitution; fifthly, comments on the similarities in dogma will be explored. Finally, in conclusion, the chapter will explore the relationship between the death of Yugoslavia and future of polyvalent federalism.

"Polyvalent" Federalism: Origins of a Term

While a relative newcomer to political discourse, the term "polyvalent" is commonplace in scientific discourses. In biology, the term has been used in conjunction with numerous fields of research, predominantly venomology; whilst in chemistry the term refers to a feature that has more than one valence. What needs to be taken from the use of polyvalent in the scientific world is the reference to "multiple" antibodies and "multiple" valency. In each case the agent has many values or meanings, or the ability to combine with more than one feature. Indeed, if two words are changed, it is in this sentence that the link between scientific polyvalency and its application to political theory can be located: "In each case the *individual* has many values or meanings, or the ability to combine with more than one *group*." What this sentence highlights is the fact that polyvalent federalism aimed at achieving a system that is better able to accommodate the intricacies and numerous interests an individual may have via the natural groupings in which he finds himself. What this idea represents is a marked shift from the social contract tradition of western liberal ideology in which the individual is reduced to a political actor in direct relation only to the state. While naturally occurring groups such as the family do exist in the social contract, they do not play a fundamental role in political, social, or economic life.

One of the first uses of the term "polyvalency" in a political arena can be found in a political discussion between Daniel Elazar and Professor Jovan Djordjević, in which the latter mentions that the Yugoslavs used Althusius as a counterbalance to Marxism (Elazar 1990). The most concerted use of the term can be found in Djordjević's 1975 article, which was based on a prior conference paper Djordjević gave in 1973.[1] The crux of Djordjević's argument was that human society was in a process of transition from "traditional" (territorial and political) federalism to a "new federalism" that is social, functional, and participatory, recently referred to as "polyvalent federalism" (1975: 77). Furthermore, this new form of federalism:

> *has some traits of the pre-nation-state era of the Middle Ages, as described in particular by the German Johannes Althusius, whose understanding of federalism is much deeper than that of Montesquieu, Madison, Hamilton and other thinkers too much concerned with legal-statist and power-ridden conceptions of federalist structure (1975: 78).*

What Djordjević offers here is an elaboration on the comments he made to Elazar in 1973; what the article does not provide are examples where Althusius, in Djordjević's view, specifically influenced Titoist federalism, a gap this chapter is designed to fill.

Given the limited references to polyvalent federalism in the academic literature, Djordjević's article is the only source for reference; but if the process of Yugoslav constitutionalism is investigated it is possible to develop a broader understanding of the essence of polyvalent federalism. Before the analysis can begin, the discussion will offer a brief introduction to Johannes Althusius' *Politica Methodice Digesta, Atque Exemplis Sacris Et Profanis Illustrata*,[2] and secondly to Edvard Kardelj's *Ways of Democracy in a Socialist Society*.

Johannes Althusius' *Politica*

The work of Johannes Althusius is little known; indeed, Daniel Elazar commented that "Althusian ideas remain peripheral, even to students of modern federalism" (Elazar 1995: 445).[3] Born in Dieden(s)hausen in the County of Wittgenstein-Berleburg in 1557, Althusius was recorded as commencing his doctorate studies in Cologne in 1581, before moving to Basel in 1586 to complete his studies in civil and ecclesiastical law. Upon completion of his doctoral studies, Althusius moved into teaching, and it was while a professor at Herborn that Althusius became a

---

1 "The Politics of Intergovernmental Relations in Federal Systems: Urban Perspectives" Temple University, 26–28th August 1973.
2 *Politics Methodically Set Forth, and Illustrated with Sacred and Profane Examples.*
3 I have discussed the main reasons behind Althusius' anonymity elsewhere (*cf.* McCullock 2006).

leading scholar in what was termed "the school of federal theology," which was the world view and the intellectual foundation (Elazar 1991: 119, 139) of Calvinist Protestantism.

It was during this period that Althusius wrote the first edition of *Politica*, in which he attacked the doctrine of undivided territorial sovereignty that had found favor through the writings of Jean Bodin. Althusius' attack centred on attributing the rightful ownership of sovereignty to the federally organized body of the people (Hueglin 1994a: 3) rather than to the Prince, as was argued by Bodin. Althusius' view was largely influenced by his desire "to rescue the autonomy" of religious and municipal self-determination from the new centralized territories (Hueglin 1994b: 82) that were beginning to emerge at that time.

Shortly after writing *Politica*, Althusius was invited by the council of Emden to become the city's Syndic in 1603. The main reason the position was offered to Althusius was that the essence of *Politica* provided the Council with a constitutional blueprint to resist the territorial advances of the Count of East Friesland, the county in which Emden was located.

Politica Methodice Digesta, Atque Exemplis Sacris Et Profanis Illustrata

Writing in a "grey" period of political thought between "past" and "present,"[4] Althusius represents the last vestiges of an alternate canon of political thought that "lost out" to the now dominant political thought that originated with Thomas Hobbes and John Locke; in this way *Politica* is based on assumptions that are often an anathema to students of contemporary political and constitutional theory.

As opposed to the abstract theory of the "state of nature," Althusius attempted to conceptualize the complex real world of the whole and of the part and the universal and particular order, as a many-layered problem requiring a multilevel constitutional solution (Hueglin 1999: 114); the essence of the Althusian system is the complex system of interaction between different levels of *consociatios*. At the base of the system are the simple and private associations: the family, or the *natural*, simple, and private association, and the collegiums or guild, which is a *civil*, simple, and private association.

This step-by-step approach to consitutionalizing "the Commonwealth" carries on when several families, hamlets, or villages join together to form the Collegium. For Althusius, this is the first example of a civil association as the common bonds that unite the differing *consociatios* are no longer reliant on blood. In this respect it is also a spontaneous and voluntary association, as it can be discontinued by mutual agreement (*Politica*: 33).

---

4   This "grey" area is best personified by Thomas Hueglin's article in the journal *Publius* (Hueglin 1979).

The next level of the system is the City, which for Althusius is an association formed by the fixed laws and composed of many families and Collegia living in the same place (*Politica*: 40). An important transformation occurs here, however. As persons coming together, they now become citizens of the same community, rather than spouses, kinsman, and colleagues. The *consociatios* have now become mixed and public (*Politica*: 40).

The next level, or Province, "contains within its territory many villages, towns, outposts, and cities united under the communion and administration of one right (*Jus*)" (*Politica*: 51). Again the main concerns of this legal order are the communion of provincial right in which the goods needed for the province are attained, and the administration of this right (*Politica*: 51).

The final level of the Althusian realm is the Universal Realm or Commonwealth:

> *In this association many cities and provinces obligate themselves to hold, organize, use, and defend, through their common energies and expenditures, the right of the realm in the mutual communication of things and services (Politica: 66).*

The bond of this Commonwealth is a tacit or expressed promise to communicate things, mutual services, aid, and counsel, and the same common laws to the extent that the utility and necessity of universal life of the realm shall require (*Politica*: 66). In other words the Commonwealth is a larger version of a province, which in turn is a larger version of a City, down to the building block of the Commonwealth – the family.

While this discussion represents a simplified version of the complex system espoused in *Politica*, it does allow an insight into a different era of political thought. The chapter now shifts its attention to introducing Edvard Kardelj to facilitate the later discussion on the Althusian influences in Titoist federalism.

Edvard Kardelj and Ways of Democracy in a Socialist Society

Born in Laibach (Ljubljana) and a teacher by training, Edvard Kardelj joined the Yugoslav Communist Youth in 1926, becoming a full member of the illegal Communist Party of Yugoslavia (the Party) from 1932. In 1930, Kardelj was tortured by the Royal Yugoslav police after being double-crossed at a communist meeting and was sentenced to two years' hard labor. Upon his release, the Party sent him to the Soviet Union, during which time he gave lectures on the Balkans. Kardelj returned to Yugoslavia in 1937, upon which he became a Member of the Central Committee, a position he would hold until his death. During the Peoples' Liberation War, Kardelj was a Member of the Supreme Command and a Member of the Main Command of his native Slovenia. After the war, Kardelj held numerous government posts and, besides his governmental roles, was the leading Marxist theoretician.

Aided by theorists such as Jovan Djordjević, Kardelj played the leading role in drafting the numerous federal constitutions.

The role of Kardelj in the Yugoslav system was best described by Slobodan Stanković, who called Kardelj "Tito's right hand; he was also his left hand, and, occasionally, even 'Tito's head' – producing theories and ideas that the aging leader then propagated in simpler terms, understandable to everyone" (Stanković 1981: 68).

Self-Management and the Political System

In 1980, the Belgrade publishing house Socialist Thought and Practice published a book entitled *Self-Management and the Political System*, which consisted of two pieces of work by Edvard Kardelj. The first, *Socialist Democracy as Practised in Yugoslavia*, written in the 1950s, refuted three common myths of the Yugoslav system: firstly, that until 1948 Yugoslavia was ideologically and politically aligned with the Soviet Union; secondly, that it was the Soviet pressure of 1948 that forced the Yugoslavs to adopt measures to eradicate bureaucracy and defend democracy; thirdly, that having embarked on this path, the Yugoslavs were bound to move towards Western bourgeois democracy (Kardelj 1980: 11). The second published work, *Ways of Democracy in a Socialist Society*, offered a definition of the idea of socialist self-management, with reference to the weaknesses of traditional "bourgeois" parliamentary democracy.

Kardelj's aim was to avoid the trappings and failings of both the conflictual system of multiparty democracy of bourgeois capitalism and the single party state system (Kardelj 1975: 41), and to create a "new historical type of democracy" which is "more progressive and more human" than parliamentary democracy (Kardelj 1975: 18). This is not to say that Titoism managed to remove *all* aspects of either parliamentary democracy or the single party state from the Yugoslav system. For Kardelj, Yugoslavia still:

> contains features of both systems. But these are no longer distinguishing features of our political system; they are only transitory and will wither away as the power of the state over society withers away (1977: 385).

In doing so, Yugoslav society was in a process of removing the remnants of the bourgeois state's political system, especially from the assembly system (Kardelj 1977: 381) and attempted to transfer power from a conflictual parliamentary to a more stable constituent base, i.e., the Worker's Committees. The conscious abandonment of Western parliamentary structures, plus the presence of the League of Communists (LCY), Kardelj argued, led:

> some foreign commentators ... to interpret our system ... as a one-party system. Such people either do not perceive the great difference between our political system and a real one-party system, or they are purposely attributing features to our system of self-management which it does not have (Kardelj 1980: 118).

Furthermore, in response to the critics of self-management, Kardelj argued that:

> *there are and will be many systems much more democratic than the bourgeois parliamentary state (Kardelj 1977: 394).*

By the time of the promulgation of the 1974 constitution, there was a high degree of pride felt by the Yugoslav elite towards their federal and constitutional arrangements, which has been described as a "Kardeljian myth of superiority" (Seroka 1993: 75).

Interpretation of the Individual: The Zoon Politikon

To fully comprehend the similarities between Althusius and Titoism it is imperative that the connection between how each system perceived the individual is clarified: indeed, the many Althusian characteristics Titoism displays is arguably based on this assumption.

Althusius developed the Aristotelian view of man as a *zoon politikon*, in which man could only realize himself within the confines of naturally occurring groups or political groupings:

> *The commonwealth, or civil society, exists by nature, and that man is by nature a civil animal who strives eagerly for association. If, however, anyone wishes not to live in society, or needs nothing because of his own abundance, he is not considered a part of the commonwealth. He is therefore either a beast or a god, as Aristotle asserts (Politica: 25).*

The *zoon politikon* is not specific to Aristotle and Althusius alone. It can be found in Aquinas, Calvin, and in Marx, and this perspective is echoed in Kardelj, when he argues that:

> *the true vehicle of social progress is not man as an abstract political citizen, but man as the exponent of an entire set of social interests (Kardelj 1980: 176).*

Furthermore, "man alone can create his own happiness, not as an individual but with other men on terms of equality" (Kardelj 1980: 67).

While in the idea of the *zoon politikon* there is no great emphasis on the individual, this does not mean that the individual does not "exist" in either Althusian or Titoist constitutionalism. Rather, the individual exists in a manner in which he can only realize himself in direct relationships with other individuals in basic groups, such as the family or guild for Althusius, or the socio-political organization or local community for Titoism, rather than as an individual in a direct relationship to the state. As Kardelj argues:

> *The [1974] Constitution bases itself on man and his authentic interests and needs, and on relationships among people resulting from their rights and mutual obligations, rather than on a relationship between man and the state (Kardelj 1980: 62–63).*

What this understanding of the individual does is put polyvalent federalism in direct theoretical opposition to the canon of federalism that was based on the work of the *Publius* authors, who in turn were influenced by the seventeenth-century English ideas of John Locke and indirectly, Thomas Hobbes. Their understanding of the individual is based on a condemnation of the notion of the *zoon politikon*. For Hobbes, using the notion as a foundation of a "Doctrine of Civill Society" is:

> *certainly False, and an errour proceeding from our too slight contemplation of "Human Nature" as the exploration into the causes of man coming together will reveal that they do so not naturally, but by accident (De Cive: 22).*
>
> ...
>
> *Againe, man have no pleasure, (but on the contrary a great deale of griefe) in keeping company, where there is no power to over-awe them all (Leviathan: 185).*

Later in Locke's work the individual chooses to join other individuals to form civil society largely to protect economic interests, but the principle is the same: the individual is theoretically stripped of all naturally occurring groups and placed in a state of nature. In this manner, the "abstract" individual has a single political bond with the state and general "abstract" representatives: a point of contention taken up by Kardelj, and a weakness consciously avoided in Yugoslav polyvalent federalism.

Having identified a notion comparable to the *zoon politikon* as forming the basis of both Althusius' work and Titoist federalism, this chapter now shifts its focus to *The Constitution of the Socialist Federal Republic of Yugoslavia Belgrade*, 1974. The first part of the investigation will focus on the articles of the constitution, while the second part will focus on the Althusian influences in the relationships and structures established by the constitution.

Althusian Influences (I): The Text of the 1974 Constitution

Althusian characteristics can be found predominantly in Part Two of the 1974 constitution: "The Social System" (articles 10–152), and focus primarily on the agreements between the individual self-managing communities. Three prominent examples are as follows:

> *Working people shall organize themselves on a self-management basis in organizations of associated labour, local communities, self-managing communities of interest and other self-managing organizations and communities, and shall specify which common interests, rights and duties they shall realize in them (article 90).*
>
> *A self-management agreement in the formation of a self-managing community of interest and its by-laws shall regulate affairs of common concern to the members of the community, the mode of decision-making regarding these affairs ... and other questions of common concern to the working people and self-managing organizations and communities organized in the community of interest (article 110).*
>
> *It shall be the right and duty of the working people in a settlement, part of a settlement or several interconnected settlements to organize themselves into a local community with a view to realizing specific common interests and needs (article 114).*

The first article demonstrates that the forming of self-managing organizations was an intentional act by a group of individuals to realize a common aim; consequently the founding of the self-managing organization is centred on these aims, a feature evident in the second article. Equally, the notion of the basic *consociatio* in Althusius is premised around a similar concept. For Althusius, each *consociatio* is founded on "what is necessary and useful for organized symbiotic life" (*Politica*: 27).

The "constitution," or self-managing agreement mentioned in articles 110 and 114, of each self-managing organization decided how best these common aims and objectives were to be achieved and by whom. Both of these aspects are mirrored in the beginning of *Politica*, in which Althusius argues:

> *The symbiotes are co-workers who, by the bond of an associating and uniting agreement, communicate among themselves whatever is appropriate for a comfortable life of soul and body. In other words, they are participants in a common life (Politica: 19).*

The examples quoted in the articles and in the supporting quote from *Politica* demonstrate a system in which the *zoon politikon* is the predominant feature. In each example the emphasis is on the individual joining with like-minded individuals for a common purpose: either specific common interests or needs in Titoism, or to "communicate amongst themselves that which is necessary for a comfortable life" in Althusius. One premise that stems from this idea is the necessity of a complex constitutional system in which the individual can achieve these common interests or comfortable life. It is to the structure and relationships established by the 1974 constitution that we now turn, and while there are several features that can be identified, only the five main features will be discussed here.

Althusian Influences (II): The Relationships and Structures Established by the Constitution

The Politicization of Society

The first common feature, and a natural outcome given the emphasis on the *zoon politikon*, is the fact that both systems "politicized" the whole of society. In the social contract theory there is the distinction between "state" and "society": "politics" is identified with the "state," while "society" is that depoliticized section inhabited by private individuals. In *Politica*:

> there is a distinction between public and private, but both are part of the political to the extent that politics is a social process of community building which extends from the organization of the family all the way to the constitution of the large commonwealth (Hueglin 1999: 77).

Similarly, the project of "constructing socialism," the cornerstone of Yugoslav society, had the direct influence of affecting "grass roots" self-management, thus turning all of Yugoslav society into a political society (Golubović 1986: 6).

An Indirect Electoral System

The second Althusian feature, and linked to the previous point, was the "indirect" electoral system. The 1974 constitution introduced an assembly system based on mandated representation. The object of this delegation system was to force the delegates to protect their primary interests first, then to look at the broader picture (Vucković 1997: 113). This was an important fact as it broke with traditional ideas of parliamentary representation, for as Kardelj explained:

> in the system of political pluralism of bourgeois society, the citizen, in elections, gives his deputy general powers to decide on all matters concerning his own and the public interests falling within the competence of parliament, whereas the worker-manager and citizen in the system of self-management pluralism gives specific powers to his delegations, or delegates (Kardelj 1980: 191).

The constitution insured that "delegates" who were given mandates by "delegations," which in turn were mandated by the voters, now officially ruled Yugoslavia. Delegates to communes elected delegates to Republican and Federal assemblies, so that Republican and Federal legislators were three stages away from their basic electorates (Lydall 1984: 103).

The key difference between the "delegate system" and a "representative system" was the "direct and virtually day-to-day responsibility of the delegates to their delegations and of the latter to the neighborhood or 'working community' that had elected them (Singleton 1976: 332–333):

> *Instead of the classical political deputy as the representative of a given political party, our delegate assembly has a collective delegation from the community of self-management interests, which acts as the spokesman for the real individual, who has specific personal and social interests (Kardelj 1980: 232).*

Under this system, elections became practical experiments in managing the welfare of the association, rather than an egotistical political contest as to who was going to exercise political power for the next n years. A key feature that was designed to ensure this "politics of welfare" was that all delegates, in addition to their political work, were required to keep their jobs, thus ensuring a process of "de-politicization" (Rusinow 1977: 331–332) as the "deprofesionalization" of power and politics should encourage only men who are engaged in creative and productive work in society to become "legislators" or "politicians" (Djordjević 1966–1967: 214).

This indirect system of governance is inherent in the entire system of Althusius. The structure of *Politica* serves to build from the lowest levels of the family and guild, to the universal association. The interesting feature here is the relationship between the different levels. Within each level there are two sets of agencies: one representing the lower levels, which must retain as much power as possible; the other representing the higher levels, whose jurisdiction is limited by the lower levels (de Benoist 2000: 33). This emphasis on the representatives being subservient to the collective is continued in *Politica*, when Althusius argues that:

> *In relation to their ownership and delegation of supreme right the united subjects and members of a realm are masters of these ministers and rectors; indeed, these administrators, guardians, and rectors are servants and ministers to these very members of the realm (Politica: 94).*

In practice, what the indirect and aggregated structure meant was that the Yugoslav federation was structured according to commune, district, autonomous province, republic, and the federation (Kardelj 1962: 164), with direct elections only possible to the level of the commune. In the Althusian universal association, only those levels below that of the city provided "the opportunity for direct participation of individuals as such in the process of rule" (Carney 1995: xix). The indirect structure is evident from the level of the city upwards, as Thomas Hueglin noted:

> *City prefects are elected by a senate whose members are in turn chosen from the city's guilds and colleges. The supreme magistrate of the realm in turn is*

> *elected by ephors who as a rule are provincial rulers or members of the estates of the realm, themselves elected or appointed (Hueglin 1999: 143–144).*

Part of the reason for the indirect electoral system in Althusius was the historical conditions of the Holy Roman Empire within which Althusius wrote, where hereditary dynastic realms were probably the norm (Hueglin 1999: 143); but what interests our discussion is the fact that the structure of the Althusian political structure is similar to that found in Yugoslavia: a "bottom-up" system, with an aggregated system of political levels, with power distributed by the notion of subsidiarity, which is the third Althusian characteristic to be found in Yugoslav federalism.

Subsidiarity

Inherent in the indirect electoral structure in Titoist polyvalent federalism was the notion of subsidiarity. This was a common feature in the Althusian system, and one that has attracted increasing attention from European Union studies:[5] indeed, Althusius could be viewed as the founder of the idea.[6] While not referring explicitly to "subsidiarity," the notion is evident in several parts of *Politica*:

> *The people first associated itself in a certain body with definite laws ... Then, because the people itself cannot manage the administration of these rights, it entrusted their administration to ministers and rectors elected by it. In so doing, the people transferred to them the authority and power necessary for the performance of this assignment, equipped them with the sword for this purpose, and put itself under their care and rule (Politica: 93–94. Emphasis added).*

Implied here is the principle that the lowest possible body takes the majority of the decisions that directly affect them, or as Lydall noted:

> *the principle that specific powers are given to the higher bodies and that all residual powers belong to those lower down (Lydall 1984: 105).*

As is evident from Lydall's quote, the notion of subsidiarity became a feature of Yugoslav federalism. With the introduction of the 1953 Constitution,[7] the Commune,

---

5   *Cf.* Friesen 2003; Hueglin 1994.
6   For an interesting discussion on the evolution of subsidiarity see Endo 1994.
7   Although the 1953 text is called a constitution for the purpose of this discussion, it was actually a series of laws aimed at reforming the constitutional system *rather than* a constitution in its own right. However, this change and reorganization was so thorough that the text is generally considered to be a new constitution (Hoffman and Warner Neal 1962: 176–179).

which was "the smallest unit of political aggregation of power" (Denitch 1977: 115), changed from "little more than docile wards under the control of the executive committees; much the same had been true for district government" (McClellan 1969: 137), to become:

> *the basic cell in society, the first level where the contradictions between the material demands of individuals and society as a whole finds its expression. The fact that the contradiction is solved here under the immediate control of the broad masses of the people has a most favourable effect in forming social consciousness (Kardelj, quoted in McClellan 1969: 137).*

Implied in this emphasis on the commune is the principle of subsidiarity, as Kardelj argued:

> *All the functions of government and administration of public affairs are carried out in the commune, except for those which, by their nature, affect the common interest of other working people and citizens of a republic or province (Kardelj 1980: 204. Emphasis mine).*

The Lack of the Need for Political Parties

The fourth Althusian feature is the lack of need for political parties: representation instead occurs within the individual consociations that could represent "real" as opposed to "abstract" views.

> *The basis of the classical system of representation (the bourgeois parliament) is the "abstract citizens" an imaginary person divorced from the fundamental social relationships in which he develops as an actual human being. Such an abstract and isolated individual can be represented only by an alienated, general deputy who pursues some sort of fictive general interest" (Todorović 1974: 2–3).*

This concept is mirrored as Kardelj argued:

> *Self-management democracy is the most suitable system for resolving conflicts and differences of this kind, because in contrast to multiparty democracy, politics are identified with the real content of self-management interests, which are pursued in various self-managing communities of interest ... and need not seek expression in the creation of political parties (Kardelj 1980: 168).*

Kardelj continued that the different interests that an individual may have are too varied and fluid to be represented by political parties and reduced to generalized political formulas. Indeed, parliamentary politics does just this and "denies the genuine expression of this diversity in the administration of society" (Kardelj 1980:

170). Furthermore, within the system of socialist self-management the "genuine political interest of the working class is unanimous" (174) and so does not require being split into artificial "parties" of representation.

The absence of political parties is also evident in Althusius. Although this feature could be explained by the fact that political parties were not a common political feature as they are a relatively recent political construct, the similarity with Titoism is that there was an overarching power that provided a framework for the different understanding of polyvalent federalism to occur. For Althusius, the Emperor and the structure of the Holy Roman Empire, including the various levels of the Empire, provided the practical framework, while theoretically there was a reliance on the Calvinist faith as providing a "life system." In the Yugoslav context the structure was provided by the party, but also by the umbrella organization, the Socialist Alliance.[8]

A Complex Separation of Powers

The fifth Althusian feature is the complex system that Althusius introduced between the Supreme Magistrate and the Ephors; each was vested with certain powers and each was designed to be the "counterbalancing" force for the other. The 1974 constitution similarly established a complicated power relationship between the executive body of the assembly, which is formed out of the executive council, and the council, which is the collegiate executive organ of the assembly of the commune (article 149). Dennison Rusinow echoes this sentiment when he highlights:

> *The system thus described [that of the 1974 Constitution] therefore included a far more complicated and multidimensional version of the American Constitution's "checks and balances" (Rusinow 1977: 328).*

Similarly in *Politica*, we find a separation more elaborate than that advocated by Locke, Montesquieu, or Madison: in fact, the Althusian separation of powers arguably has a "dual prong." The first "prong" was inherent in the residual nature of the Althusian system, as each level was dependent on the prior level for its existence.

The second "prong" is that in each level of *consociatio*, although the prefect was elected to oversee the general running of the *consociatio*, he only has power over his colleagues individually, not as a whole. In this way, although the prefect is superior, he is inferior to the Collegium that elected him and whose pleasure he must serve.

It is clear from this discussion that there are several Althusian features that were also evident in the Yugoslav federal system: the use of the mandate system representing a common collective view and forcing representatives to try to

---

8 The SAWPY, or Popular Front represented the different groups, some non-communist, which opposed the Nazis in the Second World War. By the 1980s SAWPY had some 13 million members out of a population of 23.5 million.

reconcile their communal and regional interest in decision-making is repeated in Althusius' discussion on the decision-making process in the guild and the city. Likewise, making consensus decisions the optimal form of decision-making can also be found in *Politica*. Although often derided for producing weak decisions, a consensus decision is more likely to have been thoroughly discussed and have taken into account all points of view, than if all decisions are put to a majority vote.

Althusius' and Kardelj's Dogmatic Beliefs

A final, but negative characteristic focuses on the personal traits of Althusius and Kardelj *as individuals* and continues the aim of rediscovery. As discussed above, both were involved in teaching, and both retained a theoretical aspect to their practical political life. For Althusius, his predominant aim was to rescue the autonomy of lower forms of association from the increasing centralizing tendencies; while Kardelj's aim was to ensure the structuring of Yugoslavia along self-management lines and to constantly fight against "bureaucratization" and "greater statism." The final similarity focuses on the role each theorist and their theoretical systems played in the demise of Emden and Yugoslavia.

Bearing in mind Althusius' aim to "rescue autonomy," Thomas Hueglin has argued that he:

> *continued to defend the city's autonomy even when it must have become quite clear that after the de facto demise of Imperial Power and unity only the centralized financial and military powers of the smaller territorial states could provide stability in Germany. He may therefore have – involuntarily – contributed himself to the ultimate downfall of Emden's glory, by sacrificing the city's continual economic growth for the sake of its political economy* (Hueglin 1999: 37).

What is evident here is that Althusius was a determined city politician who had a fundamental set of beliefs that were to be protected at all costs. Clearly, as Hueglin argues, Emden's immediate autonomy was far more important to Althusius than its long term stability and future, and so from the evidence presented the conclusion that Althusius' dogmatic beliefs led to the demise of the city after his death is a fair one to draw. Similarly in Yugoslavia, there has recently been a re-evaluation of the demise of Yugoslavia, focusing on the role played by Kardelj's theory.

The greatest political tension in Yugoslavia in the 1980s and 1990s was between those parties who wished to defend the constitutional structure, such as the Slovenes, and those who wished to reform the structure to stop the "erosion of the powers of the federal state" (Pavković 2004: 301), such as the Serbs. The tension reached its peak at the 14th Congress in January 1990, when the Slovenian delegation, realising that they were

> unable to defend Kardelj's doctrine of Yugoslavia from the constitutional reformists and, later, "revolutionaries" ... decided to leave Yugoslavia (Pavković 2004: 303).

Interestingly, in relation to the discussion on Althusius' staunch dogmatic beliefs above, Pavković argues that this action was:

> quite close to the spirit if not the letter of Kardelj's doctrine ... a return to a centralised Yugoslav state, from the viewpoint of this doctrine, would have been historically retrogressive and, in comparison, the dissolution of Yugoslavia appeared a preferable if not necessarily much more progressive development (Pavković 2004: 303).

In support of this claim, Dejan Jović argues that:

> Edvard Kardelj believed that the main danger to post-Tito's Yugoslavia would come from the renewal of a centralised state, either in its interwar (bourgeois) form or in a form of Soviet statist ("Stalinist" or – as Kardelj called it – "Great Statist") socialism. If this happened, Kardelj argued, the results of the Yugoslav revolution would be annulled (Jović 2003: 168).

Clearly the similarity between the collapse of Yugoslavia and the demise of Emden as a "city state" can both be attributed to the central belief of the central theoretician. Althusius resisted making Emden part of a larger centralized "German" state, while Yugoslavia was essentially undermined from the inside by the internal rivalries of the different republics that had been consolidated by polyvalent federalism, which in turn undermined the Yugoslav federal state.

Conclusion: The Viability and Future of Polyvalent Federalism

The aim of this chapter was to investigate the comments made by Jovan Djordjević with relation to the influence of the work of Johannes Althusius on Titoism, by analyzing the different aspects of the constitution through an Althusian lens. The chapter identified five main Althusian features in Titoist federalism. The secondary aims of the chapter were to link Althusius' and Kardelj's works to mainstream federal discussions. While these aims have been met, there is still an outstanding question that needs to be addressed, and focuses on the relationship between polyvalent federalism and Yugoslavia: does the bloody collapse of Yugoslavia mean that polyvalent federalism was also a casualty of the Wars of Succession?

A definitive answer to this question is impossible, but there are comments that can be made to offer some form of greater understanding. On the one hand, there is a body of literature that has been critical of the 1974 constitution (*cf.* Dimitrijević 1994), while on the other, there is considerable disagreement over the cause of the collapse of Yugoslavia, and so the 1974 constitution is partially exonerated. Dejan Jović (2001) has explored seven cited reasons for Yugoslavia's dissolution and concludes that no single cause alone can be highlighted as *the* cause of the break-up.

If a cursory glance is made across contemporary federal literature aspects of polyvalent federalism are evident, most notably in contemporary discussions on *sui generic* federalism in the European Union and the role Althusius' theory may play in aiding our understanding of such complex federal constitutional systems (*cf.* Hueglin 1994a, 1999). In this respect, while Yugoslav polyvalent federalism ended with the death of the country, maybe a polyvalent federal discussion will re-emerge in the EU: and maybe the legacy of "Althusius in Yugoslavia" will live on even after their deaths?

References

Althusius, J. (1995 [1614]), *Politics Methodically Set Forth, and Illustrated with Sacred and Profane Examples* (Indianapolis: Liberty Fund).
Bibič, A. and Graziano, G. (eds) (1994), *Civil Society, Political Society and Democracy* (Ljubljana: Slovene Political Science Association).
Bošković, B. and Dašić, D. (eds) (1980), *Socialist self-management in Yugoslavia. 1950–1980 Documents* (Belgrade: Socialist Thought and Practice).
Brown-John, C.L. (ed.) (1995), *Federal-Type Solutions and European Integration* (Lanham: University Press of America).
Burg, S. (1983), *Conflict and Cohesion in Yugoslavia: Political Decision Making Since 1966* (Princeton: Princeton UP).
Carney, F. (1995), Translator's introduction, in Althusius, J.
de Benoist, A. (2000), The first federalist: Johannes Althusius, http://www.alaindeben oist.com/pdf/the_first_federalist_althusius.pdf
Denitch, B. (1977), The evolution of Yugoslav federalism, *Publius* 7:3, 107–117.
Dimitrijević, V. (1994), The 1974 constitution as a factor in the collapse of Yugoslavia or as a sign of decaying totalitarianism (Florence: EUI).
Djokić, D. (2003), *Yugoslavism. Histories of a Failed Idea 1918–1992* (London: Hurst & Company).
Djordjević, J. (1967), Political power in Yugoslavia, *Government and Opposition* 2:2, 205–218.
—— (1975), Remarks on the Yugoslav model of federalism, *Publius* 5:2, 77–88.
Dunn, W. (1975), Communal federalism: dialectics of decentralization in socialist Yugoslavia, *Publius* 5:2, 127–150.
Elazar, D. (1990), Althusius and federalism as a grand design, http://www.jcpa.org/dje/articles2/althus-fed.htm.
—— (1991), *Exploring Federalism* (Tuscaloosa: University of Alabama Press).

— (1995), Federal-type solutions and European integration, in Brown-John, C.L. (ed.).
Endo, K. (1994), The principle of subsidiarity: from Johannes Althusius to Jacques Delors, *Hokkaido Law Review* 44:6, 652–553.
Friedrich, C. (1932), Introduction, in Friedrich, C. (ed.).
— (ed.) (1932), *Politica Methodice Digests of Johannes Althusius* (Massachusetts: Harvard UP).
Friesen, M. (2003), Subsidiarity and federalism: an old concept with contemporary relevance for political society, *Federal Governance: A Graduate Journal of Theory and Politics*, 1:1.
Golubović, Z. (1986), Yugoslav society and "socialism": the present-day crisis of the Yugoslav system and the possibilities of evolution, in Golubović, Z. and Stojanović, S. (eds).
— and Stojanović, S. (eds) (1986), *The Crisis of the Yugoslav System* (Köln: The Crisis of the Yugoslav System Research Project Crises in Soviet Type Systems).
Government of the Socialist Federal Republic of Yugoslavia (1974), *The Constitution of the Socialist Federal Republic of Yugoslavia Belgrade, 1974*, translated by Pavičić, M. (Ljubljana, Parnova: Dopisna Delavska Univerza).
Hobbes, T. (1998 [1648]), *De Cive or On the Citizen* (Cambridge: Cambridge UP).
— (1968 [1651]), *Leviathan* (London: Penguin).
Hoffman, G. and Warner Neal, F. (1962), *Yugoslavia and the New Communism* (New York: Twentieth Century Fund).
Howard, M. (2001), Market socialism and political pluralism: theoretical reflections on Yugoslavia, *Studies in East European Thought* 53, 307–328.
Hueglin, T. (1979), Johannes Althusius: medieval constitutionalist or modern federalist?, *Publius* 9:4, 9–41.
— (1994a), Federalism, subsidiarity and the European tradition, 2nd European Communities Study Association Conference, http://ecsanet.org/conferences/ecsaworld2/Hueglin.htm.
— (1994b), Johannes Althusius and the modern concept of civil society, in Bibič, A. and Graziano, G. (eds).
— (1999), *Early Modern Concepts for a Late Modern World. Althusius on Community and Federalism* (Wateroo, ON: Wilfrid Laurier UP).
Jović, D. (2001), The disintegration of Yugoslavia. A critical review of explanatory approaches, *European Journal of Social Theory*, 4:10, 101–120.
— (2003), Yugoslavism and Yugoslav communism: from Tito to Kardelj, in Djokić, D. (ed.).
Kardelj, E. (1962), Excerpt from Edvard Kardelj's Report on the Draft of the New Constitution of the SFRY at the Joint Session of the Federal People's Assembly and the Federal Board of the Socialist Alliance, in Bošković, B. and Dašić, D. (eds).
— (1975), The system of socialist self-management in Yugoslavia, in Bošković, B. and Dašić, D. (eds).

—— (1977), Excerpts from the keynote address by Edvard Kardelj delivered at the Thirtieth Session of the Presidency of the CC LCY, in Bošković, B. and Dašić, D. (eds).

—— (1980), *Self-Management and the Political System* (Belgrade: STP).

Lampe, J. (1996), *Yugoslavia as History. Twice There Was a Country* (Cambridge: Cambridge UP).

Locke, J. (1980 [1690]), *Second Treatise of Government* (Indianapolis: Hackett).

Lydall, H. (1984), *Yugoslav Socialism. Theory and Practice* (Oxford: Clarendon).

McCullock, M. (2006), Johannes Althusius' *Politica*: the culmination of Calvin's Right of Resistance, *The European Legacy* 11:5, 485–499.

McClellan, W. (1969), Postwar political evolution, in Vucinich, W. (ed).

Pavković, A. (2004), Review Article: Why did Yugoslavia disintegrate? Is there a conclusive answer? *Journal of Southern Europe and the Balkans* 6:3, 299–306.

Potts, G. (1996), *The Development of the System of Representation in Yugoslavia with Special Reference to the Period Since 1974* (New York: University of America).

Rusinow, D. (1977), *The Yugoslav Experiment 1948–1974* (London: C. Hurst & Company).

Seroka, J. (1993), Variation in the evolution of the Yugoslav Communist parties, in Seroka, J. and Pavlović, V. (eds).

—— and Pavlović, V. (eds) (1993), *The Tragedy of Yugoslavia: The Failure of Democratic Transition* (London: M.E. Sharpe).

Singleton, F. (1976), *Twentieth Century Yugoslavia* (London: Macmillan).

Stanković, S. (1981), *The End of the Tito Era. Yugoslavia's Dilemmas* (Stanford: Hoover Institution Press).

Todorović, M. (1974), Yugoslavia's new constitution, *Review of International Affairs* XXV:574, 1–4.

Triska, J. (ed.) (1968), *Constitutions of the Communist Party States* (Stanford: Hoover Institutions Publications).

Vucinich, W. (ed.) (1969), *Contemporary Yugoslavia: Twenty Years of Socialist Experiment Los Angeles* (California: California University Press).

Vucković, G. (1997), *Ethnic Cleavages and Conflict: The Sources of National Cohesion and Disintegration: The Case of Yugoslavia* (Aldershot: Ashgate).

Further Reading

Works on Yugoslav "Polyvalent Federalism"

Djordjević, J. (1975), Remarks on the Yugoslav model of federalism, *Publius* 5:2, 77–88.

Works on Althusius

Althusius, J. (1995 [1614]), *Politics Methodically Set Forth, and Illustrated with Sacred and Profane Examples* (Indianapolis: Liberty Fund).
Friedrich, C. (1932), Introduction, in Friedrich, C. (ed.), *Politica Methodice Digests of Johannes Althusius* (Massachusetts: Harvard UP).
Hueglin, T. (1992), Have we studied the wrong authors? On the relevance of Johannes Althusius, *Studies in Political Thought* 1:1, 75-93.
—— (1994), Johannes Althusius and the Modern Concept of Civil Society, in Bibič, A. and Graziano, G. (eds) (1994), *Civil Society, Political Society and Democracy* (Ljubljana: Slovene Political Science Association).
—— (1999), *Early Modern Concepts for a Late Modern World. Althusius on Community and Federalism* (Waterloo, ON: Wilfrid Laurier UP).

Yugoslavia's Constitutions

Government of the Socialist Federal Republic of Yugoslavia (1974), *The Constitution of the Socialist Federal Republic of Yugoslavia Belgrade, 1974*, translated by Pavičić, M. (Ljubljana, Parnova: Dopisna Delavska Univerza).
Triska, J. (ed.) (1968), *Constitutions of the Communist Party States* (Stanford: Hoover Institutions Publications).

Works on Yugoslavia

Bošković, B. and Dašić, D. (eds) (1980), *Socialist Self-Management in Yugoslavia. 1950–1980 Documents* (Belgrade: Socialist Thought and Practice).
Potts, G. (1996), *The Development of the System of Representation in Yugoslavia with Special Reference to the Period Since 1974* (New York: University of America).
Burg, S. (1983), *Conflict and Cohesion in Yugoslavia: Political Decision Making Since 1966* (Princeton: Princeton UP).
Lampe, J. (1996), *Yugoslavia as History. Twice There was a Country* (Cambridge: Cambridge UP).
Rusinow, D. (1977), *The Yugoslav Experiment 1948–1974* (London: C. Hurst & Company).
Singleton, F. (1977), *Twentieth Century Yugoslavia* (London: Macmillan).
Jović, D. (2003), Yugoslavism and Yugoslav Communism: From Tito to Kardelj, in Djokić, D. (ed.).

A "European" Federalism: From Altiero Spinelli to the EU Constitutional Treaty

Francesca Vassallo

Introduction

In the aftermath of the demise of the European Constitutional Treaty, scholars of European integration proclaimed the European Union (EU) project to be once again in serious jeopardy. The failed referenda in France and the Netherlands were not only a rejection of another European treaty, but a voice against possible further integration, against that long dream of a future *federally* organized continent. This time the rejection attacked directly the essence of European integration: it targeted the survival of the idea itself of a federal Union, a concept accepted by some and strongly opposed by others.

For a project that is now 50 years in the making the EU is still struggling to formally represent a clear, coherent, and generally supported organization. Besides individual leaders' responsibility for flawed designs and watered down agreements, the EU's problems derive mostly from the lack of an overwhelmingly shared interpretation of the true, basic mission integration was supposed to accomplish. In part, the main reason for such vagueness was that "federalism for the EU remains an unclear and contested concept" (Hallstrom 2003, 203), either by intentional choice or lack of preparation. Logically, the attempts made at further integration aimed at completing an organizational structure that was blurring more and more national sovereignties, in favor of a centralized source of competence. Brussels has become unequivocally more prominent than before, not because of its natural attraction as a city, but obviously as a relevant node of power, resources, and intentions. Whereas some scholars and countries side with the final idea of a federal EU structure (Burgess 2006, 237), as highlighted by the slow progress over the years towards a common currency for instance, others are still puzzled, and a few more are concerned and surprised by how fast and unexpectedly the

EU has indeed widened and deepened.[1] To some the EU is the "real deal": from a simple and straightforward identification like "a federal political system" (Christin et al. 2005, 488), to a more cautious definition like "a long-standing quasi-federal structure" (Hallstrom 2003, 54). Consequently, EU citizens' realization that the EU is now much more than the sum of its entities should not have surprised them. The federal destination was the original idea of the forefathers (Burgess 2006, 227; Spinelli 1986, XIII), even if not as clearly delineated as its current structure.

The progress European integration has demonstrated since the Treaty of Rome in 1957 would lead to the conclusion that soon enough the word "federalism" may start to be used to address the essence of the EU. As some visionaries had expected a long time ago, among them Altiero Spinelli, Jean Monnet, and more moderately Jacques Delors,[2] a more complete integration on the European continent would lead (inevitably?) to a federal system, wherein nation states have merged into a new institutional structure they participated in creating. Although the process itself has had a few ups and downs along the road, and as European political leaders and institutions struggled to form a coherent plan that would please, and maybe circumvent, national authorities in certain cases, the European *Union* has emerged, but the use of the word "federalism" has not become that much more acceptable. Despite the fact of being "federalism without a federation" (Burgess 1986, 183), the idea of a federal organization still implies a Europe of self-rule and shared-rule (Burgess 2006, 236), although by itself this definition does not define yet how dominant either component is. The balance between an interpretation of self-rule and shared-rule has kept first the European Community (EC) intact, and later the EU functioning, through the Danish NO, the British opt-outs, the repeated Irish referenda, and now the rejection of a constitutional document.

The question to be asked is: how is it possible to have a successful integration in place, without the corresponding accomplishment of a federation to allow it? On one side scholars claim the EU is the outcome of an outdated modern nation state model that is not as useful or welcomed as before (Spinelli 1986, 176–177). European integration is then the product of obsolete states, not the cause of it. On the other side, there is no "presumed antithesis between the EC and the nation-

---

1 According to Burgess (1986, 233) the revisionists have rejected the existence of a long time project, planned and envisioned since its beginning, arguing it was a sort of accident of history: "European integration was not part of a grand federal design but had emerged merely to cope with certain historically specific economic and political problems."

2 Interestingly, only a few of the more recent European leaders have been as visionary. In part because it is more difficult to be heard in a 27 member union, but also because national interests have dominated national leaders' positions when they are in Brussels. If Joschka Fisher can correctly be a name scholars have mentioned as one of the more audacious leaders, due to his 2000 speech at Humboldt University asking for the creation of a European federation (Hallstrom 2003), other names that have appeared in the literature are not so expected. "Chirac and Schröder are cautious nationalists by comparison and, ironically, Tony Blair looks like a Eurovisionary" (Fischer 2006, 274–275)!

state" (Burgess 2006, 234), so European integration is not fighting European nationalism with federalism, but actually helping the nation state cope with the changed reality (Pinder 1986, 45 speaking about Stanley Hoffmann's position). In brief, the uniqueness of the EU construction is not immune from a series of different interpretations when it comes to assess the type, level, quality, or character of federal elements the Union is evidence of.[3]

This chapter presents an overview of how the meaning of federalism has changed over time, from its original interpretation at the time of birth of the EC, to the more recent Constitutional *evil*. In particular, the focus of the discussion will be on the way leaders and scholars have assessed the possible establishment of *European federalism*, yet another ad hoc creation to explain a community that is multiple things to different actors. What was the original federal impetus some scholars underline? How has that federal connotation fared vis-à-vis later challenges? Has the federal drive gone back to its origins? The level of accomplishment of the federal character of the Union has suffered also from the type of involvement on the part of common European citizens. The incentive the original founders underlined included the full-fledged participation of Europeans as essential elements in the formation of a "United Europe." The actual development of integration itself has not conformed to that idea. As the next sections highlight, the achievement of a more integrated community has suffered from a decision made early on to focus on the elites' institutional creation rather than on European citizens' engagement.

During the first stage of integration, up to the creation of the European Union in 1992, citizens' participation was relegated to a minimum: its unfortunate consequence was a long period of political interests' quarrels that delayed many accomplishments. Finally toward the end of the first phase of integration, the direct election of the European Parliament (EP) contributed to reinvest in citizens' presence and active input. The newly decided effort progressed in part with the expansion of the competences of the EP during the second stage of integration (up until the 2004 enlargement).

As integration was progressing more successfully, the call for citizens' involvement in the European construction was not loud enough: the democratic deficit debate testifies to that. It took the third stage of integration, beginning in 2004 with the European Constitutional Treaty, to return to the idea of citizens' involvement as an integral part to a successful federal journey. As a whole the integration project has delivered many of its promises, but its recurring lack of focus on the need of a community of the citizens in Europe may make the accomplishments very fragile. The collapse of the EU Constitution referendum ratification process has caused a reconsideration of the type of integration any possibly federal Europe should need.

In order to start the debate on what federal path Europe took at the beginning of integration, the next section highlights some of the more fundamental federal ideas

---

3   See for instance Hooghe and Marks (2001) on different types of multilevel governance to explain the federal features of the EU.

the integration project was associated with: Altiero Spinelli's visionary position on European unity.

From Spinelli's Vision of the European Union (1958–1992)

The federal vision for Europe developed after the end of World War II, responding to the need for peace amidst a group of countries that had managed to destroy continental Europe twice over a 30-year period. Whether it was out of necessity or fear of a relapse once again (Spinelli 1962, 551), integration was a possible, maybe viable, option to solve multiple problems at once. Not everyone was ready for it though: US-sponsored Atlanticism was clearly predominant (Spinelli 1962, 551) due to the need for security, damaging the chances for a quicker federation of Europe. The initial steps taken toward collaboration among countries were not enough to create a stronger connection so as to prevent war ever again (Burgess 1986, 176), as naïve as that thought may have been at that time. Integration has to supersede cross-border collaboration. The benefits of federalism per se could be discussed, especially in regards to the integration of sovereign nations, but Altiero Spinelli's early passion and fight for a federal Europe has not proven to be in vain.[4] For as much as federalism cannot solve every country's problems (see Schmitter's position on the challenges federalism actually creates to democracy for instance, 2000), the current version the EU is embracing, that is, a mix of federal and confederal elements with some limitations in specific policy areas, has had its welcomed benefits: for instance, a direct voice for citizens in the direct elections of European Parliament members, the development of a common currency area that has strengthened the financial position of the EU and its Eurozone members in the world, and last, but not least, five decades of peace. If Spinelli was supporting a European federal movement based upon his theoretical[5] understanding of what federalism was supposed to bring about, its actual application was more challenging, as it required the establishment of a top-down federation, rather than a bottom-up one, as the American model had come into being (Fischer 2006, 227).

The idea of having citizens driving the momentum of European integration was exactly what Spinelli had always argued for: to give Europeans the car keys so to take the Community where Europe should have gone already. For Spinelli, citizens had to be part of the European construction (Burgess 2006, 231): an important point considering the more recent campaign of "democracy, dialogue, debate"

---

4   For further treatment of Spinelli's conception of federalism, see Chapter 18 in this volume.
5   The practical aspect of federal proposals developed only years later, when it became clear that neo-functionalism was not enough to convince European leaders to be effective. Spinelli in particular can be considered responsible for the initial draft treaty establishing the European union approved by the European Parliament in 1984, well before other EC institutions and European leaders caught up in practice to those ideas.

sponsored by the European Commission after the rejections of the Constitutional Treaty. It turned out to be also an equally relevant point in regards to the negative understanding of "EU federalism" that citizens in Europe have developed, although scholars are still trying relentlessly to make the case that "from a *normative*[6] point of view, federalism is considered to be the best approach to organizing such culturally diverse entity as the European Union" (Dosenrode 2007a, 3). The lack of people's extensive involvement in the construction of Europe contributed to form the current negative perception some EU citizens have of the Union's presence in their daily lives.

Spinelli's plea for citizens' involvement did not go far. In the end, states took control of creating a federation with the possibility of expanding a centralized decision-making process, parallel to a decentralized delivery and implementation of policies. Citizens were taken for a ride and asked to be supportive because of gradual, and at times delayed, successes. For practical purposes, like-mindedness among political leaders in Europe (Pinder 1986, 52) was more directly helpful in building the EC than a general popular consensus on a federal vision. The value of the integration process itself overtook the actual role of promoting an integrated and federal continent. The integration seemed to be more accepted, and easily reachable, as later times confirmed.

The European Economic Community evolved along institutional and policy goals that did not include directly, for the most part, citizens from that same community. Yet, the initial, naïve idea of having Europeans involved in the Community creation did not die altogether when most European leaders dismissed it. If among the integrationists Spinelli was in the minority and Jean Monnet had led the majority of Europeanists into neo-functionalism, European federalists still tried to play their game as best as they could. For instance, Spinelli attempted to exploit the slow progress (Fischer 2006, 276) that the incremental strategy of neo-functionalism could manage. The idea that European integration processes and institutions would slowly crave more integration, towards the ultimate goal line of a federal system, proved to be the case in the long term. In itself a slow progress was always welcomed, especially considering that the superior theory of a natural, inevitable success of neo-functionalism in achieving a European federation was put to the test often (Pinder 1986, 43). Neo-functionalism was indeed stoppable, and the Eurosclerosis period almost proved to have found a way. Yet, the "federal inspiration" (Burgess 1984, 347) in the midst of the confusion and incoherence of the EC did not go unnoticed.

With incremental federalism slowing down at the European level, the true, convinced federalists intervened to shake up both European institutions and leaders: if the EC could not be considered a federal state, for once it was still a "federalizing" process[7] (Fischer 2006, 228). In a more helpful way, whether incrementalism was a good strategy or not, the European federalist movement still had good opportunities

---

6   Italics in original text.
7   Very aptly Welsh (1996, 178) notes "Ever Closer Union implies a constant coming together, but there is no necessary end to the process."

to support its original cause. When events were positive and conducive to more integration and less national sovereignties, the federalists within the EC used the situation to make the case that a confederation is just necessarily a stage along the way to a federation (Burgess 1989, 13). When instead circumstances were not so favorable to Spinelli and Co., the federal movement in Europe went into a crisis exploitation mode (Burgess 1984, 340): integration could not be gradual any longer, but instead it had to leap from one major accomplishment to the next, as the series of European treaties with the Single European Act (SEA) in 1986, the Treaty of the European Union (TEU) in 1992, the Treaty of Amsterdam (TOA) in 1998 and the Treaty of Nice (TON) in 2001 showed. The gradualism of the EC had given way to the leaps that led to, and passed, the EU.

During this first phase then the motivations and the strategy employed confirmed the uniqueness of the EU pseudo-federal experiment: something hybrid, mutating on its own, definitively puzzling (Burgess 2006, 226) and therefore more difficult to assess. The multiple and vague ideas of the Union (Burgess 1984, 339) encouraged diverse interpretations that highlighted how no grand project was being orchestrated by anyone in particular. What the EC had become since the beginning was the end result of functional economic links Monnet had described as the source of a future united Europe. Even when political leaders, Eurocrats, and scholars started operating in a more federal-like mentality thanks to the incremental steps taken from 1957 through 1992, the simple word "federalism" could not fit, and neologisms came to be trendy.[8]

In brief, this very first phase of European integration ends with the determination of keeping people out and with a gamble on the success of the European institutions as chosen and directed by political elites. The second phase of integration, a closer step to a more federal Europe, resisted the urge to change course.

From Maastricht to a Stretched Union (1992–2004)

When the Treaty of the European Union (TEU) was signed in Maastricht in 1992, the simple creation of an EU, replacing the EC, was evidence that the federalist push for a federation had some weight. Yet the three-pillar structure,[9] with a combination of intergovernmental and supranational features, was not enough to make clear that the integration project was moving forward in the federal direction. As a matter of fact, Maastricht was in part considered a failure of federalism because of the intergovernmentalism of the second and third pillars (Welsh 1996, 162), and subsequently the Danish opt-outs (Welsh 1996, 170–171). More specifically, the British government did not see the United States of Europe in the TEU (Welsh 1996, 168), which was reassuring to London, but less so to

---

8   Pinder probably uses the simplest one: neo-federalism (54).
9   The economic community pillar (supranational), the common and foreign policy pillar, and the justice and home affairs pillar (both intergovernmental at that time).

all those countries who did embrace a federal continent already in the early 1990s. Equally revealing in the eyes of many who had waited for a union to take shape, Maastricht made instead an official commitment to shared rule more than to self-rule, without even mentioning the still strong institutional approach. At Maastricht, EU institutions rejoiced, in particular the EP, but EU residents were left mostly empty handed. Although European institutions started to gain powers that made them more federal in nature in specific policy-making areas, an actor like the EP was still lobbying according to its own interests: the responsibilities associated with citizens' representation were not as clear as in any federal-like system (Welsh 1996, 172). It looked like the rules of the political game had changed in part, but the actors involved were still playing based upon intergovernmental rules. Even an important treaty like the TEU could not impose a federal face and soul to a European integration project that had been many different things to many political leaders.

As this second phase of European integration started with many expectations, the then-use of the word "Union" was not enough to guarantee more forcefully the implementation of a true federal organization. Due to a backlash, in reaction to the goals of integration presented in the TEU, the federalist impetus lost cohesiveness. The ultimate outcome of "an ever closer union" became the absolute priority, whereas the federal character of the closer union was not a needed feature in the short term. If in practice Maastricht had moved Europe toward a federation, in theory the entire concept was still stigmatized. Indeed, up until the signing of the Constitutional Treaty much later, the EU successfully represented a much more forceful push towards a higher integration, maybe hoping again in the benefits of neo-functionalism: the imperceptible corrosion of the states (Burgess 1989, 11). The focus was on the integration part, not on who was coordinating the integration process.

In light of pragmatism, slowly the European project was still traveling in the same direction, without a stronger public involvement. The strengthening of the European structure's federal character did not require absolutely the development of a full-fledged federal system, since the idea of an EU does not pretend "to resemble a vast federal super-state straddling the European continent" (Burgess 1986, 182). According to some basic elements of any federal system highlighted by Schmitter (2000, 42), the TEU was indeed missing a few federal characteristics. For instance, decisional autonomy and the right to secede were not clearly presented in any document. Ultimately, the first and foremost important element dismissing the EU as a federal construction had been the lack of common, significant budgetary resources (Moravcsik 2001, 186). In consideration of the position of some concerned European political elites, the less evident the federal character of the Maastricht document, the more likely any opposition to the possibility of a slow integration without an overt federalization would be weakened. Undeniably, the second most important treaty on European integration did not have an easy life from the beginning, as it had been clear earlier that the "idea of a federal Europe is easily misrepresented as a monstrous new Leviathan Straddling Europe and ... in its single-minded pursuit of social homogeneity and cultural standardization"

(Burgess 1989, 15). For as much as initial groups of Euroskeptics, anti-integration movements, and isolated leaders with personal nationalistic agendas (à la Jean-Marie Le Pen in France for instance) resisted any attempt that could resemble a more centralized federal European government, the pro-federal supporters had never clearly agreed on what type of federalism European integration was going to follow. The Leviathan the anti-federalists were fighting in their own battles did not even exist. Supporters within the European political elites did not share a common interpretation themselves of what the Leviathan was supposed to look like.

In the end, the limitations of Maastricht were confirmation that federalism was not necessarily the final goal of integration, but still the strategy underlining the integration efforts. As it is difficult to choose a final version of federalism supporters would all agree on, it remains clear that the common position in favor of a federalization of the European Union was based on the understanding that federalism was in itself a useful process to accomplish further integration. Since "federalization is a process and not an event" (Fischer 2006, 229), the choice to implement a new European treaty, which did not go far enough in the eyes of the federalists, was a needed step to keep the everlasting dream of a federal Europe alive. By using federalism as a process, the TEU could still count on the support of all those citizens and leaders who were welcoming integration, even if they were not necessarily embracing a federal version of it. Support for further integration at large, even when not clearly federally oriented (Burgess 1989, 21), could never be bad news. From the Spinelli days, this had been the general ruse: broad support for a more integrated Europe would always help the federal idea; Maastricht was in line with this strategy.

The relevance of public support for integration *and* federalization after Maastricht became even more crucial. As previously for the other European treaties, the TEU had been once again the product of political elites' preferences in most part. For the federalist camp, this was a welcome situation: European elites had confirmed over the decades to endorse more steadily the federal view, although without mentioning the "F" word out loud. In practice, it was evident to scholars that the doubts about the federal character of the Maastricht Treaty were not a major problem in the big scheme of things, as the atmosphere in Europe at that time presented a "considerable support at elite levels for the development of a *de facto* federated form of Europe,"[10] according to Hallstrom's research (2003, 52). At the same time, assumptions about the possible support for federalism from citizens in Europe were not always confirmed. For instance, shortly before the EU Constitution was drafted, hopes for an endorsement of a federal Europe from citizens who were already living in federal states did not materialize as expected: citizens with direct experiences of federal states were not necessarily more convinced about a federal Europe (Christin et al. 2005, 497–500). Any popular movement in support of a federal Europe would have clearly helped what few European leaders were trying to accomplish, although the lack of such a strong, evident movement did not mean that federalism in Europe was doomed. Scholars such Pinder, for instance, had questioned whether indeed

---

10   Italics in original text.

a single people was indispensable in a federal organization (1986, 53). European federalism had a particular flavor and was not assuredly associated with any type of federalism, it was not unexpected for European citizens to be wary of something they did not completely comprehend.

Due to the expectations for further integration, and consequently a federal-like system in the minds of many, comparisons with other federal states (in particular the United States) did not help to grasp where exactly the EU was federal and where it was not. A comparison with a well known, typical federal system like the US one created false expectations,[11] derailing attempts to foster a better explanation of how the EU was fulfilling its full integration destiny the federalists had been advocating for. Misrepresentation of what the EU had become was inevitable then. As the integration had progressed, the rejection of the US model of federation invoked in the early stages by dedicated federalists seemed confirmed. The EU was not a simple federation, if one at all, but more something in between a federation and a confederation (Burgess 2006, 246). For others instead, the European project was on its way to "approaching statehood" (Dosenrode 2007a, 1), although this did not imply losing a national identity, just because more powers were being shared at the federal level (Dosenrode 2007b, 7). The implementation of a clear federal state from scratch is already a demanding task, when institutions have to deal with a mixed version of a subtle federalization, the challenge becomes more complicated and confused. Although the intention was there, as the EU maintained its atypical version of an aspiring federation – a "voluntary democratic federal union" (Burgess 2006, 238) – pretending to be federal and not to be federal according to the situation could not represent a solution. This type of half-commitment to federalization, as portrayed by the organization of the EU institutions with the TEU, was no longer a good strategy for the European federalists. If during the first phase of integration federalism had to be tuned and masked in the interests of a long-term victory, that temporary decision seemed instead to have buried the real meaning of the federal idea and of its value. Federalists and integrationists worked together in Brussels, sustaining each other for different reasons. Whereas the first group was providing encouragement to further integration as a way to eventually achieve a federal Europe, the second group was enjoying the aid of the federalists without necessarily the guarantee of the creation of a federal entity.

Convinced federalists did not automatically celebrate when the Treaty of Maastricht was eventually ratified and entered into effect: some of its initial intentions had been affected by the ratification and opt-out processes, according to at least one scholar causing the end of federalism: "the federal idea of a United States of Europe is dead and buried" (Welsh 1996, 178). By now it appears that what the TEU did not accomplish, later treaties did, and although Maastricht had not spelled out the word federal as much as some would have hoped for, there was indeed no need, and no hurry, for "federal state systems to be called by their real name" (Auer 2005, 423).

---

11 In part because "the evolving European model of confederal union had already replaced the classic American model of federation" (Burgess 2006, 239).

The second phase of integration confirms serious progress in the context of a more centralized Europe: the federal characteristics were becoming more evident, and the signing of two treaties, coupled with the drafting of a Constitution, suggests that the EU had continued its integration mode. Yet federalism was not openly a goal. The federal dream had somehow been muted in the interest of further integration. The EU had inched closer to evolve into a federal entity, but the arrival point was still unclear in the minds of many, including the federalist hearts in Brussels. Then the Constitution idea appeared, but it came and went too fast to replace integration with its real name of federalism.

The Deceased Constitution and Federalism (2004–2007)

The third and current stage of integration is a brutal awakening: the accomplishments of the European project over the past five decades are not enough to fool European citizens. A more federal Europe without its citizens is not necessarily the best possible option: support for the EU declines, trembles in some countries. EU leaders seem to have no choice but to correct the mistake made at the beginning of the integration project, acknowledging the indispensable element of the people in a federated Europe. Yet, the final version of the EU Constitution did not turn out to be a contract between the European (centralized) state and its citizens. Although a praised document because of its further integration accomplishments (Abromeit 2007, 48), the Constitutional Treaty evidenced once again the reiteration of increased federal features without more participation options for European citizens (Abromeit 2007, 51). Ignoring the many precedents of former federal constitutions (the American one for instance), European elites once more created a mostly top-down treaty, with a minor participation from other civil society actors. The irony was evident: the establishment of a constitutional order for Europe, with a strong impact on European citizens, but without any more venues of participation from European individuals.

Faced with the final rejection of the Constitution in two failed ratification referendums in 2005, scholars explained the need for a European constitution in two different ways. Those who had opposed a more centralized and sovereign European government used the failed Constitution to read the end of European federalism as well. Supporters of a European federation could not let anti-integration movements destroy the European Union's efforts while also damaging the federal view for Europe.

The first explanation related the push for an overall treaty to the specific circumstances of the time. With the draft of the European Constitution in 2004 European leaders who had been longing for a more federated Europe hoped to solve many problems at once. The year of the EU Constitution was also the year of the largest enlargement ever into the Union (from 15 to 25 members). As logistical problems were expected, more integration on the continent had offered once again the opportunity to convince EU member states of the benefits of a more centralized European government. A federal, centralized, coherent, and overstretching government could more easily cope with the demands and problems the Union as a whole had to deal with. The EU Constitution was therefore deemed indispensable to allow for a functioning Union that had suddenly been blown out of proportion without the proper preparation (Sbragia 2007, 5). In this case, the constitutional treaty was the ultimate example of the long-term piecemeal evolution of the European construction. The latest document signed by all EU members was a tool to realign internal devolution with an external one (Sbragia 2007, 3), and in so doing finalize the slow federal progress European integration has employed. The document was supposed to represent the finally organized and coherent process of integration, by continuing the erosion of power and rights for national authorities (Abromeit 2007, 51). In its most practical way, the constitutional treaty was a necessary tool to convince all member states that compliance with European decisions in specific areas was required (Follesdal 2006, 175), and that consequent lack of respect for the supranational character of the EU was going to have negative consequences.

The second explanation for the draft of a constitution touched instead on the grand scheme plan to create a truly federal Europe. Almost five decades after the signing of the very first integration treaty, some federalist supporters started to doubt the validity and efficacy of functionalism, as the steady push for a more federated continent. Whereas incremental steps towards a federal Europe had brought enough success to satisfy the more federalist minds among European elites, the slow pace of integration had also convinced many during the 1990s that a major switch in tone for European integration was needed and expected. Europe could not become a federal state one piece at the time, European leaders had to finally come clean and admit that their goal was a centralized, integrated, and legitimate European government. The Constitution was then the presentation of a new federal model (Burgess 2006, 245) with a clear plan on how to develop it. To some the EU Constitution symbolized the ultimate success of federalism in Europe because it was supposed to have created that organized federal structure for the European government Brussels has been waiting for since the very beginning. If a draft of a constitution is typically the very first step in the creation of a new regime, that practice was not followed on the European continent. As it has become clear, the European construction has, unsurprisingly, not really failed to follow the typical steps of nation building (Schmitter 2000, 45). The various ultimate compromises that would have easily ruined any other attempt at state creation seemed to have indeed saved the European integration project multiple times. The EU Constitution persevered in doing what all the previous European treaties had achieved: reorganizing the already existing institutions and competences so to improve the Union's functioning level. The constitutional document rearranged the pieces of the puzzle to compose a new image, using the same old pieces.

People who believed the Constitution was not simply an additional stepping stone towards integration, but instead a turning point towards a more open drive leading to a federation remained convinced that the spirit of the draft was the essence of their position. Although federalism had been presented as an important reason for the Constitution to exist (Auer 2005, 420), the concept of federalism was not clearly spelled out in the document, and to one author in particular it was also "banished" all together (Auer 2005, 421). Nonetheless, federalist supporters did not feel necessarily betrayed or pessimistic about the potential for a federal character in the constitutional draft. In the end, "what is essential is not what constitutions say, but what they do, even without saying" (Auer 2005, 423).

Any possibility of a new federal Europe due to the implementation of the next level of integration highlighted in the EU Constitution of 2004 ceased to exist as the document ratification failed. Issues such as the selection of a EU president, the more supranational character of the second pillar of Common and Foreign Security Policy, the creation of a EU foreign minister, and other elements of the Constitution prevented the EU from showing a more convincing turn toward federal organization. Although without a stronger emphasis on citizens' participation in a more centralized Europe, the end of the Constitution portrayed at first the more significant failure of a true federal Union. Only two years later, in December 2007, with the signing of the newest European treaty, known now as the Treaty of Lisbon, did federalists resurrect their hopes and dreams. The more recent treaty has embraced many of the features of the EU Constitution and it has allowed for a further attempt at bringing the EU closer to a federal state. The rejection of an open federal mission is still present, but to anti-integration movements it has become evident that the slow harmonization process is leading in one direction only. Without counting down the days towards a directly elected European executive in Brussels with sovereign powers over the residents of EU member states, federalists in Europe are now reliving the euphoria of the initial days. The very recent impetus to go back to citizens' involvement as part of a successful European integration project has brought back memories of Spinelli's vision. Although the EU cannot call itself a federal state openly, Spinelli's ideal remains a guiding principle.

Still on the Same Road?

The failed ratification of the European Constitutional Treaty initiated a discussion about the accomplishments of over five decades of integration. To some scholars and political elites, the setback from the failed Constitution represented the dissatisfaction among EU citizens who did not embrace the idea of integration, and more specifically an integration that had been slowly forming a federal entity. Although federal ideas had remained part of the long discussion over how to create a harmonized Union, an open fear of federalism per se still exists. In a certain sense, European federalism had become a victim of its own success.

On one side the neo-functional approach of inching toward a more federal Europe achieved its goal. European integration had unquestionably centralized power in Brussels, while political and economic successes had convinced national governments to release part of their national sovereignty when it came to specific policy areas. Additionally, the resilience of a federal view over time (Burgess 1986, 184) had increased people's desire for more integration. As the EU showed its potential as a political and economic entity, European citizens became more ready to release more national sovereignty to Brussels (Sbragia 2007, 6). Unwillingly, or unknowingly maybe, Europeans have been supporting integration and the formation of a European federation – particularly in regards to certain policy areas where EU nationals are convinced a European government can better perform than a national government. Sharing power within multiple layers of governance in Europe appears to be appealing and wise (Hallstrom 2003, 70).

On the other side, limited integration succeeded, but this reality also slowed down the possibility for a full and evident federal system at the EU level. Since "the EU works in practice but not in theory" (Burgess 2006, 245), the overall concept of a finally federal Europe by accident was still an ideal more than 50 years after it was developed. Through multiple stages federalism has remained an appealing end result for European integration (Moravcsik 1993, 91), although it had not achieved the ultimate outcome. During the three major phases of European integration the impact of a federal ideal changed according to the best strategy at the time. In the first phase of integration, political leaders and elites had an honest discussion about how federal the integration on the continent could be. Sincere federalists followed Altiero Spinelli's strong position for a true federal Europe, with European citizens accordingly in charge, and political elites in Brussels accountable. After a decade or so of hopes, the federalist movement in Europe realized the many obstacles to a really federal system. Ideologically, federalism was not welcomed: national governments were still chained to the value of national sovereignty. The wounds and mistrust of World War II had not disappeared. European governments could not see themselves releasing power to what could become a supranational entity. Spinelli's plan did not materialize as he wished, but the federalists chose to keep the possibilities alive by working towards European integration only. In agreement with a neo-functional interpretation of integration in Europe, the more integrated European countries planned to be, the more likely a federal structure would eventually develop. As a matter of fact, the first phase of integration ended in 1992 with the transformation of the community into the European Union: a political and economic entity that started to show a centralized decision-making power in Brussels.

The success at the end of the first phase was a confirmation that the federalists' choice of Plan B had been rewarded, although it took more than 30 years to take that step. Federalism as a second, hidden priority was effective, but time was running out. The second phase of integration continued with the choice made: gradual integration in Europe during the 1990s led to the slowed development of the second and third pillar, but new obstacles and a renewed opposition to a federal agenda made clear that the pace of integration towards a federation had been reduced considerably. The length of the first phase and the high number of problems during integration in the second phase created increasing worries for the federal movement in Europe.

The third phase of integration was cut short: the attempt to have a European Constitution to guide the EU towards a more highly integrated structure of government for the large group of EU member states failed. As the Constitution was indeed an additional momentum towards a federal entity in Europe, its spirit generated a strong opposition among anti-European integration movements. It was the federal boldness of the Constitution that in the end could be considered responsible for its own demise. From the despair from the failed ratification of the EU Constitution, European federalists were able to renew and reinvigorate the original federal message Europe had resisted during its first phase. Spinelli's insistence that Europeans must be included in the construction of a federal government echoed from Brussels after the end of the Constitution in 2005. The newly signed Treaty of Lisbon does not follow that intention though. Calls for citizens' involvement to increase the EU's accountability have not been closely followed, and the most recent attempt to move integration forward is once again short.

Federalism as part of the European integration process is much stronger today than it was at the beginning. Europe has indeed started to show features of a federal system, although with a strong insistence in its denial. European leaders still cannot openly discuss a federal European government, for fear of encouraging opposition to further integration. Slowly, but steadily, even those supporters sharing a very convinced opposition to a federal, supranational European entity cannot reject the reality of the present. The European Union today is a federal-like representation: a supranational organization in part, with a consistent impetus to expand towards other areas of decision-making. Even with Europeans mostly unable to claim their citizen position in a European government, a federal Europe is now in the making. Although five decades late, Spinelli would have approved.

References

Abromeit, H. (2007), Constitution and legitimacy, in Dosenrode (ed.), *Approaching the European Federation?* (Aldershot: Ashgate).
Auer, A. (2005), The constitutional scheme of federalism, *Journal of European Public Policy* 12:3, 419–431.
Burgess, M. (1984), Federal ideas in the European Community: Altiero Spinelli and "European Union", 1981–84, *Government and Opposition* 19:3, 339–347.
—— (1986), Altiero Spinelli, federalism and the EUT, in Lodge (ed.), *European Union: The European Community in Search of a Future* (New York: St. Martin's Press).
—— (1989), *Federalism and European Union* (London: Routledge).
—— (2006), *Comparative Federalism* (London: Routledge).
Christin, T., Hug, S. and Schulz, T. (2005), Federalism in the European Union: the view from below (if there is such thing), *Journal of European Public Policy* 12:3, 488–508.
Dosenrode, S. (2007a), Introduction, in Dosenrode (ed.), *Approaching the European Federation?* (Aldershot: Ashgate).
—— (2007b), Federalism, in Dosenrode (ed.), *Approaching the European Federation?* (Aldershot: Ashgate).
Fischer, T. (2006), An American looks at the European Union, *European Law Journal* 12:2, 226–278.

Follesdal, A. (2006), Towards a stable finalité with federal features? The balancing acts of the constitutional treaty for Europe, in Trechsel (ed.), *Towards a Federal Europe?* (New York: Routledge).

Hallstrom, L. (2003), Support for European federalism? An elite view, *European Integration* 25, 51–72.

Hooghe, L. and Marks, G. (2001), Types of multi-level governance. *European Integration Online Papers* 5 (11).

Moravcsik, A. (1993), European federalism and modern social science: a rejoinder on the Maastricht referendum, *French Politics & Society* 11:2, 85–94.

—— (2001), Federalism in the European Union: rhetoric and reality, in Nicolaidis and Howse (eds), *The Federal Vision* (Oxford: Oxford University Press).

Pinder, J. (1986), European Community and nation-state: a case for neo-federalism?, *International Affairs* 1, 41–54.

Sbragia, A. (2007), The United States and the European Union: comparing two *sui generis* systems, in Menon et al. (eds), *Comparative Federalism: The European Union and the United States in Comparative Perspective* (New York: Oxford University Press).

—— (2007), An American perspective on the EU's Constitutional Treaty, *Politics* 27:1, 2–7.

Schmitter, P. (2000), Federalism and the Euro-Polity, *Journal of Democracy* 11:1, 40–47.

Spinelli, A. (1962), Atlantic Pact or European Unity, *Foreign Affairs* 40:4, 542–552.

—— (1986), Foreword, in Lodge (ed.), *European Union: The European Community in Search of a Future* (New York: St. Martin's Press).

Welsh, M. (1996), *Europe United?* (New York: St. Martin's Press).

Further Reading

Börzel, T. and Hosli, M. (2003), Brussels between Bern and Berlin: comparative federalism meets the European Union, *Governance* 16, 179–202.

Burgess, M. (1984), Federal ideas in the European Community: Altiero Spinelli and "European Union", 1981–84, *Government and Opposition* 19:3, 339–347.

Burgess, M. (1989), *Federalism and European Union* (London: Routledge).

—— (2006), *Comparative Federalism* (London: Routledge).

Christin, T., Hug, S. and Schulz, T. (2005), Federalism in the European Union: the view from below (if there is such thing), *Journal of European Public Policy* 12, 488–508.

Dosenrode, S. (ed.) (2007), *Approaching the European Federation?* (Aldershot: Ashgate).

Fischer, T. (2006), An American looks at the European Union, *European Law Journal* 12, 226–278.

Hallstrom, L. (2003), Support for European federalism? An elite view, *European Integration* 25, 51–72.

Kelemen, R. (2003), The structure and dynamics of EU federalism, *Comparative Political Studies* 36, 184.
Menon, A. et al. (eds) (2006), *Comparative Federalism: the European Union and the United States in Comparative Perspective* (Oxford: Oxford University Press).
Ortino, S., Zagar, M. and Mastny, V. (eds) (2005), *The Changing Faces of Federalism: Institutional Reconfiguration in Europe from East to West* (Manchester: Manchester University Press).
Parsons, C. (2001), Democracy, federalism and the European Union, *German Politics & Society* 19, 103–113.
Trechsel, A. (2005), How to federalize the European Union ... and why bother, *Journal of European Public Policy* 12, 401–418.
Welsh, M. (1996), *Europe United?: The European Union and the Retreat from Federalism* (New York: St. Martin's Press).

21

From Laeken to Lisbon: Europe's Experiment with Constitutional Federalism

Martyn de Bruyn

This new Treaty is good for European citizens. It will enhance efficiency and give the Union a single voice in external relations. People will have a greater say in European policies through the reinforced powers of their directly-elected representatives in the European Parliament and the enhanced role of National parliaments.
European Commission Vice President Margot Wallström

Introduction

The ratification process of the Lisbon Treaty will not be completed before the European Parliamentary elections of 2009, however, it is unlikely that the treaty will be abandoned because of the no vote in the Irish referendum. If the Irish can be persuaded to vote affirmative on Lisbon in a second referendum, the European Union will finally be able to move away from the issue of institutional reform and focus all of its attention on more substantive issues such as energy, environment, and immigration policy. The President of the European Commission Jose Manuel Barroso has argued that the best way for the European Union (EU) to address the gap between European elites and the public is not through institutional reform but instead through good policies that affect the daily lives of EU citizens in a positive way. Institutional reform is, however, necessary to achieve policies in an ever-enlarging union. The fact that the EU has been debating its future design over the last six years shows that there are strong divisions within the union on what the future EU should look like. These divisions can best be described in the language of federalism. While some leaders are comfortable with the idea of a European federation, others remain firmly entrenched in the idea of a confederation of European nation-states.

The purpose of this chapter is to compare the Lisbon treaty with the European Constitutional Treaty in terms of federalism. In order to explore this subject, I will discuss both functional and constitutional federalism within the European context. I will argue that with the French and Dutch rejection of the Constitutional Treaty the experiment in constitutional federalism has ended. The process that started in Laeken with a declaration that called for a "different approach" to European integration, in light of the pending enlargement, has been unable to produce a different result, i.e. a European Constitution (IbR #4).[1] Lastly, I will discuss the consequences of Europe's failed experiment with constitutional federalism for the future of European federalism.

Federal, Supranational, or Multi-level Governance?

There are more definitions of federalism than there are federations in the world. Preston King defines federalism as "an institutional arrangement, taking the form of a sovereign state, and distinguished from other such states solely by the fact that its central government incorporates regional units into the decision procedure on some constitutionally entrenched basis" (1982, 77). It is important to note that federalism encompasses both federations and confederations. Federalism is an ideology that takes shape in both federation-style and confederation-style institutions.[2] Daniel Elazar describes federalism, in contrast to unitary systems, as a matrix model that "reflects the fundamental distribution of powers among multiple centers" (1997, 239). Federalism differs in this respect from devolution in which power is shifted top down from the central authority to lower level governments. According to Elazar, the European Union has actually caused a "revival of confederation" (1998, 105).[3] The unsuccessful attempt at a confederal arrangement in the United States has led many scholars to write confederacy off as an impossibility. Elazar argues that the EU has unintentionally revived, at least de facto if not *de jure*, confederalism in its practice of integration through the establishments of treaties (2001, 39).

The term supranational, rather than federalism, was used by the founders of the European Coal and Steel Community (ECSC) in the Treaty of Paris (Volcansek 2008, 24). By referring to the institution of the ECSC as supranational, the founders avoided the politically charged connotation of federalism. Monnet and Adenauer may have been interested in extending European integration from the economic to the political sphere, but they realized that this was only feasible through incremental functional steps. The use of the term federalism would have made explicit, the implicit assumption that the ECSC was only a first step towards greater European integration.

Today, scholars frequently prefer the term "multi-level governance" over "federalism." As with supranational governance, the distinction with federalism is

---

1 Internet-based References (IbR) are numbered and can be found at the end of the chapter after the standard references.
2 King distinguishes between multiple federalist ideologies (1982).
3 I will address Elazar's argument in the final section of this chapter.

more a matter of style than substance. One could say that federalism is a type of multi-level-governance. In the typology developed by Hooghe and Marks, federalism equates to type I governance (Hooghe and Marks 2003, 236). Type I multi-level governance is, according to Hooghe and Marks, characterized by general purpose jurisdictions, nonintersecting memberships, a limited number of jurisdictions, and a systemwide architecture (2003, 236–237). Under both multi-level governance and federalism, membership is nonintersecting, although competencies are often shared. The real difference is that multi-level governance does not carry the connotation of creating a European superstate. Especially type II multi-level governance, based on functional communities and a flexible policy-specific architecture, are seen as preserving rather than eroding national sovereignty (Hooghe and Marks 2003, 237–238).

I use the language of federalism in this chapter in order to highlight the new direction that the Council has chosen by attempting to further European integration through constitutionalism. As I will discuss in the next section, Europe's constitutional experiment was a clear break with the incremental functionalist past. Given the rejection by the European public of the constitutional approach, some form of functional multi-level governance may be the more feasible method of European integration.

Federalism in the European Union

The idea of a European federation predates the EU itself. In the interbellum period Richard Couenhove Kalergi published *Pan Europa* and founded the Pan-European Union. The purpose of the Pan-European Union was to provide peace and security for Europe through the creation of a customs union (Ginsburg 2007, 64). Even though the Pan-European Union was not able to prevent another war, the ideal of federalism kept alive in many resistance movements across Europe. Perhaps the most well known federalist theoreticians in the resistance movement were Altiero Spinelli and Ernesto Rossi. Spinelli and Rossi called, in their 1941 *Ventotene Manifesto*, for the creation of a European federation as the only possible successor to the nation-state (IbR #1). Similarly, the French Foreign Minister Robert Schuman in his May 9, 1950 declaration argued that "a European federation was indispensable to the preservation of peace" (IbR #2).[4] Schuman saw federalism as an antidote to nationalism that had led to two major world wars during the first half of the twentieth century.

In their response to the legitimacy crises of the nation-state, Spinelli, Rossi, Schuman, and Jean Monnet all agreed that only a federal solution would be able to prevent future wars of nationalism or imperialism in Europe. While they agreed on federalism as the best solution for European peace, Spinelli and Monnet did not

---

4   May 9th has been named Europe-day to celebrate European integration.

agree on the road towards European unification.[5] Spinelli, in his *Ventotene Manifesto*, argued: "The general spirit today is already far more disposed than it was in the past towards a federal reorganization of Europe" (IbR #1). Spinelli had hoped to bring together the anti-Nazi resistance movements across Europe and create an organization that would supersede the individual nation-states: "A free and united Europe is the necessary premise to the strengthening of modern civilization that has been temporarily halted by the totalitarian era" (IbR #1). Spinelli argued in favor of a United States of Europe, albeit based on the principle of utopian socialism and not capitalism. Spinelli's federalism can be described as constitutional federalism. He argued that it was essential to first create constitutional institutions and establish a federal *demos*. The period directly after the end of the war was a unique moment in time that provided an opportunity to transcend the nation-state in favor of a federal arrangement. Spinelli was convinced that, soon after the defeat of the Nazis, power would be returned into the hand of the traditional parties and Europe of the nation-states would remain unchanged (IbR #1). At the 1948 Hague Congress Spinelli and his supporters' hopes were dashed when the Council of Europe, instead of a United States of Europe, was founded.

Constitutional federalism is a bottom-up theory of European integration where the establishment of a constitution is the foundation of the building of the European federal structure. Constitutional federalism is based on the establishment of a covenant in which equal partners agree to form an exclusive jurisdiction in which the powers of the national government are set. Even though only the elites will actually sign the covenant, the people are the centerpiece of the constitutional document. The people are united as belonging to one national government, while their differences in culture, language, and geography are respected through the reserved powers of the territorial entities (states, provinces, regions). The assumption is made that if the people are not involved with the foundation of the federal project, they will not recognize the building that has been established in their name and for their sake. Without recognition of the building, the institution will not derive any legitimacy from the public, and the public will feel alienated from the elites and their institutions.

Jean Monnet, on the other hand, supported what has been referred to as functional federalism. Instead of creating a constitution and a set of federal institutions, Monnet believed, along the lines of the neo-functional philosophy of David Mitrany and Ernst Haas, that federalism would be established incrementally.[6] European states would cooperate in one area only to find that their cooperation would be enhanced if they simultaneously would cooperate in another area. Through a shared experience and elite socialization, Europe would incrementally develop into a federal system. The essence of the Monnet method is epitomized by Schuman when he stated: "Europe will not be made all at once, or according to

---

5   For a good discussion of the differences between Spinelli and Monnet see also Burgess (2004, 35–38).
6   See David Mitrany *A Working Peace System* (1943) and Ernst B. Haas *The Uniting of Europe: Political, Social and Economic Forces 1950–1957* (1958).

a single plan" (IbR #2). Neo-functionalism only works when all parties involved agree not to address the elephant in the room, national sovereignty.

Functional federalism is based on a top-down theory in which elites rule and the public is expected to support elite decision-making through permissive consensus.[7] Functional federalism, as opposed to its constitutional variety, is apolitical in that it relies on elite consensus and a technocratic approach to problem solving. The public is put on reserve because all attention is focused on the incremental institutionalization of the different parts of the federal body. The assumption is made that once the federal building has been established, the public will learn to appreciate it through its interactions with the institutions. As long as the institutions provide benefits to the European public in ways that cannot be achieved by individual states, the public will lose its skeptical attitude and become progressively more European. Neo-functionalists would argue that functional linkages need to be established in advance of the construction of a constitutional structure. A constitutional structure without clear evidence of how it will be able to improve the daily lives of Europeans will only alienate the public.

The "Monnet method" of functional federalism has become the standard for European integration. Between 1952 and 2001 there has never been any serious consideration of adopting constitutional federalism for Europe. It was only after the desire for a "different approach" had been voiced in the Laeken Declaration on the Future of the European Union that the idea of taking Europe to the next step in terms of federalism, from confederation to federation, by way of constitutional federalism, became a viable option (IbR #4).[8]

The Laeken Declaration on the Future of the European Union

The road to Lisbon started in Laeken in 2001 when the leaders of the European Council met to discuss the future of the European Union. The tragedy of two world wars and the looming cold war acted as impetus for European integration. The end of the cold war and the lowering of the iron curtain have provided European integration with a new momentum. In the Nice Treaty the principles of the Laeken Council, such as democracy, legitimacy, and transparency, have already been set out in the *Declaration on the Future of the Union*. The declaration also addresses the need to further clarify the status of the *Charter of Fundamental Rights of the European Union*. Finally, the declaration emphasizes the need to simplify the existing treaties and to discuss the role of the national parliaments, in particular with regard to the principle of subsidiarity, in the Union (IbR #5).

---

7   I will use the terms "functional" and "treaty" federalism interchangeably.
8   Europe's founders already had an idea that Europe would some way transform into a federal entity. However, they did not envision constitutional federalism, including a Philadelphia style convention, as the road to be taken towards that goal.

At the Laeken meeting in December 2001, it was generally accepted that Europe was standing "at a crossroads." The unification of Europe, the inclusion of central and Eastern European states into the Union was perceived as giving closure to "one of the darkest chapters of European history" (IbR #4). This meant that the expected enlargement of the Union from 15 to 25 and eventually 27, would be no ordinary case of enlargement. As the Laeken Declaration states: "At long last, Europe is on its way to becoming one big family, without bloodshed, a real transformation clearly calling for a *different approach* from fifty years ago, when six countries first took the lead" (IbR #4, italics added). The difference in the approach is significant because possibly for the first time the unification of Europe becames a goal in itself rather than being only a means towards the greater goal of peace, stability, and prosperity.

The EU has been highly successful in terms of economic integration, and moderately successful in political cooperation over the last 50 years. With the largest enlargement in European history around the corner it was argued that the treaties that have held Europe together over the last 50 years needed to be revised, renewed, or at least simplified in order for the Union to continue to function efficiently and democratically. The Union has governed for the most part of its history without any significant input from its citizens. European leaders in the Council have made the decisions with relatively little interference from public opinion. Elections for the European Parliaments are second order in nature and thus dominated by domestic politics of individual member states rather than European themes. European citizens are relatively isolated from the centre of European Union decision-making in Brussels. With regard to integration, European leaders have long been aware of a gap between the progress that has been made at the elite level, and the lack of understanding, or interest at the mass level.

In 2001, it seemed that the pending enlargement of the Union would be a good opportunity to try a new approach to European integration. Europe was to be reinvented within the context of the twenty-first century. The focus on the new EU would be to bring European institutions closer to their citizens: "The Union needs to be more democratic, more transparent and more efficient" (IbR #4). The EU can become more democratic by increasing the legitimacy of the present institutions. The EU is not per se undemocratic; it lacks legitimacy because it lacks a European *demos*. When citizens can connect to the Union and perceive it as part of and not a threat to their identity, the EU will bolster its legitimacy.

The EU can become more transparent when it makes a clear distinction between three levels of competence: exclusive competence of the Union, competence of member states, and shared competence (IbR #4). Citizens and governments ought to know in which policy areas EU competence trumps national governments and vice versa. Transparency demands that the limits of European competence are set.

Efficiency of the decision-making procedures is important because unanimity becomes more difficult to achieve with an increasing number of member states. The EU becomes more efficient when more decisions can be arrived at through qualified majority voting (IbR #4). However, efficiency also applies to the functioning of the

Commission. The Commission has been growing in size with every new member state that has joined since 1995. There are clearly more member states and candidate members in the EU than there is a need for Commissioners. The EU will function more efficiently when the principle of one state–one commissioner is abandoned. Through improvements in the areas of democracy, transparency, and efficiency, the EU expects to be ready to meet the expectations of its citizens as well as the challenges of the world around it.

From the Constitutional Treaty to the Lisbon Treaty

The Constitutional Convention was the brainchild of the former French President Valerie Giscard d'Estaing. As chair of the convention, together with co-chairs Jean Luc Dehaene and Giuliano Amato, he embarked on the most federal of all European integration projects. The idea of the convention came out of the need for institutional reform in advance of the 2004 enlargement of the union from 15 to 25 member states. For the EU to remain operational with 25 members, it was argued that it needed a new set of rules for arriving at political decisions. The existing rules, based on compromise and with a strong preference for unanimity in decision-making, it was feared, would turn the Union into gridlock with 25 members. The process of rewriting the rules became more ambitious when, under guidance of d'Estaing, it was proposed to unify the existing treaties, the Treaty on the European Union and the Treaty on the European Economic Community, into a single document. This process would not have stirred up any commotion if the resulting treaty had been referred to by any name other than "constitution."

However, the name "constitution" became attached to the unifying treaty, which set in motion a whole set of factors that were unforeseen by the members of the convention. By referring to the unifying treaty as the "European Constitution," the convention marked a shift in European integration from functional or treaty federalism to constitutional federalism. The convention set aside the five-decade-old precedent, referred to as the "Monnet method," as incremental functional integration and boldly assumed that Europe was ready for American-style constitutional federalism as had been promoted by Spinelli and other Euro-federalists in the 1940s and 1950s. As was the case in the 1950s, Europe turned out not to be ready for this momentous change in approach to its integration process. The proof of Europe's inability to change to constitutional federalism came with the ratification process, in which it would become clear how much the signatures of the individual delegates were worth.

Of the 25 nations ratifying the constitutional document, ten decided that the change from separate to a unified treaty constituted such a significant step that it ought to be ratified by referendum in addition to parliamentary vote. The reasons for organizing referendums were as diverse as the outcomes. Four out of ten referendums actually took place, but only two really mattered because of the negative result, which plummeted the union in a significant institutional crisis.[9] The French were the first to reject the Constitutional Treaty in a referendum on May 29, 2005 and the Dutch followed suit only three days later. This chapter is not the place to get into the reasoning behind the French *non* and the Dutch *nee*.[10] The rejection of the Constitutional Treaty by French and Dutch voters set in motion a period of reflection in which the different states were to decide what to do with the constitutional document.

Two decisive groups appeared in the aftermath of the no-votes. The first group, under the leadership of Spain, which successfully ratified the treaty by referendum, referred to itself as "the friends of the constitution" and argued that since a majority of the citizens of the EU had already accepted the treaty, it should be put to a second vote in France and the Netherlands (IbR #6). The second group, under the leadership of the Netherlands, argued that "the constitution is dead," and that the same document would be rejected again in a second referendum. Instead, they argued, a new document should be drafted that does not contain the same federalist language (IbR #7). When opinion polls showed that not only voters in France and the Netherlands but also in the United Kingdom, the Czech Republic, and Poland would reject the same constitution, it became evident that there was only one solution – a new treaty (IbR #7).

Under the German presidency and the energetic leadership of Chancellor Angela Merkel, the period of reflection officially ended and in the spirit of the Treaties of Rome, which celebrate their fiftieth anniversary in March 2007, the Berlin Declaration was signed (IbR #8). The declaration closed with:

> With European unification a dream of earlier generations has become a reality. Our history reminds us that we must protect this for the good of future generations. For that reason we must always renew the political shape of Europe in keeping with the times. That is why today, 50 years after the signing of the Treaties of Rome, we are united in our aim of placing the European Union on a renewed common basis before the European Parliament elections in 2009.

At the June 2007 Council meeting in Brussels, a mandate for an Intergovernmental Conference was agreed upon. In the mandate it was stated that the new "reform" treaty would do away with most of the constitutional terminology. The reform treaty downgraded the Charter of Fundamental Rights to an annex and allowed the United Kingdom and Poland to opt out of it altogether. At the Intergovernmental Conference a draft text for the reform treaty was accepted and would be voted on during the Council meeting in October 2007 in Lisbon, Portugal. The reform treaty

---

9   Spain (February 20, 2005) and Luxembourg (July 10, 2005) had successful referendums.
10 For an analysis of the failed referendums in France and the Netherlands see de Bruyn (2007), Grosskopf (2007), Moravcsik (2006), and Ivaldi (2006).

become known as the Lisbon Treaty and was signed on December 13, 2007 in the Portuguese capital.

The Lisbon Treaty and the Return to Treaty Federalism

With the conclusion of the Nice Treaty and the subsequent Laeken Declaration in 2001, European leaders have opted for a "different approach" to European integration (IbR #4). The difference in approach has been described as a change from treaty or functional federalism to constitutional federalism. The failure to ratify the European Constitutional Treaty in France and the Netherlands has led to a reversal of the new approach and a return to the old method of treaty federalism.

As stated above, federalism has always been an important end goal of European integration. The founders of the EU may have differed in their ideas on what a federal Europe should look like – capitalist for Monnet and socialist for Spinelli – but they agreed that integration was only possible in some kind of federal solution. The return to treaty federalism does not, however, mean that the principles of Laeken were also abandoned. As I discuss below, there are certainly some important differences between the Constitutional Treaty and the Lisbon Treaty, but the goals of democracy, transparency, and efficiency remain in place.[11]

Compared with the Nice Treaty, the Lisbon Treaty clearly represents a deepening of the federal relations within the Union. The European Council will be headed by a president for two and a half years instead of the a six-month rotating presidency (IbR #11 and #15). The lengthening of the term of the presidency will increase the focus of the Union and allow for long-term planning without a particular presidency/state being forced to score at least one short-term success that will mark their six months at the helm of the Union. Where the new presidency can improve domestic affairs within the Union, the new High Representative for Foreign and Security Policy will be able to represent the Union on the international scene. The new High Representative will combine the budgetary and legislative power of the external affairs commissioner with the foreign affairs cloud of the old High Representative (IbR #11 and #15). The hope is that, by uniting these two functions into one foreign affairs chief, the EU will be able to speak with the single voice in international affairs.

The European Commission will be reduced in size to 18 from 27 starting in 2014. This means that two-thirds of the members will deliver a Commissioner for a five-year period. The new Commission is expected to be more effective in decision-making when individual countries will no longer have a guaranteed option to block proposals at the initiation stage (IbR #11 and #15). The new Commission improves its connection with the European public by way of a "citizens' initiative," in which

---

11   The Lisbon Treaty is still a significant step towards a more federal Europe, compared to the Nice Treaty, even if not as significant a step as the Constitutional Treaty.

one million signatures collected allow a public interest organization to petition the Commission to initiate a certain legislative proposal.

The Council will remain the most important decision-making body in the EU. The Council will increase the number of qualified majority voting decisions. From 2014 the new double majority voting system will be used in which proposals will be accepted if they carry the support of 55 percent of the member states and 65 percent of the EU population (IbR #11 and #15). The new voting system is more proportional and gives a fairer share of the voting weights to the more populous member states. A move towards qualified majority voting decision-making in the Council reduces the number of national vetoes. The Council will also meet in public adding a level of transparency to its decision-making process that was previously unavailable. An interesting question that remains to be seen in practice is how the President of the Council and the High Representative will manage their respective competencies without trespassing on each other's territory.

The number of seats to the European Parliament will be set at 750, based on digressive proportionality which leaves the smallest state with six seats and the largest with 96. In a last minute deal, the Italian government was awarded one more Member of European Parliament, which leaves the European Parliament with 750 members plus a non-voting chair (IbR #15). The Parliament will increase its budgetary power by the removal of the distinction between compulsory and non-compulsory expenditure. With the increase in areas of competence the Parliament is becoming more similar to a legislature in any of the Union members states.

The national parliaments of the member states will be more closely involved in the EU decision-making process. The period in which a national parliament can examine community legislative acts has been extended from six (under the Constitutional Treaty) to eight weeks (under Lisbon). Furthermore, the national parliaments have received a control measure for subsidiarity in the form of a yellow card (IbR #15). A majority of national parliaments can present an opinion to the Council or European Parliament with support from 55 percent of the member states or Members of European Parliament. That the card is yellow and not red means that the national parliaments cannot block a measure, but they can ask for redress.

The *Charter of Fundamental Rights* is not included in the full text of the Lisbon Treaty. Even so, UK and Poland have claimed an opt-out from the Charter. The UK government is afraid that the Charter will alter British labor laws, while the Polish government does not agree with some of the social provisions in the Charter. Even though Poland elected Donald Tusk as new Prime Minister in October 2007, the new government did not change the Polish position (IrB #14 and #15).

Lastly, there are no references to the symbols of the EU, such as the flag, anthem, or the motto (IrB #15). This does not mean that these symbols will be discontinued; however they will not receive formal status in the treaty. There is also no reference to "an ever closer union." The most important difference between the Constitutional Treaty and the Lisbon Treaty is that the latter is not a constitutional document. The Lisbon Treaty amends the existing legal order rather than creating a new one. The Lisbon Treaty combines the Treaty on the European Union (Maastricht

Treaty) with the Treaty on the Functioning of the European Union (Rome Treaty). The non-constitutional nature of the Lisbon Treaty is important because as such it allows states to ratify the treaty by simple majority vote in Parliament instead of having to risk another referendum. The Lisbon Treaty does not differ fundamentally from the Constitutional Treaty with the few exceptions outlined above. The major differences are symbolic in that there will not be one constitutional document for Europe, the High Representative is not able to assume the title of Foreign Minister, and the symbols of the Union are not granted a formal status.[12]

The Future of European Federalism

> *It is quite possible however that the Constitution, once approved by governments, will not come into force due to problems of ratification. If that should be the case, I would expect the confederal model to emerge even without the Constitution.*
>
> Alberta Sbragia, 2004

Sbragia was correct in her prediction of the success of the European Constitution on two counts: (1) she correctly predicted problems of ratification, and (2) she correctly predicted that these problems would not derail European federalism. Even though the membership of the EU has increased to 27, without a constitution the Union is functioning very well. Since the start of 2008 the Euro-area has been increased to 15 member states, and Schengen now includes all states in central and Eastern Europe, except Romania and Bulgaria.

The July 2007 Intergovernmental Conference set up a strict mandate in advance of the October Lisbon Council meeting. While most actors involved were relieved to be able to reach a compromise, different institutions within the Union drew different conclusions based on their reading of the mandate. The Council Presidency conclusions highlight the fact that the reform treaty will not have a constitutional character. It specifies that "the Union shall act *only* within the limits of competences conferred upon it by the member states in the Treaties" (IbR #11, #20 fn. 10a). It further emphasizes that "competences not conferred upon the Union in the Treaties remain with the member states" (IbR #11, #20 fn. 10a). By focusing on competences, the Council highlighted its concern for transparency and efficiency in Europe.

The European Parliament by voice of its Constitutional Affairs Committee focused its comments on the issue of democracy and European identity instead. The European Parliamentary Constitutional Affairs Committee and its chairman

---

12 On the initiative of Germany 16 states signed a non-binding annex to the treaty in which they declared their allegiance to the symbols of the Union. The other states in support of the flag, anthem, and motto are Austria, Belgium, Bulgaria, Cyprus, Greece, Hungary, Italy, Lithuania, Luxembourg, Malta, Portugal, Romania, Slovenia, Slovakia, and Spain.

Jo Leinen express a sign of relief that the substance of the Constitutional Treaty has been salvaged (IbR #9). It also praises the language of a common approach on energy policy and climate change. At the same time, however, it "deplores" the loss of the official Union symbols, such as the flag and the anthem, and the increased number of exemptions granted to member states (IbR #9). The *Charter of Fundamental Rights* has also been relegated to a separate set of declarations. In unusually strong wording, the Committee states: "if one or more member states now claim an opt-out from the Charter of Fundamental Rights, this would represent a dramatic setback and cause serious damage to the EU's innermost sense of identity" (IbR #10). The President of the European Commission, Jose Manuel Barroso, also stated that he feels "frustrated with the number of opt-outs" (IbR #3 and #2).

The distinction between the intergovernmentalist Council and the supranationalist European Parliament cannot be expressed more clearly. Where the Council focuses on the non-constitutional character of the Reform Treaty, the European Parliamentary Constitutional Affairs Committee celebrates the fact that the European Constitutional Treaty has been salvaged. The Council further stresses transparency issues, such as the limitations put on the Union by the member states, while the European Parliamentary Constitutional Affairs Committee deplores the lack of a symbolic identity of the Union and foresees more serious problems, if in fact multiple states claim exemptions from the *Charter of Fundamental Rights*. The European Parliament, in a reaction to the dropping of the official symbols, has decided they would make more frequent use of them.

The death of the Constitutional project has also laid the ideal of a federal Europe to rest. In Lisbon Europe has ended it experiment with constitutional federalism and made it clear that a federation, *à la* the United States of Europe, is no longer its envisioned end goal. The experiment with constitutional federalism has not only shut the door on Philadelphia-style conventions but also on federation-style solutions to European integration. The EU will not transform into a *Gemeinschaft*, but will instead remain a managed *Gesellschaft* on a confederal basis (Chryssochoou 2000, 216). This means that in the EU transparency and efficiency will take precedence over democracy. It is ironic that just as scholars such as Duchacek (1982), Elazar (1998 and 2001), Sbragia (2004), and Hueglin (2000) were debating the unique nature of European treaty federalism, and the benefits of the confederal arrangements, the EU engaged in an experiment with constitutional federalism. Now that the Union has returned from its voyage into federation the arguments from the aforementioned scholars are all the more salient. Spinelli was only half right when he argued that the Monnet method would make a truly federal European Union impossible. He was right in that functional federalism will not be able to forge a constitutional arrangement or create a European *demos*. However, Spinelli underestimated the power of functional linkages to establish a working confederal system, based on national elites and consensual democracy.

References

Burgess, Michael (2004), Federalism, in Antje Wiener and Thomas Diez (eds), *European Integration Theory*. (Oxford: Oxford University Press).

Chryssochoou, Dimitris, N. (2000), *Democracy in the European Union*. (London and New York: I.B. Tauris Publishers).

De Bruyn, Martyn (2007), The EU Constitution defeated by referendum: an analysis of *non* and *nee*. Paper presented at the International Studies Association Annual Meeting, Chicago, IL.

Duchacek, Ivo, D. (1982), Consociations of fatherlands: the revival of confederal principles and practices, *Publius: The Journal of Federalism* 12:4, 129–177.

Elazar, Daniel J. (1997), Contrasting unitary and federal systems, *International Political Science Review* 18:3, 237–251.

— (1998), *Constitutionalizing Globalization: The Postmodern Revival of Confederal Arrangements* (Lanham: Rowman and Littlefield Publishers).

— (2001), The United States and the European Union: models for their epochs, in Kalypso Nicolaidis and Robert Howse (eds), *The Federal Vision: Legitimacy and Levels of Governance in the United States and the European Union* (Oxford: Oxford University Press).

Ginsburg, Roy, H. (2007), *Demystifying the European Union: The Enduring Logic of Regional Integration* (Lanham: Rowman and Littlefield Publishers).

Grosskopf, Anke (2007), Why "non" and "nee" to the EU Constitution? Reconsidering the shock of the Dutch and French referenda. Paper presented at the European Union Studies Association Biennial International Conference, Montreal, Canada.

Haas, Ernst B. (2004), *The Uniting of Europe: Political, Social, and Economic Forces 1950–1957* (Notre Dame: Notre Dame University Press).

Hooghe, Liesbet, and Gary Marks (2003), Unraveling the central state, but how? Types of multi-level governance, *American Political Science Review* 97:2, 233–243.

Hueglin, Thomas O. (2000), From constitutional to treaty federalism: a comparative perspective, *Publius: The Journal of Federalism* 30:4, 137–153.

Ivaldi, Gilles (2006), Beyond France's 2005 referendum on the European Constitutional Treaty: second-order model, anti-establishments attitudes and the end of the alternative European utopia, *West European Politics* 29:1, 47–69.

King, Preston (1982), *Federalism and Federation* (Baltimore: Johns Hopkins University Press).

Mitrany, David (1966), *A Working Peace System* (Chicago: Quadrangle Books).

Moravcsik, Andrew (2006), What can we learn from the collapse of the European constitutional project? *Politische Vierteljahresschrift* 47:2, 219–241.

Sbragia, Alberta (2004), The future of federalism in the European Union. Keynote address delivered at the European Community Studies Association Canada, Montreal Canada, May 27–29, 2004.

Volcansek, Mary, L. (2008), Judicially crafted federalism: EU and USA, *EUSA Review* 21:1, 23–31.

Internet-based References (IbR)

#1 Spinelli, Altiero and Ernesto Rossi. "Ventotene Manifesto," <http://www.federalunion. org.uk/archives/ventotene.shtml> Accessed January 5, 2007.

#2 Schuman, Robert. "Declaration of 9 May 1950", <http://europa.eu/abc/symbols/9-may/decl_en.htm> Accessed January 5, 2007.

#3 Barroso, José Manuel Durão, President of the European Commission. "The European Union after the Lisbon Treaty", 4th Joint Parliamentary meeting on the Future of Europe, Brussels, December 4, 2007. <http://europa.eu/rapid/pressReleasesAction.do? reference=SPEECH/07/793&format=HTML&aged=0&language=EN&guiLanguage=en> (European Union Homepage), Accessed January 15, 2008.

#4 Laeken Declaration on the Future of the European Union, "European Council Declarations, December 2001." <http://european-convention.eu.int/pdf/LKNEN.pdf> Accessed December 12, 2008.

#5 "Treaty of Nice: Declaration on the Future of the Union." <http://europa.eu/eur-lex/en/treaties/dat/C_2001080EN.007001.html> Accessed December 12, 2007.

#6 EurActive.com, "Friends of the Constitution want maxi-EU treaty," <http://www euractiv.com/en/future-eu/friends-constitution-want-maxi-eu-treaty/article-161233> Accessed January 12, 2008.

#7 Rennie, David. "EU Constitution is dead, says Dutch Minister," Telegraph.co.uk, <http://www.telegraph.co.uk/news/main.jhtml?xml=/news/2006/01/12/weu12.xml&sSheet=/news/2006/01/12/ixworld.html> Accessed January 14, 2006.

#8 "Declaration on the occasion of the fiftieth anniversary of the signature of the Treaties of Rome. Germany, March 25, 2007 Presidency of the European Union," <http://www.eu2007.de/de/News/download_docs/Maerz/0324-RAA/English.pdf>, Accessed March 25, 2007.

#9 "Report on the Roadmap for the Union's Constitutional Process (A6-0197/2007), Committee on Constitutional Affairs, European Parliament. May 22, 2007," <http://www.europarl.europa.eu/sides/getDoc.do?Type=REPORT&Reference=A6-2007-0197&language=EN> Accessed July 23, 2007.

#10 "Report on the convening of the Intergovernmental Conference (IGC): the European Parliaments opinion (A6-0279/2007), Committee on Constitutional Affairs, European Parliament. July 9, 2007," <http://www.europarl.europa.eu/sides/getDoc.do?type=REPORT&mode=XML&reference=A6-2007-0279&language=EN> Accessed July 23, 2007.

#11 Council of the European Union, Brussels European Council, June 21–22, 2007, Presidency Conclusions (11177/07), <http://www.consilium.europa.eu/ueDocs/cms_Data/docs/pressData/en/ec/94932.pdf > Accessed June 24, 2007.

#12 Treaty of Lisbon (OJ C306), December 17, 2007, <http://www.consilium.europa.eu /cms3_fo/showPage.asp?id=1296&lang=en> Accessed January 12, 2008.

#13 BBC News, "A close look at the reform treaty," <http://news.bbc.co.uk/2/hi/europe/6928737.stm> Accessed August 7, 2007.

#14 BBC News, "Q&A: The Reform Treaty," <http://news.bbc.co.uk/2/hi/europe/6901353.stm> Accessed July 23, 2007.

#15 BBC News, "Q&A: The Lisbon Treaty," <http://news.bbc.co.uk/2/hi/europe/6901353.stm> Accessed December 13, 2007.

#16 Hans, Barbara. "Spiegel Online, The Lisbon Coup," <http://www.spiegel.de/international/europe/ 0,1518,512446,00.html> Accessed October 19, 2007.

Further Reading

Dinan, Desmond (2006), Governance and c of the Constitutional Treaty, *Journal of Common Market Studies* 44, Supplement, 63–80.

Dosenrode, Søren (ed.) (2007), *Approaching the European Federation?* (Burlington: Ashgate).

Elazar, Daniel J. (1987), *Exploring Federalism* (Tuscaloosa: University of Alabama Press).

—— (1995), From statism to federalism: a paradigm shift, *Publius: The Journal of Federalism* 25:5, 5–18.

Maas, Willem (2007), *Creating European Citizens* (Lanham: Rowman and Littlefield Publishers).

Nicolaidis, Kalypso and Robert Howse (eds) (2001), *The Federal Vision: Legitimacy and Levels of Governance in the United States and the European Union* (Oxford: Oxford University Press).

Schmidt, Vivien, A. (2006), *Democracy in Europe: The EU and National Polities* (Oxford: Oxford University Press).

PART 5
CONTEMPORARY THEORIES OF FEDERALISM

Introduction to Part 5

Glenn A. Moots, in Chapter 22, analyzes Daniel J. Elazar's federalism in light of his covenantal political theory. Moots argues that Elazar rooted political federalism in the Latin *foedus*, a term parallel with the Hebrew word for covenant, and believed that the covenantal tradition was the most ancient of the West's political traditions. Political covenanting, according to Elazar, has two forms. Orthodox covenanting, originating in Hebrew scripture and revived during the Reformation, is explicitly theological and emphasizes God as a participant in the covenant. Weaker, more modern covenanting is not explicitly theological and, while emphasizing morality or community, may lack a divine component. Moreover, Elazar distinguishes between covenants, compacts, and contracts. Covenants include the belief that God is both a party to and guarantor of the terms of the covenant. Compacts, in which most modern constitutions are grounded, are no longer made with God but "under God." Contracts, on the other hand, are strictly private and legal in nature, lacking any emphasis on morality for their members or a divine component as a party or guarantor.

Moots argues that for Elazar, covenants, compacts, and contracts all seek liberty for their members. However, contracts emphasize a secular and individualist concept of liberty – the freedom to do as one wants – whereas covenants emphasize a communal and religious concept of liberty – the freedom to do good. Covenantal liberty, according to Elazar, must be understood as *federal liberty* and not the *natural liberty* pursued by contracts. The explicitly divine and moral dimensions of covenantal political theory qualifies it, Elazar claims, as a "political theology," and modern federalism, as a descendent of this political theology, is more than just a legal device as it requires adherence to a particular moral *ethos*. Federal arrangements in which power is distributed among the general government and the constituent governments such that shared rule is combined with self-rule, is more than simply a device to achieve other ends. Rather, federalism and its distribution of power is regarded as an end in itself, as desirable *for its own sake*. Federalism is thus an architectonic goal that embodies the moral principles of justice, liberty under law, citizen participation, and a less than absolute equality moderated by the concern for freedom and community. Moots concludes by reflecting on Elazar's thesis that America, especially the American city, is the paradigm for federalism in the modern context, and on his vision of supra-national federal solutions for persistent ethnic, linguistic, and racial conflicts in an increasingly globalized world.

In Chapter 23, Benjamin Kleinerman explores William Riker's understanding of federalism in light of Riker's turn to and development of rational choice theory. In his first and most important book on federalism, Riker, Kleinerman argues, attempts to refute two previous approaches to federalism. First, the "ideological" approach that maintained that federalism guarantees freedom, and second, the "reductionist" approach that held that certain social and economic conditions of a population allow for the rise of the federal form. Riker rejects both the "ideological" and "reductionist" claims because they ignore the political act of bargaining at the origin of the federal system. For Riker, the conditions necessary for the "bargain of federalism" to be made are essentially military; the fear of some politicians of an external military threat and the desire of others to expand their territory without conquest, leads to the political decision to adopt the federal structure. Riker therefore interprets the United States Constitution as arising from a military bargain between the separate states. The security concerns of the states, including those in the South, led them to accept a far greater degree of centralization under the national government than they would have otherwise. Thus, the federal system in the United States did not originate in the normative commitment to freedom that federalism is supposed to preserve, but is rather the product of the realist perspective of political actors pursuing what they believed was necessary for their survival. Riker goes so far as to reject any normative value to American federalism because of what he believes is its association with Southern white racists. In the United States, according to Riker, federalism does not preserve freedom but rather the dominance of the white majority over the black minority in the Southern states.

Kleinerman takes issue, however, with Riker's exclusion of the normative commitment to freedom as an explanation of the origin and continuation of federal systems. For instance, once the conditions of an external military threat or "provincial patriotism" disappear, Kleinerman asks what can explain the continuation of the federal system in the face of the dual challenges of secession and excessive centralization? Specifically, Kleinerman points to Riker's perplexity at why the Australians "bother" with federalism in absence of external threats or an explicit preference for local self-government. Kleinerman argues that Riker's initial explanation for the persistence of federalism is not the constitutional structure of the federal state or the benefits of the division and sharing of administrative responsibilities, but rather the degree of internal dissension within political parties that operate in federal systems. With highly fractious political parties, a single political party could control both levels of government but still produce dissension between state and national governments, as political actors, losing contests at higher levels of government, may find it useful to win at lower levels. Thus, although Riker points to a "political" explanation for the maintenance of federalism, Kleinerman argues that Riker will not take the next step of admitting the force of political ideas such as the value of freedom in shaping political choices. Thus, for Kleinerman, although Riker's account of federalism, influenced by his theory of rational-choice,

INTRODUCTION TO PART 5

usefully injects a dose of political realism that was missing in the administrative and economic accounts that preceded it, it still remains "reductionist" insofar as it reduces political choice to unconscious or unarticulated motivations like security concerns or the desire for power, rather than political ideas or normative commitments. Noting that Riker contradicts himself in his later work on federalism, Kleinerman concludes that Riker's theory is deficient because rational choice seeks overly simplistic explanations for political behavior. Thus, since the role of ideas in politics such as commitment to freedom which leads to federalism being valued as an end in itself, is necessarily complex, ideas must be excluded as an explanatory variable.

Alberto Majocchi, in Chapter 24, discusses the distinctive European experience of fiscal federalism in light of both classical and more contemporary theories of fiscal federalism. According to Majocchi, the classical model of fiscal federalism stipulates that in order to achieve optimal economic efficiency and maximize social welfare, economic functions should be assigned to different levels of government. The central government should be responsible for macroeconomic stabilization policy, and for income redistribution and the provision of goods and services consumed by the entire population of the state. Local governments should be responsible for the provision of goods and services whose consumption is limited to their own populations. The classical model assumes that income redistribution should be centralized as high income tax rates imposed by local government, due to the mobility of persons within a federal system, would precipitate the outflow of capital and high-income residents from the regions or localities they govern. Yet the classical model also assumes that goods and services consumed locally should be localized on the principle that those who enjoy the benefits of such public goods should be responsible for their costs. Local governments should cover such costs by relying mainly on property taxation and user fees, but this does not exclude reliance on equalization payments in which revenue is transferred from the center to the locality either through conditional or unconditional grants from the central government. Evidence showing that regional and local taxes are typically more regressive than central ones justifies the collection of national taxes and their redistribution to lower tiers of government, as well as the need to close the gap between richer and poorer jurisdictions.

A different theory of fiscal federalism, Majocchi argues, has recently been articulated to challenge the classical model. According to this new "public choice approach" to fiscal federalism, the main goal of the federal structure is to maximize the revenues extracted from the economy through a decentralized system that encourages economic competition between the localities. Inter-locality competition requires the transfer of the responsibility for and provision of public goods and services from the center to the localities, which also entails the limitation of jurisdictional equalization through central government grants. The competition imposes fiscal restraint on the public sector by restricting the expansionary tendencies of central governments and bringing both sets of decision-makers under greater public control. The citizens of one jurisdiction are encouraged to assess the performance of their government by comparing it to the performance of governments in other jurisdictions in terms of quality of services and levels of taxation. Such comparisons will induce local governments to behave as well as or better than the others to prevent outflow of capital and residents.

Majocchi argues that the European experience with fiscal federalism must be understood in light of two ongoing and simultaneous institutional changes: the upward transfer of powers from member-states to the European Union, and the downward devolution of powers within member-states from central to local governments. Thus, at the member-state or national level, the "public choice approach" to fiscal federalism is becoming predominant. According to Majocchi, this is problematic as the Treaty of Maastricht, in order to prevent excessive deficits in the member-states of the Monetary Union, sets explicit limits on the gap that can exist between government revenues and expenditures, a gap Majocchi suggests the competitive model only has a tendency to widen. At the European level, however, the Union does and should, according to Majocchi, aspire to function along the classical model of fiscal federalism. Yet the European Union contradicts the classical model in two important respects. First, responsibility for redistribution policy currently remains with the national (local) level, and not with the Union (central) level. Second, macroeconomic stabilization policy with the exception of monetary policy is also predominantly assigned to the national level rather than the Union. Thus, despite its aspirations otherwise, the European Union, like its member-states, also has a tendency to adhere to the more recent public choice approach to fiscal federalism. Majocchi concludes that therefore there is little justification for the fears of Euroskeptics that monetary union and the ensuing institutional developments such as a new EU Constitution will generate a new, strongly centralized European state. The Europe that will come into being will be federal in nature.

In Chapter 25, Gregory Marchildon argues that the rise of historically and territorially defined national minorities seeking self-determination has given rise to the practice of "post-modern" federalism. Post-modern federations attempt to reconcile unity with diversity within a peaceful, democratic political compromise that offers an alternative to violent conflict, secession, and partition. Unlike the classical federation, which tends to adhere to its originating principles as reflected in its constitution or formative documents, post-modern federations will often contradict their explicitly stated principles. Thus, in their operation, whereas classical federations are closer to what they say they are, post-modern federations are often not what they say they are; for instance, a centralized constitution may belie a decentralized reality or a formal unitary state may evolve into an informal federation. This distinction between theory and practice, Marchildon argues, goes to the heart of what post-modern federations are. Post-modern federations are defined by a constructive ambiguity or "silence of constitutions" that conceals what they actually are in order to avoid internal conflict.

Marchildon argues that consideration of the most prosperous post-modern federations such as Canada, Belgium, Spain, and the United Kingdom, in light of the wealthiest classical federations such as the United States, Switzerland, Australia, and Germany, brings to light five key characteristics of the post-modern federation. First, post-modern federations are currently undergoing rapid devolution and decentralization. Second, they reflect a high degree of formal and informal asymmetry between the sub-states. Third, they protect and promote key minority language rights. Fourth, regionally based nationalist political parties tend to supplant ideologically oriented pan-national political parties. Fifth, post-modern federations are in a continuous negotiation and struggle to construct alternatives to secession, partition, and violence. Marchildon concludes that post-modern federalism is a critique of Enlightenment universals, and suggests that post-modern federations must do without universal principles. Moreover, Marchildon argues that although the survival of such states relative to the large number of secessions in other parts of the world since the late 1980s suggests the political success of post-modern federations, such states are highly complex, contradictory, and ultimately only temporary solutions to the increasing desire for greater ethno-linguistic autonomy.

The Covenant Tradition of Federalism: The Pioneering Studies of Daniel J. Elazar

Glenn A. Moots

Introduction: The Legacy of Daniel J. Elazar

This chapter addresses Daniel J. Elazar (1934–1999), who both revived the theory of political "covenants" and also provided extensive scholarship on federalism. Elazar's theory of federalism is largely informed by his covenantal political theory, so the two shall each be given considerable attention in this chapter. Elazar also wrote extensively on comparative political systems, Jewish political thought, American politics, the politics of modern Israel, and political culture. Most of this was motivated by his theory of federalism, an idea he described as both cause and effect.

Elazar also provided counsel on active questions of federalism, including service as a consultant to governments of Israel, the United States, Spain, Canada, Italy, Cyprus, and South Africa. He directed an impressive number of colloquia, conferences, and publishing projects on federalism and covenanting. Included in Elazar's important record is the ongoing work of *Publius*, the premier academic journal on federalism. Elazar's legacy is also preserved in two organizations that he founded: the Center for the Study of Federalism at Temple University and the Jerusalem Center for Public Affairs. The former has now closed, though archived material is available. These organizations were important to the international study of federalism, led by the International Association of Centers for Federal Studies (IACFS), the Research Committee on Comparative Federalism and Federation of the International Political Science Association (IPSA) and the Forum of Federations.

Elazar rooted political federalism in the Latin *foedus*, a term often used parallel with the Hebrew word for covenant, *berith* or *b'rit*. Under federal arrangements, Elazar argues, parties bind themselves together to new unions or unities but always with the goal of preserving their own respective integrities. Elazar did not see the covenantal tradition as merely a subset of political theory, or simply a historical political theology. Rather, Elazar saw it as the most ancient of the West's great political traditions, holding it to be essentially superior to all other major political arrangements. Elazar traced the historical development of modern federal and covenantal politics into what he considered golden eras of political federalism and covenantal theory: the Protestant Reformation, with its renewed emphasis on the Hebrew model; and the American Constitution, which Elazar considered the vehicle for introducing modern federalism to the world.

Linking federalism to the work of other contemporary scholars (such as Lijphart's consociationalism), Elazar presented the federal/covenantal approach as a model for the future. Elazar explicitly prescribed federal arrangements and analysis for Yugoslavia, the European Union, Canada, the former Soviet Union, and Israel and Palestine. As ethnic identities have become more pronounced, Elazar saw federalism as an alternative to secession or antagonistic identity politics. As the modern nation-state system evolves at the regional or world level into something more cooperative, Elazar argued that only federal arrangements could solve the tension between self-rule and shared rule.

Although Elazar's extensive material is often redundant, it resists comprehensive summary or critique in a short chapter. Nevertheless, some insight can be provided. This will include the historical and theological roots of Elazar's studies, his broad definition of federalism, application to contemporary situations, his study of American federalism, and a sampling of apparent difficulties in his presentation.

Covenantal Politics as the Background to Federalism

Elazar contrasts political covenanting, classified as strong or weak, with organic or hierarchical political arrangements or those founded on conquest. Elazar also distinguishes covenanting from arrangements founded on natural law or natural right, though modern federalism (and modern constitutionalism, the descendant of historical covenanting) is not entirely exclusive of natural law or natural right (Elazar 1995, 35–51).

Elazar argues that political covenanting, among all political arrangements, is best able to fulfill political goals of liberty, equality, and justice. Elazar's studies present an entire history of covenanting, beginning with the Hebrew peoples and extending into contemporary pseudo-covenants, treaties, and trade agreements (Elazar 1998b, 101–159). He pays particular attention to both the biblical record and the most recent period of explicit and orthodox covenanting, the Protestant Reformation.

Elazar argues that while orthodox (strong) political covenanting is no longer practiced, weaker forms of political covenanting remain. Weaker forms, he argues, are evident in modern constitutionalism or theories of social contracting. Orthodox political covenanting is distinguished by an explicit theological emphasis and the assertion that God is a participant in the covenant. Weaker political covenanting may emphasize morality or community, but it lacks the explicit theological and divine component.

As we will see, Elazar's distinctions between "strong" and "weak" political covenanting raise important questions, particularly with the rise of both pluralism and explicitly secular articulations of political theory. Given the intensely religious content evident in historical political covenanting, can one even speak of an *evolving* "covenant" at all? At what point in the "evolution" of political covenanting does covenanting cease having as essential resemblance to its original articulations? What does that mean for Elazar's argument that modern federalism, particularly constitutional federalism, owes its origins to Hebrew scriptures and their political revival during the Reformation? While such problems may be detrimental for Elazar's historical argument, it has only a somewhat deleterious effect on his theoretical presentation of modern federalism.

To understand Elazar's presentation of covenanting, it is important to begin with his taxonomy of sources for modern constitutionalism. Elazar distinguishes common terms from the early history of Anglo-American constitutionalism: covenant, compact, and contract. Each, strictly considered, represents a different kind of political agreement. *Covenants* and *compacts* are presented as historically more prevalent than *contracts* and are more constitutional or public in character. Both covenant and compact are described by Elazar to include an explicit public and moral dimension.

As reciprocal instruments, covenants, and compacts bind their parties "beyond the letter of the law." By contrast, what Elazar means by "contracts" is more akin to a private device rather than the public documents that political theorists allude to when they generalize the foundations of constitutionalism as beholden to social *contract* theory. Contracts are distinguished primarily by their private and strictly legal nature (Elazar 1995, 30–32). As defined by Elazar they do not emphasize morality for their members beyond legal and minimal moral reciprocity.

Covenants, even more so than compacts, introduce a morally binding dimension above the legal dimension (Elazar 1998c, 249). Covenants are also distinguished from compacts and contracts by the belief that God is a guarantor of, or a direct party to, the relationship between parties in the covenant. Compacts, though more akin to covenants than contracts, do not explicitly include a divinely transcendent dimension and instead rely on mutual pledges and a secular legal grounding. Most modern constitutions, Elazar writes, are no longer made with God but instead "under God" (Elazar 1998c, 5). In this respect they are more like compacts than covenants.

Covenants, compacts, and contracts all seek liberty for their members, but each articulates a different relationship between liberty and morality. At the one extreme, covenantal liberty has a strong and binding communal nature, particularly under divine law. At the other extreme, contracts tend to emphasize positive law and individualistic notions of liberty. Elazar contrasts covenantal and contractual liberty thus:

> *Covenantal liberty is not simply the right to do as one pleases, within broad boundaries. Contractual liberty could be just that but covenantal liberty emphasizes the liberty to pursue the moral purposes for which the covenant was made. This latter kind of liberty requires that moral distinctions be drawn and that human actions be judged according to the terms of the covenant (Elazar 1998c, 43).*

A wider spectrum of moral license, pluralism, and tolerance is consistent with the more secular nature of contracts. Elazar argues that these two features of contracts, secularism and individualistic freedom, make it difficult for contracts to command moral unity or coherence.

This point about moral obligations is important for understanding Elazar's presentation of federalism as both a legal and ethical concept. While federalism (as a descendant of covenanting) is a legal device that protects the rights and integrity of parties to the covenant, it requires adherence to a particular *ethos*. It is this ethos which enables respect for subscribing partners to the federal arrangement and protects against encroachments on the federal agreement.

The way in which these three devices (covenant, compact, and contract) parallel, intersect, intertwine, or dominate one another has important political consequences. Each approaches the moral and legal bases of society differently and thus results in a different political theory. Covenants, compacts, and contracts resolve the tensions of political life uniquely. These tensions might include, but are not limited to: a society's conception of rights; distribution of power; the proper demands of community; and the appropriate extent of individualism. The most individualistic and secular concept is "contract" and the most communal and religious is "covenant." The contrasts between contract and covenant cannot be studied merely on a conceptual or idealistic basis. Instead, they must be studied through the experience of a particular historical reality. For Elazar that historical reality is best found in seventeenth and eighteenth century Britain and America (Elazar 1996, 60–69). Whereas modern scholars are tempted to yoke variations of consent together and look at them "backward" through the lens of liberal theory, Elazar is looking "ahead" to modern political (especially federal and constitutional) arrangements through the lens of ancient or early modern historical experience and its theological articulation.

While Elazar is on to something very valuable in theoretical terms, the precise interpretive application of this taxonomy is probably somewhat limited. It is more valuable as a theoretical tool than a means of interpreting historical documents. The test of Elazar's taxonomy, especially if one is going to use it as a tool for developing an historical theory of constitutional federalism, is whether or not his historical subjects can be said to conform to his strict categorization. If that cannot be established, and in many cases it probably cannot, the historical application would be quite limited. One cannot safely come to a particular document and impose Elazar's definition on an author's choice of "compact" over "covenant" and determine that the intent was to avoid theological significance, for example.[1] Nevertheless, the theoretical distinctions might still hold, and Elazar's work remains helpful for understanding the role of morality in federal arrangements.

Having presented Elazar's taxonomy, we now focus more closely on the consequences of a covenant for political theory and constitutionalism and federalism in particular. Elazar sees political covenanting serving three important functions which contrast it primarily with hierarchical or organic political orientations: a form of political conceptualization and mode of political expression; a source of political ideology; and a factor shaping political culture, institutions, and behavior (Elazar 1995, 35–52).

Political covenanting, Elazar argues, is unique in its reconciliation of two goals of political order: power and justice. Its conclusions and consequences are different from other types of political organization (Elazar 1995, 2–3). That reconciliation is enabled by unique political and social traditions (Elazar 1996, 6–7). A covenant is therefore more than an institutional or legal formulation. It becomes a political and social worldview (Elazar 1995, 20). Without this worldview, Elazar argues, certain institutional dimensions of constitutionalism cannot succeed. This includes the separation of powers, limited government, a jury system, and true federalism (Elazar 1995, 21).[2]

Throughout his work, Elazar uses variations of the same definition of a covenant. Following is the definition given in the first volume of his landmark work on covenanting as a political tradition:

> [A] *morally informed agreement or pact based upon voluntary consent, established by mutual oaths or promises, involving or witnessed by some transcendent higher authority, between peoples or parties having independent status, equal in connection with the purposes of the pact, that provides for joint action or obligation to achieve defined ends (limited or comprehensive) under conditions of mutual respect, which protect the individual integrities of all the parties to it.* Every covenant involves consenting (in both senses of thinking together and agreeing) and promising. Most are meant to be of limited duration, if not perpetual. Covenants can bind any number of parties for a variety of purposes but in their essence they are political in that their bonds are used principally to establish bodies political and social (Elazar 1995, 23). (Emphasis added.)

---

[1] In the case of Hobbes, for example, one could not presume that the use of the term "covenant" in *Leviathan* is intended to signify a political agreement of traditional moral and theological significance. Another example is the American Puritans, whom one would expect to conform to Elazar's taxonomy. But their civil covenants in New England do not demonstrate this. See Weir (2005).

[2] Elazar applies this to the Latin American experience and it is interesting to compare his argument with Juan Linz's for example. See also Elazar 1998b, 235.

These attributes are important politically insofar as they "establish lines of authority, distributions of power, bodies politic and systems of law ... legitimize political life and direct it into the right paths" (Elazar 1995, 1; 1998c, 101–102). The divine party to the covenant is the key to establishing the aforementioned guidelines, though Elazar also seems to think that the moral consequence resulting from divine participation may be more significant than the divine party itself.

The transcendent power subscribing to this covenant, or at least the morality binding thereby, obligates human freedom to be understood as *federal liberty* and not *natural liberty* (Elazar 1998c, 26–27; 1995, 43; Winthrop 1645). This conception of "federal liberty" is essential to understanding how Elazar presents federalism as a social (and personal) ethos as much as it is a legal and political institution. Federalism, rightly understood, is a moral commitment that preserves political community and the integrity of its members. *Federal liberty* emphasizes freedom only within the boundaries of community and moral responsibility. *Natural liberty*, by contrast, neither emphasizes nor obligates community or moral responsibility. Elazar writes, "The omnipotent Deity, by freely covenanting with man, limits His own powers to allow humans space in which to be free, only requiring of them that they live in accordance with the law established as normative by the covenant" (Elazar 1995, 43). Federal liberty calls all partners to public and private adherence to both social norms and divine moral prescriptions (Elazar 1996, 233–234). This binds the community together and transcends what may otherwise be only minimal moral obligations prescribed by legal, contractual, or private agreements.

The task of the civil magistrate under a traditional and orthodox (strong) covenant is to lead by example in fulfilling its ethical and political terms. They are to implement justice and mercy (as defined by the Deity), protect virtue against vice, and appropriately guarding against heresy. Without moral reformation, Elazar argues, no true covenant is possible. This explicit moral dimension, Elazar argues, qualifies covenantal political theory as a "political theology" (Elazar 1998c, 250).[3]

Whereas contemporary scholars, looking backward through the lens of liberal theory, might view such a broad charge as an invitation to unlimited civil power and the abuse of natural rights, Elazar sees it in quite opposite terms. He argues that covenants limit the authority of civil magistrates by defining boundaries for the use of power and by giving other civil magistrates within a federal system a common moral standard for resisting the abuse of power. Unlike other theories of political origin, there is a clear resistance theory inherent in covenantal political theory (Elazar 1996, 79). The people, or their appointed "lesser magistrates," may remove a ruler by force of arms (Elazar 1996, 247). Thus, in Elazar's study, the idea of constitutional or limited government is derived from the idea of covenants (Elazar 1995, 2).

---

3   This is a term that Elazar intends only for purposes of categorization. Although Elazar generally subscribes to Strauss's argument that revelation (as opposed to reason) is an exclusive concept, he does not mean it here as a term of exclusivity. Nor does he mean it in any way approaching Carl Schmitt's concept of "political theology," let alone Schmitt's idea of federalism.

Elazar presents constitutionalism, especially insofar as it limits civil authority, as the modern outgrowth of both medieval commonwealth theory and covenantalism. From these pre-modern and modern foundations of commonwealth and covenant came the idea of "civil society" (Elazar 1998c, xi). Elazar calls constitutionalism "a modern reinterpretation of the covenantal tradition that gave it flesh and blood and enabled it to become the instrument of liberty, equality, justice and democracy that it did" (Elazar 1998c, 5). Elazar sees a centuries-long intertwining of "covenant, natural law, and constitutionalism." This is particularly true in the case of America and other truly constitutional modern nations.

Judging the constitutional propriety of legislation, Elazar argues, is an idea rooted in both natural law and the covenant device. Testing constitutionality, Elazar argues, is the modern secular version of testing what the covenantal tradition called federal liberty (Elazar 1995, 28, 44). Federal liberty is ever mindful of political society and its need for morality and law. This distinction, Elazar argues, is at the root of our modern idea of what is "constitutional." To make a judgment of what is constitutional requires more than merely perusing a text; one must determine what is compatible with the preconditions of the political order of a civil society and what is not. Where moral constitutions may be silent on the moral preconditions of political order, pre-constitution political covenants sometimes spell those out. That is true in the case of America's Declaration of Independence, for example (Elazar 1995, 28). Elazar also makes use of natural law to a limited degree as a basis for determining "constitutionality."

In order for covenants to fulfill their function, it is important that they exhibit distinctive components. Elazar presents five broad elements necessary for covenanting and sees a clear parallel to modern federal constitutions: "Historical prologue indicating the parties involved, a preamble stating the general purposes of the covenant and the principles behind it, a body of conditions and operative clauses, a stipulation of the agreed-upon sanctions to be applied if the covenant were violated, and an oath to make the covenant morally binding" (Elazar 1995, 194–195). A sixth element may also be included, "provisions for depositing the covenant document and of periodic public reaffirmation or recovenanting" (Elazar 1995, 24, 194–195).

Consistent with the Hebrew tradition, these components define politics to consist of liberty and accountability within the context of relationships. Elazar argues:

> [A]ll covenantal political understanding revolves around similar questions of obligation and consent, free will, self-government, and political order – in other words, how are the relationships of humans one to another and to this universe and its transcendent power established and maintained so as to preserve both order and freedom, equality and opportunity, neighborliness and distinctiveness, liberty and law (Elazar 1998b, 343).

The Biblical covenants, according to Elazar have three dimensions. The first is a theological dimension wherein God is a party or witness to the covenant. The second is national-political dimension, particularly in the case of Israel. The third is a normative dimension that establishes the foundation and maintenance of justice (Elazar 1995, 86). Modern covenantal expressions recognize this divine dimension in three different ways. The first way is through explicit pronouncement that the political genesis requires the partnership and rule of God. The second way is to recognize God as a transcendent source of power over the covenant. The third way is to express a divine origin for the nature of humanity. The last type of expression is a very weak variant of covenanting and therefore closest to modern secular compacts or contracts. Nevertheless, Elazar insists that there is a kind of political theology echoed even in modern constitutions (Elazar 1998c, 251).

In addition to the divine-human relationship (a vertical relationship) is the relationship between persons and communities (a horizontal relationship). As a horizontal relationship, covenants are voluntarily created by people who have equal moral standing. The covenant, by pact and oath, creates one community (and summary institutions) respecting the integrity of each partner (Elazar 1995, 68, 179). This partnership defines and limits the powers of the parties. Through the covenant, the nation becomes a people (Elazar 1995, 178).

Not all of the covenanting societies studied by Elazar were Jewish or Christian; but all had cultural or perhaps even geographical characteristics that supported the voluntary act of covenanting. Many were involved in migration and/or had borderlands of cultural contact and interaction, another important aspect of Elazar's overall theory of federalism (Elazar 1996, 137, 337–339). Most covenanting peoples also first possessed and sustained a culture of political oaths before covenanting was understood as a religious doctrine (Elazar 1995, 24; 1996, 113, 129).

Elazar argues that cultural traditions and worldview are the key determinants in whether or not the institution of covenanting can take root (Elazar 1995, 22). Hebrew covenanting borrowed from regional cultural custom. Areas of modern covenanting embraced some critical amount of covenantal (Reformed) theology (Elazar 1995, 26). By contrast, where Greek and Roman political ideas prevailed, however, hierarchical and organic political organizations were prominent (Elazar 1996, 140). Elazar argues that covenanting societies must also possess texts to reflect their political ideals and vocabulary together with the figures, events, and concepts which embody that tradition (Elazar 1995, 5; 1998b, 353). The cultural influences (primarily social and ethical) of such a covenanting culture may often persist long after explicit covenanting practices fade (Elazar 1998b, 9).

The Decline of Political Covenanting and the Consequence for Politics and Federalism

Today, the "strong" covenanting of the Hebrews or the Protestant Reformers takes place only in church polities – if at all. In areas where strong and explicit covenantalism once ruled the political landscape, only the weakest forms of covenantalism remain. These, Elazar and his colleagues argue, are reflected in modern formulations of constitutionalism. Can one then say that political covenanting has been lost, or simply modified? What does this mean for federal arrangements as Elazar defines them? Elazar addresses these questions with both hope and skepticism.

Elazar offers a persuasive argument for the legacy of covenantalism when it is contrasted with competing models. Consent and law on the covenantal model, and not the Athenian model, is perhaps the healthiest surviving element of pre-modern politics. The covenant, argues Elazar, builds a bridge between the pre-modern and post-modern epochs. This is discernable not only in institutions but also in political culture. As evidence for this claim, Elazar cites the success that modern constitutionalism and federalism has enjoyed in countries with a Reformation covenantal tradition versus those dominated by contrasting political or religious traditions (Elazar 1998b, 7).

Can the moral vision and purpose of the old covenants be recovered in a secular age? Elazar is unclear. He suggests that civil societies can be reinvented on a similar (secular) basis (Elazar 1998b, 348). But he does not clearly spell out what that means. To complicate the question, Elazar notes that while the call for moral reformation was a source of the covenant's original vision, it was also the cause of its downfall (Elazar 1998c, 10). Persons could not always bear up under the weight of the covenant's moral obligations.

Elazar asserts hopefully, "The covenantal foundations remain and manifest themselves in those very polities even in unexpected ways in every generation" (Elazar 1998c, 6–7). Modern manifestations of federalism remain: in the language of political theory: *foedus, pactum* or *pactio, confederatio, contractus,* and *consocentio*; in the theme of "deliverance" in social contract theory; in the understanding of rights as liberties integral with justice and moral duties; in the moderate egalitarianism characteristic of modernity's rejection of organic and hierarchal arrangements (Elazar 1998b, 19, 242–248). All of this is hopeful. But Elazar warns, "When covenantal arrangements have been reduced to mechanism they offer much less to the people who use them. Often they degenerate to window dressing" (Elazar 1998b, 266, 348). Should the loss of a theo-political foundation lead to an unrealistic view of human nature or deny the moral meaning of politics, Elazar believes that true federalism, and political liberty, will be lost (Elazar 1998b, 344, 351).

Federalism in its Modern Context: Federalism as Political Institution and Political Ethos

Having studied the covenantal roots, we now turn more directly to Elazar's study of modern federalism. Like his presentation of covenants, his federal theory is both institutional and ethical. We will first examine Elazar's general theory of federalism as contrasted with other models of political organization. Next, we will see how America serves as the *sine qua non* for modern (as opposed to pre-modern or postmodern) federalism. Last, we will see how Elazar prescribes the federal model for current political dilemmas.

Elazar's theory of federalism essentially focuses on political integration. As in covenanting, federal arrangements begin when individual units combine to form a larger political unit. But in doing so, they do not lose their individual integrity; they do not become subsumed in the whole. Neither is the new political creation entirely beholden to its constituent parts. Elazar describes it as follows: "Federalism can be defined as the mode of political organization that unites separate polities within an overarching political system by distributing power among general and constituent governments in a manner designed to protect the existence and authority of both" (Elazar 1972, 2).

Federal integration, Elazar argues, distinguishes it from any kind of center-periphery model. There is no focal point or center which links units in a federal arrangement. Elazar describes this as a "matrix" model rather than a "common center" model. The emphasis in federalism is not in the strength of the center or the peripheries, but the strength of the entire network. He argues that the strength gained in a federal arrangement is gained "simultaneously and interdependently" (Elazar 1984a, 1). Thus, federalism can be called "multi-centric" rather than centralized. Elazar calls this "contractual non-centralization."

Elazar's contractual non-centralization is not simply decentralization. Whereas many conceive of decentralization as hierarchy on the pyramid model of Max Weber or Woodrow Wilson, Elazar suggests a complicated matrix emphasizing a complicated relationship between multiple centers of power on judicial, executive, and administrative concerns. Distributions of power are "differential loadings in different arenas for different purposes" (Elazar 1984b, 15–16). Constitutions provide only a frame or bones, which are then fleshed out by formal and informal institutional arrangements. These lines of communication serve as "nerves" for the system. This makes the system adaptable. It also makes a federal system, by Elazar's own admission, difficult to discuss on a theoretical level (Elazar 1984b, 16).

True federalism emphasizes self-rule and shared rule. These two principles serve as constitutional principles to distribute power among both the general governing body and the constituent governing bodies. Activities of common government are structured to maintain the integrity of the constituting elements (Elazar 1984a, 2–3). Falling back on a theological vocabulary of politics, Elazar distinguishes non-centralization from decentralization as a difference of grace and not of right. Decentralization implies the existence of a central authority that can decentralize or recentralize as it pleases. Such a central authority does not exist in Elazar's federalism. Power is diffused. Centralizing or concentrating power in a federalist system risks breaking the structure and spirit of the constitution. It negates the whole *telos* of federalism. Non-centralization applies to the United States, Canada, and Switzerland, for example. In each case, there is no central government that controls all the lines of political communication and decision-making. States, cantons, or provinces are not creatures of the federal government (Elazar 1984b 14).

Elazar is careful to distinguish federalism from its imposters. This includes the *mere application* of federal principles, as often used by large–small state relationships (especially wherein the larger may have been a colonial power), leagues (such as NATO), arrangements among local rural or metropolitan entities, or in NGOs. In those cases, formal federalism is not legally articulated or institutionalized; nor is it an architectonic principle. Federal principles are pragmatically utilized (Elazar 1984b, 24–28). Elazar also distinguishes true federalism from ineffective centralization. In the case of countries such as the UK, Belgium, PRC, Japan, or Israel, which Elazar characterizes as having unions or consociations, there is a formal agreement between entities which takes on constitutional force. There is a will toward federation but it is subordinated to other considerations (Elazar 1984b, 22). In federal countries, by contrast, it is explicitly clear that those policies judged to be "good" are those which preserve the integrity of their compound units. In countries which have a unitary organization, "good" policies encourage centralization unless there is a standing will (informal impetus) or agreement (formal impetus) to the contrary (Elazar 1984b, 22).

Federalism should also be distinguished from democracy or republicanism, though one cannot understate the close historical relationship between them. Both democracy and republicanism also exist in regimes with either ineffective centralization or what Elazar simply calls "federal principles." But it seems logical that democracy may be necessary, though not sufficient, to federal integration of power (Elazar 1984b, 47; 1976, 33–35). Elazar also compares federalism to democracy insofar as both are rich in theoretical character (Elazar 1984b, 41).

What often appears as ambiguity in Elazar's oft-repeated definitions of federalism can be attributed to his alternating between what can be called *procedural federalism* versus *substantive federalism*. Federalism must have necessary institutional (procedural) arrangements, but the essence of his federalism is more philosophical or ideological (substantive) than legal. Elazar describes federalism as both idealistic and realistic, paralleling both philosophical and legal dimensions.

It is the institutional (procedural) dimensions which provide a remedy to human nature. It is the institutional dimensions that provide guarantees for the ideological or ideal goals of federalism (Elazar 1984b, 42–45). Elazar's federalism is therefore not simply about establishing the correct lines of authority or communication. It is essentially about what Elazar calls "the institutionalization of a particular kind of relationship among the participants in political life." This makes the institutions and structures somewhat flexible so long as the substantive goals of federalism are preserved (Elazar 1984a, 2).

In substantive terms, Elazar's federalism is essentially about having *liberty* under law. It respects freedom by emphasizing both voluntary negotiated entry into federal arrangements and a certain degree of autonomy within that arrangement. Elazar describes it thus:

> *Federal principles grow out of the idea that free people can freely enter into lasting, yet limited political associations, to achieve common ends and protect certain rights while preserving their respective integrities. As*

> the very ambiguity of the term 'federal' reveals, federalism is concerned simultaneously with the diffusion of political power in the name of liberty and its concentration on behalf of unity or energetic government (Elazar 1984b, 13).

Federalism is more than just the sharing of power coupled with self-rule for the sake of other ends; rather, distribution is necessary and desirable *for its own sake*. This architectonic goal distinguishes true federalism from merely the use of federal principles.

In its broadest sense, federalism is a form of justice, emphasizing liberty and citizen participation. It cannot abandon the concern for power or justice and must always consider the relationship between the two. Federalism is also concerned with the relationship between freedom and equality, moderating each and going "against the grain of modern conceptions of absolute equality." This brings to mind the earlier discussion of federal liberty in a covenant (Elazar 1984b, 45).

Federalism in its Modern Context: The Case of America

Though Elazar lavishes praise on the Swiss commonwealth model, asserting it to have preserved and reinvented federalism in Europe, America is clearly Elazar's model for modern federalism (Elazar 2001, 43). Elazar argues that the only real pre-modern federal arrangement was confederation and that modern federalism was invented by the United States (Elazar 1998a, 42–50).

Elazar's emphasis on America demonstrates his emphasis on freedom as the goal of federal arrangements. He contrasts modern federalism, invented in America, with the "Jacobin state" as its opponent. The solution invented in America avoided the European model of the sovereign state and instead vested sovereignty in the people. Various units of government were essentially a public trust delegated by the people; multi-centralization of power represented multiple delegations. Elazar writes,

> By creating a strong overarching government, it was possible to aspire to the same goals of political unification and integration as the Jacobin state but, by removing sovereignty from the states as such and lodging it with the people, it was possible to arrange for power-sharing and to set limits on governmental authority (Elazar 1984b, 18–19).

How exactly one lodges sovereignty with the people is unclear. It is presented in the context of limiting governmental authority and multiple delegations of power. Perhaps the best way to understand this is by way of Elazar's covenant studies: inherent limits on authority exist in the voluntary creation of power and integration of political authority, rightly understood. To lodge power in the people is essentially to diffuse power and make rulers accountable.

Elazar's dual approach to federalism as both political and ethical is evident by his statement that "some have borrowed the federal structure and then not lived up to the intent at all" (Elazar 1984b, 20). This "will" to federalism can be aborted or restricted by "objective" factors – cultural, economic, military, political, or social (Elazar 1984b, 20). This parallels what Elazar said previously about factors which disable effective political covenants. On the challenge of this "dual" federalism, Elazar writes,

> *Too often today federalism is treated as simply an administrative principle or, less frequently, as a merely juridical one. The relatively few men who look at American politics with greater breadth of understanding recognize federalism as a political principle – something more than simply an administrative device or even a legal-constitutional one ... In the last analysis, however, federalism is more than simply a political principle, especially in the United States of America. It is also a fundamental principle of social organization that has to do with the relationships among individuals and families as well as governments and polities ... Americans have generally ignored federalism as a social principle because it is so deeply imbedded as such in American culture and in the psyches of American people that its social dimension is a matter of second nature, unnoticed and taken for granted (Elazar 1974, 3).*

America becomes the *sine qua non* of federalism because it succeeded in internalizing a secularized version of a religious ethos, what its earliest colonists called "federal liberty."

Elazar published extensively on the role of states and cities in American government, and these studies became the basis of collateral (and controversial) studies of political culture and urbanism. Elazar argues that local American communities have always been a three-way partnership with federal and state governments (Elazar 1962). States exist as civil societies, and their success with the larger federal unit relies on their ability to function as civil societies (Elazar 1972, 10–30). Cities demonstrate the "matrix principle" of federalism rather than a center-periphery or decentralization model. Elazar writes,

> *The American anti-city is a particularly appropriate institution in a federal system where the diffusion of power is counted as a positive good, though not for the reasons generally used to justify locally-centered government. While Americans have an ideological predilection for emphasizing the primacy of local government, in fact, they have not hesitated to utilize the power of government on all planes – federal, state, and local – to secure their political ends. At the same time, they have continued to emphasize the principle of local control over all government activities within the community, regardless of their official point of origin (Elazar 1987, 21).*

American cities are a reflection of the American political ethos, what Elazar calls "the classic American sense of politics, power and justice." This original persuasion is "federal democracy." American proclivities for migration and historical agrarian patterns stand in contrast to the European model, founded on the classical idea of the *civitas* wherein the city was the center of the political order; the American city has as its model the Israelite city-building described in the Bible. Tying together what he says elsewhere about the significance of civil society in federalism, Elazar argues, "The city in this country, as in ancient Israel, developed not to be the state but to fulfill certain functions for an existing civil society which could best be fulfilled by bringing people together in relatively dense population groups where they could interact socially and commercially" (Elazar 1987, 17–18). The growth and effective organization of American cities to accomplish their assigned tasks is, for Elazar, a demonstration of the value of this American ethos.

American cities, an essential part of American federalism, cannot be compared to, let alone measured against, European cities. Elazar writes,

> *The bulk of the massive literature on the American city ... is, in certain respects, misleading if not wrong. The literature is misleading because, as it relates urbanization in America to the general phenomenon of urbanization, it ignores, glosses over, or simply refuses to understand the particularly American character of the American city and special frontier setting in which American cities have developed and must function ... The agrarian commitments of American culture are deliberately carried over into the American city (Elazar 1987, xi).*

Elazar's ensuing discussions of everything from urban renewal, neighborhood government, and the grid system of streets and roads attempts demonstrates the political culture and values integrated into every facet of American political life.

"Federal democracy" or "federalistic individualism," especially in the American experience, is presented by Elazar as a political ethos. It stands contrast or opposition to populism and participatory democracy, liberalism and conservatism, pluralism and juridical democracy. The latter have all claimed to be the American political vision, Elazar writes, but they are not authentic. Federal individualism provides an orientation different from ideologies such as "radical individualism, collectivism, corporatism" (Elazar 1987, vii, xx, 10–17).

A clear example of federalism as both ethos and institution is demonstrated during the Civil Rights movement. The success of the movement was not dependent on superior federal force. Rather, as he argued in 1972, it depended on the successes of local enforcement and local sentiment (Elazar 1972, 6–10). Unwritten constitutional traditions also become important here (Elazar 1972, 36). American federalism can be termed a "national political culture" which is a "synthesis of three major political subcultures that jointly inhabit the country, existing side-by-side or even overlapping." These cultures are nationwide, but each subculture is tied to specific sections of the country, reflecting streams and currents of migration. Elazar identifies three cultures: *individualistic, moralistic,* and *traditionalistic.* Each of these represents a "particular synthesis of the marketplace and the commonwealth" in approaching politics. This involves yet another of Elazar's trademark matrices, demonstrating the relationship between efficiency, commerce, legitimacy, and agrarianism. Political culture is also a factor in intrastate cohesion, an essential component of federalism (Elazar 1972, 10–30, 84–178, 196–198).

Testing and Contesting Elazar on Political Culture

In arguing how culture accounted for political variables such as participation, party, policy, and bureaucracy, Elazar offered ideal types as representatives of political culture (individualistic, moralistic, and traditionalistic). The "individualistic" political culture views political participation as a means of improving one's social and economic position, paying less attention to traditional expectations for government. Corruption is likely overlooked, government services (bureaucracy) minimal, and parties strengthened by coalitions of groups seeking political advantage. Broad political participation is not emphasized. (Civil society is a means rather than an end.) By contrast, a "moralistic" political culture encourages much broader participation and emphasizes the role of government as an agent of common good. A "traditionalistic" political culture encourages participation among elites and maintains the status quo. It minimizes the role of parties, popular participation, and bureaucracy, though not for the same reasons as the individualistic subculture (Elazar 1970; 1972; 1984d). Lieske, citing Press and VerBerg, summarizes Elazar to link culture with "(1) what state and local governments do, (2) how they are organized, (3) what political rules they observe, and (4) who participates in the political process" (Lieske 1993).

Elazar's study of political culture echoes three of his leitmotifs. First, it explains politics and policy in terms of moral and social characteristics, recalling covenant theory. Second, it demonstrates how federal subunits (regions defined by states) accommodate different cultures and political goals. That accommodation of diversity, Elazar argues, is an advantage of federalism. Third, Elazar's study of political culture addresses the substantial import of migration patterns. Migration is not only relevant for understanding Elazar's theory of federalism and covenant, it is essential for his understanding of *American* federalism.

Elazar's studies of political culture are not substantially empirical, relying on matrices rather than statistical investigation. His geopolitical designations are based on no empirical data other than migration patterns, personal observations, interviews, and other scholarly studies of regions or groups. And it is arguably guilty of overgeneralization and imprecision, particularly given that it remained unchanged for decades. It was left to others to test or update the relationships Elazar asserted. Over 100 studies have subjected Elazar's thesis or a subcultural variation to empirical tests. (Kincaid and Lieske 1991) Together with Elazar's own work, these replies played an important role in the revival of political culture studies during the 1980s (Wirt 1991).

Overall, the response to Elazar's work has been mixed. Johnson complains that the unidimensionality of Elazar's categories fails to preserve the notion of three separate cultures (Johnson 1976). Some have found Elazar's classification of cultures to be helpful in explaining participation, bureaucracy, or public programs (Sharkansky 1969; Kincaid 1980; Herzik 1985). Sharkansky (Sharkansky 1969) empirically operationalized Elazar's assertions, creating the "Elazar–Sharkansky Political Culture Scale" used in subsequent studies (Ritt 1974; Sigelman 1976; Weber and Shaffer 1972; Dean 1980; Fitzpatrick and Hero 1988; Joslyn 1980; King 1994; Wirt 1991). Elazar's taxonomy has also been used in various studies of policy and party (Paddock 1998; Lamis 1990; Fitzpatrick and Hero 1988; Hero and Fitzpatrick 1986).

Those who have tested relationships between cultural patterns and mass opinion have found only weak or negative relationships (Nardulli 1990; Kincaid 1980; Schiltz and Rainey 1978; Lowery and Sigelman 1982; Joslyn 1980). But these studies are not without their critics, and those criticisms offer important insights into the study of political culture. Savage argues that there are serious flaws in Schiltz and Rainey, for example: survey problems, creating a straw man hypothesis, poor statistical analysis and presentation and "a rummage-sale approach to the study of political culture demonstrating an altogether inadequate conceptualization of the research problem at hand." Furthermore, Savage argues, Schiltz and Rainey provide only a passing mention of analyses supportive of Elazar. This includes not only Sharkansky's study, but other empirical studies along the same lines (Luttbeg 1971; Monroe 1977; Savage 1973; 1975; 1977; 1981, 331–332). Critiquing Schiltz and Rainey's approach to CSEP data as a "bargain basement" approach to discerning correlations, Savage suggests that confirming ideal types (such as Elazar's) requires a different kind of methodology. By "rummaging about" in the CSEP dataset, they use inadequate formulations of Elazar's theory and uncritically accept CSEP data ambiguously. Savage suggests that for their purposes, the R-methodological (normative) perspective is inferior to Q-methodology (ipsative) perspective, which points to comparison of communities as whole arrays of attributes. These factors, Savage argues, disable their study from being a critical test of Elazar's assertions (Savage 1981, 335–336).

Some tests of political culture deliberately parallel Elazar's. Johnson tested Elazar's indices based on 1906–1936 religious census data, using discriminant analysis. Using religion as his key variable, he is "mildly successful" in replicating Elazar's classification of states by dominant political culture. Significant correlations in the predicted direction are found for six dependent variables: government activities, local emphasis and administration of programs, innovative activity by the government, encouragement of popular participation in elections, popular participation in elections, and party competition. Hypothesized relationships were not supported for two dependent variables: centralized governmental decision-making and the importance of political parties (Johnson 1976). Morgan and Watson re-examined this relationship using 1980 religious affiliation data. This study was also successful in confirming many of Elazar's assertions (Morgan and Watson 1991). This direct use of religion as a variable may be read different ways. Insofar as religion was implicitly underlying Elazar's ideal types, it can be read as a confirmation of those types. On the other hand, what if directly correlating religion is more efficient? If so, this may not so much confirm Elazar's classifications as complicate or replace them. Morgan and Watson argue that using religious data as proxy for state political culture "avoids reliance on a single linear scale in which political culture remains invariant over time," and is also less "vulnerable to the charge of being impressionistic." Furthermore, it is data available by county, permitting intrastate analysis.

Lieske and Kincaid propose the development of new subcultural measures in addition to religious affiliation. They also offer an improved and more empirically substantial methodology. They directly measure what Elazar considered sources of political culture: racial origin, ethnic ancestry, religious affiliation, and social structure (Lieske and Kincaid 1991). One major advantage of their approach, they argue, is addressing the problem of circularity. Lieske writes, "This focus would exclude from the derivation of any new measures the confounding "manifestations" and "effects" of culture, i.e., political behavior and institutional arrangements" (Lieske 1993, 889). In a subsequent study, Lieske creates subculture algorithms which are more statistically reliable, reflect current cultural conditions, distinguish differences down to the county level, and reflect "nonpolitical" measures (Lieske 1993, 889–892). The approach here is not to directly test Elazar's overall argument, but rather to make it more precise and empirical. Using principal component and cluster analysis, Lieske provides a helpful contribution to political culture which summarily confirms the seminal nature of Elazar's study of American political culture.

There remains the question of timeliness and currency. Do cultural patterns established at the turn of the century have staying power in comparison with the institutions or policies with which they are linked? Furthermore, while Elazar addresses the importance of elites in a traditionalist culture, his overall taxonomy seems to make little distinction between elites and mass sentiment (Welch and Peters 1980; Kincaid 1980; Kincaid 1982; Lowery and Sigelman 1982). Berman asks whether the cultural values that Elazar identifies ever really had much effect on the political attitudes of the general public or whether these public attitudes are more appropriate for identifying contending elites. To test this question, Berman focuses on the relationship between culture and mass sentiment on various issues during the progressive era in the first decades of the twentieth century. He argues, "Assuming that the cultural patterns identified by Elazar actually existed, they would have been relatively fresh during this period, especially in western states. During this era, moreover, issues which logically evoke cultural divisions along the lines identified by Elazar were unusually salient" (Berman 1988, 169). Relying on Sharkansky's cultural index scale, Berman considers how various ballot proposals concerning participation, regulation, taxation, and government ownership fared in elections between 1912 and 1916. He concludes both that Elazar's theories do have some utility in understanding voter positions during the progressive era and also that cultural variables were important below the elite level. But overall, Berman argues that there is want of a strong relationship and also that other variables need to be taken into account in discerning the voting habits of a particular region.

Furthermore, he believes that the weak to mild effect of culture on the electorate during the progressive era would only weaken over time (Berman 1988, 176–179).

Contemporary Applications for Federalism

Federalism today is found in associated state arrangements, common markets, consociational polities, unions, and leagues. These, together with functional authorities and condominium, are all post-modern applications of the federal principle (Elazar 1984a, 4). These post-modern applications, some of which are cast as modern versions of the old confederalism, are offered by Elazar as phenomena of globalization and the successor to the nation-state and statism. Though these post-modern applications are not the equivalent of modern federalism on the American model, Elazar does consider them to be a legitimate form of federal democracy, albeit with its own strengths and weaknesses (Elazar 1998a, 5). Modern confederation brings the advantages of federalism without the threat of tighter union (Elazar 1998a, 41).

Whereas federalism was applied most specifically to nation-states, the new post-modern and confederal arrangements apply to inter-nation-state unity (Elazar 1998a, 23–24, 40). Pre-modern confederations (then termed federations) were predicated on virtue, security, or prosperity, in some combination. With the rise of modern federalism (such as in America), constituent polities focused on virtue while general governments concentrated on interests. Within transnational and transconfederal leagues, the post-modern epoch places responsibility for virtue with the constituent or federated states while the large federations and "sovereign" states share responsibility for security and economic affairs (Elazar 1998a, 51).

This "new" incarnation of federalism strives to enable security, economic integration, and the protection of human rights. These three interests serve states, commercial actors, and individual citizens respectively. The new confederal arrangements also differ from the old federal nation-state arrangements insofar as they emphasize not the enlargement of states but their transformation. States now strive to be autonomous jurisdictions within a larger system wherein they participate in decision-making but yet give up some capacity for unilateral action. This differs from the old desire to emphasize sovereignty and self-sufficiency above all (Elazar 1998a, 4). In a federal polity, the federal government can reach directly to its citizenry; confederal government must reach individuals only through federal polities. A federation is concerned with preservation of individual liberty. Confederation places greater emphasis on preservation of local liberties of constituent polities. Federation is possible only where a common law binding all citizens is possible. Confederation is viable to establish federal ties where parties can only tolerate specific and limited common laws (Elazar 1998a, 74).

Elazar argues that the nation-state model is increasingly obsolete and must give way to the new and better federal arrangement (Elazar 1982). Only federal solutions can resolve seemingly intransigent political problems arising from conflicting national, ethnic, linguistic, and racial claims. Elazar argues that confederalism (the new confederations) is the best way of engaging globalization to curb its economic excesses, support federal democracy and human rights, and balance individual and group (Elazar 1998a, 5–6). It is a largely post-modern development in part because of the post-modern "legitimation of ethnic identity." By ethnic, Elazar means racial, linguistic, ethnocultural, tribal, and religious identity. Federalism, in the national sense, can become very problematic for navigating ethnic assertions and resurgences, especially in cases of what Elazar calls "highly egocentric ethnonationalist statism." Federal solutions are adaptable, and can be used in ethnically heterogeneous regions (Elazar 1991, 7–8, 40–60). But they will only succeed if their subscribers believe that the advantages of interdependence supercede the desire for separate ethnic identity (Elazar 1998a, 19–21, 200). This is especially true in case of Israel, an area of particular concern to Elazar (Elazar 1991).

Federalism is, as Elazar sees it, the most "just" resolution of these problems in the service of attaining "local and world peace." Here again, Elazar falls back on his theological vocabulary. The peace to which he alludes is exemplified in the Hebrew *shalom*, a cognate of the Hebrew *brit*: peace and "covenantal wholeness" (Elazar 1984a, 3–5).

References

Berman, David R. (1988) Political culture, issues and the electorate: evidence from the progressive era, *The Western Political Quarterly* 41, (March), 169–180.

Dean, Gillian (1980) The study of political feedback using nonrecursive causal models: The case of state divorce politics, *Policy Studies Journal* 8 (Summer), 920–927.

Elazar, Daniel J. (1962) *The American Partnership: Intergovernmental Co-operation in the Nineteenth-Century United States*. (Chicago: University of Chicago Press).

—— (1970) *Cities of the Prairie*. (New York: Basic Books).

—— (1972) *American Federalism: A View from the States*. (2nd edn) (New York: Thomas Y Crowell Company).

—— (1974a) First principles, in Elazar (ed.) (1974b).

—— (ed.) (1974b) *The Federal Policy. A Publius Publication*. (New Brunswick, NJ: Transaction Books).

—— (1976) *The Ends of Federalism: Notes Toward a Theory of Federal Political Arrangements*. Working Paper Number 12. (Philadelphia: Temple University/Center for the Study of Federalism).

—— (ed.) (1982) *Governing Peoples and Territories*. (Philadelphia: Institute for the Study of Human Issues).

—— (1984a) Introduction, in Elazar (ed.) (1984c).

—— (1984b) The role of federalism in political integration, in Elazar (ed.) (1984c).

—— (ed.) (1984c) *Federalism and Political Integration*. (Lanham, MD: University Press of America).

—— (1984d) *American Federalism: A View from the States*. (3rd edn) (New York: Harper and Row).

—— (1987) *Building Cities in America: Urbanization and Suburbanization in a Frontier Society*. (Lanham, MD: Hamilton Press).

—— (1991) *Two Peoples – One Land: Federal Solutions for Israel, The Palestinians, and Jordan*. (New York: University Press of America).

—— (1995) *Covenant and Polity in Biblical Israel: Biblical Foundations and Jewish Expressions*. The Covenant Tradition in Politics, Vol. I. (New Brunswick, NJ: Transaction Publishers).

—— (1996) *Covenant and Commonwealth: From Christian Separation Through the Protestant Reformation*. The Covenant Tradition in Politics, Vol. II. (New Brunswick, NJ: Transaction Publishers).

—— (1998a) *Constitutionalizing Globalization*. (New York: Roman and Littlefield Publishers).

—— (1998b) *Covenant and Civil Society: The Constitutional Matrix of Modern Democracy*. The Covenant Tradition in Politics, Vol. IV. (New Brunswick, NJ: Transaction Publishers).

—— (1998c) *Covenant and Constitutionalism: The Great Frontier and the Matrix of Federal Democracy*. The Covenant Tradition in Politics, Vol. III. (New Brunswick, NJ: Transaction Publishers).

—— (ed.) (2001) *Commonwealth: The Other Road to Democracy. The Swiss Model of Democratic Self-Government*. (New York: Lexington Books).

Fitzpatrick, Jody L. and Hero, Rodney E. (1988) Political culture and political characteristics of the American states: A consideration of some old and new questions, *Western Political Quarterly* 41, 145–53

Hero, Rodney E. and Fitzpatrick, Jody L. (1986) State mandating of local government activities: An exploration. Paper presented at the annual meeting of the American Political Science Association, Washington DC.

Herzik, Eric (1985) The legal–formal structuring of state politics: a cultural explanation, *Western Political Quarterly* 38 (September), 413–423.

Johnson, Charles A. (1976) Political culture in American states: Elazar's formulation examined, *American Journal of Political Science*, Vol. 20, No. 3 (August), 491–509.

Joslyn, Richard (1980) Manifestations of Elazar's political subcultures, *Publius* 10 (Spring), 37–58.

Kincaid, John (1980) Political cultures in the American compound republic, *Publius* 10 (Spring), 1–13.

—— (ed.) (1982) *Political Culture, Public Policy and the American States* (Philadelphia: Institute for the Study of Human Issues).

—— and Lieske, Joel (1991) Political subcultures of the American states: State of the art and agenda for research. Paper delivered at the annual meeting of the American Political Science Association, Washington DC.

King, James D. (1994) Political culture, registration laws, and voter turnout among the American states, *Publius* 24 (Fall), 115–127.

Lamis, Alexander (1990) *The Two Party South*. (New York: Oxford University Press).

Lieske, Joel (1993) Regional subcultures of the United States, *The Journal of Politics*, Vol. 55, No. 4 (November), 888–913.

Lowery, David and Sigelman, Lee (1982) Political culture and state public policy: The missing link, *Western Political Quarterly* 35 (September), 376–384.

Luttbeg, Norman R. (1971) Classifying the American states: An empirical attempt to identify internal variations, *Midwest Journal of Political Science* 15 (November), 703–721.

Monroe, Alan D. (1977) Operationalizing political culture: The Illinois case, *Publius* 7 (Spring), 107–120.

Morgan, David R. and Watson, Sheilah S. (1991) Political culture, political system characteristics, and public policies among the American states, *Publius* 21, 31–48.

Nardulli, Peter F. (1990) Political subcultures in the American states: An empirical examination of Elazar's formulation, *American Politics Quarterly* 18, 287–315.

Paddock, Joel (1998) Explaining state variation in interparty ideological differences, *Political Research Quarterly*, Vol. 51, No. 3 (September), 765–780.

Press, Charles and VerBurg, Kenneth (1983) *State and Community Governments in the Federal System.* (2nd edn) (New York: Wiley).

Ritt, Leonard G. (1974) Political cultures and political reform: A research note, *Publius* 4 (Winter), 127–133.

Savage, Robert L. (1973) Patterns of multilinear evolution in the American states, *Publius* (Spring 1973), 75–108.

—— (1975) The distribution and development of policy values in the American states, in *The Ecology of American Political Culture: Readings*. Edited by Daniel J. Elazar and Joseph Zikmund II. (New York: Crowell), 263–283.

—— and Gallagher, Richard J. (1977) Politicocultural regions in a Southern state: An empirical typology of Arkansas counties, *Publius* (Spring), 91–105.

—— (1981) Looking for political subcultures: A critique of the rummage-sale approach, *The Western Political Quarterly*, Vol. 34, No. 2. (June), 331–336.

Schiltz, Timothy D. and Rainey, R. Lee (1978) The geographic distribution of Elazar's political subcultures among the mass population. *Western Political Quarterly* 31 (September), 410–415.

Sharkansky, Ira (1969) The utility of Elazar's political culture: A research note, *Polity* 2 (Fall), 66–83.

Sigelman, Lee (1976) The curious case of women in state and local government, *Social Science Quarterly* 56 (March), 591–604.

Weber, Ronald E. and Shaffer, William R. (1972) Public opinion and American state policy-making, *Midwest Journal of Political Science* 16 (November), 683–699.

Weir, David A. (2005) *Early New England: A Covenanted Society.* (Grand Rapids, MI: William B. Eerdmans Publishing Company).

Welch, Susan and Peters, John G. (1980) State political culture and attitudes of state senators toward social, economic welfare, and corruption issues, *Publius* 10 (Fall), 59–67.

Winthrop, John (1645) *A Little Speech on Liberty.*

Wirt, Frederick M. (1991) "Soft" concepts and "hard" data: a research review of Elazar's political culture, *Publius* 21 (Spring), 1–13.

Further Reading

Elazar, Daniel (1987) *Exploring Federalism*. (Tuscaloosa: University of Alabama Press).
—— (1995) "Federalism," in *The Encyclopedia of Democracy*, Vol. 1–4, edited by Seymour Martin Lipset. (Washington, DC: Congressional Quarterly).
—— (1998) "Covenant," in *Encyclopedia of Politics and Religion*, edited by Robert Wuthnow. (Washington, DC: Congressional Quarterly).
—— (2002) *Kinship and Consent: The Jewish Political Tradition and its Contemporary Uses*. (Lanham, MD: University Press of America).
—— (2003) *The Metropolitan Frontier and American Politics*. (Piscataway, NJ: Transaction Publishers).

23

ASHGATE
RESEARCH
COMPANION

William Riker's "Rationalist" Federalism

Benjamin Kleinerman

Although William Riker contributed much to the study of federalism, he is better known for his contributions to and development of the more general field of rational choice theory in the study of politics. While arising out of the study of economics, Riker was perhaps not simply boasting when he wrote: "I believe our group at Rochester ... was the core of the political science part of the movement." To a significant degree, then, one can neither summarize nor evaluate his account of federalism without at the same time discussing rational choice theory. To elucidate his theory of federalism, we must understand something about his viewpoint on the usefulness of "theory," as he understood it, in the study of politics. That being said, to a significant degree, Riker's interest in federalism predates his interest in rational choice theory – the latter interest, as he also admits, did not develop until after he had already written a considerable amount in the political science field (Riker 1997, 194). Thus, one can justly say that Riker understood federalism apart from, or at least without the initial help of, his adoption of the method of explanation employed by rational choice. For this reason, Riker's understanding of federalism may cast as much light on his approach to rational choice as vice versa. In fact, Riker's understanding of federalism not only casts light on his approach to rational choice, it also helps to reveal both the strengths and the limitations of this theoretical approach to the study of politics.

Riker's most important book on federalism came out in the 1960s in the midst of his turn to rational choice theory. In the first place, *Federalism: Origin, Operation, Significance* offers a strident argument against two previous manners of understanding federalism, that is, the "ideological" and the "reductionist" fallacies. The ideological fallacy "is the assertion that federal forms are adopted as a device to guarantee freedom" (Riker 1964, 13). Riker claims that it is neither true empirically that the federal form has guaranteed freedom nor true that "uninformed constitution-writers" have believed "they were providing for freedom simply by making the federal bargain." According to Riker in this book, the creation and the maintenance of federalism has absolutely nothing to do with the preservation of freedom. Alongside the "rather crude ideological fallacy is the subtler and initially more impressive reductionist fallacy." By this theory, the social and economic conditions of any given population create the conditions for the federal form. So, quoting Karl Deutsch, a leading proponent of this theory, there are nine "essential conditions for an amalgamated security-community." Riker claims this theory bypasses "the political," because it bypasses "the act of bargaining itself." Although it shows the social and economic conditions that might make federalism appealing, "it leaves out the crucial condition of the predisposition to make the bargain" (15–16).

According to Riker, the necessary conditions for the "bargain of federalism" are both essentially military. "The politicians who offer the bargain desire to expand their territorial control" and "the politicians who accept the bargain ... are willing to do so because of some external military-diplomatic threat or opportunity" (12). Much of the book aims to prove this thesis about the necessary conditions for the formation of federalism. The thesis itself illustrates well the critical starting point of the "Rochester" school of rational choice theory. While derived from economics, their argument, as in this specific case, departs from economics in emphasizing the essentially political nature of political decisions. As Riker says in a footnote in a different context, they deny any economic theory that is "wholly deterministic." He continues: "Deterministic philosophies are inhumane in that they deny human decision" (Riker 1997, 201). Economic conditions may predispose people to make certain political decisions, but the decision itself stems from an intentional "free choice." In adopting the federal bargain, the presence of both a military threat and a desire to expand without conquest creates a political decision. According to Riker, federalism arises neither from an excess of politics (the "ideological" fallacy), nor from an absence of politics (the "reductionist" fallacy). Instead, it arises from an eminently realist awareness that political actors must possess of that which is necessary for their individual survival.

By this argument, the United States Constitution, on which Riker focuses most of his attention both in this book and in his later work, arises from a military bargain between the separate states. Their security concerns were sufficiently pressing that they were willing to accept a far greater degree of centralization than they would have otherwise. For the same reason, the South becomes unwilling, Riker sometimes suggests, to maintain the federal form in the decades leading up the Civil War. The collapse of the acceptance of the federal form in the South arises from the lack of an external military threat that would make federalism necessary. To note this, however, begs a question that Riker never fully answers, either in this book or in his later work. If a necessary condition is the presence of an external threat, absent this condition, why does only the South, and not the North, desire to leave the "federal bargain?" This is to say that, while Riker shows some of the necessary conditions, for the "federal bargain," he does not show all of them. Or, he shows a necessary but not the sufficient condition for the "federal bargain." In fact, in rejecting the "ideological fallacy" from the very beginning, Riker has deprived himself of an additional explanatory variable. And what is interesting about this rejection is that it is an explanatory variable that explains both his initial distaste for federalism and his later embrace of it.

Riker's federalist model has complete "peripheralization" at one side and complete "centralization" at the other. Complete "peripheralization" occurs when the attachment to and sovereignty of the states becomes sufficiently high as to cause there to be no longer an effective central government. Complete centralization occurs when the national government assumes effective control over all governmental functions. Given these two extremes, the question then becomes: what causes the sustenance, or lack thereof, of the "federal bargain?" Although Riker admits the force of what he calls sometimes "provincial patriotism" in contributing to "peripherilization" and admits the force of nationalizing interests who aim at greater centralization, he remains, especially in this early book, unwilling to admit the role that the idea of federalism itself might play as an explanatory variable. Most telling in this respect is his discussion of Australia. Noting that "Australians have seldom voted … for the frequently proposed (from the center) constitutional amendments to increase federal functions at the expense of the states," he is perplexed by such votes because they seem "to express more a preference for local self-government than a provincial patriotism." He writes immediately thereafter, "Australia seems less in need of appeasing subordinate patriotisms than any other government. One wonders, indeed, *why they bother* with federalism in Australia" (Riker 1964, 113; italics mine). Having ruled out the possibility that the "ideology" of federalism plays any role in explaining either its creation or its sustenance, Riker cannot now see the very explanation for why Australians "bother" with federalism. His exclusion of "ideology" as an explanatory variable in the federalist choice is self-fulfilling: Riker "proves" its truth, not because it is true but because he excludes any evidence which would prove its falsity.

What is most perplexing about Riker's argument in this respect is that the ideology of federalism explains both his rejection of the federal form in this book and his admitted embrace of the federal form 20 years later. In this book, he rejects the normative value of federalism because of its association with Southern white racists. He writes: "If in the United States one approves of Southern white racists, then one should approve of American federalism. If, on the other hand, one disapproves of the values of the privileged minority, one should disapprove of federalism. Thus, if in the United States one disapproves of racism, one should disapprove of federalism." For Riker, federalism is not worth keeping because its only effect "is a system of minority decision that imposes high external costs on everybody other than the minority" (155). But, as Riker emphasizes, such normative judgments come only at the end of the book, set apart entirely from the descriptive judgments of the rest.

In his later book on American federalism, a collection of his life's work on the subject, he admits to a "variation in my ideological judgment" since the publication of his first book. Describing this variation in his own outlook from a New Dealer in the 60s to a liberal anti-statist in the 80s, he describes the reasons one would have differing ideologies on federalism: "Since federalism restrains the national government by setting the scene for conflicts between the states and the nation, the appropriate stance for a New Dealer is to seek to eliminate federalism. On the other hand, the liberal goal of protecting rights from governmental attack justifies restraints like federalism and separation of powers that occasion intergovernmental and interbranch deadlocks." He continues: "Given my ideological shift, I have also changed my evaluation of federalism" (Riker 1978, xiii). That is, he here admits that, at least in his personal case, his evaluation of federalism is profoundly influenced by ideology. In other words, he admits to the political import of the ideology of federalism in his own acceptance of it but still seems to want, for the most part, to exclude such ideology from his "political" explanation of its sustenance. This is to say that, even as Riker points to a "political" explanation capable of doing justice to human choice and intention, he seems ultimately unwilling to take the next step, which would be to admit the force of political ideas in shaping political choices. His reductionism is less "reductionist" than the economic theories he criticizes, but it still remains so insofar as it ascribes political choice to unconscious or unarticulated motivations like security concerns or "provincial patriotism" rather than to conscious or articulated motivations like a belief that the national government can best accomplish political change or the belief that the federal form protects rights or makes possible local self-government. And, as I will suggest later, there is simply no necessary reason why rational choice theory, the theory out of which this account of federalism comes, must reduce political motivations in this manner.

The problem of the "rationalist" account of intentions is well illustrated by one of Riker's other major contributions to the study of federalism. He argues persuasively that the formation of the United States invented a new form of federalism, different from and superior to all of the forms that preceded it. It is the federal form invented by the United States that has been copied by so many governments in the last 200 years. For this reason, it is critical to the development of federalism throughout the world that the members of the Constitutional Convention created the form of federalism that they did. Where the federalism that preceded their invention "was a highly peripheralized federation," they created a "centralized national government modified with provisions to preserve the states" (20, 30). This invention is significant, Riker argues, not just for the United States but for the rest of the world because it allows the expansion of states without either conquest or the sacrifice of some amount of local sovereignty.

Not only did the founders invent a new form of federalism, but those who think that the progressive centralization of power in the United States departs from the founders' intentions misunderstand their invention. Riker argues that a significant centralization of power has always been implicit in the Constitution that they created. Rather than departing from or changing the form they created, the centralization of power over the course of American history has merely fulfilled the founders' intentions. In fact, Riker suggests that the founders were "mostly intent on centralizing at the expense of federalism" (41). Moreover, they were so intent on centralization that, so far from intending successfully to reinvent federalism, "it is hardly possible to attribute its success to the prescience of the framers." In making this argument, Riker also seems interested in claiming that the founders persisted in their desire for centralization. To the extent that the founders did not centralize completely, it was because they had to make concessions to the partisans of provincial patriotism. Riker's account of the development of federalism seems to have room for essentially two opposing motivations: the centralizers who want complete control at the national level and the provincial partisans who want complete control at the state and local level. The "federal bargain" emerges because security concerns cause the provincial partisans to be willing to make some concessions to the centralizers.

Riker seems unwilling to brook the possibility that, even if they did not initially intend the federal form (an argument that, on its own, he does not so much prove as assert), the American founders, at least, may have come to embrace their creation. In other words, a more accurate description of the politics of the American founding and beyond would have to make room for some middle-ground partisans of federalism itself. That there might be partisans of federalism would, as I have already said, help to solve one of the questions that Riker never answers sufficiently: why does federalism persist even after the conditions for the initial bargain that brought it into existence have disappeared? If provincial patriotism disappears, why doesn't everyone become a centralizer? If provincial patriotism persists and the security concerns disappear, why doesn't the "federal bargain" collapse?

In Riker's original book on federalism, he does attempt to answer that question by finding what he calls "a sufficient (but not necessary) condition" of the maintenance of federalism. This condition comes not from the institutional structure of the federal state but from its party structure. Riker writes: "The federal relationship is centralized according to the degree to which the parties organized to operate the central government control the parties organized to operate the constituent governments." He continues: "This amounts to the assertion that the proximate cause of variations in the degree of centralization (or peripheralization) in the constitutional structure of a federalism is the variation in the degree of party centralization" (Riker 1964, 129). What does this mean? To explain, an example would help. Riker notes that the Soviet Union, as a federal state, had, at least on paper, numerous federal guarantees to the various states within it. Yet, despite those constitutional guarantees, there was no effective federalism in the Soviet Union. To explain this absence, Riker cited the uniformity of the party structure. Such constitutional guarantees are meaningless in the Soviet Union not because it is an autocratic state as such but because of the unity and centralization of its single-party control.

For this reason, to see if federalism is effective, Riker argues, one must look not so much at the constitutional guarantees of federalism but at the instances of friction between the states and the central government. In states like the United States with party structures that are much less centralized and where there is much more ideological disunity, there is a far greater degree of tension between the federal government and the states. In fact, Riker suggests that presidents articulate ideological agendas precisely so as to create a manner in which to unify their political parties across the disunity inherent in the federal structure. As stated already, Riker wants to assert that party peripheralization and disunity is a cause, rather than a consequence, of the persistence of federalism. In other words, federalism persists in the United States not because of either its constitutional guarantees – look at Russia – or because of the "ideology" of federalism but because the United States has political parties characterized by a significant degree of internal dissension. This internal dissension produces the possibility that majority winners at the national level will not necessarily be able to command the obedience of even members of their own party who are majority winners at the state level. Thus, even if a political party controlled both all of the state and all of the national levels of government, there could still be dissension between the state and national governments. Riker claims that the opposition depends "on a partisan difference between the central and constituent leadership."

In arguing for the centrality of political parties in maintaining federalism, Riker does not simply dismiss the social conditions of any given state. He writes: "It is true that federalism is maintained by the existence of dual citizen loyalties to the two levels of government." But such, he claims, is "almost a tautology." While what Riker calls "background social conditions" certainly play a role in maintaining the federal bargain, "the structure of the party system" is the "main variable intervening between the background social conditions and the specific nature of the federal bargain." This means that, as important as background social conditions might be, they do not play a direct role in the maintenance of the federal bargain. The extreme example is helpful in seeing the consequence of this claim. Riker would suggest that, if a given party system is significantly centralized and unified, the federal bargain will also be centralized even if there is a significant amount of dual loyalty to the state and the national levels. Dual loyalty may contribute to the degree of party centralization but it does not directly affect the federal bargain.

In emphasizing the centrality of political parties as an explanatory variable, Riker decidedly rejects what he calls the "administrative theory of federalism." By this theory, the persistence of federalism derives from the "division and sharing of administrative responsibilities" (135). The central government is maintained by "administrative centralization" and "the sharing of administration is what is supposed to preserve the guarantees to the states." Riker claims there is absolutely no evidence for the explanatory power of either of these theories. Federalism is not maintained because of an attachment to abstract theories regarding the division of administrative labor. Riker's rejection of the administrative theory reveals him at his most strident. He writes: "Unfortunately, most American students of the subject have been deeply attracted to the theory; hence it has tended to obscure constitutional realities. I will be content if this essay has no other impact but to disabuse scholars of their faith in the clearly false administrative theory of federalism" (84).

Much is revealed by Riker's stridency in rejecting the administrative theory of federalism. Riker's account of federalism, in particular, and rational choice, in general, aims to impart a level of realism to the account of political institutions that it felt missing in the formalistic accounts that preceded it. For instance, describing K.C. Wheare's survey of federalism in his bibliographic section, "Suggestions for further reading," Riker writes: "It is highly legalistic in tone and displays very little understanding of political realities." He celebrates essays by David Truman and Edward Weidner for "transcending both the legalistic and the normative categories in which federalism is usually discussed" (157). Riker rejects completely such legalistic and normative accounts of federalism that fail to pay attention to what could be called the "facts on the ground." The administrative theory, as Riker understands it, asserts that federalism persists because it needs to persist so as to share the various functions of government. The sharing of the various functions of government is both functionally necessary and normatively good. But, for Riker, political reality rarely obeys either functional necessity or normative goods. Instead, it obeys a logic of political choice by which the results of politics follow from the aims of politicians within an institutional environment that constrains those aims. So, to discuss the maintenance of federalism, one must ignore normative or functional concerns about the sharing of administration and focus solely on why political actors have found it useful to maintain.

Thus, Riker suggests that political actors who have either lost on or been left out of decision-making at a higher level find the opportunities afforded by the lower levels of the federal state attractive. Federalism is maintained because political actors find it useful to win at lower levels when they have lost at higher levels. As such, they have no attachment to the principle of federalism itself – hence, the irrelevance of the administrative theory; they are attracted only to the opportunities that the institutions of federalism have afforded them. The discussions of federalism prior to Riker's ascribed the "ought" of federalism to the "is" of its maintenance. By contrast, in this book, he claims it is maintained for reasons having nothing to do with the attraction or lack thereof to its principles. He is strident against the administrative theory because he is strident against the claim that the normative principles of political scientists, i.e. federal administration is good because it shares responsibilities, have any explanatory power in describing political reality.

However, Riker's account of institutions seems to change over the course of his life so that, as has already been indicated, the stridency of his position modifies. In his later work, The *Development of American Federalism*, while he would still reject legalistic or normative theories that ascribe the "ought" of politics to the "is" of politics, he does write: "Institutions, once consciously formed, continually influence – with participants often unaware – the formation of the tastes of the next generation so that its members in turn clarify and render consistent the essential features of the institution as initially constructed" (Riker 1978, ix). The earlier Riker seemed to understand the institutions of federalism entirely in terms of their effect on political action. Political actors, unattached to the institutions as such, embraced the institutions or rejected them depending on their political wants. These political wants are entirely extrinsic to the institutions of federalism themselves. Now, Riker seems to admit the political power of federalism in its own right. Institutions can shape tastes. This concession means that, though it still would not be the case the federalism is maintained because political scientists think it ought to be maintained, it might be the case that a belief in the administrative theory of federalism among political actors themselves has contributed to the maintenance of federalism. The institutions of federalism do not simply constrain or provide opportunities for political losses and gains, they also create their own politics.

So, for instance, as Riker presents federalism in the first book, it merely provides the opportunity for Southern racists to maintain the oppression of blacks in the Southern states they control because they have lost this opportunity at the national level. In embracing the principles of federalism, they do so not because they love state sovereignty but because they want to oppress blacks in their states. As he presents it in this later book, the institutions of federalism are capable of shaping political tastes. It is now possible to embrace federalism as an end in itself and to reject the complete centralization of power neither because one wants to achieve other political ends nor because one possesses some irrational form of provincial patriotism.

This discontinuity between Riker's earlier and his later treatments of federalism holds in other areas as well. In characterizing the thesis that holds together the variety of essays that makes up his later book on federalism, Riker writes that one of his aims was to define "federalism as a constitutional form, not as mere administrative centralization." As a constitutional form, he examines, for instance in a paper that he co-authors with William Bast and includes in this book, the extent to which presidents have been able to exert an influence in congressional nominations. The constitutional form of federalism seemed to preclude the kind of national leadership that would exist if presidents were able more consistently to exert influence in congressional nominations. Because members of Congress are seeking election or reelection in races that are always and inherently about a large portion of local issues, they find that presidents are unable in many circumstances to exert influence on these races or even, in some cases, that attempts to exert influence have a reverse effect on the outcome of the election. As such, this indicates that the constitutional form of federalism changes the dynamics and the possibilities of national leadership.

But, whereas in the earlier book, he had argued that the persistence of federalism was a consequence of the disunity and decentralization within political parties, this argument seems to indicate that federalism, as a constitutional form, produces such disunity and decentralization. As he writes in the commentary before a section of the earlier book that is included in the later book: "There has been neither political nor constitutional unification because the separation of powers and the framers' kind of federalism have kept political parties local." In other words, whereas he had previously rejected the possibility that federalism itself could cause its persistence, he now seems willing to entertain this possibility. In fact, he writes: "Centralized federalism has been in fact self-perpetuating" (218). Constitutional forms do not simply alter political events; they also create their own.

Given these changes in his position, however, it is strange that Riker neither perceives nor admits to them. Instead, in the case both of his commentary on his earlier argument regarding political parties and his description of the formative influence of institutions, Riker suggests that his argument has remained constant throughout. Characterizing the point from which he began in the 1950s, he writes: "I assumed as an axiom that institutions are self-perpetuating" (ix).

But how can this be true given his argument in his first substantial book on federalism? In that book, so far from assuming that institutions are self-perpetuating, he seems almost perplexed at the survival of federalism long after the conditions that made the "federal bargain" necessary. Perhaps, however, insofar as Riker's understanding of federalism antedates his turn to rational choice theory, this contradiction can be explained by an excess of stridency that accompanied his initial turn to a more economic manner of thinking. This is to say that perhaps Riker overstated and even misstated his arguments regarding federalism in his 1964 book because he had found a new way of approaching all political questions. After all, he does not say that his initial assumption about federalism in the 1950s stemmed from his theoretical approach. Instead, as he admits in the article mentioned earlier, he had not yet found that theoretical approach in the 1950s when he initially makes these assumptions about federalism. What is interesting then is that, as he now understands his intellectual journey, his initial assumptions have survived his theoretical turn, rather than, as in the 1964 book, being drastically changed by it. In other words, it seems his initial pre-theoretical understanding of federalism was more correct than his 1964 "theoretical" understanding.

If this is true, what does it say about the worth of rational choice theory for, in this specific case, our understanding of federalism and, in the more general sense, our understanding of politics? Given the analysis I have offered here, one might be tempted to conclude that it detracted from as much as it contributed to Riker's understanding of federalism. However, it is still surely the case that Riker's "rationalism" provided a useful corrective to the excesses of legalism and normativism that preceded him in 1964. By focusing our attention on the action of politics, rather than its optimal organization or its laws, Riker's theoretical model helps us to create an account of federalism that, as he says, constitutes a "fairly considerable advance" (xiii). Rather than either concluding that federalism exists because it ought to or that federalism exists because economic conditions make it necessary, Riker makes us realize that federalism can only come into being if some set of political actors want it to come into being. Political institutions can arise only from the intentions of political actors. Insofar as this emphasis on intentions derives from rational choice, we can see how useful rational choice is as a corrective to the determinism inherent in other explanations of political behavior. If the political actors in the Constitutional Convention had not arrived at the "federal bargain" as a palliative to the provincial interests while still achieving, to the extent possible, their vision of centralization, then centralized federalism, as much as it might have been the correct answer to their problems, would not have been created. This is to say that the real contribution of rational choice is no more than, but also no less than, the insight that political results can only arise from political intentions, as they are constrained by a given political environment. Riker and the Rochester school he creates help us to see that a real explanation of politics must be essentially political, taking into account the political wants of all those involved.

Given this, however, why is it that, in the throes of this new approach to politics, Riker seems more reductionist in his account of federalism? In other words, if rational choice helps us to focus our attention on the eminently political nature of political events, why is it that Riker seems so interested in ruling out a certain portion of politics in his 1964 book? To answer this question adequately would go beyond the bounds of this chapter. It is helpful, but by no means sufficient, to note, as Riker does, that rational choice arises from economics. And, perhaps both because of its roots in economics and because it seeks "parsimony" in its political explanations, there is a tendency within rational choice to try to find an overly simplistic explanation for any political behavior. Thus, it is far simpler, for instance, to suggest that federalism arises from a bargain struck between the centralizers and the provincialists than to suggest that the bargain itself created its own set of partisans. Moreover, insofar as the role of ideas in politics is necessarily complicated and contested, rational choice, as a method of explanation that aims for the status of science, tends to want to downplay or eliminate their importance as causal factors.

The economic model tends to posit simply self-interest, or surplus maximization, for its explanation of human behavior and so its adoption by rational choice has tended to cause it to seek the same sorts of motivations. But Riker and the Rochester school, more generally, have consistently maintained that to explain political behavior, they both need not and cannot reduce human motivations to the same overly simplistic matrix of self-interest. Instead, as Riker emphasizes in one of his most useful articles on this question, even suicide can be analyzed rationally so long as the human being is rational in the manner in which he seeks this end (Riker 1990, 173). In short, rational choice simply provides a manner of analyzing the ways in which human beings seek indeterminate and widely varying ends in an instrumental fashion. Politics necessarily involves a wider range of ends than economics and so must incorporate a wider range of motivations.

Given this admission, it is not the case that Riker's later discussion of federalism contradicts his adoption of rational choice. Instead, it seems to indicate the evolution of his understanding of rational choice itself. He came to see that there was no necessary reason why his adoption of rational choice should exclude the assumptions he made at the beginning of his study of federalism. Instead, he implicitly realized that he must accommodate the arguments of rational choice to the truth about the explanation of federalism. As an explanatory model of political behavior, rational choice cannot simply exclude those assumptions that aid in explanation. Though an attachment to the idea of federalism is a necessarily more complicated explanation, it cannot simply be excluded because of its complications. In fact, Riker seems to have come to see what he would not admit in his 1964 book: that one cannot explain the persistence of federalism except with some incorporation of an attachment to the idea itself.

Thus, though Riker would not have admitted this, he came to see that there was at least a kernel of truth in the arguments that had been advanced within administrative theory. Though he would (and should) reject any claim that federalism persists because it is the most rational manner in which to organize a large state, he would no longer reject the claim that federalism persists, at least in part, because many politicians think it is the most rational manner in which to organize a large state. In helping us to see that federalism only persists so long as it is seen as good, Riker provides a tremendous insight into our understanding of federalism.

Riker's other significant addition to our understanding of federalism derives from his intimate understanding of American federalism. Although it is ultimately insufficient as an explanation of the whole cause of the "federal bargain," Riker's military argument provides an important insight into the origins of federalism. He shows persuasively both that security concerns were preeminent in the minds of those who accepted or sought federalism at the American founding and that security concerns have also been preeminent in the minds of those who have copied the American example of centralized federalism since. Given a set of provincial states with significant autonomy but common security concerns, a federal state is likely to form when people become sufficiently concerned about their security. Of course, because Riker does not ascribe to a principle of political determinism, a federal state will not necessarily form given those conditions. Moreover, it would be extremely unlikely to form were it not for the American invention of "centralized federalism." Since what came before was not the form of federalism that we now know throughout the world, other states might not have arrived at this principle of "centralized federalism" on their own. Thus, for Riker, the creation of the American form of federalism stands as a watershed event in the history of federalism. The American founders did not, Riker suggests, copy other forms of federalism that came before it. Instead what they invented was so entirely new as to make federalism as we know it entirely impossible without their invention.

References

Riker, William H. 1964. *Federalism: Origin, Operation, and Significance*. Boston, MA: Little, Brown, and Company.
— 1978. *The Development of American Federalism*. Boston, MA: Kluwer Academic Publishers.
— 1990. Political science and rational choice, in *Perspectives on Positive Political Economy*, eds James E. Alt and Kenneth A. Shepsle. Cambridge, UK: Cambridge University Press.
— 1997. The ferment of the 1950s and the development of rational choice theory, in *Contemporary Empirical Political Theory*, ed. Kristen Renwick Monroe. Berkeley, CA: University of California Press.

Further Reading

Amadae, S.M. 2003. *Rationalizing Capitalist Democracy: The Cold War Origins of Rational Choice Liberalism*. Chicago, IL: University of Chicago Press.
Ferejohn, John A. and Barry R. Weingast (eds) 1997. *The New Federalism: Can the States be Trusted?* Palo Alto, CA: Hoover Institution Press.

Green, Donald P. and Ian Shapiro. 1994. *Pathologies of Rational Choice Theory: A Critique of Applications in Political Science*. New Haven, CT: Yale University Press.
Johnson, Kimberley S. 2007. *Governing the American State: Congress and the New Federalism, 1877–1929*. Princeton, NJ: Princeton University Press.
Riker, William H. 1982. *Liberalism Against Populism: A Confrontation between the Theory of Democracy and the Theory of Social Choice*. San Francisco, CA: W.H. Freeman.
—— 1986. *The Art of Political Manipulation*. New Haven, CT: Yale University Press.
—— and Peter C. Ordeshook. 1973. *An Introduction to Positive Political Theory*. Englewood Cliffs, NJ: Prentice-Hall.
Rose, Jurgen and Johannes Ch. Trout (eds). 2002. *Federalism and Decentralization: Perspectives for the Transformation Process in Eastern and Central Europe*. New York, NY: Palgrave.
Shepsle, Kenneth A. and Mark S. Bonchek. 1997. *Analyzing Politics: Rationality, Behavior, and Institutions*. New York, NY: W.W. Norton & Company.
Wibbels, Erik. 2005. *Federalism and the Market: Intergovernmental Conflict and Economic Reform in the Developing World*. Cambridge, UK: Cambridge University Press.
Zimmerman, Joseph F. 1992. *Contemporary American Federalism: The Growth of National Power*. Westport, CT: Praeger Publishers.

Theories of Fiscal Federalism and the European Experience

Alberto Majocchi

The Classical Model of Fiscal Federalism

Within the global field of public finance, fiscal federalism addresses the vertical structure of the public sector, and the model to which the literature refers is that built initially by Musgrave (1959) and then developed by Oates (1972). In this model the economic functions are assigned to the different levels of government according to a scheme where the central government has basic responsibility for macroeconomic stabilization and for income redistribution. In addition to these functions, the central government provides goods and services consumed by the entire population, while local governments provide goods and services whose consumption is limited to their own population. These conclusions follow from some very simple assumptions:

- The redistribution function should be centralized because the mobility of persons – which increases as the size of the territorial area diminishes – may cause locally implemented redistribution policies to fail. In fact, any jurisdiction which unilaterally imposes higher taxes on the rich encourages the loss of mobile resources, including both capital and high-income residents. Alternatively, jurisdictions which unilaterally offer large subsidies to the poor will attract outsiders to share the benefits. Consequently, where the intention is to adopt a strongly redistributive policy, the financial resources will be lacking because expenditure is very high and the tax base has shrunk, while in the other areas the budget will show a substantial surplus because the tax base has expanded.
- The stabilization function should also be centrally managed. The reason in this case is the greater effectiveness of fiscal policy, which depends on the propensity to import and, therefore, on the level of the multiplier. Lower levels

of government are more open to trade. Consequently, expenditure remaining equal, a larger amount of benefits in terms of income and employment will arise outside the territorial area in which the resources necessary to finance expansionary policy have been collected. In the presence of strong positive externalities, the supply of the public good "stabilization" may therefore be sub optimal.
- Only the allocative function should be distributed geographically, because the task of supplying public goods should be assigned to the level of government within whose territory the majority of the benefits of spending occur. Hence, the production of local public goods should be undertaken by the lower levels of government, in that "a varied pattern of local outputs in accordance with local tastes will be Pareto superior to an outcome characterized by a centrally determined, uniform level of output across all jurisdictions" (Oates 2005, 353).

This proposition, well known as the Decentralization Theorem, correctly recognizes that output of some local public goods can produce interjurisdictional spillover benefits, i.e. benefits for residents in other jurisdictions. If these external effects are limited, they could be internalized, according to the traditional Pigouvian theory, through subsidies provided by a higher level of government. However, when public services are pure public goods for which the marginal cost of adding another user will be zero, or when external benefits are large or the benefits extend nationwide, the production of public goods becomes a task of the central government since a decentralized production of these goods, characterized by large positive externalities across jurisdictions, will yield a sub optimal level of output.

The Decentralization Theorem assumes that the alternative to the local provision of public goods is a centrally determined uniform level of public output. This assumption is based on two arguments: the first is that local governments are closer to their constituencies, and therefore have more in-depth knowledge of the local preferences. Instead, it is difficult for the central government to determine the different preferences of all the jurisdictions. The second argument is that there is a political constraint – the need to avoid any discrimination between different local or regional authorities – which induces the central level of government to provide a uniform level of output to all the local units.

A further argument in support of the assignment of the allocation function to the local authorities as far as the provision of local public goods is concerned is linked to the well-known Tiebout (1956) model, in which households are assumed to be freely mobile. They shop among local jurisdictions and select the community of residence that offers their preferred package of local public goods, taxes, and regulations. In this institutional structure, if any jurisdiction were to provide public services inefficiently, households would move to another jurisdiction. Tiebout's competition then produces a Pareto-efficient outcome since people sort themselves into groups that are homogenous in their demands for local services. As the Decentralization Theorem clearly shows, the more homogenous local jurisdictions are in their demands, and the greater the variation in these demands across local jurisdictions, the larger the welfare gains from decentralization. Hence the Tiebout argument strengthens the validity of the Oates model.

According to Oates, therefore, there are solid economic reasons for preferring a federal structure of the state. This structure, in fact, is optimal not only because of the political benefits that it brings by guaranteeing greater democracy through the creation of a pluralist, and therefore competitive, system, but it is so also from an economic point of view (Breton and Scott 1978) in that it complies with Wheare's (1963, 10) recommendation that "by the federal principle I mean the method of dividing powers so that the general and regional government are each, within a sphere, co-ordinate and independent."

Wheare's institutional vision must be kept in mind if the optimal economic constitution is to be defined, since, according to Oates, a federal model guarantees effective coordination, and therefore unity, as far as stabilization and redistribution policies are concerned, and the independence of the various tiers of government in the allocation branch of the government. In this regard, territorial differentiation in the production of public goods is the necessary condition for the maximizing of social welfare.

The Financing of Local Governments with Own Resources and Intergovernmental Transfers

The principle of fiscal equivalence implies that, within a given jurisdiction, the costs of providing public goods should be covered by those that enjoy their benefits. This prompts the question known in the literature as the "tax assignment problem" (McLure 1983): what are the taxes best suited to financing the different levels of government?

The idea in the mainstream literature is generally that benefit taxation should be the rule at the local level. This implies that local governments should rely mainly on property taxation and user fees, while the use of redistributive taxes – like the progressive income tax – should be assigned to the central level of government. An important corollary to this contention concerns environmental taxes (Brosio 2006). If the tax base is related to the territory, or land use, the tax should be assigned to the local level. A relevant example is road pricing. Taxing the use of roads is a kind of benefit taxation because the environmental benefits (less congestion, less pollution) are mainly enjoyed by residents in the area. Energy taxation could be established at the central level, since the benefits (less emissions of greenhouse gases, less acidification) are enjoyed by everybody, while an additional local tax on the same tax basis is likewise justified since local pollution diminishes.

Here, the main concern regards the possible distortions due to the decentralized taxation of mobile tax bases. Local governments operate in settings where economic units are able to move rather freely among jurisdictions. Hence, taxes may give rise to distortions in resource allocation. If capital – which is quite mobile – is taxed at the local level, the outcome may be capital outflows and the inefficient location of this production factor. As Oates stresses, this does not mean that mobile units should not be taxed at the local level, but "that on efficiency grounds decentralized governments should tax mobile economic units with benefit levies" (Oates 1999, 1125).

Reliance on benefit taxes at the local level does not exclude the use of intergovernmental transfers. These are justified for at least three reasons. The first of them is the existence of benefits external to the jurisdiction. If these are not internalized, the production of public goods will be sub optimal. The second is that fiscal equalization across jurisdictions is necessary to reduce excessive differences in per capita income among different areas. Given the same fiscal effort, the jurisdiction where the level of per capita income is higher will be preferred both by the rich and the poor because the revenue from local taxes, and therefore the output of public goods, will be higher. Horizontal equity is violated since households are treated differently according to their location or residence (Boadway 2006). A lump-sum grant from the central to the regional or local government is therefore justified on both equity and efficiency grounds, for otherwise the gap between the level of economic activity in the poor jurisdiction and the national average will constantly widen. The third reason is that there is no perfect correspondence between expenditures and revenues raised at the different levels of government, and this disequilibrium must be covered by a transfer of resources from the central government to the local ones.

Grants may be either conditional, with restrictions on their use by the recipient, or unconditional, so that they can be used for any purpose. Conditional grants should be utilized in the form of matching grants to internalize benefits engendered for residents of other jurisdictions, when the grantor guarantees a certain share of the expenditure. This is a sort of Pigouvian subsidy whose purpose is to incorporate external benefits into the economic calculations of the decision-maker; and the matching rate should reflect the extent of the spillovers.

Unconditional grants are normally used for fiscal equalization on the basis of an equalization formula related to the fiscal need or the fiscal capacity of the recipient jurisdiction. In the absence of such grants, the gap between rich and poor jurisdictions will widen, whilst grants could produce a more level playing field. But the primary justification for fiscal equalization is still the one based not on efficiency, but on equity grounds. According to Oates (1999, 1128) "the prescriptive theory of intergovernmental grants thus leads to a vision of a system in which there exists a set of open-ended matching grants, where the matching rates reflect the extent of benefit spillovers across jurisdictional boundaries, and a set of unconditional grants for revenue sharing and, perhaps, equalization purposes."

Local governments could be funded through revenue sharing as well. This implies that the central government collects taxes whose revenue is in turn redistributed to the local or regional levels. There is a large body of evidence that regional and local taxes are normally more regressive than the central ones, and this justifies the collection of national taxes and their redistribution to the lower tiers of government. Furthermore, if the administration of local taxes is inefficient, it makes sense for central government to collect tax revenues for, and then transfer grants revenue to, regional and local governments. To avoid the risk that moral hazards generate inefficient behaviours by local governments – which view such transfers as "blank cheques" issued by the central government – they should be linked to the rates of taxes determined by local authorities.

The New Theory of Fiscal Federalism

A different view of fiscal federalism has been pioneered in the literature by Brennan and Buchanan (1980) and Breton (1998). It envisions the public sector as a Leviathan whose main goal is to maximize the revenues extracted from the economy. From this perspective, decentralization is a device to restrict the expansionary tendencies of the government. Competition among local authorities can limit the capacity of a monopolistic central government to increase its control over the economy's resources and "offer partial or possibly complete substitutes for explicit fiscal constraint on the taxing power" (Brennan and Buchanan 1980, 184).

According to the "public choice approach," a decentralized system produces, through competition, control over decision-makers (Breton 2006). This is because when the citizens of one jurisdiction appraise the performance of their government by comparing it with the performance elsewhere but at the same jurisdictional level, they will induce their government to behave as well as (or better than) the other ones in terms "of levels and qualities of services, of levels of taxes or more general economic and social indicators" (Salmon 1987, 32).

This is a controversial issue with regard to the European experience, because the Treaty of Maastricht does not consider fiscal competition to be a mechanism adequate to control the gap between revenues and expenditures at the level of member-states joining the Monetary Union, and it has set an explicit limit in order to prevent any excessive deficits. Whilst some states have been explicitly in favour of fiscal competition among the different member-states, the prevailing view has been that the risks of a "race to the bottom" engendered by fiscal competition should be avoided by adopting a cooperative approach.

In an important survey of theories on fiscal federalism, Inman and Rubinfeld (1997, 47) remark that "for most economists, the principle of economic federalism, with its recommended institutions of competitive decentralized local governments and a strong central government to provide pure public goods and control intercommunity externalities, essentially defines what federalism is about. However, the principle has had only mixed success as a guide to economic policy. Its strength has been to articulate how fiscal competition among decentralized local governments can ensure the efficient provision of congestible public services; several recent studies offer empirical support for the proposition that competitive local governments do provide citizens the public services they want at the lowest cost."

On the other hand, cooperative federalism assigns all public goods and the control of intercommunity externalities locally, unless local governments voluntarily agree to do so centrally. But even agreements among few jurisdictions often fail to achieve fully efficient outcomes, and the macro-management of the economy can also be regarded as the response of the central government to a failure of Coasian bargaining among the local authorities. With reference to the European experience, Collignon (2003, 108) shows the conditions necessary for member-state governments to voluntarily co operate in order to supply European collective goods: "1) if the benefits for one government are less than the total cost of providing the European good, there is a rational incentive to this government not to participate in the EU's provision of the collective good and to 'free ride'; 2) the larger the number of the EU member-states, the less likely they are in providing the collective goods."

Finally, Inman and Rubinfeld define democratic federalism as a system that "unlike economic federalism does not implicitly assume that the central government will provide public goods and regulate interjurisdictional spillovers efficiently. In contrast to cooperative federalism, only majority-rule – not unanimity – is required to make a decision. Democratic federalism seeks to balance the potential efficiency gains of greater centralization in a world of local spillovers and pure public goods against the inefficiencies which might arise when a central legislature sets policies" (Inman and Rubinfeld 1997, 51). Close account should be taken of this approach in the ongoing discussions on the new Lisbon Treaty and the development of fiscal federalism in the perspective of a European Constitution (Collignon 2003).

The Distinctiveness of the European Experience

Assessment of the prospects for European fiscal federalism must start from the premise that Europe is at present undergoing two simultaneous institutional changes: on the one hand, an upward devolution of powers from member-states to the European Union; on the other, a downward transfer of powers from states to local governments. The current political debate does not generally take account of this simultaneity, and the two processes are studied separately. In particular, whilst close consideration is made of the increasing decentralization of government functions, insufficient examination is made of the new constraints – and the new opportunities – that membership of the European Union entails for all lower levels of government.

The decentralization of functions from the central state to local government is a process ongoing in almost all the member-states of the European Union: new competences are attributed to infra-state levels (Breton and Fraschini 2003), and in parallel, albeit in different ways according to the country, the resources necessary to meet spending requirements are transferred. At the same time, apparent at European level is a model of fiscal federalism which reflects the classic definition by Oates (1999), but with original features connected with the distinctive experience of the European Union.

As a matter of fact the Musgrave–Oates theoretical model is contradicted by the current distribution of functions within the European Union (Tabellini 2001) in two main respects:

- Redistribution policy is, and presumably will remain at least in the foreseeable future, assigned to the national level, not to the Union. Since Pauly's (1973) celebrated essay on redistribution as a local public good, the literature has put forward various theoretical reasons for this choice, which seems necessary in Europe given the marked differences that persist at national level in social preference functions concerning the optimum level of redistribution.
- But stabilization policy, too, is predominantly assigned to the national level. It is true that the management of monetary policy has by now been transferred to the European level, but the Treaty of Maastricht gives the European Central Bank solely the task of ensuring price stability, whilst in regard to stabilization policy the Treaty merely states that this must be pursued through the coordination of national policies.

The building of Europe is a process in constant evolution. Hence it may happen that this allocation of functions will change over time. It is possible that the European experience may generate a new model for the assignment of governmental economic functions: one which is more federalist, and which grants a greater role to the lower levels of government in regard to redistribution and stabilization. Should this happen, it will obviously be necessary, on the one hand, to strengthen the decision-making capacity of the European institutions, and on the other, to introduce mechanisms for effective coordination not only between the European Union and the member-states, but also with regional and local governments.

As regards stabilization policy, the Oates model envisages that this function should be undertaken at the supranational European level, for a stabilization policy managed at national level is largely ineffective, given the macroeconomic externalities that it produces. Indeed, since the creation of the monetary union, currency management has been assigned to the European level of government. But national fiscal policy, too, is already subject to numerous restrictions. Firstly, owing to the constraints of Europe-level fiscal harmonization, taxes cannot be freely varied. Secondly, as regards public spending, its expansionary effects tend largely to be transferred to the other member countries, given the extent of interdependence now achieved. Thirdly, budget balances are conditioned by the Maastricht constraints and the rules set out in the Stability Pact, which significantly condition the flexibility of fiscal policy at the member-state level.

It follows from these remarks that stabilization policy should necessarily be transferred to the European level, and the literature puts forward various arguments in support of this conclusion. Firstly, national governments are prepared to produce an amount of the public good "stabilization" which falls short of that deemed optimal by the European Union, because stabilization policies tend to exert their effects in the other countries belonging to the Union. Secondly, in the event of asymmetric shocks, automatic stabilization is excessive, and therefore more deflationary than necessary, because it does not take account of the negative external effects that it generates.

A second reason for assignment of stabilization policy to the European level concerns the operation of Ricardian equivalence. In this case, agents anticipate the effects of intertemporal stabilization on their tax liabilities, thereby dampening the impact on aggregate expenditure of variations in the net balance of taxes and transfers. Bayoumi and Masson (1998) have shown that, in Canada, the impact of a deficit in the provincial budget on consumption within the province is only equal to between one-third and one-half of the expansionary effect of an equivalent federal deficit in the same province. Finally, also the mobility of tax bases within a monetary union may reduce the effectiveness of a stabilization policy at regional level (Torres and Giavazzi 1993).

The Coordination of Fiscal Policies

The debate about stabilization policy within Europe has produced important innovative ideas, especially in those countries where there is strong resistance against relinquishing national autonomy in the management of stabilization policy. In his discussion of whether responsibility for such policy should be transferred to Community level, Leeftink (2000) concludes to the contrary, because the financial discipline imposed first by the Maastricht constraints and then by the Stability Pact have already significantly strengthened the effects of automatic stabilization. Consequently, in his view there is no convincing economic argument for strengthening the coordination of policies. Nevertheless, closer coordination of the economic policies of the member-states belonging to the monetary union has already been initiated by the Maastricht decisions intended to ensure a more effective stabilization policy.

As regards fiscal policy in particular, there are two main arguments in support of coordination, and therefore against unrestrained fiscal competition among member-states. Firstly, in the presence of closer integration among member countries, and especially greater mobility of the factors, fiscal competition may progressively reduce tax rates, with the consequent impossibility of financing a level of public spending deemed desirable. The coordination of fiscal policies, with rates sufficiently high to generate the requisite tax yield, may therefore be the suitable arrangement. Likewise, whenever it seems possible to obtain increased efficiency through a common management of taxation, it is advisable to assign a proportion of the tax yield to European level, i.e. to create a system of revenue-sharing between the European Union and national governments.

The second argument in favour of coordination concerns the existence of externalities which render uncoordinated policies sub optimal. In general, this may happen if the benefits of public spending extend beyond national boundaries, if there are increasing returns to scale in the production of public services, or if fiscal policies have macroeconomic external effects. However, once the need for closer coordination of fiscal policies within the European Union has been recognized, the debate shifts to how such coordination can be achieved in practice (Masson 2000).

In general, three models of coordination are available. Firstly, the member countries may decide to harmonize their spending and taxation policies. There is already a notable level of VAT harmonization in Europe. By contrast, attempts to harmonize taxation on financial incomes have to date been unsuccessful, and there is scant coordination of social policies, despite the attempts recently made by the Luxembourg European Council. It seems unlikely that further harmonization can be achieved without substantial institutional strengthening of the Union so that it is able to influence the decisions of member-states, also through the use of suitable financial incentives. A striking example is provided by the hitherto unsuccessful attempt to achieve the close harmonization of excise duties, in particular through the creation of a common system of energy taxation.

Secondly, it may be decided to launch a common action run directly by an European institution. In this case the coordination would very strong, and it would represent an important step towards creation of a system of fiscal federalism.

Thirdly, coordination may involve a mechanism of multilateral surveillance over national fiscal policies, although without binding constraints on the exercise of national sovereignty or a significant increase in the size of the European budget. Coordination would therefore result from a system of peer pressure. But there would be no guarantee that the final outcome would be any different from that forthcoming from an uncoordinated system.

As the institutional development of the European Union proceeds, it is likely that the three models of coordination will coexist until the final stage of a federal system has been reached: there will be harmonization in some areas, multilateral surveillance and peer pressure in others, and in yet others some embryonic form of fiscal federalism. The problem is determining in which of the traditional sectors of public finance – allocation of resources, stabilization and redistribution of income – intervention through a European fiscal policy is necessary, given that there exist substantial externalities which, according to the subsidiarity principle, render national-level fiscal policies ineffective.

Approval of the Stability and Growth Pact has greatly restricted the scope for autonomous stabilization policy at national level if a country is hit by an exogenous asymmetric shock when it is already close to the deficit level set by the Pact. It has been proposed in the past that this limitation could be overcome by creating a European Unemployment Fund. First mooted in the MacDougall Report (European Commission 1977), this idea has been subsequently taken up by other authors with a view to introducing an automatic stabilizer at European level (Melitz and Vori 1992; for more critical treatment see von Hagen and Hammond 1997). It is true that, as for example Fatás and Mihov (1999) have shown, the volatility of output is lower in countries where the share of public spending in GDP is high, as in the European countries. Yet this argument does not seem decisive as regards stabilization, given that other authors have stressed that high public spending may have negative effects on development (Masson 2000), and that there is, moreover, strong political pressure to reduce expenditure to rebalance budgets structurally and thus comply with the constraints imposed by the Stability Pact.

The Maastricht Model

In the end, the Maastricht model (Treaty on European Union 1992) comprises significant innovations in the field of stabilization policy, but it also has a serious shortcoming. The model is important because it does not transfer stabilization policy in its entirety to the European level but leaves responsibility for it to national governments, merely stating that the European level should ensure the coordination of national economic policies. It thus seeks to avert the risk of asynchrony in stabilization policies – whereby one country adopts an expansionary policy while another country pursues a restrictive one – and uses the multilateral surveillance mechanism to steer national economic policies towards convergent objectives.

This therefore appears to be a significant deviation from Oates's theoretical model. The European experience does not deem it necessary to transfer the direct management of stabilization policy to the supranational level. Stabilization policy is in fact managed by member-states, although its coordination is to be ensured at supranational level. This provision means that "the budgeting may be done on a national and regional level, while the aggregate fiscal policy stance needs to be set at the European level" (Collignon 2003, 137). Yet there is a decisive shortcoming in the Maastricht model, and it consists in the fact that coordination must be ensured by the Council of Ministers, where decisions on fiscal policy are subject to the rule of unanimity. And this rule can guarantee neither the democracy nor the efficiency of decisions. Hence at European level also decisions on fiscal matters should be taken by majority vote in the future, and no longer unanimously, in accordance with the rules of democratic federalism. However, this outcome is still very distant, even after the innovations that should ensue from ratification of the Treaty of Lisbon.

If Europe is able to generalize the rule that decisions are taken by majority vote, important innovation may come about at European level in the management of stabilization policy, in that it will be predominantly managed by member-states through the coordination method, and coordination will be effective to the extent that majoritarian principle is applied. Also without direct intervention through the European budget, and therefore with the limited resources available at present, there will be neither the current time delays nor the current inefficiencies; and an embryonic common economic policy will finally be in place, rather than a mere sum of national policies. Obviously, once the federal stage has been reached, and when the European budget is of adequate size, European resources will efficaciously supplement national resources in the management of stabilization policy, thereby heightening its efficiency.

Redistribution Policy

With regard to redistribution, it is widespread within member-states but still limited at European level. The reason that it should be increased is the fact that fiscal capacity varies across countries owing to their different levels of per capita income. Consequently, in order to furnish the same level of services, governments must impose different tax rates, thereby favouring the mobility of factors for fiscal reasons, a system which is inefficient because it entails real costs in terms of resources. From this point of view, redistribution appears justified. Moreover, redistribution may serve the purpose of increasing solidarity among the countries belonging to the European Union, and thus promote further integration. However, from both these points of view there does not at present seem to be scope for increasing redistribution processes within the Union (Masson 2000).

Interpersonal income redistribution did not originate as a public policy; rather, it was initially managed by private agents and was founded upon the sense of solidarity. The latter is stronger at local level where face-to-face relationships predominate, but it tends to diminish as the territorial area increases, because solidarity springs from interdependence among utility functions and there is a positive external effect if poverty is reduced. If the redistribution function is assigned to the higher level of government, the amount of the redistribution tends to decrease because, at this level, it is more difficult to foster a real sense of solidarity. It is thus necessary to return, in a certain sense, to the origins of redistribution policy, but without losing the efficacy achieved at national level through creation of the large-scale social security systems that characterize the European model. Interpersonal redistribution should therefore in principle be entrusted to the lowest levels of government, which for that matter are already those most concerned with it.

Instead, significant responsibilities for the territorial redistribution of income should be assigned to the higher level of government, and therefore to the European level. It is necessary to ensure that also poorer areas can enjoy certain minimum standards in the level of public services, so that at least potentially equal opportunities are afforded to all persons resident upon the territory of the European Union. There is consequently an important distinction between the territorial and personal redistribution of income. The European level must undertake territorial redistribution so that equalizing transfers ensure that all areas of the European Union offer equal opportunities (minimum levels of healthcare, education, and so on) and certain basic services are furnished uniformly. The member-states and local communities, for their part, must maintain their responsibilities for the management of social policy and the redistribution of personal income – according to the preferences of each community – while averting the perverse effects in terms of mobility envisaged by the theoretical model of fiscal federalism. The European Union seems already to be moving towards this structure of redistribution policy by intervening substantially in territorial redistribution through the Regional Fund and the Structural Funds. But it does not concern itself with personal redistribution, which should remain largely the competence of the lower levels of government, even if reform of social security systems should seek to ensure that their structure is such to increase mobility through the standardization of benefits without producing significant net flows among countries (Masson 2000).

The New Model of Fiscal Federalism

The role of the European budget is extremely limited as regards the allocative function, given that its size is equal to around 1 per cent of European GDP. The production of public goods and services has historically been undertaken primarily by the state. But today it appears more uniformly distributed among the different levels of government, albeit with marked differences within the Union. In the allocation branch – bearing in mind that a substantial increase in expenditure on a European foreign and security policy is unavoidable in the future, but politically difficult in this phase of the integration process, after the collapse of the European Constitution in the referendum held in France and Netherlands – there are good reasons for the transfer to European level of higher education, since it has significant cross-border externalities, and for the creation of infrastructures with features that make them essential in an European context. Also the common financing of expenditure on research and development is desirable, given that its benefits are not typically manifest at the national level alone. There are probably other sectors in which greater intervention by the European budget is justified; yet it is not in the allocative sector that the future development of the Union's public finance of the union will concentrate.

In conclusion, since the allocative function is largely assigned to the national level of government, the model of fiscal federalism apparent within the European Union is more decentralized than in the theoretical model developed by Musgrave and Oates. Hence, there seems to be little justification for the fears that the creation of the monetary union and the ensuing institutional developments may generate a new, strongly centralized state (Tabellini 2001). The Europe that will come into being will be federal in its nature. The problem is that today this federal structure – able to ensure both efficiency and the maximum possible decentralization of governmental economic functions – does not yet exist. Hence substantial problems may arise during this transitional phase, and particularly as regards the effectiveness of stabilization policy.

As regards redistribution, a first step towards structural reform has been accomplished with creation of the Monetary Union, in that most of the member-states have definitely relinquished monetary sovereignty and, therefore, the possibility of financing redistributive policies with the issuance of money. Today incisive redistribution measures can be financed only to the extent that it is possible to build the consensus necessary for their financing out of taxes – or at any rate by levying the higher taxes which will be necessary in the future to service the new debt produced by welfare policies. On the other hand, welfare services are increasingly allocated to the market or to non-profit organizations, which operate mainly at local level and can be supported by tax benefits decided at national level.

As for stabilization, an increasing proportion of total public spending is now handled by lower levels of government. This therefore raises the problem not only of ensuring efficient economic policy coordination – which is still the only means to manage the Economic Union – at the level of the Union, but also at national level, the purpose being to prevent financially autonomous local governments from increasing expenditure during periods of expansion and reducing it during recessionary phases, with pro-cyclical effects. The task of the state is therefore to manoeuvre transfer policy in such a way as to prevent the onset of these perverse effects.

The Financing Structure of the Lower Levels of Government and the Institutional Mechanism for Resources Distribution

A further problem is defining the optimal financing structure for the lower levels of government. First to be pointed out is that it now seems widely accepted that local public expenditure should be financed by taxes collected in the territorial area where most of benefits from the spending occur. Also from this point of view, European experience appears highly diversified. But a common problem still persists. The assignment to lower levels of own taxes may ensure autonomy, but it must be supplemented by equalizing transfers for two reasons: on the one hand, the more financial autonomy increases, the greater the need for a system of equalizing transfers; on the other, the allocation of own taxes to regional and local governments does not guarantee that the dynamics of the revenues will exactly correspond to the dynamics of spending by these levels of government whilst also ensuring the minimum output of the local public goods which the state intends to guarantee throughout the country because it regards them as merit goods.

But the optimal level of transfers cannot be decided independently by the state, for this would seriously curtail the decision-making autonomy of local governments. The aim should therefore be to define a system of public finance governance which ensures participation by lower levels of government in both definition of the equalizing transfers and the assignment of resources to supplement own resources. This institutional mechanism is guaranteed in a federal system like Germany's, in which the Länder participate in decisions by the Bundesrat on the assignment of resources. But in unitary states, once state law has defined the assignment of own resources and transfers, any variation is subject to a further decision by the state, which is generally under the obligation to conduct only non-binding consultations.

The form taken by the institutional mechanisms regulating the distribution of resources is also important for assessment of possible solutions to the problem of the different kinds of competition – vertical and horizontal – that may arise within a system of fiscal federalism. The former, which is normally considered more important, presupposes that the taxpayer is unique and is subject to an overall tax burden consisting of the sum collected by the state and the lower levels of government. Consequently, if the amount of spending is freely decided by each level, which must then collect the necessary resources in accordance with the principles of fiscal federalism, the quantity of resources usable by the other levels is automatically defined once the overall tax burden deemed acceptable in a particular political context has been determined. In this case too, therefore, coordination among the different levels of government appears unavoidable.

References

Ahmad, E. and Brosio, G. (2006), *Handbook of Fiscal Federalism* (Cheltenham: Edward Elgar).
Bayoumi, T. and Masson, P. (1998), Liability-creating versus non-liability-creating fiscal stabilisation policies: Ricardian equivalence, fiscal stabilisation and EMU, *Economic Journal*, 1–20.
Boadway, R. (2006), Intergovernmental redistributive transfers: efficiency and equity, in Ahmad, E. and Brosio, G. (2006), 355–380.
Brennan, G. and Buchanan, J. (1980), *The Power to Tax: Analytical Foundations of a Fiscal Constitution* (Cambridge: Cambridge Univ. Press).
Breton, A. and Scott, A. (1978), *The Economic Constitution of Federal States* (Toronto: University of Toronto Press).
—— (1998), *Competitive Governments: An Economic Theory of Politics and Public Finance* (Cambridge: Cambridge Univ. Press).
—— and Fraschini, A. (2003), Vertical competition in unitary states: the case of Italy, *Public Choice*, 114(1–2), 57–77.
—— (2006), Modelling vertical competition, in Ahmad, E. and Brosio, G. (2006), 86–105.
Brosio, G. (2006), The assignment of revenue from natural resources, in Ahmad, E. and Brosio, G. (2006), 431–458.
Collignon, S. (2003), *The European Republic. Reflections on the Political Economy of a Future Constitution* (London: Federal Trust).
European Commission (1977), *Report of the Study Group on the Role of Public Finance in European Integration* (MacDougall Report), Brussels.
Fatás, A. and Mihov, I. (1999), Government size and automatic stabilizers: international and intranational evidence, Cepr Discussion Paper 2259 (London: Centre for Economic Policy Research).
Hairaut, J.-O., Hénin, P.-Y. and Portier, F. (eds) (1993), *Business Cycles and Macroeconomic Stability: Should We Rebuild Built-in Stabilisers?* (Boston: Kluwer).
Inman, R.P. and Rubinfeld, D.L. (1997), Rethinking Federalism, *Journal of Economic Perspectives* 11(4), 43–64.
Leeftink, B. (2000), Rules versus flexibility. Does the Stability Pact limit budgetary stabilisers?, in Fiscal Sustainability, Proceedings of the Perugia Workshop, Bank of Italy, 20–22 gennaio 2000.

Masson, P. (2000), Fiscal policy and growth in the context of European integration, IMF Working Paper 133.

McLure, C.E., Jr. (ed.) (1983), *Tax Assignment in Federal Countries* (Canberra: Australian National University).

Melitz J. and Vori, S. (1992), National Insurance against unevenly distributed shocks, Cepr Discussion Paper 697 (London: Centre for Economic Policy Research).

Musgrave, R. (1959), *The Theory of Public Finance* (New York: McGraw-Hill).

Oates, W.E. (1972), *Fiscal Federalism* (New York: Harcourt Brace Jovanovich).

—— (1999), An essay on fiscal federalism, *Journal of Economic Literature* 38, 1120–1149.

—— (2005), Toward a second generation theory of fiscal federalism, *International Tax and Public Finance* 12, 349–373.

Olson, M., Jr. (1969), The principle of "fiscal equivalence": the division of responsibilities among different levels of government, *American Economic Review* 59, 479–487.

Pauly, M. (1973), Income redistribution as a local public good, *Journal of Public Economics* 2, 35–58.

Salmon, P. (1987), Decentralization as an incentive scheme, *Oxford Review of Economic Policy*, 3(2), 24–43.

Tabellini, G. (2001), *The Assignment of Tasks in an Evolving European Union* (Milan: Univ. Bocconi).

Tiebout, C. (1956), A pure theory of local expenditures, *Journal of Political Economy* 64, 416–424.

Torres, F. and Giavazzi, F. (eds) (1993), *Adjustment and Growth in the European Monetary Union* (Cambridge: Cambridge Univ. Press).

Treaty on European Union (1992), in *Offical Journal of the European Communities*, August.

von Hagen, J. and Hammond, G. (1997), Insurance against asymmetric shocks in a European Monetary Union, in Hairaut, J.O., Hénin, P.Y. and Portier, F. (1997).

Wheare, K.C. (1963), *Federal Government* (London: Oxford University Press).

Further Reading

Akai, N., Nishimura, Y. and Sakata, M. (2007), Complementarity, fiscal decentralization and economic growth, *Economics of Governance*, 8(4), 339–362.

Aronsson, T. and Blomquist, S. (2008), Redistribution and provision of public goods in an economic federation, *Journal of Public Economic Theory*, 10(1), 125–143.

Brueckner, J.K. (2006), Fiscal federalism and economic growth, *Journal of Public Economics*, 90(10–11), 2107–2120.

Brülhart, M. and Jametti, M. (2006), Vertical versus horizontal tax externalities: An empirical test, *Journal of Public Economics*, 90(10–11), 2027–2062.

Chari, V.V. and Kehoe, P.J. (2007), On the need for fiscal constraints in a monetary union, *Journal of Monetary Economics*, 54(8), November.

Cheikbossian, G. (2008), Rent-seeking, spillovers and the benefits of decentralization, *Journal of Urban Economics*, 63(1), 217–228.

Claeys, P., Ramos, R. and Suriñach, J. (2008), Fiscal sustainability across government tiers, *International Economics and Economic Policy*, 5(1–2), July, 139–163.

Colciago, A., Moscatelli, V.A., Rosele, T. and Tirelli, P. (2008), The role of fiscal policy in a monetary union: are national automatic stabilizers effective?, *Review of International Economics*, 16(3), August, 491–610.

Enikolopov, R. and Zhuravskaya, E. (2007), Decentralization and political institutions, *Journal of Public Economics*, (91)11–12, 2261–2290.

Gonçalves Veiga, L. and Pinho, M.M. (2007), The political economy of intergovernmental grants: Evidence from a maturing democracy, *Public Choice*, 133(3–4), 457–477.

Hallerberg, M., Strauch, R. and von Hagen, J. (2007), The design of fiscal rules and forms of governance in European Union countries, *European Journal of Political Economy*, 23(2), June, 338–359.

Köthenbürger, M. (2007), Ex-post redistribution in a federation: Implications for corrective policy, *Journal of Public Economics*, 91(3–4), 481–496.

—— (2008), Revisiting the "decentralization theorem" – on the role of externalities, *Journal of Urban Economics*, 64(1), 116–122.

Lundholm, M. (2008), Decentralizing public goods production, *Journal of Public Economic Theory*, 10(2), 259–279.

Mazzaferro, C. and Zanardi, A. (2008), Centralisation versus decentralisation of public policies: does the heterogeneity of individual preferences matter?, *Fiscal Studies*, 29(1), 35–73.

Oates, W.E. (2008), On the evolution of fiscal federalism: Theory and institutions, *National Tax Journal*, 61, June, 313–334.

Peralta, S. (2007), Political support for tax decentralization, *Journal of Public Economic Theory*, 9(6), 1013–1030.

Thornton, J. (2007), Fiscal decentralization and economic growth reconsidered, *Journal of Urban Economics*, 61(1), 64–70.

—— and Mati, A. (2008), Fiscal institutions and the relation between central and sub-national government fiscal balances, *Public Finance Review*, 36(2), 243–254.

Tommasi, M. and Weinschelbaum, F. (2007), Centralization vs. decentralization: a principal-agent analysis, *Journal of Public Economic Theory*, 9(2), 369–389.

Postmodern Federalism and Sub-State Nationalism

Greg Marchildon

The emergence of the postmodern federation directly relates to the rise of historically and territorially defined national minorities seeking a high degree of self-determination. Central states facing such movements have relied heavily on the political instrument of federalism to reach an accommodation with their territorially based national communities. In effect, the postmodern federation attempts to channel ongoing tensions between unity and diversity into a peaceful and democratic political compromise rather than the potentially violent conflict of secession and partition (Schertzer 2008; Guibernau 2006). According to Moreno (1994), the federalist paradigm is "an indispensable tool for social and political accommodation." At the same time, the ongoing compromise between the central state's desire for territorial integrity and security with a territorially encompassed minority's aspiration for greater autonomy and self-determination is complex, contradictory and very temporary.

Unlike the postmodern federation, the classical federation generally adheres to its originating organizing principles as reflected in the constitution or other formative documents. In contrast, the reality of postmodern federation will often contradict its originating conceptions; for example, a centralized constitution belies a decentralized reality or a formal unitary state evolves into an informal federation. Although some asymmetry can be found in all federations, it nonetheless remains true that the classical federation eschews asymmetry among its constituent units while the postmodern federation more readily accepts, and exhibits, a high degree of formal and informal asymmetry among its constituent sub-states (Watts 2005). In postmodern federations, the history of the country itself is highly contested. Rival narratives of the historical experiences of nationalities within the same country often contradict the broader historical narrative of the country as a whole.

The ethno-linguistic tensions inherent in postmodern federations are often channelled into active nationalist movements that continually challenge old assumptions, political compromises and institutions underpinning the state. There is no lasting equilibrium in a postmodern federation as the status quo is constantly subject to revision. In order to forestall secessionist movements and the breakup of the existing state, central political elites are driven to new accommodations and new institutions, including new federal institutions and approaches. At the same time, regional political elites representing national minorities obtain enough power, privilege and recognition within the existing political system to be satisfied with pursuing a more gradualist project of greater autonomy and self-determination rather than immediate independence (Guibernau 2006). These same sub-state political elites may also fear the consequences of full state independence in terms of losing privileged access to markets, the benefits of collective security or the creation of new minority problems in the event of partition.

The term "postmodern" was first used shortly after the Second World War to describe modern architecture but was soon applied to art, music and literature and then in numerous other contexts in an effort to distinguish the new styles then emerging from the modernistic styles before them. In this spirit, Daniel J. Elazar (1998) used "postmodern" as a modifier for federalism. However, postmodern must mean more than the fact that it defines something that post-dates modern. A postmodern knowledge construct itself, Wikipedia posits the following: "Largely influenced by the disillusionment induced by the Second World War, postmodernism tends to refer to a cultural, intellectual, or artistic state lacking a clear central hierarchy or organizing principle and embodying extreme complexity, contradiction, ambiguity, diversity, and interconnectedness or interreferentiality."[1]

To work as a useful metaphor, postmodern federalism must at least allow us to distinguish one type of federalism from another (Stewart 1982). Drawing from a comparison of Canada (1867), Belgium (1993), Spain (1978) and the United Kingdom (1998) – four prosperous postmodern federations or incipient, quasi-federations, to four wealthy classical federations – the United States (1789), Switzerland (1848), Australia (1901) and Germany (1949) – I hypothesize five key features as characteristic of the postmodern federation. In all cases, the postmodern federation is: (1) undergoing recent devolution and decentralization; (2) reflecting a high degree of formal and informal asymmetry; (3) protecting and vigorously promoting key minority language rights; (4) experiencing the rise of regionally based nationalist political parties and the decline of ideologically oriented pan-national political parties and (5) constantly struggling to construct alternatives to secession, partition and violence. While there are also important constitutional, political and administrative differences among Canada, Belgium, Spain and the United Kingdom, the main purpose of this chapter is to explore the extent to which they share the characteristics of a postmodern federation.

Before reviewing each of the five characteristics, it is worth mentioning that classical federations have a higher degree of constitutional federalism – as defined by their institutions and decision rules – than postmodern federations. Based upon 13 different features and a 20-point scale, Requejo (2006) calculated that the United States (15.5), Switzerland (15), Germany (14) and Australia (14) all had a higher degree of constitutional federalism than Canada (13), Belgium (11), Spain (6.5)

---

1   http://en.wikipedia.org/wiki/Postmodernism: accessed on 26 Jan. 2008.

and the United Kingdom (5). In their constitutions, institutions and rules, classical federations are closer to what they say they are, while postmodern federations are often not what they say they are. More precisely, postmodern federations prefer not to say what they are in order to avoid internal conflict. This is the – some would say *constructive* – ambiguity that goes to the heart of the postmodern federation (Erk and Gagnon 2000). Calling this the "silence of constitutions," Michael Foley (1989) uses some memorable phrases to describe this uncertain and imprecise state of affairs, including studied inattention, dormant suspension, convention of non-exposure, strategic oversight and protective obfuscation.

Rapid Devolution and Decentralization

Contrary to more classical and modern federations, postmodern federations have witnessed a rapid or sudden decentralization of power and responsibility from the central government to sub-state units. It is not the degree of decentralization that separates the postmodern federation from the classical federation; rather it is the rapidity of change from a relatively more centralized structure (whether a federation or not) to a more decentralized federation or quasi-federation. While classical federations have a relatively stable relationship between centralization and decentralization irrespective of where they sit on the spectrum, postmodern federations undergo rapid decentralization in a relatively short period of time. In absolute terms, for example, based upon Requejo's (2006) 20-point decentralization scale, both Spain (10.5) and the United Kingdom (8.5) are less decentralized than Australia (12) and Germany (12) while Belgium (14) is equal to Switzerland (14) and Canada (16.5) is more decentralized than the United States (14.5). But while the classical federations have moved little along the scale of centralization–decentralization, the postmodern federations examined here have all experienced a rapid movement towards a more decentralized state during the past half-century and even the past decade.

This decentralization has been political, administrative and fiscal in nature. While the word "decentralization" is generally used in the context of formal federations such as Canada and Belgium, the same process is often described by the word "devolution" in previously unitary countries such as Spain and the UK. Part of the reason lies in the more technical meaning of the word "devolution", which is defined as an extreme form of administrative – rather than political – decentralization (Rondinelli 1983). For this reason, the term "devolution" may seem less threatening to political elites desperate to avoid the charge of politically decentralizing the state (Laffin and Thomas 1999). In reality, however, the full-fledged definition involving varying degrees of political, administrative and fiscal decentralization applies as much to Spain and the UK as it does to Canada and Belgium.

Since the early 1960s, Canada has undergone major political, administrative and fiscal decentralization. This development is mainly the result of two ethnonationalist projects within the country. The first and most long-standing is the province of Quebec's ongoing evolution as a sub-state protecting the interests of its French-speaking majority population. In the last decade, all provinces, especially Quebec (which has led the process) have obtained additional authority and control over economic and social programmes, including immigration and labour market policy. Finally – and despite a temporary reduction of federal transfers to provincial governments in the mid-1990s – provinces have been increasing their share of fiscal resources, both own-source and total, relative to the federal government since the 1950s (Marchildon 1995; Requejo 2006).[2] The second, more recent, development is First Nation and Inuit communities establishing the right to self-government, aided by the constitutional entrenchment of Aboriginal rights in section 35 of the Constitution Act of 1982 as well as the Supreme Court's subsequent interpretation of that section as well as indigenous treaty rights (Hylton 1999; Kelly and Murphy 2005). In effect, a third order of constitutional government is emerging which impinges on the jurisdiction of the federal and provincial governments that, prior to 1982, were the two exclusive orders of government recognized under the constitution of Canada.

With its secession from the Netherlands in 1830, Belgium was established as a unitary state. Beginning in the early 1970s, Belgium began its gradual transformation to a federation with authority and responsibility flowing from the centre to the two major linguistic (French and Dutch) communities and the Flemish and Walloon regions (Hooghe 2004; O'Neill 1998). This constitutional–political decentralization has been accompanied by administrative and fiscal decentralization, although this was more limited relative to Canada in part because of Belgium's Bismarckian social insurance arrangements that are less statist than Canada's social programmes (Béland and Lecours 2007). This decentralization was triggered by the conflict between two ethno-linguistic communities, the Dutch-speaking Flemish and the Walloon-speaking French. This conflict drove the "divided house" unitary state towards a federal "solution", one in which each group obtained responsibility and authority over areas of language and culture as well as aspects of social and economic development each deem critical to their respective futures (Stroschein 2003).

Spain has also witnessed a rapid evolution from the highly centralist state under the Franco dictatorship to the current period beginning with the new Spanish Constitution and the adoption of a quasi-federal structure in 1978 (Colomer 1998). Since the early 1980s, decentralization has continued, led by the Basques and Catalans who have sought increased political and administrative (programme) responsibilities as well as a greater share of fiscal resources. The 17 autonomous communities saw their share of total government expenditures increase from a miniscule 2 per cent in 1981 to 15 per cent by 1990 (Agranoff 1996). This percentage

---

2   Using Requejo's (2005) 8-point scale with more points allocated to sub-states with higher ratios of own-source state revenues to total revenues, Canada's provinces have one of the higher legislative power scores (7) among sub-states in federations in the world.

share continues to grow despite the central government's reticence to share fiscal resources.

Following referenda in Scotland and Wales in 1997 and the Good Friday Agreement attempting to end political violence in Northern Ireland in 1998, the United Kingdom has begun its own devolutionary journey (Gamble 2006; Bogdanor 2001). All three regions have elected assemblies and home civil services. In particular, Scotland achieved a high degree of autonomy very quickly relative to Northern Ireland and Wales (Leeke et al. 2003). Due to sectarian conflict, the evolution of self-government for Northern Ireland has followed a more tortured path. In December 1999, the power to administer many of Northern Ireland's domestic affairs including social, educational and cultural policy as well as responsibility for rural, regional and agricultural development was devolved from the Westminster Parliament to the Northern Ireland Assembly. Although devolution has been suspended on three occasions since that time, the Northern Ireland Assembly was restored in May 2007.

Formal and Informal Asymmetry

Contrary to classical federations in which power and responsibility is equally apportioned among sub-states to the greatest extent possible, postmodern federations tend to exhibit a higher degree of asymmetry among the sub-states. McGarry (2005) defines asymmetrical federalism as a "situation in which one region of the country enjoys a distinct form of autonomy, and often a distinct constitutional status, from other parts". While all federations exhibit some asymmetrical features, they generally pale in comparison to the asymmetries in postmodern federations, driven as they are by the minority national communities, particularly those operating through established sub-states.

Classical federations tend to eschew asymmetrical arrangements for a number of reasons including the fact that they are perceived to threaten existing norms concerning democratic equality, liberty and accountability. They fear that asymmetry, rather than preventing the breakup of the state, only serves to facilitate secession by encouraging sub-state nationalism and ethnocentric behaviours (Anderson 2004; McGarry 2005). While most federations may go to great lengths to avoid or mitigate asymmetries, postmodern federations seem to be driven to asymmetry even while recognizing the inevitable costs involved in such a strategy, costs they are willing to incur in order to manage separatist demands and prevent a breakup of the larger state. Moreover, asymmetry may be supported by nationalist sub-state governments as preferable to symmetrical decentralization because this recognizes the privileged national status of the sub-state relative to other sub-states within the same federation: after all, such sub-states demand recognition as nations, not simply as sub-states with a degree of autonomy within a given federal framework.

Although Quebec has been unsuccessful in getting formal constitutional recognition for its status as a nationalist homeland for French-Canadians resident in Quebec, it has received considerable political support for this status, including a resolution that "the Québécois form a nation within a united Canada" that was approved by all political parties in the Canadian House of Commons in November of 2006. Beyond the symbolic, numerous asymmetric legislative and funding arrangements pertaining to Quebec have accumulated since the 1950s. From special tax point arrangements in which the federal government has ceded unique tax room for the government of Quebec to separate national legislation including the Quebec Pension Plan which has been running parallel to the Canada Pension Plan since the mid-1960s (Boadway and Hobson 1993; Béland and Lecours 2006), the Canadian state has made numerous asymmetric accommodations to meet nationalist demands from the province of Quebec. Beyond Quebec, growing asymmetry of a more formal type can be seen in the establishment of a separate Inuit "homeland" with the carving out of the new territory of Nunavut in 1999 and the signing of the Nisga'a Treaty in British Columbia in 2000 (McGarry 2005).

The greater congruence of the Flemish community to the Flemish territory (region) relative to the Walloon community and region, as well as the lack of a territory (region) for an officially recognized German-speaking community, produce both formal and informal asymmetries within the Belgian federation. In addition, the "ordinances" of the Brussels regional parliament are judicially inferior to the "decrees" passed by the regional parliaments in Wallonia and Flanders (Swenden 2002).

Following the new constitution of 1978, the new Spanish quasi-federation began its life with a high degree of *de jure* asymmetry as the historic communities of the Basque Country, Catalonia and Galicia received far more powers than the remaining 14 autonomous communities. In part, this was a consequence of the powers such communities enjoyed during the period of the Second Republic in the 1930s (Agranoff 1996). This asymmetry was exacerbated by the demands of the historic communities for fiscal resources at the very time that the new autonomous communities were being established. Despite the fact that formal asymmetries continue to persist in linguistic policy, health policy and taxation, the gap in asymmetries among the autonomous communities has narrowed with time as the central government has transferred more power and fiscal resources to the remaining sub-state governments increasing overall decentralization (Colomer 1998). In response to this, the Basque Country and Catalonia in particular have demanded extra powers from Madrid in recent years in a bid to separate themselves from the other autonomous communities (Agranoff 2005).

Devolution in the United Kingdom has been asymmetrical from its inception in the late 1990s. Scotland, Northern Ireland and Wales each have unique electoral arrangements that have replaced the United Kingdom's first past the post system (Jeffery and Wincott 2006). Each of the constituent units has different powers and responsibilities. While Scotland and Northern Ireland have a number of features in common – both have legislatures which pass primary as well as secondary legislation in areas not reserved for Westminster as well as separate executives accountable to their respective legislatures – there are important differences. For example, while the Scottish Parliament can legislate on criminal justice and policing, the Northern Ireland Assembly cannot. The National Assembly for Wales includes both parliamentary and executive functions in a single legal body but the Assembly can only make delegation legislations (regulations) within the framework of the laws of the Westminster Parliament (Leeke et al. 2003). Of course, the one outstanding exception to devolution is England itself. No separate English parliament or separate English region(s) have been established (Jeffery and Wincott 2006).

Linguistic Protection and Promotion

In contrast to postmodern federations, most classical federations continue to adhere to the idea of the homogenous nation-state with "common institutions functioning in a common language" (Costa 2003, 413). Although Switzerland is an exception, the idea of single, common language, connected to a single national identity, remains powerful in classical federations such the United States, Australia and Germany.

In contrast, postmodern federations are compelled to make major adjustments for minority nationalists and their languages in sub-state territories. At the same time, nationalist elites have used the legislative power of the sub-state to protect and promote their languages in government, education, culture and business, encouraging a renaissance in the use of these minority languages in recent years. While postmodern federations are generally multi-lingual federations, special status is accorded to the minority languages that are (or aspire to be) majority languages within territorially defined sub-states. Since language goes to the heart of cultural identity as defined by the minorities which define postmodern federations, control over language is central to their nation-building projects, including the linguistic assimilation of immigrants and newcomers.

In Canada, language has (arguably) become more important than religion or even ethnicity in terms of the identity of those living within territorial boundaries of Quebec (Oakes 2004). Beginning in the Quiet Revolution of the early 1960s in Quebec, the geographical and linguistic descriptor "Québécois" increasingly supplanted the older ethnic descriptor of "French Canadian". In the mid to late 1960s, the federal government transformed itself into a bilingual (French–English) state while the Quebec government passed a law making French the official language in Quebec in 1977 and promoted its use by requiring businesses to use French signage. The protection of language was used as the principle justification for the "distinct society" clause in the failed constitutional negotiations of the late 1980s (Marchildon 1996). Beyond Quebec, the territory of Nunavut, as the homeland of the Inuit, was created as an officially bilingual (Inuktituk–English) state in 1999.

Likewise, Belgium has seen a transformation from an officially unilingual (French) unitary state to an officially bilingual (French–Dutch) unitary state and then to a federation in which language is controlled by two levels of governance, one based on single language communities (French–Dutch–German) and one based on the unilingual regional governments of Wallonia and Flanders. Beginning in the 1930s and reinforced in the 1960s, Belgium has adhered to a strict policy of regional unilinguism. This policy promotes linguistic homogeneity in the Walloon and Flemish regions, thereby transforming linguistic concerns into territorial issues (Hooghe 2004).

Although the sole official language of the Spanish state is Castilian (Spanish), the autonomous communities of the Basque Country, Catalonia and Galicia preserve and promote their own languages to an extent that would have been unthinkable in Franco's Spain during the Franco dictatorship between 1939 and 1975. Although Spanish is legally required to be an official language alongside Basque, Catalan and Galician, these minority languages have become the language of government as well as the majority languages within the three autonomous communities. In Catalonia, for example, Catalan stands as an official language along with Spanish and (since 2006) Aranese. However, Catalan is the language of almost all government services, education and culture. Moreover, businesses in Catalonia have been required by the Catalan government to display all information in Catalan (Costa 2003).

Unlike the situation in Spain, English remains the dominant language in Scotland, Wales and Northern Ireland. At the same time, considerable – some would say heroic, others would argue doomed – efforts have been made by the sub-state governments in Scotland and Wales to revive their respective Celtic languages. Although most business in the Scottish Parliament is conducted in English, Gaelic debates are actively encouraged. And while Welsh is a distinctly minority language within the territory of Wales, the Welsh Assembly Government has recently produced a national action plan to achieve a bilingual (English–Welsh) country including language funding through the Welsh Language Board sponsored by the Welsh Government.

Regionally-based Nationalist Parties

In postmodern federations, political parties tend to fragment along sub-state and minority nationalist lines. In classical federations, such as Germany (Christian Democrat–Social Democrat), Switzerland (Christian Democratic–Social Democratic–Free Democratic–Swiss People's Party), Australia (Conservative–Labour) and the United States (Republican–Democrat), parties are divided along an ideological right–left spectrum. In addition, party identity and rivalry easily translates from the central government to the sub-state level. However, in postmodern federations, party identity at the centre in postmodern federations generally differs substantially from party identity at the sub-state level. Moreover, nationalist parties can be right-wing or left-wing and have fewer objections to forging coalitions with parties of opposing ideological stripe when support can be obtained for more nationalist objectives (Erk 2005). Regional and ethno-linguistic divisions in postmodern federations promote a welter of political parties capable of challenging and supplanting traditional political parties. Many of these parties have an explicit objective of gaining more power from the central government in favour of a sub-state. Some explicitly promote a form of ethnic-linguistic nationalism while others have openly secessionist objectives and a few political parties (generally banned) are committed to using non-parliamentary means, including violence, to attain the objective of full national independence. Whatever their objective, these political parties continually pressure for major institutional and fiscal changes, making it almost impossible for postmodern federations to adhere to the status quo for any length of time.

In Canada, nationalist parties have long played an important role at the provincial level of government in Quebec. With the rise of the openly secessionist Parti Québécois and the separation of the Liberal Party of Quebec from the Liberal Party of Canada in the 1960s and 1970s, the discourse shifted from a debate between federalists and nationalists to one between nationalists and separatists (secessionists) within the province of Quebec. Since that time, the Parti Québécois (PQ) has sponsored two referenda, one in 1980 and a second in 1995, advocating the independence of Quebec. Although both referenda were defeated, separatists came so close to winning the second that the federal government launched a reference case to the Supreme Court of Canada on the legality of secession and passed a federal law (called the Clarity Bill) delimiting the terms upon which it would recognize any future, successful referendum (Aronivitch 2006). Unhappy with the failure of constitutional change by the early 1990s, a coalition of federal politicians from Quebec formed the Bloc Québécois (BQ), a separatist party operating at the federal level. Since the election of 1993, the BQ has represented a majority of Quebec seats in the federal Parliament.

Similar to Canada, Belgian politics has witnessed a major sea change in terms of the alignment of political parties since the early 1970s. Traditional pan-Belgian political parties have been fragmented. Eight separate Flemish and French-speaking Social Democratic, Christian Democratic, Liberal and Green parties have replaced the four federal versions of these same parties. Flemish nationalism is associated with the political right while Walloon nationalism is associated with the political left (Erk 2005). Flemish parties do not appeal to French voters, while French parties do not compete for votes from Flemish voters. The result solidifies a "two solitudes" approach in Belgian politics which bifurcates all issues and policy responses along language community and region (Swendon 2002).

In Spain, federal politics continues to be dominated by mainstream pan-Spanish parties polarized between left (Spanish Socialist Workers' Party or PSOE) and the right (People's Party or PP). In the early stages of devolution, however, smaller nationalist parties operating at the national level, such as the Catalan Democratic Convergence (CiU) and the Basque Nationalist Party (PNV), were instrumental in pushing for the decentralization of the Spanish state. In fact, the constitution of 1978 was a compromise between the two sides (Colomer 1998). The CiU and the PNV are both conservative parties representing a broad range of constituents, from those satisfied with current autonomous community arrangements to secessionists. Both have held power for extensive periods in their respective autonomous communities while the Galician Nationalist Bloc (BNG) has only recently managed to join the government as a junior member in a coalition with the regional version of PSOE.

Although devolution has only just begun in the United Kingdom, it has already had a significant impact on political party development in the devolved regions if not on UK-wide elections where the traditional Labour–Conservative duopoly continues to dominate. While the previously separatist Scottish Nationalist Party (SNP) predates devolution, it now holds the largest block of seats in the Scottish Parliament (Holyrood) coming out of the election of May 2007. In addition to the traditional strength of mainstream political parties – Labour, Conservative and Liberal Democrat – the mixed member proportional representation system has encouraged the participation of tiny Scottish-flavoured niche parties such as the Scottish Green, Scottish Senior Citizens, Scottish Christian and Scottish Socialist. Following the 2007 election in Wales, no party held a majority of seats and the mainstream Welsh Labour Party entered into a coalition with the Welsh nationalist party, Plaid Cymru, to form a new government. In Northern Ireland, the election in March 2007 and the negotiations which followed produced a power-sharing government between the two parties with the largest blocks of votes – the Democratic Unionist Party, historically associated with the Protestant majority, and Sinn Féin, historically linked with the Catholic minority and the Irish Republican Army.

Intra-State Federal Accommodation versus Secession, Partition and Violence

In *Modernity and Self-Identity*, Anthony Giddens (1991) argues that postmodernism remains at it essence a type of (and perhaps extreme) critique of Enlightenment universals. In this sense, postmodern federalism is federalism without universals. It has no single defining theory or national narrative but one in which alternative theories and narratives operate side by side in a given country. Given rival interpretations held within a single polity, it is always risky, if not dangerous, for any central government to impose a single vision or theory of federalism on the population. Facing duelling interpretations and histories within itself, the postmodern federation must remain as pluralistic as possible to prevent sub-state nationalism from becoming secessionist.

The most striking feature of postmodern federations is the struggle of their central governments to construct democratic alternatives to secession, partition and possible organized violence. In the four postmodern federations examined here, the central state always faces the constant prospect of secession or partition. Organized violence has also been a significant part of the very recent history of some of these countries. In some cases, such as the Basque Country and Northern Ireland, violent opposition to the existing democratic order, remains a very real threat to those who wish to work within the federalist framework (Mansvelt Beck 2008).

To counter such threats, postmodern federations must be highly flexible in terms of their constitutional principles and their accommodations. They cannot afford to be universalist in their approach. In such countries, the political elites, whether representing the central state or the sub-states encompassing national minorities, struggle to find a compromise between solutions which, on the one hand suit all sub-states, and those which, on the other hand cater to the aspirations of the "national" sub-states. Of course, nationalist parties and nationalist sub-state governmental demands for greater autonomy will continue despite concessions by central governments. Therefore, the process of finding compromise continues almost indefinitely.

There are two main vehicles to achieve this ongoing compromise. One is through representation within the central legislative system while the other is through executive-style intergovernmental negotiations. Classical federations tend to institutionalize federal relations in central legislative bodies to a greater extent than postmodern federations which tend to rely more heavily on intergovernmental executive decision-making. Moreover, intergovernmental linkages within postmodern federations are less institutionalized and less subject to decision-rules than in classical federations (Bolleyer 2006a and 2006b). The result is that executive leadership at the sub-state and central government levels plays a critical role in determining the compromises reached in postmodern federations.

The inherent flexibility of postmodern federalism is also its greatest weakness in the sense that it makes it nearly impossible for central governments to plan for the future much less engage its own "nation"-building agenda. Gamble (2006) describes the United Kingdom as lacking overall direction since devolution began, decrying the fact that the central government's approach creates ambiguity, asymmetry, muddle and inconsistency. This same criticism might easily be applied to the central governments of Canada, Belgium and Spain. Nevertheless, the reality is that a more coherent direction from the centre, particularly one that emanates from a *supra*-state nationalism, will be in direct conflict with the narrative and assumptions of increasingly vigorous sub-state nationalisms. Moreover, the imposition of greater centralization or authoritarianism is more likely to drive nationalists into the secessionist camp than it is to preserve national unity. In such circumstances, accommodation through greater devolution and decentralization may be the only sustainable option to keeping the country together.

At the same time, the process is not as open-ended as it sounds. Sub-state nationalist leaders can take a "certain comfort" from their gradualist nation-building projects by retaining the democratic support of the majority within their regions even while benefiting from the power, prestige and recognition that comes from operating within the political status quo (Guibernau 2006, 72). They often respond by marginalizing the nationalist forces supporting outright and immediate independence and, even more so, those forces supporting collective violence (Mansvelt Beck 2008). Even for those nationalist parties supporting separation, in Quebec and the Basque Country for example, the trend has been to support qualified independence – one which retains significant linkages with the country from which it proposes to secede.

Has the constant accommodation of postmodern federations succeeded? Based upon the continuance of such states relative to the large number of secessions in other parts of the world since the late 1980s, the answer is yes. Based on the decline in the level of violence in Northern Ireland and the Basque Country, the answer would also have to be yes. Based on the extent to which a compromise has been found between the ability of sub-state nationalities to pursue a larger degree of self-determination as measure by language, culture and business, the answer would again have to be yes. But there are no guarantees concerning the future and it seems possible, perhaps even likely, that certain sub-states in these postmodern federations will eventually attain the status of associated states if not fully independent states in the future.

References

Agranoff, R. (1996), Federal evolution in Spain, *International Political Science Review* 17, no. 4, 385–401.

—— (2005), Federal asymmetry and intergovernmental relations in Spain, Institute of Intergovernmental Relations Asymmetry Series, no. 17 (Kingston, ON: Institute of Intergovernmental Relations Asymmetry Series).

Anderson, L.M. (2004), The institutional basis of secessionist politics: federalism and secession in the United States, *Publius: The Journal of Federalism* 34, no. 2, 1–18.

Aranson, P.H. (1990), Federalism: the reasons of rules, *Cato Journal* 10, no. 1, 17–38.

Aronivitch, H. (2006), Seceding the Canadian way, *Publius: The Journal of Federalism* 36, no. 4, 541–64.

Béland, D. and Lecours, A. (2006), Sub-state nationalism and the welfare state: Québec and Canadian federalism, *Nations and Nationalism* 21, no. 1, 77–96.

—— (2007), Federalism, nationalism and social policy decentralization in Canada and Belgium, *Regional & Federal Studies* 17, no. 4, 405–19.

Boadway, R. and Hobson, P. (1993), *Intergovernmental Fiscal Relations in Canada* (Toronto: Canadian Tax Foundation).

Bogdanor, V. (2001), *Devolution in the UK* (Oxford: Oxford University Press).

Bolleyer, N. (2006a), Federal dynamics in Canada, the United States, and Switzerland: how sub-states' internal organization affects intergovernmental relations, *Publius: The Journal of Federalism* 36, no. 4, 471–502.

—— (2006b), Intergovernmental arrangements in Spanish and Swiss federalism: the impact of power-concentrating and power-sharing executives on intergovernmental institutionalization, *Regional and Federal Studies* 16, no. 4, 385–408.

Collomer, J.M. (1998), The Spanish "state of autonomies": non-institutional federalism, *Western European Politics* 21, no. 4, 40–52.

Costa, J. (2003), Catalan linguistic policy: liberal or illiberal?, *Nations and Nationalism* 9, no. 3, 413–32.
Elazar, D.J. (1998), *Constitutionalizing Globalization: The Postmodern Revival of Confederal Arrangements* (Lanham, MD: Rowman and Littlefield).
Erk, J. (2005), Sub-state nationalism and the left–right divide: critical junctures in the formation of nationalist labour movements in Belgium, *Nations and Nationalism* 11, no. 4, 551–70.
—— and Gagnon, A.-G. (2000), Constitutional ambiguity and federal trust: codification and federalism in Canada, Spain and Belgium, *Regional & Federal Studies* 10, no. 1, 92–111.
Foley, M. (1989), *The Silence of Constitutions: Gaps, "Abeyances" and Political Temperament in the Maintenance of Government* (London: Routledge).
Gamble, A. (2006), The constitutional revolution in the United Kingdom, *Publius: The Journal of Federalism* 36, no. 1, 19–35.
Giddens, A.J. (1991), *Modernity and Self-Identity* (Cambridge: Polity).
Guibernau, M. (2006), National identity, devolution and secession in Canada, Britain and Spain, *Nations and Nationalism* 12, no. 1, 51–76.
Hooghe, L. (2004), Belgium: hollowing the center, in Amoretti, U. and Bermeo, N., eds, *Federalism and Territorial Cleavages* (Baltimore: Johns Hopkins University Press).
Hylton, J., ed. (1999), *Aboriginal Self-Government in Canada* (Saskatoon: Purich).
Jeffery, C. and Wincott, D. (2006), Devolution in the United Kingdom: statehood and citizenship in transition, *Publius: The Journal of Federalism* 36, no. 1, 1–18.
Kelly, J.B. and Murphy, M. (2005), Shaping the constitutional dialogue on federalism: Canada's Supreme Court as meta-political actor, *Publius: The Journal of Federalism* 35, no. 2, 217–43.
Laffin, M. and Thomas, A. (1999), The United Kingdom: federalism in denial?, *Publius: The Journal of Federalism* 29, no. 3, 89–108.
Leeke, M., Sear, C. and Oonagh, G. (2003), *An Introduction to Devolution in the UK*, House of Commons Library Research Paper 03/84 (London: House of Commons Library).
Mansvelt Beck, J. (2008), The Basque power-sharing experience: from a destructive to a constructive conflict?, *Nations and Nationalism* 14, no. 1, 61–83.
Marchildon, G.P. (1995), Fin de siécle Canada: the federal government in retreat, in McCarthy, P. and Jones, E., eds, *Disintegration and Transformation: The Crisis of the State in Advanced Industrial Societies* (New York: St. Martin's Press).
—— (1996), An attempt to reconcile the irreconcilable, *Inroads* 5, 98–104.
—— and Maxwell, E. (1992), Quebec's Right of Secession under Canadian and international law, *Virginia Journal of International Law* 32, no. 3, 583–623.
McGarry, J. (2005), Asymmetrical federalism and the plurinational state, working position paper prepared for the 3rd International Conference on Federalism, Brussels, 3–4 March 2005.
Moreno, L. (1994), Ethnoterritorial concurrence and imperfect federalism in Spain, in de Villiers, B., ed., *Evaluating Federal Systems* (Dordrecht: Martinus Nijhoff).
—— (2002), Decentralization in Spain, *Regional Studies* 36, no. 4, 399–408.

—— Arriba, A. and Serrano, A. (1997), Multiple identities in decentralized Spain: the case of Catalonia, Instituto de Estudios Sociales Avanzados (CSIS), Working Paper 97–06.
Oakes, L. (2004), French: a language for everyone in Québec?, *Nations and Nationalism* 10, no. 4, 539–58.
O'Neill, M. (1998), Re-imagining Belgium: new federalism and the political management of cultural diversity, *Parliamentary Affairs* 51, no. 2, 241–58.
Requejo, F. (2006), Federalism and democracy: the case of minority nations: a federalist deficit, Political Theory Working Paper, Departament de Ciències Polítiques I socials, Universitat Pompeu Fabra (Barcelona: Departament de Ciències Polítiques I socials, Universitat Pompeu Fabra).
Rondinelli, D.A. (1983), Decentralization in developing countries, World Bank Staff Working Paper 581.
Schertzer, R. (2008), Recognition or imposition? federalism, national minorities, and the Supreme Court of Canada, *Nations and Nationalism* 14, no. 1, 105–26.
Stewart, W.H. (1982), Metaphysics, models, and the development of federal theory, *Publius: The Journal of Federalism* 12, no. 2, 5–24.
Stroschein, S. (2003), What Belgium can teach Bosnia: the uses of autonomy in "divided house" states, *JEMIE – Journal of Ethnopolitics and Minority Issues in Europe* 3, open access electronic journal: http://www.ecmi.de/jemie/download/Focus3-2003_Stroschein.pdf.
Swendon, W. (2002), Asymmetric federalism and coalition-building in Belgium, *Publius: The Journal of Federalism* 32, no. 3, 67–87.
Watts, R.L. (2005), A comparative perspective on asymmetry in federations, Institute of Intergovernmental Relations Asymmetry Series, no. 4 (Kingston, ON: Institute of Intergovernmental Relations).

Further Reading

Agranoff, R., ed. (1999), *Accommodating Diversity: Asymmetry in Federal States* (Baden-Baden: Nomos).
Buchanan, A. (1991), *Secession: The Morality of Political Divorce from Fort Sumter to Lithuania and Quebec* (Boulder: Westview Press).
Burgess, M. (2006), *Comparative Federalism: Theory and Practice* (London: Routledge).
Duffy Toft, M. (2003), *The Geography of Ethnic Violence: Identity, Interests and Indivisibility of Territory* (Princeton: Princeton University Press).
Erk, J. (2007), *Explaining Federalism: State, Society and Congruence in Austria, Belgium, Canada, Germany and Switzerland* (London: Routledge).
Gagnon, A. and Tully, J., eds (2001), *Multinational Democracies* (Cambridge: Cambridge University Press).
—— Guibernau, M. and Rocher, F., eds (2003), *The Conditions of Diversity in Multinational Democracies* (Montreal: Institute for Research on Public Policy).

Guibernau, M. (1999), *Nations without States: Political Communities in the Global Age* (Cambridge: Polity Press).

—— (2004), *Catalan Nationalism: Francoism, Transition and Democracy* (London: Routledge).

Hannum, H. (1996), *Autonomy, Sovereignty, and Self-Determination: The Accommodation of Conflicting Rights* (Philadelphia: University of Pennsylvania Press).

Keating, M. (2001), *Nations against the State: The New Politics of Nationalism in Quebec, Catalonia and Scotland*, 2nd ed. (London: Palgrave).

—— (2005), *Plurinational Democracy: Stateless Nations in a Post-Sovereignty Era* (Oxford: Oxford University Press).

Mansvelt Beck, J. (2005), *Territory and Terror: Conflicting Nationalisms in the Basque Country* (London: Routledge).

McRoberts, K. (1997), *Misconceiving Canada: The Struggle for National Unity* (Toronto: Oxford University Press).

Moreno, L. (2001), *The Federalization of Spain* (London: Frank Cass).

Requejo, F. (2001), *Democracy and National Pluralism* (London: Routledge).

Seymour, M., ed. (2004), *The Fate of the Nation State* (Montreal and Kingston: McGill-Queen's University Press).

Watts, R.L. (1999), *Comparing Federal Systems*, 2nd ed. (Montreal and Kingston: McGill-Queen's University Press).

PART 6
REGIONAL EXPERIENCES OF FEDERALISM

ASHGATE
RESEARCH
COMPANION

Introduction to Part 6

The final Part of this research companion is devoted to examining the practical experiences of federalism in a global context. We see the federal principle employed to a variety of purposes including promoting economic and political development, harmonizing cultural diversity, transforming constitutional traditions, and defining the scope of federal–state or provincial power. This Part reconsiders both familiar and less familiar case studies of functioning federal systems, as well as analyzing the limits and possibilities of federalism in regions scarcely thought of in terms of federalism.

For instance, in Chapter 26 Sara Jordan examines the African experience of federalism in light of the indigenous influences on its development. Jordan argues that contrary to the typical view, federalism in Africa is not an inheritance from the colonial legacy. Rather the ideas of federalism, and most notably confederation, are structures of government indigenous to the history of the state and society in Africa. In particular, she identifies strong federal elements in the native African idea of empire – very different from the western view – that is essentially the "culmination of successive acts of confederation." Jordan examines in detail the historical examples of Pharonic Egypt and the Asante Empire of West Africa, and finds a "confederative cycle" in operation, according to which the consolidation of kinship groups into larger units including tribes and tribal associations gradually evolved into confederated states with important federal elements such as common administration and governance institutions. The legacy of the Asante and ancient Egyptian empires is not only the modern African characteristic of political organization suffused with the values of community, but also a flexible and federalistic approach to the concept of the state acquired prior to colonization.

In the following chapter, Haig Patapan turns our attention to Australia. He argues that whereas the nation-building purposes behind the origin of Australian federalism are well-documented, the less obvious, but no less significant, impact federalism had on the transformation of traditional Westminster constitutionalism has received much less attention. Patapan demonstrates that the introduction of an essentially American conception of federalism into Australia dramatically altered the fundamentally British traditions of parliamentarism and common law that characterized colonial constitutionalism. The transformation of Australia's constitutionalism produced by this innovation took and continues to take three main forms. First, the development of the Australian idea of the constitution as a single authoritative piece of constituent legislation can be traced back to the federal origins of the commonwealth. Second, the practice of judicial review – unknown in the British tradition of parliamentary sovereignty – emerged in Australia primarily as a means to resolve disputes about the demarcation of federal and state powers. Finally, Patapan argues American style federalism brought to Australia an idea of rights that placed greater emphasis on individual rights than in the colonial constitution and jurisprudence. As Patapan reveals, Australian federalism always involved more than just structural issues of commonwealth–state relations. Federalism produced nothing less than a transformation of Australian constitutionalism that continues to impact modern Australian politics today.

In Chapter 28 Akhtar Majeed analyzes the most populated federal state in the world: India. The central challenge to Indian political organization is, of course, the nation's stunning diversity with a plethora of distinct cultural, linguistic, religious, and regional identities. Majeed identifies the Indian national government's response to this diversity as what he terms "cooperative federalism." Cooperative federalism is not a rigid structure for the division of power between the national government and sub-national units. Rather it is a federal arrangement designed to encourage a process of power sharing that enables reconciliation of internal diversity within a political constitutional framework. Majeed highlights the role played by India's constitution in the recognition of minority group rights and in the organization of democratic processes to promote "shared rule," as opposed to simple majority rule, on the basis of the widest possible consensus. In India, Majeed argues, the federal constitution is the foundation for a "self-equilibrating" political system designed to prevent the dominance of one party or one interest. Shared rule involving the national government and the constituent states is intended to encourage diversity, while providing common goals and purposes as well as political accountability. Balancing the power of strong states with a solid parliamentary center establishes a mechanism to reduce regional and economic disparities through fiscal federalism. Thus, in India, Majeed proposes, federalism involves more than a structural division of power: it is a principle of social and distributive justice.

Julián Durazo Hermann continues this theme of federalism as an instrument of economic and political development in his examination of the Latin American experience of federalism in Venezuela, Mexico, Argentina, and Brazil. In Chapter 29, Hermann considers the development of Latin American federalism in terms of theory, practice, and historical experience. He illustrates how federalism has been as an important, but ambiguous, principle in Latin America operating on the levels of theoretical doctrine modified from the American model, constitutional design and practice regulating the relations of the national and sub-national units, as well as in terms of political practice and public policy. In the course of this analysis, Hermann highlights major differences, as well as sources of continuity, among the four federal Latin American states he considers. He demonstrates that whether it is with respect to recent moves towards decentralization in the region or relating to its role in promoting the democratic process and economic development, the federal structure

INTRODUCTION TO PART 6

in Venezuela, Brazil, Argentina, and Mexico has played a pivotal role contributing to the stability of the broader political systems during periods of regime change. Hermann concludes by considering the continuing role of federalism as a mechanism of state-building in the region for the present and foreseeable future.

In Chapter 30 Khalil Habib turns to the Middle East, a region of the world that has attracted a great deal of attention in recent times, especially with respect to the obstacles and possibilities facing the prospect of democratization in the Arab world. Habib, however, offers a novel perspective by framing this discussion in terms of the possibility for federalism, frequently seen as a strong correlative for democracy, in the region. He argues that new light is shed on the question of democracy and federalism in the Middle East by investigating the great medieval Arabic political philosopher Ibn Khaldun. Khaldun, Habib argues, reminds us that the possibility of federalism and democracy in the Middle East must be understood in the context of the relation between Islam and the deeply rooted pre-Islamic Bedouin tribal attitudes toward authority. He contrasts the success of American federalism, which following Tocqueville he attributes to the separation of church and state and the doctrine of "self-interest rightly understood" inherited from the liberal natural rights tradition, with the Islamic fusion of the religious and secular. In the freedom loving character of the loosely organized Bedouin tribal system, Khaldun identified a potential indigenous source for federalism that is in deep tension with the centralizing thrust of Islamic politics. It is, however, in Khaldun and Habib's view the triumph of Islam over Bedouin tribalism that gives the Middle Eastern conception of politics its distinctive character. In contrast to Arab tribal culture, which resists any central authority, Islam presents a transcendent claim that political sovereignty cannot be divided or understood as a product of human contrivance and consent. Habib concludes with a caution that contemporary proposals for democratic decentralization in the Middle East "must first address any form of federalism from the perspective of Islam, rather than to fit Islam into the perspective of Western federalism."

In Chapter 31 Jack Wade Nowlin examines recent developments in federalism and American constitutional law with an analysis of the main elements and impact of the "New Federalism" of the Rehnquist Supreme Court (1986–2005). As Nowlin observes, while the US Supreme Court has long played a role in preserving the "federal balance" between national and state power, in the decades following the New Deal the Court typically disclaimed the power to enforce federal limits on the power of the national government. The "New Federalism" of the Rehnquist Court broke this period of passivity from the court on federal matters as it introduced a set of judicially enforceable constitutional doctrines recognized by the Court that sought to reinvigorate federal limits on the national government. Nowlin examines the main areas of the "New Federalism" including the Rehnquist Court's use of the commerce clause, the anti-commandeering principle, as well as a narrow interpretation of the 14th Amendment and the abrogation of state sovereign immunity in its efforts to place federal limits on congressional authority. Nowlin concludes by speculating whether the new federalism is the start of a "legal counterrevolution," a last holding action before the doctrine of judicially enforceable federal limits on the national government disappears for good, or perhaps will have a lasting impact lying somewhere in the middle.

Federalism in Africa: An Indigenous Idea with a Colonial History

Sara Jordan

Introduction

As with so many ideas and artifacts emerging from African societies, the construction of African politics bears a consistent relationship to a mythical politics of the West. Throughout later recorded history, as trade routes circumnavigating the African continent proliferated, travelers' accounts of strange and often terrible cultures emerged as the pattern of relating Africa to the west (Davidson 1991, 4–5). In much of the comparative politics literature, it seems little has changed. Those engaged in the study of "Africa" often paint the continent with one large brush, a point that generates inevitable political and scholarly errors (Hyden 2006, 1–4). The persistence of ideas of a single Africa or a unitary Africanity is not the proper subject of the following analysis, but it is important to declare at the outset that when using the continental term, I mean Africa as an ideal, similar to the way that we might describe the European ideal.

This chapter is an effort to add to the description and theorization of African politics. The first, descriptive, goal is to show how the relational definition of modern African federalism is historically inaccurate. The primary contention of this chapter is that federated African states are not vestiges of the colonial legacy, nor are present federal states using these structures as attempts to ameliorate residual problems from the colonial "scramble for Africa." Federalism and the associated ideas of confederation and empire are structures of government indigenous to the history of state and society in Africa.[1] The second goal of this chapter is to elaborate upon a new theory of historical political organization, which I call the confederative

---

1 In *Indigenous African Institutions* (2nd Edition), Ayittey hints to such a conclusion, though he does not make this point explicitly (Ayittey 2006, notably 105–133, 233–263).

cycle, taken from the historical progression of politics on the African continent.[2] To construct this theory, I reexamine the history of two vibrant civilizations in Africa – that of dynastic Egypt and that of the modern Asante Empire – as archetypes of this mode of political organization.

Federalism, Confederation, and Empire

The concepts of federalism, confederation, and empire come from the study of these political forms in the global West. Notably, our understanding of federalism and confederation comes from the study of European and American systems.[3] What we know of Empire comes primarily from our understanding of Greece, Persia, and Rome, and more recently Tsarist Russia, the Ottoman Empire, and the British Empire (Motyl 1999, 127). Yet the reliance on the histories of these areas as the agar for the growth of these concepts places a burden upon their use in alternative contexts. Thus a historian of ideas may argue that the use of the concept of confederation outside of the western European context exemplifies "conceptual stretching" (Hyden 2006, 234–236; Sartori 1970).

A drastic reworking of the definitions themselves is beyond the ambit of this chapter, thus I present some initial definitions of these concepts below.

Federalism

As in the descriptions of Dahl, we may define federalism as merely an institutional form; a collection of states around a single, unifying legal document:

> *By federalism I mean a system in which some matters are exclusively within the competence of certain local units – cantons, states, provinces – and are constitutionally beyond the scope of authority of the national government, and where certain other matters are constitutionally outside the scope of the authority of the smaller units (Dahl 1989, 197).*

Alternatively, federalism may be merely the absence of a unitary system.

> *In unitary systems, local units are merely creations of the national parliament, fully subject, in a constitutional principle at least, to its control. The national government delegates authority to local governments; it does not alienate its authority. Thus the constitutional arrangements would permit the national*

---

2   The importance of confederation in African politics is not a new point. Ayittey (2006) and Heath (2001; pen name of Michael Van Notten) make this point as well.
3   See Levy 2007 for an extensive bibliography on the topic of federalism. See also Elazar 1974 and 1987 for a thorough elaboration on federalism in these contexts.

demos to exercise control over the agenda of political life (Dahl 1989, 197–198).

A more thorough definition may offer that federalism is the institutionalization of the will of the people to govern themselves through the most proximate, local means possible. In this vein, ought we think of federalism as the secular expression of subsidiarity?

> *Subsidiarity is the doctrine ... that political decisions ought to be made at the most local level possible, so as to encourage participation and policies that better match local needs, desires, and conditions (Levy 2007, 462).*

Following Acton, we might offer that federalism is the mode of political organization that allows for the preservation of unique cultural, ethnic, or linguistic affiliations within the context of a whole.

> *Private rights, which are sacrificed to the unity, are preserved by the union of nations. No power can so efficiently resist the tendencies of centralization, of corruption, and of absolutism, as that community which is the vastest that can be included in a State, which imposes on its members a consistent similarity of character, interest, and opinion, and which arrests the action of the sovereign by the influence of a divided patriotism (Acton 1985, 424–425).*

A synthesis of the above points yields the following provisional definition: a federal system includes the presence of multiple, distinct self-governing units under the aegis of a supra-organizational power. This form preserves sub-group distinctions and communicative power through institutions that elaborate a legally or otherwise normatively binding statement of the principles of relationship that govern the whole and its parts.

Confederacy

Conceptually and practically, confederacies are more diffuse than federations. Confederations are politically fluid organizations, as seen in the distinctions between the internally focused and unequal Iroquois Confederation, the pluralistic Dutch confederation of Althusius, and the externally focused, equal confederation of the United States.

Following Tilly (1975), we might conceptualize confederation as the first step in the generation of states. Or following Althusius, we may offer that confederation is:

> *Where [the] central government really was founded upon a confederation of provinces diverse in religion, language and national sentiment. Althusius'*

> *description of the state as a community in which several cities and provinces have bound themselves by a common law offered a better principle for limiting the power of a magistrate than a theory which contemplated a union of individuals under a sovereign ruler (Sabine 1963, 419).*

Confronted with the term confederacy we may call to mind the definition offered by Crémer and Palfrey (1999):

> *We model a confederation as a collection of districts, together with rules for the aggregation of preferences of the members of various districts, which produces policy outcomes that can vary across districts. The districts can be thought of as regions, provinces, counties, villages, or other well-defined decentralized political units. The large body is referred to as the "confederation", and it can be thought of as any political unity that contains some collection of smaller political units (69).*

To understand adequately the purposive nature of confederation, rather than federation or imperialism, it is necessary to go further than this minimalist definition of confederation. We may find a more thoroughgoing definition of confederation, in the unlikely places of the Iroquois confederation (Lutz 1998) and the American "Articles of Confederation [and Perpetual Union]."[4]

As Lutz describes it, the Iroquois confederation – a document of much historical concern for its relationship to the American "Articles of Confederation" – was [initially] an oral and unequal agreement between tribes for the purpose of protection and internal unity (1998, 100). Lutz describes the contours of the Iroquois confederation in the following way:

> *One distinctive characteristic of the Iroquois Constitution was that, contrary to the Confederation's reputation, its primary purpose was to maintain peace among its members, not to coordinate outward action. A second distinctive characteristic ... is that it was not composed of equals. A third distinctive characteristic ... was a nondemocratic means for selecting Confederation leaders, which also did not provide any sure political means for their removal. A fourth distinctive characteristic was an unusual provision that permitted adding members to the Confederation Council who excelled in virtues defined by the shared culture, but particularly those who distinguished themselves in war. A fifth distinctive characteristic was a set of provisions that not only laid out a policy of defense imperialism but also institutionalized and justified wars of annihilation on defensive grounds (Lutz 1998, 101–102).*

The idea of confederation reflected in the Iroquois context is useful as an example of an unequal, defensive, confederation guided by the need to maintain internal unity

---

4   The text used in this analysis is drawn from http://www.usconstitution.net/articles.html. Last retrieved on December 22, 2007.

among members. As I will demonstrate in subsequent sections, the persistence of inequalities among the members of an act of confederation is noteworthy in the context of African confederation as well.

To elaborate on the more unusual case of confederation among equals, it is helpful to examine the basic expectations of confederal actors enshrined in the "Articles of Confederation." We find the basic expectations reflected in Articles II, III, and IV:

> *Article II. Each state retains its sovereignty, freedom, and independence, and every power, jurisdiction, and right, which is not by this Confederation expressly delegated to the United States, in Congress assembled.*
>
> *Article III. The said States hereby severally enter into a firm league of friendship with each other, for their common defense, the security of their liberties, and their mutual and general welfare, binding themselves to assist each other, against all force offered to, or attacks made upon them, or any of them, on account of religion, sovereignty, trade or any other pretense whatever.*
>
> *Article IV. The better to secure and perpetuate mutual friendship and intercourse among the people of the different States in this Union, the free inhabitants of each of these States, paupers, vagabonds, and fugitives from justice excepted, shall be entitled to all privileges and immunities of free citizens in the several States; and the people of each State shall free ingress and regress to and from any other State, and shall enjoy therein all the privileges of trade and commerce ....*

Whether between equals or unequals, it is critical to the construction of the confederative cycle to point out that the act of bringing together political organizations for the purpose of mutual benefit – the act of confederation – precedes the formation of a federation and even the formation of an empire. Despite their loose contours, confederations are the foundations of most modern political systems (Tilly 1975).

Empire

The relationship between confederation and federation seems ready enough. What of the relationship between these two political forms and the apical form, empire?

For a definition of empire, I rely upon Hardt and Negri's "conceptual rather than historical" characterization.[5]

---

5   Some aspects of this definition are echoed in Motyl's definition: "Empires, then, are structurally centralized political systems within which core elites dominate peripheral societies, serve as intermediaries for their significant interactions, and channel resource and information flows from the periphery to the core and back to the periphery. Although empires invariably develop legitimating ideologies, they are associated, not

> *The concept of Empire is characterized fundamentally by a lack of boundaries: Empire's rule has no limits. First and foremost, then the concept of Empire posits a regime that effectively encompasses the spatial totality, or really that rules over the entire "civilized" world. No territorial boundaries limit its reign. Second, the concept of Empire presents itself not as a historical regime originating in conquest, but rather as an order that effectively suspends history and thereby fixes the existing state of affairs for eternity. ... Third, the rule of Empire operates on all registers of the social order extending down to the depths of the social world. Empire not only manages a territory and a population but also creates the very world it inhabits. It not only regulates human interactions but also seeks directly to rule over human nature. Finally, although the practice of Empire is continually bathed in blood, the concept of Empire is always dedicated to peace – a perpetual and universal peace outside of history (Hardt and Negri 2000, xiv–xv).*

The lack of boundaries and totalizing impulse of empire does not arise spontaneously – it is constituted through the generation of political and social power established in earlier organized forms. At its beginning, middle, and end, empires cannot outrun their genetic constitution, the DNA of which includes the previous confederal agreement.

For the purposes of present argument, empire is the culmination of successive acts of confederation. The initial confederation becomes federated, joins to other organizations through a confederal association, expands the federal power to these new spheres, and ultimately the consensus of the federation becomes the power that drives the emergence of the empire. Within the final stage of empire, the federal constitution becomes the expression biopower and ideology (Hardt and Negri 2000, 23–24; Motyl 1999, 133–134).

The Confederative Cycle

The relationship postulated between confederation, federation, and empire, follows loosely the Aristotelian description of an evolutionary political cycle; the relationship posited here is one of evolution, decline, and reemergence. It is important to recall here again the distinction between confederation and federation. The confederative act is not a legal–constitutional one – it is more temporary, ad hoc, often plagued by inequalities, and "purposive." The act of federation is a legal–constitutional one where a confederation makes the terms of its existence clear and, potentially, permanent, rather than as the original confederative catalyst wanes. In the context of federalism, we may say that a federated state views itself as an independent part of a whole. In the context of empire we may say that a state views itself as a subjugated part of a

---

defining characteristics of empire" (1999, 128). The role of ideology in the definition of empire is the key difference between these two descriptions.

reluctant whole. In the confederate system, partners ally for a purpose commonly decided amongst the members, and members view themselves as constituent and willing parts of a whole. While the cobbled together membership of an empire may disintegrate spectacularly given the weakening of the center's power, a federation or confederation is less likely to collapse dramatically due to the weakening of the center (Motyl 1999, 128–137). Indeed, in the context of a confederacy, the collapse of the center means the collapse of the meanings shared between the confederating partners and a fundamental shift in the relational identity of members of the alliance.

Evolution

In the African context, the evolutionary stage of the cycle transits in the following way: the confederation of kinship groups for mutual benefit and protection is followed, through the evolution of a strong pattern of leadership – a chief – by the codification of power in a constituted federation. As the federation seeks to increase its power or expand its resources (population or productive), this federation may take on a more imperial character. As seen in the evolution of dynastic Egypt (which will be taken up in more detail below), the desire to consolidate then expand the economic preeminence of the Nile civilizations vis-à-vis the Nubian, Libya, Sinai, Hyksos, and other "Asiatic" peoples,[6] led to the evolution of some of the defining characteristics of empire as described above.

Decline

Most empires disintegrate through the concatenation of internal and external pressures. Within the Egyptian empire, the confederation of internal groups opposed to the empire eventually create a federation of opposed "heretics" or revolutionaries.[7] Externally, as the empire increases its expansionist tendencies and emerges as a regional hegemon, related competitor groups may confederate in opposition to the empire.[8] The break-up of an empire may involve the collapse into a federation or a confederation, depending largely on whether the catalyst of collapse comes from inside or outside of the empire itself.

---

6 "Asiatic peoples" is a classificatory term used by scholars of Egypt's early dynasties to denote those people from beyond the Sinai Peninsula.
7 In an empire with the same religious–political architectonics as Egypt and other African states, like the Mali and the Asante, to go against the state is to go against the religion as well. Politically opposed groups may, indeed, be heretics.
8 The confederation of the peoples of Nubia (Kush) to repel the power of the ascendant Egyptians is an example (see Davidson 1991, 56–59, 64–69).

The Ashgate Research Companion to Federalism

Reemergence

Prior to the colonial take-over, the collapse of empires in Africa was due largely to internal reasons, resulting in the emergence of a provisional political anarchy. The anarchic condition, or the pre-confederal order, is that of multiple kinship groups locked into a mutual struggle. The attempt to resolve this struggle may result in the generation of multiple loose confederacies and thus the cycle begins anew.[9]

Figure 26.1 is a visual representation of the confederative cycle, which may serve as a useful heuristic.

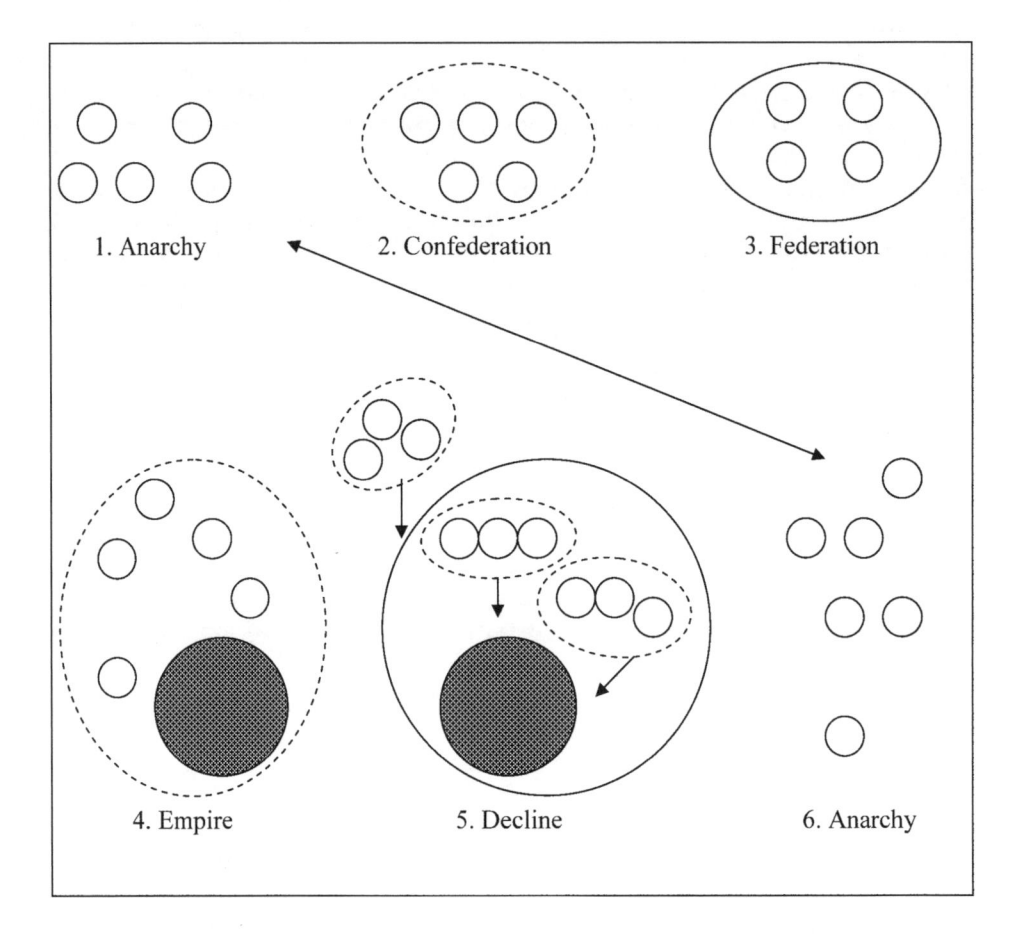

Figure 26.1 The confederative cycle

---

9   Motyl arrives at a similar conclusion in the context of Tsarist Russia and Soviet history (1999).

Roots of the Confederative Cycle in Africa

What can be said about the relationship between confederacy, federalism, and empire in historical Africa? States as geographically definitive units for the delineation of the legitimate use of force have little historical relationship to African politics. This is due to the strongly communitarian nature of African politics and the expression of political communitarianism through reliance on mutual associations (Wingo 2006, 453–457). African communitarianism is, as Masolo (2006, 483–499) makes clear, a unique system requiring separate forms of analysis and commendation.

Its contours are roughly as follows: first, the kinship unit (nuclear and immediate extended family) forms the basis of all political organizations. Second, the primary kinship unit is the extended group, what might be called a homestead or sub-village, cooperative group. This second level, importantly, is not a "tribe." The tribal level – that of a sociopolitical unit that recognizes itself in relation to other similarly constituted, competitive, or contractually cooperative groups – is the third significant level of political expression of African modes of community. Using a modern example from Leopold Senghor's African socialism, the uniqueness of African communitarianism becomes apparent:

> *I would say that the latter [the collectivist European society] is an assembly of individuals. The collectivist society inevitably places the emphasis on the individual, on his original activity and his needs. In this respect, the debate between "to each according to his labor" and "to each according to his needs" is significant. Negro-African society puts more stress on the group than on the individual, more on solidarity than on the activity and needs of the individual, more on the communion of persons than on their autonomy. Ours is a community society. This does not mean it ignores the individual, or that collectivist society ignores solidarity, but the latter bases this solidarity on the activities of individuals, whereas the community society bases it on the general activity of the group (Senghor 1964, 93–94; quoted in Masolo 2006, 489, emphasis in the original).*

Within the tribal level, we find a broad swath of organizational types across the continent. Significantly, each contains a religious–political, apical figure – a chief, broadly understood. This chief, contrary to early travel narratives and missionary reports, is not often a despot as his rule is contingent on his ability to generate the cooperative support of the subgroups around him. It is the political role of the chief to maintain this confederation of village cooperatives and to serve as the repository of the law (Ayittey 1999, 88–91 and 2006, 143–185; McCarthy 1994, 227–231; Teffo 2006, 445–448; Wamala 2006, 436–441). The embodiment of the law in the person of the chief, such as in the context of the Asante discussed below, transforms what would only be a homestead of confederated bodies into the larger political unit – a federated tribe. The tribal level is also part of a larger federated structure bearing many of the same organizational features. This fourth level of politics – the tribal association – is the closest approximation to the "state" in historical Africa.

As seen in the case of the Asante in particular, the larger Asante group is a loose federation of related (Akan) tribes under a politically and religiously significant leader – the Asantehene. The subgroups, "tribes" perhaps, are free to associate amongst themselves and may form internal confederations that may, eventually, pose a problem to the larger tribal federation as a whole. The constitution, and importantly the dissolution of this group, is dependent upon confederation groups' consent, not any larger or more powerful, coercive force.[10]

Empire, Federation, and Confederacy among the Egyptians and Asante

Many significant studies of African political organization come from anthropological and demographic studies, such as the influential studies compiled by Fortes and Evans-Pritchard (1970) and Stevenson (1968). Yet much of this literature on African politics remains "anthropological" and explicitly dedicated to describing political organizations. Here, I attempt to review the history of two societies – the early Egyptians and the modern Asante – from the perspective of the political theorist and historian.

Egypt of the Dynastic Period[11]

What we know of the politics of ancient Egypt is colored by the western fascination with "oriental despotism"; western visions of Pharonic politics are orientalist in the extreme (Said 1978). Calling to mind the Narmer (Menes) Palette, we envision Pharaohs as despots who smite prisoners and enslave their people to satisfy cravings for the accumulation of power and commodities.[12] Certainly the megalomaniacal

---

10 See Sarbah (1996) for an excellent description of this process in the context of the Fante, a group related to (geographically, linguistically, and ultimately, politically) to the Asanti.
11 We commonly refer to Egypt and the "Egyptians" as "outside" of Africa (Davidson 1991, 64). However, reflecting upon the recent evidence describing the panoply of genetic variation amongst peoples on the African continent, we might suggest that the racial and ethnic make up of early Egypt is the archetype of modern Africa (Kittles and Weiss, 2003). Thus, it is reasonable to begin this abbreviated analysis of the political history of the continent with the Egyptians as truly foundational for the continent.
12 The Narmer Palette is one of the earliest artifacts is and one of the most famed artifacts from the pre-dynastic/early dynastic period of Egypt. For a brief summary and plate of the Narmer palette, see Shaw 2004, 1–10; see also plate 21 in Daumas 1965 and associated explanation.

Ramses II fits this model, but what of the politics of the remainder of the 3000 years of Ancient Egyptian, or maybe it is best to refer to this as Kemet, history?[13]

We have little record of the earliest (first to sixth) dynasties of Egypt. Even nimble scholars of Egyptian history and politics, such as François Daumas, are left with only bare scaffolding for their suppositions and conjectures. In the extended, multi-century period of Kemet politics, what emerges from the Nile valley is a vibrant political system with both pre-modern and modern trappings. The pre-modern trappings of the empire of Kemet we can categorize under the broad heading of politico-religious mysticism. Certainly the Pharaohs maintained a mystical, godlike aura around them, but this was hardly the fullness of true Pharonic power; religious and sacro-political sanctions were but one arm of the Pharaoh's monopoly on the legitimate use of power (Daumas 1965, 129–149, 247–250). The economic and military–imperial arm of Pharonic power was the other.

In any basic Egyptian history book, we are told the tale of the unification of Upper and Lower Egyptian kingdoms under the rulership of Menes in the first dynasty, or circa 3200BCE (Daumas 1965, 37 and 551; but see Emery 1961, 27–29 for a discussion of the difficulty of these dates). The purposes of unification and the nature of early unified politics are largely unrecorded, but we do know that the Upper kingdom retained significant power relative to the Lower kingdom.[14] The task left for the political historian is to imagine the reasons for unification. This can be pieced together with some reliability if we examine the context of the context in which the Egyptian dynasty emerged.

Even in the shadowy first through sixth dynasties, we have records of a society seeking internal stability in the face of multiple external pressures, such as the rise of multiple competitor states. A motivation for internal consolidation, Ward (1963) suggests, were the pushes against Egyptian economic supremacy in the region from the peoples of the Libyan plains, the Nubians (Kush), Mediterranean states, and peoples from the Sinai Peninsula. Though recorded history suggests that Kemet was not under significant, coordinated siege until the late Old Kingdom (sixth dynasty), such a suggestion is likely incomplete. For example, recorded conflicts between the peoples of "miserable Kush" and the Upper kingdom occur around 3200BCE (Adams 1984; Davidson 1991, 54–59). Also previous Nubian incursions up the Nile or Mediterranean trading expeditions down the Nile had occurred, and importantly had provoked Egyptian military responses (Davidson 1991, 56–57; Asante and Abarry 1996, 446–448). A safe conjecture for the purposes of unification of the Upper and Lower was for the protection of Kemet's position as an economic

---

13   Asante and Abarry 1996, 6–7.
14   There are multiple renderings of the beginnings of unified Egypt, some more strange than others. Despite the problems of his book (such as the assumption of the imposition of Pharonic rule by an invading master race) Emery's brief recount of unification, its problems, and its artifacts, is interesting and useful (1961, 38–105). See Shaw 2004, 10–16 and Daumas 1965, chapter 3 "Trois Mille ans d'Historie" for other analyses and useful indications on the purposes and problems of unification. Neither is complete.

power.[15] This had secondarily important effects of strengthening the ties between the Kemet peoples as an ethno-linguistically similar group in distinction from the different groups of the Kush and the "Asiatics."

Just as we have limited information about the causes of unification, we have sparse records of the difficulties surrounding the unifications of the states, though we have some record of battles between the two kingdoms from Heirakonpolis (Emery 1961, 42–43). The results, however, seem clear. As suggested by Ward:

> *In Predynastic times, Egypt possessed a largely indigenous culture developed within the Nile valley. ... Predynastic settlements also flourished in the north (that is, from the Fayum northward) at the Fayum, Merimde, El Omari, Maadi and possibly at Heliopolis. By the end of the Predynastic age, the southern culture had spread northward making Egypt a fairly unified cultural complex. Whether or not this cultural unity was accompanied by political unity is still open to question (Ward 1963, 2–3).*

Contrary to Ward's position on the openness of the political question, it seems logical to conclude that the cultural homogeneity of northern and southern Egypt, the expansionist moves of the South against the North, and the increasing pressures from external actors, all led to the establishment of some manner of unrecorded terms of confederation of the Egyptian peoples. Each of these conditions, external pressure, cultural similarity, and differentiation of power between closely associated actors suggests that the generation of a political confederation is likely. Likewise, artifacts suggesting that the kings of the Upper kingdom had to engage in conciliatory politics with the Lower suggests that all was not easy between the two unequal partners of the newly formed kingdom (Emery 1961, 42–51).

From the standpoint of political categorization then, we might categorize the pre-dynastic (Naqaba 1, 2, 3) periods as one of emerging confederation between the two kingdoms. Emerging from a decentralized system, the earliest recorded dynasties represented a confederal and emerging federated unity of states. Later Old Kingdom dynasties, specifically from the fourth through the sixth, we might describe as the emergence, dominance, and demise of the federated imperial state on the continent, complete with the common imperial trappings of colonization and expansionist military incursions into neighboring states. Table 26.1 offers some preliminary categorizations of the dynasties according to this model.

The discrete historical causes of confederative transition in each dynasty are beyond the scope of detail I can provide here, so I will focus, for the purposes of example, on the first confederative cycle lasting form the first through the eleventh dynasties.[16]

There are almost no records of any sort – either textual or archaeological – from the First Intermediate Period (dynasties seven through ten), but it can reasonably

---

15 Though see Daumas 1965, 247–252 for an explanation for unification based upon religion.
16 But see arguments by Kemp 1983 and 1989 for some hypotheses.

Table 26.1 The confederative cycle in Egyptian dynastic history

Dynasties	Years Beginning	Years Ending	Categorization
I- III	~ 3200BCE	2600BCE	Confederation/ Federation
IV- VI	2600BCE	2200BCE	Empire, Internal Confederation
VII- X	2200BCE	2000BCE	Decline & Anarchy, Emerging Confederation
XI- XII	2000BCE	1800BCE	Weak Federation
XIII-XVII	1800BCE	1600BCE	Decline & Anarchy, Emerging Confederation
XVIII- XX	1600BCE	1000BCE	Federation Empire
XXI- XXX	1000BCE	332BCE	Internal Confederation, Eclipse

be inferred that the weak and divided Egyptian dynasties were in no position to undertake either slaving operations or mineral enterprises abroad.

The restoration of unified control in Egypt under the eleventh dynasty (ca. 2000BCE) was followed very shortly by the reemergence of Egyptian colonial ambitions in the south, in a radically new and more overt form. After a series of massive military incursions – obviously a renewal of the earlier slave raids – the pharaohs laid formal claim to the territory between the First and Second Cataracts, and they proceeded to fortify the region around the Second Cataract with a chain of the mightiest fortifications ever seen in the ancient world (Adams 1984, 44).

The confederal cycle as seen in the period of dynastic history in question can be traced as follows. Subsequent to the loose unification of the two kingdoms in the first dynasty, the Pharaohs sought to consolidate their newly formed kingship federation into a more stable political system, particularly in light of the increasing external powers – the Nubians, the Libyans, and the "Asiatics." The accumulation of external pressures, along with the codification of particular laws and protocols of kingship in the second dynasty paved the way for the opening of the first period of true Egyptian imperial ascendance in the third dynasty (Emery 1961, 38–111). The ascendance of the empire under Djeser led to the spectacular rulership of Snefru and the other fourth dynasty kings. It was during the fourth dynasty that the most well known of Egyptian cultural artifacts – the pyramids of Giza and the Sphinx – were constructed. These spectacular artifacts were made possible only through the political and economic stability enjoyed by the fourth dynasty. As described by Daumas, it was in the fifth dynasty that the early Egyptian empire reached its apogee and began to decline into the decadent and destabilized sixth dynasty (1965, 552). In the fifth dynasty, the Egyptians continued to pursue the expansion and consolidation of their empire vis-à-vis the surrounding states, including greater pushes into Nubian territory and the establishment of mining and exploratory towns as far as the Second Cataract and well into the Sahara. But these expensive expeditions led to the weakening of the Pharaoh and the eventual collapse of central Egyptian authority in the sixth dynasty through the combination of internal revolution and incursions by the Asiatics (Adams 1984, 42–44; Daumas 1965, 552). The dynasties of the First Intermediate Period were a time of relative anarchy as multiple regents declared rulership over their feudal states. In the ninth and tenth dynasties, for example, the Pharaohs Akhotes 1 and 3 re-conquered parts of the former empire, the western Delta and Thebes, respectively. It was not until the eleventh dynasty that the power of the Egyptian empire again showed itself (Daumas 1965, 43–81, 550–554; Kemp 1989, 31–44; Shaw 2004; Ward 1963). The full unification of the empire under the eleventh dynasty and the inauguration of the Middle kingdom was rather short lived as it was a mere 250 years later in the fourteenth dynasty that the Hyksos conquered leading to the Second Intermediate Period. Thus, in a period of approximately 1500 years, the peoples of the Nile delta transited through the full confederal cycle – the period of emergence, decline, reemergence, and subsequent decline.

Such a rendering of the politics of ancient Kemet may provoke some pause among scholars of political history and political science, specifically, given the sparse record. Such is the nature of Egyptology (Shaw 2004, 157–158). Thus, to substantiate the earlier and foundational claim that the confederative cycle seen in dynastic Egypt is characteristic of a great many African states, I turn now to a more contemporary example, that of the Asante empire (variously: Ashante, Asanti, Ashanti) of west Africa.

The Asante Empire

Like the Mali empire and others in the history of Africa, the history of the Asante empire traces that of the empire of dynastic Egypt. We can view these empires through the lens of the confederative cycle as well. Prior to (around) 1690, the Asante were a group of minimally coordinated, but cultural-linguistically similar Akan peoples. As minimally coordinated groups sought to increase their own holdings, the region began to destabilize and warfare became a more common occurrence.[17] It was not until the convening of the first tribal council at Kumase that the peoples managed to create a union – a confederation – to protect the mutual benefit of the member nations. Soon after the establishment of the confederation (though we do not know how soon), the confederation became more properly federal under the

---

17 The importance of warfare in the establishment of the Asante and Mali empires of west Africa contradicts the hypotheses put forward by Herbst (1990) that warfare is not as essential to the formation of states in Africa as it is in the formation of European states.

Charter of the Golden Stool (Davidson 1991, 53–55). Under the federated structure of the Charter of the Golden Stool, the Asante empire blossomed.

> *Without any doubt, one of the most impressive aspects of Asante history is the systematic development of a national ideology and the elaboration of complex social and political institutions for the management of society's affairs. Outstanding early rulers like Osei Tutu (ca 1695–1717), Opuku Ware I (1717–1750), Ose Kwadwo (1764–1777), and Osei Bonsu (1801–1824) created an elaborate military organization and a sophisticated centralized bureaucracy to ensure order, stability, and effective administration in the huge empire. They also used diplomacy, kinship ties, religious oaths, and the ideology of the Golden Stool to bind together the chiefs and officials in the central government (Aidoo 1977, 1).*

Like dynastic Egypt, the territory of the Asante Empire was blessed with significant internal agricultural and mineral wealth, matched only by the wealth available to regional competitor states. But, unlike Kemet, the Asante's basic political formation was not so strongly monarchic (Pharonic), though the similarities between the Pharaoh and the Asantehene (Asante chief) merit some discussion. Like the Pharaoh, the Asantehene enjoys both religious and political significance and power. Unlike the Pharaoh, the Asantehene is subject to the internal review and possible deposition through the expression of displeasure from lower chiefs of the federated states that make up the Asante empire.[18] The Pharaoh, unlike the Asantehene, served as the repository of Egyptian religious and practical law. The Asantehene, on the other hand, serves as the highest adjudicator and protector of the 77 laws recorded in the Charter of the Golden Stool, and while he enjoyed religious significance, he was not a complete religious ruler, sharing those duties with the Dente oracle (Maier 1981). But, though the Pharaoh had the consultation of the vizierate and his court,[19] the Asantehene was part of the ruling council or the Asantemanhyiamu (Asante parliament of chiefs) (Boahen and Webster 1970, 118–120). Though the two enjoyed religious and political significance, the Pharaoh came closest to the notion of the despotic ruler while the Asantehene came closest to the ideal of the constitutional monarch (Davidson 1991, 385–388).

---

18 "This [Asante] empire, that stretched over much of what is now called Ghana, consisted of two parts: Metropolitan Asante and Provincial Asante. Metropolitan Asante included the amanot or 'true' Asante states clustered around Kumasi. The principal amantowhere the five Oyoko states of Kumasi, Nsuta, Juaben, Bekwai, and Kokofu; an important non-Oyoko amanto state was that of Mampong. Most of these states lay within about thirty-forty miles radius from the capital, Kumasi, and its inhabitant considered themselves to be of the Asante tribe; that is owing allegiance to the 'golden stool.' Provincial Asante consisted of vassal tribes" (Ayittey 2006, 241).

19 The power of the vizierate is open to some question, though we do have some first hand indications from the (auto)biographical accounts of court insiders and viziers such as Weni and Harkhuf, viziers from the sixth dynasty (Asante and Abarry 1996, 446–451).

"The first feature to note about the Asante system is that it was based on decentralization, which gave a large measure of local autonomy to the smaller units" (Busia 1967, 29, quoted in Ayittey 2006, 242–243). Though the Asantehene is the apical leader, the Amanhene (which included the chiefs of the amanto or true states), the Asanteman (Asante people), and the Asantehemaa (Queen mother of the Asante) check his use of power. As Aidoo offers,

> The Asantehene's power was constitutionally and religiously circumscribed. First, he had to maintain a balance of power and interests with the Asantehemaa who was his real or classificatory mother or sister. Theoretically, the Asantehemaa was a co-ruler, and she had a well defined constitutional and political role. ... Thus the Asantehene and Asantehemaa were the joint hereditary rulers of all the ruling groups at the apex of power. ... The second most important group at the apex were the Amanhene of the federated states. They shared authority with the Asantehene and Asantehemaa and regarded them jointly as primus inter pares. The Amanhene derived their power from their own local royal matrilineages. They held their lands absolutely, ran their own local administrations, and had immediate control over their fighting men (1977, 10–11).

Yet, far from being completely subservient, the Asantehene are state heads, free to engage in diplomacy on behalf of their people (Adjaye 1985). The chiefs of the states, however, are also free to collaborate in order to depose despotic leaders or realign themselves if the opportunity was right. The extent of freedom of the (metropolitan and provincial) state chiefs under the guidance of the Asantehene is made clear by Davidson 1992:

> While the concept of a national unity framed upon an overarching rule of law [Charter of the Golden Stool] was modified to the extent of allowing non-Akan subject peoples to maintain their own separate charters of identity, the acknowledged spokesmen of these subject peoples were obliged to recognize the supremacy of the Golden Stool and its inherent charter. They had to attend the odwira, or annual yam festival, this being a means of insisting on the primacy of national over subnational rights and obligations, and... performed as an embodiment o the "overriding national purpose" (Davidson 59–60).

The role of the Asantehene and Asantehemaa, though occupied by co-regal persons, serve in a capacity roughly equivalent to that of a modern federal government constitution – they must protect the Golden Stool[20] as the symbol of Asante power, preserve the legality of the Charter of the Golden Stool, co-issue relevant laws for member states and adjudicate law within and between said relevant member states,

---

20 The Golden Stool, as related by Davidson, is the symbol of the Asante nation, much like the English Crown (1992, 56–57). For a more incisive view of the function of the Golden Stool in Asante law, see Chazan (1978).

along with the Amanhene. They can be brought to Council by a dissatisfied state and deposed by the same Amanhene if they fail to perform their expected functions or step out of line with the expectations of the Asanteman, or Asante people.[21] This form of decentralization, based upon the non-legal agreement between groups, constituted the Asante as a confederal, perhaps federal if we consider the role of the Asantehene as protector of the original confederating document, state.[22]

As the Asante empire stabilized and grew, the political structure suffered from the intrigues of power and the flux of internal secessionist movements (Ayittey 2006, 289). In a particularly important historical case, that of the attempt by the Dente Bosomfo (or the priest of the Dente oracle in Krachi) to challenge and secede from the greater Asante federation, the Asantehene had to face down a direct, internal threat from the separatist Bron confederation (Maier 1981). The empire withstood this and other secessionist movements and was certainly an apical state in the region at the time of British occupation. The empire transited through the three major stages of the confederative cycle – emergence, decline, and reemergence – throughout its approximately 200-year known history. It was not until the overwhelming pressure of the British did the empire finally collapse (Davidson 1992, 66–73).

Prior to the British dispossession and colonization of the Asante in 1895–1896, they functioned as a true nation state. Like the Egyptian dynasties, whose history was thwarted by the incursions of Alexander in 332BCE, the Asante's eventual political might and history, and their autonomous progression along the unique confederative cycle of is resigned now to being a counterfactual mystery.

The Reinvigoration of Federalism as the Reinvention of Indigenous Democracy

Federalism, as Levy (2007) reminds us, is a form of government that allows us to vote with our feet if we are displeased with the system of government in our present location. While the Theibout sorting hypothesis was constructed in the context of urban–exurban migration in America, the hypothesis is explanatory for the patterns of historic, democratic federalism in Africa. As with the historical movement of the Akan people into the Asante confederation, the choice of the people was to move into an area with a stable system. The peoples of the present day nation of Ghana, far before the introduction of the sorting hypothesis, were "voting with their feet" and voting for a people-centered pattern of government. Thus, we might conclude that one of the original purposes of federalism in Africa

---

21   Such a system was not uncommon in the remainder of the West African region during the seventeenth, eighteenth, and nineteenth centuries (Casely Hayford 1911, quoted in Ayittey 2006, 243).
22   A similar argument is made by Busia 1951, Carlston 1968, 125–130, and Ayittey 2006, 242–243.

was the provision of choice. In indigenous societies, the people were the authors of their own government, not the king or chief. While the king or chief did hold tremendous, sometimes God-like power, their position in the kingdom was based upon the acceptance of their people. If a king or queen failed to protect and provide for their people, they could be removed. Or, alternatively, the people would remove themselves from the kingdom.

In the indigenous form of African federalism, states entered into an alliance – a confederation – that provided for their protection from the negative effects of lawlessness and from the influence of other societies. In the context of pre-colonial Africa, the purpose of federalism was not solely government stability but the protection of necessary components of a stable community life. Once it was clear that the alliance was sufficient for these two tasks, the state could rise in power to the status of an empire, taking part in its own forms of colonial expansion. The African state, prior to colonialism was a form of political organization suffused with the values of community and the vagaries of historical cycles. Any further studies of federalism or the politics of the continent must take these considerations into account.

References

Acton, Lord J. E. E. D. ([1862] 1985), Nationality, in Fears, J. R. (ed.) *Selected Writings of Lord Acton, Vol. 1*. (Indianapolis: Liberty Fund), 409–433.
Adams, W. Y. (1984), The first colonial empire: Egypt in Nubia, 3200–1200BC, *Comparative Studies in Society and History*. 26:1, 36–71.
Adjaye, J. K. (1985), Indigenous African diplomacy: an Asante case study, *International Journal of African Historical Studies*. 18:3, 487–503.
Aidoo, A. A. (1977), Order and conflict in the Asante Empire: a study in interest group relations, *African Studies Review*. 20:1, 1–36.
Asante, M. K. and Abarry, A.S. (1996), *African Intellectual Heritage: A Book of Sources*. (Philadelphia: Temple University Press).
Ayittey, G. B. N. (1999), *Africa in Chaos*. (New York: St. Martin's Press).
—— (2006), *Indigenous African Institutions*, 2nd Edition. (Ardsley, NY: Transnational Publishers, Inc.).
Boahen, A. A. and Webster, J. B. (1970), *History of West Africa*. (New York: Praeger).
Busia, K. A. (1951), *The Position of the Chief in the Modern Political System of the Ashanti*. (Oxford: Oxford University Press).
—— (1967), *Africa in Search of Democracy*. (London: Routledge).
Carlston, K. S. (1968), *Social Theory and African Tribal Organization*. (Chicago: University of Chicago Press).
Chazan, N. H. (1978), The Africanization of political change: some aspects of the dynamics of political cultures in Ghana and Nigeria, *African Studies Review*. 21:2, 15–38.

Crémer, J. and Palfrey, T. R. (1999), Political confederation, *Political Science Review.* 9:1, 69–83.

Dahl, R. A. (1989). *Democracy and its Critics.* (New Haven: Yale University Press).

Davidson, B. (1991), *African Civilization Revisited.* (Trenton, NJ: Africa World Press, Inc.).

—— (1992), *The Black Man's Burden: Africa and the Curse of the Nation-State.* (New York: Times Books).

Daumas, F. (1965), *La Civilisation de l'Egypte Pharaonique.* (Paris: Arthoud).

Emery, W. B. (1961), *Archaic Egypt.* (Baltimore: Penguin Books).

Elazar, D. J. (ed.) (1974), *The Federal Polity.* (New Brunswick, NJ: Transaction Books).

—— (1987), *Exploring Federalism.* (Tuscaloosa, AL: University of Alabama Press).

Fortes, M. and Evans-Pritchard, E.E. (eds) (1970), *African Political Systems.* (Oxford: Oxford University Press).

Hardt, M. and Negri, A. (2000), *Empire.* (Cambridge, MA: Harvard University Press).

Heath, F. D. (2001), Whither Somaliland? Tribal society and democracy. *Somaliland Forum* [website], (Last retrieved 12-21-2007), http://www.somalilandforum.com/articles/whither_somaliland.htm.

Herbst J. (1990), War and the state in Africa, *International Security.* 14:4, 117–139.

Hyden, G. (2006), *African Politics in Comparative Perspective.* (Cambridge: Cambridge University Press).

Kemp, B. J. (1983), Old Kingdom, Middle Kingdom and Second Intermediate Period, in Trigger, et al. (eds), 71–174.

—— (1989), *Ancient Egypt: Anatomy of a Civilization*, 1st Edition. (London: Routledge).

Kittles, R. A. and Weiss, K. M. (2003), Race, ancestry and genes: implications for defining disease risk, *Annual Review of Genomics and Human Genetics.* 4, 33–67.

Levy, J. T. (2007), Federalism, liberalism, and the separation of loyalties, *American Political Science Review.* 101:3, 459–477.

Lutz, D. S. (1998), The Iroquois Confederation Constitution: an analysis, *Publius.* 28:2, 99–127.

Maier, D. J. E. (1981), The Dente Oracle, the Bron confederation, and Asate: religion and the politics of secession, *The Journal of African History.* 22:2, 229–243.

Masolo, D.A. (2006), Western and African communitarianism: a comparison, in Wiredu (ed.), 483–499.

McCarthy, S. (1994), *Africa: The Challenge of Transformation.* (London: I. B. Tauris & Co.).

Motyl, A. (1999), Why empires reemerge: imperial collapse and imperial revival in comparative perspective, *Comparative Politics.* 31:2, 127–145.

Sabine, G. H. (1963), *A History of Political Theory*, 3rd Edition Revised. (London: George G. Harrap & Co.).

Said, E. W. (1978), *Orientalism.* (New York: Pantheon Books).

Sarbah, M. (1996), On the Fante National Constitution, in Asante and Abarry (eds), 462–469.

Sartori, G. (1970), Concept misformation in comparative politics, *American Political Science Review.* 64:4, 1033–1053.
Shaw, I. (2004), *Ancient Egypt: A Very Short Introduction.* (Oxford: Oxford University Press).
Stevenson, R. F. (1968), *Population and Political Systems in Tropical Africa.* (New York: Columbia University Press).
Teffo, J. (2006), Democracy, kingship, and consensus: a South African perspective, in Wiredu (ed.), 443–449.
Tilly, C. (ed.) (1975), *The Formation of National States in Western Europe.* (Princeton, NJ: Princeton University Press).
—— (1975), Reflections on the history of European state making, in Tilly (ed.), 3–83.
——, Kemp, B. J., O'Connor, D., and Lloyd, A. B. (eds) (1983), *Ancient Egypt: A Social History.* (Cambridge: Cambridge University Press).
Trigger, B. G. (1983), The rise of Egyptian civilization, in Trigger, et al. (eds), 1–70.
Wamala, E. (2006), Government by consensus: an analysis of a traditional form of democracy, in Wiredu (ed.), 435–442.
Ward, W. A. (1963), Egypt and the East Mediterranean from predynastic times to the end of the Old Kingdom, *Journal of the Economic and Social History of the Orient.* 6:1, 1–57.
Wingo, A. H. (2006), Fellowship associations as a foundation for liberal democracy in Africa, in Wiredu (ed.), 450–459.
Wiredu, K. (ed.) (2006), *A Companion to African Philosophy.* (Oxford: Blackwell Publishing).

Further Reading

Works on Historical African Politics

Ajayi, J. F. A. (1989), *UNESCO General History of Africa: Africa in the Nineteenth Century until the 1880s.* Volume 6. (UNESCO and Berkeley: University of California Press).
Boahen, A. A. (1985), *UNESCO General History of Africa: Africa under Colonial Domination.* Volume 7. (UNESCO and Berkeley: University of California Press).
Ki-Zerbo, J. (1981), *UNESCO General History of Africa: Methodology and African Prehistory.* Volume 1. (UNESCO and Berkeley: University of California Press).
Mokhtar, G. (1981), *UNESCO General History of Africa: Ancient Civilizations of Africa.* Volume 2. (UNESCO and Berkeley: University of California Press).

Introductory Texts on Politics and Political History in Africa

Ayittey, G. B. N. (1993), *Africa Betrayed.* (New York: Palgrave Macmillan).

—— (1999), *Africa in Chaos: A Comparative History.* (New York: St. Martin's Griffin).
—— (2006), *Indigenous African Institutions.* (Ardsley, NY: Transnational Publishers).
Davidson, B. (1959), *Lost Cities of Africa.* (Boston: Back Bay Books).
—— (1978), *A History of West Africa: 1000–1800.* (London: Longman Group).
—— (1989), *Modern Africa: A Social and Political History.* (London: Longman Group).
—— (1991), *African Civilization Revisited: From Antiquity to Modern Times.* (Trenton, NJ: Africa World Press).
—— (1993), *The Black Man's Burden: Africa and the Curse of the Nation-State.* (New York: Times Books (Random House)).
—— (2001), *Africa in History.* (London: Weidenfeld & Nicholson).
Mazrui, A. A. (1980), *The African Condition: A Political Diagnosis.* (Cambridge: Cambridge University Press).
—— and Levine, T. K. (1986), *The Africans: A Reader.* (Westport CT: Praeger).
—— and Mazrui, A. M. (1999), *Political Culture of Language: Swahili, Society and the State.* (Binghamton, NY: The Institute of Global Cultural Studies).
—— Laremont, R. R., Kalouche, F., and Falola, T. (eds) (2002), *Africa and Other Civilizations: Conquest and Counter-Conquest.* (Trenton, NJ: Africa World Press).

Works on Political Science in Africa

Bates, R. H. (1981), *Markets and States in Tropical Africa.* (New York: Cambridge University Press).
Bayart, J-F. (1993), *The State in Africa: The Politics of the Belly.* (London: Longman Group).
Bratton, M. and van de Walle, N. (1997), *Democratic Experiments in Africa.* (New York: Cambridge University Press).
Clark, J. F. and Gardiner, D. E. (eds) (1997), *Political Reform in Francophone Africa.* (Boulder, CO: Westview Press).
Dia, M. (1996), *Africa's Management in the 1990s: Reconciling Indigenous and Transplanted Institutions.* (Washington, DC: World Bank).
Herbst, J. (2000), *States and Power in Africa: Comparative Lessons in Authority and Control.* (Princeton, NJ: Princeton University Press).
Hyden, G. (2006), *African Politics in Comparative Perspective.* (Cambridge: Cambridge University Press).
—— and Venter, D. (eds) (2001), *Constitution-Making and Democratization in Africa.* (Praetoria: Africa Institute of South Africa Press).
Kennedy, P. (1988), *African Capitalism: The Struggle for Ascendancy.* (Cambridge: Cambridge University Press).
Laitin, D. (1992). *Language Repertoires and State Construction in Africa.* (New York: Cambridge University Press).
Sandbrook, R. (1982), *The Politics of Basic Needs: Urban Aspects of Assaulting Poverty in Africa.* (London: Heinemann).

—— (1985), *The Politics of Africa's Economic Stagnation*. (Cambridge: Cambridge University Press).
Van de Walle, N. (2001), *African Economies and the Politics of Permanent Crisis, 1979–1999*. (Cambridge: Cambridge University Press).
——, Ball, N. and Ramachandran, V. (eds) (2003), *Beyond Structural Adjustment: The Institutional Context of African Development*. (New York: Palgrave).
Villalon, L. A. and Huxtable, P. H. (eds) (1998), *The African State at a Critical Juncture: Between Disintegration and Reconfiguration*. (Boulder, CO: Lynne Rienner).
Young, C. (1994), *The African Colonial State in Comparative Perspective*. (New Haven: Yale University Press).

Australian Federalism: An Innovation in Constitutionalism

Haig Patapan

The Commonwealth of Australia came into being on 1 January 1901. On that day the former colonies of New South Wales, Victoria, South Australia, Queensland and Tasmania, "agreed to unite in one indissoluble Federal Commonwealth." The new Australian Constitution, drafted in the course of public conventions and finally adopted through referenda, transformed the former colonies into states, preserving as much as possible their constitutions. It also brought into being a new federal government made up of a new parliament and executive, as well as a new federal judiciary. From this perspective the rather spare and prosaic provisions of the Constitution confirm the Australian founding to be, in essence, a federation, where colonial concerns regarding defence and economic efficiency were accommodated while retaining as much as possible their Westminster inheritance. Accordingly much of the scholarship on Australian constitutionalism, and indeed the bulk of its constitutional litigation, has concerned aspects of Australian federalism; scholarly debate has been dominated by the problem of commonwealth–state relations, the judicial resolution of such disputes, and the far-reaching political and public policy consequences of these debates.

The founding as a federation – something obvious and undeniable – is also in one sense unhelpful for understanding Australian constitutionalism. The reason for this is that by concentrating on this aspect of the founding and therefore the Constitution, we are distracted from seeing something that is of equal consequence – the founding was a revolutionary moment in Australia. Of course the founding was not revolutionary in the sense that it was a radical break from Britain: it is enough to recall that Australia is still a monarchy, and that the Constitution, though autochthonous, was finally enacted as a British Act of Parliament. Rather, it was revolutionary in the subtle yet profound way it transformed orthodox Westminster constitutionalism.

It is generally accepted the Australian founding is an admixture of British and American influences. Yet the fundamental changes introduced by the adoption of federalism has been insufficiently appreciated. In this chapter we will explore the changes in constitutionalism introduced into Australia through the means of American federalism, regarded by the American founders as an innovation in modern political science. To do so, we will first examine the complex nature of orthodox colonial constitutionalism, the tradition that shaped and informed the colonial founding and which continues to influence modern Australian constitutionalism. As we will see, this colonial constitutionalism is itself constituted by a number of traditions, the most significant of which include parliamentarianism and the common law. Having examined the dynamic tensions within colonial constitutionalism, we then examine the extent to which federalism was understood by the American founders as a modern innovation to secure republicanism. In the final section the chapter will look at three specific aspects of constitutionalism – the idea of constitutionalism itself; judicial review; and rights – to explore how the innovation of federalism has transformed Australia. Seeing Australian federalism as more than matter of federal–state relations, as an innovation in constitutionalism, I suggest, is important not simply for historical reasons, but because it provides important insights into an innovation that continues to shape and influence the contours of modern Australian politics.

Parliamentarianism, the Common Law and Colonial Constitutionalism

To understand the innovation that was federalism, it is necessary to appreciate the character of the constitutionalism that informed the Australian colonies. This task is made difficult, however, by the limited extent of the scholarship on the different traditions that influenced colonial rule before federation.[1] Certainly there is comparatively little research on the way indigenous traditions have shaped Australian constitutionalism.[2] Of the British inheritance, much more research is needed into the theoretical sources that influenced colonial, and subsequently Australian constitutionalism.[3] What is clear, however, is that the colonial founding was shaped by many traditions, some of which were at considerable tension. In this context it is sufficient if we sketch two major – and contending – sources of these traditions to show the dynamic tensions within the orthodox constitutionalism.

---

1 See generally Castles (1982); Hirst (1988); Irving (1997); Martin (1969); La Nauze (2001); Gascoigne (2002).
2 See in this context the High Court's decision in *Mabo* (*Mabo v Queensland (No 2)* (1992) 175 CLR 1) and Russell (2005).
3 Of the recent scholarship that attempts to examine these theoretical influences see, for example, Warden (1993); Meale (1992); Melleuish (1995); McMinn (1994); MacIntyre (1991); Aroney (2002); Brown (2004).

Captain Cook took possession of the eastern coast of Australia on behalf of the Crown in 1770. But the colony of New South Wales was secured only after its subsequent possession and settlement by Governor Philip at Sydney Cove on 26 January 1788. Though initially a penal colony, by 1828 Imperial Legislation defined New South Wales and Tasmania as settled colonies. Representative government was attained in the colonies in 1842, and in 1850 the *Australian Constitution Act (No 2)* (UK) introduced responsible government by giving authority to the Legislative Councils of New South Wales, Tasmania, South Australia and Victoria to establish bicameral legislatures and to fashion their own constitutions (Castles 1982; Windeyer 1962; Lumb 1983).

This "Westminster" inheritance of parliamentary and responsible government, the initial model for the colonies that was subsequently retained in the new state and Commonwealth governments, relied to a large extent on conventions. The monarchy was, in Bagehot's terms, the "dignified" part of the constitution. The efficient consisted of the Cabinet, "a hyphen that joins, a buckle that fastens," the legislative and the executive (Bagehot 1963, 68). Drawn from and enjoying majority support in the popularly elected house, ministers in Cabinet were individually and collectively responsible to that house of parliament for the administration under their control. Under ministerial control, these officials holding independent and permanent tenure were selected on grounds of ability and expertise to be loyal, confidential advisers and servants of the ministers of the day. The conventions of British constitutionalism, especially of responsible government, thus animated the formal structures of the British parliamentary representative system made up of the Crown, the House of Commons and the House of Lords. Even at the time of Bagehot this account of the Westminster system was no more than an ideal – according to Crossman (in Bagehot 1963, 35), the extension of suffrage, party machines and a large independent civil service had transformed Bagehot's account of Cabinet government. Nevertheless it was this concept of parliamentary and responsible government that dominated many aspects of the Australian founders' understanding of the ideal form of political arrangements. Consequently, it was these ideas that shaped the way they anticipated and responded to changes and innovations in constitutionalism (see generally, Parker 1982).

The Westminster tradition we have outlined above co-existed – and at times was in tension with – another tradition that had its origins in Britain, namely that of the English common law.[4] The dominant understanding of the "common law", influenced by legal realists, is that it is "judge-made law", the exercise of personal discretion by judges and the judiciary.[5] In contrast, the older "declaratory" theory of

---

4   For an earlier formulation of this discussion see Patapan (2005).
5   The American jurist and Supreme Court justice, Oliver Wendell Holmes, argued in his famous work *The Common Law*, that what was historically understood as the common law was no more than the incremental exercise of personal discretion by judges and the judiciary (Holmes 1881). Legal realism, in the form of Roscoe Pound's sociological jurisprudence, was introduced into Australia by Julius Stone: see Mason 1996; Gleeson 1999; Fullagar 1993; Kirby 1983.

the common law denied that judges made the law; rather, they applied precedents that were appropriate to the case at hand. Thus it was the judge's duty to discover, not invent, what law governed the case at hand. The written evidence of the common law was to be found in the record of cases previously decided. Where a case was genuinely novel, the judge was to proceed by analogy to the appropriate precedent, on the basis of the common law maxim that a precedent that ran against reason was no law. According to Sir Edward Coke, renowned common-lawyer who had sat as chief justice of the Court of Common Pleas (from 1606) and as chief justice of the King's Bench (from 1613), the common law was the "perfection of reason". But this reason was not any one individual's reason. As he writes in his famous and influential *Institutes*, "for reason is the life of the law, nay the common law itselfe is nothing else but reason; which is to be understood of an artificiall perfection of reason gotten by long study, observation, and experience, and not every man's naturall reason" (I *Inst.* 97b; Coke 1832; Stoner 1992, 23).[6]

According to this common law tradition, the common law as a body of law entered colonies with its first settlers as their "inheritance and birthright".[7] But this common law did not simply define the terms and concepts that would subsequently be used in federation.[8] More radically, it was the source of all legal authority. To understand what this means, it may be useful to refer to the opinion of Sir Owen Dixon, Chief Justice of the Australian High Court and regarded as one of greatest common law jurists.[9] Dixon claimed that the common law was an "ultimate constitutional foundation" (Dixon 1957). Unlike the American model, according to

---

6   The realist attack on this tradition can be traced from Holmes' realism, back to Bentham's attack on the confederacy of "sinister interest", to Blackstone's attempt to reform the common law, finally to its origin in Hobbes' critique of the common law.

7   In contrast, the "reception date" for statutory law was established for New South Wales and Van Diemen's Land by the *Australian Courts Act* 1828 (Imp) as those laws and statutes in force in England on 25 July 1828 (so far as they could be applied). This was also the reception date for Victoria and Queensland as a result of their separation from New South Wales. The reception date for South Australia is 28 December 1836, and for Western Australia, 1 July 1829 (Zines 1999, 3). For detailed accounts of the reception of the common law see Castles (1982) and Windeyer (1962). For the history of the reception of representative and responsible government in the colonies see Melbourne (1963) and McMinn (1979).

8   The Constitution is much indebted to the common law, using many of its terms and concepts, including the powers, privileges and immunities of the executive (s 61); the meaning of trial by jury (s 80); the office of the Speaker (ss 35–37, 40); and the legal remedies of prohibition, mandamus and injunction (s 75 v) (Saunders 2003, 230; Zines 1999, 15).

9   In the 35 years he spent on the Court, first as justice in 1929, and subsequently as Chief Justice from 1952 until his retirement in 1964, he left an impressive and influential legacy in the interpretation of the Constitution and the common law in Australia. He was considered as "perhaps the most distinguished exponent in the world of the common law" (Lord Diplock) and as "one of the greatest common lawyers of all time" (Lord Pearce). For these and other assessments see Stephen (1986, 293).

Dixon, "In Australia we subscribe to a very different notion. We conceive a state as deriving from the law; not the law as deriving from a State."

> *We do not of course treat the common law as a transcendental body of legal doctrine, but we do treat it as antecedent in operation to the constitutional instruments which first divided Australia into separate colonies and then united her in a federal Commonwealth. ... The anterior operation of the common law in Australia is not just a dogma of our legal system, an abstraction of our constitutional reasoning. It is a fact of legal history (Dixon 1943, 199).*

According to this view, parliamentary sovereignty itself revealed the primacy of the common law: "It is not the least of the achievements of the common law that it endowed the Parliament which was evolved under it with the unrestricted power of altering the law" (Dixon 1935, 40). It is because the common law is the source of the authority of the Parliament at Westminster – the English constitution forms a part of the common law – that Australia had as its ultimate constitutional foundation the common law.

As the antecedent jurisprudential principle for the Australian founding, the common law shapes the nature of Australian institutions and how they are to be understood and interpreted by the judiciary.[10] For example, the common law supported the view that the Australian Constitution was an act of Imperial Parliament.[11] It also accounted for the importance accorded to the *Australia Acts 1986* enacted simultaneously by the United Kingdom and the Commonwealth, in effect severing legislative authority of Westminster Parliament over Australia.[12] Importantly, the common law defined the nature of the judiciary: where the Constitution has as its foundation the common law, the High Court, in interpreting the Constitution, is in effect a common law court; the court interprets the Constitution primarily to dispose a dispute; it will not give advisory opinions;[13] its decisions are never prospective.[14]

---

10 On the importance of the common law for the institutions of government, ranging from the principle of parliamentary sovereignty to responsible government see Saunders (2003, 229–231).

11 See, for example, Windeyer (1962); Latham (1961); Mason (2000) and generally Winterton (1998).

12 In arguing that parliamentary sovereignty is a child of the common law, these decisions reveal popular sovereignty as founded upon the common law.

13 Unlike the Canadian Supreme Court, the High Court has held that it will not provide advisory opinions; the Court will not hear a matter unless there is a dispute or controversy where some immediate right, duty or liability needs to be established by the determination of the Court: *Crouch v Commissioner for Railways (Qld)* (1985) 159 CLR 22.

14 In striking down a provision as unconstitutional, the Court has held that such invalidity exists from the beginning or is *void ab initio*: see *South Australia v Commonwealth* (1942) 65 CLR 373; *Victoria v Commonwealth* (1975) 134 CLR 338; Mason (1989). In rejecting

This necessarily brief account of only two, albeit major, strands of colonial constitutionalism – parliamentary responsible government and the common law – reveals the complexity, and the dynamic tensions, within the orthodox constitutionalism that could trace its origins to the early British history. It was this rich tradition that was soon to be transformed by the innovation that was federalism.

Australian Federalism

The comprehensively popular or democratic character of the Australian founding becomes evident when we examine the drafting of the Australian Constitution, and especially the role of the major conventions – the National Australasian Convention of 1891 and the Australasian Federal Convention of 1897–8.[15]

After Henry Parkes' famous Tenterfield Oration favouring a national government, the National Australasian Convention was held in Sydney from 2 March to 9 April 1891. Forty-five delegates from seven colonies, including New Zealand, attended the Convention, drafting the first, and influential, version of the Constitution.[16] For various reasons, however, the federation cause was not resumed until the Australasian Federal Convention, which met in three sessions, in Adelaide and Sydney (1897) and finally in Melbourne (1898).[17] The significant feature of this Convention, which drafted the final version of the Constitution, was that its delegates were elected by the people.[18] Importantly, after the Convention adopted the draft of the Constitution of the Australian Commonwealth, it was put to the people in the form of a referendum on the Constitution Bill.[19] When the bill was amended to take into account certain concerns of New South Wales, it was again put to the people in 1899, where it was endorsed by all the states

---

prospective invalidity, the Court adopts the common law view that it interprets and declares the law, rather than making it.

15 For first hand accounts of the Australian founding see, for example, Deakin (1944); Moore (1902); Wise (1913). For more contemporary accounts see La Nauze (1972); Crisp (1990); Irving (1999); Williams (2004).

16 The reasons for federating (principally economic, military and immigration) can be discerned from the resolutions proposed by Parkes at the Sydney Convention in 1891.

17 The official record of the Convention Debates are in Craven (1986) and electronically at http://www.aph.gov.au/Senate/pubs/records.htm and http://setis.library.usyd.edu.au/oztexts/index.html.

18 A conference at Corowa in 1893 had devised the "Corowa Plan" for a new popular constitutional process. In 1897 popular elections returning ten delegates from each state were held in New South Wales, South Australia, Victoria and Tasmania. The Western Australian parliament appointed its delegates and Queensland did not send any representatives.

19 The referendum took place in all states but Western Australia and Queensland. It was unsuccessful in New South Wales.

except Western Australia.[20] As this brief account of the making of the Constitution indicates, in the popular election of delegates for drafting the Constitution and in its final endorsement by the people through referenda, the Australian founding revealed and confirmed its democratic credentials.[21]

The Convention debates reveal the profound difficulties of federation, especially of fashioning new institutions and allocating powers and responsibilities while retaining as much authority in the states as possible. Where the orthodox constitutionalism confronted the new demands of federalism, the founders did not attempt to resolve these problems in abstract, theoretically, in the way, for example, *The Federalist Papers* (Hamilton et al. 1982) sought to argue for federation in America.[22] Rather, the Australian debates reveal attempts to reconcile different theoretical positions in the specific context of practical and institutional arrangements. For example, the major issue that divided the 1891 Convention, jeopardizing federation itself, concerned the Senate's powers regarding amendment and rejection of money bills, which appeared to be inconsistent with the convention of responsible government where the lower house was to predominate. After intense negotiations in Adelaide in 1897, the "compromise of 1891" was adopted, restricting initiation of money bills to the House of Representatives and forbidding the Senate from amending taxation bills. Similarly, it was not clear whether federalism would, in the words of Hackett, "kill responsible government" (Convention Debates, Sydney, 1891, 280). Sir Samuel Griffith in the 1891 Convention had proposed to leave the question open by providing that the executive *may* sit in Parliament. By the time of the 1897–8 Convention there was strong support for retaining responsible government, described by Sir Isaac Isaacs as the "keystone of this federal arch". Accordingly the requirement that the executive sit in Parliament was retained (Convention Debates, Adelaide, 1897, 169).

American Innovation

The discussion above shows how the founders suspected that federalism was innovative, yet attempted to resolve any possible tensions pragmatically, by modifying institutions or devising new ones. But what was innovative about federalism? If one were to understand federalism simply in terms of the allocations of powers between the states and the new commonwealth it may be possible to

---

20 Western Australia held its referendum on 31 July 1900.
21 Even when the bill was taken to the United Kingdom for its passage as an Act of Parliament, the delegates strongly resisted changes to its terms. On the nature of the compromise regarding the High Court provisions see Deakin (1944, 155–6). For a discussion of the limited conception of "the people" see, for example, Irving (1996).
22 For an exception see, for example, Cockburn's defence of the English constitution as natural, as opposed to manufactured, "rigid and written" American Constitution (Australasian Federation Conference, Debates, 1890, 135).

separate the innovations of federalism into changes that were due to federalism itself, for example, the introduction of another parliamentary body in the commonwealth, and in those innovations incidental to federalism, for example, that a new constitution was needed to implement federalism. Such an approach, though tempting, tends to deny something fundamental to the American federalism that the Australian framers used as their model, namely, the view that federalism itself was part of a larger experiment in democratic government.

We can see this more clearly when we examine the American founders' conceptions of federalism. According to Publius in *The Federalist Papers* the founding represented a political experiment, not only for the benefit of Americans, but for all of humanity (*Federalist 1*) (Hamilton et al. 1982).[23] The question to be tested was the very possibility of republicanism itself; whether it was possible to have a politics founded on "reflection and choice" instead of "accident and force". In testing the possibility of free government, Americans had before them the grand history and ancient models of republicanism. Yet the founders did not simply take their bearings from the past; the founding was not only politically, but also theoretically revolutionary: modern republicanism was founded upon natural rights.[24] Natural rights, informed by the modern political thought of Locke, Montesquieu and Hume, and not divine, ancestral and traditional authority, was the foundation of modern republicanism. These rights, discerned by unassisted human reason ("self-evident" truths) and "inalienable", included the individual liberty to pursue happiness. Accordingly, they determined the character, extent and end of government. Thus government was founded on a social contract or "instituted" by the consent of equal, rights-bearing individuals, to secure these rights, and no more. Where governments exceeded this authority, natural rights also guaranteed a right of revolution.[25]

Because "advocates of despotism" relied on historical accounts of republican disorders to question not only republican government but all free government, another starting point was needed to found modern republics, one that had been developed in modern political thought. Modern political thought questioned the ability of individuals to dedicate themselves to the common good. Much safer, it was argued, to rely on a Machiavellian "realism" – that "it is necessary to whoever disposes a republic and orders laws in it to presuppose that all men are bad".[26]

---

23 These were 85 letters by "Publius" (Alexander Hamilton, James Madison and John Jay) published in New York newspapers in December 1787 urging the voters of the state of New York to ratify the proposed Constitution of the United States. On the status of *The Federalist Papers* as a rhetorical and philosophical work see generally Epstein (1984).

24 The revolutionary nature of the American founding can be seen in the introductory words of the *Declaration of Independence*, which inaugurated a *novus ordo seclorum*, or a "new order of the ages". The motto on the obverse of the Great Seal was suggested by Charles Thomson in June 1782.

25 On the Lockean influence on the founding see generally Zuckert (1994; 1996); Pangle (1988).

26 "Men never work any good unless through necessity": Machiavelli, *Discourses on Livy*, Book I, Chapter 3.

In Hume's much admired reformulation, it was "a just *political* maxim, *that every man must be supposed a knave*". For Publius this was the realistic and therefore safe political maxim that men are not angels (*Federalist 51*). Human knavishness, apparently fatal to liberty, was to be transformed by the "Inventions of prudence" to counter the "defect of better motives" and establish modern republicanism. These inventions drew upon improvements in the science of politics that yielded new discoveries and perfected principles "imperfectly known by the ancients":

> *The regular distribution of power into distinct departments – the introduction of legislative ballances [sic] and checks – the institution of courts composed of judges, holding their offices during good behaviour – the representation of the people in the legislature by deputies of their own election – these are either wholly new discoveries or have made their principal progress towards perfection in modern times (Federalist 9; Hamilton et al. 1982, 38).*

To this list Publius added the enlargement of the republic into a "one great confederacy", that is, federalism. Unlike ancient republics, the modern federal republic of the United States would have extensive territory, a consequence of the principle of passion countering passion, applied in terms of ambition countering ambition in government, to overcome the perennial problem of "faction" in the governed. Faction, though traditionally based on the divisions between rich and poor, also included the modern problem of religious "enthusiasm". A commercial republic with an extensive territory would, in addition to the benefits of greater security without, multiply faction and thereby ameliorate both forms of potential divisiveness. Thus the American founding, an innovation in politics and an experiment in free government, was a modern founding; the modern diagnosis of the deficiencies of ancient thought and classical republicanism, and the new means of improving on their deficiencies, captured the founders' imagination and instructed their actions.

Federalism itself, in this account, was one part of a much more ambitious experiment in republicanism, an innovation to test the possibility of people ruling over themselves by election and choice, without descending to constant dissolution and war. Each aspect of American founding, brought together, established a comprehensive political device to solve the political problem of securing republicanism. It was this innovation in modern politics that was introduced into Australia by American federal constitutionalism. Did the Australian founders appreciate the extent of this innovation? Some, for example Inglis Clarke, the Tasmanian Attorney-General who was one of the major contributors to the 1891 draft and a great admirer of America, certainly did. Others no doubt saw the innovations in the context of specific institutional tensions, as we have noted above. Perhaps for most, however, what was foremost was not the theoretical issues at stake, but exploiting the advantages of federation to solve immediate and pressing economic and security problems.

Transforming Colonial Constitutionalism

To appreciate the extent to which to federalism was innovative it is useful to examine in greater detail specific theoretical changes that were introduced at the founding. Clearly a comprehensive enumeration is not possible in this context. In what follows we will briefly review the core concept of constitutionalism, and its related ideas of republicanism, judicial review and natural rights, to examine the nature of the innovations that federalism introduced to colonial constitutionalism. As we will see, these innovations were adopted extensively or in part, depending on the extent to which they challenged the orthodoxy. Moreover, the continuing tensions between traditions often became a matter for resolution by the judiciary, which until recently tended to favour the orthodox colonial constitutionalism and its presuppositions.

Constitutionalism

The very concept of constitutionalism – of a constitutive legal enactment, derived from the people, that places limits on government – was a federal innovation. Strictly speaking Britain did not have such a foundational enactment – its constitution was an amalgam of conventions and a number of significant historical agreements and Acts, such as the Magna Charta, the Bill of Rights and the Act of Settlement. Colonial constitutionalism was of course familiar with constitutions, but only as enactments by Imperial Parliament founding the colonies and allowing them increasing independence and authority. Thus in this context the Australian Constitution was, simultaneously, section 9 of the British *Commonwealth of Australia Constitution Act 1900*, and an enactment by the people of the colonies to establish a new nation. This tension and ambiguity between a British parliamentary conferral of authority, and a popular "Australian" limitation on governmental authority, can be seen most clearly in the political problem of who was sovereign in Australia. The formal authority of the United Kingdom Parliament was evident in the Constitution itself, as well as the subsequent enactments such as the *Statute of Westminster 1931* (UK) and the *Australia Acts 1986* (UK and Cth), which confirmed the gradual evolution of Australia into an independent nation.[27] After all, the Constitution did speak of a "subject of the Queen" (section 117). Yet it could not be denied that the means by which the Constitution was drafted and accepted, as well as its provisions, also recognized and established popular sovereignty in Australia. "Whereas the People", its very first words, signalled the decisive importance of the people. Consistent with the intention of the preamble, the people are essential for the parliamentary democracy secured by the Constitution: it is the people who choose members of the House of Representatives and senators (sections 7; 24). Importantly,

---

27 The *Australia Acts 1986* were identical provisions enacted by the United Kingdom Parliament and the Commonwealth, declaring that United Kingdom Parliament could no longer legislate for Australia.

it is only the people (as "electors") who can alter the Constitution (section 128). The scholarly debate as to whether Australia was a federal republic from its inception indicates the tension between this colonial understanding of constitutionalism, where parliament is sovereign, and the sovereignty of the people, an innovation introduced by federal constitutionalism.[28]

Judicial Review

These different conceptions of constitutionalism were also evident in the founders' understanding of judicial review. As we have seen the founders sought to secure what Publius called one of the new discoveries of political science – separation of powers – into the Constitution. Though its adoption was resisted and limited by the principle of responsible government, so that the executive and the legislative were not strictly separated in Australia, in one respect separation was wholly successful: the "Judicature" was entrenched in the Constitution (chapter 3). Along with the establishment of a new High Court of Australia, the Constitution secured the appointment, tenure and remuneration of the judiciary. Importantly, one of the most significant roles assigned to the new Court was that of determining constitutional disputes.

For the founders, judicial review was a natural and necessary consequence of federalism. How would the inevitable problems, doubts and disputes regarding the federal demarcation of powers be resolved? The answer appeared simple once the Constitution was seen as a legal enactment: the judiciary, and specifically the new High Court, was best placed to determine the meaning of the Constitution. It was qualified to undertake such a legal task, and it was sufficiently independent to assure a fair outcome. Judicial review was indistinguishable from the way common law adjudication proceeded, and was identical to the role of the Judicial Committee of the Privy Council, the ultimate source of appeal for constitutional and general legal disputes.[29] This view and understanding of judicial review was incapable of seeing the democratic problem of judicial review as articulated in the American Supreme Court decision of *Marbury* v *Madison*. In terms of federal constitutionalism, judicial review meant the striking down (for being inconsistent

---

28 See generally Winterton 1992; Warden 1993; Galligan 1995; Williams 1995; McKenna 1996; Wright 1998, 2000 and 2001; Meale 1992; McKenna and Hudson 2003.

29 One of the important changes made in London in the course of enacting the Constitution bill was to retain appeals to the Privy Council. This was supported by the British Colonial Office, a group of colonial Chief Justices and retired judges, as well as English investors: see generally La Nauze (1972, 173, 220–2, 248–9). Appeals to the Privy Council were gradually limited: *Privy Council (Limitation of Appeals) Act* 1968 (Cth), the *Privy Council (Appeals from the High Court) Act* 1975 (Cth). The *Australia Acts* 1986 abolished the remaining avenues of appeal to the Privy Council so that by 1986 the High Court was effectively the final court of appeal in Australia. In theory a right of appeal to the Privy Council remains under s 74 of the Constitution but because it requires a certificate from the High Court it is effectively obsolete.

with the constitution) of a democratic enactment by an unelected judiciary. As such it represented a profound challenge to the principle of popular sovereignty. In Australia this understanding of judicial review assumed greater prominence as the High Court's federal jurisprudence increasingly challenged the Labour government's post-war social policy (see generally Galligan 1987). But the full extent of the tensions between the two approaches to judicial review would not become marked until the 1990s, where the Mason High Court became increasingly concerned with rights and freedoms, augmenting its federal judicial review with a jurisprudence that placed greater emphasis on the rights and freedoms secured in the Constitution (see generally Patapan 2000).

Rights

Of course rights as such were also an innovation introduced into the Constitution. The Australian founders did not adopt comprehensive bill of rights in the Constitution; certainly there is no mention of "nature's rights" or "inalienable rights". Colonial constitutionalism could not comprehend the idea of limiting parliamentary sovereignty in such a way. Liberty was secured by allocating the greatest authority to parliament and reviewing it through responsible government; certainly not by limiting or restraining such authority by appealing to "nature" or some other higher principle. Such "distrust" of parliament was considered an American innovation (see, for example, Moore 1902; Galligan et al 1990). Yet primarily due to the influence of Andrew Inglis Clark, whose republican sympathies meant that he followed the American model as closely as possible, a number of individual rights were enacted in the Constitution.[30] The requirement of acquisition of property on just terms (s 51 xxxi); the requirement of trial by jury for indictable offences (s 80); freedom of religion (s 116), and limits on state discrimination based on residence (s 117) are some of the provisions in the Constitution that seek to secure individual rights. The tensions between these different conceptions of rights can be most clearly seen in the High Court's jurisprudence. These rights were initially given limited scope by the High Court, which tended to interpret them in the spirit of colonial constitutionalism, especially the concepts of parliamentary sovereignty, responsible government and the common law. In its more recent rights-based jurisprudence, the Court expanded its understanding of such rights, but in doing so insisted on their procedural rather than natural rights or human rights based provenance.[31]

---

30 On Inglis Clark generally see Howard and Warden (1995); Reynolds (1958); Williams (1995) and Patapan (1997).
31 For a general discussion of rights and the constitution see Patapan (1997; 2000); Williams (2002).

Federalism as Innovative Constitutionalism

Australian federalism is generally understood in terms of state–commonwealth relations. As a consequence scholars have defined federalism in terms of a struggle between centripetal and centrifugal forces that result in "coordinate"; "cooperative" or "coercive" federalism. Mathews (1980), for example, divides Australian federalism into distinct periods, characterized by coordinate federalism (1900 to 1920); cooperative federalism (1920–1940); coercive federalism (1940–1945); co-ordinate federalism (1950–1975) and new federalism (from 1975) (see also Mathews 1977; Starr 1977; Parker 1977). More recently, the Hawke and Keating period has been described as "collaborative federalism" (Painter 1998), and the Howard period as "regulatory federalism" (Parkin and Anderson 2007). These accounts of federalism are undeniably useful, especially in understanding public policy initiatives. In neglecting the larger theoretical framework of Australian federalism, however, they have in effect entrenched a limited and limiting pragmatic approach to questions concerning federalism (Hollander and Patapan 2007).

In this chapter we have explored the innovation that is federalism in the light of the American founding, and within a larger context of the dynamic tensions within colonial constitutionalism between parliamentary and common law traditions. As our examination of constitutionalism, judicial review and rights indicates, understanding federalism as an innovation provides profound insights not only into the theoretical provenance of the founding, but in important practical aspects of governance. The innovative nature of federalism is not merely a matter of historical curiosity, of concern for historians of constitutionalism or of ideas; it has immediate and practical consequences for Australian political life. The tensions we have noted between various streams of constitutionalism continue to animate, and in important respects shape and influence Australian politics and public policy. One need only consider the nature of the continuing debates regarding, for example, republicanism, indigenous and individual rights and freedoms, judicial politics, to see how the formulation of contending arguments reveal the persistence and power of these fundamental tensions. A more subtle awareness of the innovation that was and is Australian federalism therefore provides an essential starting point for a more comprehensive, theoretically informed, appreciation of modern Australian politics.

References

Aroney, N. (2002), Imagining a Federal Commonwealth: Australian Conceptions of Federalism, 1890–1901, *Federal Law Review* 30: 2, 265–94.

Brown, A.J. (2004), One continent, two federalisms: rediscovering the original meanings of Australian federal ideas, *Australian Journal of Political Science* 39:3, 485–504.

Bagehot, W. [1867] (1963), *The English Constitution* (Ithaca, New York: Cornell University Press).
Castles, A. (1982), *An Australian Legal History* (Sydney: Law Book Co.).
Coke, E. [1628] (1832), *The First Part of the Institutes of the Laws of England; or, a Commentary Upon Littleton.* Charles Butler ed. Volume 1, 19th ed. corrected (London: Clarke).
Craven, G. (ed.) (1986), *Official Record of the Debates of the Australasian Federal Convention* (Sydney: Legal Books).
Crisp, L. F. (1990), *Federation Fathers* (Carlton: Melbourne University Press).
Deakin, A. (1944), *The Federal Story: the Inner History of the Federal Cause* (Melbourne: Robertson & Mullens).
Dixon, O. (1935), The law and the constitution. In Dixon (1997), 38–60.
—— (1943), Sources of legal authority. In Dixon (1997), 198–202.
—— (1957), The common law as the ultimate constitutional foundation. In Dixon (1997), 203–218.
—— (1997), *Jesting Pilate and Other Papers and Addresses.* Collected by Judge Woinarski, 2nd ed. (Buffalo, New York: William S. Hein & Co.).
Epstein, D. (1984), *The Political Theory of the Federalist* (Chicago: Chicago University Press).
Fullagar, I. (1993), The role of the High Court: law or politics? *Law Institute Journal* 67:72–73.
Galligan, B. (1987), *Politics of the High Court: A Study of the Judicial Branch of Government in Australia* (St Lucia: University of Queensland Press).
—— et al. (1990), Australian federalism and the debate over a Bill of Rights, *Publius: the Journal of Federalism* 20:4, 53.
—— (1995), *A Federal Republic: Australia's Constitutional System of Government* (Cambridge: Cambridge University Press).
Gascoigne, J. (2002), *The Enlightenment and the Origins of European Australia* (Cambridge: Cambridge University Press).
Gleeson, A.M. (1999), Legal oil and political vinegar, Address to the Sydney Institute, Sydney, 16 March.
Hamilton, A. et al. [1788] (1982), *The Federalist Papers* (New York: Bantam).
Hirst, J.B. (1988), *The Strange Birth of a Colonial Democracy: New South Wales 1848–1884* (Sydney: Allen & Unwin).
Hollander, R. and Patapan, H. (2007), Pragmatic federalism: Australian federalism from Hawke to Howard, *Australian Journal of Public Administration*, 66(3): 280–297.
Holmes, O.W. (1881), *The Common Law* (Boston, Mass.: Little, Brown and Company).
Howard, M. and Warden, J. (eds) (1995), *An Australian Democrat: The Life, Work and Consequences of Andrew Inglis Clark* (Hobart: Centre for Tasmanian Historical Studies).
Irving, H. (ed.) (1996), *A Woman's Constitution?: Gender & History in the Australian Commonwealth* (Sydney: Hale & Iremonger).
—— (ed.) (1997), *To Constitute a Nation* (Cambridge: Cambridge University Press).

—— (1999), *The Centenary Companion to Australian Federation* (Cambridge: Cambridge University Press).
Kirby, M. (1983), Law reform as "ministering to justice," in Blackshield, A. R. (ed.) *Legal Change: Essays in Honour of Julius Stone* (Sydney: Butterworths).
La Nauze, J.A. (1972), *The Making of the Australian Constitution* (Melbourne: Melbourne University Press).
—— (2001), *No Ordinary Act: Essays on Federalism and the Constitution.* Irving, H. and Macintyre, S. (eds) (Carlton, Vic.: Melbourne University Press).
Latham, J. (1961), Interpretation of the Constitution, in Else-Mitchell, R. (ed.) *Essays on the Australian Constitution* (Sydney: Law Book Co. of Australasia).
Lumb, R.D. (1983), *Australian Constitutionalism* (Sydney: Butterworths).
Macintyre, S. (1991), *A Colonial Liberalism* (Melbourne: Oxford University Press).
Mason, A. (1986), The role of constitutional court in a federation: a comparison of the Australian and the United States experience, *Federal Law Review*, 16:1–28.
—— (1996), The judge as law-maker, *James Cook University Law Review*, 3:1–15.
—— (2000), Judicial review: a view from constitutional and other perspectives, *Federal Law Review* 28:2, 331–43.
Mason, K. (1989), Prospective overruling, *Australian Law Journal* 63:526–531.
Mathews, R. (1977), Innovations and developments in Australian federalism, *Publius* 7:3, 9–19.
—— (1980), *Federalism in Australia and the Federal Republic of Germany: A Comparative Study* (Canberra: Australian National University Press).
McIlwain, C.H. (1947), *Constitutionalism: Ancient and Modern* (Ithaca, New York: Cornell University Press).
McKenna, M. (1996), *The Captive Republic: A History of Republicanism in Australia 1788–1996* (Cambridge: Cambridge University Press).
—— and Hudson, W. (2003), *Australian Republicanism: A Reader* (Carlton, Vic.: Melbourne University Press).
McMinn, W.G. (1979), *A Constitutional History of Australia* (Melbourne: Oxford University Press).
—— (1994), *Nationalism and Federalism in Australia* (Melbourne: Oxford University Press).
Meale, D. (1992), The history of the federal idea in Australian constitutional jurisprudence: a reappraisal, *Australian Journal of Law and Society* 8:25–29.
Melbourne, A.C.V. (1963), *Early Constitutional Development in Australia*, 2nd ed. (St. Lucia: University of Queensland Press).
Melleuish, G. (1995), *Cultural Liberalism in Australia: A Study in Intellectual and Cultural History* (Cambridge: Cambridge University Press).
Moore, W.H. (1902), *The Constitution of the Commonwealth of Australia* (London: John Murray).
Painter, M. (1998), *Collaborative Federalism: Economic Reform in Australia in the 1990s* (Cambridge: Cambridge University Press).
Pangle, T.H. (1988), *The Spirit of Modern Constitutionalism: The Moral Vision of the American Founders and the Philosophy of Locke* (Chicago: Chicago University Press).

Parkin, A. and Anderson, G. (2007), The Howard government, regulatory federalism and the transformation of commonwealth–state relations, *Australian Journal of Political Science* 42:2, 295–314.

Parker, R.S. (1977), Political and administrative trends in Australian federalism, *Publius* 7:1, 35–52.

—— (1982), The evolution of British political institutions in Australia, in Madden, A.F. and Morris-Jones, W.H. (eds), *Australia and Britain: Studies in a Changing Relationship* (Sydney: Sydney University Press), 117–34.

Patapan, H. (1997), The dead hand of the founders? Original intent and the constitutional protection of rights and freedoms in Australia, *Federal Law Review* 25:2, 211–36.

—— (2000), *Judging Democracy: The New Politics of the High Court of Australia* (Cambridge: Cambridge University Press).

—— (2005), The forgotten founding: civics education, the common law and liberal constitutionalism in Australia, *Griffith Law Review* 14:1, 91–107.

Reynolds, J. (1958), A.I. Clark's American sympathies and his influence on Australian federation, 32 *ALJ* 62.

Russell, Peter H. (2005), *Recognizing Aboriginal Title: the Mabo Case and Indigenous Resistance to English-Settler Colonialism* (Toronto: University of Toronto Press).

Saunders, C. (2003), Future prospects for the Australian Constitution, in French, R. et al. (eds), *Reflections on the Australian Constitution* (Sydney: The Federation Press), 212–35.

Starr, G. (1977), Federalism as a political issue: Australia's two "new federalisms," *Publius* 7:1, 7–26.

Stephen, N. (1986), Address by His Excellency the Right Honourable Sir Ninian Stephen upon the occasion of the commemoration of the 100th anniversary of the birth of Owen Dixon. University of Melbourne, 28 April, in Dixon (1997), 283–302.

Stoner, J.R. Jr (1992), *Common Law and Liberal Theory: Coke, Hobbes, and the Origins of American Constitutionalism* (Lawrence, Kan.: University Press of Kansas).

Warden, J. (1993), The fettered republic: the Anglo-American commonwealth and the traditions of Australian political thought, *Australian Journal of Political Science*, 28:Special Issue, 83–99.

Williams, G. (1995), A republican tradition for Australia?, *Federal Law Review* 23:1, 133–48.

—— (2002), *Human Rights Under the Australian Constitution* (South Melbourne: Oxford University Press).

Williams, J. (1995), With eyes open: Andrew Inglis Clark and our republican tradition, *Federal Law Review* 23:2, 149–179.

—— (2004), *The Australian Constitution: a Documentary History* (Carlton, Vic.: Melbourne University Press).

Windeyer, I. (1962), A birthright and inheritance: the establishment of the rule of law in Australia, *Tasmania Law Review* 1, 635–69.

Winterton, G. (1992), Modern republicanism, *Legislative Studies* 6:2, 24–6.

—— (1998), Popular sovereignty and constitutional continuity, *Federal Law Review* 26:1, 1–13.
Wise, B. (1913), *The Making of the Australian Commonwealth* (New York: Longmans, Green and Co.).
Wright, H. (1998), Sovereignty of the people – the new constitutional Grundnorm?, *Federal Law Review* 26:1, 165–194.
Wright, J.S.F. (2000), The nature of the Australian Constitution: the limitations of the institutional and revisionist approaches, *Federal Law Review* 28:3, 345–64.
—— (2001), Anglicizing the United States Constitution: James Bryce's contribution to Australian federalism, *Publius: the Journal of Federalism* 31:4, 107–29.
Zines, L. (1999), The common law in Australia: its nature and constitutional significance, *Law and Policy Paper 13* (Leichhardt, NSW: The Federation Press in association with the Centre for International and Public Law, ANU).
Zuckert, M.P. (1994), *Natural Rights and the New Republicanism* (Princeton: Princeton University Press).
—— (1996), *The Natural Rights Republic* (Notre Dame: University of Notre Dame Press).

Further Reading

Blackshield, T. et al. (2001), *The Oxford Companion to the High Court of Australia* (Oxford: Oxford University Press).
—— and Williams, G. (2006), *Australian Constitutional Law and Theory: Commentary and Materials*, 4th ed. (Annandale, NSW: The Federation Press).
Collins, H. (1985), Political ideology in Australia, *Daedalus* 114:1, 147–69.
Craven, G. (ed.) (1992), *Australian Federation: Towards the Second Century* (Carlton, Vic.: Melbourne University Press).
—— (2001), A liberal federation and a liberal constitution, in Nethercote, J.R. (ed.), *Liberalism and the Australian Federation* (Annandale: The Federation Press).
Crisp, L.F. (1983), *Australia's National Government* (Melbourne: Longman Cheshire).
Davis, S.R. (1995), *Theory and Reality: Federal Ideas in Australia, England and Europe* (St Lucia: Queensland University Press).
Deakin, A. (1944), *The Federal Story: the Inner History of the Federal Cause* (Melbourne: Robertson & Mullens).
Detmold, M.J. (1985), *The Australian Commonwealth: a Fundamental Analysis of its Constitution* (Sydney: Law Book Co.).
Galligan, B. (1993), Australian federalism, in Marsh, I. (ed.), *Governing in the 1999s: An Agenda for the Decade* (Melbourne: Longman Cheshire).
—— and Mardiste, D. (1992), Labor's reconciliation with federalism, *Australian Journal of Political Science* 27:1, 71–86.
—— and Walsh, C. (1990), Australian federalism: developments and prospects, *Publius: the Journal of Federalism* 20:4, 1–17.

—— B. and Wright, J.S.F. (2002), Australian federalism: a prospective assessment, *Publius: the Journal of Federalism* 32:2, 147–166.

Gillespie, J. (1994), New federalisms, in Brett, J. et al. (eds), *Developments in Australian Politics* (South Melbourne: Macmillan Education Australia).

Goldsworthy, J. (1992), The constitutional protection of rights in Australia, in Craven (1992), 151–8.

Holmes, J. and Sharman, C. (1977), *The Australian Federal System* (London: George Allen & Unwin).

Jaensch, D. (ed.) (1977), *The Politics of "New Federalism"* (Adelaide: Australasian Political Studies Association).

Keating, M. and Wanna, J. (2000), Remaking Federalism?, in Keating, M. et al. (eds), *Institutions on the Edge? Capacity for Governance* (St. Leonards: Allen & Unwin).

La Nauze, J.A. (2001), *No Ordinary Act: Essays on Federation and the Constitution*. Irving, H. and Macintyre, S. (eds) (Carlton: Melbourne University Press).

Maddox, G. (2005), *Australian Democracy in Theory and Practice*, 5th ed. (Frenchs Forest, N.S.W.: Pearson Education Australia).

Martin, A.W. (ed.) (1969), *Essays in Australian Federation* (Melbourne: Melbourne University Press).

Painter, M. (1998), Public sector reform, intergovernmental relations and the future of Australian federalism, *Australian Journal of Public Administration* 57:3, 52–63.

—— (2001), Multi-level governance and the emergence of collaborative federal institutions in Australia, *Policy and Politics* 29:2, 137–50.

Parkin, A. and Anderson, G. (2007), The Howard government, regulatory federalism and the transformation of commonwealth–state relations, *Australian Journal of Political Science* 42:2, 295–314.

Quick J. and Garran, R.R. (1901), *The Annotated Constitution of the Australian Commonwealth* (Sydney: Angus & Robertson).

Sawer, G. (1969), *Modern Federalism* (London: Pitman Publishing).

Stokes, G. (2004), The "Australian settlement" and Australian political thought, *Australian Journal of Political Science* 39:1, 5–22.

Storing, H.J. (1981a), *What the Anti-Federalists Were For* (Chicago: University of Chicago Press).

—— (ed.) (1981b), *The Complete Anti-Federalist* (Chicago: University of Chicago Press).

Wheare, K.C. (1963), *Federal Government*, 4th ed. (Oxford: Oxford University Press).

Winterton, G. et al. (1999), *Australian Federal Constitutional Law: Commentary and Materials* (Pyrmont NSW: LBC Information Services).

India: A Model of Cooperative Federalism

Akhtar Majeed

Generally, most federations, whether dualist or integrative in their underlying design, provide for some form of accommodative governance, sharing of institutions and some forms of joint action. A dimension that needs to be discussed is the various different ways in India in which institutions and tiers of government work with each other and with others across jurisdictional boundaries, interact to manage inter-jurisdictional conflict and tension, the techniques and structures of interaction, and accountability and transparency. The actual operation of the Indian federation should be categorized not in terms of rigid structures for the division of powers, but as involving a process that enables reconciliation of internal diversity within the federal framework. Power-sharing, cooperation and accommodation are more effective, cheaper and lasting methods of accommodation for developing plural societies, as found in India. They become a meeting point for antagonistic groups and seemingly irreconcilable positions.

A country the size of a continent, with an area of 1 265 000 square miles and a population of over a billion, India is an extremely plural society, with 22 national languages and some 2000 dialects, a dozen ethnic and seven religious groups fragmented into a large number of sects, castes and sub-castes, and some 60 socio-cultural sub-regions spread over seven natural geographic regions. The existence of such identities, and such perceptions, cannot be wished away. A viable and successful polity must recognize these identities, respect them and must accommodate them. The Constitution of India has done just that and, in this way, through the assurance of providing Good/Quality Governance, and cooperative federalism, has become the best guarantee for a viable and vibrant nation. In multi-cultural, multi-ethnic and plural societies, like India and many others, social justice, economic progress and political democracy can be achieved only through an accommodation of diverse interests and identities.

As the society in India is plural, whereas the nation-state is uniform and polity is federal, the potential for strife and frictions are all too obvious. A plural society has been guaranteed by the Constitution of India in a self-equilibrating system, which does not allow one group or one party or one interest any enduring dominance. The Constitution describes India "a Union of States" and this implies the indestructible nature of its unity (*Ref.* Preamble to the Constitution of India). Some countries' political systems do not accommodate diversity, however, the Indian system does not treat plural diversity as a threat to integration of the nation. In India, the desire to identify some common goals and purposes, and to establish not just political legitimacy but political accountability, has become the basis of nationhood. If power is properly shared and varied interests are accommodated, there need not be any threat to power. The Indian federal mechanism is intended to provide precisely the same. In the above context, the Indian federal Union was formed by reconciling various visions, diversities, ideologies and influences. The federal Union was formed with some basic objectives: (i) to put in place a mechanism of federal governance with a strong parliamentary centre, (ii) to guarantee cultural autonomy to regions with strong linguistic, religious, tribal and/or territorial identities, (iii) to create a mixed economy with sectors demarcated for state and private enterprise, and (iv) to reduce regional and economic disparities through fiscal federalism and planning. As the Indian constitutional structure has shown, it is possible to respect cultural diversity without having to fear wrecking the nation-state. Ultimately, it is not just the question of majority–minority in a plural society; it is the question of social and distributive justice in a liberal democracy. If a democracy is not receptive to various identities in a plural society then it remains only a majoritarian democracy that "disprivileges" minorities. The viable alternative is that which has been provided under the Constitution of India (*Ref.* Articles 25 to 30 of the Constitution of India). Since the democratic procedures and institutions, in the normal course, would work in a manner that would be disadvantageous to the minorities, the state has ensured special provisions for the protection of minority rights.

Recognition of minority rights in the Constitution of India is important in this context. This does not create any conflict between the group rights of minorities and individual rights. Nevertheless, some sort of group rights have to be reorganized, compatible with individual rights. This is a combination of multi-layered federalism, democracy compatible with federalism, acceptance of multiculturalism and acceptance of minority rights compatible with individual rights (Sheth and Mahajan 1999) This is how apprehensions regarding cultural identities in a federal democracy are assuaged. This is the method of governing in the form of a "cooperative federalism", within the hierarchical social order that exists in India. The primary purpose of democratic procedures is not the rule of the majority but a shared-rule by achieving the widest possible consensus. When the decision-making processes are decentralized, the result is a consensual democracy which is much more stable in societies that are multi-ethnic, multi-cultural and are diverse, as in India.

Before independence, sub-nationalist identities were not even adequately realized. It was much later on that it was realized that federalism could be a good device for solving the problems based on ethnicity, language and others if these ethnicities are territorially identifiable.

Self-Rule and Accommodation Through States' Reorganization

In India, the federal constituents are states, which are the unit of self-rule through which autonomy of the society (in terms of maintenance of identity and assured development) operates. People having a distinct socio-cultural identity, concentrated in few contiguous districts within the existing state-systems, sought a separate state in order to preserve, protect and promote their identity. They believed that a separate state would provide them with a political identity and a constitutionally documented institutional space for interest articulation and protection within the broader territorial state In India, the unit of "self rule" may be: (i) a fully fledged state, (ii) autonomous region or regional councils with adequate legislative and executive powers within the existing states in which they are included, (iii) district development councils with adequate authority over local planning for the people located in "ethnic enclaves" of an otherwise composite state or (iv) granting of Union Territory status to city regions, strategically important regions or sub-regions and to those areas which are extremely backward (governed directly by the Union Government, Union Territories were created for small areas having special cultural heritage or for an area coming under inter-state dispute). Statehood may be granted to those regional communities which do qualify the three-point criteria of: (i) administrative and political manageability involving closer contact between the people and their elected representatives, (ii) techno-economic viability and (iii) socio-cultural homogeneity (in terms of tribes/jatis, language/dialect, belief system/religious communities and ethnic identities). In order to promote federal stability at the macro level, the institutions of shared rule such as Zonal Councils, Inter-State Councils, etc., were activated. These institutions are advisory or recommendatory bodies, facilitating inter-state cooperation and coordination in the areas of national and regional planning and development.

Arguments in favour of the formation or reorganization of states have been, among others, geographical proximity, a common language, similar usages and customs, comparable socio-economic and political stages of development, common historical traditions and experiences, a common way of living, administrative expediency and, more than anything else, a widely prevalent sentiment of "togetherness", that is, a sense of identity (Khan 1992, 109). In the competition for resources, the regions used several benchmarks to establish their identity. They were language, culture, economic advancement, administrative coherence, and even the socio-economic backwardness of the region (due to its being part of a bigger regional unit). Regional movements sparked demands for the formation of new states, and for the reorganization of existing states. These demands did not usually go beyond claiming resource-sharing within the broader national context. In this, language was often the symbol giving expression to these aspirations. A close scrutiny of state-formation in India would reveal that, together with languages, many variable and critical factors like ethnic-*cum*-economic consideration (Nagaland, Meghalaya, Manipur and Tripura); religion, script and sentiments (Haryana and Punjab);

language-*cum*-culture (Maharashtra and Gujarat); historical and political factors (Uttar Pradesh and Bihar); integration of princely states and the need for viable groupings (Madhya Pradesh and Rajasthan) and of course, language-*cum*-social distinctiveness (Tamilnadu, Kerala, Mysore, Andhra Pradesh, Assam, Bengal and Orissa) have played a decisive role in the composition of the Indian federation. A successful working of India's federal nation would involve administrative sub-division of larger states on the principles of regional autonomy and regional identity. The large, composite, states face problems of governance, and their very size may hamper economic development. Today's Uttar Pradesh, Bihar, Madhya Pradesh and Rajasthan provide examples of states with problems. When the people are made partners in governance, the nation as such is strengthened. Comparable development is possible elsewhere with the decentralization of power, and may lessen the demands for separate states. One should not rush to assume that granting more administrative and fiscal powers to the states, or creating a large number of states, may weaken the country.

States need to be reorganized in a manner which may accommodate and institutionalize various sub-regional identities. One way could be to identify a "four variables" basis for reorganization: administrative convenience, economic viability, similarity in the developmental needs of a sub-region and cultural-linguistic affinity. On this basis, even if more states are formed, it would only be strengthening "the self-rule, shared-rule" principle of cooperative federalism. And that would provide quality governance, as well.

Cooperation in the Jurisdictional Distribution

In view of historical traditions of centralization of power and authority, the operative principle in the making of India's Constitution was that a government was best when it was able to bring about social transformation. Hence, the framers of the Constitution and the subsequent law-makers consciously ensured that the overwhelming majority of powers and authority was kept with the Union government, with the result that there is "blood pressure at the Centre and anemia at the periphery", resulting in morbidity and inefficiency. Equally important, the country's diversity and socio-economic conditions, coupled with the ideological influences of socialism, drove the Constitution towards a kind of organically unitary federalism in the name of justice, equality and rights protection.

However, the wide powers given to the Union, and limited powers given to the states must not be seen in terms of "either or federalism" of the past, which rested on a dichotomy between the Union and the states (Majeed, 2005, 74). The two should not be seen as competing centres of power but as co-partners in the task of nation building. The Union has been assigned the duty of nation-building, maintenance of unity, protection of territorial integrity of the country and maintenance of constitutional-political order throughout the country. The states are to cooperate with the Union in the performance of these functions and in discharging their own constitutional duties with regard to subjects that are local. But as soon as any subject ceases to be "local", the Union would intervene to legislate on that subject.

The Indian Constitution would seem, in the end, to create a "cooperative union" of states rather than a dual polity. What is being observed now is federal restructuring through politically developed rules and conventions, without disturbing the basic scheme of the Constitution. The actual working of cooperative federalism in India has entailed the Union's exercising its influence rather than its constitutional authority. Exigencies of coalition politics have forced the Union and state governments to share power. The Union has more often played the role of a facilitator in inter-state disputes than that of an arbitrator. A redistribution of powers – through decentralization and the devolution of authority from the Union to states and from states to local bodies and municipalities – is facilitating the attainment of the objectives of the Constitution: unity, social justice and democracy. Any federal system is a device of shared governance, and the Constitution of India envisages a "creative balance" between the need for an effective union and effectively empowered states. There is a paradigm shift from the principle of dual federalism (with each tier of government exercising its own powers) to cooperative federalism (with the federal and state governments interacting with each other in the formulation and implementation of public policy). India is one such example of cooperative federalism with variations in the degree in which policy areas are handled by different tiers of government. Overall, the impression is that inter-governmental relations in India focus more on the needs of the citizens, particularly in welfare policy areas, rather than on questions of turf and jurisdiction.

For power sharing a sense of accommodation needs to be there, and a paradigm shift is needed in which democracy need not be just representative but participatory, and that is the direction towards which Indian federalism is now moving. In the constitutional scheme of distribution of responsibilities, the persistent theme revolves around cooperative federalism. If the lower/sub-federal level (*panchayats*, urban local governments) depend on the higher levels of government, for money and resources, the latter (Union and state governments, both) depend on the former for providing services to the people.

The practical importance of the concurrent list (when adopted in any federation) lies in the fact that the vesting of the same type of power in two parallel agencies carries, within it, the seeds of a possible conflict. This implies that the Constitution should provide, in advance, a mechanism for resolving such conflict. In India, the Constitution primarily seeks to incorporate such a mechanism: (i) The co-existence of Union and state laws in a particular area can give rise to litigation. Such problems arise either because the Union or a state may illegally encroach upon the province of the other (parallel) legislature, or they may arise because (though there is no encroachment, as such, on each other's sphere), the two laws clash with each other. (ii) The two situations are, strictly speaking, different from each other; and in India they are judged by two different tests. Where the subject matter of the legislation in question falls within either the Union list or the state list only, then the question is decided with reference to legislative competence. One of the two laws must necessarily be void, because (leaving aside matters in the concurrent list), the

Indian Constitution confers exclusive jurisdiction upon Parliament for matters in the Union list and upon a state legislature for matters in the state list. The Union is not empowered to interfere in any matter pertaining to the exclusive concern of a state. The correct doctrine applicable in such cases is that of *ultra vires*. Since one of the two laws must be void, the question of inconsistency between the two has no relevance. Only one law will survive; the other law will not survive, because *ex hypothesis*, it has no life. (iii) In contrast, where legislation passed by the Union and the state is on a subject matter included in the concurrent list, then the matter is not determined by applying the test of *ultra vires* because the hypothesis is that both the laws are (apart from repugnancy), constitutionally valid. In such a case, in the Constitution of India, the test to be adopted is that of repugnancy.

It is obvious that, where either the Union or the state legislature proposes to enact a law, it must, in the first place, decide whether it has legislative competence with reference to the subject matter of the law.

Features of Fiscal Federalism

Sharing among regions is not unique to federations. What makes the Indian federation different is not the fact of interregional redistribution per se, but the fact that it is explicit (Vithal and Sastry 2001, 255). Indeed, the analogue between inter-regional sharing within a federation and that within a unitary state in part accounts for the use of the financial arrangements of the unitary state as a benchmark for judging inter-regional sharing in a federation.

Inter-regional fiscal sharing schemes take different forms in different federations, depending especially on the nature and extent of the fiscal responsibilities assumed by the regions. Unlike the Indian one, regions in such federations have significant expenditure responsibilities, but rely on the central government for their finances. Financing can be formula-based or can have significant discretionary elements. In India, inter-governmental fiscal sharing schemes essentially complement policies implemented by the various levels of government and apply intact regardless of the extent of vertical redistribution pursued by governments. They can be looked at as policies that facilitate the decentralization of fiscal responsibilities, ensuring that the benefits of decentralization are achieved without compromising national objectives of efficiency and equity.

An important feature of India's fiscal federalism is revenue sharing between the Union and the states. Finally, Parliament is empowered to make such grants as it deems necessary to providing financial assistance for any state in need. Such grants can be block grants or specific categorical grants. There is a clear vertical imbalance between (i) the powers of taxation assigned to the Union and the states and (ii) the social and economic responsibilities assigned to the states; that is, the states' responsibilities exceed their own-source revenues. But the Finance Commission, the Planning Commission and the National Development Council provide mechanisms for periodically correcting this imbalance and for allowing the states to better discharge their responsibilities. These forums cater to the grievances of the states, which they redress to the extent possible.

The Constitution provides that the distribution between the Union and the states of the net proceeds of taxes that are to be divided between them, and the allocation between states of the respective shares of such proceeds, shall be done on the recommendations of a Finance Commission that is appointed by the president every five years. The Commission also recommends the principles that should govern grants-in-aid to the states. The grants are both a means to assist development schemes in states lacking adequate financial resources and an instrument to exercise control and coordination over the states' welfare schemes.

The following provisions of the Constitution are noteworthy in this connection.

> 1. There are duties levied by the Union but collected and appropriated by the States.
>
> 2. There are taxes levied and collected by the Union but assigned wholly to the States.
>
> 3. There are taxes levied and collected by the Union and distributed between the Union and the States. This is the position of taxes on income other than agricultural income.
>
> 4. There are taxes and duties which are levied and collected by the Union and may be distributed between the Union and the States if Parliament by law so provides.
>
> 5. Parliament is empowered to make such grants as it may deem necessary to give financial assistance to any State which is in need of such assistance. Such grants may either be block grants or specific grants.

It appears as if there is a clear vertical imbalance between (i) the powers of taxation assigned to the Union and the states and (ii) the social and economic responsibilities assigned to the states; that is, the states' responsibilities exceed their own-source revenues. This arrangement is intended to permit each order of government to do what it is thought to do best; that is, it recognizes that the Union is perhaps in the best position to collect certain kinds of taxes and to expend and redistribute tax revenues for equitable purposes nationwide, while states and their local governments are in the best position to manage developmental programs and to deliver most services because they are closest to the people.

Resource transfers authorized on the recommendations of the Finance Commission are known as statutory grants; those authorized on the recommendations of the Planning Commission are known as discretionary grants. When grants to states are recommended by the Finance Commission, which is a statutory body, the Union government is constitutionally obligated to authorize the grants; hence the Union's authority with respect to grants does not add to its powers. But discretionary grants recommended by the Planning Commission, which is not a statutory body, are at the discretion of the Union government and thus political in nature. As such, they are criticized for causing states' abject dependence on the Union: a dependence that is said to further enable the Union government to discriminate between states. Plan grants provided are 50–50 matching grants, which means that the Union government issues a grant equal to the sum that the state has raised through its own resources. It also means that states have to fall in line with Union policies, priorities and preferences in issuing matching grants and also dovetail their own funds to Union allocations.

Local-Level Governance

There is a third tier of Indian federal structure, comprised of local governing bodies. Part IX of the Constitution outlines the framework of institutions of rural self-government: a three-tier system of units known, in ascending order, as the village, intermediate and district *panchayats*. This system came into existence with two basic objectives: (i) democratic decentralisation and (ii) local participation in planned programmes.

Part IXA of the Constitution sets forth the framework of urban local government. Three types of institutions of local self-government have been provided for urban areas, namely *nagar panchayats* for transitional areas (i.e., areas that are being transformed from rural to urban), municipal councils for small urban areas and municipal corporations for large urban areas. Every state is obliged to constitute such units. Local government remains an exclusive state subject. The Constitution provides for direct election of local bodies, in urban and rural areas, every five years. The other noticeable provisions are:

(ii) *reservation of seats for women and for scheduled castes and tribes;*
(iii) *a State Finance Commission to ensure financial viability of these institutions;*
(iv) *devolution of powers and responsibilities to the local bodies with respect to:*
   (a) *preparation of plans and implementation of schemes for economic development and social justice.*
   (b) *devolution of financial powers to the local bodies,*
   (c) *endowment of these institutions with powers, authority and responsibility to prepare plans for economic development and community welfare programmes for revenue raising responsibilities.*

Panchayats and local urban bodies have now been given powers and responsibilities to plan and execute economic development programmes, social justice and the implementation of schemes listed in the Constitution. These activities include: antipoverty programmes such as the Integrated Rural Development Programme, land improvement, minor irrigation, social forestry, small scale and cottage industry; primary and secondary schools, non-formal education, technical training; health and sanitation and family welfare; social welfare, welfare of weaker sections, public distribution systems and women's and children's development; roads, housing, drinking water, markets, electrification, maintenance of community assets, etc. But local bodies have such a limited scope for revenue generation and relatively vast area of jurisdiction, that they are perennially dependent upon the states for the latter's grants. Local bodies have to depend almost entirely on state governments for discharging responsibilities assigned to them. The constitutional difficulty is in the fact that devolution of powers and responsibilities for *panchayats* are listed but an elaborate scheme has not been provided regarding their sources of finance. Thus, what has been organized is the assignment of functions but not the resources. Further, because state governments are reluctant to part with revenue-generating powers, fiscal autonomy is actually denied to the *panchayats* and urban local bodies (Shah 2006).

In this constitutional scheme of distribution of responsibilities, the persistent theme revolves around cooperative federalism. If the third tier (*panchayats* and urban local governments) depends on the other two tiers of government for money and resources, the latter (Union and state governments) both depend on the former for providing services to the people.

Cooperative federalism can succeed only if a fair balance is maintained between the claims of diversity and the requirements of unity. If those are absent, whatever mechanisms of inter-governmental relations are devised remain non-functional and ineffective. The constitutional provisions stipulate that the state shall decide resource transfers to local bodies. Any transfer mechanism increases the dependence of local level units. Local units are expected to collect taxes because they are "self-governing units", but the system works on the principle of "you collect and I will transfer". However, the core principle of governance is that the government should meet its expenditure or, at least, revenue on core services should come from its own resources. This should be by right and not through the benevolence of any other government. What needs to be transferred is a power to collect resources, to garner resources and the power to tax. Unless that is there, local units remain locally dependent units, not local self-governing units.

Decentralized and grass-roots planning and implementation are features of shared governance; this, in turn, reflects the correct image of federal governance. Social federalism cannot be sidelined in the name of political federalism. Local bodies in India function more closely with community-based organizations, with the user-groups or stakeholders in development. The starting point is not just the distribution of functions but in transferring functions to these bodies and allocating funds to them, thus making them competent to perform the functions constitutionally assigned to them.

Cooperative Federalism

After the States Reorganisation Act 1956, five zonal councils were set up, each composed of the chief ministers of the states in a council's zone, the development ministers and chief secretaries of these states, and a member of the Planning Commission, with each council headed by the Union's home minister. The zonal councils are intended to: (i) foster the psychological integration of the country by mitigating regional consciousness, (ii) help the Union and state governments to evolve uniform social and economic policies, (iii) assist with effective implementation of development projects and (iv) evolve a degree of political equilibrium among the regions of the country. The Autonomous District Councils (ADCs) provide in-built safeguards in the Constitution which maintain and strengthen the rights of minority and micro-minority groups while empowering them with greater responsibilities and opportunities, for example, through the process of central funding for planned expenditure instead of routing all funds through the state governments. They play a central role here by developing a process of public education on the proposed changes, which would assure communities of protection of their traditions and also bring in gender representation and give voice to other ethnic groups.

Union–state cooperation, as worded in the Constitution, leaves ample scope for conflict over interpretation of definitional phrases. The Constitution, therefore, allows the president to establish an Inter-State Council (ISC) to work out modalities for continuing cooperation and to forge procedures for coordination between the Union and the states as well as among the states themselves. The text is so phrased as to allow the council to discuss, debate and recommend suitable policy measures on any subject. There is scope for enlarging the ambit of the council, as it would be lawful for the presidential order "to define the nature of the duties to be performed by it and its organization and procedure". As an advisory body, the council may inquire into disputes that "have arisen between states"; investigate and discuss subjects "in which some or all of the States, or the Union and one or more of the States, have a common interest"; or recommend better coordination of policy and action on any subject necessitating interaction between the Union and the states. For smooth running of federal relations, the starting point has to be adding to the competence of the ISC. Since the ISC is an advisory body, it is difficult to assess the efficacy of its policy performance. And, for the same reason, its cost-effectiveness also cannot be determined. A solid institutional structure for inter-governmental cooperation has not emerged. The ISC needs to be included in the process of central legislation over matters in state lists. In such cases, not only should there be informal consultations between the Union and the states, but also the central government should place the proposal before the ISC before such legislation is introduced. The jurisdictional competence of the ISC needs to be extended so as to enable it to review every bill of national importance or which is likely to affect the interests of one or more states before it is introduced in Parliament or a state assembly. There should be no limitation on the ISC that it can consider only political issues. The Union's directions to a state government, under any of the Articles, ought to be issued in consultation with, and with the approval of, the ISC. Since the purpose of setting up the ISC was to facilitate the Union in its coordination activities, it cannot discharge its function without being a body for securing cooperation between two levels of government as well.

Because Union grants are routed through central ministries to their counterparts in the states, each Union ministry is in a position to use the strings of financial power to superintend, direct and control the corresponding state department. In this way, besides the territorial or horizontal federation set up by the Constitution, a sort of vertical federation has come into being. Various ministries of the government of India issue grants to corresponding ministries of state governments and, in this way, they are in a position to dictate and supervise departments of state governments. A vertical federation has resulted in which, through matching grants, the departments of central and state governments on the same subject form a unit for the purposes of programmes and expenditure on the same. Yet, there is a kind of subsidiary element in different units of the constituent federal system. The mechanism of inter-governmental relations in India are tilted in favour of the Union government. There are inter-governmental institutions meant to exercise some uniformity in administrative relations. The hegemony or the dominance of the Union governmental institutions over the state governments is meant to bring about some kind of uniformity of standards in administrative procedures. In some respects, states have also acquired certain say in matters that were traditionally the domain of the Union. One reason is the regional parties sharing political power in the Union. In terms of foreign affairs, states that have economically performed well, and have attracted Foreign Direct Investment, have influenced the foreign economic policy of the Union. States are now more conscious of their role in foreign affairs with neighbouring countries as well as international organizations like WTO, World Bank, ADB, etc. Thus, inter-governmental relations reflect both the tendencies of conflict and cooperation, and they keep changing.

There are both formal institutional and informal political arrangements for Union–state coordination. Among the formal mechanisms are the Planning Commission, Finance Commission, National Development Council, Inter-State Council, National Integration Council, zonal councils, tribunals for adjudicating specific disputes, and various commissions and committees to look into specific aspects of Union–state relations. The informal mechanisms include ministerial and departmental meetings, conferences of constitutional functionaries and of political executives, and the governors' and chief ministers' conferences that are convened by the president and the prime minister. These informal arrangements are aimed at laying down procedural norms of conduct, particularly over such issues as the sharing of central taxes and the Union's intervention in states' affairs, and at evolving a common policy on such trans-governmental issues as the environment, communications and health. Similarly, such informal mechanisms evolve conventions of governance on questions of states' rights, inter-state trade and commerce, sharing of river waters, inter-state communications and other matters.

It can be said that, in India, instruments of inter-governmental cooperation have not been successful and effective because the required decentralization has not been possible due to India's administrative centralization and earlier central planning structures. Cooperative federalism, as envisaged by the Constitution, is possible when these inter-governmental institutions become effectively operative. A mechanism for inter-governmental cooperation can succeed if it does not have to depend on other executive organizations for implementing its decisions. It needs to be pointed out that issues of economic planning and development cannot be settled through institutions set up be the central government, such as Planning and Finance Commissions. They require coordinated efforts and for that cooperated federal arrangements are needed, which role can best be provided by concerted ventures of the National Development Council and the ISC.

In the debates on federalism, special attention needs to be given – but often is not in India – to the importance of inter-governmental relations and mechanisms for resolving contentious issues between different tiers of government. Such academic attention is particularly needed for plural societies where different socio-economic interests vie for political control of the national polity. Inter-governmental agencies have generally operated outside the framework of the Constitution. At least in India, the inter-governmental agencies have not acquired the functional relevance visualized in the Constitution. The recommendations of inter-governmental agencies, in India, have lacked any force and have not been in a position to cope with the inter-jurisdictional strains of the Indian federal set-up. This is due to the ad hoc style of their functioning and this has eroded their credibility. Cooperative federalism can succeed only if a fair balance is maintained between the claims of diversity and the requirements of unity. If those are absent, whatever mechanisms of inter-governmental relations are devised remain non-functional and ineffective.

What is now called competition in India's negotiated/cooperative federalism actually developed as a result of the emergence of coalition politics and power-sharing. In this way, the Union and the states, under the impact of competitive party politics and increasing regionalism, have become more like coordinate centres of power. Howsoever strong the position of the Union in planning, programming and financing, the execution of plans and projects rests in the hands of state governments. No other large federal government is as dependent as India's on theoretically subordinate, but actually rather distinct, units responsible to a different order of government for so much of the administration of what are recognized as national programmes. In the final analysis, the authority organically exercised in New Delhi is influence rather than power.

The Indian Constitution would seem, in the end, to create a "cooperative union" of states rather than a dual polity. What is being observed now is federal restructuring through politically developed rules and conventions, without disturbing the basic scheme of the Constitution. The actual working of cooperative federalism in India has entailed the Union's exercising its influence rather than its constitutional authority. Exigencies of coalition politics have forced the Union and state governments to share power. The Union has more often played the role of a facilitator in inter-state disputes than that of an arbitrator. A redistribution of powers – through decentralization and the devolution of authority from the Union to the states and from the states to the *panchayats* and municipalities – is serving to facilitate the attainment of the objectives of the Constitution: unity, social justice and democracy.

References

Khan, Rasheeduddin (1992), *Federal India: A Design for Change* (New Delhi: Vikas).
Majeed, Akhtar (2005), *Federalism Within the Union: Distribution of Responsibilities in the Indian System* (New Delhi: Manak).
——, Ronald R. Watts and Douglas M. Brown (2006), *Distribution of Powers and Responsibilities in Federal Polities* (Montreal: McGill-Queens).
Shah, Anwar (ed.) (2006), *Local Governance in Developing Countries* (Washington, DC: World Bank).
Sheth, D.L. and Gurpreet Mahajan (1999), *Minority Identities and the Nation-State* (New Delhi: Oxford).
Vithal, B.P.R. and M.L. Sastry (2001), *Fiscal Federalism in India* (New Delhi: Oxford).

Further Reading

Austin, Granvile (1999), *Working A Democratic Constitution* (New Delhi: Oxford).
Bakshi, P.M. (2009), *The Constitution of India* (New Delhi: Universal Law Publishing Co.).
Basu, D.D. (2002), *Introduction to the Constitution of India (19 edn)* (New Delhi: Wadhwa).
Jenkins, Robert (2004), *Regional Reflections: Comparing Politics Across India's States* (New Delhi: Oxford).
Kincaid, John and G. Alan Tarr (2003), *Constitutional Origins, Structure and Change in Federal Countries* (Montreal: McGill Queens).
Kirpal, B.N. et al. (2000), *Supreme But Not Infallible: Essays in Honour of the Supreme Court of India* (New Delhi: Oxford).
Majeed, Akhtar, Ronald R. Watts and Douglas M. Brown (2006), *Distribution of Powers and Responsibilities in Federal Polities* (Montreal: McGill-Queens).
Majeed, Akhtar (2005), *Federal India: Design for Good Governance* (New Delhi: Manak).
Noorani, A.G. (2000), *Constitutional Questions in India* (New Delhi: Oxford).
Om Prakash Mathur (2006), Local government organization and finance: Urban India, in *Local Governance in Developing Countries*, ed. Anwar Shah (Washington, DC: World Bank).
Rao, Govinda and Nirvikar Singh (2005), *Political Economy of Federalism in India* (New Delhi: Oxford).

Verney, Douglas (2003), From quasi-federation to quasi-confederation? The transformation of India's party system, *Publius: The Journal of Federalism*, Vol. 33 No 4, Fall.

Vora, Rajendra and Anne Feldhaus (2006), *Region, Culture and Politics in India* (New Delhi: Manohar).

Federalism:
The Latin American Experience

Julián Durazo Hermann

In spite of strong political controversies and sometimes contradictory practice, Latin America has the longest historical experience with federalism after the United States. In 1811 Venezuela became the second modern country to adopt federalism. Mexico followed (albeit hesitantly) in 1824, Argentina in 1853 and Brazil in 1890. Despite other profound changes in their political systems, these four countries have formally and continuously been federations since the late nineteenth century (Griffiths and Nerenberg 2002).

While I concentrate in this chapter on the contemporary elements of Latin American federalism, it is important to keep in mind that the region's understanding of federalism is profoundly influenced by its historical experience. Since it is impossible to cover all relevant aspects of Latin American federalism within the limits of this chapter, I concentrate on three dimensions, each of which will constitute a separate section.

The first is the doctrinaire dimension of Latin American federalism, where I explore the fundamental principles of federalism as understood in Latin America and their relationship with the region's most important federal model: the United States. The second dimension is the constitutional dimension, in which I assess the way federal systems are actually constituted in Latin America. In so doing, I will attempt to determine the extent to which Latin American subnational states can actually engage in autonomous policy initiatives and institutional reform – a major advantage of federalism, according to the *Federalist Papers* (Hamilton et al. 1788, no. 45).

The third dimension is political and addresses the relationship between federalism and the broader political system. While many authors assert that federalism is indissolubly associated with democracy (Hamilton et al. 1788, nos. 39 and 62; Ostrom 1991, 223; Beaud 1998, 95), all four Latin American federations have experienced prolonged periods of authoritarian rule while maintaining at least a nominal federal structure. It is thus evident that federalism has some political value in Latin America beyond the simple apportionment of jurisdiction.

In this chapter I analyze the theory and practice of federalism in four Latin American countries from a comparative perspective. In so doing, I attempt to portray the way the always complicated relationship between federal theory and federal practice plays out in Latin America with a view to contributing to our broader understanding of federalism.

Latin American Doctrines of Federalism

Is there a Latin American doctrine of federalism? How has it evolved? What is its content? In this section, I seek to identify whether a coherent corpus has emerged in this respect, independent of the questions of whether and how it is actually enforced, which I address in the following section.

Given the geographical and historical proximity, it is not surprising that US theories of federalism – primarily as expounded in the *Federalist Papers* (1788) – has profoundly influenced the conception of federalism in Latin America. This influence extends beyond the doctrinaire dimension and spills over into the actual constitutional texts (González Oropeza 1995).

In both the United States and Latin America (and also in Canada), federalism appeared not only as a mechanism to divide (and share) power along territorial lines, but also – and foremost – as a state-building technique. Across the hemisphere, federalism was seen as a way to fill the power vacuum generated by independence and the collapse of the previous political systems (Chevrier 2006). In this context, the embryonic regional governments established during the late colonial period (*intendencias* in Spanish America, *províncias* in Brazil) were seen as the relative equivalent to the founding US colonies (Lee-Benson 1955).

In Latin America, federalism was also perceived as a way to protect the country's territorial integrity. The loss of Paraguay and Uruguay and of California and Texas are directly related to the debate surrounding the adoption of federalism in Argentina and Mexico, respectively, and also contributed to their definitive conclusion in favour of a federal system (Floria and Belsunce 1992; Vázquez 2000). In Brazil, secessionist menaces were more diffuse, but also present (Love 1993). Venezuela, on the contrary, broke from the Great Colombia in response to its centralizing policies (Brewer-Carías 2002).

At first, all four Latin American federations followed the US model of dual federalism quite closely. This model assumes that subnational states, which are *de jure* symmetrical, pre-exist the federation, grants them extensive institutional and political autonomy in both executive and legislative affairs and assigns them residual jurisdiction. Consequently, the federal and subnational levels are presumed to be separate and relatively unrelated spheres of government (Watts 1999).

The Latin American federations also reproduced the US bicameral legislature, in which the Senate is the locus of territorial representation on an equal basis. Furthermore, US federal doctrine is constantly used as an interpretive guide, both in judiciary adjudication and in scholarly research (Tena y Ramírez 2007).

Nevertheless, US federal principles and institutions were not adopted uncritically nor without debate. More importantly, they were moulded by distinct political practices. Subsequent evolution has further diverged from the original US model (Bidart Campos 1993; Souza 2005a).

The most notable difference, and a feature common to all four Latin American federations, is the constitutional status of municipalities. Whereas municipalities are absent from the US constitutional text and are assumed to be the creatures of subnational government, the Latin American federations follow the colonial Iberian model (see, for instance, Spanish Constitution of 1812, arts. 309–323), which grants municipalities constitutional recognition and assigns them both jurisdiction and fiscal resources, effectively transforming them into a third tier in intergovernmental relations (Carmagnani 1993). Argentina, which had not originally granted its municipalities constitutional recognition, did so in the late 1980s – although at subnational, not federal, behest (Bidart Campos 1993).

Another important difference relates to the constitutional amendment procedures. Mexico follows the US model of requiring subnational ratification of amendments approved by the federal Congress but abandoned the possibility of convening a constitutional convention if a comprehensive reform was envisaged in the 1960s (Mexican Constitution, art. 135). In Argentina, on the other hand, only an ad hoc constitutional convention can amend the Constitution (Argentine Constitution, art. 30). While the United States have never resorted to this mechanism, it has been used several times in Argentina, most recently in 1994 (Patroni 2002).

In Brazil, the reform of the federal Constitution is entirely in the hands of federal organs, although it must be adopted in two separate votes (Brazilian Constitution, art. 60). In Venezuela, all constitutional reforms (adopted either by the National Assembly or by a Constitutional Convention) must be ratified in a referendum (Venezuelan Constitution, title 9). While these Constitutions do not formally involve subnational participation in the amendment process, some authors argue that their stringent reform procedures protect federalism nonetheless (Rosen 1994).

Originally, all Latin American federations conceived the Senate as the locus of formal subnational representation in the federal legislature and granted equal membership to each subnational unit, in keeping with the US model. In 1996, however, a constitutional reform broadened the Mexican Senate so as to include members elected by proportional representation on a national list. The argument behind the reform was to improve opposition representation in the Senate. However, the principles of federalism were completely absent from the debate (Mizrahi 2002).

In a more radical decision, the 1999 Venezuelan Constitution squarely abolished the Senate, arguing the duplication of representation principles was unwarranted, as both assemblies ultimately represented the people (Núñez Nava and Matos Mosquera 2006). Instead, the Venezuelan Constitution provides for a Federal Government Council, integrated by appointed representatives from all three levels of government – federal, state and municipal – to fulfill intergovernmental oversight and coordinating functions (art. 185). While this Council gives more weight to subnational units than previous intergovernmental fora, it has no legislative powers (Matheus Iriarte and Romero Ríos 2002).

Long before the abolition of the Senate, Venezuela had departed from the original US model. In 1961 it became the only Latin American federation to formally abandon dual federalism and opt for the collaborative model, in which the federation concentrates general legislative powers but subnational states are empowered to exercise executive authority in accordance with their particular conditions (an arrangement similar to that observed in Austria and Germany based on the principle of subsidiarity [Watts 1999]). The break became complete with the adoption of the 1999 Constitution, which explicitly emphasized the collaborative nature of Venezuelan federalism, established a constitutionally mandated intergovernmental forum (the Federal Government Council) and abolished the Senate and all forms of subnational representation in the federal legislature (Núñez Nava and Matos Mosquera 2006).

The most important differences between Latin American federalism and its US model, however, lie in the realm of constitutional interpretation, rather than in the constitutional text itself. The imperatives of state-building – a crucial issue in nineteenth-century Latin America – and of conducting a state-led economic development strategy – a defining feature of the region during the twentieth century – led Latin American interpretations of federalism, both judicial and scholarly, to give the federal government a preponderant role that the US federal government would never acquire (Carmagnani 1993).

While centralization appears a natural development in revolutionary Mexico, where it was also an important contributor to pacification after the war (Hernández Chávez 1993), it was also a major part of state-building under both populist and military regimes in Argentina and Brazil (Bidart Campos 1993; Camargo 1993). In Venezuela, centralization actually was perceived as a bulwark for democracy against the authoritarian threats of subnational *caciques* (Penfold-Becerra 2004). The rise of the so-called imperial presidencies in Latin America, which further concentrated power in the federal executive, reinforced the trend (Carmagnani 1993).

In spite of this centralizing trend, which became reflected in the growing list of concurrent and exclusive federal powers and in the liberal resort to the doctrine of federal implicit powers, the federal nature of each of the Latin American federations was never called into question (at least in the twentieth century). Moreover, subnational units always remained largely responsible for guaranteeing local governance (Medina 1997). I will return to this point in the third section of this chapter.

Regime change in Latin America has recently led to intense reflection on the nature of federalism and its relation to the broader political system. The outcomes have been different, however; whereas in Mexico the most important changes were related to political practices and constitutional interpretation without formal reform (Díaz-Cayeros 2004), in Brazil the reaction to the centralizing experiments of the military regime led the 1988 Constituent Assembly to declare that the federal character of the country was not subject to constitutional amendment (Souza 2005a). Even in Venezuela, where the federal structures of the country have been the object of profound reforms, both in the 1960s and since the late 1980s, no new comprehensive federal doctrine seems to have appeared (Brewer-Carías 2002; Penfold-Becerra 2004).

In conclusion, the doctrinaire dimension of federalism in Latin America is directly related to the original US model, although it does not follow it strictly. Moreover, its evolution has been markedly different. However, the original US doctrines of federalism have not been substituted by a Latin American corpus; rather, changes have been both incremental and pragmatic. The ongoing debate on the nature of federalism in all four Latin American federations reflects this tradition, despite significant institutional innovation.

Constitutional Features of Latin American Federalism

In this section, I describe how the principles of federalism, as described above, are translated into political reality in the Latin American federations. In so doing, I address the question of whether subnational units can engage in autonomous institutional reforms or undertake independent policy initiatives.

Based on the assumption that the states precede the federation, the US Constitution provides no explicit guidance regarding the institutional framework of the US states, beyond guaranteeing them "a republican form of government" (art. 4:4). Although this assumption was accepted by the Latin American federations, their constitutional provisos provide on occasion extensive guidance as to the form and content of a country's subnational institutions.

In Mexico and Argentina, subnational units are nominally sovereign in their internal affairs, beyond the obligation to adopt a republican form of government (Argentine Constitution, art. 122; Mexican Constitution, art. 40). They have thus been free to exercise important institutional innovation – as demonstrated by some Argentine provinces' decision to constitutionally recognize their municipalities (Bidart Campos 1993).

Recent developments in Mexico, however, have led the federal Constitution to impose a number of provisos upon subnational states, most notably regarding the composition of their legislatures (the obligation to include members elected by proportional representation) and the nature of their judiciary (the obligation to have a judicial adjudication system for electoral disputes) (Andrade Sánchez 1997). In implementing these mandates, however, Mexican states have demonstrated an important degree of differentiation (Eisenstadt and Rionda 2001).

In contrast, constitutional constraints in Brazil and Venezuela impose a substantial degree of homogeneity on subnational institutions. In both countries, the length of the gubernatorial and legislative terms, the unicameral character and the size of the state legislatures, as well as the electoral procedures to be used are all determined by the federal Constitution (Brewer-Carías 2002; Boschi 2004).

In Brazil, moreover, attempts by some of the larger states to develop differentiated institutions have been struck down by the Supreme Court, thus further dampening subnational initiatives (Souza 2005b). In contrast, the 1999 Venezuelan Constitution represents an improvement *vis-à-vis* its 1961 predecessor, which made both governors and mayors presidential appointees that served at pleasure, thus cancelling any potential for subnational autonomy (Porras Ponceleón 2002).

As in the original US model, each subnational unit in Argentina, Brazil and Mexico has its own judiciary system, which adjudicates issues arising from subnational legislation. In all cases, however, the federal judiciary retains important review powers and may overturn certain subnational judicial decisions. In contrast, Venezuela does not have a subnational judiciary system, in consonance with its collaborative model of federalism, where legislation (and, consequently, adjudication) is largely a federal affair (Rosen 1994).

Within this rather constrained institutional environment, subnational units could still undertake autonomous policy initiatives. This, according to the *Federalist Papers* (1788, no. 45), is a major advantage of federalism, since it allows for extensive policy experimentation, while constraining the results to a limited territorial area. If the innovation is successful, it may be easily emulated elsewhere.

In Latin America, however, this has seldom been the case. Although the federal constitutions (with the exception of Venezuela) assign residual jurisdiction to the subnational units, their casuistic nature – a feature common, although not exclusive, to all Latin American constitutions – has given rise to long and detailed lists of exclusive and concurrent federal jurisdiction items, especially in areas concerning economic development or otherwise defined as strategic, thus substantially limiting subnational autonomy (Griffiths and Nerenberg 2002).

The doctrines of federal primacy, through which federal law supersedes subnational law, and of implied powers, which allows for the expansion of federal jurisdiction into new areas by claiming they are necessary to fulfill its explicit mandates, further constrain subnational policy initiative (Watts 1999). While these doctrines are not exclusive to Latin American federalism, their aggressive use under the imperial presidencies, upheld by judicial adjudication, has had profound effects on subnational autonomy (Carmagnani 1993).

In Venezuela, the collaborative model of federalism makes the state governments the natural agents of the federation at the subnational level (art. 165). This is also the case of the Argentine Constitution (art. 128), while in Brazil, it is secondary legislation and Supreme Court jurisprudence that has enacted this state of affairs, even if it contradicts the otherwise dual nature of their federal systems and further limits subnational autonomy by diverting time and resources to the enforcement of federal mandates (Souza 2005b).

A development common to all Latin American federations, and one which may alter the very nature of federalism in the region, is the rise of decentralization. Originally rather limited in the various constitutional texts, given the dual nature of Latin American federalism, decentralization allows central governments (including those in unitary countries) to delegate the actual delivery of public services to other levels of government while retaining responsibility for setting and enforcing common standards. The principle of subsidiarity is often invoked in this context (Oxhorn et al. 2004).

While Venezuela has long adhered to this model of collaborative federalism, the other Latin American federations have recently taken explicit steps in this direction. The Argentine and Brazilian constitutions make subnational governments the formal executors of federal legislation (at least in some areas). In Mexico, the federal Constitution mandates since the early 1980s that the federation and the subnational states coordinate – nominally on equal footing – their policies in a number of areas, including fiscal and economic planning, health and education (Aguilar Villanueva 1996).

Decentralization and coordination both increase subnational responsibilities but limit political initiative, especially if the federation imposes common standards. Important problems may also arise if they result in unfunded mandates (Flamand Gómez 1997).

For subnational units, the possibility to actually engage in autonomous policy initiatives depends on their access to sufficient unconditional economic resources. In all four Latin American federations, however, this access is restricted, although fiscal federalism has recently become a major political issue and important reforms have taken place in all four countries.

Under the 1961 Constitution, Venezuelan states were wholly dependent on a constitutionally mandated, but conditional revenue-sharing scheme. Although the 1999 Constitution did not substantially expand state jurisdiction (including fiscal capacities), it assigned 30 per cent of the new value-added tax to states and municipalities, as well as a much larger share of oil royalties. Nevertheless, oversight by the Federal Government Council and other constitutional bodies limits discretionary subnational spending (art. 167).

In Brazil, the 1988 Constitution translated its mandate to be a bulwark against renewed authoritarian practices and its conviction that centralization was an authoritarian device into an extensive fiscal decentralization scheme that made subnational states and municipalities the recipients – but not the collectors – of the bulk of the country's taxes, including the value-added tax (title 6). Regional equalization schemes were also significantly expanded. However, there was no simultaneous transfer of responsibilities and it soon became clear that, given the economic situation, the constitutional fiscal scheme was not viable (Rezende 1996). In the midst of the crisis, the federal government managed to centralize certain tax revenues – in exchange for assuming most state debts. The agreement, however, was temporary and has been renegotiated several times, pending a definitive solution (Samuels and Mainwaring 2004).

Despite the constitutional right to levy their own taxes, Mexico's subnational states became increasingly dependent throughout the twentieth century on federal transfers to finance their expenditures. Following the adoption of constitutionally mandated fiscal coordination in 1980, federal transfers increased to 82 per cent of state revenue. Although these transfers were intended to compensate states for the loss of autonomous revenue sources, a significant portion of them are conditional, thus imposing federal priorities and standards upon subnational governments (Aguilar Villanueva 1996). As a result of the growing strength of the federal opposition parties at both the federal and subnational level, subnational states have successfully negotiated further unconditional federal transfers, including oil royalties for the first time. Nevertheless, the states' autonomous taxation capabilities remain very limited and therefore subject to the political vagaries of fiscal federalism (Sobarzo 2005).

In Argentina, the Constitution assigns jurisdiction over most tax sources to the provinces. Nevertheless, limited subnational capacity and intense federal pressure since the 1930s have led to a number of "co-participation agreements", through which the provinces transfer tax jurisdiction to the federation in exchange for participation in broader revenue-sharing schemes. Moreover, the Supreme Court has further limited subnational taxation powers by invoking the commerce clause (Bidart Campos 1993). In any case, chronic instability has led to the emergence of a relatively inefficient fiscal system, with low returns for both the federation and the provinces (Melo 2005).

Except in Argentina, all new fiscal arrangements in the Latin American federations include an important municipal dimension that has strengthened the three-tiered nature of Latin American federalism. Following these reforms, municipalities received both autonomous sources of revenue and an increased share of federal and subnational transfers. While the municipalities' financial autonomy is far from secure, the principle seems firmly established.

Although all four Latin American federations present very significant cases of de facto asymmetry, they remain symmetrical *de jure*, at least in constitutional terms (Agranoff 1999). Nonetheless, the rise of decentralization and coordination, implemented in the name of subsidiarity through casuistic intergovernmental agreements, has led to the emergence of substantial sub-constitutional asymmetry in all four federations. Nevertheless, with the exception of Venezuela, the dual nature of federalism has not been explicitly debated (Gutiérrez González 2005; Souza 2005a).

Whatever their level of development, subnational institutional autonomy and policy initiatives can ultimately be trumped by direct federal intervention in (or takeover of) subnational political systems should peace, order or the republican form of government be threatened. This possibility, absent in the US Constitution (although art. 4:4 is often invoked in this context), is explicitly present in all four Latin American federations and was abundantly used throughout the twentieth century, although mostly for strictly partisan motives rather than for constitutionally justified reasons (González Oropeza 1987).

Nevertheless, federal intervention has been the object of constant criticism, as it very evidently subverts federalism. In the two countries where federal intervention was most common, Argentina and Brazil, constitutional amendments were passed (in 1994 and 1988, respectively) to curtail unjustified federal intervention by increasing legislative oversight, even if the executive retains the declaratory power (Patroni 2002; Souza 2005b). Furthermore, in the case of Brazil, discussion and approval of all constitutional reform initiatives are suspended for the duration of federal intervention (art. 60:1).

In Venezuela, the 1999 Constitution attributed oversight of federal intervention not only to the National Assembly, but also – and concurrently – to the Supreme

Court (title 8, chapter 2). In Mexico, article 76:5 makes the federal legislature responsible for declaring federal intervention (although in practice the procedure was always adopted under executive initiative). After a particularly controversial episode in 1975, the federal Congress enacted a secondary law providing for the specific criteria needed in order to declare federal intervention (González Oropeza 1987). As a consequence of this law, no new federal interventions have taken place.

The constitutional dimension of Latin American federalism provides a mixed picture. Despite the broad powers contained in the original constitutional provisos, subnational states have lost substantive autonomy in all four federations after being – explicitly or implicitly – designated as regional agents of the federal government. Nevertheless, the growing restrictions on federal intervention powers have increasingly protected whatever autonomy subnational units have, especially against purely partisan motives.

Future perspectives are also mixed. While recent trends in fiscal federalism tend to strengthen both subnational units and municipalities, if not by granting them autonomous sources of revenue, at least by expanding their part in the revenue-sharing schemes, the rise of ad hoc decentralization programmes have represented a new, not always welcome burden on subnational budgets and agendas. In conclusion, subnational institutional autonomy and policy initiative are limited at best and only ambiguously provided for by the Latin American federal constitutions.

The Political Dimension of Latin American Federalism

It is clear from the foregoing discussion that the Latin American federations do not wholly fulfill the requirements of the classic definitions of federalism (Riker 1964; Wheare 1967, other chapters in this volume). Nevertheless, federalism remains a prominent feature in these countries' political systems and a subject of much political debate. Thus, rather than dismissing the Latin American federations as "false federations" (Wheare 1967), we should attempt to explain the persistence of the federal model – whatever the practice – in these four countries for over a century.

In this section, I argue that, beyond its institutional functions, federalism plays a crucial political role in all four Latin American federations: the presence of both federal and subnational levels of governments provide for governance guarantees and power-sharing arrangements that are crucial to the functioning of the broader political system. In my view, it is these features – rather than abstract ideological principles or constitutional provisos – that explains the tenacious persistence of federalism in the region.

As mentioned above, federalism was conceived in Latin America – as elsewhere – as a state-building instrument (Chevrier 2006). In Latin America, the weak nature of state inherited from the colonial period (furthered weakened in Argentina, Mexico and Venezuela by prolonged independence wars) meant that, if the large territorial units were to be preserved, regional stakeholders were to be explicitly included in the new power-sharing arrangements. In this context, federal institutions are a way of granting official recognition to independent and pre-existing structures that need to be politically accommodated (Mallon 1994).

State-building and state penetration of society – Latin America's major political tasks during the nineteenth century – were thus accomplished with the participation of regional actors and structures. A pattern then emerged in which regional leaders served as intermediaries between the national (federal) government and local societies (some of which were not fully integrated into the natural cultural and linguistic mainstream, as in the case of indigenous regions). In exchange for their services, these regional leaders – commonly known as *caudillos* in Argentina, *coronéis* in Brazil and *caciques* in Mexico and Venezuela – received federal recognition and substantive autonomy in those areas not directly appropriated by the federation (Falcón 1994; Gibson and Falleti 2004).

This pattern continued well into the twentieth century. As shown above, the growth of the federal state – as required by the state-led development model – was made at the expense of formal subnational jurisdiction. Nevertheless, the need for intermediation did not subside, as state penetration of society remained incomplete. Moreover, certain *caciques* proved adept at using modern structures to renew their patrimonial control over their subnational states (Pansters 2005).

Even in Mexico, where for most of the twentieth century the choice of subnational governors was effectively in the hands of the President through the hegemonic party (the PRI), regional elites were allowed a say in the process, though their preferences were not always satisfied. Moreover, specific subnational circumstances were always taken into consideration, as the federation sought to avoid – or defuse – governance problems in the states (Langston 1997).

While federalism in Latin America thus protected social diversity, it did so by preserving traditional domination structures that conflict with federalism's purported democratic character (Beaud 1998). Furthermore, during the twentieth century, Latin America saw the emergence of authoritarian versions of federalism, in which subnational states and their leaders, with their extensive social networks and their control over local governance, became crucial elements in the coalitions supporting them (Hagopian 1996; Salmerón Sanginés 2000).

All four federations attempted to reduce their dependence on subnational political support by creating and controlling functionally organized social groups with little territorial links through the development of state corporatism (Schmitter 1974). While not completely fruitless, these efforts failed in relieving federal dependence on territorial intermediation (Hagopian 1996; Medina 1997).

The relationship between federalism and the regime change process of the 1980s and 1990s in Latin America is thus ambiguous. Many subnational leaders were (and remain) suspicious of the process and have thus not supported it wholeheartedly.

As a result, authoritarian enclaves have emerged in all four Latin American federations. Not only have certain old regional intermediation networks reasserted themselves but, given the increasing political uncertainty at the federal level, subnational authoritarian elites have been capable of eliciting federal tolerance for their practices despite substantive democratic reforms.

On the one hand, regional governance remains in the hands of the subnational states and the federations are unable to forego their collaboration in this respect. Thus, subnational elites have substantial clout in mediating federal interference in their affairs. On the other, some parties (such as the PRI in Mexico) are dependent on their regional bases for their continued electoral success and must thus defend their subnational governments against potential federal intervention despite their spotty records (Gibson 2005).

Moreover, the retreat of the federation from a number of policy areas (because of decentralization, as discussed above, or simply as a result of the neoliberal development strategies followed since the late 1980s) and the unravelling of state corporatism has allowed subnational states to expand their authority and, in some cases, impose undemocratic reregulation schemes. The resources obtained under the new revenue-sharing arrangements have reinforced the subnational units' capacity to sustain these experiments (Snyder 2001).

Nevertheless, federal structures are also associated positively with democratization. In Brazil, the newly elected governors of the most populous states were instrumental in organizing the massive demonstrations that finally led the military to hand over power to civilians in 1985 (Abrucio 1998). In Venezuela, the election of state governors for the first time in 1989 was seen as the first step towards the end of partitocracy and the elected state governors are now seen as a potential bulwark against Hugo Chávez's populist excesses (Porras Ponceleón 2002).

In Mexico, the election of the first opposition governor in 1989 was also perceived as a major breakthrough in the democratization process. Moreover, the new governor's decision to create a subnational voters' register with stringent standards (including a photo ID) was seen as crucial in the federation's decision to follow suit (Espinoza Valle 1996).

In all four cases, subnational leaders have gained new relevance as federal political actors (Gibson 2005). Several former state governors have been elected President (Fernando Collor de Melo in Brazil in 1990, Vicente Fox in Mexico in 2000, Néstor Kirchner in Argentina in 2002).

While regime change has significantly altered the operation of federalism in Latin America, it has not fundamentally transformed its nature. Subnational units and municipalities – and their leaders – have always been important political actors. The new fiscal schemes, which increase subnational and municipal participation in revenue-sharing arrangements, are reflective of their increasing clout in the political system.

Nevertheless, even under this new state of affairs, Latin American subnational units remain largely dependent on federal transfers, a great many of which are conditional in nature. Moreover, subnational jurisdiction remains ambiguous in all four countries and both constitutional interpretation and judicial adjudication in this respect have systematically favoured the federation.

Consequently, a shift in the power equilibrium may again concentrate both formal power and material resources in federal hands. In any event, subnational states and municipalities will remain relevant political actors, as their power resides less in legal structures and material resources than in social networks and political intermediation. As the main channels of state penetration in local society – especially in highly diverse areas – and as guarantors of regional governance, subnational states have an undisputed place in the Latin American federations.

The Features of Latin American Federalism

In its doctrinaire dimension, Latin American federalism largely follows the original US federal doctrine, adapted to local conditions. Subsequent amendments to the nature of federalism have been pragmatic rather than doctrinaire in nature, giving rise to occasional contradictions (such as the simultaneous persistence of the principle of subnational residual jurisdiction and the constant resort to the doctrine of federal implied powers, both in scholarly interpretation and in judiciary adjudication).

The most striking doctrinaire difference between Latin American federalism and the US model is the specific inclusion of municipalities – inherited from colonial law – as a constitutive element of federalism, thus giving rise to three-tiered federations. Consequently, municipalities are integral players in intergovernmental relations, most notably in fiscal federalism. Constitutional recognition of municipalities is no longer unique to Latin America, as later federations, such as Germany (1948, arts. 28–29) and India (1950, part 9), have also given municipalities explicit constitutional recognition, if not always formal standing as an independent tier of federalism.

Latin America's pragmatic approach to federalism is most visible in its constitutional dimension. While the casuistic nature of the constitutional text as well and the frequent amendments are also part of the Iberian legal tradition, federalism and its structures have been treated as subordinate to the country's priorities at any given time: to state-building in the nineteenth century and to state-led economic development for most of the twentieth century. As a result, subnational institutional autonomy and policy initiative have been substantially restricted. The new developments in fiscal federalism, with their reliance on federal transfers and significant conditionality, have only partially reversed the trend.

In conclusion, the political dimension is the most important one in Latin American federalism. Despite its ideological and technical shortcomings, federalism has always been a critical element in the operation of the Latin American federations' political systems. This feature, which at least partially explains the region's pragmatic approach to federalism, has been present since the adoption of Latin America's first federal constitutions in the early nineteenth century and is crucial in explaining both state-building and the preservation of social diversity in the Latin American federations. Moreover, recent political changes associated with democratization (but not necessarily democratic themselves) have strengthened this trait. Federalism in Latin America thus remains a power-sharing and coalition-building institution.

Reflecting on the theory of federalism under the light of the Latin American experience, it is evident that we must go beyond the simple study of federal doctrines, jurisdiction apportionment or representative institutions and conceive federalism as a pragmatic governance instrument. After all, the value of any federal structure is measured by its contribution to the stability of its broader political system. Current scholarship is already moving in this direction, but much more research is needed.

References

Abrucio, Fernando (1998), *Os barões da federação: os governadores e a redemocratização brasileira*, São Paulo, Universidade de São Paulo – Hucitec.

Agranoff, Robert (1999), Power shifts, diversity and asymmetry, in Robert Agranoff (ed.), *Accommodating Diversity: Asymmetry in Federal Countries*, Baden-Baden, Nomos.

Aguilar Villanueva, Luis (1996), El federalismo mexicano: funcionamiento y tareas pendientes, in Alicia Hernández Chávez (coord.), *Hacia un nuevo federalismo?*, Mexico City, Fondo de Cultura Económica – El Colegio de México, 109–152.

Andrade Sánchez, Eduardo (1997), *La reforma política de 1996 en México*, Mexico City, UNAM (*Cuadernos Constitucionales México – Centroamérica*, no. 25).

Argentine Constitution (*Constitución Nacional de la República Argentina*) (1853), as amended.

Austin, Granville (1999), *Working a Democratic Constitution: A History of the Indian Experience*, Oxford, Oxford University Press.

Beaud, Olivier (1998), Fédéralisme et souveraineté, *Revue de droit public*, 83:1, 84–122.

Bidart Campos, Germán (1993), El federalismo argentino desde 1930 hasta la actualidad, in Marcello Carmagnani (coord.), *Federalismos latinoamericanos: México, Brasil, Argentina*, Mexico City, Fondo de Cultura Económica – El Colegio de México, 363–396.

Boschi, Renato (2004), Instituciones políticas, reformas estructurales y ciudadanía: dilemas de la democracia en Brasil, *Política*, 42, 281–308.

Brazilian Constitution (*Costituição da República Federativa do Brasil*) (1988), as amended.

Brewer-Carías, Allan (2002), Venezuela, in A. Griffiths (dir.), and K. Nerenberg (coord.), *Guide des pays fédérés 2002*, Montreal–Kingston, McGill–Queen's University Press, 376–389.

Camargo, Aspásia (1993), La federación sometida. Nacionalismo desarrollista e inestabilidad democrática, in Marcello Carmagnani (coord.), *Federalismos latinoamericanos: México, Brasil, Argentina*, Mexico City, Fondo de Cultura Económica – El Colegio de México, 300–357.

Carmagnani, Marcello (1993), El federalismo: historia de una forma de gobierno, in Marcello Carmagnani (coord.), *Federalismos latinoamericanos: México, Brasil,*

Argentina, Mexico City, Fondo de Cultura Económica – El Colegio de México, 397–416.

Chevrier, Marc (2006), La genèse de l'idée fédérale chez les pères fondateurs américains et canadiens, in Alain Gagnon (dir.), *Le fédéralisme canadien contemporain: Fondements, traditions, institutions*, Montreal, Presses de l'Université de Montréal, 19–61.

Constitution of India (1950), as amended.

Constitution of the United States of America (1787), as amended.

Díaz-Cayeros, Alberto (2004), Do federal institutions matter? Rules and political practices in regional resource allocation in Mexico, in Edward Gibson (ed.), *Federalism and Democracy in Latin America*, Baltimore, Johns Hopkins University Press, 297–322.

Eisenstadt, Todd, and Luis Miguel Rionda (coords.) (2001), *Democracia observada: las instituciones electorales locales en México*, Guanajuato, Universidad de Guanajuato.

Espinoza Valle, Víctor (1996), Alternancia y liberalización política. El PAN en el gobierno de Baja California, *Frontera Norte*, no. 16, 21–35.

Falcón, Romana (1994), Force and the search for consent: The role of the *Jefaturas Poíticas* of Coahuila in national state formation, in Gilbert Joseph and Daniel Nugent (eds), *Everyday Forms of State Formation: Revolution and the Negotiation of Rule in Modern Mexico*, Durham, Duke University Press, 107–134.

Flamand, Laura (1997), *Las perspectivas del nuevo federalismo: el sector salud. Las experiencias en Aguascalientes, Guanajuato y San Luis Potosí*, Mexico City, CIDE (Documento de trabajo AP-55).

Floria, Carlos, and César García Belsunce (1992), *Historia de los argentinos*, Buenos Aires, Larousse.

German Constitution (*Grundgesetz für die Bundesrepublik Deutschland*) (1948), as amended.

Gibson, Edward, and Tulia Falleti (2004), Unity by the stick: Regional conflict and the origins of Argentine federalism, in Edward Gibson (ed.), *Federalism and Democracy in Latin America*, Baltimore, Johns Hopkins University Press, 226–254.

Gibson, Edward (2005), Boundary control: Subnational authoritarianism in democratic countries, *World Politics*, 58, 101–132.

González Oropeza, Manuel (1987), *La intervención federal en la desaparición de poderes*, Mexico City, UNAM.

González Oropeza, Manuel (1995), *El federalismo*, Mexico City, UNAM.

Griffiths, A. (dir.) and K. Nerenberg (coord.), (2002), *Guide des pays fédérés 2002*, Montreal–Kingston, McGill–Queen's University Press.

Gutiérrez González, Juan Marcos (2005), United Mexican States, in John Kincaid and Alan Tarr (eds), *Constitutional Structure and Change in Federal Countries*, Montreal–Kingston, McGill–Queen's University Press, 208–238.

Hagopian, Frances (1996) *Traditional Politics and Regime Change in Brazil*, Cambridge, Cambridge University Press.

Hamilton, Alexander, James Madison and John Jay (1788), *The Federalist Papers*, ed. by Clinton Rossiter, New York, Mentor, 1961.

Hernández Chávez, Alicia (1993), Federalismo y gobernabilidad en México, in Marcello Carmagnani (coord.), *Federalismos latinoamericanos: México, Brasil, Argentina*, Mexico City, Fondo de Cultura Económica – El Colegio de México, 263–299.

Langston, Joy (1997), *The PRI Governors*, Mexico City, CIDE (documento de trabajo EP-66).

Lee-Benson, Nettie (1955), *La diputación provincial y el federalismo mexicano*, Mexico City, El Colegio de México.

Lerner, Emilia (1993) El federalismo argentino, *América latina hoy*, 6, 28–32.

Love, Joseph (1993), Federalismo y regionalismo en Brasil, 1889–1937, in Marcello Carmagnani (coord.), *Federalismos latinoamericanos: México, Brasil, Argentina*, Mexico City, Fondo de Cultura Económica – El Colegio de México, 180–223.

Mallon, Florencia (1994), Reflections on the ruins: Everyday forms of state formation in nineteenth-century Mexico, in Gilbert Joseph and Daniel Nugent (eds), *Everyday Forms of State Formation: Revolution and the Negotiation of Rule in Modern Mexico*, Durham, Duke University Press, 69–106.

Matheus Iriarte, Milagros, and María Elena Romero Ríos (2002), El federalismo en el Estado venezolano, niveles territoriales y relaciones intergubernamentales, *Ciencias de gobierno*, no. 11, 27–50.

Medina, Luis (1997), *La división vertical de poderes: el federalismo*, Mexico City, CIDE (documento de trabajo EP-70).

Melo, Marcus André (2005), O leviatã brasileiro e a esfinge argentina: os determinantes institucionais da política tributária, *Revista brasileira de ciências sociais*, 58, 91–128.

Mexican Constitution (*Constitución Política de los Estados Unidos Mexicanos*) (1917), as amended.

Mizrahi, Yemile (2002), Le Mexique, in A. Griffiths (dir.) and K. Nerenberg (coord.), *Guide des pays fédérés 2002*, Montreal–Kingston, McGill–Queen's University Press, 268–283.

Núñez Nava, Rosa, and Gabriela Matos Mosquera (2006), El Estado federal unicameral: nuevo paradigma del federalismo, *Provincia*, special number, 218–238.

Ostrom, Vincent (1991), *The Meaning of Federalism*, San Francisco, ICS Press.

Oxhorn, Philip et al. (2004), *Decentralization, Democratic Governance, and Civil Society in Comparative Perspective: Africa, Asia, and Latin America*, Washington DC, Woodrow Wilson Center Press.

Pansters, Wil (2005), Goodbye to the *Caciques*? Definition, the state and dynamics of *Caciquismo* in twentieth-century Mexico, in Alan Knight and Wil Pansters (eds), *Caciquismo in Twentieth-Century Mexico*, London, Institute for the Study of the Americas, 349–376.

Patroni, Viviana (2002), Argentine, in A. Griffiths (dir.), and K. Nerenberg (coord.), *Guide des pays fédérés 2002*, Montreal–Kingston, McGill–Queen's University Press, 44–59.

Penfold-Becerra, Michael (2004), Federalism and institutional change in Venezuela, in Edward Gibson (ed.), *Federalism and Democracy in Latin America*, Baltimore, The Johns Hopkins University Press, 197–225.

Porras Ponceleón, Temir (2002), Venezuela: les ambiguïtés de la 'révolution bolivarienne', *Problèmes d'Amérique latine*, no. 39, 3–23.

Rezende, Fernando (1996), El federalismo fiscal en Brasil, in Alicia Hernández Chávez (coord.), *Hacia un nuevo federalismo?*, Mexico City, Fondo de Cultura Económica – El Colegio de México, 225–241.

Riker, William (1964), *Federalism: Origin, Operation, Significance*, Boston, Little, Brown and Co.

Rosen, Keith (1994), Federalism in the Americas in comparative perspective, *Inter-American Law Review*, 26:1, 1–50.

Salmerón Sanginés, Pedro (2000), El partido de la unidad nacional (1938–1945), in Miguel González Compeán and Leonardo Lomelí (coords.), *El partido de la Revolución*, Mexico City, Fondo de Cultura Económica, 150–199.

Samuels, David, and Scott Mainwaring (2004), Strong federal constraints on the central government and economic reform in Brazil, in Edward Gibson (ed.), *Federalism and Democracy in Latin America*, Baltimore, Johns Hopkins University Press, 85–130.

Schmitter, Philippe (1974), Still the century of corporatism?, *Review of Politics*, 36, 85–131.

Snyder, Richard (2001), *Politics after Neoliberalism: Reregulation in Mexico*, Cambridge, Cambridge University Press.

Sobarzo, Horacio (2005), Federalismo fiscal en México, *Economía, sociedad y territorio*, special number, 103–121.

Souza, Celina (2005a), Federal Republic of Brazil, in John Kincaid and Alan Tarr (eds), *Constitutional Structure and Change in Federal Countries*, Montreal–Kingston, McGill–Queen's University Press, 76–102.

—— (2005b), Federalismo, desenho constitucional e instituições federativas no Brasil pós-1988, *Revista de Sociologia e Política*, 24, 105–121.

Spanish Constitution (*Constitución Política de la Monarquía Española*) (1812).

Tena y Ramírez, Felipe (2007), *Derecho constitucional mexicano*, Mexico City, Porrúa (39th ed.).

Vázquez, Josefina Zoraida (2000), Los primeros tropiezos, in *Historia general de México – versión 2000*, Mexico City, El Colegio de México, 525–582.

Venezuelan Constitution (*Constitución de la República Bolivariana de Venezuela* [1999], as amended).

Watts, Ronald (1999), *Comparing Federal Systems*, Montreal–Kingston, McGill–Queen's University Press.

Wheare, K.C. (1967), *Federal Government*, Oxford, Oxford University Press.

Further Reading

Carmagnani, Marcello (coord.) (1993), *Federalismos latinoamericanos: México, Brasil, Argentina*, Mexico City, Fondo de Cultura Económica – El Colegio de México.

Gibson, Edward (ed.) (2004), *Federalism and Democracy in Latin America*, Baltimore, The Johns Hopkins University Press.

González Oropeza, Manuel (1995), *El federalismo*, Mexico City, UNAM.

Griffiths, A. (dir.) and K. Nerenberg (coord.), *Guide des pays fédérés 2002*, Montreal–Kingston, McGill–Queen's University Press.

Hernández Chávez, Alicia (coord.) (1996), *¿Hacia un nuevo federalismo?*, Mexico City, Fondo de Cultura Económica – El Colegio de México.

Kincaid, John, and Alan Tarr (eds) (2005), *Constitutional Structure and Change in Federal Countries*, Montreal–Kingston, McGill–Queen's University Press.

Lee-Benson, Nettie (1955), *La diputación provincial y el federalismo mexicano*, Mexico City, El Colegio de México.

Oxhorn, Philip et al. (2004), *Decentralization, Democratic Governance, and Civil Society in Comparative Perspective: Africa, Asia, and Latin America*, Washington DC, Woodrow Wilson Center Press.

Riker, William (1964), *Federalism: Origin, Operation, Significance*, Boston, Little, Brown and Co.

Rosen, Keith (1994), Federalism in the Americas in comparative perspective, *Inter-American Law Review*, 26:1, 1–50.

Venezuelan Constitution (*Constitución de la República Bolivariana de Venezuela*) (1999), as amended.

Watts, Ronald (1999), *Comparing Federal Systems*, Montreal–Kingston, McGill–Queen's University Press.

Wheare, K. C. (1967), *Federal Government*, Oxford, Oxford University Press.

Federalism or Islam?
Ibn Khaldun on Islam and Politics

Khalil Habib

Despite the complexity of the federal system of government in the United States of America, those men and women who actively participate in the daily administration of governing are able to do so relatively smoothly. The separation of powers, along with the separation of church and state, allow this federal system of government to weave many diverse people and 50 states into a fairly peaceful coexistence. This federalist form of government, presupposing a separation of church and state, is at least worthy of note, if not awe and admiration.

Yet can the spirit of such a federal constitution be exported to or emerge by itself in Islamic states? American foreign policy is increasingly pre-occupied with spreading or encouraging modern Western forms of democracy and or some form of federalism throughout the Middle East. Several decades ago riches from oil, the rise of local nationalism, and the spirit of self-determination swept through the Arab world promising a future of greater freedom. Despite the influx of "Western Ideas," however, there is hardly a country in the Middle East today with freedom of speech, stable democratic elections, or individual rights guaranteed and protected under the law (Pryce-Jones 1989, 1–21, 402–406). Will political reforms along Western styled models threaten the Middle East more than its own tradition has? Is democracy destined to succeed or to fail in that troubled region? Recent attempts to introduce democratic forms of federalism in the Middle East have not been encouraging (see Lewis 2004, 113–119). Why should this be?

The purpose of this chapter is not to provide an exhaustive answer, but rather to recast the question in a new light by investigating Ibn Khaldun's (1332–1406) views on Islam and politics. Although he wrote in the fourteenth century, Ibn Khaldun's work is more relevant to our times than it has been for many generations. Because Ibn Khaldun examines the often neglected but deeply rooted character of pre-Islamic tribal attitudes and their tension with politics and Islam from the vantage point of one who is *within* the Islamic Middle East, he ought to be an important resource and guide for us. At this stage as several nations in the Middle East attempt a liberal reordering of their regimes, the perspective of a historian "who could look back upon seven centuries of Arab history" (Patai 2007, 20) may help us gain the needed distance for political debate.[1] Ibn Khaldun's book the *Muqaddimah* (1377) offers an appreciation of the Muslim world, which is still pertinent today, and which Arnold Toynbee compares to "the work of Thucydides or the work of Machiavelli for both breadth and profundity of vision as well as for the sheer intellectual power" (in Issawi 1958, 1).

My approach is largely conceptual and my principal purpose will be to present Ibn Khaldun's views on religion and politics as briefly as the subject allows. Although I shall only occasionally allude to contemporary concerns, and at no point discuss them systematically, nonetheless, they should be kept in mind. Before turning directly to Ibn Khaldun, I shall first examine the religious and philosophical ideas behind the American model of federalism. Throughout this section, I shall contrast the separation of church and state in the West to the Islamic idea of God and politics whereby religious and secular authority is identical. The second part of the chapter turns directly to Ibn Khaldun's major work, the *Muqaddimah*, which I shall take on its own terms, approaching the author's arguments from within his own thought. The spirit of democratic federalism, it will be seen, requires what Tocqueville refers to as "self-interest rightly understood," the belief in citizenship, the separation of church and state, and an enlightenment teaching informing those beliefs. These are concepts foreign to Ibn Khaldun's Islam.

The American Model

> *The Constitution of the United States [is] the best of all known federal constitutions ...*
> *The Constitution of the United States is like one of those beautiful creations of human diligence which give their inventors glory and riches but remains sterile in other hands.*
>
> Alexis de Tocqueville, *Democracy in America*

Is a federal constitution transferable to other cultures or peoples? In his noble book, *Democracy in America* (1835), Alexis de Tocqueville (1805–1859) argues that the advantages the Americans derive from a federal system of government are "not given to all peoples to enjoy" (Tocqueville 1969, 164). This is because, according to Tocqueville, a country's political order always accompanies a commonly held belief in God:

> *There is hardly any human action, however private it may be, which does not result from some very general conception men have of God, of His relations*

---

[1] It goes without saying that any attempt to discuss a "culture" requires generalization.

> *with the human race, of the nature of their soul, and of their duties to their fellows. Nothing can prevent such ideas from being the common spring from which all else originates (1969, 442–443).*

Tocqueville points out that the 13 colonies, which simultaneously jettisoned the English yoke at the beginning of the nation's founding, "had the same religion, language, and mores, and almost the same laws" (1969, 112). The common religion was, as it still is, Christianity. Although many denominations of Christianity exist in America, Tocqueville reports that all agree that the complete separation of church and state is "the main reason for the quiet sway of religion over their country." He adds, "That throughout my stay in America I met nobody, lay or cleric, who did not agree about that" (1969, 295). Tocqueville even contrasts Islam with Christianity:

> *Muhammad brought down from heaven and put into the Koran not religious doctrines only, but political maxims, criminal and civil laws, and scientific theories. The Gospels, on the other hand, deal only with the general relations between man and God and between man and man. Beyond that, they teach nothing and do not oblige people to believe anything. That alone, among a thousand reasons is enough to show that Islam will not be able to hold its power long in ages of enlightenment and democracy, while Christianity is destined to reign in such ages, as in all others (1969, 445).*

Two centuries later, Bernard Lewis argues that the "idea that religion and political authority, church and state are different, and can or should be separated – is, in a profound sense, Christian" (Lewis 2002, 96). This separation developed out of the history of European Christianity: "The persecutions endured by the early church made it clear that a separation between the church and state was possible; the persecutions inflicted by later churches persuaded many Christians that such a separation was necessary" (Lewis 2002, 96–99).

At the center of this issue within Christianity, Lewis explains, is the passage in Matthew 22:21, where "Christ is quoted as saying, 'Render therefore unto Caesar the things which are Caesar's; and unto God the things that are God's'" (2002, 97). Controversy surrounds the exact meaning of this passage; nevertheless, "for most of Christian history it has been understood as authorizing the separate coexistence of two authorities, the one charged with matters of religion, the other with what we would nowadays call politics" (Lewis 2002, 97).

No such division between religion and politics exists in Islam. Muhammad was, unlike Christ, a founder of both a religion and a polity (Medina) and head of a vast and expanding empire. At no time did Muhammad or his successors "create any institution corresponding to, or even remotely resembling, the church in Christendom" (Lewis 2002, 99). For that matter, Lewis continues, "There are no parliaments or representative assemblies of any kind, no councils or communes, no chambers of nobility or estates, no municipalities in the history of Islam; nothing but the sovereign power, to which the subject owed complete and unwavering obedience as a religious duty imposed by the Holy Law" (Lewis 1958, 318–319).

While Christianity seems to be the necessary condition for the emergence of democracy and a federal system, it is obviously not its sufficient condition. Tocqueville's reflections on the failure of the Mexican constitution of 1824 to establish a successful federal constitution modeled after the United States drives this point home. Mexico, a largely Christian nation, lacked an enlightened understanding of "self-interest rightly understood,"[2] and consequently an imported democratic federal system, according to Tocqueville, did not take root there:

> The Mexicans, wishing to establish a federal system, took the federal Constitution of their Anglo-American neighbors as a model and copied it almost completely. But when they borrowed the letter of the law, they could not at the same time transfer the spirit that gave it life. As a result, one sees them constantly entangled in the mechanism of their double government. The sovereignty of the states and that of the union, going beyond the spheres assigned to them by the constitution, trespass continually on each other's territory. In fact, at present Mexico is constantly shifting from anarchy to military despotism to anarchy (Tocqueville 1969, 165).[3]

The Western separation of church and state that we know today emerged only after a long and difficult contest between religious and political authority. The development of early Christian dogma within the context of Roman secular law, which was largely indifferent to religion, lays down a model of church–state relations that still continues. As Roger Scruton argues, ideas such as Saint Augustine's (354–430) distinction between two kingdoms, Pope Gelasius I's (d. 496) doctrine of the "two swords ... that of the Church for the government of men's souls, and that of the imperial power for the regulation of temporal affairs," culminate in Marsilius of Padua (1275–1342) declaring that "it is the state and not the church that guarantees the civil peace, and reason, not revelation, to which appeal must be made in all matters of temporal jurisdiction" (Scruton 2002, 4). The medieval distinction between *regnum* (kingship) and *sacredotium* (priesthood) and the important developments that took place long before the Reformation and the Enlightenment have no parallel in the Islamic world.

The European enlightenment and its emphasis on scientific development, David Pryce-Jones writes, "laid the foundation of European dominance of the world of Islam." He cites names like "Galileo, Newton, Descartes, Hooker," and the Royal Academy, a group of enlightened thinkers and "institutions projecting their societies out of the fixed religious doctrines of the past and into the different harness of reason and discovery whose purpose ... was the 'mastery of nature'" (Pryce-Jones 1989, 58–59). The extraordinary success of the scientific project and the spread of enlightenment ideas allowed European society to begin a flourishing of artistic and scientific development that worked to their own advantage by "objectifying and

---

2   I owe this point to Mark Kremer.
3   Tocqueville's views on Mexico are, I believe, outdated. Although Mexico today is hardly despotic, it nevertheless is closer to an oligarchy than democracy.

universalizing all knowledge" (Pryce-Jones 1989, 59). By contrast, Ibn Khaldun, writing in the fourteenth century, comments on a contrary intellectual trend among his fellows living under Islam: "The practice of the arts is in general very limited in the countries where the Arabs are indigenous and in the areas which they have conquered since the promulgation of Islam. Consider, on the other hand, how the arts are flourishing in the countries inhabited by the Chinese, the Hindus, the Turks and the Christians, and how the other nations derive goods and foodstuffs from them" (Pryce-Jones 1989, 59).

One of the most important products of the enlightenment is the notion of the modern liberal state, the purpose of which is to safeguard individual rights such as free speech, property, life, liberty, and pursuit of happiness. These ideas were promulgated most notably by Thomas Hobbes (1588–1679) and John Locke (1632–1704), animated by the need to create a government founded on the consent of the governed to secure the confidence and loyalty of its citizens. In order to educate human beings towards peace, and thereby overcome religious wars, Hobbes, for instance, teaches that all moral opinions reflect only the individual's arbitrary desires and aversions. Hobbes thereby strips religious and philosophical authorities of absolute authority over notions such as Good and Evil for the sake of which they persecute others. Hobbes teaches that our most powerful passion is the fear of violent death. Our enlightenment consists in our acknowledgement of this powerful passion as our fundamental nature and, consequently, our understanding of the civil state as the means to security. Having interpreted morality in terms of the passions, Hobbes can lay the foundation for the modern state.

Out of Hobbes' understanding of human fear, Locke and later thinkers develop a new understanding of sovereignty on which to build the state. Since all human beings are, by nature, born to the same desire for self-preservation, they are by nature free and equal. Their wills belong to themselves and, consequently, legitimate government must have its source in their will, or consent. This consent is to citizens' advantage because the state exists to protect our individual private property and security. By obeying the state's authority, we obey our own enlightened will and interests. This is what Tocqueville refers to as "self-interest rightly understood" (Tocqueville 1969, 525–528).[4]

This spirit of "self-interest rightly understood" underpins the federalist system of government. Tocqueville notes,

> *In the federal system [of the United States] one finds some accidental defects deriving from the laws; these can be put right by the lawgivers. There are others, inherent in the system, which cannot be eliminated by the peoples who have adopted it. Therefore these people must find within themselves the strength necessary to support the natural imperfections of their government*

---

[4] According to Tocqueville this also explains the absence of democracy in Russia, which he characterizes as "America minus the Enlightenment and liberty" (Tocqueville 1958, 3:164). See Letter to Beaumont, 3 Nov 1853 13, 3:164 in *Oeuvres Completes*. Edited by J.-P. Mayer. 18 vols. Paris: Gallimard, 1958–1998.

> ... whatever one does, therefore, the federal system rests on a complicated theory which, in application, demands that the government should use the lights of their reason every day (Tocqueville 1969, 164).

Liberal democracy presupposes both the belief that the political sphere is a vital, autonomous realm of human activity, and, also an enlightened teaching of citizenship that informs that belief. Democracy expresses the will of the people, rather than the will of God, and therefore depends on the notion of citizenship. Yet Lewis informs us that "there is no word in Arabic, Persian, or Turkish for 'citizen.'" The closest cognate means "compatriot" or "countryman." Our English word citizen derives from the Latin *civis* and the Greek *polites*, which means one who participates in the affairs of the *polis*. Lewis contends that there is no parallel "in Arabic and the other languages because the idea – of the citizen as participant, of citizenship as participation – is not there" (Lewis 1996, 52–63). This is why Tocqueville notes, that "the Turkish peoples have never taken any part in the control of their society's affairs; nevertheless, they accomplish immense undertakings so long as they saw the triumph of the religion of Muhammad in the conquests of the sultans. Now their religion is departing; despotism alone remains; and they are falling." How, he asks "can liberty be preserved in great matters among a multitude that has never learned to use it in small ones" (Tocqueville 1969, 94)?

Moreover, in a liberal democracy founded on enlightenment ideas, according to Tocqueville,

> Everything in such a government depends on artificially contrived conventions, and it is only suited to a people long accustomed to manage its affairs, and one in which even the lowest ranks in society have an appreciation of political science. Nothing has made me admire the good sense and practical intelligence of the Americans more than the way they avoid the innumerable difficulties deriving from their federal Constitution. I have hardly ever met one of the common people in America who did not surprisingly and easily perceive which obligations derived from a law of Congress and which were based on the laws of his state and who, having distinguished the matters falling within the general prerogatives of the Union from those suitable to the local legislator, could not indicate the point where the competence of the federal courts commences and that of the state court ends (164–165).

The idea that "everything in such a government depends on artificially contrived conventions" (164) and "the idea that any group of persons, any kind of activities, any part of human life is in any sense outside of the scope of religious law and jurisdiction is alien to Muslim thought" (Lewis 2002, 100). From the perspective of Islam, there is "no human legislative power, and there is only one law for the believers – the Holy Law of God, promulgated by revelation" (101).

Islam is rooted in the submission to the one and only God. He alone is the sole sovereign and the sole source of law and only His will is behind the events of history. It is the duty of His faithful to bring to the rest of the world His final message. Consequently, as Roger Scruton argues, the universal significance of Islam "regards territorial jurisdiction and national loyalties as compromises with no intrinsic legitimacy of their own" (Scruton 2002, 125). Territorial and national loyalties might divide the faithful, weakening the sovereignty of Islam. Scruton writes:

> *Although there have been attempts to manufacture nationalisms both appropriate to the Islamic temperament and conducive to a legitimate political order, they have fragmented under the impact of sectarian or tribal allegiances, usually giving way to military dictatorship or one-man, one-family, or one-party tyranny. Islam itself remains, in the hearts of those who live under these tyrannies, a permanent call to a higher life, and a reminder that power and corruption will rule in this world until the reign established by the Prophet is restored (125–126).*

This struggle between Islam and tribal allegiances runs throughout Islamic history and is one of the greatest themes in Ibn Khaldun's sociology, to which we now turn.

Islam and the Bedouin Legacy

"God distinguished man from all the other animals by an ability to think which He made the beginning of human perfection and the end of man's noble superiority over existing things," writes Ibn Khaldun (M II, 411).[5] The ability to reason (*quwwa natiqq, virtus rationalis*) enables human beings "to obtain their livelihood, to co-operate to this end with his fellows, and to study the Master whom they worship" (M I, 175). Through the intellect, we can gain knowledge of "a certain order" in the universe, of which we are a part, and understand our relation to it and seek and discover the "causes and things caused;" through the intellect, we can understand, perceive, and come to know the "existence of essences beyond" the realm of sense perception of particular objects (M I, 194). Reason is, therefore, the "principle of man's perfection" (M I, 90).

All political communities come into being for the sake of life, Ibn Khaldun writes, but their end is the good life, a goal that is not evident in man's cruel, nomadic beginnings. Ibn Khaldun supports Royal Authority as the highest potential specific to humans and the end to which all human associations aspire (M I, 92, 284ff, 336–337; II, 119): "Royal authority is a noble and enjoyable position. It comprises all the good things of the world, the pleasures of the body, and the joys of soul" (M I, 123).

---

5   Khaldun 1958, *Muqaddimah*, volume II, 411. Hereafter in text and notes references to Ibn Khaldun's *Muqaddimah* will be of the following form: first M, for title, followed by volume and page number. All quotations by Ibn Khaldun are from the translation of *Muqaddimah* in Rosenthal 1958.

The good life consists in the blessed contemplation of the "world of eternity" (M I, 161). This blessed contemplation can only take place if humans understand their greatness: political associations can promote the conditions that allow the good life to occur. Our social organization, Ibn Khaldun instructs, is necessary because "man is a political animal" (M I, 89). He warns that "this situation is not at all understood by the great mass" (M I, 123).

According to Ibn Khaldun, Islam is a unifying element for the Arabs because they "can attain [Royal authority] (only) once their nature has undergone a complete transformation under the influence of some religious coloring that ... causes the Arabs to have a restraining influence on themselves and to keep people apart from each other" (M I, 307). Human beings perfect themselves within cities, and the Bedouin Arabs are desert people. They need the assistance of Islam:

> *Arabs can obtain royal authority only by making use of some religious coloring, such as prophecy, or sainthood, or some great religious event in general. The reason for this is that because of their savagery, the Arabs are the least willing of nations to subordinate themselves to each other, as they are rude, proud, ambitious, and eager to be the leader. Their individual aspirations rarely coincide. But when there is religion (among them) through prophecy or sainthood, then they have some restraining influence in themselves. The qualities of haughtiness and jealousy leave them. It is, then, easy for them to subordinate themselves and to unite (as a social organization) ... (M I, 305).*

Centuries of pre-Islamic nomadic habits may have "developed social and psychological attitudes preventing them from creating a civilization and driving them to destroy the civilizations they may dominate" (Mahdi 1964, 199). Once Islam is intertwined with politics, Ibn Khaldun informs us, a great civilization is possible because:

> *... religious coloring does away with mutual jealousy and envy among people who share in a group feeling, and causes concentration upon the truth. When people (who have a religious coloring) come to have the (right) insight into their affairs, nothing can withstand them, because their outlook is one and their object one of common accord. They are willing to die for (their objectives) ... the dynasty they attack may be many times as numerous as they. But their purposes differ, in as much as they are false purposes, and afraid of death. Therefore, they do not offer resistance to (the people with a religious coloring), even if they themselves are more numerous. They are overpowered by them and quickly wiped out ... (M I, 320).*

But, Ibn Khaldun argues, when "religious coloring" is destroyed,

> *The power (of the ruling dynasty) is then wiped out. Superiority exists then merely in proportion to (the existing) group feeling, without additional*

> *(power of) religion. As a result, the dynasty is overpowered by those groups (up to this time) under its control that are equal or superior to it in strength. It had formerly overpowered the groups that had stronger group feeling and were more deeply rooted in desert life, with the help of the additional power that religion had given it (M I, 321–322).*

The contest between tribal and religious authority is to the Middle East what the contest between political and religious authority has been to the West: it is, for Islam, what Pryce-Jones (Pryce-Jones 1989, 27) calls a "power-challenge dialectic" that runs throughout Arab history and can be seen throughout Ibn Khaldun's *Muqaddimah*. Deeply rooted tribal identities resist reform and outside influences. "Islam was originally such a threat ... Teaching that men were equal before God, Islam was a creed carrying reformist implications for tribalism" (1989, 27). Joining the community of the faithful entails leaving behind one's tribal loyalties and identity. At the time of the Prophet Muhammad's revelation of Islam, Arab tribes spread their religious loyalties among various pagan beliefs or half-hearted Judaism or Christianity: the "welding of the community of Islam released human energies which had been hitherto suppressed in scattered tribalism" (27). In order to grasp the importance of Islam for Ibn Khaldun's thought, it is necessary to turn to his discussion of Bedouin and sedentary society.

Bedouin versus Sedentary Life

According to Ibn Khaldun, human life moves between two poles: the primitive, nomadic life (*umran badawa*) of necessity and the sedentary life (*hadara*) of leisure; between Bedouin wandering and urban sedentary life; between barbarism and civilization. The development of full humanity requires the overcoming of the primitive nomadic life, not simply because a life devoted to necessity is undesirable for its own sake, but because the goods of the soul cannot come into existence without a life settled enough to allow the soul to rule over the body. For Ibn Khaldun, our full humanness can only thrive in an urban, political situation.

Ibn Khaldun describes the Bedouin as a tribal, nomadic people. They possess a strong social solidarity, ambition, fortitude, and endurance in plenty. They are loyal, courageous, bold, and ferocious. They use all their qualities to survive successfully in the unforgiving deserts, and they almost always bring disaster to those they encounter along their way. By contrast, he writes, the sedentary "people have no desire for the desert condition" (M I, 253). They live in urban settings and readily submit to political authority, which the rule of law in a populous city necessitates. They enjoy a life of relative peace and the fruits of a productive economy that make possible intellectual pursuits such as the arts, the sciences, and philosophy. But tranquility destroys fortitude which is necessary for defense. Consequently, they almost always find themselves victims of Bedouin conquest.

Ibn Khaldun warns that sedentary life is given to "luxury and success in worldly occupations and to indulgences in worldly pleasures" (M I, 254). The city of luxury estranges its inhabitants from the "ways and means of goodness ... Eventually they lose all sense of restraints" (M I, 254). They also lose the taste for freedom because, explains Ibn Khaldun,

> *They are sunk in well-being and luxury. They have entrusted defense of their property and their lives to the governor and ruler who rules them, and to the militia which has the task of guarding them. They find full assurance of safety in the walls that surround them, and the fortifications that protect them ... They are carefree and trusting, and have ceased to carry weapons. Successive generations have grown up in this way of life. Eventually, this has come to be a quality of character (M I, 257).*

By contrast, the Bedouin tribal unity preserves a certain rough virtue which stems of necessity. They are

> *alone in the country and remote from militias. They have no walls and gates. Therefore, they provide their own defense and so do not entrust it to, or rely upon others for it. They always carry weapons ... They go alone into the desert, guided by their fortitude, putting trust in themselves. Fortitude has become a character quality of theirs, and courage their nature. They use it whenever they are called upon or an alarm stirs them (M I, 257–258).*

It is the cruel life of the desert that endows the Bedouin with a taste for freedom, Ibn Khaldun continues:

> *It is difficult for [the Bedouin] to subordinate themselves to each other, because they are in a state of savagery [and freedom]. Their leader needs them mostly for the group spirit that is necessary for purposes of defense. He is, therefore, forced to rule them kindly and to avoid antagonizing them. Otherwise, he would have trouble with the group spirit, and (such trouble) would be his undoing and theirs. Royal leadership and government, on the other hand, require the leader to exercise a restraining influence by force. If not, his leadership would not last (M I, 306).*

Although today Bedouins make up not more than 10 per cent of the population of Arab countries, (Patai 2007, 78), their ethos and moral principles continue to dominate the Arab world in general (Berque 1964, 174). Patai advises that the Bedouin mindset is still a strong force today in Arab culture, and that "it still ... upholds the same values, and has preserved even in its religious life many pre-Islamic features" (Patai 2007, 82). According to Ibn Khaldun, the only possible force to counter the tribal ferocity of the Bedouin is Islam, which can unite them into a cohesive whole. Their inner fortitude and moral character make them more "prone to lead a virtuous life when it is preached to them" because, he says, "no people are as quick (as the Arabs) to accept (religious) truth and right guidance" (M I, 306). It is Islam alone that can provide the inspiration to link the sedentary urban civilization to the strong social solidarity of the Bedouin, who in turn gain meaning from serving the higher religious law.

To emphasize this last point Ibn Khaldun draws attention to the achievement of the Muslim community when tribal spirit (*asabiyaa*) adopted Islam. The inspired unity under Islam caused the Arabs to "be willing to die for" their new religious identity. Tribal disunity was replaced by certain "submissiveness and obedience" awed by "extraordinary miracles and other divine happenings" (M I, 320).

Barbara Stowasser draws a distinction between the submissiveness and obedience to Islam of the Bedouin to the lassitude of the comfortable city dweller whose fortitude was destroyed through luxury. The courage and fortitude of the early believers "strengthened and enhanced" the fortitude of the early Muslim community (Stowasser 1983, 10). Ibn Khaldun explains,

> ... the [Bedouins] around Muhammad observed the religious laws, and yet did not experience any diminution of their fortitude, but possessed the greatest possible fortitude. When the Muslims got their religion from the Lawgiver (Muhammad), the restraining influence came from themselves, as a result of the encouragement and discouragement he gave them in the Qur'an ... which their firmly rooted (belief in) the truth of the articles of faith caused them to observe. Their fortitude remained unabated, and it was not corroded by education or authority [or urban comfort] ... (M I, 260).

The truth of Islam's articles of faith offered the early Muslim community a social cohesiveness and transcendent common purpose that allowed a great empire to be established in the name of Allah. Unity added to courage brought vast conquest.

Islam also introduced the distinction between legitimate and illegitimate empire. According to Stowasser, a legitimate empire works towards the fulfillment of divine commands in which Royal authority is exercised in the name of God (Stowasser 1983, 11). According to Ibn Khaldun,

> ... when the Lawgiver (Muhammad) censures royal authority, he does not censure it for gaining superiority through truth, for forcing the great mass to accept faith, nor for looking after the (public) interest. He censures royal authority for achieving superiority through worthless means and for employing human beings for indulgence in (selfish) purposes and desires ... If royal authority would sincerely exercise its superiority over men for the sake of God and so as to cause those men to worship God and to wage war against His enemies, there would not be anything reprehensible in it ... (M I, 416–7).

Stowasser interprets the above passage from Ibn Khaldun in the following way: legitimate ends are those that draw inspiration from Allah; illegitimate desires are worldly when they stray from Islam. Thus, for Ibn Khaldun, a separation between church (Islam, Allah) and the state (worldly concerns) would separate God's unifying and overruling purpose from our worldly ambitions. The latter can never, for Ibn Khaldun, be considered legitimate ends for virtuous humans to pursue. Wealth in itself is not an evil provided that it is acquired for the sake of God, as in the early Abbasid dynasty: "Amassing worldly property ... did not reflect [poorly upon the early Muslims] ... since their expenditures followed a plan and served the truth and served the purpose of attaining the other world" (M I, 420–1). However, when the later generations of the Abbasids began to be "concerned only with the gratification of their desires and with sinful pleasures ... and enmeshed in worldly affairs of no value and turned their backs on Islam ... God permitted them to be ruined, and (He permitted) the Arabs to be completely deprived of their power, which he gave to others" (M I, 424). This is Allah's punishment for illegitimate pursuits.

Royal Society can only be legitimate to the degree to which it is lawful and in accordance with *sharia*, the law of God. Islamic communities that fail to be a lawful will be punished by God (Stowasser 1983, 23). A community's distance from Islam results in corruption, then disintegration, factionalism, and dissent. After the influence of Islam and its followers faded, Ibn Khaldun writes, "the affairs took again their ordinary course":

> *The Arabs ... neglected the religion ... forgot political leadership and returned to their desert. They were ignorant of the connection of their group feeling [asabiyaa] with the people of the ruling dynasty, because subservience and lawful (government) had (now) become strange to them. They became once again as savage as they had been before ... power passed altogether out of their hands. Non-Arabs took over the power in their stead. They remained Bedouins in the desert, ignorant of royal authority and political leadership. Most Arabs do not even know that they possessed royal authority in the past, or that no nation had ever exercised such (sweeping) royal authority as had their race (M I, 307–308).*

Once again, tribal loyalties reemerged (M I, 170). Ibn Khaldun states that,

> *... after the removal of its prophet, a religious group must have someone to take care of it. Such a person must cause the people to act according to the religious laws ... he stands to them in the place of their prophet, in as much as he enjoins the obligations which the prophet had imposed upon them [for] ... the human species must have a person who will cause them to act in accordance with what is good for them and who will prevent them by force from doing things harmful to them. Such a person is the one who is called ruler (M I, 472–473).*

In Islam, unlike Christianity, "religious and secular authority does not merely coexist, but are identical, since the supreme office in the community includes all other offices" (Stowasser 1983, 23). According to Ibn Khaldun, this unity of religious purpose extends to religious war:

> *In the Muslim community, the holy war is a religious duty, because of the universalism of the Muslim mission and (the obligation to) convert everybody to Islam either by persuasion or by force (M I, 473).*

This singularity of purpose requires, according to Ibn Khaldun, a unity of rule where "caliphate and royal authority are united in Islam" (M I, 473). There is no separation between religious and secular powers, as Ibn Khaldun notes, in Judaism and Christianity. He observes that:

> *the holy war was not a religious duty to [Christianity and Judaism], save only for purposes of defense. It has thus come about that the person in charge of religious affairs in [Judaism and Christianity] is not concerned with power politics at all. (Among them) royal authority comes to those who have it – by accident and in some way that has nothing to do with religion. It comes to them as the necessary result of group feeling, which by its very nature seeks to obtain royal authority, as we mentioned before, and not because they are under obligation to gain power over other nations, as is the case with Islam. They are merely required to establish their religion among their own people (M I, 473–474).*

As Muhsin Mahdi (Mahdi 1964, 247) points out, Islam must not "distinguish between affairs of the spirit and the affairs of the world." He asserts that "religion must be politicized" and goes on to explain that it is out of this religious heritage that Muslims philosophers like Ibn Khaldun write. This is why the Islamic community makes no distinction between secular and religious power, and why it can unify in holy war: "the religious principle behind the historical fact that the Prophet and his true successors in the leadership of the Islamic community aspired to have both religious and political authority, while the leaders of other religious communities [such as Judaism and Christianity] did not have to be concerned with political affairs" (1964, 247). In other words, Islam combines church and state, serving the political role in the Islamic state that democratic federalism plays in America.

Conclusion

Ibn Khaldun helps us to see that the Middle East is a tribal culture that is opposed to any central authority unless it is imposed by God (Islam). His analysis of the tensions between tribalism and Islam reveals an enduring political problem and reflects a radically different vision of the nature of humankind, God, and politics from that of the West.

Islam has lived through a different religious history from Christianity. The Arabs share a very different culture from the West; consequently, the problems and solutions to government are perceived differently from the West. In the United States, American federalism divides sovereignty between the states and the federal government and does so within the framework of its constitution founded on the enlightened consent of the governed. This democratic phenomenon arises from a shared Christian history, as well as commonly held beliefs about God and politics that grew out of the horrors of religious wars in Europe and the ensuing Enlightenment ideas, rather than from some vast, universally experienced past or universally accepted beliefs about God and politics.

In Islam, it has been seen, sovereignty cannot be divided, for it is God's alone, and politics is never a separate or autonomous realm of human activity, as it is under American federalism. As Ibn Khaldun pointed out, Islam depends on the will of the one supreme God only, above all, and not on the will of any of His faithful or on enlightened self-interest, as has developed in Western cultures.

The Islamic approach to politics derives from the religion and the experience of past generations of Muslims, just as the triumph of American federalism marks the transformation of the separation of church and state in Christendom into a form of constitutional democracy in the United States. Any attempt to answer the question with which we began must first address any form of federalism from the perspective of Islam, rather than to fit Islam into the perspective of Western federalism.

References

Berque, Jacques. 1964. *The Arabs: Their History and Future*. New York: Praeger Press.
Issawi, Charles. 1958. [1377] *An Arab Philosophy of History: Selections from the Prolegomena of Ibn Khaldun of Tunis (1332–1406)*. London: John Murray Press.
Khaldun, Ibn. 1958. [1377] *Muqaddimah*, 3 vols. Franz Rosenthal, trans. Princeton: Princeton University Press.
Lewis, Bernard. 1958. Communism and Islam. *The Middle East in Transition*, Walter Laqueur, ed. London: Routledge and Kegan Paul, 318–319.
—— 1996. Islam and liberal democracy: A historical overview. *Journal of Democracy* 7:2, 52–63.
—— 2002. *What Went Wrong?* Oxford: Oxford University Press.
—— 2004. *The Crisis of Islam*. New York: Random House.
Mahdi, Muhsin. 1964. *Ibn Khaldun's Philosophy of History: A Study in the Philosophic Foundation of the Science of Culture*. Chicago: University of Chicago Press.
Patai, Raphael. 2007. *The Arab Mind*. Long Island City: Hatherleigh Press.
Pryce-Jones, David. 1989. *The Closed Circle: An Interpretation of the Arabs*. New York: Harper Collins.

Scruton, Roger. 2002. *The West and the Rest: Globalization and the Terrorist Threat*. Wilmington: Intercollegiate Studies Institute Press.

Stowasser, Barbara Freyer. 1983. *Religion and Political Development: Some Comparative Ideas on Ibn Khaldun and Machiavelli*. Washington: Center for Contemporary Arab Studies, Georgetown University.

Tocqueville, Alexis de. 1958. [1853] *Oeuvres completes*, 18 vols. J.-P. Mayer, ed. Paris: Gallimard. Letter to Beaument, 3 Nov 1853 13, 3:164.

—— 1969. [1835]. *Democracy in America*. J.P. Mayer, trans. George Lawrence, ed. San Francisco: Harper and Row, vol. 1.

Further Reading

Al-Azmeh, Aziz. 2003. *Ibn Khaldun: An Essay in Reinterpretation*. Budapest: Central European University Press.

Anderson, Norman. 1976. *Law Reform in the Muslim World*. London: Athlone Press.

Baali, Fuad. 1988. *Society, State, and Urbanism in Ibn Khaldun's Sociological Thought*. New York: State University of New York.

Binder, Leonard. 1988. *Islamic Liberalism: A Critique of Development Ideologies*. Chicago: University of Chicago Press.

Cook, Michael. 2001. *Commanding Right and Forbidding Wrong in Islamic Thought*. Cambridge: Cambridge University Press.

Enan, M.A. 1993. *Ibn Khaldun His Life and Work*. India: Ashref Lahore Press.

Eulau, Heinz H.F. 1941. Theories of federalism under the Holy Roman Empire. *American Political Science Review* 35:4 (August), 643–664.

Fromkin, David. 1990. *A Peace to End All Peace: The Fall of the Ottoman Empire and the Creation of the Modern Middle East*. New York: Avon Books.

Gauchet, Marcel. 1997. *The Disenchantment of the World: A Political History of Religion*. Oscar Burge, trans. Princeton: Princeton University Press.

Gibb, H.A.R. 1962. *Studies in the Civilization of Islam*. London: Routledge and Kegan Paul Ltd.

Hobbes, Thomas. 1996. [1651]. *Leviathan*. Richard Tuck, ed. Cambridge: Cambridge University Press.

Hourani, Albert. 1962. *Arabic Thought in the Liberal Age: 1798–1939*. Oxford: Oxford University Press.

Hudson, M. 1980. Islam and political development. *Islam and Development*. J.L. Esposito, ed. Syracuse: Syracuse University Press.

Kedourie, Elie. 1992. *Politics in the Middle East*. Oxford: Oxford University Press.

Lewis, Bernard. 1988. *The Political Language of Islam*. Chicago: University of Chicago Press.

Madison, James, Alexander Hamilton and John Jay. 2001 [1778]. *The Federalist Papers*. Indianapolis: Liberty Fund.

Mortimer, Edward. 1982. *Faith and Power: The Politics of Islam*. London: Faber and Faber.

Rosenthal, Erwin. 1958. *Political Thought in Medieval Islam: An Introductory Outline.* Cambridge: Cambridge University Press.
Ruthven, Malise. 1984. *Islam in the World.* Harmondsworth: Penguin.
Quran. 1999. Sayed A.A. Razwy, ed. Abdullah Yusuf Ali, trans. Tahrike Tarsile. Media.

The Rehnquist Court and the "New Federalism"

Jack Wade Nowlin

The U.S. Constitution establishes a federal form of government with political authority in the United States divided between the national government and the 50 state governments. The questions surrounding the precise contours of the "federal balance" struck between national power and state power by the Constitution have been a subject of continuing and evolving controversy since the ratification of the Constitution. The authority of the Supreme Court to resolve these questions has also been a subject of ongoing controversy – with the Supreme Court sometimes aggressively asserting the power to enforce federal limits on the national government and sometimes passively disclaiming such power. The "New Federalism" of the Rehnquist Court (1986–2005) refers to a set of judicially enforceable constitutional doctrines recognized by the Supreme Court over the last two decades which reinvigorated federal limits on the national government of the United States. As such, the Rehnquist Court's "New Federalism" has raised – once again – fundamental questions concerning the federal balance and its judicial resolution.

The "New Federalism" of the Rehnquist Court finds its expression in several distinct areas of constitutional law: the scope of Congress' power to regulate interstate commerce under Article I of the U.S. Constitution; the scope of congressional power to "commandeer" or otherwise induce state legislatures and executives to enact or enforce laws according to federal specifications; the scope of Congress' power to enforce Section One of the Fourteenth Amendment through the passage of civil rights legislation under Section Five of the Fourteenth Amendment; and the scope of congressional power to abrogate or eliminate "state sovereign immunity," the immunity each state has, as a sovereign, from being sued by citizens without the state's consent. Each of these areas of the "New Federalism" deserves elaboration.

The Commerce Clause

A major "New Federalism" doctrine recognized by the Supreme Court in the Rehnquist Court era involved the revival of judicially enforceable limits on the scope of Congress' power to regulate interstate commerce under Article I of the U.S. Constitution. The text of Article I – read in conjunction with the Tenth Amendment – grants to Congress power over national or *inter*state commerce and reserves power over local or *intra*state commerce to the individual states. Given the potential sweeping scope of the power to regulate commerce, the distinction between national power and state power in this area is of central importance to maintaining the federal balance. Indeed, as recently as the mid 1930s, the Supreme Court actively enforced constitutional limits on the congressional power to regulate commerce, attempting to distinguish what was truly national or interstate commerce from what was truly local or intrastate commerce and thereby preserve the federal balance between national and state regulation of the economy.

The Court in this era, for instance, recognized the power of Congress to regulate channels of interstate commerce (such as interstate waterways, railways, and highways), instrumentalities of interstate commerce (such as locomotives or other vehicles used in interstate shipping), and items in the "stream" or "flow" of interstate commerce (such as commodities in the process of shipment across state lines); but the Court rejected the view that Congress has the power to regulate the local or intrastate production of commodities and their ultimate local or intrastate sale.[1] Therefore Congress could regulate the interstate shipment of commodities such as coal or poultry but not their local production before entering the stream of interstate commerce or ultimate local sale after leaving the stream of interstate commerce.

However, under the political pressures generated by the Great Depression in the 1930s, the Supreme Court appeared to abandon active judicial enforcement of federal limits on Congress' power to regulate the economy. By 1942, in *Wickard v. Filburn*, the Supreme Court was willing to uphold congressional regulation of even purely local production of very small amounts of wheat.[2] The Court in *Wickard* held that while the congressional regulation at issue was not limited to a channel of interstate commerce, an instrumentality of interstate commerce, or an item in the stream of interstate commerce, it was nonetheless within the broad scope of Congress' power to regulate interstate commerce. The Court justified this expansive reading of congressional commerce power by asserting that even modest local production of wheat – in the aggregate and across the nation – can affect national or interstate wheat prices and therefore that the congressional regulation of such production concerns interstate commerce. Since virtually any activity in the aggregate across the nation can affect the national economy in some respect, *Wickard* was widely understood at the time as a final confirmation of the

---

1   See, e.g., *Carter v. Carter Coal Co.*, 298 U.S. 238 (1936); *A.L.A. Schecter Poultry Corp. v. United States*, 295 U.S. 495 (1935).
2   317 U.S. 111 (1942).

Court's unwillingness to invalidate acts of Congress under the interstate commerce clause. After *Wickard*, the category of national or interstate commerce appeared to be legally unbounded.

In 1995, however, the Rehnquist Court revived judicially enforceable limits on Congress' commerce power and invalidated a congressional statute on commerce clause grounds for the first time in almost 60 years. In *United States v. Lopez*, the Supreme Court struck down the federal Gun-Free School Zones Act of 1990, which prohibited possession of a firearm near a school, as exceeding the scope of congressional authority under the commerce clause.[3] The Court in *Lopez* first observed that it had never specifically extended the understanding of the scope of the national commerce power to criminal statutes that did not regulate a form of economic activity, an unlikely form of "commercial" regulation. The Court then justified its invalidation of the Gun-Free School Zones Act on the grounds that if the Court were to view a purely criminal statute regulating non-economic activities as a regulation of "interstate commerce" under *Wickard*'s aggregation principle, then the Court would have obliterated *any* distinction between national and local power. Finally, the Court carefully distinguished *Wickard* on the grounds that *Wickard* had involved a clearly economic activity – production of wheat, a commodity for which there is a national economic market.

The Court in *Lopez* thus limited *Wickard*'s deferential aggregation principle to economic activities and refused to extend that standard to criminal statutes involving non-economic activities. In 2000, the Supreme Court in *United States v. Morrison* further confirmed the vitality of this revived limit on congressional power by invalidating the Violence Against Women Act (VAWA) on essentially the same grounds: VAWA, like the Gun-Free School Zones Act, was a criminal statute regulating a non-economic activity – gender-motivated crimes of violence – and therefore exceeded the scope of Congress' commerce power.[4] In both cases, the Court observed that Congress could add a jurisdictional element to its criminal statute limiting the application of the statute to cases where there is a specific tie to interstate commerce – such as a crime involving channels of interstate commerce, instrumentalities of interstate commerce, or items or persons associated with the stream of interstate commerce.

The precise nature of the distinction between the economic activities which Congress has broad authority to regulate under *Wickard* and the non-economic activities which Congress has little or no authority to regulate through criminal statutes under *Lopez* (at least absent proof of a specific link to interstate commerce under a jurisdictional element) has remained an elusive one. In *Gonzales v. Raich* in 2005, the Supreme Court divided over whether the congressional Controlled Substances Act (CSA) – which prohibits cultivation, possession, and use of marijuana – exceeded the scope of the national commerce power as applied to medical uses of marijuana authorized by state law.[5] The majority in *Raich* analogized the issues

---

3   514 U.S. 549 (1995).
4   529 U.S. 598 (2000).
5   545 U.S. 1 (2005).

to those of *Wickard*, concluding that both cases involve congressional regulation of an economic activity: production of a commodity for which there is a national market, an illegal market in *Raich* and a legal market in *Wickard*. Thus the Court applied *Wickard*'s deferential aggregation standard and upheld the application of the CSA to medical use of marijuana authorized by state law. The dissenters in *Raich* emphasized the criminal nature of the statute and questioned whether cultivation and possession of small amounts of marijuana for medical purposes constitutes an economic activity. These Justices would have invalidated the application of the CSA to medical use of marijuana on grounds similar to those in *Lopez*.

The Anti-Commandeering Principle

A second "New Federalism" doctrine recognized by the Supreme Court in the Rehnquist Court era is the anti-commandeering principle. This principle prohibits the national government from appropriating the legislative and executive processes of the state governments. The basic requirements of the anti-commandeering doctrine are simple: Congress may not require state legislatures to enact state laws or require state executive officials to enforce federal laws. Such congressional requirements of state political action are viewed by the Court as unconstitutional "commandeerings" of state political institutions. Thus, for example, while Congress may use its commerce power to enact a national speed limit on interstate highways as channels of interstates commerce, it may not enact a law requiring state legislatures to enact such speed limits as matters of state law, and it may not enact a law requiring state executives (such as state law enforcement officers) to enforce any congressionally enacted national speed limit.

The Supreme Court first clearly established the anti-commandeering doctrine in 1992 in the case of *New York v. United States*.[6] The Court in *New York* invalidated a part of a congressional regulatory scheme over low-level radioactive waste disposal that "commandeered" state legislatures by requiring them in effect to pass radioactive waste disposal legislation according to federal standards or to legislate to assume legal liability for the undisposed radioactive waste in their respective states. Because both these choices Congress extended to the states appropriated or conscripted the state legislative process by requiring the states to enact legislation, the Supreme Court struck down this part of the regulatory scheme as a form of unconstitutional commandeering. The anti-commandeering doctrine was then reaffirmed and expanded in 1997 in *Printz v. United States*.[7] The Court in *Printz* invalidated a section of the Brady Handgun Violence Prevention Act, congressional gun control legislation, which "commandeered" state executive officials by requiring state officials to enforce the Brady Act's requirement of a background check on prospective purchasers of handguns.

---

6   505 U.S. 144 (1992).
7   521 U.S. 898 (1997).

THE REHNQUIST COURT AND THE "NEW FEDERALISM"

The Court in *New York* and *Printz* grounded the anti-commandeering principle in the sovereign dignity state governments retain in the federal system established by the U.S. Constitution, a dignity that would be compromised if the national government could simply treat states as subordinate administrative units by ordering them to enact state laws or enforce federal laws. The Court located this structural principle of state sovereign dignity in the text of the Constitution – both in the limited delegation and enumeration of congressional powers in Article I and in the Tenth Amendment, which states that all powers not delegated to the national government are reserved by the states. The Court's opinion in *New York* also cited preservation of the structure of federal democracy as a further justification for the anti-commandeering principle, particularly the importance of maintaining clear lines of national and state political accountability so that voters will know which institutions are responsible for which laws. Finally, the Court in *Printz* cited an additional justification for the prohibition of congressional commandeering of state executives: the preservation of the national separation of powers and the concern that Congress – in the absence of such an anti-commandeering prohibition – could use state executive resources as a substitute for the national executive and thereby "shatter" the unitary national executive.

The anti-commandeering principle as an aspect of the "New Federalism" left in place what has been called the Constitution's scheme of "cooperative federalism." The Rehnquist Court's anti-commandeering principle did not disturb the power that Congress often has to offer incentives to states to cooperate with the national government by adopting laws that meet federal standards or by enforcing federal laws. These incentives include the "carrot" of federal financial subsidies and the "stick" of federal preemption of state laws. It has long been established that Congress has very broad authority to spend for the "general welfare,"[8] and the Rehnquist Court has reaffirmed that Congress – under the federal structure of the Constitution – may condition federal spending on the state enactment of laws which adhere to a national standard as long as three requirements are met. First, Congress must state unambiguously the condition that attaches to the receipt of federal funds. Second, there must be a sufficiently close relationship between the interest furthered by the condition and the interest furthered by the spending to justify the condition as an attempt to induce state cooperation in attaining the purpose of spending. Third, the condition must amount to no more than mere national "pressure" on the states to legislate rather than national "compulsion." In the view of the Court, Congress may place such limited conditions on the state receipt of federal funds consistent with respect for the sovereign dignity of states to legislate within their own spheres of authority.

For instance, in *South Dakota v. Dole*, Congress conditioned the provision of a portion of national subsidies for state highway construction upon state adoption of a national minimum age requirement for the purchase of alcohol.[9] The Court upheld this act of conditional spending for the three reasons stated above. First, the Court

---

8   *United States v. Butler*, 297 U.S. 1 (1936).
9   483 U.S. 203 (1987).

found that Congress had clearly stated the condition that attached to the spending. Second, the Court concluded that a sufficiently close relationship existed between the purpose of the condition (furthering highway safety by reducing incidents of drunken driving associated with driving across state lines to take advantage of varying state drinking ages) and the purpose of the spending (promoting highway safety through the provision of highway construction funds) to justify the condition as congressional encouragement of state cooperation in achieving the broad goal of the spending program: greater highway safety. Third, the Court found that the condition constituted mere congressional pressure on states to legislate rather than any form of compulsion because the condition affected only 5 percent of federal highway funds each state was to receive. Thus Congress, as the Court recognized in *New York*, will often have the power to offer substantial financial incentives to states to enact state laws following national standards or to enforce national laws.

Moreover, under the Supremacy Clause of Article VI of the U.S. Constitution, congressional legislation preempts or trumps state legislation when the two conflict. Congress, when acting within the scope of its delegated and enumerated powers, may choose conditionally to preempt state legislation – offering states the opportunity to regulate within guidelines set by the national government or suffer the alternative of displacement of their own laws by direct federal regulation. Congress, for instance, could give the states the choice of adopting and enforcing state speed limits on interstate highways consistent with standards set by Congress or face the preemption of state regulation of interstate highways by a federal regulatory scheme consisting of a national speed limit and a national highway patrol to enforce it. In the Court's view, this scheme of "cooperative federalism" is consistent with respect for the states as sovereign entities within the Constitution's architecture of government.

Finally, the Court in *New York v. United States* distinguished the impermissible act of commandeering of state political processes from the constitutionally permissible act of applying a general regulatory statute to similarly situated private and state actors. For instance, in *Garcia v. San Antonio Metropolitan Transit Authority* in 1985, the Court upheld the application of provisions of the congressional Fair Labor Standards Act (FLSA), such as the establishment of a minimum wage, to state – as well as private – employers. The Court viewed this national regulation of state employment as consistent with respect for the federal constitutional design.[10] Notably, *Garcia* overruled an earlier decision, *National League of Cities v. Usery*, in which the Court had invalidated the application of provisions of the FLSA as applied to state employment in "traditional governmental functions."[11] The Court in this earlier decision had agreed that the FLSA was within the scope of the congressional interstate commerce power, but the Court also concluded that the Constitution's federal structure prohibits Congress from regulating state employers in core state functions as if they were merely private employers. The Court in *National League of Cities* viewed such regulation as inconsistent with the sovereign dignity of states

---

10   469 U.S. 528 (1985).
11   426 U.S. 833 (1976).

under the Constitution's federal architecture. The *Garcia* Court's justifications for overruling *National League of Cities* and upholding the application of the FLSA even to state employers in areas of traditional state concern were the general unwisdom of judicial enforcement of federal limits on Congress and the difficulty of defining clearly an area such as "traditional governmental functions."

Clearly the Rehnquist Court's "New Federalism" has doctrinally eroded *Garcia* by rejecting both its main justifications – in favor of active judicial enforcement of federal limits on Congress even at the cost of some legal uncertainty in defining the contours of national and state power. Even so, the Rehnquist Court declined to overrule *Garcia* and simply limited its application in *New York* to those cases where Congress has subjected states to "generally applicable laws" that regulate "private parties" as well as state actors. In sum, Congress may not commandeer a state legislature by, say, requiring a state to enact a state minimum wage law, but Congress, under *Garcia*, may use its interstate commerce power to establish a national minimum wage that applies to both private employers and state employers, congressional action that will inevitably require some action in the state political processes to ensure that the national minimum wage requirements are met by the state acting as employer.

The Section Five, Fourteenth Amendment, Enforcement Power

A third major "New Federalism" doctrine concerns the scope of Congress' power to enforce the constitutional rights found in Section One of the Fourteenth Amendment through the passage of civil rights legislation under Section Five of the Fourteenth Amendment, which expressly grants Congress the power to enforce Section One through appropriate legislation. The scope of Section One, Fourteenth Amendment rights subject to congressional enforcement under Section Five of the Fourteenth Amendment is now quite broad. As originally written and ratified in the eighteenth century, the Bill of Rights – with its celebrated guarantees of freedom of speech and the free exercise of religion – applied to only the national government. However, in the aftermath of the American Civil War, the Fourteenth Amendment was written and ratified as a source of new constitutional limits of the power of the states and a source of new national powers to enforce those limits on state governments. Section One of the Fourteenth Amendment contains both the Equal Protection Clause and one of the Constitution's two Due Process Clauses. The Fourteenth Amendment Due Process Clause has been held by the Court to "incorporate" by reference most of the provisions of the Bill of Rights – including rights of freedom of speech and religion. As a result of this "incorporation," these provisions of the Bill of Rights now limit the authority of the 50 state governments as well as the national government. Therefore Congress has power under Section Five to pass civil rights legislation designed to enforce on the states the constitutional rights in Section One, including the incorporated rights of the Bill of Rights such as the free exercise of religion. Obviously, the scope of this congressional power over the states implicates the constitutional structure of federalism.

In *City of Boerne v. Flores* in 1997, the Rehnquist Court clarified that substantial judicially enforceable limits on Congress' use of its Section Five enforcement power do exist.[12] In *Boerne* the Court invalidated a congressional statute entitled the Religious Freedom Restoration Act (RFRA) as it applied to the 50 states for exceeding the scope of congressional power under Section Five of the Fourteenth Amendment. *Boerne* ultimately turned on the question of the relationship of the Court's understanding of religious freedom protected by the First and Fourteenth Amendments and the statutory right created by Congress in RFRA. In 1990, the Supreme Court in *Smith* confronted the question of the meaning of the Free Exercise of Religion Clause of the First Amendment – a provision incorporated by the Due Process Clause in Section One of the Fourteenth Amendment and thus applicable to the 50 states.[13] The Court decided in *Smith* that the Free Exercise Clause – with one or two narrow exceptions – requires nothing more than that criminal laws be generally applicable and neutral with respect to religion. In *Smith* the Supreme Court upheld a law that criminalized hallucinogens as applied to members of the Native American Church, a group which uses the hallucinogen peyote as a sacrament. The Court upheld the law at issue because it was generally applicable and religion-neutral: it did not target religious drug use but merely placed an incidental burden – however substantial – on the practices of the Native American Church as part of its general restriction on drug use.

The *Smith* decision modified and in effect largely overruled an earlier case, *Sherbert v. Verner*, that held that even religion-neutral laws that incidentally burden religion in a significant way must meet a form of the constitutional test known as strict scrutiny – i.e., the laws must be narrowly tailored to serve a compelling state interest – or such laws violate the Free Exercise Clause.[14] *Smith* thus represented a narrower interpretation of the scope of the constitutional right to the free exercise of religion than the one previously endorsed by the Court in *Sherbert*. Congress responded to *Smith's* new and narrower understanding of religious freedom by passing RFRA, which reinstated by statute *Sherbert's* broader strict scrutiny test for the free exercise of religion. Congress justified RFRA in part as an exercise of Congress' Section Five power to enforce on the states through legislation the constitutional rights found in Section One of the Fourteenth Amendment, the latter including the First Amendment's Free Exercise of Religion Clause through the doctrine of incorporation.

In *Boerne*, the Rehnquist Court invalidated RFRA, as applied to the 50 states, on the grounds that it exceeded Congress' Section Five Enforcement power. The Court first held that congressional legislation passed under Section Five to enforce

---

12   521 U.S. 507 (1997).
13   *Employment Division, Department of Human Resources of Oregon v. Smith*, 494 U.S. 872 (1990).
14   374 U.S. 398 (1963).

a Section One constitutional right must reflect the Supreme Court's interpretation of the Section One constitutional right – not a different interpretation preferred by Congress but rejected by the Court. Significantly, the Court also held that a congressional statute may sweep beyond the Court's conception of the precise scope of the Section One constitutional right, but the statute may do so only in order to prevent or to remedy the violation of that constitutional right as understood by the judicial branch. The Court in *Boerne* held that such legislative sweep beyond the scope of the Court's conception of the Section One constitutional right must be "congruent and proportional" congressional response to the danger of state violation of the Section One right as the scope of that right is understood by the judiciary.

The Court applied this analysis to RFRA and concluded that RFRA's protective strict scrutiny standard was not designed in a "congruent and proportional" manner to prevent or remedy state violations of the constitutional right to the free exercise of religion as defined narrowly by the Court in *Smith*. Rather, the Court concluded that Congress in RFRA was merely expressing its disagreement with the Supreme Court over the correct interpretation of the Free Exercise Clause and that Congress was further attempting to impose its more rights-protective view of the proper interpretation of the free exercise of religion on the 50 states through Section Five of the Fourteenth Amendment. RFRA, in short, was not designed in a proportional and congruent manner to prevent or remedy violations of the free exercise of religion as defined by the Court in *Smith*. Rather, RFRA was designed simply to change the scope of the right back to the *Sherbert* strict scrutiny standard rejected by the Court in *Smith* and to enforce that change on the 50 states. The Court thus concluded that RFRA, as applied to the states, exceeded the scope of Congress' Section Five enforcement power in violation of the Constitution.

The Rehnquist Court justified *Boerne*'s "congruence and proportionality" standard as one necessary to preserve the preeminence of the Supreme Court over Congress in constitutional interpretation and also to preserve state legislative autonomy from undue interference by Congress. Under the principle of the separation of powers, the Court reasoned that judicial determinations of the meaning of the Constitution, including the rights contained in Section One of the Fourteenth Amendment, are authoritative over Congress because the judicial power includes the power to decide with ultimacy what the law of the Constitution means. And under the principle of federalism, Congress may use its Section Five enforcement power to vindicate the Court's understanding of Fourteenth Amendment constitutional rights found in Section One, but not to impose mere congressional policy preferences on the 50 states. The *Boerne* standard, then, is grounded in both the separation of powers and federalism.

Precisely what constitutes a "congruent and proportional" use of Congress' Section Five power has remained a source of controversy on the Court, though a fairly clear pattern has emerged. The Court extends greater latitude to Congress under Section Five when the Section One right or interest Congress is vindicating receives heightened forms of protection under the Supreme Court's precedents. For instance, the Supreme Court's jurisprudence under the Fourteenth Amendment

Equal Protection Clause has evolved into a "tiers of scrutiny" analysis with the tier or form of scrutiny depending upon the kind of state classification involved. State laws that classify on the basis of age or disability receive only rational basis review, the lowest form of scrutiny, and must be found merely rationally related to a legitimate state interest in order to be upheld by the federal courts. State laws that classify on the basis of gender receive intermediate scrutiny, and such classifications must be found substantially related to an important state interest in order to be upheld. And state laws that classify on the basis on race receive strict scrutiny and must be found necessary to a compelling state interest to be upheld. Under these tiers of scrutiny, the vast majority of laws can pass rational basis review but would also fail under the more rights-protective strict scrutiny standard. When Congress is acting under Section Five to limit age or disability discrimination, classifications that need only pass rational basis review to be upheld, the Court has given little deference to Congress under *Boerne*'s proportionality and congruence analysis. Therefore Congress can do little in these areas under Section Five beyond simply prohibiting the constitutionally "irrational" discrimination the Court considers unconstitutional under rational basis review. But when Congress is acting under Section Five to limit by statute forms of discrimination that trigger heightened protection under the Court's tiers of scrutiny, the Court has granted substantial deference to Congress under *Boerne*. In these areas, Congress can sweep well beyond prohibiting by statute only what the Court considers unconstitutional state discrimination under intermediate or strict scrutiny. Congress can even place affirmative obligations on the state to prevent or remedy potential constitutional violations.

For instance, in the *Hibbs*, a case in 2003 concerning gender classifications that trigger the heightened protection of intermediate scrutiny, the Court upheld under *Boerne*'s analysis a congressional statute which mandates that state employers grant an equal amount of substantial family and medical leave to both male and female employees.[15] While it is quite clear that the Equal Protection Clause in no way requires that states extend any family and medical leave in employment at all, the Court upheld this congressional action because it was "congruent and proportional" to the goal of preventing and remedying unconstitutional state gender discrimination. The Court reasoned that if Congress had simply mandated or allowed greater family and medical leave for women than for men this would have reinforced the archaic gender stereotype of women as primary care-givers and would also have stigmatized female employees as a drain on workplace productivity. The Court reasoned further that if Congress had simply prohibited gender discrimination in granting family and medical leave, states might then have opted to grant little or no such leave to state employees. This choice by states would adversely affect women who, as a group, remain the primary family and medical care-givers and do so, in part, because of past and present state action reinforcing gender stereotypes. Therefore, the Court upheld Congress' mandate that states grant an equal minimum of family and medical leave to their employees, male

---

15   *Nevada Department of Human Resources v. Hibbs*, 538 U.S. 721 (2003).

and female, as a "congruent and proportional" response to unconstitutional state gender discrimination.

Abrogation of State Sovereign Immunity

The last major "New Federalism" doctrine concerns the scope of congressional power to abrogate or eliminate "state sovereign immunity," the immunity each state has, as a sovereign, from being sued by a citizen without the state's consent. While the sovereign immunity of the national government has remained largely uncontested, both the doctrine of state sovereign immunity and the scope of congressional power to abrogate that immunity remain sources of controversy in American constitutional law. The primary significance of these questions lies in the form of lawsuit a citizen must use to seek redress when a state violates federal statutory or constitutional rights, an issue which will often determine the precise nature of the remedies the citizen can expect to obtain. A central question here is whether a citizen may sue the state directly and thereby obtain access to the state's treasury to fund any award of money damages the citizen may receive or whether the citizen must sue – instead of the state itself – *state government officials*, officials who may have limited monetary resources, who may not be subject to financial indemnification by the state, and who may possess certain forms of immunity which limit their liability.

In 1793, the U.S. Supreme Court in *Chisholm v. Georgia* held that individual states constituting the United States were not in fact "sovereign" within the federal constitutional design and therefore did not possess the immunity from suit by citizens that sovereigns traditionally had under English common law.[16] *Chisholm* was an unpopular decision, and elected officials responded by writing and ratifying the Eleventh Amendment, which overturned the specific holding of *Chisholm* and (re)established a form of state sovereign immunity. Notably, the express language of the Eleventh Amendment extends sovereign immunity only to the kind of case at issue in *Chisholm*, cases involving a suit against a state by citizens of *another* state or foreign state. The Eleventh Amendment thus did not address the question of a state's sovereign immunity from lawsuit by its own citizens. In 1890 the Supreme Court in *Hans v. Louisiana* held that the Constitution's federal design preserves the basic attributes of state sovereignty and thus that state sovereign immunity extends to suits against a state by citizens of that state as well as citizens of other states and foreign states.[17] The text of the Eleventh Amendment, then, is illustrative rather than exhaustive of the sovereign immunity states possess as part of the federal structure of the Constitution.

State sovereign immunity has been long considered part of the federal structure of constitution by the federal courts, but it is not absolute. Congress has the power,

---

16   2 U.S. (2 Dall.) 419 (1793).
17   134 U.S. 1 (1890).

at least in certain circumstances, to abrogate that immunity and authorize citizen lawsuits against unconsenting states, suits barred by state sovereign immunity. In *Fitzpatrick v. Bitzer* in 1976 the Supreme Court held that Congress may abrogate sovereign immunity when Congress is using its Section Five, Fourteenth Amendment power to enforce by appropriate legislation Section One, Fourteenth Amendment constitutional rights.[18] Congress, then, may authorize a citizen suit against an unconsenting state as long as Congress is using its Section Five power to enforce a constitutional right found (directly or indirectly through the doctrine of incorporation) in Section One of the Fourteenth Amendment.

The Court in *Fitzpatrick v. Bitzer* justified this position by observing that the fundamental purpose of the Fourteenth Amendment was to alter the original federal constitutional design: Section One of the Fourteenth Amendment created new constitutional rights against state governments thus limiting state authority, and Section Five of the Fourteenth Amendment placed new power in the hands of Congress to enforce those rights on the states through the passage of civil rights legislation. Any recognition of an absolute form of state sovereign immunity not subject to congressional abrogation would frustrate this purpose. Therefore the Court concluded that the Fourteenth Amendment implicitly grants to Congress the power to authorize citizen lawsuits against unconsenting states when the object of the lawsuit is the vindication of constitutional right citizens possess against their state government by virtue of the Fourteenth Amendment.

Whether Congress can use its Article I powers – such as the commerce power – to abrogate sovereign immunity has proved to be more controversial. It is well established that Congress can use its commerce power to create federal statutory rights against state governments as long as the creation of the federal statutory right remains within the scope of Congress' delegated and enumerated powers in Article I – such as the power to regulate interstate commerce – and complies with the Court's anti-commandeering principle. Further, these commerce-based statutory rights against state governments may be much broader in scope than the federal constitutional rights against state governments that individuals possess under provisions of the Constitution such as the Fourteenth Amendment. For instance, the Fourteenth Amendment Equal Protection Clause, as interpreted by the Supreme Court, prohibits only constitutionally "irrational" state discrimination against individuals on the basis of their age or disability, the lowest level of constitutional protection in the Court's traditional tiers of scrutiny analysis. Therefore, states engaging in constitutionally "rational" discrimination on the basis of age or disability are not violating the Fourteenth Amendment, though such discrimination may be highly objectionable as a matter of political morality. Congress, then, may use its commerce power over the economic activity of employment to prohibit by statute "rational" forms of employment discrimination on the basis of age or disability that Congress finds morally objectionable. When Congress does so, it creates federal statutory rights under the commerce clause against discrimination in employment, statutory rights which may sweep well beyond the narrower

---

18   427 U.S. 445 (1976).

federal constitutional rights available under the Fourteenth Amendment. Moreover, under *Garcia* and *New York*, Congress may create such rights against states as long as the rights are applicable to private actors as well. In sum, then, while certain forms of discrimination by states are not unconstitutional under the Fourteenth Amendment, Congress may prohibit them by statute as long as Congress is acting under a delegated power such as that over interstate commerce and in compliance with the anti-commandeering principle.

The question then arises: may Congress abrogate state sovereign immunity when Congress is using an Article I power such as the commerce power to create federal statutory rights that extend beyond the constitutional rights established by the Fourteenth Amendment? In *Pennsylvania v. Union Gas* (1989), the Court concluded that Congress may indeed abrogate sovereign immunity using the very broad congressional power over interstate commerce.[19] A plurality of the Court justified this holding by citing the breadth of the congressional power over interstate commerce. A power so broad in scope, the plurality reasoned, must include the power to abrogate state sovereign immunity.

However, in *Seminole Tribe of Florida v. Florida* in 1996, a majority of the Court rejected this argument and held that Congress may not use an Article I power such as the commerce power to abrogate sovereign immunity.[20] The Supreme Court in *Seminole Tribe* observed that Congress' Article I commerce power and state sovereign immunity were both intended as part of the original federal design of the Constitution. As parts of the same original constitutional design, the Court reasoned, Congress' Article I commerce power must have been intended to be exercised in a manner consistent with state sovereign immunity – not in contravention of it. The Court thus concluded that Congress cannot use the commerce power to abrogate state sovereign immunity. As a result of this ruling, commerce-clause based statutory rights may be vindicated only by forms of lawsuit consistent with respect for sovereign immunity – such as a citizen suit against state government officials. The Rehnquist Court in *Seminole Tribe* distinguished *Fitzpatrick v. Bitzer* on the grounds that the Fourteenth Amendment – unlike the commerce clause – was intended to modify the original constitutional design and to provide to Congress, at least implicitly, the power to abrogate sovereign immunity when Congress acts to enforce the Fourteenth Amendment. In sum, then, Congress may abrogate sovereign immunity under its Section Five, Fourteenth Amendment enforcement power, but Congress may not abrogate sovereign immunity under its Article I powers such as the commerce power.

The interaction of these doctrines has created a number of cases where a congressional statute's creation of civil rights is clearly within the broad scope of Congress' power but the statute's abrogation of sovereign immunity to vindicate those rights is not. This occurs because Congress may use its commerce power to prohibit many forms of state discrimination that are not unconstitutional under the Fourteenth Amendment. Therefore many congressional anti-discrimination

---

19   491 U.S. 1 (1989).
20   417 U.S. 44 (1996).

statutes creating statutory rights are within the scope of the congressional commerce power but are outside the scope of the congressional Section Five enforcement power. In these instances, Congress has the authority to pass the anti-discrimination statute (acting under the commerce power) but not the authority to abrogate sovereign immunity (since Congress is acting under the commerce clause, not under Section Five). A number of the Court's recent cases have thus involved the narrow but important issue of whether a congressional prohibition of discrimination uncontestedly within the scope of the congressional commerce power is also within the scope of congressional power under Section Five, which would allow Congress not only to prohibit the state discrimination but also to abrogate state sovereign immunity so that citizens may directly sue states when states violate the statute.

The Supreme Court in *Garrett* in 2001 faced just such a case.[21] At issue was the abrogation of sovereign immunity under the Americans with Disabilities Act (ADA), which required specified private and state employers to make affirmative "reasonable accommodations" for disabled workers. The ADA's anti-discrimination/ accommodation requirements are clearly within the scope of the congressional commerce power (because they regulate the economic activity of employment under *Wickard* and *Lopez*) and are not otherwise barred by principles of federalism such as the anti-commandeering principle (because the ADA is a general regulation applying to both private and state actors under *Garica* and *New York*). Congress, however, may not use the commerce power to abrogate sovereign immunity. Therefore in order to justify the abrogation of sovereign immunity the ADA's requirements must fall within the scope of the congressional Section Five enforcement power in light of *Boerne*'s "congruence and proportionality" analysis. The Court held in *Garrett* that the ADA is outside the scope of congressional power under Section Five because the ADA's affirmative requirement of "reasonable accommodation" of disabled employees is not a "congruent and proportional" response to the minimal danger of constitutionally "irrational" – and thus unconstitutional – state discrimination. In sum, the ADA's basic accommodation requirements are constitutional because they fall within the scope of the congressional commerce power and are consistent with the anti-commandeering principle, but the ADA's abrogation of sovereign immunity is unconstitutional because the ADA's requirements fall outside the scope of the congressional Section Five enforcement power. Congress can thus create a right to "reasonable accommodation" for disabled workers against private and state employers but may not authorize citizen suits against unconsenting states for a violation of these rights. Other forms of lawsuit consistent with respect for state sovereign immunity must be used.

---

21 *Board of Trustees of the University of Alabama v. Garrett*, 531 U.S. 356 (2001).

Conclusion

Perhaps the most distinctive feature of the Rehnquist Court is its "New Federalism": the Court's revival of judicially enforceable federal limits on the power of the national government, a course of action which reversed a half-century or more retreat in American constitutional law away from enforcing such limits. Across a wide range of issues – the scope of the congressional commerce power; the anti-commandeering principle, the scope of Congress' Section Five enforcement power, and the abrogation of state sovereign immunity – the Rehnquist Court displayed a new resolve in asserting the judicial power to defend a foundational principle of the U.S. Constitution: Federalism. The Rehnquist Court's "New Federalism" may be the start of a legal counter-revolution; or it may represent a mere last holding action before judicially enforced federal limits on the national government disappear from the legal landscape forever; or it may be something in between. Only time – and the future decisions of the U.S. Supreme Court – will tell the tale.

Further Reading

Calabresi, Stephen. 2001. Federalism and the Rehnquist Court: A normative defense, 574 *Annals of American Academy of Political & Social Science* 24.

Epstein, Richard. 2006. The federalism decisions of Justices Rehnquist and O'Connor, 58 *Stanford Law Review* 1793.

Fallon, Jr. Richard H. 2002. The "conservative" paths of the Rehnquist Court's federalism decisions, 69 *University of Chicago Law Review* 429.

Kramer, Larry. 2000. Putting the politics back into the political safeguards of federalism, 100 *Columbia Law Review* 215.

Massey, Calvin. 2002. Federalism and the Rehnquist Court, 53 *Hastings Law Journal* 431.

Prakash, Saikrishna B. and John C. Yoo. 2001. The puzzling persistence of process-based federalism theories, 79 *Texas Law Review* 1459.

Rossum, Ralph A. 2001. *Federalism, the Supreme Court and the Seventeenth Amendment: The Irony of Constitutional Democracy* (Lexington Books, 2001).

Yoo, John C. 1997. The judicial safeguards of federalism, 70 *Southern California Law Review* 1311.

Conclusion

Ann Ward and Lee Ward

From classical and biblical antiquity to the contemporary world, federalism has been and remains a permanent political possibility for the arrangement of human society. As this volume amply demonstrates, it is hard to think of many important political thinkers who did not at some stage in their careers reflect seriously upon the virtues and defects of federalism. We have seen how the theory and practice of federalism has developed and evolved in tandem over the centuries. From the loose confederations of independent city-states in antiquity, to the complex relations of secular and religious institutions in the Bible, and the Catholic and Reformation thinking derived from this tradition, we see federalism in its various diverse forms mold and shape beliefs about the nature of a good society. In early-modern Europe we see a new and distinctively modern idea of federalism emerge from a colossal intellectual struggle with the predominant theory of unitary sovereignty that is absolute and indivisible.

The early American Republic presented this new idea of modern federalism in its most ambitious form up to that point in time with the creation of a modern liberal democratic state based on the principle of constitutional federalism. Whereas America profoundly clarified the distinction between confederation and a new idea of the federal state, a distinction present but often implicit in early-modern European thought, nineteenth- and twentieth-century European federal theory and practice established the outlines of a restored or refurbished version of the older idea of federation, this time adapted to the complex political realities of modern Europe. Contemporary federal theory and practice are, then, both the inheritors of a rich legacy of federal experience and at the same time sources of constant innovation in the federalist tradition.

Despite the considerable developments in federalism over the centuries, the claims put forth as to the superiority, or at least the value, of federalism as a model for political society have remained remarkably stable for a very long time. Federalism has, and continues to be, praised for its ability to provide for common defense and security, to protect civil and religious liberty, to promote an ideal of self-government consistent with cultural, ethnic, linguistic, and regional distinctiveness, and its capacity to institutionalize efficient administration, especially in large complex nations. These claims reflect both an empirical and a normative dimension of the various phenomena described by the concept of federalism. Or to put it another way, what we have seen through the course of this volume is that federalism includes an instrumental element relating to structures and processes, in addition to representing an end in itself.

The conceptual distinction between the instrumental, and for want of a better term "deontological," aspect of federalism is very real, but so too is the undeniable relationship between the dual characteristics of the federal idea. In being both a way to design institutions and a way of thinking about and approaching the political world – what Preston King and Michael Burgess identify as the relationship between federation and federalism (King 1982, Burgess 2006) – federalism is both instrumental to specific goods, while simultaneously being the embodiment of a certain conception of the good simply. It is the complex relation between these dimensions of federalism that makes it such an important, but nevertheless elusive, subject for the student of political things. In this volume we have seen federal thinking impacting unitary states and regions of the world with little formal experience of federalism, even as we considered long established federal states and federations struggling with the challenges posed to national cohesion by federal pressures. The federal cloak of many colors seems at times to more closely resemble an entire complex, multi-hued ensemble.

While it is wise to avoid trying to define federalism rigidly or to reduce its many complex experiences to a few representative types, it is perhaps fair to observe that historically the test for the importance, or even viability, of the federal model of government rests on a range of variables. These typically include a federation's duration, prosperity, cohesiveness, equitable distribution of wealth and power, its capacity to protect human rights and civil liberties, and its ability to harmonize sub-national self-government with the needs of national unity. However, perhaps the most definitive conclusion we can draw from this volume is that the real measure of the value and importance of federalism is the persistent desire of human beings from a diverse array of national, ethnic, cultural, religious, and historical backgrounds to choose to live in and maintain federal systems. In both its instrumental and deontological sense, federalism stands or falls on the basis of its capacity to promote human flourishing.

The meaning of human flourishing is, of course, the subject of intense philosophical and even metaphysical debate. Human flourishing may be a feature of the stable, and indeed unchanging, properties of a fixed human nature, or it may be a historically contingent concept constantly adapting to the conditions of cultural and temporal relativity produced by the development, progressive or regressive, of human society. Obviously a volume on federalism could not hope to resolve this philosophical debate. However, defenders of federalism can at least look to the collected studies presented herein as proof that federalism as a political construct animated by a flexible and experimental spirit is uniquely attuned to the intellectual and practical contours of this debate about the nature and requirements of human flourishing. In this age of deepening globalization marked by ever greater economic and political integration, as well as ever greater cultural homogenization, it is possible that federalism will prove ultimately to be, like traditional empires, an outmoded and illegitimate form of political organization. Then again, this volume has tried to suggest that admirers of federalism may have reasonable confidence that in a world of increasing interconnectedness, federalism may become an even more attractive and important political option for societies in the future.

References

Burgess, Michael. 2006. *Comparative Federalism: Theory and Practice*. New York: Routledge.

King, Preston. 1982. *Federalism and Federation*. London: Croom Helm.

Index

(References to illustrations are in **bold**)

Adams, John 196, 212
   Rutherford's influence 62
Africa
   communitarianism 471
   diversity 463
   federalism 459, 479–80
      see also confederative cycle
Africans, in Jefferson's federalism 217
Agamben, G. 299
Albertus Magnus 34
Alcibiades, and destruction of Athens 26–7
Alcmaeonidae family 17
Althusius, Johannes 13, 331
   censura concept 76, 83–4, 87
   consociation 71, 76–80, **81**, 82–7, 280, 334, 339
      levels 334–5
   covenantalism 41, 55
   federalist thought 41–2
   Hueglin on 345
   on inequality 82
   man, as *zoon politikon* 337
   Politica 75, 78, 83, 84, 87, 333–5, 339, 340, 341, 342, 344, 345
   on politics 76
   symbiotic association doctrine 55–6
   Yugoslav Constitution (1974), influences 338–46
American Civil War 171, 172, 195, 201, 234, 237, 238–9, 262–3, 414
   see also slavery
American Constitution
   10th Amendment 216
   14th Amendment 194, 203, 234–5, 238, 551
      Supreme Court, enforcement power 557–61, 562
   17th Amendment 194, 203
   amendments 185
   Antifederalist critique 170, 195–7
   compact theory of 221
   elections 188–9
   federalism, extent of 272
   Framers 172, 173, 176, 191, 225, 226, 232, 236, 237, 241, 246
   Hume's influence 121
   as military bargain 414, 423
   powers, state/national distribution 202
   President's power 184–5
   slavery in 273–4
   and the Supreme Court 199, 203, 205–6
   taxation power 187–8
   Tocqueville on 171, 200–1, 228
   see also Articles of Confederation
American federalism
   Americanness of 231–5
   Elazar on 402–5
   European federalism, comparison 359
   features 169
   mixed nature of 169–70, 193–4
   present-day 202–6
   as republican experiment 492–3
   and secession 172, 237
   sovereignty 548
   Tocqueville on 197–200, 225–41, 286–7, 539–40
   see also American Constitution
American Founders 121, 124, 125, 134, 272, 417, 423, 486, 492

American Union 171, 201, 217, 221, 225, 230, 232, 234, 264
Amsterdam, Treaty of (1998) 356
ANC (African National Party) 256
Andreotti, Giulio 327
anti-republicanism, in Jefferson's federalism 218–19
Antifederalists
    American Constitution 170
    "aristocratic" government, fear of 204
    Bill of Rights 193, 203–4
    critique of American Constitution 195–7
Aquinas, Thomas 12, 14, 31
    federalism, approximation of 39–40
    on hierarchies 38, 39–40
    on the *polis* 35, 36–7
    on self-sufficiency 37–8
    typology of societies 38–9
    works
        De Regno 34–5, 37
        Summa Theologiae 34
Argentina, federalism 519, 524
Aristotle 22
    polis, theory 35, 36
armed forces, Montesquieu on 115–16
Aroney, Nicholas 12, 14
Articles of Confederation (US) 169, 173, 175, 180, 188, 265
    defects 247, 271–2
    main features 467
    see also American Constitution
Asante empire
    Charter of the Golden Stool 477, 478
    confederative cycle 476–9
association, Rousseau on 140–1
Athenians, political virtue 111
Athens
    democracy, emergence 17–18
    destruction, and Alcibiades 26–7
    as "idea" 18
    imperialism 21, 22–3
Atlanticism 354
Australasian Federal Convention (1897-8) 490
Australia
    colonization 487
    Commonwealth formation 485
    constitutionalism 486
    federalism 415, 459–60, 490–1
        as innovative constitutionalism 497

Australian Constitution 485
    English common law input 487–9
    judicial review in 495–6
    major conventions 490–1
    rights 496
    sovereignty 494–5
    Westminster model 487

Baker, J.W. 53
Bamberg, S. 62
Barrera, Guillaume 279
Barroso, Jose Manuel 367, 378
Beaud, Olivier, *Théorie de la Fédération* 294
Bedouin
    Ibn Khaldun on 543–4, 545
    tribalism, and Islam 461, 541–3
    vs sedentary life 543–7
Belgium
    decentralization 444
    Flemish community 446
    language protection 448–9
    nationalist parties 449
berith 52, 391
    see also foedus
Berlin Declaration (2007) 374
Bill of Rights (US) 215, 557, 558
    Antifederalists 193, 203–4
Bodin, Jean 5, 334
    Six Books of the Republic 94
    on sovereignty 94
        responses to 94–5
Bradford, William 62
Brandt, Willy 326
Brazil, federalism 519, 521–2, 523, 527
Bretton Woods system 323, 324
Brewster, William 62
Brownson, Orestes 237
"Brutus" (Antifederalist) 196, 197, 203
Bryce, James 4
Buchanan, James, on secession 267–8
Bullinger, Heinrich 13
    on the covenant 53, 54
    influence on Knox 56
    theologico-political federalism 56
Burgess, Michael 1, 3, 4, 568
Bush, George W. 202
Buthelezi, Mangosuthu 256

Cabell, Joseph 212, 213
Calhoun, John C.

nullification 245, 246
  on slavery 246
  theory of federalism 171–2, 245, 247–58, 292
    concurrent majority principle 172, 248, 250, 251, 252
    consensus rule 248–9, 256–7
    majorities 248
    significance 255
    state veto rights 247–8
  works
    A Discourse on the Constitution 246
    A Disquisition on Government 246
Canada
  federalism 271
    decentralization 443–4
    First Nation community, self-government 444
    Inuit community
      asymmetric status 446
      self-government 444
  see also Quebec
Castaldi, Roberto 280
censura concept, Althusius 76, 83–4, 87
centralization
  France 283
  Proudhon on 287–8
Charles IV, Holy Roman Emperor 92
Charter of Fundamental Rights, opt-outs 376, 378
Chávez, Hugo 527
Christian Commonwealth 14
Christianity, Islam, comparison, Tocqueville on 537
church, state separation 12, 35–6, 57, 538
  Tocqueville on 537
Cicero, Marcus Tullius, on social covenanting 50
citizen, term 540
citizenship, and democracy 540
civic virtue 169
Civil Rights Act (1964) 194
Cleisthenes 17
collegia, in Althusius's consociation 77–8, **81**, 86
Colorni, Eugenio 316
Common Band, Scotland (1557) 56, 57
communitarianism, African 471
compacts 385, 393
conciliar movement 12, 41

confederacy 176–7
  definition 466
confederalism
  EU as 368
  and globalization 409
confederation 32, 76
  characteristics 292
  definitions 465–6
  empire, relationship 468
  federalism, distinction 289–90, 291, 468–9
  Iroquois 466
  proposal, Yugoslavia 254–5
  purpose 293
  types 285
  see also Articles of Confederation (US)
confederative cycle 468–72, 479–80
  African roots 471–2
  Asante empire 476–9
  decline 469
  Egyptian dynastic period 473–6
  evolution 469
  model **470**
  reemergence 470
consensus rule
  Calhoun's federalism 248–9, 256–7
  Roman Republic 249
consociation
  Althusius 71, 76–80, **81**, 82–7, 280, 334, 339
  heresy 83–4, 84–5
  Lijphart's model 172, 245, 250–1
  Northern Ireland 251
  religion 80–6
  schools, purpose 86
Constant, Benjamin 283
  federalism 284–5
constitution
  connotations of term 373
  English 114, 115
Constitutional Convention (US) (1787) 125, 126, 175, 176, 189, 190, 215, 416, 421
constitutionalism 494–5
  Elazar on 397
  innovative, Australian federalism as 497
contracts 385, 393
contractualism 49
Cooper, Robert 17
Coppet Group 284

covenantal political theology 13
covenantalism
    Althusius 41, 55
    Puritanism 57–8
    Scotland 56–7, 58–9
covenanting
    political, Elazar 395–9
    social, Cicero on 50
covenants
    Biblical 49, 51–2
        as basis of federalism 392–9
        Book of Judges 51
        Bullinger on 53, 54
        creationist basis 63
        definition 13, 53, 385, 395–6
        Deuteronomy 51, 52
        Elazar on 397–8
        Genesis 52, 53–4
        and idolatry 52
        Israel 51
        Psalm 89
        in Reformational thought 53
    Bullinger on 53
    moral dimension 393
Crawford, William 218
Cullen, Daniel 73
Cusanus, Nicolas 12, 31
    De Concordantia Catholica 41
    federalist thought 41

Darius, King of the Persians 19
Daumas, François 473, 475
Davis, Rufus 4
de Coulanges, Fustel, *La Cité antique* 289
de Freitas, Shaun 12, 13, 14
de Klerk, F.W. 255, 256
de la Court, Pieter, *True Interests* 97
de Tracy, Destutt 214, 222
DeBruyn, Martyn 281
decentralization
    Belgium 444
    and federalism 43
    Spain 444–5
    UK 445
Decentralization Theorem 426–7
Declaration of Independence (1776) 173, 228, 237, 265, 272
Delian league, and Athenian imperialism 22–3
Delors, Jacques 352

democracies, Hamilton on 126
democracy
    Athens 17–18
    and citizenship 540
    consociational model 172, 245, 249, 250–1
    and federalism 297, 298, 310–11, 430
    federalism, distinction 401
    and homogeneity 303–4
    liberal, Tocqueville on 540
    and military effectiveness 18, 19
    parliamentarism, opposition 302–3
    republic, distinction 178
    Schmitt on 302–4
    Westminster model 249
Demos, and *Nomos* 304
Deutsch, Karl 414
Diderot, Denis 144, 145, 146, 147
Diodotus 25, 27
Djordjević, Jovan, *Remarks on the Yugoslav Model of Federalism* 331
Douglas, Stephen 273
Dred Scott decision 194, 268, 274
Duchacek, Ivo 4
Duguit, Léon 283
Duplessis-Mornay, Philippe 13
    Vindiciae Contra Tyrannos 55
Dutch Republic 71, 72, 93
    federalism 95, 97–100, 118
    Stadtholderless period 97
    see also Holland

ECSC (European Coal and Steel Community) 319, 368
ECU (European Currency Unit) 324
EDC (European Defence Community), proposal 319, 320
EEC (European Economic Community) 321, 322
  neo-functionalism 355
Egypt, dynastic period, confederative cycle 473–6
Einaudi, Luigi 316
Elazar, Daniel 1, 3, 6, 34, 50, 51, 52, 75, 331, 368, 385
    on the American city 403–4
    on American federalism 402–5
    on Biblical covenants 397–8
    on constitutionalism 397
    legacy 391

political covenanting 392–9
　　decline 398–9
　　strong/weak varieties of 392–3
　　on political culture 405–8
　　　criticism of 405–6
　　theory of federalism 400–2
　　works
　　　Covenant and Commonwealth 49
　　　Covenant and Polity in Biblical Israel 49
empire
　　concept 468
　　confederation, relationship 468
EMS (European Monetary System) 324
English Civil War, Hume on 122
The Enlightenment, and European flourishing 538–9
EP (European Parliament) 323, 324, 325, 372
　　direct election 353
　　Lisbon Treaty (2007) 376
　　Treaty of European Unity (1984), adoption 326
EPC (European People's Congress) 321
EU (European Union)
　　as confederalism 368
　　creation 353
　　distribution of functions 431
　　enlargement 360, 373
　　federalism in 369–71
　　fiscal federalism 388, 430–8
　　fiscal policies
　　　coordination 432–4
　　　　benefits 432–3
　　　　models 433
　　　redistribution policy 435–6
　　Stability and Growth Pact 433–4
　　stabilization policy 431–2, 434, 437
　　subsidiarity 371, 376, 433
Europe, Council of 318–19, 370
European Commission 373
　　proposed reduction 375
European Constitutional Treaty (2005)
　　Dutch rejection 374
　　failure of 281, 351, 353, 358, 363–4
　　as federal model 361–2, 373
　　French rejection 374
　　Lisbon Treaty (2007), comparison 376–7
　　need for 360–1
　　ratification process 373–4
　　top-down structure 360
European federalism 281
　　American federalism, comparison 359
　　benefits 354
　　citizen's involvement 354–5
　　Constitutional Treaty, as model of 361–2
　　future 377–8
　　incrementalism 355–6
　　Movimento Federalista Europeo 317
　　origins 354
　　as process 358
European integration 281, 351, 352–3, 362–3, 368
　　early phase 354–6
European Union, Treaty *see* Maastricht
European Unity, Treaty (1984) 326
Evans, M.S. 50

family, in Althusius's consociation **81**, 86
Federal Convention *see* Constitutional Convention (US)
federal republic, Montesquieu on 107–8, 117–18
federal state, unitary state, distinction 292–3
federalism
　　administrative theory of 418–19
　　Africa 459, 479–80
　　in Althusius's thought 41–2
　　in Aquinas's thought 39–40
　　Argentina 519, 524
　　asymmetrical 445–7
　　Australia 415, 459–60, 490–1
　　benefits of 567–8
　　Brazil 519, 521–2, 523, 527
　　Calhoun's theory 171–2, 245, 247–58, 292
　　Canada 271
　　　see also Quebec
　　characteristics 246
　　classical, postmodern, comparison 442–3
　　comparative approach 4
　　competitive 206
　　conceptual diversity 2
　　concurrent majority principle 172, 248, 250, 251, 252
　　conditions for formation 414
　　confederation, distinction 289–90, 291, 468–9

in Constant's thought 284–5
constitutional 370, 371, 442–3
    and the Lisbon Treaty (2007) 375–7
contradictions 175
cooperative 430
    India 460, 507, 512–15
covenantal roots 392–9
current relevance 1
in Cusanus's thought 41
and decentralization 43
definitions 33–4, 49, 137, 368, 400, 464–5
and democracy 297, 298, 310–11, 430
democracy, distinction 401
and difference 137–8
Dutch Republic 95, 97–100, 118
Elazar's theory 400–2
in the EU 369–71
extent of, in the American Constitution 272
in *Federalist Papers* 176–91
feudal
    and absolute monarchy 131
    amd the perfect commonwealth 131–2
    in Hume's thought 122, 129–33
    Maastricht Treaty 388
    Majocchi 387–8
    role of barons 130, 133
fiscal *see* fiscal federalism main entry
and the French Revolution 284
functional 370, 371
German Empire 101–4
and globalization 408
Greek city states 15, 16–17, 21, 27, 28
in the Hebrew Republic (OT) 99
in Herodotus's *Histories* 16–17
Hugo on 101–2
and human flourishing 568
in Hume's perfect commonwealth 72–3, 122, 123–9, 133–4
and individuals 226
Jefferson's theory 170–1, 210–23
as justice 402
in Kant's thought 73–4, 155–63
Latin America 460–1, 518–29
Le Fur on 289–94
and leadership 16–17, 20–1
Leibniz on 103–4
Lincoln's 172–3, 262–3, 270–1

Mexico 286, 519, 521, 523–4, 526, 527, 538
military, *Federalist Papers* 182
models 246–7
Montesquieu on 16
as multi-level-governance 369
and the nation state 408–9
origins 12, 14
Poland 145
polyvalent *see* polyvalent federalism main entry
postmodern 388–9, 408–9
    classical, comparison 442–3
    decentralization 443
    devolution 443
    features 441–2, 450–1
    flexibility 451
    formal/informal asymmetry 445–7
    linguistic protection/promotion 447–8
    regional nationalist parties 448–50
psychology of 182–3
in Quidort's thought 40–1
republicanism, distinction 401
Riker's theory 414–20
in Rousseau's thought 73, 137–42, 147–8
Schmitt on 306–11
scope 3
and secession 261, 263
secular 76–80
as social contract 146
and sovereignty 142, 290
    reconciliation 104
Spinelli's 316–28
Spinoza on 99–100
as subsidiarity 433
theologico-political 54–5, 63
    Bullinger 56
    in early American history 61–3
    Rutherford 58–61
theorists 3
Venezuela 519–20, 521, 522, 523, 524–5, 527
Yugoslavia 253–5
see also American federalism; European federalism
Federalist Paper no. 1: 492
Federalist Paper no. 9: 117–18, 121, 123, 126, 169, 175, 176–7, 177–8, 183–4
    on democracies 126

nationalist vision 184
on republican government 121
Federalist Paper no. 10: 195–6, 248
Federalist Paper no. 15: 179
Federalist Paper no. 16, national principle 179–80
Federalist Paper no. 39: 193, 246, 272
Federalist Paper no. 43: 266
Federalist Paper no. 44: 188
Federalist Paper no. 45: 522
Federalist Paper no. 62: 189
Federalist Papers
    federalism in 176–91
    military federalism 182
federations, modern 43
Fenna, Alan 75
Festival of Federation 284
Fiorina, Morris 202
First Nation community, Canada 444
fiscal equivalence, principle 427
fiscal federalism
    classical model 387, 425–7
    EU 388, 430–8
    India 508–10
    lower levels of government 437
    Maastricht Treaty (1992) 388, 429
    new model 436–7
    new theory 429–30
    public choice approach 387–8, 429
    resources distribution, mechanisms 437–8
    varieties of 508
Flinn, R. 59
foedus 32, 33, 139, 385, 391
    see also berith
Foley, Michael 443
Fott, David 72
France, centralization 283, 290
    Tocqueville on 286
French Revolution, and federalism 284
Friedrich, Carl Joachim 4, 49, 75

Gelon of Syracuse 20–1
German Empire 71
    federalism 101–4
    political form 92–3, 101
    Pufendorf's criticism 96
Germanic Confederation (1815) 290
Gerson, Jean 41

Giddens, Anthony, *Modernity and Self-Identity* 450
Gierke, Otto von 75, 293
Giscard d'Estaing, Valéry 324, 373
globalization
    and confederalism 409
    and federalism 408
Golden Bull (1356) 92
Good Friday Agreement, Northern Ireland (1998) 172, 252–3, 445
    consociational democracy 251
Gough, J.W. 59
The Social Contract 49
government
    energy in, need for 181–2, 187
    functions, Montesquieu on 113
    monarchical, Montesquieu on 114–15
    powers
        Montesquieu on 112, 114, 117
        separation of 114
Great Society, economic program 194
Greek city states, federalism 15, 16–17, 21, 27, 28
Greve, Michael 203
Grotius, Hugo
    De Jure Belli et Pacis 95
    natural law theory 95
    on sovereignty 95

Haas, Ernest 370
Habib, Khalil Marwan 461
happiness, in Jefferson's federalism 214–15
Harrington, James, *Commonwealth of Oceana* 123
Hartford Convention (1814-15) 219
Hassner, Pierre 143, 145, 147–8
Hebrew Republic (OT), federalism 99
Helvetian Confederation 285, 290
Henderson, Alexander 58
heresy, consociation 84–5
Hermann, Julian Durazo 460
Herodotus, *Histories* 11, 15, 16–17
hierarchies, Aquinas on 38, 39–40
Hindenburg, FM von 305
Hirschmann, Ursula 316
history, and Kant's federalism 161
Hobbes, Thomas 5, 539
    political system 152–3
    social contract theory 42
Holland, dominance in Dutch Republic 93

Holy Roman Empire *see* German Empire
homogeneity, and democracy 303–4
Hooker, Thomas 62
House of Representatives (US) 196
Hueglin, Thomas 3, 75, 341
   on Althusius 345
Hugo, Ludolph 91
   De Statu Regionum Germaniae 101
   on federalism 101–2
human flourishing, and federalism 568
human nature, in Kantian thought 154
human rights
   in Kant's federalism 158–9
   see also rights
Hume, David
   on the English Civil War 122
   History of England, feudal federalism in 122, 129–33
   "Idea of a Perfect Commonwealth" 72, 121–2
   perfect commonwealth 72–3, 122, 123–9, 133–4
   and feudal federalism 131–2
   on republican government 132
   US Constitution, influence on 121
Hyneman, Charles 62

Ibn Khaldun 461, 535
   on arts in Islam 539
   on the Bedouin 543–4, 545
   on holy war 547
   Muqaddimah 536, 543
   on reason 541
   on royal authority 541–3, 545–6
India
   Constitution 506, 509, 514–15
   cooperative federalism 460, 507, 512–15
   fiscal federalism 508–10
   Inter-State Council 512–13
   local-level governance 510–11
   plurality 503–4
   states, self-rule 505–6
   Union government/states, power sharing 506–8
Indian Constitution 506
the individual
   and federalism 226
   and sovereignty 539
   in Titoism 337–8
inequality, Althusius on 82

Inuit community, Canada 444
   asymmetric status 446
Iroquois confederation 466
Islam
   arts, Ibn Khaldun on 539
   basis of 540–1
   and Bedouin tribalism 461, 541–3
   Christianity, comparison, Tocqueville on 537
   sovereignty 546–7, 548
Israel, and the covenant 51

Jacobinism 284
Jay, John 169, 175, 176
Jefferson, Thomas 196
   Kentucky Resolutions 216, 219, 221
   the people, trust in 211
   on republicanism 210
   on separation of powers 211–12
   theory of federalism 170–1, 210–23
      and Africans 217
      anti-republicanism 218–19
      challenges to 215–20
      contradictions 221
      current relevance 222–3
      happiness 214–15
      liberty 213–14
      and Native Americans 217, 218
      practicality 215–20, 221–2
      secession 218, 219
      security 213, 218, 221–2
      slavery 219, 220
      and states' admission 217
      strict construction doctrine 215–16
      war 221–2
Jellinek, Georg 290, 291, 292
Jordan, Sara 459
Jordan, Will 72, 73
judicial review, Australian Constitution 495–6
justice, federalism as 402

Kalergi, Richard Couenhove, *Pan Europa* 369
Kant, Immanuel
   critical turn 152
   federalism 73–4, 155–63
      distinctiveness 162–3
      and history 161
      and human rights protection 158–9

international 156–7, 160–1
    NATO-type defense system,
        comparison 160
    realism 162–3
    UN system, comparison 158–9
on human nature 154
on the moral politician 154, 155, 161–2
purpose 151–2
on republican government 154–5,
    159–60
Rousseau's influence 152
works
    Critique of Judgment 151
    Critique of Practical Reason 151
    Critique of Pure Reason 151
    Idea for a Universal History 156, 161
    Metaphysics of Morals 157
    Perpetual Peace 161
    Theory and Practice 161
on world government 156–7
Kardelj, Edvard 6, 280, 281
    life 335–6
    on self-management 332, 336–7, 343
    works
        *Self-Management and the Political
            System* 336
        Socialist Democracy 336
        Ways of Democracy 332, 336
Kentucky Resolutions, Jefferson 216, 219,
    221
Kercheval, Samuel 211
King, Preston 4, 32, 368, 568
Kleinerman, Benjamin 386
Kleon 25
Knippenberg, Joseph 73, 74
Knox, John, Bullinger's influence 56
Koch, Bettina 71

Laeken Declaration (2001) 371–3, 375
Lafayette, Marquis de 219
Latin America, federalism 460–1, 518–29
    American influence 518–19, 520, 528
    centralization tendencies 520
    constitutional features 521–5
    decentralization, rise of 522, 523, 524
    doctrines 518–21
    features 528–9
    federal supremacy 522
    municipalities 519
    political dimension 525–8

law cases
    *Board of Trustees of Univ of Alabama v.
        Garrett* (2001) 564
    Brown v. Board of Education (1955) 194
    Chisholm v. Georgia (1793) 561
    City of Boerne v. Flores (1997) 558, 559,
        560
    Fitzpatrick v. Bitzer (1976) 562
    Garcia v. San Antonio Metropolitan TA
        (1985) 556, 557
    Gonzales v. Raich (2005) 553, 554
    Hans v. Louisiana (1890) 561
    Marbury v. Madison (1803) 495
    National League of Cities v. Usery (1976)
        205, 556
    Nevada Dept of Human Resources v. Hibbs
        (2003) 560
    New York v. United States (1992) 554, 556
    Pennsylvania v. Union Gas (1989) 563
    Prigg v. Pennsylvania (1842) 274
    Printz v. United States (1997) 554
    Seminole Tribe of Florida v. Florida (1996)
        563
    Sherbert v. Verner (1963) 558
    South Dakota v. Dole (1987) 555
    United States v. Lopez (1995) 205, 553,
        554
    United States v. Morrison (2000) 205, 553
    Wickard v. Filburn (1942) 202, 552, 553,
        554
Lawler, Peter Augustine 171
Le Fur, Louis 6, 279
    federal state, unitary state, distinction
        292–3
    on federalism 289–94
    on sovereignty 291–2
    Thesis of 1896 289–94
        criticism of 294–5
leadership, and federalism 16–17, 20–1
Leibniz, Gottfried von 91
    De Suprematu Principum Germaniae 102
    on federalism 103–4
    on sovereignty 102–3
Lewis, Bernard 537, 540
liberty
    contractual 394
    covenantal 394
    in Jefferson's federalism 213–14
    natural vs federal 396
    Proudhon on 288

Lijphart, Arend
    democracy, consociational model 172, 245, 249, 250–1
    majority rule 250
    minority veto 250–1, 256
Lincoln, Abraham
    Cooper Union speech 273
    federalism 172–3, 262–3, 270–1
    Lyceum Address (1838) 200
    secession crises 263–74
        speeches 264, 267, 268–70
    on slavery 269, 273
Lisbon Treaty (2007) 281–2, 362, 430
    and constitutional federalism 375–7
    European Constitutional Treaty (2005), comparison 376–7
    European Council 375, 376
    European Parliament 376
    provisions 375
    ratification 367, 377
Locke, John 539
    Second Treatise of Government 42
    social contract theory 42–3
Louisiana Purchase 171, 209, 210
    problems 217–18
Lutz, Donald 62
Lycian republic 117, 118
Lycurgus
    economic reforms 110
    social reforms 110–11
Lydall, H. 342

Maastricht Treaty (1992) 281
    federalism 357–8
        fiscal 388, 429
    ratification 359
    stabilization policy 434
    three-pillar structure 356
McAllister, D. 51
McCullock, Matthew 280
MacDonald, Sara 11, 12, 14
McGarry, J. 445
McNamara, Peter 170, 171
Madison, James 125, 126, 169, 175, 176, 184
    Federalist no. 10: 177, 248
    Federalist no. 14, democracy/republic distinction 178
    Federalist no. 39: 246, 272
    Federalist no. 43: 266
    Federalist no. 51, division/separation of powers 178
Magna Charta 130
Mahdi, Muhsin 547
Majeed, Akhtar 460
Majocchi, Alberto, fiscal federalism 387–8
majority rule, Lijphart on 250
Mandela, Nelson 256
    Long Walk to Freedom 257
Manent, Pierre 237
Marathon, battle 18, 19, 27
Marchildon, Gregory, post-modern federalism 388–9
Mason, R. 57, 63
Mathie, William 172, 173
Melian dialogue 26
Merkel, Angela 374
Mexico, federalism 286, 519, 521, 523–4, 526, 527
    Tocqueville on 538
military effectiveness, and democracy 18, 19
Miltiades 19
Milton, John 58
Missouri Compromise (1820) 219, 222–3, 273
Mitrany, David 370
Mitterand, François 324, 326
money, Montesquieu on 112
Monnet, Jean 319, 320, 352, 355, 369, 370
Montesquieu, Baron de 15
    on armed forces 115–16
    on federal republics 107–8, 117–18
    on federalism 16
    on government functions 113
    on Greek democracy 108
    on monarchical government 114–15
    on money 112
    on nobility, role of 114–15
    on political
        liberty 113
        survival 112
        virtue 109–10, 111
    on regimes 108
    on republican government 112, 114, 117
    on republicanism 112, 210
    Spirit of the Laws 11, 72, 107, 108, 116, 210
Moots, Glenn A. 385

moral politician, in Kantian thought 154, 155, 161–2
More, Thomas, *Utopia* 123
Moreno, L. 441
Morgan, E.S. 58, 62
Moro, Aldo 324
Movimento Federalista Europeo 317
multi-level-governance, federalism as 369
Mycale, battle 21
Mytilene, debate about 25–6, 27

Narmer Palette 472
nation building, in Rousseau's thought 144
nation state, and federalism 408–9
National Australasian Covention (1891) 490
national identity, construction 143–4
National Party, South Africa 255–6
national principle, *Federalist* 16: 179–80
nationalism, in Rousseau's thought 143–9
Native Americans, in Jefferson's federalism 217, 218
NATO-type defense system, Kant's federalism, comparison 160
natural law theory
    Grotius 95
    Pufendorf 95
natural right, in Rousseau's thought 145–6
neo-functionalism, EEC 355
New Deal program (US) 194, 201–2
New Orleans, Battle of (1814) 218, 219
Nice Treaty (2001) 356, 371, 375
Nomos 301–2
    and *Demos* 304
Northern Ireland
    Assembly 446
        concurrent majority principle 252
    consociation 251–2
    Good Friday Agreement (1998) 172, 252–3, 445
    taxation 445
Nowlin, Jack 461
nullification 171–2, 216
    in Calhoun's thought 245, 246
    controversy 201–2
    doctrine 199

Oates, W.E. 425, 427, 428, 430, 434
Ottoman Turks, Tocqueville on 540

Pan-European Union 369

Papen, Franz von 305
parliamentarism, democracy, opposition 302–3
Partito d'Azione 317, 325
Patai, Raphael 544
Patapan, Haig 459
Patrici, Nicolas 279, 280
Peloponnesian War 11, 15, 16, 22, 27
perfect commonwealth, Hume 72–3, 122, 123–9, 133–4
Pericles, funeral oration 24–5
Persian Wars 11, 15
Pertini, Sandro 316
Pflimlin, Pierre 327
Philadelphia Convention *see* Constitutional Convention (US)
Philip of Macedon 111
philosophy, theology, distinction 32, 35
Plato, *Republic* 27, 123
Plattner, Marc 143, 145
Plutarch, *Life of Lycurgus* 110
Poland, federalism 145
polis
    Aquinas on 35, 36–7
    Aristotle's theory 35, 36
politeuma, in Althusius's consociation 78, 79, **81**, 86, 87
politia, in Althusius's consociation 79–80, **81**, 86
political culture, Elazar on 405–8
political liberty
    Montesquieu on 113
    threats to 114–15
political right, in Rousseau's thought 139, 144, 146, 147, 148
political survival, Montesquieu on 112
political system, in Hobbes's thought 152–3
political virtue
    Athenians 111
    conditions for 111
    Montesquieu on 109–10, 111
politics, Althusius on 76
polyvalent federalism 280, 281, 331, 338
    origins of term 332–3
    viability of 346–7
Progressive movement (US) 201
Proudhon, Joseph 284, 285
    on centralization 287–8
    Du Principe Fédératif 287
    on liberty 288

on self-government 288
province, in Althusius's consociation **81**
Pryce-Jones, David 538, 543
public choice approach, fiscal federalism 387–8, 429
"Publius" (Federalists) 169, 171, 176, 177, 178, 180, 181, 182, 183, 185, 186, 189, 190, 492
Publius journal 391
Pufendorf, Samuel 5
   German Empire, criticism of 96
   natural law theory 95
   Present State of Germany 96
   on sovereignty 95–6
Purcell, E. 202
Puritanism, covenantalism 57–8

Quebec
   asymmetric status 446
   federal transfers to 444
   language protection 447
   nationalist parties 449
   and right to secession 261–2, 449
Quidort, Jean 12, 31
   federalist thought 40–1

Raath, Andries 12, 13, 14
rational-choice theory, in Riker's federalism 386–7, 421–2
Read, James H. 171
reason, Ibn Khaldun on 541
rebellion, secession as 172
Reformed Christianity 13
regimes, Montesquieu on 108
Rehnquist Court (1986-2005) decisions 551–65
   14 Amendment, section 5, enforcement power 557–61, 562
   anti-commandeering principle 554–7
   interstate commerce regulation 552–4
   Religious Freedom Restoration Act, invalidation of 558, 559
   State Sovereign Immunity, abrogation 561–4
Rehnquist, William H. 461
religion, in Althusius's consociation 80–6
Religious Freedom Restoration Act, Rehnquist Court invalidation 558
republic, democracy, distinction 178
republican government
   English 114
   expansion possibilities 178–9
   Hamilton on 121
   Kant on 154–5, 159–60
   powers, Hume on 132
republicanism
   American federalism as experiment in 492–3
   federalism, distinction 401
   Jefferson on 210–11
   Montesquieu on 112, 210
rights, Australian Constitution 496
   see also human rights
Riker, William 3, 6
   theory of federalism 414–23
      as constitutional form 420
      military bargain 414, 423
      and rational choice theory 386–7, 421–2
      role of political parties 418
   works
      Development of American Federalism 419
      Federalism 413
Riley, Patrick 75, 138, 139
Robbins, Lionel 316
Rollier, Mario Alberto 317
Roman Republic 188
   consensus rule 249
   downfall 213
Rome Treaty (1957) 352
Roosevelt, Franklin 201–2
Rossi, Ernesto 316, 369
Rossi, Pellegrino 284
Rossiter, C. 62
Rossum, R. 203
Rousseau, Jean-Jacques
   on association 141–2
   federalism 73, 137–42, 147–8
      and sovereignty 142
   Kant, influence on 152
   on nation building 144
   nationalism 143–9
   on natural right 145–6
   political right 139, 144, 146, 147, 148
   on war 140
   works
      Considerations on the Government of Poland 283
      Discourse on Political Economy 148

Plan for a Constitution for Corsica 143
Principes de Politique 284
Social Contract 138–9, 140, 141, 142, 147
Rusinow, Dennison 344
Rutherford, Samuel 13, 53
   influence on Adams 62
   theologico-political federalism 58–61

St Pierre, Abbé de 139
   European federation, vision of 73, 141, 142, 146
   Project for Universal Peace 141, 142
Salamis, battle 18
Sbragia, Alberta 377
Schaefer, David Lewis 170
Schengen Agreement (1985) 377
Schmitt, Carl 6, 279–80
   on democracy 302–4
   on federalism 306–11
      antimonies 308–10
   on the political 301–2
   on sovereignty 298–301
   works
      Der Hüter der Verfassung 305
      Die geistesgeschichtliche Lage 302
      Politische Theologie 298
      Verfassungslehre 305
Schuman, Robert 369, 371
Schwab, George 299
Scotland
   covenantalism 56–7, 58–9
   Parliament 445, 446
Scruton, Roger 538, 541
SEA (Single European Act) (1986) 356
secession
   and American federalism 172, 237
   basis for 265–6
   Buchanan on 267–8
   and federalism 261, 263
   in Jefferson's federalism 218, 219
   Lincoln on 263–75
   as rebellion 172
   right to, Quebec 261–2, 449
   South Carolina 263, 265, 269
security, in Jefferson's federalism 213, 218, 221–2
self-government, Proudhon on 288
self-management
   Kardelj on 332, 336–7, 343
   Yugoslavia 280–1, 339
self-sufficiency, Aquinas on 37–8
Senghor, Leopold 471
separation of powers 114
   Jefferson on 211–12
   Madison on 178
Silving, H. 51
slavery
   in the American Constitution 273–4
   Calhoun on 246
   in Jefferson's federalism 219, 220
   Lincoln on 269, 273
   Tocqueville on 239, 240
social contract, federalism as 146
social contract theory 49
   Hobbes 42
   Locke 42–3
social reforms, Lycurgus 110–11
societies
   Aquinas's typology 38–9
   plural 249–50
Solemn League and Covenant (1643) 13, 58, 61
South Africa 255–8
   minority veto proposal 256, 258
   National Party 255–6
South Carolina 237, 271
   secession bid 263, 265, 269
sovereignty
   American federalism 548
   Australian Constitution 494–5
   Bodin on 94
      responses to 94–5
   definition 298–9
   doctrine 94
   and exception 298–300
   and federalism 142, 290
      reconciliation 104
   Grotius on 95
   and the individual 539
   Islam 546–7, 548
   Le Fur on 291–2
   Leibniz on 102–3
   mixed 94
   Pufendorf on 95–6
   Schmitt on 298–301
   Spinoza on 98
Spain
   asymmetric federalism 446
   decentralization 444–5
   language diversity 448

nationalist parties 449–50
Spinelli, Alterio 6, 280, 352, 354, 355, 369
   achievements 327–8
   American contacts 322
   European Commissioner 323
   federalist activities
      1943-45: 317–18
      1947-54: 318–20
      1954-61: 320–1
      1961-70: 322–3
      1970-76: 323–5
      1976-86: 325–8
      constitutional 370, 371
      shaping of 316
   health 327
   life 316
   political activity 317–18
   works
      Marxist politics and federalist politics 316
      PCI che fare? 326
      The Eurocrats 322
      The European Adventure 324
      The United States of Europe 316
Spinoza, Benedict 91, 97–8
   on federalism 99–100
      in Hebrew Republic (OT) 99
   on sovereignty 98
   Theologico-Political Treatise 99
Stowasser, Barbara 545
subsidiarity 71, 76, 222, 281, 326, 520, 522, 524
   EU 371, 376, 433
   federalism as 433
   Yugoslav Constitution (1974) 342–3
Supreme Court (US)
   and the American Constitution 199, 203, 205–6
   antisegregation decisions 194
   jurisdiction 189–90
   New Federalism 461, 551
   see also Rehnquist Court (1986-2005)
supreme magistrate (*summus magistratus*),
      in Althusius's consociation 80, **81**, 82

taxation, local/national levels 427–9
Taylor, John 210
Taylor, Quentin 169
Temple, William 93
theology, philosophy, distinction 32, 35

Thucydides, *Peloponnesian War* 11, 15, 22
Tiebout model 426, 427
Tindemans, Leo 324
Titoism 332, 336, 346
   individual in 337–8
Tocqueville, Alexis de 138, 170, 284, 285
   on the American Constitution 171, 200–1, 228
   on American federalism 197–200, 225–41, 286–7, 539–40
      church, state separation 537
      dissolution, tendency towards 235–8
      large/small, advantages 228–31
      local institutions 227, 232–3
      North v. South 239–40
      as particularly American 231–5
      theory of 227–31
      uniformity of opinion 228
   Democracy in America 193, 197, 201, 225, 238, 240, 536–7
   on French centralization 286
   Islam/Christianity comparison 537
   on judicial restraint 199–200
   on liberal democracy 540
   on Mexican federalism 538
   on the Ottoman Turks 540
   on slavery 239, 240
   on township government 198
township government, Tocqueville on 198
Toynbee, Arnold 536
Truman, David 418

UK
   devolution 445
      asymmetrical 446–7
   nationalist parties 450
UN system, Kant's federalism, comparison 158–9
United Provinces *see* Dutch Republic
Utrecht, Union of (1579) 93, 97

Vassallo, Francesca 281
Vaughan, C.E. 140
Venezuela, federalism 519–20, 521, 522, 523, 524–5, 527
Ventotene Manifesto 316, 369, 370
Voting Rights Act (1965) 194

Waitz, Georg 4

Wales, Assembly 445, 447
War of 1812: 217
war
   in Jefferson's federalism 221–2
   in Rousseau's thought 140
Ward, Ann 11, 12, 13, 72
Ward, Lee 71–7
Ward, W.A. 474
Watts, Ronald 3, 4
Weidner, Edward 419
Weimar Republic 304–5
Westminster Assembly (1643-46) 56, 58
Westminster model
   Australian Constitution 487
   democracy 249
Westphalia, Peace of (1648) 92
Wheare, K.C. 3, 4, 418, 427
Wilson, Woodrow 201
Winthrop, Delba 237
world government, in Kantian thought 156–7

Xerxes, King of the Persians 16

Yenor, Scott 72, 73
Yugoslav Constitution (1974) 253–4, 337, 338
   Althusian influences 338–46
      absence of political parties 343–4
      indirect electoral system 340–2
      politicization of society 340
      separation of powers 344–5
      subsidiarity 342–3
   federalism 253–5
   self-management 280–1, 339
Yugoslavia
   breakup 255, 347
   confederation proposal 254–5
   see also Titoism

Ziblatt, Daniel 4
Zulu Inkatha Freedom Party 256